STRAW PLAITING

HERBERT PRESS
Bloomsbury Publishing Plc
50 Bedford Square, London, WC1B 3DP, UK
29 Earlsfort Terrace, Dublin 2, Ireland

First published in Great Britain in 2023

A catalogue record for this book is available from the British Library

ISBN: 978-1-7899-4075-6; eBook: 978-1-7899-4076-3

2 4 6 8 10 9 7 5 3 1

Produced and designed for Bloomsbury by Plum5 Limited

Printed and bound in China by RR Donnelley Asia Printing Solutions Limited

MIX
Paper | Supporting responsible forestry
FSC® C144853

Front cover image: Basket made from straw plait by Ann Young of Aldbury, Hertfordshire. (CTLC 90/38)

STRAW PLAITING

HERITAGE TECHNIQUES FOR HATS, TRIMMINGS, BAGS AND BASKETS

VERONICA MAIN

ILLUSTRATED BY HELEN CHAPMAN

HERBERT PRESS

LONDON • OXFORD • NEW YORK • NEW DELHI • SYDNEY

For all the straw plaiters who have gone before.
May your skills and diligence finally be respected.

Made by Lucy Barlow using plait made by Veronica Main, the hat was hand-stitched.

CONTENTS

ACKNOWLEDGEMENTS

Without the support, patience, and love of my husband and children who have endured my passion for straw throughout the years this book would not have been possible.

Wardown House, Museum and Gallery, Luton, Bedfordshire is where I began my dedicated research of the extensive hat industry and headwear collections and its associated specialist library amassed through the efforts of **Thomas Wyatt Bagshawe, Charles Freeman** and **Dr John Dony**. **Marian Nichols** and **Rachel Heyburn** who at that time were the Principal Museum Officers gave me endless advice and encouragement. They enabled a grant from the **Pilgrim Trust** and with **The Friends of Luton Museums, The Worshipful Company of Feltmakers, The Rotary Club of Luton, Kate Beakes, Leslie and Amy Coburn, Jean Davis, László Gróf**, **Ray Nichols** and **Joan Ruck** were instrumental in assisting me through those early years. Throughout my journey **Elizabeth Adey** has given helpful guidance.

As the book became a reality, the **Culture Trust Luton** staff have played an important part. **Elise Naish** has been magnificent in searching out hidden information. From the very beginning **Chris Grabham** has been fundamental to the completion of this project and I will forever be grateful. **Mary Love** arranged photography of museum objects by **Phil Giles** of **Pan 3Sixty**. Access to Thomas Wyatt Bagshawe's research archive was granted with kind permission of **T. W. Bagshawe's family**. **The family of Richard Durler** kindly gave permission to include his remarkable images taken in Japan.

Tony Horn facilitated my access to Luton's hat companies who shared vital information. Tony and many others I met in those early years are no longer with us, but it gives me great delight that I can still count **John Horn** of Barford Brothers as well as **Richard Horn** and **Nicholas Horn** of Baxter, Hart and Abraham as friends and great supporters of my work.

I was awarded a **Queen Elizabeth Scholarship** and later a **Wingate Scholarship** which enabled research in former worldwide centres of the hat industry. Through this my close association at first with **J. Rudolf** and **Jackie Isler** now continues with **Jacques Isler** and **Andrea Isler.** They enabled in-depth research at **Strohmuseum im Park**, Wohlen, Switzerland where **Petra Giezendanner**, the Museum Director gave assistance. The research of **Margitta Hansel**, **Peter Bacon** and **Andreas Tomczak** has revealed much new information about the German industry. In the United States, **Linda Meeker, Nancy Meeker**, **Nancy Rexford** and **Jan Huss** helped me to access important museum collections. More recently **Pamela Burnside** and **Patricia Glinton-Meicholas** have introduced me to Bahamian straw work and to the artist **Kim Smith**. **Sue Brian** is keeping the skills and knowledge of cabbage tree hats alive in Australia and has been of enormous help in tracing references.

There are many people around the world who have assisted me in so many valuable ways. You are not named but you will know your part and that I will forever be thankful for your generosity, kindness, hospitality and trust in sharing knowledge and advice.

As the manuscript was prepared **Heather Beeson** painstakingly worked through my plait instructions. Her diligence, tenacity and dedication have been remarkable, and I am thrilled that she is now an accomplished plaiter. **Jim Cornish** came to my rescue by drawing important images so I could show what would be otherwise inaccessible. I am in awe of the illustrations created by **Helen Chapman** who was infinitely patient and precise as she brought the plaiting techniques to life. At Bloomsbury/Herbert Press **Jayne Parsons** and **Caroline Guillet** have been both supportive and understanding throughout the editorial process for which I am very grateful. My thanks to **Jasmine Parker** who produced the stunning cover. **Andy Chapman** at Plum5 has brought my research to life through the book's design. Finally, but definitely not least, thank you to everyone in the marketing, publicity and sales teams who have brought this book to you.

Daniel Carpenter and **Mary Lewis** of **Heritage Crafts** continue to fight for greater recognition of many endangered heritage skills. I hope their ongoing work, the support of all who have enabled my research, and this book, will be a big step towards preserving straw plaiting for future generations.

FOREWORD

I first met Veronica in the early 1980s when a colleague and I had been tasked with finding suitable craftspeople who would be willing to act as demonstrators at the newly opened Craft Museum and Gardens in Stockwood Park, Luton, now known as the Stockwood Discovery Centre. Visiting a large craft fair, we were struck, not just with her evident high level of skill, but also her ability to communicate her love of this humble material which was so important to the economy of the town and its surrounding countryside. She became one of our most popular demonstrators. She also became a lifelong friend.

I was, at that time, Luton Museums Keeper of Social History, a role which encompassed an enormously wide range of subjects, including the subject of this book, part of the fascinating world of the hat industry. My mentor in my early years at the museum was Dr John Dony (1899–1991), the distinguished botanist, and author of many books and articles. He was the honorary Keeper of Botany at the museum, but he was also an authority on local history and particularly the hat industry, his doctoral thesis resulted in a book *A History of the Straw Hat Industry*, 1942 which was rarely far from my desk during all my years at the museum. It was John who took me round my first hat factory where Salvation Army bonnets were being made around felt makers and dye works. He recalled seeing some of the last local plaiters at work in the 1930s, but, like so many before, he said that their fingers moved so quickly he could not really see what they were doing. It was a craft on the verge of extinction.

Veronica has sometimes said that I plant seeds in her head and watch them grow. When she started by demonstrating corn dolly making at Stockwood, I planted a seed which grew and grew to an extent which I never believed would be possible. Only a few examples of straw plaits were on display in the museum, together with splitters, mills and a sorter, the basic tools of the trade, but there were hundreds more in store, not just from Britain, but from around the world, trade sample books from China and Italy, exhibition samples from Japan, even cabbage tree plaits from Australia, as well as many examples of Swiss straw work. All these caught her eye and imagination and so began an exploration which led firstly to Veronica's book on the Swiss industry, and which has culminated in this book. Many others have written about straw plaiting, but only from the point of view of a social, economic or fashion historian; none from the maker's position. I will not forget her amazement when she began reading the evidence given by straw plaiters to various government commissions in the nineteenth century. Here were the voices of women and children who practised this craft, and who relied on it to supplement their families' meagre incomes; the results of their skill, although visible in the museum collection, were in danger of being lost forever – but not if Veronica had anything to do with it! Her enthusiasm knew no bounds, and her love of travel combined with an inquiring mind, tenacity, and love of the subject made her the ideal researcher.

Determined that the skills of the plaiters should not be forgotten, we embarked on a book together, which would provide a historical background for straw plaiting, a catalogue of the museum's collection of plaits together with instructions for making many of the plaits. As we worked, it soon became apparent from the growing number of appendices and the frequency of changes having to be made, that the project was too vast for us to cope with at that time, and that we were only skimming the surface. The project was shelved, for there was so much more to discover, if the subject was to be given the full attention it so richly deserved. That has now happened, though as readers will find, there are still many pathways to explore.

The seed which I planted has now grown into this carefully researched account of straw plaiting, its history and practice. This book goes far beyond what we originally envisaged. It includes both the story of the industry and the techniques which will enable exact replication of the multifarious plait patterns from many parts of the world. For creatives and design makers, it provides an exciting starting point for the development of an ancient practice, perhaps using new and different materials or recycling old ones. For those who pursue the history of costume and fashion, it will provide new and detailed insights into their subject. For those who find the terms 'straw plaiter' or 'straw drawer' while researching their family history, they will have a greater understanding of what their ancestors did for a living. They might even try to emulate them, all the instructions are here, and in so doing they will learn something of the skills that were needed to turn straw into gold.

Marian Nichols
Formerly Principal Museums Officer
(Collections), Luton Museums.

INTRODUCTION

Straw plaiters probably had no idea of the extent to which their livelihoods were affected by politics, governments, taxes and world events, they only knew that sometimes their work received a good price, and at other times a poor price. They may have heard suppliers and dealers talk about foreigners and competition, but I believe they would have been amazed to know the global extent of straw plaiting, and to realise how similar and yet how different it was from their local knowledge and personal experiences. Had they been privy to this information, with access to today's technology could they have changed the trade's course and ultimately their demise? Heritage Crafts' Red List of Endangered Crafts classifies *Straw Plaiting for the Hat Industry* as Critically Endangered. Worldwide only a few traditional plaiters are still working which makes it vital to record the industry's history, skills and techniques, but most importantly to share this knowledge.

This book charts the plaiting industry's development. It introduces the principal players of the commercial world stage and explains how they interacted and developed. Plaiters in each centre had their characteristic skills and used various types of straw for their products. Straw is not just 'straw'. All too often when plait is mentioned it is assumed to be made from wheat but that is far from true, even from the earliest times. In the industry it was any available fibre, either natural or manmade, which could be transformed into a commercially viable hat, bag, basket or other product.

Diversity and development were crucial, and as commentators frequently noted the trade was at the constant mercy of fashion. The development of plait patterns and products is complex, with some centres being famous for their specialism. To understand the trade, it must be observed from many international perspectives rather than by only taking the British viewpoint. I do make the plea that when information is found it is understood within the context of international trade rather than as the isolated work of one area.

Terminology is a pitfall waiting to engulf researchers as they try to interpret written accounts of the industry. Plaiting, braiding or weaving? These terms were used interchangeably within the trade to describe very different types of straw products. My years of study to investigate and unravel the secrets of materials, products and techniques is why this book has been so long to develop. As I searched more widely, my research conclusions were often contradicted, so I had to continue. In passing on the information I have gathered I do not want to create further confusion so have adopted a simple hierarchy of terminology. What I refer to as straw plaiting is known in the United States and many other countries as straw braiding or straw weaving. Separation of products and clear definitions will enable readers to develop a deeper understanding of the subject.

Whilst much has been written about the plaiters' social and economic conditions, the techniques used to create plait patterns and colourways were not deemed worthy of close consideration. The few accounts that do exist were usually written by observers rather than practitioners; outsiders who could not fully comprehend what they were witnessing. Plaiting instructions were usually passed on by demonstration rather than in any written document, so as plaiters died their skills died with them. Precious surviving examples of their work are in the collections at Wardown House, Museum and Gallery, Luton, Bedfordshire; Strohmuseum im Park, Wohlen, Switzerland; Sensler Museum, Tafers, Switzerland; Musée gruérien, Bulle, Switzerland; Museo della Paglia e dell'Intreccio, Signa, Italy and Musée d'Eben, Bassenge, Belgium. In Germany I discovered a wealth of information at an exhibition, Stroh zu Gold, Moritzburg, where examples of plaits from various museums in Saxony were displayed. In the United States, Killingly Historical Society, Connecticut holds two important straw objects, and Framingham Historical Society and Old Sturbridge Village, Massachusetts both have significant collections of plaits and artefacts of the trade. Although many other organisations hold only one or two surviving examples, when considered as part of a larger collective they help to build a clearer understanding.

By using these sources and many archives, libraries and much more, I have been able to replicate plait patterns taking care to record individual techniques and variations. It would have been easier to use my own methods but apart from lacking authenticity, it would have failed to appreciate the history and essence of these plaits. This amazing worldwide trade still has many stories to be told. If readers feel sufficiently inspired to keep these skills alive, and if with renewed interest straw plaiting can be removed from its current critically endangered status to a less precarious classification, I will have succeeded.

Veronica Main MBE

Terminology

The use of plait and braid interchangeably creates confusion when classifying straw products. Within North America the original term plait has largely been forgotten as has the word's pronunciation. Plait should be spoken to sound as in cat or mat. This is more obvious when seeing the original spelling which was plat or occasionally platt. Throughout this book the term plait and braid are used to signify that within the hat industry these are two different products. Weaving, another term interchanged with braiding or plaiting creates confusion when understanding accounts of the hat industry. To provide a clear understanding throughout this book the following definitions have been applied:

Plait	An interlaced structure made by hand. Can be made from any odd or even number of working ends.
Braid	An interlaced structure made by machine.
Loom-made braid	Made with a silk, cotton or silk/cotton warp. The weft may incorporate a variety of materials often within one product.
Woven	Hand woven with a bias to form a hat body such as a Panama hat or an English Brazilian hat.
Straw	Used as a generic term in the trade, but where possible in this book the type of straw is specified to enable understanding.
Straw hat	Within the industry the term was used to indicate a lightweight summer hat that could be made using a variety of methods from a wide range of materials.

Abbreviations

CTL Culture Trust Luton

CTLC Culture Trust Luton collection

Pictured in January 1922, Luton plait dealer Frank Dawson stands alongside an unnamed elderly plaiter, who is making a plait. Her plait is to be made into a hat for Princess Mary's wedding trousseau.

CHAPTER ONE

STRAW PLAITING IN GREAT BRITAIN

Straw plaiting has always been a complicated story to tell as it is part of a world-wide straw hat industry closely linked to fashion and its changing trends. No centre worked in isolation because copying new patterns, colourways and materials brought profit and success. That there was straw plaiting and straw hat production in most countries is understandable, since within society the wearing of hats was *de rigueur*. As this chapter reveals, external influences constantly played a part in the trade's development in Great Britain.

The early years

By the late 1400s various snippets of evidence indicate an organised trade importing straw hats from Italy and the Low Countries, yet currently there are no indications of any organised home-based industries of straw hat making or straw plaiting. During the 1500s wills and inventories list hats, but there is no clue if these were imported or home-produced. Dr John Dony's book[1] hinted at home production when he wrote of Martin Johnson of Gueldres, 'a strawen hat-maker or splyter hatmaker', being granted a letter of denization in 1530.[2] Since these documents were generally granted to wealthier immigrants it may be reasonable to assume this was an established business. The description splyter hatmaker probably indicates that Johnson was producing hats made from wood chip which is occasionally referred to as wood plait. Intermittent references throughout the eighteenth and nineteenth centuries indicate that chip or wood plait was a significant element of the straw hat industry.

One theory frequently cited claimed that during the early 1500s the craft was introduced into England by Mary Stuart (Mary, Queen of Scots from 1542–1587). In the 1930s this theory was thoroughly investigated by Thomas Bagshawe, Luton Museums' first director, Charles Freeman, curator, and later by their colleague Dr John Dony all of whom found no supportive historical evidence for this theory.[3] The original story appeared in the book written by Agnes Strickland in 1852.[4] She claimed that Mary: 'Engaged a company of the Lorraine straw-plaiters to return with her to her own country in order to instruct her countrywomen in their simple art; and thus was the first straw hat manufactory established in Scotland.' Strickland continued that the colony struggled until Mary's son James (King James VI and I) took, 'a kindly interest in his unfortunate mother's straw-plaiters.' She attributed this information to a pamphlet on female employment and domestic manufactures written by Mrs Mooney, wife of an Irish Clergyman.[5] In 1878 when Edward, Prince of Wales visited the town, Luton hat manufacturers were happy to perpetuate the story. The Address delivered on behalf of the Corporation and Straw Hat Manufacturers began: 'We would remind your Royal Highness that 273 years have passed since our town was honoured by presence of Royalty, in the person of His Majesty King James the First to whom we owe the introduction into this district of the manufacture of straw plait. . . '[6]

Local manufacturers disagreed about the reliability of these claims, with one of the pioneers and most esteemed of the early hat manufacturers, John Waller, refusing to accept the theory and making many counter arguments.[7] Despite evidence this romantic story continues to be widely circulated.

During the 1600s, whilst it seems probable the making of straw hats, bags, baskets and other items continued and was developing into a more organised trade, more frequent reports did not appear until the 1700s. A book published in 1715[8] included reference to Isabel Denton living in Beeston, near Leeds in Yorkshire. Denton and her partners were said to be earning a living from dealing in hats of some 'seven thousand pounds per annum' which seems an enormous amount for the time. It continued that in the same way that 'bone lace' had been affected by foreign influences, so had straw hats which were now made of 'wood pelt (sic) imported from beyond the Sea'[9] and stated that Denton first invented 'Straw Hats and Baskets.' Hopefully he was implying that she first introduced them into Beeston rather than to the whole country which would be inaccurate.[10] It is logical to conclude that manufacture was occurring elsewhere, and there must be other undiscovered documents which would enable researchers to build a picture of straw plaiting and hat making throughout the whole of Great Britain.

Another notable mention of straw hats which is frequently cited appears in the diaries of Samuel Pepys when he wrote of a visit to Hatfield on Sunday 11 August 1667: 'Being come back, and weary with the walk, for as I made it, it was pretty long, being come

Cruikshank's 1796 drawing shows what are described as 'Itinerant Dealers in Dunstable Ware.' It appeared in Eccentric Excursions or Literary and Pictorial Sketches of Countenance, Character, and Country in Different Parts of England and South Wales *by G. M. Woodward.*

back to our inne, there the women had pleasure in putting on some straw hats, which are much worn in this country, and did become them mightily, but especially my wife.' Frustratingly, it does not tell us if the hats had been made locally or were imported. In his diary entry of 24 January 1667 Pepys recorded a visit to the theatre where after the performance he was joined by one of the actresses who in her stage costume was 'dressed like a country-mayde with a straw hat on.' It may be possible to deduce that at this time the wearing of straw hats was associated with country folk rather than fashion.

Growth of the industry into Hertfordshire is often attributed to the information that in 1680 Tring was granted a market where straw plait was permitted to be sold on a Friday morning. A transcript of the original document does not specifically mention straw plait, it simply describes the selling of all manner of cattle, sheep and corn. In 1900 revised byelaws relating to the newly built market mentioned straw plait, even though by that time the trade was in rapid decline. Perhaps the wording of this revision has been mistakenly assumed to be the wording of the original documents.[11]

In 1681 Thomas Baskerville[12] observed at Dunstable that 'some people of this town are very curious in making straw hats and other works of that nature.' Observing what must have been a prominent occupation it shortly precedes a petition presented in 1689. The industry had reached a sufficient size and organisation within the south east Midlands to give workers confidence to petition Parliament against a bill which would have enforced the wearing of woollen hats at certain times of the year. The straw workers claimed that 14,000 persons were dependent on their industry. They claimed that if the bill were passed, it would lead to their 'utter ruin and undoing' not only to the straw hat makers but also to the farmers supplying the straw, sales which gave them 'considerable advantage.' The petition was successful, but threats to the straw hat industry had not diminished.

Development in the 1700s

Plaiting was frequently associated with poverty and the workhouse where it was one of the skills encouraged as a means of making the poor self-sufficient and less of a burden on the parish. There are several references including Toddington in Bedfordshire, where in the period 1714 to 1715 Churchwardens paid for Dorothy Powell's hatting straws and the Overseers of the Caddington workhouse in Bedfordshire paid for the straw and for pressing (blocking) the hats made there.

Representatives for the straw workers in the south east Midlands presented a second petition to Parliament in 1719. This time they pleaded for assistance against importations to prevent the workers facing destruction of the trade and becoming dependent upon their parishes. The document stated that the threat came from, 'great Quantities of chip and of shaving from Holland, which is plaited and a sort of Platt and Hats from Leghorn, and other places the Duties which amounts to but an Inconsiderable Sum.' The petition explained what may have been lost by the men, women and children, aged from four to four-score years, if imports took over. In their spare hours the farmers' wives, children and servants could earn £10, £20 or £30 per annum which helped them pay their rent. A penny-worth of straw could earn eight, nine or sometimes ten shillings. It concluded the brief account of the work by saying that every week they carried the hats for sale to market. It is interesting to note that the petition spoke of the workers selling finished hats not just plait. This time the petitioners were less successful, as imports continued to increase during the 1700s despite imposition of restrictive import duties. Dony did not include the following information in his book but in private notes prepared for various talks, he stated that, 'Luton and its hamlets of Leagrave,

Limbury, East and West Hyde sent their petition in on 3 February. At the end of the month, however, the merchants of Bristol also petitioned Parliament, anxious to encourage the trade with Bermuda from where many of the hats came from – two sides to every question!'

Another short-lived threat arose in 1724 with an application for a patent that also resulted in a petition to Parliament. William Heaton wanted to claim rights for making hats with 'a Vegitable called Bent or Straw' that would produce hats much finer than the Leghorn and Bermudas. Articles appeared in various newspapers[13] stating they 'hear from Hemel Hempsted, Luton, Dunstable and Redbourn where many thousands of poor people are employed in platting wheat straw, and this has been an occupation for more than one hundred years.' The report concluded that the petition was delivered and refused which brought great joy. John Oldmixon, writing in 1735,[14] recounted additional concerns including that he had been told at Hemel Hempstead that £100 a week had been turned in a market day on the sale of straw hats. Dony added that another reason for refusal was that Heaton's patent infringed Thomas Masters' patent issued in 1716 (see Chapter Two, page 27).

During the 1700s the straw industry must have grown significantly since it regularly attracted the attention of travel writers, many of whom recorded their observations. Daniel Defoe, in his *Tour thro' the Whole Island of Great Britain*[15] noted that the 'Manufactures of Straw-work, especially Straw Hats . . . is greatly increased within a few Years past.' In 1746 the writer of *The Agreeable Historian or the Complete English Traveller*[16] tells us that: 'about Dunstable and Luton they make straw hats and other things of that sort, which manufacturers find business for several thousand people.' In 1748, Pehr Kalm, a traveller, scientist and student of Linnaeus, provided perhaps the most comprehensive account[17]. For about three weeks, spanning March to April, he stayed in Little Gaddesden, Hertfordshire to study the rural economy and way of life. He recorded the dress of the women in the village and commented that they always wore a straw hat which 'they have made themselves from wheat straw and are pretty enough.' Kalm observed several women 'very busy

Made from eleven-end and seven-end plaits, this bonnet dates from 1835. It was made for a lady in Hockcliffe, Bedfordshire by the Dunstable hat manufacturer Benjamin Bennett. (CTLC L/153/34)

making straw hats which they afterwards sent hither and thither to be sold.' He noted that only wheat straw was used and then described its preparation and bleaching. While able to record these parts of the process, he wrote: 'The particular manner in which this plaiting is afterwards done cannot so clearly be described in words.' It was a difficulty commonly encountered in later years by many other writers.

While evidence indicates a home trade of plaiting straw into hats and other items, and Dunstable and Hemel Hempstead are mentioned as places where such goods were sold, there appears to be no specific centre where the plaiters sent their finished work. In fact, they appear to have been sold directly through local markets. Home-produced hats were not the only source available to the trade, great quantities were being imported primarily from Italy, Bermuda and the Bahamas. Dony investigated the Trade Returns to study imports of hats during the 1700s but from the available data was not able to specify the origin of these imports. His list begins in 1721 when 7,117 hats were imported. By 1725 the figure had risen to 34,063 and by 1760 to 477,024, which is the zenith of the import trade. Numbers then erratically declined into the early 1800s. He concluded that in the 1600s the British straw hat industry was small, providing the needs of local demand, then in the 1700s gradually expanded but he madeto the point that compared the industry and products of Tuscany, the home market probably served the 'cheaper demands of the market.' Even with the increase in home production the import figures indicate a high demand for hats and Dony noted that official import figures for the period 1759 to 1766 showed an annual quantity of about 1,400,000 hats, which are listed as being chip and straw.[18]

Development in the 1800s

Towards the end of the 1700s, the plaiting and making of straw hats as one process within the family or community, with makers selling directly at market, began to decline. While this combined work was to continue into the 1800s, a gradual change began. The process of straw plaiting became a separate occupation and production of hats rather than a greater range of straw products became the focus. During the French and Napoleonic wars at the end of the 1700s and into the early 1800s the English straw plaiting and hat making industry expanded rapidly, making it of considerable economic and social importance to the region. The fine Italian hats were expensive and difficult to obtain, and presumably disruption in Bermuda and the Bahamas restricted those exports, but hats were still imported from there and Denmark, Germany, Flanders, France and

This drawing, published in the 1882 Cassells Family Magazine *accompanied an article about straw plaiting.*

Gibraltar. A paper presented to the Society of Arts in 1805 records a total of nearly 30,000 dozen imports between 1794 and 1803.[19]

The market demanded hats to be like those of Italy where they were made from fine Tuscan straw, but the home-produced wheat straw was thick and produced a relatively coarse plait. Experiments were made with grasses, rye and new varieties of wheat in attempts to emulate the fine, delicate Italian plaits. The most well thought out of these was expedited by Thomas Waller who took out a patent in 1826[20] to employ Tuscan wheat straw, but to use 'the upper part nearest the ear of the straw instead of the lower part.' The main result of his work was development of an eleven-end plait which was sewn into a hat known in the trade as the Tuscan grass bonnet. According to Thomas Austin, this received royal patronage and became very fashionable.[21] Having achieved greater importance, straw plaiting began to be recorded separately, but was still regarded as an occupation for the poor, often undertaken by children as well as adults and with attempts at organised trades as it spreads around Britain. The Society of Arts, in London, offered monetary premiums and medals, and the Society for Bettering the Condition of the Poor organised workrooms to encourage growth. The efforts of these Societies, especially the latter, led to many smaller and in most cases short-lived plaiting industries springing up around the country. There are records of the industry in Cornwall, Devon, Wiltshire, Dorset, Kent, Suffolk, Norfolk, Warwickshire and in the Orkney and Shetland islands. László Gróf[22] noted that the 1841 English and Welsh census recorded plaiters as listed in all but three central Welsh counties. Fleeting references to straw plaiting in north Wales occur sometimes mentioning working with wild grasses, but there is no indication of any organised trade. *The Workwoman's Guide* author, when discussing the making of English Imitation Leghorn plaits referred to plaiting in Ireland using crested dog's-tail grass, which she said the Irish called 'trawnyeens.'[23] It was 'being made up by the Irish, and is said to become a productive manufacture.' No evidence has yet been found to indicate an organised industry. Growth of the industry attracted the attention of national figures such as Arthur Young, William Corston, Joseph Lancaster and William Cobbett who each played their part in promoting and recording the trade. In 1861, its first year of publication, *The Queen Magazine*[24] published an article which stated that 80,000 English plaiters, women and children, produced 200 million yards of plait each year. This would equate to 2,500 yards from each plaiter who would have to have made nearly seven yards every day of the year.

Straw plait schools

While throughout the 1700s plaiting provided a means for the poor to pay their keep in workhouses,[25] from the first years of the 1800s until the 1870s many children in the straw plaiting areas attended plait schools where they were supervised by the plait mistress or, more rarely, master.[26] The British system of plaiting schools is the most widely recorded. However, the organisation of children into specific groups where their main daily occupation was plaiting with some education was commonplace throughout the straw plaiting areas of Europe. A straw plait school was said to have been introduced into a village in the Swiss canton Aargau in 1807,[27] while in Bohemia and Saxony during the 1800s the government funded plaiting schools.[28]

As to how much plait was expected of each child, in 1843 a report stated, 'Children generally plait in schools, a task of so many yards being set to them by the parents, and the duty of a mistress is to act the part of an overlooker in a factory, and see the proper amount of work is done.'[29] Plaiting schools possibly existed earlier, but the first currently known in England is in 1801. The school was established by William Corston who because of his enterprises became a plait dealer, opening a warehouse in Ludgate Hill, London under the company name of

Corston and Shackle where the plaits produced at his workrooms in Fincham, Norfolk were sold. He claimed the sale price averaged not less than two shillings and sixpence a score. In 1804, reported in an account published in 1805, he was awarded a gold medal by the Society of Arts for specimens of rye straw and rye straw plait made by his workers. His paper to the Society detailed the cultivation processes and his estimates for the financial benefits of his enterprise. His correspondence concluded in December 1805 with a plea that if the Government would allow 1,000 acres of Bagshot Heath in Surrey to be cultivated with rye, it would provide employment for 5,000 poor children.

Corston formed an association with Joseph Lancaster, supporting the latter's method of education. In Lancaster's book published in 1807[30] Corston contributed a lengthy section to support the inclusion of straw plaiting within the education scheme, claiming it would support the 'female poor.' As to how widely instruction in straw plaiting was introduced into the curriculum is unclear and there were those who believed the idea was unsound. Editorial in the *Belfast Monthly Magazine*[31] argued strongly against including within the Lancastrian system the teaching of straw plaiting and other skills, saying it would be detrimental to the trade since plait would be widely available and consequently become worthless.

Corston was also involved with The London and Dublin Societies for Bettering the Condition of the Poor.[32] This was a Society that became very active in using straw plaiting as a means for generating income. During September 1801 a lengthy report details a scheme to assist local spinners in Avebury, Wiltshire whose previous trade in the area had ceased, to learn the plaiting of split straw. A person, perhaps Corston or someone associated with his attempts, came from London to provide instruction. By August 1802 their plaits were sold in London and Bath raising about £80 per month which was extrapolated within the report to amount to £1,000 a year. The enterprise was considered so successful that it was recommended the scheme should be extended to other towns in Wiltshire. Later volumes of the Society's reports recorded that children were making straw plait in their schools around the country. In Cheltenham whole straw was being plaited for baskets that were then sold at reduced prices to the poor of that district. In Campsall School, near Doncaster, girls under the age of eight were required to take an examination in which as well as writing, they produced specimens of straw plait, seaming, hemming, stitching, marking their initials, darning and making a buttonhole. Prizes were awarded to successful girls.

The Society's reports also expressed concern about the wisdom of enabling young girls to earn, good income and the writers discussed the potential evils of enabling straw plaiting as an occupation. Such discussions were to continue throughout the 1800s. Had straw plaiting succeeded in being assimilated into a nationwide formal system of education then it may have enjoyed a higher level of repute instead of falling into dame schools and unofficial village workrooms. The plaiting schools of the south east Midlands were the subject of many government investigations during the 1800s. The often high earnings and independence of the young people able to make a living, in the good times of the trade, presented a perceived threat to the social order which was witnessing civil unrest in other parts of society. There was little hope that the various reports would support the enterprises and a concern they would use their findings to justify reduction in the poor rates paid.

Most plait schools were in small cottage rooms, but separate buildings were occasionally used with some specifically constructed for the purpose. The rooms were, on average, between

10–13 feet long (approximately 3–4 metres) with low ceilings and often only one window and door. At the height of the busy season the room was the daily workplace for between 20–30 children, occasionally more. 'We sit very screwed at school' said one 12-year-old of her plait school in 1864. Supervised by a village woman known as the plait mistress, attendance started at about three years old and by the age of five a child was expected to make a marketable plait. The first lesson was recorded as learning to make a plait variously called twittle twattle, widdle waddle or Jacob's ladder which was a loose plait of three straws. The second lesson was to make a hen's ladder, a plait of four straws, and the third to make a perfect plait of seven straws. The plait mistress ensured the children made the amount of plait set for them by their parents. The charge for attending plait school ranged between one and three pennies, and the children had to pay for their straw. After these deductions the remaining money resulting from sale of the plaits could be kept. Plaiting was considered a skill that was essential to learn, as was pointed out in 1882. 'At four or five years a child which could not "do its fives," that is to plait five straws together, was looked upon as a greater dunce than one who at ten did not know its alphabet.'[33]

It was not until 1838 that the first Government Report[34] revealed official details of the conditions of these schools, although it is important to appreciate there were political motives behind these reports meaning they probably recorded the worst. Major J G Burns presented a report in 1843 to the Children's Employment Commission based on evidence collected from individual plaiters and visits to a 'very great number of the straw plait schools.' In a few of them reading was taught once a day, but Major Burns described plaiting as a complete bar to 'anything like education, for as soon as children can use their fingers, they are put to it.' In 1867, George Culley stated that: 'Although there is a pretence of teaching the children to read, the teachers themselves are often unable to do that which they profess to teach the children to do, and the reading is reduced to the repetition of a few verses of the Bible which they all know by heart. In some plait schools there is not even this pretence, and the result is that a great many children (girls especially) are growing up without any education.'[35]

Even the youngest children assisted in the production process. Anne Tompkins, plait mistress at Houghton Regis in Bedfordshire, described how the youngest children in her school clipped off the ends of the straw after it had been plaited. 'Lizzie Ibbins there, who is between two and three years old is clipping some plait made by her sister elsewhere. Lizzie Cook, who was three last month I think, can clip her ten (yards) in the day, which Lizzie Ibbins has never done yet . . . In clipping, the scissors sometimes hurt their fingers, and some have to put two in to be able to hold them. They are very troublesome, and I have to use the stick a great deal more than I like.' Mr J. E. White, who was Tompkins' interviewer, observed that he had seen infants of two, three and four years old in the schools, with their scissors tied to their bodies with which they clipped off the straw ends.[36] The plait mistresses and the parents believed that for the children to become good, proficient plaiters they had to start learning at a very early age, so that their supple young fingers could become accustomed to the repetitious movements of plaiting.

With such large numbers of very young children confined within a small space for many hours each day, discipline was a feature of the daily routine. Sometimes the presence of a stick or cane in the corner of the room provided sufficient deterrent, but occasionally it was used. Schools known for strict discipline were more popular amongst the parents than lax ones, since the children would produce more plaits for the parents to sell. Parents also exercised discipline as recorded in the evidence of Sarah Meager who was seven years old. 'If I do "five" mother says I am a good girl; she doesn't hit me, the mistress sometimes does.'[37]

In a change from the very first educational attempts which were only for girls, both boys and girls attended plait school. Boys generally took up farm work at 10 or 11 years old, but in times of good trade and high demand they returned, as would their fathers and brothers. Usually, however, the majority of plaiters above the age of 10 were female. Some of the girls stayed at the plait school until well into their teens. Older children attended plait school in the evenings as well as during the day, working from 6pm until 9 or 10pm. During the day the hours were usually 9am until 12pm and from 2pm until 5pm. Children who went to the parish or 'reading' school, or who were at work during the day, also attended the evening school at times of high demand. Children at plait schools could earn significantly more than those at the lace schools, making plaiting the preferred occupation.

Viewed from a neighbouring property, plaiters stand outside the Harrow Inn, Akeman Street in Tring. Some work as they chat and look along the road.

These plaits were made in the 1800s and are interesting as there are a range of patterns, many of which were still being made in Italy in the early 1900s.

During a day at school a 10-year-old was expected to make about 30 yards of simple plait. Making intricate patterns, fine split straw and Tuscan plaits made with bents took longer but according to seasonal demand fetched higher prices. It is difficult to determine what they earned at school, especially since the term child encompassed the 4-year-old just learning to plait and the 14-year-old who could earn as much as an adult plaiter. Fear of the 'Relieving Officer,' who may have removed or reduced any assistance a family received, may have created a reluctance to reveal their true earnings. This apprehension may be indicated during the cross-questioning of the evidence offered by Mrs Chandler.[38] She told the inspector that a child of eight years would earn one shilling and three pennies, but this amount was later reduced to nine pennies per week. The investigation ended in some confusion as the committee tried to make sense of the estimates of earnings which the various interviewees provided. From each child's earnings money had to be deducted for straw as well as for the school fee. Four children in one family 'can make six shillings a week by plaiting straw when the straws are all paid for,' however in another section of the same report in a generalised statement, children were said to make three to four shillings a week.[39]

Accounts of conditions in the schools described them as 'close and offensive.' Warmth was necessary to 'insure sufficient suppleness of the fingers' and therefore in cold weather 'every breath of air is carefully excluded.' To help keep themselves warm many children used 'dicky pots', small earthenware jars or tins containing wood, coal or charcoal to provide extra heat. The smoke and fumes from these would have done nothing to improve an already unpleasant atmosphere. Concerns about the overcrowding of small rooms and lack of ventilation providing 'bad air' was frequently raised in the reports and did appear to have caused genuine concern for the welfare of the children. It was noted that whilst plaiting was not an unhealthy occupation compared to others in the area, there was a tendency for children to suffer from stomach and catarrhal problems which was attributed to the practice of damping the straws in their mouths.[40] Since the straws were bleached with sulphur and one account stated that 'brimstone and vitriol are, I believe, used to prepare the straws, possibly something worse,'[41] there may have been some truth in this concern.[42] It was also said the children suffered cut lips and fingers from the sharp edges of the split straws.

Clearly, some control of the plaiting schools was needed but the existing legislation was ambiguous as to their status. The Workshop Regulation Act of 1867 provided a clearer position, but the local authorities had no means of enforcing the Act, and the factory inspectorate was already overworked. A Parliamentary paper of 1867[43] stated that the chief constable of Buckinghamshire had established 1,457 children attended 102 schools in the central and south-eastern part of the county and if trade was good, attendance could increase by 30 or 40%. Dony estimated that there may have been 600 schools with an attendance of 10,000, possibly increasing to 13,000 at times of good trade. Despite a test case in 1871,[44] abuses continued but the education legislation finally offered more forceful means to control the plait schools.

The plaiters' lives

By 1851, nearly 80% of the total workforce of straw plaiters lived in the south east Midlands, with over 10,000 in south Bedfordshire alone, but figures do not adequately express how much straw plaiting dominated everyday existence. Nearly all aspects of social and economic life in the area were intimately bound up with the fluctuating fortunes of the straw plaiting and hat-making industries. The seasonal nature of the trade was intensified by the whimsical demands of fashion, but when plaits were 'good' everything else was abandoned for them, much to the disapproval of some commentators. Many were concerned by the social, moral and educational problems supposedly caused by straw plaiting. Wives were said to often keep their earnings secret from their husbands. Worse still, the women had an alternative occupation that could stop them from going into service. The high earnings and the independence of the women caused authors of these reports, usually male, considerable problems, for these were circumstances regarded as incompatible with the accepted view of women at the time. The lack of a factory-type discipline also appalled the onlookers; unlike pillow lace making, straw plaiting could be done almost anywhere, in the house or outside, walking about, sitting still or gossiping over the garden gate. These fears were summed up in evidence submitted to commissioners in 1868[45] which included a chain of correspondence from Rev. Richard Gee, vicar of Abbots Langley, Hertfordshire who said that 'Plait is not an unmixed evil which some of my neighbours consider it. It is preferable to the field work, as less unfeminine and to the lace work more prosperous . . . It is not unhealthy nor is it even sedentary. It saves the family much pressure when the husband (say in winter) is out of work. I write thus because I believe these advantages are often overlooked. As a diocesan Inspector I am aware of some of the difficulties it presents in the way of education . . . I am sensible of the evils, or rather the dangers, of plait. They may, most of them, be traced to the disinclination which it causes in young women to go into service. They stay at home, independent of their parents as regards earnings, and therefore control. They put what they do earn on their backs, and become vain and over-dressed.' Charles Knight commented following a visit to Luton in 1861 that 'Here, as at other straw-plaiting towns . . . high wages would allow cottage girls to dress like ladies.'[46] Whilst in this instance he was referring to the girls who had migrated to the town to work as better paid bonnet sewers and other jobs within the factories, this typifies the critical comments made. He also expressed dismay that when the downturn of trade came, they would be 'little fitted for domestic service.'

In the mid 1800s an average week's earnings from plaiting was five shillings (25p)[47] but a good worker could earn more during a busy season and according to the plait pattern being worked. An adult plaiter and her children could double the family income, which within an area where the average wage of an agricultural labourer was 10 shillings (50p) a week, it was little wonder that other household duties were put to one side at those times. The plaiter's life was not an easy one and so it is of little surprise that the ambition of many was to become a bonnet sewer, a better paid and more reliable trade that could be done at home or in a factory.

Having made the plait, it had to be sold for the best possible price. Some plaiters living in villages that were some distance from the nearest plait market would sell their plaits within the village in exchange for one or two 'pottle loafs.' In some villages where the workers had a good reputation, the plait dealers would travel to them and buy at their door. While this meant they may receive slightly less for their plaits, it sometimes saved long early morning walks to reach a market. If the plaiter was making a coloured plait, then the dealer would usually supply the straws and commission plaits for the following week. Plaiters in less respected villages, or those with less reputation for fine work, had to walk to their local plait markets located in many of the towns. Austin,[48] in 1871, recalled earlier times when markets began at 7 o'clock in the morning and may have been as much as 12 miles from the location of the dealers or plaiters. Not only the plaiters walked to market; he described a plait dealer dying on Dunstable Downs before dawn as he attempted to walk to Hemel Hempstead market.

An account by Charles Knight[49] provided a vivid account of the Luton open air market in 1861 saying that the market bell rang at 9 o'clock and within an hour or two the street was empty, the plaiters either having sold directly to bonnet makers or to dealers. Each town's market was held on a different day of the week but although a higher price might have been achieved if the plaiter arrived early, it would have been amongst great competition with others and the plaiter would have had to be willing to barter fiercely. Most plait markets were held outside until the opening of the Luton Plait Halls in 1869. Austin[50] carefully described a visit he made to the new halls and estimated that, within half an hour of the market bell sounding, 2,000 people filled the space, buying from the dealers who had already acquired their stock of plaits. At the Waller Street entrance to the halls stood 'rows of poor plaiting women who hoop upon their arms the week's labors of themselves and children, patiently waiting till the first rush of business is over.' He stated that whilst this was 'the original way in which plaits were bought, and is still in vogue in the neighbouring markets', now fewer plaiters came to sell at market, instead selling directly to the dealers who visited the local plaiting villages.

Straw plaiting in the Orkney and Shetland islands

Albeit for a relatively short time, an industry in the Orkney and Shetland islands reached a high standard of work by copying the highly prized Tuscan plaits and bonnets. Early in the 1800s the skills were introduced into the islands by a Scottish company, Muirs of Greenock. In Lerwick 50 girls were working at straw plaits, earning one penny a yard. They could earn between 10 pennies and one shilling and sixpence a day.[51] In the Orkneys the industry was on a much larger scale employing between 1,200 and 1,400 people by 1814[52], rising by the 1840s to over 2,000 plaiters. The greatest concentration of plaiters was in the town of Kirkwall.

At first imported Italian straws were used and then islanders grew and prepared their own fine rye straw grown specifically for plaiting. It was sown thickly to make the straw grow long and fine. The best plaiters used the finest straw, while beginners and the less skilled used the thicker, lower part of the stem. The locally grown rye straw was said to be more durable than the straw imported from Italy.

At its height, about 7,000 people worked in the industry, both plaiting and bonnet sewing, as well as growing and preparing the straw. The industry was not without its achievements. In 1823 Muirs were presented with the Ceres Medal of the Society of Arts for a 'hat face and thirty score of plait of different qualities.'[53] At the Great Exhibition of 1851, Muirs exhibited examples of plaits and bonnets made from rye straw grown in the Orkneys, while Mrs John Rendall of Stromness received a medal for samples of Tuscan plaits suitable for bonnets. 'Specimens of 11 straws, fine Tuscans, and of 15 straws, coarse Tuscans. Grown and dressed in Orkney and plaited by the female inhabitants.' Charles Still from Kirkwall was another exhibitor at the Great Exhibition, with a display of straw plaits for making bonnets.

However, fashions change, the duty on foreign plaits and hats was reduced and technology was introduced into the Luton hat industry. As the competition increased, straw plaiting and bonnet sewing gradually declined in the Orkneys and Shetlands. When Muirs opened a branch in Luton, the island's industry diminished rapidly[54], although there were other companies involved in these enterprises[55]. Luton straw hat manufacturer, Arthur Tansley, reported that in 1859 the quantity of plait made in the Orkneys was very limited.[56] Having died out in the Shetlands in 1841, it disappeared entirely from the islands by the 1870s. Despite the excellent quality produced, they were too far away from the main trading markets to continue.

This hat from the mid 1800s is trimmed with two-end plait, palm flowers and natural foliage. While its provenance is unknown, it may have been made in Massachusetts. (DH2094)

CHAPTER TWO

STRAW PLAITING IN THE ATLANTIC ISLANDS AND NORTH AMERICA

Unlocking information about straw industries is challenged by the ever-changing terminology used in contemporary reports and accounts. It appears correspondents did not appreciate the nuances of different products nor take note of the techniques employed. The process of linking surviving artefacts with written information is especially difficult when examining the straw industry of the United States, which is a far more complex story than perhaps at first obvious. The chapter begins with an account of the introduction and development in the Atlantic islands of Bermuda and the Bahamas, from where the trade was taken into the United States.

Bermuda and the Bahamas

Sybilla[57] Masters of Pennsylvania is cited as being the first 'American' woman to be granted patents although they had to be registered in the name of her husband Thomas. When investigated further the story is not straightforward and leads to a far wider picture of international trade and the spread of straw plaiting from Bermuda into North America and England.

Sybilla was born in Bermuda, married Thomas Masters, also a Bermudian, before emigrating to Philadelphia in 1687.[58] Thomas Masters was to become one of the most important men in the city and he and Sybilla were friends with William Penn and his family. The Masters' social importance provides an indication as to why Sybilla's attempts to secure patents would have been taken more seriously than those of others. By the 1680s straw plaiting of a variety of products made from palmetto leaves was well established in Bermuda.[59] In a dissertation by Anna Saskia Wolsak, she surmised that plaiting skills may have been brought to Bermuda by the first English or Scottish settlers. Plaits, hats, baskets and dressing boxes were being sent to America, the Caribbean and England. Sybilla would have been aware and is assumed to have been a skilled maker with a good knowledge of this island industry and its importance within the trading structure.[60] It should be noted that by the 1690s Bahamian products were already being sent to Pennsylvania.

Her first patent was for a new way of milling corn which she named Tuscarora rice and hoped to sell in England as a form of corn (maize) that would survive the long voyage. This patent was finally granted in 1715, however, the grits or cornmeal did not please the English taste and the project was unsuccessful. It was her second patent[61] which is relevant to this subject as it relates to the manufacture of palmetto palm. It stated: 'With great charge, paines and expence, invented and brought to the perfeccon. A new way of working and staining in straw, and the plat and leaf of the palmetta tree, and covering and adorning hatts and bonnetts in such a manner as was never before done or practised in England or any of our plantacons.' Initially both her patent applications failed, and she took the bold step of travelling to London, leaving behind her five children. This was a time when women could not be granted a patent, and the entire process was complicated and expensive for the patentee since it involved both considerable fees and bribes.[62] Presumably she hoped that Queen Anne would personally grant her permission, but by the time her first patent was granted in 1715 and the second in 1716, it was in the reign of King George I.

At this time although patents could cover genuine inventions, they were frequently used to control trade. Patents were granted for a period of 14 years and within that time Masters could organize and control the Bahamian straw industry. As Wolsak indicated, it seemed she was an entrepreneur rather than an inventor.[63] Having established that by the time of Masters' application the making of straw plait from palmetto was a well-established trade in Bermuda, it called into question her claim that her patent was for a method 'never done or practiced in England or any of our plantacons.' Perhaps true of England but not of her homeland where it was a well-organised industry.

Masters was to remain in London until 1716, presumably until after her second patent had been granted by King George I and perhaps this gave her the confidence to open a shop in Catherine Street in the Strand. An announcement in the *London Gazette*, 18 March 1716, said: 'The West India Hat & Bonnet' shop is selling hats and bonnets from one shilling upwards, as well as 'dressing and child-bed baskets, & matting made of the same West India for chairs, stools, & other beautiful furniture for the apartments of persons of quality, etc.' The success of her patent application and of her enterprise resulted in the growth of the island's industry, a boom which was to continue until 1730, ten years after Masters' death.

John Hope, the Governor of Bermuda between 1721 and 1727, wrote, 'English ladies never thought themselves handsome or well-dressed unless they had a small Bermuda hat.'[64] A costume dictionary defined a Bermuda hat as '1st half 18th century. Female. Of straw for country wear' and included a detail of an advertisement taken from the *New England Weekly Journal*, 1727, 'Women's Hatts made of fine Bermuda Platt.'[65] The Court Records of the Old Bailey[66] provided an interesting source of information, and whereas the theft of straw hats was mentioned in earlier cases, on 7 December 1720 John Antony and Ann Collins were accused of stealing 15 Bermuda straw hats with a value of 39 shillings. In 1726 there were two cases where Bermuda hats and plaits were listed amongst the stolen goods. Witness accounts said the Bermuda hat was lined with blue silk.

There is a second, less documented, exponent of straw plaiting in Bermuda, who as a contemporary of Masters deserves mention. Mrs Martha Hayward, née Carter, claimed to have sent a hat that she made to Queen Anne that won her favour. Hayward lived on the island of St David's and was known to plait for a living. According to island folklore a young French woman had travelled to Bermuda with her fiancé and was desirous of a lace hat of the type worn in France. One was fashioned for her using local

The elaborate lace-like pattern and the frame on which it is supported has been made from a yet unidentified plant fibre. It certainly is of a quality to present to Queen Anne.

materials. Whether Haywood and Masters worked together and whether the sending of a hat to the Queen links to the making of a lace-like hat for the French woman will never be known. What we do know is that the period of Haywood's activity does date to the same period as Masters' activity with straw and her promotion of the industry.

In museum collections in America and England there are surviving examples of elaborate lace-like women's hats variously attributed to the seventeenth and eighteenth centuries but about which very little else has been discovered. The lace structure is made from plant fibre and is supported by a cane-like frame of fine stems. This form of straw hat would have been something quite different from hats in common circulation and would have created considerable interest.[67] Although the hat held at Hatfield House is attributed to Queen Elizabeth I, perhaps most significantly and importantly is the story of the hat held in the collection at Hereford County Museum. This is said to have belonged to Queen Anne (1665–1714) and may be associated with Thomas Foley (*c*.1670–1737) who was a member of the English parliament. He was a commissioner on the Board of Trade and then Auditor of the Imprests so would have been acutely aware of the trade to and from Bermuda. Documentation held by the Foley family stated he gave the hat to Queen Anne when she visited his house. Given his links with Bermuda and her travels, it does seem likely that their paths would have crossed at some points in their lives and there appears to be some credibility to the provenance of this one hat.

Made in the Bahamas this Harl Taylor bag incorporates a variety of plaits made on the islands.

Wolsak wrote that the Bermudian trade boom with England ended in the 1730s. However, although trade may have declined, it still existed. In 1760 the Society of Arts offered a premium of £20 for the largest quantity of Bermuda plaits, not less than one ton in weight, imported from Bermuda or the Bahamas, and in announcing another premium for a straw hat to rival the Leghorn, promised a double premium if it was made from 'Bermudan plaits.' During the 1700s 'thousands of yards of plaits' were sent to America.[68] At the Great Exhibition of 1851 an exhibit from Bermuda included palmetto braid and arrowroot which were described as the two important exports.[69] In 1862 a visitor to Bermuda wrote, 'Baskets beautifully decorated with straw leaves and flowers, are also an article of manufacture, and command a high price.'[70] The industry continued without note until around the 1930s when the work seems to have been lost. Today, the skills are being revived on the islands.

Bahamas

Straw plaiting, hat and basket making are said to have come from Bermuda to the Bahamas in 1724 when George Phenney, who was the Governor between 1721 and 1728, brought a Bermudian woman to teach the skills to the Bahamians.[71] Very little early history appears to exist, and it seems the Bahamas worked in the shadow of the Bermudan industry but continued to trade with the Carolinas. According to the organisation Creative Nassau, it was not until tourists began to visit the islands in the 1860s that the trade revived.[72] In the 1920s when cruise ships began to visit, the occupation of plaiting received a boost through the sale of hats, bags and baskets. It is claimed that during their time on the island, the Duke and Duchess of Windsor saw the need to promote and support this occupation for the islanders, seeing it as a useful source of income. The Bahamians had built the sheds and stalls in Rawson Square which form the famous Nassau Straw Market. This continues to be a tourist destination, and visitors can buy straw plaited items made on the islands thanks to the initiatives of Creative Nassau, who are planting palms, arranging workshops and supporting sellers.[73]

United States

The straw hat industry of the United States was a diverse industry where many techniques and materials were used. Starting in the first colonies on the eastern seaboard, as the first settlers moved across the continent opening new states, the skills travelled with them. Enterprises were to remain on the level of individual makers producing for personal or local use, while in New England it was to grow to a large and internationally important industry.

Palmetto and palm-leaf

Atlantic island trade brought palmetto weaving into the southern states in the late 1600s. Wolsak claimed that export of palmetto leaves from Bermuda to New England for women to make up had reached a size sufficient to warrant the introduction of laws banning export.[74] Imports spread northwards into Pennsylvania and New England. The writer of *Hats and their Manufacture*[75] stated that in 1826 the making began in Massachusetts and by 1830 their value was estimated at $10,000,000, and exports reached $500,000. In 1831 two million hats were made and sold. While making in Massachusetts may have begun at this time or at least become sufficiently significant to attract attention, it almost certainly appears to have existed in New England much earlier. In the accounts it is unclear how the workers were making the hats, whether from plaits or woven in the style of a Panama hat, since examples of both survive. As the industry grew the material was referred to as palm-leaf rather than palmetto possibly indicating imports from several places, including Cuba which is frequently mentioned in accounts. The weaving of palm leaves into hats was not exclusive to the United States, it was an established skill in Central and South America and in the Far East. In St Albans,

This palmetto hat, from about 1863, was made in Brunswick County, North Carolina by a woman who could not afford the expensive store hats.

Hertfordshire, England, there was a large trade of 'Brazilian hat making' using palm said to have come from Brazil, but probably sourced from elsewhere. The town's trade was lost to Nancy, France where similar hats were being made.

Thomas Dublin[76] has undertaken an intensive study of the outworking of the trade in Fitzwilliam, Massachusetts, detailing how the palm was handed out and paid for by the local store owner. He describes how the trade increased between the 1820s and 1850s. By the 1850s, Whittemore, the store owner who was controlling the local workers, 'employed more than 800 hatmakers who produced 80,000 hats annually.'[77] The trade spread to other towns in Massachusetts, and in neighbouring Royalston some research has been undertaken into a general and palm hat industry store opened by Franklin Gregory in the early 1800s.[78] By the 1830s the store had been taken over by Joseph Estabrook and Joseph Raymond. Surviving store records for the period 1838 to 1843 show trade in hats made by local people. As with the trade in Fitzwilliam, hats appear to have been traded for goods from the store.

Hats made in these towns were sent to the southern states and all indications were of a major industry that had spread throughout this part of the state and into neighbouring New Hampshire. In the town of Amherst, the L M Hills Company, founded in 1829, was claimed to have been the largest in Massachusetts by 1869, making about 100,000 dozen palm-leaf hats each year.[79]

There are many examples of hats made from palmetto surviving in museum and historical society collections along the eastern seaboard. They show the use of palm leaves being woven into a hat shape, being woven on a loom or made into a plait that was then stitched into a hat shape. The overall shape of the hats made from plaits tends to be similar, but the finish and trimming show a great variety which does address the social history of each hat, from its wear by plantation workers in the southern states to an item of fashion further north.

Loom-woven straw

Before examining straw plaiting it is necessary to first return to the beginning of the 1800s and look at another aspect of the straw industry. Whereas Sybilla Masters gained her patent in the name of her husband Thomas, Mary Dixon Kies was the first American woman to gain a patent in her own name. Her patent in 1809 was for the weaving of straw with silk or thread, unfortunately little more is known since her patent was one of many destroyed in the Patent Office fire that occurred in 1836.

These two samples of woven straw fabric made by Mary Kies were donated to Danielson Library Connecticut by her great-granddaughter.

Two samples of her work do survive in the collection of the Killingly Historical and Genealogical Center.[80] Killingly had an established textile weaving industry making it probable that Kies had existing knowledge of weaving, but what made her decide to adapt the process for straw may never be understood. In Europe straw was being woven into sheets with split straw forming the weft, and silk the warp. The sheets were cut into the required pattern, shaped, and stitched into a bonnet. It may have been that she was aware of these novelties and their popularity. Her invention does not appear to have been taken up with the millinery trade and in 1837 she died a pauper. Weaving of palm, chip and straw did continue throughout the 1800s, the sheets being cut to form the iconic Quaker bonnet style. A loom and samples of the loom-woven straw braids can be seen at Fruitlands Museum, Harvard, Massachusetts.

Straw plaiting

The introduction of straw plaiting to imitate the hats being imported from England and Italy appears to have begun in New England in the 1700s, but as to who may have introduced it, and where and when the introduction occurred is a matter of great speculation. The common thread for the various stories is that after some young girls had seen and been envious of an imported straw hat, they sought to copy and make it. Caroline Sloat repeated the story of Sarah Anna Emery of West Newbury, Massachusetts being the first person to have succeeded in this task but continued by acknowledging 'The histories of such towns as Framingham, Wrentham, Westborough, Norton and Mansfield trace their hat industries back to enterprising young women who mastered the craft and taught their peers.'[81] Barbara Gorely Teller built on this statement in her series of articles.[82] Elizabeth Whitney née Fay was claimed to have been plaiting straw and making hats in Westborough in the 1760s and into the 1770s. Sarah Peabody of West Newbury was said to have made hats from oat straw and taught her niece, Sarah Ann Emery née Smith to plait. At Framingham in the 1780s, 'Mrs Joseph Bennet and her daughter Betsey were making them to order before 1800.'[83] Yet another Framingham woman, Mrs Mary Rice, claimed in 1800 to have earned $340 making braid and sewing it into hats.[84] About this time, Hitty Eames was said to have taken straw from the best bed to plait. Betsey Baker née Metcalf was the most well known of all these early makers but her claim to be the first can be contested; her story is like all the others. In about 1797 or 1798 she saw a hat in the shop of Naomi Whipple and wanted to copy it, so took oat straw from her father's fields and taught herself to make a seven-end plait. She went on to share the skills with others, causing the trade to spread throughout New England in the early years of the 1800s.

Gorely Teller wrote of children also making plait with 'two yards being expected of 7-year-olds and 10 yards for 10-year-olds on non-school days. The yardage was measured by homemade yard-sticks or by hanging the braid out of an upstairs window until it reached the ground or the doorstone.' She continued by saying a woman was expected to make 20–30 yards a day, and additionally provided the information that by 1850 12 different patterns were made, some of which are on display at Framingham Historical Society, Massachusetts. The *Columbian Reporter* in January 1831 contained an advertisement: 'Straw: 250 lbs superior braiding straw this day received and for sale by Geo. Leonard, 2d. P.S. Cash or goods, at the most reduced prices given for good diamond or leghorn braid.'[85] Just as with the palm-leaf industry in the early days the straw plaiters traded their work for goods from the local store.

The interest and development occurred at a time when imports from Europe were restricted due to wars and prices were high. Europe was to continue its influence on the development of the skills for as

It has not been fully established how diverse and significant straw loom weaving was in New England. Narrow loom-woven braids were made in Massachusetts hat factories and the weaving of bonnets and other products continued in the Shaker communities into the 1900s.

long as a demand for hats continued. The growing trade began to attract some concern since women were earning reasonable amounts and becoming independent. In 1825 an essay was published which warned of the dangers of straw plaiting.[86] Its subtitle was, 'An historical account of the introduction of the manufacture, its effect upon the Employments, Dress, Food, Health, Morals, Social Intercourse, &c. of the inhabitants of the several Towns in which it has been carried on; with Moral, Political and Miscellaneous Remarks.' This title set the tone for the judgement contained within, despite the author acknowledging that in 1804 the ladies of Wrentham used the income from the bonnets they had made to purchase an 'elegant organ' for their Congregational Society. The footnote stated that in 1823 the organ was moved from its 'proper and conspicuous place' and taken to one of the back pews where it stands as a 'monument of industry and enterprise as well as of vanity and folly.'

Imitation Leghorn

Sophia Welles née Woodhouse of Wethersfield, Connecticut (1799–1883) was another enterprising straw worker. Influenced by the fine Italian straw and the method of stitching the plait together edge to edge, she rose to prominence when in 1819 and again in 1820 she won a prize for her grass bonnet at the Hartford County Society for Promoting Agriculture and Domestic Manufactures. Using grass that grew locally she prepared and plaited it, then sewed it together edge to edge to create an illusion that the bonnet was made from a continuous sheet of straw. Only a slight ridge indicated where the plait was joined to form the hat. Since the Society of Arts in London were offering premiums for the best imitations of Leghorn hats, Woodhouse sent samples with an explanation of her work. The committee reported that they 'received with pleasure communication from Miss Woodhouse, the daughter of a farmer residing at Weathersfield in the State of Connecticut, stating she had manufactured some bonnets in imitation of Leghorn, from the stems of a species of grass growing spontaneously in that part of the United States, and popularly known by the name of Ticklemoth.' It continued by saying she has sent a bonnet and 'dried specimens of the entire grass', accompanied by a certification to confirm they were genuine signed by a Hartford Justice of Peace. The judges concluded the bonnet was superior to Leghorn in its fineness and colour. They awarded her a 'Large Silver Medal and Twenty Guineas', on the condition that she would supply the committee with seed and knowledge of the processes she used to bleach the straw. In December 1821 she wrote to the committee explaining the growing season was past, but she was sending some grass from the last growing season. She pointed out that she was unable to send much seed since the grass was not propagated, it just grew wild.[87] Interestingly, although the Society of Arts Transactions stated that the grass was ticklemoth, other accounts said it was spear grass or red top. In 1824 two farmers in Winslow, Buckinghamshire, England were awarded a premium of 20 guineas by the Society of Arts for growing a crop of ticklemoth grass from seed collected in Connecticut in 1822. The seed produced from the project was sent to 'our friends on the continent.'[88] This enterprise may have been instigated by the work and promotion of William Cobbett whose son James was in New York. William sent him to visit Woodhouse to learn more about her techniques and to collect seed. James sent back a sample of grass and plait and Cobbett identified the grass as Poa Pratensis. In a long article in the American Farmer, 1824, the manufacture of grass bonnets was discussed at length and the author concluded ticklemoth was Agrostis Alba, which is now identified as *Agrostis gigantea*, black bent or redtop.

Not only was her work drawing attention in London, one of Sophia's hats was sent to the wife of John Quincy Adams, then President of the United States, who remarked it was 'an extraordinary specimen of American Manufacture.'[89] Another hat was sent to Dolley Madison, wife of President James Madison. With her husband Gurdon Welles[90], Sophia was granted a patent on 29 December 1821 for her 'new and useful improvement in the manufacture of Grass bonnets and hats.'[91] She went on to set up a workshop for the manufacture of straw hats and employed local Wethersfield women. One, Marie Francis, produced three hundred bonnets in one summer.[92] Following a fire Sophia closed her business in 1835.

Lucy Burnup was granted a patent in February 1823 for 'Hats, weaving grass.' Usually referred to as the Burnap sisters of Merrimack, New Hampshire they rose to some prominence for selling their Leghorn bonnets for $40–50. There was some competition with the Connecticut makers, since in 1821 their hats made from local grasses were said to be 'very superior to the one lately sent to England from Connecticut.'[93]

The *New England Farmer*, 1824, included an article[94] which quoted from the *National Gazette of Philadelphia*: 'It is stated, that in the counties of Worcester, Middlesex, Norfolk and Bristol, Massachusetts, there have been manufactured about 300,000 bonnets in a year, at an average of $2.75 per bonnet, amounting to $825,000, employing 25,000 persons, most of whom were females from the ages of four to twenty years. Those employed in plaiting straw have been able to support themselves, and in many instances, to assist those of their immediate family.' The report did not state if all the bonnets were made from local plait but did continue by identifying the real threat posed by the importation of hats from Italy 'at all prices.' A plea to restrict the trade was made to Congress but rejected. One of the clauses of the appeal was to cite the imposition of the restrictive import taxes levied by the British on American hats and bonnets. The British Government's argument was that in the year ending 5 April 1823, 176,045 American hats and bonnets and 3,512 lbs of straw plait were imported. It was feared that trade with England would never be restored. It seems that following the American Civil War the manufacture of straw plaits was almost lost. Hat production became confined to large factories that were supplied with imported plaits from the Far East and Europe.

Canada

The USA and Canada appear to be closely linked by the manufacture of the Mackinaw hat. Although little is now known or understood about this type of straw hat, from the 1850s into the early 1900s it attracted a large proportion of the North American hat trade. In the early years of its introduction the plaits were made up in Framingham, Massachusetts, however, manufacture also appears to be closely associated with Baltimore, Maryland.

The most detailed information appears in William Tufts Brigham's book, *Baltimore Hats Past and Present*[95] where he wrote it was previously known as the Canada hat being made in 'lower or eastern Canada.' This hat was considered low quality. Both the Canada and Mackinaw hats are made from plaited wheat straw grown in Michigan and in the lands reaching into Canada, and the best quality Mackinaw plaits were said to come from the Lousseux family. The popularity of these hats, and their move away from being a country, harvest-time hat appears to have occurred in the 1830s with sales gradually increasing until the 1870s when they were also sold extensively throughout the state of New York. In November 1914, The *Hatters' Gazette* drew on information contained in Brigham's book whilst adding an additional broader trade insight. It added that the success of the Mackinaw hat transformed the fortunes of Baltimore. The *Hatters' Gazette* reported that the Mackinaw hat 'transformed the erstwhile sleepy little hamlet of Baltimore into the great city that it is today. So much for the power of

Made by Rachel McLeod for a 1927 Women's Institute exhibition, this straw hat was entered as a 'Thrift Exhibit' but was not accepted as the judges did not believe it had been made at home by Rachel using straw grown on the family farm. The straw was dyed red but that has faded and was split using the tool shown on page 103.

the hat!'[96] One Baltimore hat manufacturer said that in the year 1872–3 he sold upwards of 9,000 hats. The same manufacturer, R J Taylor was quoted as saying the Mackinaw had been sold to the exclusion of all other straw hats for 30 consecutive seasons with no reduction of popularity.

The same report stated that the name Mackinaw is a trade name rather than providing any indication of its place of origin, and claimed that the name was probably not in common use until after 1855. It confirmed the information from Brigham's book that the Canada hat was inferior to the Mackinaw, and the latter name was used to represent superior quality suitable for 'genteel wear.' One reason for this difference was the source of wheat. That of the eastern provinces was of poor quality and colour while that from the western areas 'was clear and white in colour, possessing a brilliant enamel which imparted a beauty that rendered the Mackinaw so famous. . .' Information as to what the Mackinaw plait may have been is found in a photograph in the *Hatters' Gazette* where it is included in a group of plaits. The pattern shown is a folded edge four-end plait of what appears to be whole straw.[97] The description provided in the article called the plait 'supple and light' but then created great confusion by claiming it was originally a product of central America which contradicted all other information. It also stated that the plait was now made in Japan and used for boaters and soft hats in the Panama style.[98] Various types of four-end plait were made in Japan, but there is currently no indication that any were called Mackinaw plait and it is unclear as to whether the pattern shown was the only one used or if it was one of many.

Apart from the limited information about the Canada and Mackinaw hat, there is currently little evidence about any more general organisation of straw plaiting and hat making in Canada. Plaiting appears to have supplied local areas rather than an industry organised for export, except for the Canada and Mackinaw hat trade.

To date, most available information suggests limited straw plaiting and hat making in Nova Scotia. The county of Lunenburg was a centre of straw plaiting and hat making so it is perhaps not surprising to learn that the first immigrants arriving in the mid-1700s were from Germany and Switzerland, two established plaiting areas. In her book *Handwoven Hats*, Joleen Gordon cites a reference from 1830 which stated that the new Scottish settlers were wearing hats made from native straw plaited by their children.[99] The hats were made of wood chip and of locally grown rye straw, but production remained limited, not reaching any size until the 1850s when a display of grass bonnets and hats was exhibited at the 1851 Great Exhibition in London. They featured amongst a wide range of items from Nova Scotia.[100] Hats and bonnets made from native grasses were submitted for awards at international and regional exhibitions during the later 1850s and 1860s at which time they won various awards. The two women mentioned in these enterprises were Mrs Ann Begg of Onslow and Eleanor Turner of Shubenacadie. Later, while others took up the challenge, by the 1890s straw plaiting and hat making appears to have disappeared.[101]

The interconnection of European straw industries is beautifully shown in these women's shoes made for indoor wear. They date from the 1840s. The uppers are made using Italian plait and they are trimmed with Swiss loom-woven products. (CTLC 1c/19/28)

CHAPTER
THREE

STRAW PLAITING IN EUROPE

There are undoubtedly more stories to reveal from sources of undiscovered information about the European industries, but the loose terminology used to describe products and techniques, combined with translation into English, creates challenges. What has been uncovered raises awareness of lost or barely surviving industries whose true size, scope and output may never be fully appreciated. This chapter does not attempt to provide a complete account of all European histories, that information awaits discovery by future scholars.

Italy

Italy is perhaps the oldest centre of straw plaiting and possibly the greatest influence on the early straw industry in Britain and many other countries. One writer indicated that as early as the 1600s a small quantity of hats originating from the town of Signa were imported into England through the port of Livorno, known by the English as Leghorn.[102] Signa grew into an important centre of straw plaiting and hat production during the 1700s.[103] The industry's development was complex with frequent impositions of import duties and wars badly affecting trade in different periods.

A report in the British Government's Colonial Office Blue Book written by Consul-General Colnaghi[104] provides a fascinating and detailed account of the Italian straw hat industry. He stated that although by 1575 a Corporation of Merchants of Straw Hats in Florence was recorded, the industry only began to flourish at the beginning of the 1700s when Domenico Michelacci 'introduced or perfected the culture of spring wheat "grano marzuola" sown thickly.' Shortly after 1714 the first experiments took place around Signa. Michelacci was also claimed to be the first person to establish an export trade with England, and by 1731 had opened a factory in Signa. A document from 1757 stated that the export of hats to England provided the Tuscan Grand Duchy with a profit of 70,000 scudi. By 1771 profits had risen to 100,000 although it is not clear if this is only for exports to England.[105]

Not only were the English good customers from the earliest times, but Thomas Vyse was also one of the first traders to introduce the Leghorn hats into London around 1804, and then set up business in Florence in 1827, possibly Brozzi. In about 1845 he opened a second branch in Prato. The endeavours of Thomas Vyse brought fresh impetus to the trade.[106] *The Anglo-Florentines* by Diana and Tony Webb investigated in detail the Vyse family's part in the Italian hat industry.

In 1810 Guiseppe Carbonari of Leghorn established himself in Signa, to the northwest of Florence. He introduced a new wide-brim hat, a *fioretti*, that became extremely popular throughout Europe. While continuing to trade with England he also set up commerce with France and Germany. Between 1816–18, his enterprise caused the industry to spread to Brozzi, Sesto, Campi, Carmignano, Pistoia and Prato.[107] In 1818 40,000 women and girls were employed in the trade until a rise in orders from England between 1819 and 1822 increased employment to 60,000. He began an export trade to America in 1822 which raised the number to 80,000. The plaiting districts grew, and new villages were built to cope with the influx of workers.[108] Plaiters earned relatively high wages and there was prosperity in the region. By comparison, in 1861, which was considered the peak of employment in England and Wales, it was recorded that 30,235 people were employed as plaiters.[109] Carbonari remained in business until 1828.

Import duties and restrictions on exports caused peaks and troughs in the trade. This was particularly apparent at the time of the Napoleonic Wars, when attempts at tax avoidance encouraged smugglers to conceal hats under their clothes or wear several tightly stacked so they appeared as a single hat. The fineness of the Italian product was due to the straw and method of construction, stitching together edge to edge. The hat appeared as one piece with the only indication of the stitching being a slight ridge at each join. This process was described in the trade journals as knitted straw. The plait was stitched either into a small cone shape or into a flat shape. The flat shape was a large circle of the stitched plait. To make a bonnet, one flat was cut in half and then stitched to a hood. By 1827 both fashion and competition created a need for change. The eleven-end plait introduced by Thomas Vyse and sewn into a hat by overlapping, became a staple product of the Italian industry for several years.

Other Italian centres

In the province of Bologna (Emilia-Romagna region), probably from about 1780 they began to make plaits and by the early 1800s produced thirteen-end and seven-end plaits made from locally grown and prepared straw. The town of Monghidoro was the centre for local production with at least one factory producing a range of straw articles. The 1899 statistics for the province of Bologna indicated that there were 3,000 plaiters who worked for an average of 200 days a year. In nearby villages there were 3,360 plaiters who worked on average 190 days a year.[110] Accounts suggest the plaits being made in this area were coarser than those made around Florence so were called *pedal*, to differentiate them from the fine *punte* straw of other villages.

Marostica in the region of Veneto is another important area which produced a range of products. As with Monghidoro their products were sent to Florence and then exported. Information provided by the Ecomuseo sulla lavorazione della paglia (Ecomueum for Straw Working) in Marostica stated that straw plaiting began in 1667 and by 1840 about 3,000 workers produced 704,000 pieces, or hanks of plait. One reference claimed that a seven-end plait as narrow as 3 mm was made here. Their local speciality was the *capotte*, a straw hood, and exports from this area to New York began in 1850.

Located on the eastern side of Italy in the Marche region, the towns of Montappone, Falerone, Massa Fermana, Monte Vidon and Corrado are less well documented. Claims were made that an industry was established before the 1800s, but I have not found

Thought to have belonged to Sarah Handforth who was from a Cheshire farming community, this bonnet from around 1835 is made from Tuscan straw plait. It will never be possible to know if the plait was made in Italy or Great Britain. (CTLC 33/61)

supporting evidence. What is clear is that plaiting and hat manufacturing was well established by the 1850s; however, available statistics only refer to hat making which continues in the towns today.

Export of straw

An aspect of the Italian trade which has remained relatively hidden is the production of plaiting straw for export. Following the Italian successes including the growth of an export market to America, the English virtually stopped buying hats and increased their purchase of straw. This coincided with various moves to produce 'English Leghorn' to compete with the Italian product. This enterprise avoided the associated import costs and was easier for English companies to control. Seeing the British success, and instead of importing hats, the Germans, French, Swiss and Americans began to purchase straw.[111] Olivia Rucellai wrote in her book that the town of Empoli exported half its straw, and of the other half one-third was exported as plait and two-thirds as hats.[112] Dony collated official British trade returns which is assumed to include imports of straw from Italy.[113] In 1827 £435 was imported rising to £6,050 in 1829 and in 1836 nearly £500,000. Statistics indicate that enterprising Luton traders had seen an import/export opportunity and were re-exporting.

Switzerland

This innovative industry had centres in the Onsernone valley (canton Ticino), the Rafzerfeld (canton Zürich), Gruyères (canton Fribourg), Seetal (within the cantons Aargau and Luzern) and the Freiamt (canton Aargau). Supplied with products from the other areas, Wohlen (Aargauer Freiamt region) was the historic centre and became of worldwide importance.

Onsernone, canton Ticino

This canton, founded in 1803 being on the southern border of Switzerland, has a long association with Italy's northern regions. This geographic closeness may explain why a straw industry was introduced in the 1500s as an alternative occupation to farming. There was a pattern of permanent and seasonal migration to Piedmont, Lombardy, Florence and Flanders, where locally made hats, bags and baskets were sold in the 1600s.[114] Growth is indicated by the account that in 1757 four traders from the village of Loco, accompanied by 44 porters, were caught trying to smuggle 10,000 hats into Italy.[115]

Villagers worked rye straw into a variety of whole straw plaits but there seems to be no evidence of split straw plait production. Giovanni Bianconi wrote that in winter, both for company and to save on heating and lighting, the villagers would come together in one room to plait. He also claimed that in 1870, twelve million metres of plaits were made at a price of two francs per 100 metres, a length that could be made by two very skilled people in one day. To make even a simple plait using thick straws would entail long hours of work.

Gruyères, canton Fribourg

Development within this relatively small region may have been associated with the growth of the Aargovian industry as links between the two were recorded in 1815. Much of the work from this region, as of that from Onsernone, remained largely unrecognised since Wohlen traders placed the samples in sales books without reference to their origins.

The first hatmaker in the area who is said to have come from or to be associated with the Alsace, was recorded in 1769.[116] However, another story claimed that in the late 1700s, a woman called Anna Raemy from the village of Planfayon,[117] needed but could not afford a new basket so made her own from straw plaits, causing the introduction of an industry.[118] The 1811 cantonal census listed 25 merchants and 25 hatters. By 1842 the cantonal census recorded 515 plaiters in the villages of Vaudens, LaRoche, Avry, Vuippens and Cerniet, where 384 of the total number lived. Between 1860–80 the number grows from 1,000 to 1,300. Such was the importance of straw plaiting that, in 1888, a vocational school to teach and train plaiters to make many types of straw products was established.

Dyed straw was introduced in the 1830s, leading to the making of split and whole straw speckled patterns alongside the natural and single colour plaits already produced.[119] By the 1850s various plaiting materials were combined to create new patterns.[120]

Made for the Exposition Universelle of 1855 in Paris, this table cover which was exhibited and won a medal, shows the ingenuity and skills of straw workers in canton Aargau.

At the height of the industry villages to the south of Gruyères became established as a plaiting area. Two villages within the Pays-d'Enhaut probably developed as plaiting centres early in the 1800s with the majority of plaiters living and working in Château d'Oex and Rougement. This was a poor area so the prosperous work of plaiting must have been an attractive option.[121]

Wohlen, canton Aargau

The medieval origins of the industry are often attributed to the return of Swiss mercenary soldiers from Italy. In 1593, the Zurich barbers were reassured of their rights to manufacture plaited straw hats, but by 1660 they appear to perceived a threat. Villagers from Hägglingen and Dottikon, through their administrative centre of Bremgarten, which were hat making villages close to Wohlen, sent a petition to the bailiff of Zurich pleading for them to be allowed to sell their hats in the city. In 1744 Wohlen was firmly established and by 1786 salesmen were sent out to neighbouring countries. During the 1800s they were travelling extensively throughout Europe, Great Britain, America and Russia. Peter Isler of Wohlen was granted a passport to Germany and the 'pre-Austrian lands' to carry out his business in the straw plait trade for six months. An account book from the joint company of Wohler, Bruggisser, Isler showed trade primarily with Paris, but also with Hamburg, Dresden, Berlin and Bremen, as well as with Leipzig and Vienna in 1815. In 1812 an order of 293 dozen hats was sent to Paris.[122] The hats were made of plaits described as seven-end, ring, saw plait, bögli, spitzli, mirror plait and four hälmigs.[123] While some were widely known, others made from split straws must have been novel and exciting for the fashion trade. Researchers have surmised that inspiration for these products came from passementerie embellishments produced in France as there are similarities.

The Swiss researcher Gottlieb Rodel in his book, *Die Strohindustrie*,[124] provided accounts of individual villages detailing the companies and products made in each. It shows just how diverse and integrated into the area the straw trade had become. Rapid growth in the Rafzerfeld and Freiamt lead to the introduction of plaiting schools thanks to a collaboration between the Isler company and Pastor Alois Röthelin. Although other schools had been opened in Fribourg in 1816, Berne in 1820 and Luzern in 1838,[125] three schools, or trading houses, in Niederschongau, Oberschongau and Ruedikon/Metmenschongau were organised with a list of 16 rules intended to ensure good morals and order.[126] The schools were for girls of all ages, but only for boys under the age of 14 and they were not for school-age children when the normal village school was open. Rule eight stated that a daily school prayer would be said morning and evening, and decent songs would be sung throughout the day. Students were required to be as clean as possible 'both in their bodies and their suits.' 'Everyone should endeavour to keep the plait clean and to make beautiful plait, taking as much care as possible with the plaiting material and not throwing the useless under the table or chairs but laying them neatly aside.'

Repeated concerns expressed inferiority of rye straw due to its colour, and the belief was that rye could not compete with the beautiful wheat plaits from Belgium, Saxony, Italy and England. A quickly implemented solution was to use a black dye made from logwood and galls in 1810 and this led to the introduction of dyeworks in 1833. By the 1840s the trade expanded from Wohlen to neighbouring towns in the area, but rye straw did not take pale colours successfully and so the suggestion was made to urge local farmers to grow wheat. At Bremgarten these encouragements fell on deaf ears, and the farmers' refusal was met with dismay, possibly because traders foresaw the need to import straw. They imported Italian straws and later, when prices permitted, wheat straws from England.

Concern about importing supplies and competition with other centres perhaps encouraged the industry leaders to begin to use new materials. Manila hemp was the first imported material to be introduced, arriving early in the 1820s and by 1829 it was being made into a product called 'hanf patent', which was a woven tape or sheet then plaited. Loom-made braids or bordüres were introduced in about 1820; made using straw, silk, cotton and horsehair, they became a staple product of the industry. During the 1830s horsehair was introduced by Augustus Bell of Luzern, who, inspired by hair-work, used the horse tail to make tubular braids on a hand-operated braiding machine. He later produced bordüres. In the 1840s a family in the Rafzerfeld possibly introduced the most ingenious product, a two-ply straw thread called Schnürli or Drähtli. They were perfectly suited to rye straw and could be used in a myriad of products. Finally, the companies had found a range of products that resolved their long-held concerns.

Germany

An 1897 article in the *Hatters' Gazette*[127] stated that straw plaiting was introduced from provinces of the Austrian Empire. First into Bohemia, then spreading northwards across the border with Germany to Saxony until by the 1500s plaiting was prevalent in a large area of the southern edges of Saxony. Several stories, including that of its introduction during the 1600s into Lindenberg in the Allgäu region of Bavaria, claimed that the industry arrived from Italy via Austria and into Germany through horse dealers who learned the skills in Italy and introduced them on their return.[128]

In the 1700s a Saxon industry was established around Pirna and Dohna, southeast of Dresden spreading to the Erzgebirge (Ore Mountains) region and along the border of Northern Bohemia, now part of Czechia. The export trade of Saxon straw plaits to foreign competitors became detrimental to the hat making areas, leading in 1748 to the issue of a royal warrant.[129] The export of finished straw hats produced in Saxony was more profitable than the export of straw plaits. The exportation of plaits was therefore a threat to prosperity, as they were not then available to the hat makers.

Growth in the 1800s

From the 1700s straw plaiting supplemented family income in the Saxon areas from other sources of work such as mining, agriculture and the making of wooden toys and decorations. The seasonal nature of agriculture and uncertainty of mining meant the economic importance of other activities such as wood and straw work might compensate for income fluctuations. Later in the 1700s as mining declined in the Erzgebirge, the straw industry became increasingly important with communities organising themselves into 'plaiting villages' or 'sewing villages' where the hats and bonnets were made. Dealers visited villages to collect finished work that was taken to the nearby sewing villages, or to the manufacturers in Dresden. In the 1800s it was estimated there were about 50 Saxon villages with about 5,000 workers and by the end of the 1800s the number had risen to about 150 villages employing 10,000 workers.[130]

Children began to learn to plait from about three years old, but what is quite different from the British system is that official plaiting schools were organised in the main plaiting villages. A *Hatters' Gazette* article[131] stated that the 'committee for the advancement of home industries' established the first schools in northern Czechia, such as in a village now known as Cinovece or BöhmischZinnwald, which is to the south of the Saxon town of Altenberg, and Vysoké nad Jizerou, formerly known as Hochstadt, which is about 100 miles to the east of Zinnwald. This organised and better regulated school system ensured the production of high-quality plait. Straw plaiting schools existed in Saxony from around 1830 until 1910.

This willow, rush and plait basket was purchased in Berne, Switzerland but may have been made in the Black Forest in the late 1800s. The originally blue dye has faded to purple on both the willow and speckled straw plait.

Workers in the Erzgebirge were described as 'simply cottage workers, and the management of the whole industry lays in the hands of the dealers.' Some plaiters sold to the local shopkeeper or innkeeper who acted as the middleman, while others sold to what are described as 'itinerant buyers of restricted means' who wandered from house to house. Dealers working for larger companies were mainly located in the towns of Geising and Altenberg and visited the plaiting villages at the beginning of the season. The *Hatters' Gazette* article stated that the number of plaiters located in Saxony and Bohemia 'may be safely estimated as 20,000 to 30,000, mainly women who have begun as children and continue plaiting until their old age.' The height of the plaiting season was October until Christmas which was the time of highest earnings since work had to be ready for export and delivery to America. The workers came together to work in a single room called a 'Rockenstube' to share the light and heat, and, the article stated, may work from 'early dawn until late at night, often indeed, until midnight, or even till 2 a.m.' Work continued in the villages throughout the year, although the price achieved for plait tended to drop off later in the season.

The German straw industry had always produced a diverse range of products, and workers in Lindenberg im Allgäu and nearby Heimenkirch began production of what they called Drohdelschnüre, or straw strings for the Wohlen trade. By 1853 it was reported that almost everyone in the towns was producing these threads to the detriment of hat production. An account said that 'everyone is drohdeling.'[132]

Black Forest

The Black Forest was another centre of straw industry that seems to have attracted attention in England. A long account in *All Year Round* reflected on Alois Faller and Mathäe Tritzcheller, who it claimed were the founders of straw hat making and straw plaiting, and their trade links between Lenzkirch and Italy.[133] Another article about the Black Forest industry appeared in *Girl's Own Paper*[134] and was then repeated in the *Hatters' Gazette*. The worthy and flowery article provided an account of the life of girls in the Black Forest where they were taught needlework, embroidery, knitting and straw plaiting alongside more formal education. It claimed that straw plaiting was introduced into Triberg in 1694 when glassworkers brought with them a straw hat from Switzerland. In 1826 more than 1,500 women in Triberg were straw plaiters and according to the article the number had increased to 6,000 in 1885. The *Hatters' Gazette*[135] published a second article which stated that straw plaiting was in 'the Gutach Valley of Triberg, and Hornberg, extending as far down as Hausach' and claimed various types of straw were being plaited. It named 'Italian straw, rice straw from Italy and Southern Europe, the beautiful Panama fibre of the ribbed leaf of the Bombomaxa (Luduvica Palmata), the Guayaquil grass, the Pitta, and other similar materials, and the Bast or inside bark of the linden and other trees have been introduced and manufactured into hats, cigar cases, bags, satchels, and other braided articles.' It continued by saying that many a Panama hat, supposed to be real, had been made in the Black Forest.

North Germany

The town of Twistringen to the southwest of Bremen was another centre of straw hat making. Straw plaiting was established in the mid 1700s and by the middle of the 1830s 25 to 30% of the town's population were plaiting straw. Their straw industry was to diversify in many novel directions including the mass production of a straw sleeve for bottles, and drinking straws made from natural straw.[136] The *Hatters' Gazette* stated that this was also an English trade where the straw or 'pipe that is unsuitable for plaiting is exported in large quantities to America for cocktail straws.'[137]

The Low Countries and France

In Belgium legend states that in the Middle Ages the landlord from the village of Glons returned from a pilgrimage to Rome bringing with him a straw hat and introduced a local industry. Two iconic paintings from the 1400s confirm links between Italy and the Low Countries. Art historians studying Pisanello's *The Virgin and Child with Saints* (circa 1440),[138] which clearly depicts Saint George wearing a plaited straw hat, have discovered documents indicating that straw hats were in fashion at that time and known in Italy as Flemish hats.[139] Furthermore, *Portrait of Giovanni Arnolfini and his Wife*, painted by Jan van Eyck[140] (1435), reveals that Arnolfini's dramatic black hat is made from plait. It has been established that Arnolfini was an Italian working in Bruges. While it is unclear if the hats were made in Flanders or Italy, it may be possible that an already established industry was of sufficient importance to merit mention in the later Liege charter of 1453. The city's charter lists plaiting in the villages of Wonck, Bassenge, Roclenge, Glons and Elmaille as well as others along the river Geer.

A priest, Ervard Ramoux, was appointed to the village of Glons in 1784 which was at that time the centre of the straw plaiting industry. With the help of Nicholas Delvenne, the village school master, it was claimed that Ramoux transformed the fortunes of the area and promoted the industry of straw hat making. The joint efforts enabled local development that spread to other parts of Belgium, Holland, northern Germany and France.

A *Hatters' Gazette* article[141] stated that in 1880 it was estimated some 40,000 people were involved in

Made from fine Belgian spilt plait, the bonnet's silk ribbons are held in place with pins. It is lined with plain blue silk and dates from about 1815. (CTLC 2018/36/1)

straw plaiting, and there were no less than 6,000 hat sewers generating an annual income of four million francs. At the time of the article, the village of Roclenge was said to be the centre of the industry, however its proximity to the other villages should be noted.

Surviving evidence shows that the women and children plaited a variety of patterns using either whole or split straw. They were carried to the manufacturer each week and the price achieved was subject to supply and demand, just as in other plait markets. The 'workmen' were often paid in coffee, rice and other articles rather than money, which was observed as being fairly administered by the larger manufacturers, but was sometimes used as a means of suppression.

There were complaints of short measure of the finished lengths which was a problem also commonly noted in other plaiting centres throughout the 1800s. Principal manufacturers held a congress and agreed that plaits of nine to ten straws would be sold in 56-metre lengths, comprising two pieces each of 28 metres. Plaits of 11 and 15 straws would be sold as a 12-metre length. White or coloured plaits 'which are subject to contraction' would have a deduction of 4% allowed. A short account in the October issue of the 1885 *Hatters' Gazette* stated that in the valley of the Geer, while the women made the fine plaits and the children the coarse plaits, the older men clipped the ends and prepared the plaits. The younger men stitched the plait into hats and in January some four or five thousand men travelled to Germany, Holland and France where they worked to make hats.[142]

The extent of export rather than production for home consumption may be inferred in 1896 when a local parliamentary representative complained that the industry of the Vallée du Geer was mostly ignored in Brussels and Liège, but attracted customers from England, Holland, France, Italy and America.[143] What must have been an influential centre within the hat industry embraced the making of machine-made braids at the beginning of the 1900s, but after the First World War, [144] straw plaiting disappeared, and hat manufacture was affected.

Development in France

While France had a large hat manufacturing and millinery industry, straw plaiting does not appear to have been organised. John Dony stated that in 1792 there was a centre in Septfonds, in the Garonne valley near Toulouse.[145] Popular legend said that the industry was founded around 1818 by Pétronille Cantecor who was married to a Septfonds man. She and her husband set up a hat making business and commissioned local people to make straw plaits. Some versions of the story say that the first hat was made from rushes to be worn by horses. In 1796 she registered with the local Chamber of Trades presumably indicating her company was of some importance in the area. Her family continued the trade and in the first half of the 1800s were sending hats to Lyon, Nancy, Grenoble as well as Britain.[146] It appears that the local plaits were rather coarse and the hat making industry grew throughout the 1800s by relying on the import of plaits from Italy, Belgium and Switzerland rather than from the assistance of locally made plaits.[147] Three, five, seven, nine and eleven-end plaits were made in the area and taken for sale to a market at Puylaroque to the north of Septfonds. Plaiting continued well into the 1900s with both wheat and rye straw grown for the purpose. Today there are still a few plaiters working for personal satisfaction rather than commercial enterprise.

Centres of straw plaiting in the twenty-first century

Even the mighty world-dominating commercial plaiting industry of China is in decline as costs and hat production changes. There are a few centres in Europe operating on a low-scale local commercial production and these are noted in the following sections.

The Iberian Peninsula

The *Hatters' Gazette* published a short account of the Spanish palm-leaf hat industry including the statistics that between three and four million hats were exported to New York in 1904. The work was in southern Spain and it was stated that 'thousands of families, from grandfather to children, not yet in their teens, are from January to December engaged in working the palm into shape.'[148] This appears to indicate that the hats were woven into hoods or capelines rather than of plaits, and that the workers seemed to be bringing their finished hats to Malaga.

A traditional women's hat is still plaited, sewn and finished in the Cáceres province, in the Extremadura in western Spain. Workers in the town of Montehermosa continue to make a spectacular hat that local historians[149] believe did not appear until around 1888 and grew in popularity in the twentieth century. The plaiters use rye straw grown locally that is prepared, then plaited into a seven-end plait which is used to create the hat body. Lengths of two-straw plaits are used alongside woollen pompoms, mirrors, beads and fabric to trim the hat. The wearing of the hat and its making were described by Ruth Matilda Anderson who watched the maker Señora Máxima use three types of plaits: *trenza* (seven-end), *picado* (rustic) and *cordon* (cordinette).[150]

Straw hats of a local traditional style are also made in and around Ávila, Castilla y León where local people are keeping the skills alive. The hat features highly elaborate trimmings but is less colourful than that of Montehermosa since only natural coloured straw trimmings are added. The features of this hat are the coils of split straw set around the side of the high square crown. A two-straw plait arranged in decorative patterns decorates the wide brim of a hat body made from plaits.

In Portugal, a small industry survives in the region of Braga where attempts are being made in the towns of Golães and Fafe to teach and pass on the information.[151] One account says a variety of plait patterns are still made. When visiting Fabrica de Chapeus, a maker of the famous Madeiran straw boater in St Maria, Funchal in 2015, I was told that they were still using plaits made in Fafe. In the workroom there was a stack of many long hanks, each probably 20 metres long, which were said to have been made in 2012 and 2013.

Romania

There are snippets of information and occasional memories of people in the hat making districts that there was an organised straw hat industry in the early 1900s, with companies using local and imported straw plaits. Today straw plaiting survives in Romania within the northwest and central areas which villagers refer to as Transylvania. Here straw plaiting and hat making are found in the counties of Mures, Harghita and Cluj. In the first years of the twenty-first century wood chip plait was being produced in villages around Brasov. However chip plaits made from poplar wood are now principally made in Maramureş. Various types of wheat straw are used for plaiting in Transylvanian villages, and when I visited in 1999 there were six patterns being made in large quantities: the seven, the eleven, the Rece also known as lace or soldier's lace which is a four-end rustic plait, the Lyukas, the batwing and an open-ventilated plait.[152] A round spiral plait made using either five or six ends is used as a hat band. The hats, mainly men's hats, are produced to supply local demand which is declining as baseball caps are preferred over traditional styles.

Possibly made in the 1960s, this hat may originate from Castilla y León. Now in a fragile condition, the seven-end and four-end rustic plait hat is trimmed with split straw curls, two-end plait, coloured paper now faded and a circular mirror placed centre front. (CTLC 2015/150)

In an attempt to earn a living, plaiters and hat sewers turned to making decorative objects such as this diorama. The man plays a violin while the dog jumps up. The maker used imported scraps of plait and braid alongside locally made plait. (CTLC L/12/37)

CHAPTER FOUR

THE DECLINE OF THE STRAW PLAITING INDUSTRY

The causes of the decline are complex and cannot be attributed to just one change in the trade, it was a combination of many events leading to an evolution. It has often been stated that cheap imports from the Far East brought about the end of the straw hat industry, but they created quite a contrary result: they began the demise of straw plaiters but ensured growth and prosperity for hat manufacturers. In the movement towards free trade, import duties imposed in the early years of the century were gradually reduced, being finally repealed in 1861 which coincided with a widespread adoption of new hat production machinery.

Chinese straw plait

Chinese plaits were first imported into Great Britain during the 1850s; however, for reasons that are currently unclear, the Board of Trade Returns indicated that these imports into Britain were not successful. Chinese plaits were however being imported successfully into America at this time. By 1870 import levels were significant and hat manufacturers were delighted by the quality and colour of the plaits. A representative of Munt, Brown and Co., London said that 'One advantage of the moderate price the Chinese plait is offered is that in cheapening the cost of straw hats it encourages and secures a larger demand, thus benefitting the hat trade in general.'[153] The delight was not to continue for long since in March 1874 a trade report said that 'The demand for Canton plaits has fallen off considerably: without crimping it looks very plain and heavy, the colour being bad when compared with English straw; its use for ladies hats will be very limited.'[154]

The first imported Chinese plait was known as Canton,[155] named after the Chinese port of export rather than the areas of the manufacturing villages. There were several plaiting centres over 1,000 miles north of Canton in the provinces of Shandong, Henan, Hebei and Shanxi.[156] In hat trade market reports, the imported plaits' sizes, qualities and prices arriving from various ports were published. The provinces where the straw was being plaited were agricultural, producing mainly cereal crops.

Of them, Shandong was the most important region, with German financiers building a railway to connect inland Shandong with the port of Tsingtao.[157] This move caused export to increase until it became more important than Chefoo[158] which stopped exporting plaits in 1914. Shanghai and Canton, both British ports, continued their importance.

Deanie Neuhofer, a textile enthusiast, knew of my research and was so excited to see straw plaiters during a visit to the Dali Yunnan province in 1989 that she sent me a photograph. They are making a seven-end plait.

Since it was the only occupation in many areas – other than growing cereal crops – plaiting carried on throughout the year. Work only stopped for a few weeks while the harvest was gathered. A report written in 1908 said that the best plaits were made in the spring, summer and autumn when the climate was moist. During the winter the air was extremely dry, the low temperatures were believed to be detrimental to the quality of plaits, and the fires in the plaiters' homes were said to damage the plaits by marking them with smuts.[159] 'Men, women, and children, are engaged in plaiting. Hardly a villager can be seen without his bundle of straw under his arm walking about the streets or sitting upon the door-step.' These are almost identical words to those used when describing the English plaiters. In the province of Shandong, the region of Laichow[160] had a reputation for producing the best quality plaits and within today's hat industry some types of Chinese plait are still referred to as Laichow or Laichow mottled.

At first the plaits imitated the seven-end either with or without a twist edge. Next came the four-end rustic plaits plaited with natural-coloured straws later incorporating black and navy straws. Encouraged by samples supplied from the European traders, patterns were copied and in about 1874 splitters were sent to China so that plaiters could produce split straw and fancy plaits which were particularly popular in the United States.[161] Chinese plaiters were judged to be good at imitating European plaits, and although not innovative, they could supply considerable quantities of a new design to the manufacturers in England within 12 months of the first samples being sent.[162] Chinese plaits were made of wheat straw and in later years also from barley, rice straw, rush and wood chip, which was perhaps influenced by the Japanese.[163] The 1908 report states that according to the width, and presumably the complexity of the pattern, a plaiter would take two to six days of work to make 60 yards of a plait 10–11 mm wide. A plait 5–6 mm wide

Originally thought to be a poor joining method, this type of join is where two lengths, perhaps made by different plaiters, were joined to make the marketable length. This Chinese plait was made in the 1930 or 1940s. (CTLC 12/31/41)

would take five or six days. The narrowest possible plait was 3 mm and the widest 30 mm.

In imitating plaits, there was one technique which the Chinese initially failed to observe. Instead of regularly joining in new straws along the length, they added new straws in what was commonly termed 'sets and runs', with joins to all the working ends being made in consecutive sequence. Dealers and manufacturers disliked this, complaining that the appearance was ragged and the plait weak where it was joined. Some of the weakness may have been created by the European and American straw brokers' unregulated purchasing practices. Plaiters sold their plaits by the Chinese foot[164] and made pieces ranging from a few feet to several yards. The brokers sorted the pieces into different qualities before joining them together into 30-, 60- or 120-yard lengths to form a single hank. The hanks were packed into quantities of 240 pieces then wrapped in coarse fabric ready for shipping. Being more valuable, split and fancy plaits were packed in boxes of 480 pieces.[165]

As early as 1887 reports stated that the 'quality has fallen off, the product is uneven and irregular, and the bundles are rarely of proper lengths. The buyers in the home markets are dissatisfied, the trade has become unsound, the losses have become so continuous the foreign merchants are beginning, after their disagreeable experiences, to regard the article with some suspicion and disgust. If the Japanese people should enter as competitors and carry on the manufacture and sale in a reasonably honest spirit, the trade will go to the land of the Rising Sun.'[166] By 1889 there were complaints that in recent years the Chinese had overproduced to a point that no more products could be absorbed by the British and United States markets. As a result, the prices dropped, and complaints of short measure and poor quality persisted. There was even a warning that should these bad practices continue dealers would refuse to continue the trade.[167] It was claimed that some bales of plaits suffered sea damage although one report stated that in the early days of trading, bales were purchased by weight so some sellers moistened the plait before packing.

By the time the shipment arrived at its destination the plait was rotten.[168]

Poor quality did not stop the manufacturers since Chinese imports supplied 'the sweating part of the straw trade. The common rough straws are sold for as low as threepence or fourpence a piece even for girls' hats, and for very little more roughly got up men's, with a piece of tape around them, such as the miscalled 'planter's' hat.'[169] Quantities of imports were vast, the same report stated that 'most of the plait comes from China . . . over 80,000 bales of Chinese plait were imported into the country last year.' Chinese imports were profitable not only for the purpose of making up cheap goods, but for the practice of re-exportation, much of it trading back and forth to the United States. This practice was examined by Catherine Robinson in her 2016

During the 1920s, Richard Durler, of his family's important Luton company, travelled to Japan to see the Japanese working methods first hand. He must have been shocked and yet delighted as to how the making of straw plaits was organised.

thesis which delved deeper into this historical period and the effects of Chinese trade on the Luton hat industry.[170]

Early in the 1900s trade continued to be mercurial, but as much as the traders felt they suffered, the Chinese also experienced problems of international conflict and competition when the Japanese entered the market. Today straw plaits are still made in China within areas such as Laichow (Laizhou), but production is declining and many of the fancy and split straw patterns are no longer made as production turns to the weaving of straw hoods.

Japanese plait

Whereas the *Hatters' Gazette* frequently published articles of complaint and concern about the China trade, when mentioned, Japan attracted either neutral or relatively positive comment.

Japan may have exported plaits and straw hats for the European market from the 1830s[171] however it was not until the opening of Japan to the west in the 1850s that trade opportunities developed. Exports to the United States started in 1882 with a shipment of 11,000 pieces, each piece 60-yards long. The following year 30,000 pieces were sent, rising spectacularly in 1884 to 250,000 pieces with the prediction of the figure rising to one million pieces.[172] The plaits were made from wheat straw and manufactured in Omori, between Tokyo and Yokohama. The American Consul-General concluded that 'The Japanese braid produced by some of our large dealers in the United States is the very finest to use . . . fast taking the place of the celebrated Mackinaw braids, which, for so long a time, have commanded the highest prices in the markets.' Given the close association of the United States and British straw traders, the British must have seen advantageous opportunities in this new source of supply. John Dony said that the first large quantities of Japanese plaits were not sent to England until 1891[173] but this does not rule out the possibility of supplies having entered Great Britain via the United States prior to that date. Indeed, the *Hatters' Gazette* reprinted an article from *Strohhut Zeitung*, the German hat industry trade journal, which stated that Japanese wheat straw plaits met with good sales in London during 1886. However it seems that demand outstripped supplies: 'the diversity of requirements as to shape and colour were not to be properly supplied by the existing arrangements as to production.'[174] Enterprising Japanese individuals had developed a large plaiting establishment which included a bleaching and dyeing plant at Kanangawa called Kakinuma Mugiwara Shokai or Kakinuma Wheat Straw Company. It employed 300 of the country's most skilled plaiters, brought together from all parts of Japan, and already orders for 200,000 rolls of plaits had been received. Alongside the making and export of plaits, the Japanese were developing a hat manufacturing industry. In 1888 one half of the plaits produced were used within the country for making hats and other products. The writer claimed that the first customer was the United States. However, now that large quantities were being sent to Great Britain and France from 13 houses, or plaiting establishments, in Yokohama, it was noted that 'This industry has developed in direct competition with the Chinese, but the Japanese product is of superior quality.' Exports reached one million bundles, having risen from 5,000 in 1882.[175] Even though it was acknowledged that the Japanese product was superior, according to import records published in the *Hatters' Gazette*, total Japanese imports into England never overtook those from China between 1894–1900,[176] even after the signing of the Anglo-Japanese Treaty of 1894. A Consular Report outlined how the growth of the Japanese industry affected the Chinese trade from Chefoo, stating that the Japanese 'produce a splendid plait . . . they are favoured with better straw . . . the conditions under which they work are much more practical and better regulated than any the Chinese care to try.'[177]

This boater was made in Luton from Japanese barley straw rustic plaits. It has a cane or corded brim edge and was made by A. E. Olney of Luton for the Harrow School uniform. (CTLC 142/57)

Barley straw and boaters

The Japanese also used barley straw, which became extremely popular. Tatsuaki Morimoto wrote [178] that production began in 1887 with the formation of two houses, or factories, within the Okayama prefecture, and was funded with local support. Producing plaits and preparing them for shipping was organised into a factory structure where output, quality and dispatch could be controlled. While there was some home production, the factory organisation was in stark contrast not only to the production arrangement but also to other centres where the work was done at home. As Robinson stated, 'Japanese workers . . . thrive on pattern change.'[179]

With the development of factories, production increased rapidly but trade was always dependent on a successful harvest, and trading conditions were affected by what was happening in China. There had been some criticism of short measure which the Japanese traders quickly implemented through Articles of Association which specified how each 18-yard long piece would be wound. [180] Examples in the CTL collections include beautifully presented pieces tied with tape. Plait was shipped to England, the United States and Hong Kong (China) from where it would have been shipped onwards to European centres. Wheat and barley were only two of the materials; wood chip, hemp and other grasses were also plaited, and were sometimes mixed within one plaited pattern.

By 1900 the *Hatters' Gazette* reported that 'Rustic plait is very popular, of every 1,000 hats 999 are rustic, of every 100 hats 99 are Japanese.'[181] The barley straw provided a lightweight plait ideally suited to the production of men's boater hats and a correspondent remarked to the *Hatters' Gazette* that he had fully intended to purchase a boater made from English plait but chose a Japanese one since the weight and appearance were far superior.[182] Rustic plaits were supplied in a variety of widths and grades under imported names. For first quality: Imperial Crown, Lion, Rose and Eagle, and for second quality: Sun, Peacock, Lily and Hawk.[183]

The Japanese appear to have understood the criticisms levelled at the Chinese and determined not to make the same mistakes. There were frequent competitions for plaiters, and in the early 1900s the Japanese began to exhibit at international trade shows in the United States and Europe.[184] In 1910 at the Japan–British Exhibition, several associations in addition to individual manufacturers exhibited, and examples of the plaits displayed are held in the CTL collections. Constant improvement of their product seems to have been a continuing aim. Within an article in 1913 a journalist declared that 'The trade spread to Japan which today stands foremost in the world for plait production.'[185]

Trade in Japanese wood chip plaits amounted to about 25% of the overall production and continued into the mid 1900s. The wood chip was described as coming from pine, spruce, cypress and cedar trees. Sometime around 1910 they began to produce machine-made braids using hemp fibre, some of which was grown locally, but they may also have imported Manila hemp.

This is another of the series of images taken during Durler's trip to Japan. In this image, the finished plait is being carefully wound around a frame to ensure the measured length is correct.

Mechanisation of the industry

That a regular supply of cheap plaits was an advantage for companies but not for plaiters does not appear to be perceived as a problem. This was clearly indicated by Frank Thirkell[186] who gave a remarkable interview to the New York Herald in July 1890. He said that the English industry is in no way threatened by the Chinese competition and there was really no cause for alarm. 'It is just 20 years ago since I first introduced into this country plaited straw from China. At that time we had 20 factories at Luton employing altogether some thousands of hands. Now we have only three factories; though I need hardly say that difference does not signify any falling-off in our business.' He agreed that Chinese imports contributed to the decline of plaiting but argued that the chief reason for their misfortune was the introduction of the straw hat sewing machine.

English plaits were normally made in scores (20 yards), but it was common practice for the poorest plaiters to sell five- and ten-yard lengths. Plaits from Europe were normally supplied in 50-metre pieces, while Chinese and Japanese wheat straw plaits were in 60 metres, and sometimes up to 120 metres. Longer lengths reduced the amount of joining and speeded production. English plaiters were urged to change their established practice but all pleas fell on deaf ears. They felt their diminishing income would take longer to earn if the piece length was extended.

Photographed in about 1907 in a small Luton hat sewing room, workers sew hats. They were working with a range of plaits and braids sourced from around the world. On the floor there is a bag of braid and above it a metal mill.

Sewing machines

Domestic machines could stitch together lengths of plaits into parallel strips that were cut to shape and hand-stitched together.[187] The Luton company Munt and Brown introduced machines in 1869–70 but were not pleased with the results and stopped the trial.[188]

Mr Stratford, who was the Luton Singer sewing machine sales representative, and Jeffrey Eustace, a local manufacturer, began to make modifications to the machine and in about 1874 Stratford's wife, Elizabeth, was given a friendly challenge to sew a hat working from the crown outwards towards the brim. She made part of a hat using coarse plaits and the following day stitched a complete hat using a 'fine make of English China Purl.'[189] Work to improve the machine continued and Harry Inwards wrote: 'In 1874 Mr Henry Bland, a Luton mechanic, turned his attention to making alterations to the Willcox and Gibbs domestic machine, in order to render it more suitable for sewing straw plait . . . He took out patents to cover his improvements which were subsequently acquired by Willcox and Gibbs.' In 1875 the Willcox and Gibbs 10 Guinea machine was introduced. It was capable of stitching both fine and coarse plaits with a visible chain stitch. In about 1879 the Willcox and Gibbs 17 Guinea machine was introduced.[190] Singer also started to sell a sewing machine that could produce this type of work, and the German Grossman company introduced the Dresdensia visible stitch machine that sold at a lower price.

The French Légat sewing machine, introduced in 1875, was a 'hand-stitch' machine forming a short top stitch and long under stitch. Girls were sent to Paris to learn how to use them, which created great excitement.[191] However, only 40 machines were purchased, and they were not widely adopted in the industry due to their high price and ongoing maintenance costs.[192] Machines increased efficiency and provided 'the ability to produce a dozen hats in the same time as one made by hand-sewing.'[193] Although liked, they were not entirely successful since the stitches became dirty, so development continued.

A German machine made by Kurtz was introduced in 1877, but although it was a 'hand-stitch' machine, and the sale price was low, little else is known. Thirkell travelled to New York in the 1870s to purchase an American machine that was claimed to produce a concealed stitch at a time when no other existed, and Vyse purchased the patent rights. Initially, 30 machines were purchased and set up in their Luton factory, and by 1878 40 were installed, driven by steam.[194] They did indeed produce a concealed stitch, provided that the hat was stitched from the brim in towards the crown. This method restricted the number of shapes that could be sewn therefore was not successful. In 1878 Edmund Wiseman patented his concealed-stitch machine which used two needles to create the desired small stitch on the top surface of the hat and long stitch underneath. It successfully stitched fine plait but was less reliable with coarse plait. Wiseman worked with Willcox and Gibbs to make the machine self adjusting, so it could suit all types of straw. This machine became known as the box machine. The *Hatters' Gazette* predicted that 'With such a really splendid machine, the straw trade everywhere will largely increase their trade and their profits. . .'[195] An advertisement published the previous month detailed the machine's efficiency. A long list of benefits included:

- It was easy to learn.
- It could sew 1,000 stitches per minute.
- It could sew a hat in two minutes.
- It could sew 142 hats in a day.
- It used 20% less thread.[196]

Many types of machines were introduced for specific hat making processes but the final iconic model, the German Anita machine, was introduced in 1920. It made a visible zigzag stitch allowing plaits to be stitched edge to edge rather than overlapping.

Blocking machines

Now that plaits could be quickly stitched, other improvements were required to speed up production. To shape a straw hat, a hat block was required,[197] as well as some form of hot or cold press. While this was suitable for factory use, in their homes, families were still making the plaits, sewing and pressing them into shape either using a slicken stone or a mallet. A slicken stone was a smooth stone or glass, shaped like a darning mushroom. Later, with some care, so as not to scorch the straw, they used flat irons.

In the first half of the 1800s various inventors made improvements to speed up the process including, in 1815, Thomas Scorrar, who claimed that his invention was capable of blocking 50 hats a day instead of the 20 using the existing machinery.[198] When blocking became a factory process, it was a well-paid and respected trade. A blocker in the 1860s could expect to earn 20 to 30 shillings a week. The first machines were screw presses until about 1868 when a French inventor introduced a machine that used hydraulic pressure. The *Illustrated London News* provided a good account witnessed at the Vyse factory: 'After the plait has been sewn into hats or bonnets, these are stiffened by being passed through a solution of gelatine and dried. As they are somewhat shapeless, they are now pressed into shape, either by being pressed by hand with a heavy iron on blocks of the required shape, or by means of machine power. In the latter case heated zinc moulds, of various shapes and sizes, as the demand of fashion requires, are used, and, the hat being placed in the mould, heavy pressure is applied from above. In the process of "crimping", in addition to pressing the hat into shape, the mould impresses a pattern onto the straw . . . the protuberance shown on the under surface of the upper part of the machine is a part of a bag made of stout india rubber and this, when the mould is closed by the upper part of the machine being lowered and

A Luton hat manufacturer's hat blocking room pictured in 1907. The same machines and techniques are still being used today in the manufacture of hats.

securely fastened, fits into the interior of the hat. This bag is then distended by water forced into it by the action of condensed air, and a pressure of many tons thus brought to bear on the hat, which is forced to take the impress of the zinc mould.'[199]

Another blocking machine, still widely used in today's hat industry, was originally called a French Press and is operated by gas or electicity.[200] The hat is placed into the larger pan and then the smaller one of the same shape is pressed down.

Improved transport

Improvements to manufacture brought the potential to sell more hats, but that required the introduction of the railway. Dunstable, Luton and St Albans were the main centres of the straw hat manufacturing industry, with Luton eventually becoming the largest of the three towns. The railway came to Dunstable in 1848 and Luton in 1858, thus aiding the rapid development of the home, and in particular foreign, trade which occurred in the 1860s. The introduction of the railway, while bringing great benefits, needs to be balanced with the improvements to production rather than being cited as the principal reason for changes to the industry.

Effect on the plaiters

Improvements to hat production were not exclusive to Luton. All other centres were introducing improvements and plaiters everywhere experienced a dramatic loss of income causing them to either switch to factory work or to find other employment.

Great Britain

This statement appeared in the *Hatters' Gazette*: 'The Luton Plait Halls show the production of 10,000 plaiters weekly but large quantities are foreign plait. Only ⅙th of the quantity is home produced.'[201]

Thirkell, when asked about the effect of Chinese imports on prices, said that 'The price of one bundle of plaited straw, which twenty years ago, would have cost 4s 6d, is now just 4½d' (22.5 pence reduced to just under 2 pence.) The interviewer asked if 'It may be concluded then, Mr Thirkell, that these rumours as to the impending extinction of the straw-plaiting industry in England are unfounded?' Thirkell replied that 'demand for these goods is so great that many thousands of people are still profitably employed at the industry in England, and doubtless will be for so many years to come.'[202] His thoughts were not only to prove incorrect, they were not substantiated by statistics. The Luton Chamber of Commerce produced startling figures: in 1871, 48,863 were engaged in the straw trade in England and Wales, and in 1881, the number had decreased to 30,984.

Good times for the manufacturers but the *Hatters' Gazette* wrote that 'changes had tended towards the depletion of our country villages, and to the centralisation of the population in the towns . . . it is certainly deplorable to notice the signs of decay in some of our large villages . . . which some 15 or 20 years ago were prosperous.'[203] A plaiter in Hemel Hempstead making seven-end split plaits said she had to provide herself with 'a mill costing 2s 6d, and a machine, 4d, for splitting the straws. A bundle of white straws cost 5d, and one of blue straws 3d, which must be bought from the dealer to whom the plait is sold.' She explained that if the straw was good it might make five score (100) yards of plait, and if the plait was exceptionally good she would receive 4d per 20 yards. 'If I commence about nine in the morning and leave off at nine at night, doing some housework between whiles, I can do 25 yards which will bring me in clear about threepence.' She concluded that it was poor pay, but she had children to look after, and there was nothing else she could do.[204]

By 1886 reports concluded that the home plaiting industry was 'almost ruined' due to the 'excellent quality' Canton plaits imported at such low prices. In St Albans plaits had been used to make baskets and bags since the 1870s, an occupation that was to continue until the end of the century with workers using offcuts to make a range of decorative products. This was considered a great benefit in the earlier years for both plaiters and sewers. 'Our trade in baskets is as flourishing as ever, and this is the only set-off the poor plaiters get, for if the straw was only used for hats their work would be bad indeed.'[205]

Germany

By the middle of the 1800s hat production in Saxony was increasingly concentrated into factories, where larger numbers of people were employed in straw plaiting and hat sewing under one roof. New factories were opened in towns in and around Dresden[206] but the *Hatters' Gazette* reported in 1887 that the plaiting industry around Dresden was no longer remunerative due to Chinese imports. Statistics in the *Hatters' Gazette* recorded that in the German straw hat industry in the 1880s, 40% of hats were sewn from local products, but by 1890 it was only 11.5%, falling dramatically to 4.4% in 1895. By 1900 straw plaiting was no longer a significant industry due to imports from Japan.[207]

Italy

Despite the variety and quality of products, and their popularity within fashion, by 1886 little optimism existed concerning the prospects of the Italian industry. The Chinese, who had already copied some plain plaits, began to copy the newer Italian fancy patterns. Three years after its introduction in 1882, the Chinese flooded markets with their copy of *ginocchiello*, causing a significant price drop.[208] Competition from imported Chinese plaits was fierce and exports of some types of Italian plaits ceased because of this competition. Seven-straw *pedal* and Tuscan ends were still popular, but some feared supply would outstrip demand for the product. Local people, described as peasants, had taken up plaiting to supplement their incomes and were willing to sell their products at lower prices than the professional plaiters.[209] This situation caused complaints, then protests as the plaiters' incomes dropped. Linari wrote that there were a total of '84,558 (females 80,160, males 4,398) all in the province of Florence. Of these 19,059 are peasants, 65,499 being real professional plaiters.'[210] These circumstances led to strikes and riots in 1896, but nothing could prevent the impending spectre of an industry's demise. Olivia Rucellai provided figures indicating the dramatic change of fortune. Between 1880–2 the value of plait was about 2,000 lira per quintal. In 1895 it had fallen to 500 lira. She added that a 120-yard length of seven-end Chinese plait could sell for as little as one lira. In 1897 a customs tariff imposed by the United States further impacted the industry. The plaiters had protested and demanded action to support them, and the Minister for Agriculture and Commerce agreed to identify causes and propose resolutions. A range were offered, but perhaps the most shocking proposal for plaiters was to reduce the number of plaiters from 80,000 to 40,000. The changes did work, and the industry revived in the early years of the 1900s.[211]

Switzerland

Switzerland developed a diverse industry throughout the 1800s, so while the straw plaiters in canton Fribourg were affected, the industry centred in Wohlen continued to thrive, its decline not coming until the last half of the twentieth century. No matter how good the plait was, it could be quickly copied by the Chinese at a far lower price, and patterns created by the Japanese were unlike anything seen before. Joseph Reichlen provided statistics of the decline. The peak of trade in the area was reached before the American Civil War when the annual income generated from the straw trade reached fr.1,800,000. He stated that in 1881, plait from China, Italy and Belgium flooded the markets causing a decline, however thanks to support from companies in Bulle, income had grown back to fr.1,500,000 and the straw industry employed about 15,000 people in 1891. These figures probably included all people involved in the straw industry since he stated that Gruyère accounts for ⅓ of this figure.[212] By 1900 other reports say there were fewer than 400 plaiters around Gruyère and located in just five villages. With the assistance of continuing support from the Bulle company Gretener, and later from Sidonie Romanens in Sorens, some plaiting continued for a few more years. New factories producing food products were being introduced into the area and the plaiters found work at first in the factory producing condensed milk, and then in the chocolate factories.[213]

Attempts to revive plaiting

Just as the Italians had been advised to work new types of plaits and to be innovative, the English plaiters were given similar instructions as early as 1881. 'It is a misfortune that amongst the hundreds of straw plaiters so few are able to adapt themselves to the requirements of the trade. . . Surely our plaiters have as much ingenuity as the Italian peasantry. . . It would be worth the trouble and expense to send out two or three of our skilled plaiters, who could impart their knowledge on their return.'[214] The proposal was not implemented.

Three years later in 1885, the *Hatters' Gazette* published a scathing judgement made by Mr Wright to the Luton Chamber of Commerce: 'I fear that our plaiters have much to blame themselves for in this matter; their work has often been done slovenly and most unsatisfactorily, they have made no great effort to produce novelties in design, preferring to earn poor wages rather than disturb the even tenor of their way.' Given these attitudes it is perhaps surprising that any attempt would have been made to support the plaiters, but it was the catalyst for action as Wright considered part of the problem was a lack of structured education in the art of plaiting.[215]

Two remarkable suggestions to counter the decline were made firstly in 1891 when it was suggested that properly trained teachers should be brought from Switzerland and Germany.[216] The second in 1899 when the *Hatters' Gazette* repeated a rumour circulating around the town that 5,000 Japanese plaiters should be brought to Luton to produce plaits since this would make their plaits more easily available to the trade and they would be able to produce the elaborate new patterns required for fashionable hats.[217] Perhaps having heard of the Japanese competitions held for plaiters, competitions for local plaiters were organised in villages and a major exhibition was held at the Luton Plait Halls in 1885 to encourage and display their skills. The aim was to move ahead of the Chinese and Japanese by creating new plait patterns, and to improve the quality to the standard of Switzerland and Italy.

Many correspondents maintained that the closure of the plait schools after the 1870 Education Act caused the decline in the industry. However, while certainly a factor, it was not the main cause. Beginning in 1891, there were various valiant attempts instigated by the Luton Chamber of Commerce and Council's Education Committee to restore the industry, with the hope that if the scheme could employ '10,000 women in the villages and each could earn five shillings a week,' it would generate sufficient money to 'benefit directly and indirectly nearly every trade within the county.'[218] The idea was to set up specific classes, at first for the primary school teachers so they could teach the children in their classes, then continue the training as children progressed through school. For older girls it was intended that they would attend plaiting classes held in local villages. The educational authorities in the plaiting areas appointed instructors in 1892 who were to visit various villages, at first in Bedfordshire, and then into Buckinghamshire, with the plan to not only teach plaiting, but also to teach the art of design and to use a far wider range of materials. Buckinghamshire reported that there were about 150 pupils on a waiting list, although plaiting was being taught in several schools.[219] In 1894 the *Hatters' Gazette* reported that schemes had been introduced into Leeds and Bradford where the Bedfordshire instructors had published a booklet containing instructions for a series of simple plaits based on Japanese designs. The plan attracted attention from around the country with enquiries arriving from Lancashire, Dorset and Birmingham although it is not known if these schools did introduce the schemes. Weekly classes did spread to Hertfordshire and Cambridgeshire in 1897. However, praise for the scheme was not universal. Miss Crouch reported to the Technical Committee that she thought the 'girls should be encouraged to go into service rather than idle about at their doors, plaiting which led them to neglect their homes, and tended to immorality.'[220] Annual exhibitions of the plaiters' work were held, and the Bedfordshire County Education Report from 1896–7, says that 52 entries were received that were 'of very great merit . . . better than they [the judges] had ever before seen executed by English plaiters . . . of such excellence.'[221] Prizes were awarded for their plaits made with wheat, chip, manilla, gimp and other materials, but the plaiters expressed disappointment that orders were not forthcoming.

The Bedfordshire Education Report of 1899–1900, made the encouraging claim that once again at least a few plaiters were making their living from plaiting, and that their work was of high quality. That appeared to change in the 1900–1 report. While still praising and promoting the scheme, a downturn in the trade had reduced demand for their products.

The British Straw Plait Association (later Company) was formed in 1896 as the direct result of the Bedfordshire County Council's efforts. It had a dual purpose: to put the plaiters in touch with the market and to enable them to receive improved wages. At the time of its instigation there were 100 workers at four centres in Bedfordshire 'whilst a far greater number have been employed in the neighbouring county of Bucks.'[222] The Association's chairman was Harry Inwards who worked in the hat trade. Initially the Association had success and later reported in 1898 that between January and June hundreds of women were making plaits of superior designs, and were earning between four and seven shillings a week. This was short-lived and the venture was wound up in 1899.

In 1902 a school of plaiting design was opened in Luton with the award of eight scholarships to attend a two-week course. This appeared to mark a change in the format of the scheme. Instead of classes being offered in villages, now tuition was given in Luton. Technical education in plaiting was still being discussed in 1903, but the earlier enthusiasm was lacking, and the old criticisms of the plaiters' abilities to confront their opposition were once again voiced. The following year the report failed to make any mention of straw plaiting.

This decorative basket from 1889 has been made using a wide variety of materials including chip, palm, bast, hemp and cereal straw. (CTLC 2/38/59)

CHAPTER
FIVE

PLAITING MATERIALS

Within the hat industry straw has always been used as a generic term rather than referring to a single material. To understand this facilitates the appreciation of materials used in the construction of straw headwear. During the 1700s, chip, knotted bast, cane and horsehair are all mentioned as hat materials. A rare woven horsehair hat is in the collection at Colonial Williamsburg, VA, United States,[223] and an equally rare cane hat is in the collections of the Museum of London. Whichever material was used, the intended outcome was the production of a lightweight hat or bonnet made from an easily available natural fibre. By the later 1800s, alongside natural fibres, new manufactured materials were introduced. This chapter explores plaiting materials used in previous centuries.

Made in the 1700s this large split cane hat is woven using a basket making technique. It is lined with cream silk in the crown and red silk on the underside of the brim. The brim edge has been covered with a silk brocade.

Cereal crop straws

Wheat

Wheat plaits were recorded from the 1700s and the most universally used type as it is flexible, easy to split and bleach, and takes dyes successfully.

White Chittum and Red Lammas are two spring wheats documented in south east Midlands references, but it is probable other types were also used. Arthur Young wrote of varieties called Rivet, Burwell (named after its place of origin in Cambridgeshire), and Day's Snout, which he stated grew around St Albans and Hitchin. A footnote added that this variety may also have been known as Pirks or Pirky.[224] Edwin Grey also mentioned the use of a variety called Golden Drop which was grown at Rothampsted.[225]

The chalky soil of the south Midlands is credited with producing high quality straw for plaiting, which some attribute to the proportion of silex in the straw.[226] Although supply is largely attributed to the Chilterns, straw dealers would travel to other areas, including Reading, Berkshire and to 'the chalk hills south of the Thames' to purchase straw.[227] There appears to have been some competition between the shires of Bedford, Hertford, Oxford, Buckingham and Essex regarding the quality of the straw. English plaiting straw was exported to Switzerland for their plaiters to use. However, straw grown in Essex was considered poor quality and lacking lustre due to the heavy clay and stony soil in which it was grown. There may have been some justification for these reports since some plaiters in Essex are said to have preferred to purchase their straw from the market in Hitchin, Hertfordshire.[228]

William Wilshere of Hitchin recorded the economic factors involved in selling straw in 1816[229]: '12 acres produced about 38cwts. of straw fit for plaiting, which sold at prices varying from 20s. to 32s. a cwt. This gave a profit of £60 from the 12 acres when allowance has been made for the expenses of drawing and preparing the straw.' He then detailed the economics of preparing the sheaves: '3 sheaves of wheat straw in 1816 of an average quality weighed 42 lbs, with the ears cut off 23 lbs. The straw drawn for platts (after cutting off the ears) 13 lbs. Flag and other refuse 6 lbs. The produce, when cut into lengths and prepared for platting was 3 lbs. Coarse worth some 2s 6d, some 9d per lb, on an average 7½d, [total] 1s 10½d 1¼ lbs fine at 1s 6d [total] 1s 10½d.' Total value 3s 9d. Later in his records he calculated that 'A pound of split straw of good quality is sufficient for from 80 to 100 yards of plat which will make two bonnets – weighing from 2 to 3 ounces each – many are much finer and lighter – and more are coarser. 10 yards per day of good plat is a fair day's work, it now sells at about 2s 6d per score, giving the platter something more than 1s per day net, some earn double and others not above half as much.'[230] In 1852 plaiting straw was still attracting a good price: 'straw brings from £6 to £8 a ton, it is as valuable by the acre as corn.'[231]

Such was the regard for Italian straw that publications frequently reported on its methods of cultivation, saying that not only was the warm and sunny Italian weather perfect, but the soil also provided ideal growing conditions. Domenico Michelacci is credited with adapting the method of sowing grain at high density to ensure development of the stem rather than the seed head. The name of the variety of wheat varies between publications, William Cobbett and Linari called it *triticum oestivum* whilst the Society of Arts in London referred to it as *grano marzolano* and the *Hatters' Gazette grano marzuolo*.[232] Another variety, *triticum turgidum*,[233] was described as a bearded spring wheat similar to that grown in England.[234] Once cut the straw was left in the field to dry, provided there was no rain or dew, then bundled and taken for preparation. While wheat may have been used by the 1700s it should be noted that in 1611 Thomas Coryat[235] remarked that

Harvesting tall growing wheat straw using a reaper binder. Photographed in Staffordshire, England.

around Turin he saw both rye and wheat growing, and given their later propensity to plaits with a far wider variety of straws, the idea that they may have used rye should not be ruled out.

In 1829 on a visit to Tring, Hertfordshire, William Cobbett was appalled to find local traders in the town selling imported Tuscan straws to local plaiters.[236] He implored local farmers to follow his instructions and produce fine straw to stop imports. According to Grey, in about 1867 experiments to grow Italian wheat were undertaken at Rothamsted Experimental Station, Hertfordshire, but there is no indication of success.[237]

Rye straw

Unlike wheat, varieties of rye were not mentioned in accounts during the 1700s and 1800s. Rye grows taller than wheat and can produce slender stems that are both strong and wiry, qualities that are not suitable for all plaits. When bleached it has a darker sheen than wheat. While rye grown in the Swiss climate and soils was considered less than successful, that grown in other countries was considered perfectly suited for the plaits.

Experiments using rye were made in the early 1800s by William Corston[238] who felt it would provide effective competition to the Italian products. *The Workwoman's Guide*[239] stated that rye straw was considered the best for plaiting but was more difficult than wheat to obtain. 'Soft good, coloured straws should be chosen, as free from blight and spots as possible.' Plaiters in the Orkney islands first relied on straw being sent from London,[240] but later, rye straw grown in the Italian manner – by sowing the seed close together to produce fine straws – was used. James and Andrew Muir in their submission of plaits and hats to the Society of Arts in 1827, explained that they were made from rye straw grown on the islands; they had '40 bolls sown for straw, which was put in five or six Scotch acres.'[241]

Barley straw

The Japanese industry appears to be the only one which used barley on a commercial scale. Farmers in Bedfordshire and Hertfordshire grew barley for malting but there are no contemporary references to the use of barley straw for commercial plaiting. Arthur Young wrote that Zealand winter barley was grown around Aldbury, Hertfordshire, but the grain was bad, and he concluded that barley was 'very uncertain on chalk.'

Rice straw

The *Hatters' Gazette*, and no doubt other European

hat industry journals, often referred to rice plaits. There is confusion as to what was meant by this term since it could refer to a plait pattern or to the type of straw. Piedmont is one of the historic rice-growing areas in Italy, and is a region named in one of the earliest references to straw plaiting and hat making. Rice straw is soft and flexible so it does seem probable that it would have been used in some centres.

Grasses

Documents from the 1800s frequently refer to wild grasses as bents. This may now be an obsolete word referring to meadow grasses or it may have some association with bennet grass which Cobbett referred to in his correspondence. The grasses used were often only known by their local names which can create confusion when interpreting accounts. The collection of specimens of 'Italian grasses used in the Italian industry to make hats and trimmings' held in the CTLC includes examples of rye, various types of wheat, oats and wild grasses such as *briza maxima* amongst others. Oats are not often mentioned in accounts, but in *Little House in the Big Woods* by Laura Ingalls Wilder, Laura described the oat harvest, then watching her mother plait the oat stems into seven-end plaits and a nine-end plait with a notch edge that were later sewn into hats.

William Cobbett was prolific in his experiments with native English grasses, and these are recorded both in his extensive correspondence with the Society of Arts, London between 1822–3, and in his book *Cottage Economy*. His experiments included the following grasses (current names are shown in brackets): *Melica caerulea* or purple melica (Molinia caerulea), *Agrostis stolonifera* or fiorin grass (creeping bentgrass), *Lolium perenne* or ray grass (perennial ryegrass), *avena flavescens* or yellow oat-grass, *cynosurus cristatus* or Crested dog's-tail, *anthoxanthum oderatum* or Sweet vernal-grass, *Agrostis canina* or brown bentgrass (dog bentgrass).[242]

Maria Edgeworth described the use of crested dog's-tail grass in her writings,[243] saying that a local Irish lady had taught several girls to prepare the grass and make the bonnets. The author of *The Workwoman's Guide* appears to have read, or at least heard of this book, since she referenced Maria's words.

Of the many types of water grasses, sedges and rushes that have been used for plaits in Italy, sala, a type of rush collected from the Fucecchio marshes to the west of Florence, was introduced later in the 1800s. It was used for making bags, shoes and the soles of slippers in the 1940s.[244]

This collection of grasses represents varieties used in the Italian straw industry.

Chip, bast and raffia

Chip

As one of the earliest materials used in the making of hats and bonnets, wood chip has almost been forgotten, which is surprising given its importance and widespread use in the hat industry until the 1960s. In Great Britain chip was sourced from willow and poplar, while in Europe it came from lime or linden.[245] In Japan, pine, spruce, cypress and cedar were used. Chip could be bleached and took dye very well due to its porous surface. In the 1850s many chip plait bonnets were painted with whitewash for a bride to wear. Strips were either woven on a loom into a sheet known as a willow square, or made into plaits.

Bast

Bast is a commonly used generic term which causes much confusion in both documentation and identification of examples. At times the word was used to refer to chip and at others to raffia. A common definition of bast is as the fibrous inner layers of a plant encompassing various types of wood and palm. The Swiss researcher Rodel applied the name bast to a wide range of materials in his recording of those used in the Swiss hat industry.[246] Depending on its plant origin, bast varies greatly in its appearance, sometimes open and fibrous, sometimes dense and solid, like wood. In the mid 1890s an entirely new product was introduced, Cuba bast, which Rodel said came from *hibiscus elatus*, a small tree of the mallow family.[247] The strips were immersed in acid until only the soft tissue dissolved, leaving a skeletal outline. As with so many products used in the hat industry, although seemingly only associated with Cuba, the palm was probably sourced from various locations.

Raffia

This material should probably appear within the following section on palm, but it is so frequently confused with bast that it is included here. Rodel, writing in 1960, cited two sources: 'raphiabast' from the 'raphia ruffia' plant, and raffia *pedunculata*. It appeared that this material was introduced into the hat industry in the later 1800s as a substitute for Russian bast, the inner bark of the Russian lime, which was difficult to obtain during the Crimean War. Raffia is obtained from a particular type of palm growing in the southern hemisphere, particularly in Madagascar and the Seychelles. A sample of plait from the early 1900s made in the Seychelles, from what is recorded as 'raphia', appears to have been made from fibre obtained from a vein of the plant. Its appearance is unlike soft garden raffia which is a broad tape. Raffia takes dye easily and produces a lightweight product that was eminently suitable for the fashionable large hats popular in the Edwardian era. During the early 1900s raffia became a popular material for ladies wishing to make their own hats and a wide variety of useful items. To add to the confusion of defining and identifying raffia, products made from paper and viscose amongst others are today sold as raffia.

Palms

Globally palm must compete with wheat straw to be the most widely used material in the hat industry since many parts of the plant are used. Palm leaves formed a large part of the industry in the United States. In the Bahamas and Bermuda palmetto palm was recorded as being used in the early years of the industry, but today the indigenous silver top palm, *coccothrinax argentata*, is used by the islands' workers – although the supply of this palm is in decline. One account published online in 2014 quoted a plaiter as saying she remembered mixing coconut and silver top or just using coconut to make a plait.[248]

There are hundreds of suitable varieties growing around the world and the industry journals include reports of them being sourced from China, Borneo, the Philippines, the West Indies, Brazil, British Honduras and many other countries. Whatever

Most plait pattern names are now forgotten but in the Bahamian islands they keep them alive. The board shows some of the patterns still being made in the Bahamas.

Work in progress. Sue Brian works to keep the skills of making Australian cabbage tree hats alive by teaching the techniques of making them and speaking about their history.

the species used, it is usually an easily available indigenous palm from which the new growth of an unopened leaf is cut with great care not to damage the plant. According to the type of palm either the central vein or stem can be retted into fibres, or the leaves can be used whole or split.

Cabbage tree palm

The use of the cabbage tree palm, *Livistona australis*, is ingrained in Australian social history. The true beginnings of this industry are yet to be fully understood, and while the skills would have been introduced through the settlers, to link the hat only to this part of society perhaps does not represent the entire story. They are commonly associated with Sydney, but there may also have been significant production in Tasmania since in 1847 they were advertised for sale in local newspapers.[249] Arthur Tansley implied that some Australian cabbage tree hats,[250] and both plaits and hats made from cabbage tree palm, were imported into England and exhibited in the 1862 International Exhibition held in London. Exhibits, all of which were given honourable mentions, were sent from New South Wales by a farmer and painter, and from Victoria by what are listed as 'Destitute Children', whose exhibit was described in the Exhibition notes as 'Cabbage Tree plait, plaiting well-made and of good colour.' A second exhibit of plait from Victoria was sent by an individual called Duffin.[251] The CTL collections include seven examples of four-end rustic plaits and two miniature hats made in Sydney that were displayed at this exhibition.

Other materials

Almost any flexible and durable tape has been worked into a plait at some stage in the last 150 years.

Paper

The use of paper strips can be dated back to the later 1700s at a time when paper was made from rag so had a greater strength. In 1804 a British patent was granted to George Simmonds for 'manufacturing hats, bonnets, and other useful articles of paper, and rendering the same waterproof when required.'[252] He explained that the 'Sheets of paper are cut into strips and woven, matted or plaited into sheets or squares after the manner of cane or chip, or into the shape of the article required.' He also described plaiting the strips into narrow strips in the manner of straw or Leghorn plait. In today's hat industry many hats are made from a Japanese product called Toyo paper.

A loom-woven sheet of hemp (weft) and silk/cotton (warp) stiffened, cut into strips, then plaited.

Cotton tape.

Artificial silk tape.

Ramie tape and felt.

Bast (pink) and Sala.

Yedda tape and artificial tortoise shell.

Whalebone

One of the more unusual historical materials was whalebone, or baleen. Whalebone is occasionally mentioned during the 1800s. In 1806 a patent was issued for processing baleen so that it could be made into plaits for making 'hats, caps for men and women' as well as a wide variety of other uses.[253] A hat in the costume collection of the Los Angeles County Museum of Art dating from 1816–17 is made from dark-coloured baleen that has been plaited into a four-end rustic plait.[254]

Musa textilis

Many plant fibres were manufactured into tapes. *Musa textilis*, a member of the abaca family, is one of the most significant. From its introduction into Switzerland in 1825, by 1840 under the name Manila hemp, about 4,000 tons of hemp fibre were being processed within the industry each year.[255] It is still in use in the hat industry today as machine-made braids and as the popular hat material known as sinamay. A Swiss product called Patent Hemp, in Switzerland called 'hanf patent', was introduced in 1829 by the Bruggisser company of Wohlen. The hemp threads were woven into a length of fabric with hemp as the weft and silk as the warp. The woven piece was passed through a gelatine bath, dried, then passed under cutting rollers where it was cut into strips that were then plaited. This product was the forerunner of the lames or tapes made from long fibres laid side by side that were to enter the market as both plaiting and machine-braid materials later in the century.

Cotton

Cotton lames for the hat trade were first created in Alsace and exhibited at the 1862 International Exhibition in London where they won an award. The Swiss manufacturers of the Seetal region saw an opportunity and by 1867 had perfected their own version of the glued cotton tape. Cotton was the first fibre that could provide a pure white product, something that was desirable for hat fashion at that time. Later the Swiss manufacturers went on to mix hemp with cotton in the lames, a product that became extremely popular in the 1890s.

Ramie

Sometimes referred to as China Grass, ramie comes from the plant *Boehmeria nivea* and variety *tenacissima* which is a member of the nettle family. After combing, the short and silky fibres are glued together and according to the purpose of the finished product, may be stiffened. The sheet is then cut into strips to be worked on a braiding machine or plaited by hand. Ramie was introduced into the Swiss industry in the 1890s causing some sensation as its light weight and sheen were much admired. When dyed the fine fibres could be put together into a tape to create an ombré effect which had never been seen before.

In 1928, following the introduction of cellophane into the materials manufacturing industry, the ramie tape was covered with cellophane on one side to create a new product called neora. As more producers started to make this new product, many trade names appeared. In 1935 cellophane was used to cover both sides of the tape and this product was given the generic name of faltbandel; one of its trade names was Rio. Multiple variations were to follow as many more tapes made from a variety of products including, silk – then artificial silk and viscose products including visca – began to appear in the early 1900s.

This photograph was one of a series taken at Pitstone Farm, Buckinghamshire to show straw preparation. Here, David Cook is seen cutting the straws to shorter lengths.

CHAPTER SIX

STRAW PREPARATION

Before the process of plaiting could begin, the preparation of cereal crop straw was an interconnected industry requiring many processes. In the early years of the English industry some plaiters bought straw direct from the farmers, but later, as the number of plaiters increased, and as the areas in which they lived spread further afield, they purchased prepared bundles from plait markets, dealers or even from the local shop where they could also take finished plaits in exchange for provisions.

This chapter includes an account of the straw bleaching and dyeing industry which was a critically important element of the trade. The demands of fashion were such that the plait dealers supplied the plaiters with coloured straws and instructed them as to the required pattern colourway. Close links and fierce competition existed between the bleaching and dyeing companies of Great Britain, Switzerland, Germany and France. Many foreign companies had branch offices in Luton and St Albans where they received new colours and patterns, which were quickly copied. The *Hatters' Gazette* regularly published new dye recipes and reported on improvements that would have been read closely by the bleaching and dyeing departments of larger hat manufacturers.

Harvesting

The harvested fields of the 1800s were different from those of today, with a smaller size and the crops growing much taller. Harvesting using sickles and scythes was a laborious task necessitating the involvement of many people to cut, gather into sheaves, and tie. With the gradual introduction of harvesting machinery, first the reaping machine introduced to some farms in the 1800s, then the development of a reaper binder that cut and then tied the straw into sheaves, the necessary manpower required to bring in the harvest reduced. While plaiting straw was not a separate crop in England, care had to be taken during harvesting as damaged straws could not be used. Following cutting and binding, the sheaves were stooked or shocked. In this process, several sheaves – the number varied throughout the country and according to the crop – were stood with the uppermost heads leaning against each other so air could pass between and start drying the straw. Sheaves were turned regularly to prevent the inside of the stook to develop mould. The shorter time it was left in the field, the better, since leaving it for too many days risked discoloration by rain and dew. The historian Frederick Davis wrote that after harvest the straw was 'stored away in barn or ricks, like other agricultural products.'[256]

Sometimes tenant farmers were forbidden by their landlords to sell straw for plaiting. It is unclear if this was provoked by jealousy that the tenant could earn more money, or whether it was enforcement of the deep-seated belief that what grew on the land should be returned to the land the next year. William Wilshere,[257] in a journal entry dated January 1817, calculated that a profit of £60 could be made from the straw of 12 acres of plaiting straw. The fact that the crop was both grown for grain and plaiting did create a conflict since by the time the grain was ready for harvest, it was past its best as a plaiting straw. The plea of Corston and others in the early years of the 1800s was that the straw should not be grown for grain, but that the seed should be sown on poor ground which would only provide enough growth for the stem rather than a seed head.

From the early 1700s, the efforts of Domenico Michelacci led the Italian farmers in a different direction. They were encouraged to produce straw specifically for plaiting rather than for grain. This form of dedicated cultivation brought both admiration and a world trade for their Tuscan straw. An 1897 Foreign Office Report recorded that plaiting straw was grown on land owned by farmers or by a group of men known as 'terraticanti, who rent land for the purpose.' The report, which was written at the time when the Italian industry was in decline, also provided the information that, some years before the report was written, 'the district of San Miniato . . . more than 12,000 sacks of seed per annum were sown, in 1896 only 300 sacks were employed for this purpose.'[258] The Italian climate allowed the hand-cut straw to be laid out to dry in the field for a few days before being gathered into small bundles known as manate. In another report on the Florentine industry,[259] Consul-General Colnaghi provided more detail by saying that the small bundles were spread out fan-shaped in the field, left for four or five days, then turned and left for another few days by which time the straws had taken on a light yellow colour.

Drawing

On 2 December 1816 William Wilshere wrote that 'two labourers (this a.m.) began at 9 this morning and before dark had drawn 30 sheaves of an average bulk and appearance as to goodness (two of them being rejected as not worth the labour) the 28 produced 95 lb of drawn straw – considerably more than 3 lb per sheaf.' He also gives details of the work of drawing straw: 'A man used to the work will easily draw 8 lb of straw, in its rough state, in an hour or 64 lbs will be an easy day's work.'[260] Davis, writing in 1874, and whose work may possibly have been the basis for later accounts, called these labourers straw factors and provided a description of their work. 'Each sheaf is taken between the knees, and the straws are drawn out a handful at a time; the wheat ears are then cut off and are ready for the flail; the two upper joints of the straw are preserved for plaiting, the other, or root joint, being cast away; they are then tied into bundles varying in weight from eighteen to thirty pounds.'[261]

An occupation referred to in the census records as straw cutter may also have been carried out by the drawer. Accounts normally refer to the straw being cut to shorter lengths 9–10 in (23–25 cm) long. The *Saturday Magazine* stated that the top three joints could be used if the straw was very good, but the top two joints are more normally used. After the heads had been removed, the article continued, small bundles were sometimes sold 'in the rough' to plaiters for 'twopence per pound.'[262] If the plaiters

Harvesting in the fields of Bramingham to the north of Luton. As far as the eye can see, there are rows of sheaves and at the back of the field you can see some straw ricks.

had the money they usually bought readily prepared straws which cost more but saved considerable preparation time each week.

Sorting

Following the drawing process, although the straws were now the same length, free from leaves and usually from nodes, their thickness still varied. To make a good plait it was essential to sort the straw otherwise the plait would be an uneven width along its length and unsaleable. An account published in 1805[263] stated that 'The straw should be as free from blight and spots as possible, and small, short, soft straws are reckoned the best. The straw is cut or broken at the joints, and the outer covering being removed, is sorted to equal sizes, and formed in short bundles of eight or ten inches in length, and a foot in circumference.' This appears to imply that the straw had been sorted into bundles of similar thickness, but other accounts are less clear. This account does not mention any equipment therefore the straws may have been hand sorted. Sorting can be a hand process; various accounts suggest that hand sorting was undertaken by some plaiters in Essex, and this method is still being used by plaiters in Transylvania.

The first mention of a sorting machine appeared in Tansley's paper to the Society of Arts in 1860: 'Of late years, sorting is performed by a hand-machine similar to a sieve; the straws, being held in any upright position, fall through holes of a uniform size.'[264]

The sorter incorporated metal grids set into a wooden frame. The number of grids varied, and the CTL collections have examples of straw sorters with one to four spaces into which different sized grids could be inserted. Bundles of straws were tapped over the grids, which varied in the spacing of wires, and the straw fell through, down the respective chute into bins below. Once sorted they were tied into bundles of a diameter of about 15 cm (6 in.). Some references spoke of the bundles having a circumference of two hand spans. From this stage onward the straws were called stubs or pipes.

The Saturday Magazine provided two interesting pieces of information. First that the bundles of straw

Pitstone Farm, Buckinghamshire. The rake was used to remove loose weeds and flag before the task of drawing begins. The heads have already been cut off.

purchased at market by plaiters may not have been sorted, so this had to be done at home. The second indicated that the process of sorting was undertaken at several stages, not only for size, but for the quality of straws. The first time was after the drawn (headless) straw had been bleached and before they were cut to their eight- to ten-inch lengths and made into bundles of 'ten inches round.' Once the plaiters had purchased the bundle they would check before plaiting or splitting for the following faults: '1st Black-haud, spottiness or spot; 2nd Red-haud, which is also a fault spoiling the appearance of the plat; 3rd Bruised straw; 4th Jointed straw; 5th Crooked straw.' The plaiter would then sort the straws into three or four sizes.[265] Davis, however, provided contradictory information, saying that the straw factor cut the straws to their length of about nine inches then sorted them through the grids after which they were steamed with the fumes of sulphur. Then a second 'final sorting takes place when all the spotted and discoloured straws are thrown out (these are useful for making into plait for dyeing).'

In Italy the process of sorting was organised on a larger scale using a mechanised process to shuffle the bundles of straws through the grids. The size of grids reflected the size of straw, their size ranging between 0.8 mm to 3 mm. Colnaghi described the complicated mechanical process which revealed that the heads were still on the straw at this stage. They were then sorted into different lengths before being bundled and only then were the heads removed. [266] One of the machines is displayed in the straw museum in Signa, Italy[267] where it is said the straw-sorting machines were introduced in 1827.[268]

Preparation of palm

The process of preparing palm is less complex. In a talk to the Royal Australian Historical Society in 1919 Campbell stated that 'The material used was the young unexpanded leaves of the cabbage-tree palm, which formed an article of commerce then. The immature leaves were dipped in boiling water, which unfolded the sections and toughened and bleached them.'[269] This preparation process is found throughout the various centres of palm plaiting, with the unopened new shoot taken from the plant.

Bleaching

Bleaching, steaming, stoving and sulphuring were terms used in different plaiting areas to describe the same process. In warmer climates straw could be bleached in the sun and many experiments were tried in England in the early 1800s, but the weather made them unreliable.[270] Bleaching with sulphur or brimstone provided a simple and inexpensive method of improving the straw. This work was either undertaken by those who had prepared the straw, or by the plaiters in their homes, which perhaps explains the variations found within accounts.

Pehr Kalm recorded his observations of bleaching in Little Gaddesden, Hertfordshire, in 1748. He saw bundles of straws, which were cut to to length, dipped in water and, after a piece of sulphur contained in a dish was set on fire, the straws were set above the can then covered with a cloth. 'The vapour and smoke from the sulphur makes the straw in these bundles much whiter than it naturally was before.' Joseph Lucas, who translated Kalm's account in an 1892 publication,[271] added a footnote: 'In Ivinghoe village, Sept. 1882, sulphur about the size of a walnut is laid in a shallow circular iron pan, shaped like a scale and, nearly 6 inches diameter and about ¼ inch deep. This is set on to the live coals which are contained in a circular iron pan 6 inches diameter at top, and 2 inches deep, narrowing toward the bottom. The whole apparatus is called the "Steam-pan" and is bodily put into a box or can with the straw round it, and covered over as described by Kalm.'

Accounts vary as to when the straw was bleached, some claimed that the English straw was bleached before it was drawn and sorted; others that bleaching took place after it was drawn, or even later, after it had been drawn and cut. To spend time bleaching the straw while it still had its outer leaves in place seems inefficient since the unwanted leaves and flag would also be bleached; however this process also fumigated the straw and there may have been occasions when this was necessary. Bleaching the bundles of straw, cut to their shorter length, but not necessarily sorted first, first appeared in an account in 1805 and was then repeated in subsequent accounts describing methods of straw preparation.

The chamber used for bleaching could be an old chest or barrel rather than a specifically made box. Examples do not survive in England but can be seen in collections in European and New England museums and historical societies. The surviving boxes have a wide variety of sizes, not all sufficiently large to contain a full length sheaf; however, one report stated that the bleaching box could take up to 200 lbs of straw at a time. *The Workwoman's Guide* provided a drawing of a bleaching box, a small dish to hold the hot embers, and the grid that the straw stood on. The author's directions stated that the tied bundles of straw must first be washed in hot water containing 'soap, pearlash and sugar of lead', after which they were placed in what she described as the 'fumigating box.' The tightly tied bundles had to be placed with care, so they didn't 'fall upon the lighted brimstone and catch fire.' She wrote that they should remain in the box for 12 to 18 hours before being removed, cleaned with a cloth and tied back into bundles.[272]

In Transylvania the plaiters also used a variety of boxes; they ranged from purpose-made bleaching cupboards built from wood or brick, to an old wooden wardrobe.[273] Without providing an explanation, one maker bleached bundles straight from the field while others bleached cut straws, both sorted and unsorted. After plaiting, the smoking, as they called the process, was repeated once the hat was made. Since the process is noxious the box had to be without gaps. The straws were first rinsed in cold water, but one plaiter in Transylvania insisted on using milk, saying the resulting colour was superior. The straws were drained, then stood upright on the rack. If a plait was being bleached it was hung. Many of the boxes had a small gap at their base with a sliding door through which the pan of embers was placed. A piece of sulphur ignited by the hot embers was inserted under the grid before the box was sealed and covered with a heavy damp cloth or blanket. This was to prevent fumes escaping during the process which could take up to 24 hours. Even that time may not be sufficient to achieve the desired shade in which case the whole procedure was repeated.

Commercial bleaching

In the 1890s bleaching with sulphur was still in use in at least one Luton bleaching and dyeing works. An account in *Luton Illustrated* described the process on an industrial scale: 'The works proper are on the ground floor, and consist of wash-house, bunch-house, and stringing house, fitted with steam boiling apparatus, and surrounded by 14 sulphur boxes, used to bleach the straw after washing, also for finishing. These boxes are all connected with a shaft for letting off the vapour when opening, thus avoiding the fumes coming to the faces of the workpeople, and also for enabling the boxes to be cleared at once.'[274]

The sulphuring process was not entirely risk free. The *Hatters' Gazette* described the equipment and stated that the process took three to four hours. It then cautioned that: 'The sulphur must be used sparingly and must be well distributed in the vessel; for, if a large quantity is used in a thick layer, the flame rising too high gives the straw a black colour, which cannot be removed by any means whatever.' The time quoted for bleaching seems to be rather short since other accounts indicate that the process could take up to 24 hours. *The Penny Cyclopaedia* provided a very similar account, saying that if the sulphur was burnt too quickly the straw would develop black, burned spots.

Whilst the sulphuring process was widely known, other processes, introduced later in the 1800s, were closely guarded with secrecy. Inwards wrote that in about 1852 Mr Welch of Welch & Sons patented bleach which was called the 'Luton Bleach.' After washing, the plait was immersed in a bath of weak oxalic acid, then fumed with sulphur, hung out in the sun to dry, then fumed with sulphur again. Inwards noted that 'In those days nearly all bleaching was done by the actual manufacturer of the hats, it was only when the trade began to move by leaps and bounds that works entirely for bleaching purposes were established.'[275]

The *Hatters' Gazette* reported a bleaching process using 'Aqueous of liquid sulphurous acid.'[276] It specified a recipe then gave details of a long and complicated method of bleaching which took five to six days in total. The process appears to bleach using chlorine which would make the straw very brittle, therefore the assumption must be that the straw being bleached was a tough plait. The *Hatters' Gazette* also stated that chlorine could give the straw an undesirable yellow colour if too much chemical was used. In fact, chlorine was later found to be a most unsuitable chemical to use on straw since it caused the straws to become brittle and break.

Later in the 1800s Luton dominated the European bleaching and dyeing trade, buying unbleached plaits from China, bleaching them in Luton and selling them on to the North American and European hat manufacturing centres. This situation created some irritation and friction. Lye & Sons of Luton[277] provided an account of the introduction of a new commercial method of bleaching straw which was to replace the original use of sulphur. 'The introduction of the first Monopol bleach[278] on straw plait by the use of hydrogen peroxide as a bleaching agent satisfied a long felt want of the manufacturers of straw hats in 1892 and lead to a rapid extension of the firm's business, especially to America.' The story of how they came to discover hydrogen peroxide as a bleaching agent is amusing. The account began by saying that the Italians knew the method for this way of bleaching, but kept it secret. On a trip to Paris, Mr W T Lye 'saw a product called Eau-de-Javel advertised in a hairdresser's window for the bleaching of human hair and conceived the idea of trying it out on straw plait.' This claimed that the experiment was the key to successfully bleaching straw plaits by the universally known 'Monopol process.' Despite the company pride shown by Lye, it must be pointed out that there were other commercial trade names for similar bleaches such as A1 and Diamond and there were continual attempts to improve bleaching processes.

Luton Illustrated, describing the bleaching processes at the Luton company Hucklesby and Co., mentioned that 'a new bleaching process by which China straw is now made available for white hats, and though we are not aware of the secret of the operation, we understand that it has had a very favourable influence in still further advancing the trade of the firm and enhancing their reputation.'[279]

Commercial bleaching is still carried out in Luton by the company Barford Brothers. In the 1990s Tony Horn, the then Chairman of the company, explained the bleaching method. The straw was first washed to remove dirt and grease, then submerged in a bath of hydrogen peroxide heated to 140°F, then left to cool overnight. The following day it was rinsed and placed in a bath of cold acid (type not specified) to neutralise the straws, then rinsed again. If the straw was to be dyed it was submerged and held in a dye bath for two hours before a final rinse and drying.

Dyeing

An article in the *Hatter's Gazette* reported: 'Straw dyeing is perhaps as difficult a branch of the dyer's art as any other kind of dyeing. This is due to the peculiar character of the material, the fact that the straw contains an outer coating of a mineralized nature which does not take kindly to dyes.'[280] The bleaching and dyeing trades were closely linked since many types of straw had to be bleached before they could be successfully dyed. In the early years of the 1800s, dyeing was limited both by fashion and the restrictions of vegetable dyes. It was not until the mid 1850s, with the introduction of aniline dyes, that this part of the industry experienced a dramatic change and dyers developed exquisite skills to produce hundreds of shades. This was one of the most secretive sectors of trade since plait and hat colours followed fashion trends. It was an area where companies enjoyed a considerable export trade, in part due to fluctuations in import and export tariffs. Given the importance of coloured plaits and the number of hats made from them, it is perhaps surprising that so few hats survive.

The lack of extant evidence, and the fact that early photographs were in black and white, has created a false impression of straw hats in the 1800s, and that in turn has created an inaccurate understanding of hat fashion. Trade reports in the *Hatter's Gazette* repeatedly referred to the fickle nature of fashion. Colour trends could change within weeks and should there be a death in the Royal Family the trade was badly affected, since a period of mourning would be declared and all plaits and hats would have to be dyed black. Unless they were willing to earn less money by making utilitarian plaits supplying the lower end of the market, plaiters could never anticipate demand and make up stock in advance due to this constant threat.

Plaiters normally purchased, or were supplied with, readily dyed straws from the dealers who would also frequently instruct them on the required plait

Pictured at Ivinghoe, Buckinghamshire the women are sorting the bundles of straw to an evenly matched thickness.

pattern and colour or colours required. Single colour plaits were normally produced by dyeing whole lengths of finished plaits, but some patterned plaits, which were loosely structured, could not withstand the violence of the dyeing process and were made with previously dyed straws. Straws and plaits were often bleached before dyeing, so pale and pastel colours were more effective.

The process of dyeing was a trade within the hat industry rather than being a home-based process. This contrasts with the dyeing of palms which appears to have been undertaken on a smaller scale and seems to have been a home-based occupation using domestic and natural dyes. In both Australia and the Bahamas there were stories[281] that to 'dye' palm black it was hung in a chimney space or held over a smoky flame. On questioning the practice in Australia, I was directed to an 1896 article in the *Evening News*, Sydney that included this explanation: 'Its newness, too, was always a source of anxiety to the wearer. Even as a meerschaum pipe claims no respect until it is colored, so the cabbage-tree did not bear the true hall mark until tanned and weatherworn. It looked as though it had been through many moving incidents by flood and field. Hanging a new hat in a chimney – one of the wide bush chimneys where the beef used to be hung to smoke – was allowable, but no other artificial means were permitted.'[282] It appears that the intention was to age rather than to dye.

The straw industry in the Bahamas has been revived relatively recently, so commercial dyes for home use have always been widely available. Rosemary Brice in the Bahamas shared the information that to create colour, plaiters use fabric dyes for the straw. She stated that the two exceptions were for obtaining brown and black. To obtain brown was as simple as using the dried palm known as brown peel, rather than fresh palm. For black they used the smoke from an oil lamp. She said it is a 'long, tedious process to use the soot from the oil lamps to blacken the straw.' Currently there is no evidence of the North American commercial palm industry using dyes, but absence of evidence does not exclude its existence.

Natural dyes

The earliest reference so far located for the dyeing of straw dates to 1799. This was a period when straw was widely used for the ornamentation of clothes. The article provided instructions for dyeing barley straw a 'beautiful yellow.' After boiling in 'clear lye' the instructions said to 'add as many French beans as will bring them to the colour desired.' Then instructions continue to add brazilwood to dye the straw red. To dye the straw blue, litmus was added[283] and to dye the straw green, it was first dyed blue and then the yellow was boiled in.[284]

Before the introduction of aniline dyes, the industries of England and Europe relied on the relatively limited capabilities of natural materials. Inwards writes that using them was complicated, involving the use of mordants so results were unpredictable.[285] A document of reminiscences written by an employee of Skilbeck Brothers Limited[286] gave detailed information about the origins and uses of various natural dyes for both straw and felt.

- Brazilwood, which produces violets, greys and black.
- Madder, one of the oldest known dyestuffs which can be used to produce a range of colours: purple, orange, red, yellow, and brown.
- Fustic produces yellow and was mixed with other dyes to create shades.

The writer stated that the logs of fustic came from the West Indies, Mexico and Cuba, then were chipped in Luton. There then followed a list of other dyestuffs used in the Luton hat trade: cochineal (which went out of fashion following the introduction of aniline dyes), cudbear, a lichen, annatto, verdigris or acetate of copper, barwood, indigo and galls.

The Workwoman's Guide included two recipes for dyeing straw black. 'Three quarts of water, three quarts of urine, three quarters of a pound of logwood, half a pound of alum, quarter of a pound of copperas, three or four nut galls. Boil the water, urine, logwood, alum, and nut galls together a quarter of an hour, then add the copperas and boil the whole half an hour, afterwards put in the straw, and let it boil six hours. Let the straw remain in the dye till quite cold, then take it out, spread it on a tray or board to dry in the air, turn it every day for a fortnight, then rub each straw with an old linen duster, tie the straw in bundles, and keep in a damp place. It should be used up quickly, or else it will decay, without being stiffened.' A second recipe in the book was slightly different and included instructions for stiffening the straw by steeping gum arabic in small beer[287] and wetting the straw with this solution. The caustic nature of the ingredients listed make it easy to understand why black straw on early hats so often shatters, meaning so many no longer exist.

The earliest references to commercial dyeing in Luton refer to a Mr Randall opening dye works in Sundon in about 1845. Inwards explained that prior to this first organisation into a separate associated industry, dyeing had been undertaken by individuals on a small scale. He also stated that in the early years the only colours produced were black, a very

A collection of natural dyestuffs used in the Luton hat industry. The bottom right box contains sulphur and in the centre box there is Verdigris.

A collection of dyestuffs derived from coal tar and used in the Luton hat industry in the early 1900s.

poor brown and a dark blue. *The Penny Cyclopaedia*[288] provided details of dyeing straw, attributing the information to Dr Ure. He stated that blue was given by working indigo into sulphuric acid, yellow from turmeric, red by boiling hanks of red wool or by using cochineal with salt of tin and tartar. He also mentioned that brazilwood and orchil were also used.

Thomas Lye Senior first had a business in Kirkby Malzeard, near Ripon, buying plaits and hats from the local people and travelling to Luton to sell them. He also had a small dye yard. It was his sons, Thomas and John, who set up business in Luton probably in the early 1850s. Trading as a manufacturer, their first premises were in Wellington Street; however the partnership did not last and Thomas set up his own business as a dyer in Guildford Street possibly around 1855 or 1856,[289] moving to the site in Wardown Park in 1857. Apparently his first success was a grey 'which no other competitor had attempted' stated Inwards. Called 'Quaker Grey,' it was a fashion success. According to the Lye publication, Lye's talent was to produce a range of shades and to copy 'particular colours from natural dyestuffs.' Lye's supremacy in the trade continued throughout the 1800s.

One of the main problems with natural dyes is that they are not colourfast, meaning that some surviving hats that were originally made from coloured straws may have faded. Lack of colourfastness, alongside the limited colour range and presumably the variability of the dyeing process, probably all provided incentives for manufacturers to find new ways to dye straw.

Chemical dyes

This was a vitally important trade within the hat industry. Many of the larger hat manufacturers had their own dyeing sections and the industry's trade journals published new dye recipes and developments during the 1800s. This was an exciting time with the introduction of aniline dyes, derived from coal-tar, and later vat dyes. The first aniline or synthetic dye was accidentally discovered by William Perkin in 1856. He originally called his invention aniline purple but from 1859 the names mauve or mauveine were widely used. Later Carl Gräbe and Carl Lieberman in Germany were the first to discover alizarin. These were then quickly followed by the introduction of many other colours. Although not completely colourfast they were less susceptible to fading; however, their greatest benefit was reliability, meaning not only were the colours good, but they could also be reproduced accurately. Following these developments, Lye's quickly introduced mauve and various shades of violet to their trade offering, and then introduced even more new colours. A report published in 1887[290] listed many colours, some produced by a wide range of dyestuffs: 'Straws there were bleached and unbleached, dyed and undyed, coarse and fine, whole and split, and few prettier sights could anywhere be seen than the collection of dyed straw shown by a local firm comprising over two hundred distinct shades, all of which had been dyed within the week . . . Golds, fawns, greys, steels, reds, blues, greens, and yellows were there in profusion; and the newer shades including heliotrope, old rose, Tonquin brown, olive, myrtle, light Tuscan, terra cotta, coral and Lord Randolph Churchill primrose.' The previous year the company had produced 547 different colour shades for an exhibition. In 1899 they won a gold medal for their exhibit of 1,100 graduated shades displayed at an exhibition in Paris.

George Gage[291] was granted a patent for dyeing straw or straw plaits in 1860. His patent provided a method of producing mauve and magenta. He concluded by providing instructions for dyeing split straw which he explained took the dye only on the inner pith side; the outer, shiny, enamelled side of the straw staying uncoloured to produce a speckled plait. In a conversation with Tony Horn,[292] he recalled using this method in the 1950s and calling it double dyeing. Acid dye was used to dye the outer, shiny side of the split straw plaits and vegetable dye to dye the pithy inside surface. The vegetable dye did not affect the results of the acid dye. The CTLC include plaits made by Hannah Freeman of Finchingfield, Essex who used a commercial clothes dye to produce the same effect.

Many novelty dyeing techniques were introduced at the very end of the 1800s and Inwards[293] described some of the most popular methods. To produce a mottled effect bundles of straw pipes were stood upright in the dye bath and the dye allowed to run through them. They were dyed on the inside and on the outside where they did not touch another straw. Water was run through to create shading. Straws were also dyed with more than one colour; the straw or plait was dyed and then a second colour dye was sprayed or splashed on to the surface. This effect can be seen on some of the Japanese plaits in the CTL collections. The Japanese were the masters of unusual dyeing techniques, surpassing the Germans who had until that time been considered the most proficient. Lye's were one of many companies throughout Europe that developed an iridescent effect on straws by overdyeing the straw with several colours.

The myth of the Aylesbury prune

One story which regularly circulated in the south east Midlands plaiting areas tells of the use, during the late 1800s and early 1900s, of what are variously called plums, prunes or damsons to dye straw plaits. The late-ripening plums were known locally as prunes and were widely grown in Buckinghamshire and Bedfordshire. The subject was comprehensively investigated in an article by local historian Mary Farnell[294] who found no substantiation for the claims and yet the story continued to circulate. In the earliest days of the plaiting industry when hats were made in small numbers, perhaps within family groups, or when plaiters produced their own hats, they may have used local dyestuffs to colour the straw; however, this would have been unusual. When asked if plums would dye straw, and if he had any knowledge of them being used particularly during the Second World War, the late Tony Horn could not provide any substantiation of the claims.

It is rare to find an image of a plaiter using a mill in their home. The size of bundle she is passing through the rollers indicates the amount of plait she will be making.

CHAPTER SEVEN

TOOLS OF THE TRADE

If you could afford to buy plaiting straws and had knowledge of patterns, you needed very few tools. To earn the most money, you had to make split straw plaits, so a splitter, which could be as simple as a pin for splitting palm or a more elaborate tool for cutting wheat or rye, was essential. Plaiters were working to the precise instructions of the plait dealer therefore had to make accurately sized plaits. Better paid split straw plaits required the cutting of whole straws into a specific width, usually between 1–2 mm. Although the straws were sorted into bundles of a similar size, the straw supplied by the dealer, or purchased from the market, varied and plaiters never knew the straw diameter of the bundles for purchase. To consistently cut a whole straw to the required splint width, they needed a range of splitters with different numbers of cutting fins.

Plaiters also needed an efficient means of softening the straw splints before beginning to plait. Various designs of mills, either designed to hang on a wall or to be a floor-standing device, are found in British, European and North American plaiting centres. The mill was also used to flatten, stretch and beautify finished plaits. Both these essential tools could be shared between the family or within groups of plaiters when they worked together.

The splitter

Thomas Bagshawe and Charles Freeman undertook considerable research into the origins of the splitter, but surprisingly although having researched extensively, they seem to have failed to appreciate the full significance of their findings. In *The Romance of the Straw Hat*,[295] they published a truncated explanation which has become a much repeated story. They omitted their belief that the straw splitter had been adapted from an earlier tool. Documents in the Bagshawe Collection Archive[296] provided evidence of an evolution from the basketmakers' osier cleave or cleaver to the straw splitter of the 1800s. Although at the time they did not realise it, a cleave that they had found bore remarkable similarities to the early forms of straw splitters found in both France and Switzerland. We will never know if they found a drawing in Diderot and Alembert's Encyclopaedia of 1751[297] which showed a metal tool for splitting hard woods intended for cabinet work. It was more compact than an osier cleave but had the same cutting fins. Both types lacked the guiding point found in later forms of straw splitters.

Through auction in 1950, they purchased what they described as a 'basket-maker's cleave. 3-wing,' possibly made of yew, inscribed on the shoulder 'Pavlvs Bopp 1654 and on the wings: P 1 C 6 P 54.'[298] They also discovered two small bone tools in a Suffolk Museum which were recorded as 'implements used for splitting straws. Used in fancy work.' No date was provided, and the definition of fancy work is not recorded.

Four versions of early cleaves and splitter

Bagshawe and Freeman thought this may be Flemish but used in England. Length: 6.7 cm (2.6 in.).

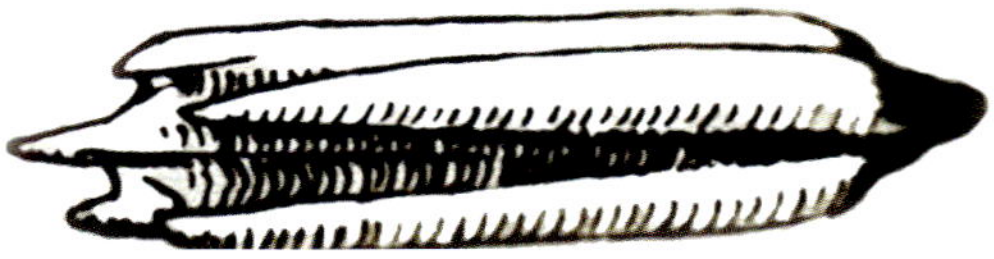

Bone splitters found in Suffolk. It has four 'wings.' Length: about 4.5 cm (1.75 in.).

Horn splitter believed to have been made and used by prisoners at Yaxley barracks. Length: 6.5 cm (2.6 in.).

A Swiss bone splitter with twelve cutting fins. Note how this example has a short guide point. Length: 6.5 cm (2.6 in.).

First introduction

By the 1600s, straw marquetry, also called laid work, was a popular commercial trade in France, the Low Countries, Italy, Germany and Great Britain. The work involved cutting whole straw stems into splints of an equal width. A reliable tool to speed up this work would have been of enormous benefit to the workers.

In December 1860, Alfred John Tansley presented a paper to members of the Society of Arts and wrote of the splitter:[299] 'it is generally supposed that the French[300] prisoners at Yaxley Barracks, near Stilton, first made it in bone, between the years 1803 and 1806. It was about two inches long, brought to a point, behind which a set of cutters was arranged in a circle.' This theory of invention by prisoners held in detention at depots within Great Britain between 1797–1814 is regularly repeated. Amongst the wide range of goods that prisoners were producing were those decorated with straw marquetry. While the prisoners may have made splitters, they may have used existing knowledge of a tool but without further evidence it may have to be accepted they created some form of new design.

On examination of the facts, what is less likely is that at the beginning of their incarceration they were splitting straw to make straw plaits. A bonnet believed to have been made by prisoners at the Yaxley Barracks in the collections at Peterborough City Museum was made from fine whole straws very similar to Tuscan straws.[301] The Waller family, Luton hat manufacturers, were illicitly trading in straw plaits and hats, supplying straw to the prisoners. There were soon attempts to restrict this trade, which was argued would create unfair competition for the English plaiters. After the introduction of trading bans, collusion between the guards and prisoners enabled trade to continue for some time before being stopped in about 1807. Given the evidence of the surviving hat, and the demand for imitations of Italian products in this period, the straw they used was imported from Italy rather than being split. Italy was the one centre not needing a splitter because they used fine straw, and it was only later in the 1800s, with the introduction of loom-woven straw and horsehair braids, that a splitter was required.

In France there was a type of straw splitter only 34 mm long (1.25 in.), made from wood, but possibly of bone and horn as well. Although of a similar design to a cleave, it had a pronounced guiding point that inserted into the hollow stem to hold the straw in place as it split. Very little information has so far been found about this type of splitter. Without citing their original sources, some references claimed that they dated to the 1700s, others to the 1800s. These are the splitters that may have been known to the prisoners, and since they could be easily carved from bone or horn, or whittled from wood, they were easy to make. If a straw splitter already existed at this time and was successfully being used for marquetry, its full potential would only be realised when split straw was needed for plaits or other uses.

In the 1780s and 1790s, and perhaps in part due to the influx into London of French émigrés, decorating straw embroidery on clothes became very fashionable. It was used for men's waistcoats, shoes and dresses. *The European Magazine* and *London Review* reported on these fashionable introductions, firstly in 1783[302] in an article: 'The crapes and gauzes were very much ornamented with straw in different colours; this beautiful invention is now arrived to its highest perfection, but we should be sorry to see it long in use, as it must hurt the needle-workers in embroidery severely . . . Straw, flowers and gauze are worn in every part of dress, particularly in dress caps.' The next month there was a second article: 'Straw! Straw! Straw! Everything is ornamented with straw from the cap to the shoe buckle; and Ceres seems to be the favourite idol with

Made from hard wood, these decorative splitters, with their long guiding point, split straw very effectively. Each one is about 3.5cm (1.4in.) long.

not only the female, but with the male part of the fashionable world, for the gentlemen's waistcoats are ribbed with straw, and they look as if they had amused themselves in Bedlam for some time past, manufacturing the flimsy doublet.' In France silk and straw fabrics woven on a loom were being manufactured and the straw industry in Switzerland was developing. By examining all this information, it appears that rather than being invented sometime between 1785 and 1805, as claimed by many writers, an existing tool was introduced into wider use.

The Penny Cyclopaedia[303] included an account of the introduction of the straw splitter, which they called a 'machine.' The author wrote that the operation of splitting straw and using the narrow splints, or slips of straw, in lieu of whole straws, was introduced at the end of the 1700s. Before the introduction of the splitter, straw was split with knives by hand which 'was both tedious and unsatisfactory, since it gave no security for the uniform width of the splints upon which the beauty of the plat greatly depends.' The article continued that his informant was a correspondent from Watford who stated that 'his father Thomas Simmons (now deceased) was residing when a boy, about the year 1785,[304] at Chalfont St Peter's, Buckinghamshire, and that when amusing himself one evening by cutting pieces of wood, he made an article upon which he put a straw, and found that it divided it into several pieces. A female who was present asked him to give it to her, observing that if he could not make money of it, she could. She had the instrument, and gave the boy a shilling. He was subsequently apprenticed to a blacksmith; and, on visiting his friends, he found them engaged in splitting straws with a penknife. Perceiving that the operation might be much better performed by an apparatus similar to that which he had made some time before, he then made some machines of iron on the same principle.'

In 1801, Arthur Young writes that 'the instrument for splitting straw was invented about a year since, and has had a great effect; before, they were forced to pick small straws, and could neither make the works they effect now, nor execute so well.'[305] During the first years of the 1800s the splitter was introduced into workhouses and even into prisons. The Bedford Quarter Session Report of 1804 stated, that 142 straw splitting machines were purchased for the county gaol (Bedford) and prisoners were put to plaiting to earn their keep.[306] Reports from the London and Dublin Societies[307] state that 'It is about five years since the manufactory of split straw was introduced into this country by Mr Simpson of Lillypot Lane, near Wood Street.' This clearly was a reference to the Simpson and Ibester patent of 1800,[308] which does not explain how the straw was split, or mention use of a specific tool. These accounts appear to agree that in 1800 a splitter was introduced into the hat industry.

The Saturday Magazine, 1833[309] added to the story of Thomas Simmons, making the claim that 'the ingenuity of the inventor (a great benefactor to his country,) was rewarded by realising a fortune of £30,000; and from that time may be dated the use of the plat made from divided straws.' The claim of great rewards was both repeated and dismissed in subsequent reports, with the son of Thomas Simmons saying that 'so far from raising a fortune . . . it realised one shilling.' The large sum of money quoted may reflect the monetary benefit to the entire industry rather than to Simmons.

Design evolution

In *Dunstaplelogia*[310] Charles Lamborn provided the following account: 'According to the evidence of Agnes Ashwell, now widow Siret living in an adjoining village, the first splitters were made by the French prisoners, about the year 1805, and were of bone, one inch and a-half in length with the cutting knives at the end; the straw being put on the point was thrust over the splitter, something in the same way as osiers are now split by basketmakers. Norman, a blacksmith, living upon the spot now occupied by Mr Joseph Guttridge's farm, made an improvement by working the machine in iron, but still retained the upright position; subsequently Janes, another blacksmith turned the end at right angles and formed an elbow about half-an-inch in length, and brought it to a point, placing the fangs or cutting knives at the lower end in the form of spokes, by which the straw is divided into as many portions as desired. His machines were still made of iron, and very similar to those now in use, differing only in the metal used, brass being much cheaper, though far less durable. The enormous price of these machines prevented them from getting into general use as much as two guineas having been paid for a single instrument. Another improvement was made in 1815. A circular piece of wood containing four or five small holes, into which were fixed iron splitters, in the form of spokes on a wheel, with spikes to run down the straw, thus placing a whole set of machines in one frame.'

Marian Nichols,[311] former curator at Luton Museums, said that John Dony was sceptical about the accuracy of Lamborn's information; however a search of the national census and local records seems to provide some credibility for the individuals mentioned and

Lamborn's data collection methods. Agnes Ashwell was a plaiter living in Edlesborough and both she and her children, and later grandchildren, were listed as plaiters in the 1841, 1851 and 1861 census records. Norman may have been Henry Norman, a blacksmith living at Hudnall in the parish of Edlesborough, whose wife and daughters were plaiters. Janes being a common local name is more difficult to trace; it might have been James Janes, living in Edlesborough, buried in Dunstable, whose sons James and Benjamin were listed as blacksmiths in later census records. Lamborn's account provided a logical progression from a splitter, shaped like an osier cleave, to a splitter on a stem or handle, and finally to the frame where the cutting fins were placed within the wooden stand.

His description links to bone splitters found in Switzerland and possibly elsewhere. Gotlieb Rodel provided one of two accounts so far found.[312] He stated that they were made by many men in the village of Egliswil, canton Aargau, but failed to provide any dates for their production. He also wrote that the men of the town arranged manufacture and sale of the splitters but did not reveal the scale of this trade. Joseph Reichlen claimed that Jean Jelk of Planfayon, canton Gruyère, invented an instrument called a splitting iron and seemed to indicate this occurred in the first years of the 1800s, and he believed the tool enabled a rapid progression of the industry. No description of the tool was provided. The link to Switzerland was possibly part of the story missed in Bagshawe and Freeman's research and was perhaps why there was some distrust of Lamborn's account.

Splitter designs constantly evolved in the 1800s. An account of straw work in Dunstable, published in 1825,[313] described the splitter being used: 'they saw a young woman, by pushing them through a hollow tube, bring each of them into five or six delicate narrow lengths. It was still beyond their comprehension how this could split them so completely, all of a size, and so perfectly straight at the edge . . . We were then shewn that, within that tube, a little way down, there were several small, thin, and very sharp blades fixed in the sides, so that no straw could get through the tube without meeting them, and being cut by them from end to end; these lengths, so prepared, are called splints.'

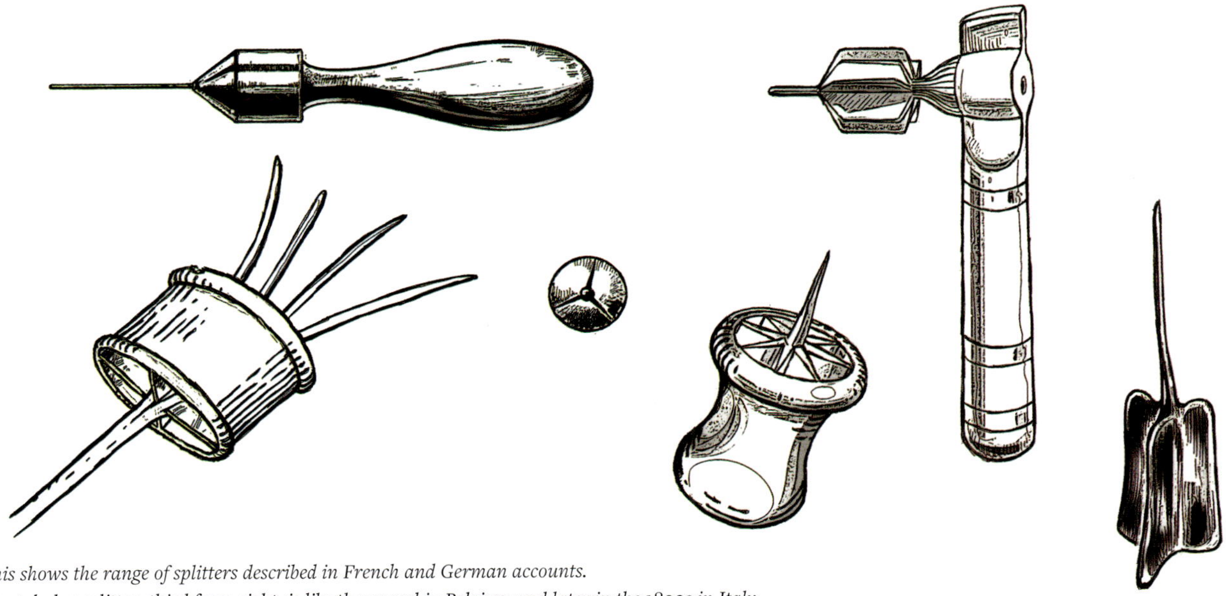

This shows the range of splitters described in French and German accounts.
The tubular splitter, third from right, is like those used in Belgium and later in the 1800s in Italy.

Similarly designed, tube splitters were used in the French, Swiss, German and Belgian plaiting industries. An essay included drawings and the description of a newly improved splitter developed by Messieurs Laselve and Chastaing, producers of straw and silk fabrics in Lyon.[314] This design had metal cutters enclosed within a circular wooden frame. A similarly designed splitter was included in *The Girl's Own Paper*'s account of straw plaiting in the Black Forest.[315] One online source stated that the splitter was introduced into the Black Forest industry by Obervogt Huber in 1806.[316] It seems that more than one design may have been available in Germany and probably elsewhere since a publication of 1821 described a splitter with a handle.[317] The Ottmar Reich hat company centenary book published in 1938 included images of splitters used in the Lindenberg industry during the 1800s. Two are like the Swiss splitter, one of them had an extremely long guiding point, the third had its cutting fins housed within a wooden tube.[318]

No clear information has been found to indicate when a splitter was first used in Belgium. Records in the *Hatters' Gazette* and other sources indicate that from the early 1800s Belgian plaiters were highly respected for their split straw plaits. This provides indication that a splitter must have been in use by that time.

The metal splitter was described in *The Saturday Magazine*: 'there are two kinds. One kind, probably the earliest, consists of a pointed wire, upon which the straw is forced; it then comes in contact with 4, 5, 6, 7, 8, 9, 10 or 11 sharp divisions (the numbers 5, 6, 7 are the most usual), which divide the straw into so many equal parts. These instruments have handles, and are made of either brass or iron; some are made more crooked than others the price is from twopence upwards.' *The Workwoman's Guide*[319] published in 1840 reported that they 'may be procured with almost any number of wire or divisions, from two up to seven or eight. The machine, which is nothing but crossed wires or divisions in iron, is set into a wooden handle, through which the straw is pressed, and thus divided into an equal number of splints or split straws. These machines cost from 2d to 8d each.'

It is rare to have the pot used to hold the range of splitters needed. The detail of the splitter shows how repeated use wears away the metal fins. Eventually the fin will break, and the splitter will be useless.

Two splitters have been found in Canada. The first iron example was made by a blacksmith living near Penobsquis, New Brunswick, Canada. At one end it has four fins and at the other three. It was owned and used by Rachel Loretta Branscombe McLeod. *See page 38.*
The second splitter which has five cutting fins was made by Hugh Ackland in the 1830s from a penny, then attached to an iron shaft. He emigrated from Ireland in about 1819 but no family association to hat making is known. Perhaps his wife Mary made hats for herself and their children.

Metal splitters also appear in North America. As to whether they were locally made or imported is not usually known. Two exceptions exist in Canada, one in Nova Scotia and the second in Ontario, and both are extraordinary homemade splitters. The first example was smithied in the 1800s in Penobsquis, New Brunswick. It is made of iron and is a double-ended splitter, one end has four cutting fins and the other three. The second, in the collections of the Carleton Place and Beckwith Heritage Museum,[320] was made by Hugh Ackland an immigrant from Borrisoleigh, County Tipperary, Ireland who arrived in the area in about 1819. Currently no information links him to straw hat making.

Bone splitters

Seringe, in his essay of 1828 entitled *Mémoire sur la Culture et Emploi des Céreales*, included a drawing of what he described as a Swiss or Fribourg splitter which was a bone splitter set onto a wooden handle. This was like those found in various museums in canton Fribourg, Switzerland and in Essex, England. Chalkley Gould[321] presented a paper in which he expressed his view that the Essex plaiters preferred to use a bone splitter. 'Of late years the bone engine has entirely disappeared, and present day plaiters on the borders of Bedfordshire have told me that they have never used, or even seen, other than metal engines . . . yet it cannot be 30 years since an old

English bone splitters were usually attached to a wooden shaft, but there were design variations.

dame at Little Maplestead told me she had tried them new-fangled iron things and did not hold with them; bone for her.'

In 1907, Miller Christy[322] stated that he was told by a Mr Bingham that 'Up to 30 years or so ago, thrifty labourers used to supplement their weekly wage by making, out of beef shank bones, the little bone instruments called by them engines, which were used for splitting the straw. These were made in sets of six or seven, each one having a different number of cogs (or wings) intended to split the straw into four, five, six, seven, eight, nine, or ten strips, according to the fineness required. A good workman could make three or four engines in an evening, and they sold at a penny or three-halfpence each. Great care was needed in order to make each of the radiating cogs the exact size required and all the same distance apart. Later on, bundles of straws, already split, were bought from Dunstable, and the making of these engines came to an end.'

Gould also included a description of men making the splitters. From an ox shank-bone obtained from a butcher, the hardest part was made into cubes or dice, then with a penknife and narrow chisel fashioned into an 'engine.' After fitting it into a wooden handle it was sold to the plaiter for 1d, or more according to the number of 'cutting cogs.' R. W. Rowe claims that in Essex splitters were either homemade or bought from travelling gypsies and pedlars, but he provided no sources for this information.[323] As with the blacksmith-made metal splitters, many variations are found with the bone splitters.

Frame splitter

Said to have been introduced in about 1815, this type houses a varying number of splitters within a wooden frame. These were more expensive to buy but if a plaiter could afford one then it must have been a relief to have all the splitters easily to hand and not to have to search for an individual splitter. The skill of the plaiter when using a frame splitter was described in *Cassell's Family Magazine*, 1882: 'experienced splitters know their holes as well as bagatelle-players know the numbers of the cups into which their balls may go.'[324]

It is described by *The Saturday Magazine* as 'consists of the point and sharp part let into wood. Several instruments, as the Nos. 4, 5, 6 and 7, are in one piece of wood. This latter instrument sells, in white wood or oak, for one shilling and upwards; in mahogany somewhat dearer.'[325]

Other than indicating its practicality, no accounts explain the derivation of a frame splitter, and none provide explanation for attribution to 1815. A reference needing further research is in a German publication[326]. In about 1815 the German plaiters around Lindenberg wanted to improve the existing form of splitter with one that could split several straws at the same time. This led to a collaboration with a London trading company called Hoole that produced iron and steel products. London Trade Directories of this period list two cutlers with the name Hoole, including Stephen Hoole trading in Oxford Street in 1810. He was listed as a 'razor-maker, engraving-instrument-maker, and cutler.' Is this a connection to its development?

There is a great variation in shapes and sizes of frame splitters. Most appear to be homemade rather than crafted and may have been made to the specification of the plaiter. The smallest holds two cutting fins and the largest eight within a single frame.

The CTLC include a selection of frame splitters each one with the name of its maker stamped. The names are Green and either J Austin or Austin. It is widely assumed that the maker J Austin lived in Akeman Street, Tring. Indeed, there was a woodturner working there in the 1800s, but it should be noted that Austin is quite a common name and national census records list others who were turners or carpenters living in and close to Tring. If the maker listed in the census records is indeed James Austin of Akeman Street, he was not born until 1805 or 1806 so would not have been making and selling his splitters in 1815 which is the attributed date of introduction. By 1834, aged about 29, he was listed in Pigot's Directory as a wood turner. This information could indicate that any frame splitter marked J Austin was made after the 1820s. He continued in trade until the 1870s when in his sixties. Jean Davis[327] wrote that the Austin splitters were filed from a French nail, but she did not disclose where she collected this information.

Other preparation tools

The Ottmar Reich book included a wooden block called a 'Strīchar.' It was 'used to flatten overly coarse straws and judging by the wear and tear many of this type must have been used.'[328] It seems that in Germany some whole straw was softened and flattened by using this tool.

In 1898 Louis Edgar Andés[329] implied that German plaiters were using the entire top section of the straw which varies in width between the *punte* and *pedale* ends. To correct the uneven width, after splitting the splints were put through a 'slitting comb between flat rollers.' This process was not mentioned elsewhere.

Another splitting process was described in the *Hatters' Gazette*, the whole straw being 'flattened and straightened at the same time,' then 'split into several strips by being passed once more between the piece of leather and a small steel plate with several teeth.'[330]

THE IDYLL OF THE PALM-LEAF HAT.—From a Design by J. N. Hyde.—See Page 287.

This detailed drawing appeared in Frank Leslie's Illustrated Newspaper, *1871 It clearly shows a hat being woven from what is described as palm leaf. The palm is being split with a fork-like tool Another woman is weaving rather than plaiting a hat.*

Splitting palm

It is surprising that although the making of woven Brazilian hats was a large and significant trade in St Albans, very little was written about their making. It is assumed that the palm must have been split using a tool like those used in the other centres where palm hats were being made. In the Bahamas, Bermuda, southern United States and various Caribbean Islands, where plaits are still being made from local palms, the prepared leaf is split with a pin or knife. In the 1800s when the industry was of far greater significance, other forms of tools were used to split the palm leaf quickly and effectively. An illustration which appeared in *Frank Leslie's Illustrated Newspaper* showed two young women making a palm hat. In the doorway, a young boy was delivering another bundle of leaves, a seated woman was hand-weaving a hat, and the standing woman was intently splitting a leaf which was held down onto the table by a splitting tool shaped like a comb. As she drew the leaf under the splitting comb, her right hand grasped and pulled the split leaf.

There was a second type of straw and palm splitter which is more commonly found, particularly in the collections of historical societies in New England. Advertisements appeared in the *New England Farmer* and other newspapers from about 1818.[331] A description of this design of straw and palm splitter appeared in a German publication of 1821 which called it a Saxon straw splitter.[332] That the American straw splitter was significantly different from those used in Europe reflects the nature of the North American straw industry, where the use of palm was possibly a larger industry than that involving wheat, oats and rye.

Another fascinating type of palm splitter was discovered during an archaeological exploration of the Hyde Park Barracks in Sydney. This splitter has a wooden handle broadening into a head into which sharp blades have been inserted. Hyde Park Barracks were built between 1817–19 to house government-assigned convicts. The last convicts left in 1848 after which the building became a home for destitute women and orphan children.[333] Many plait fragments of four-end rustic plaits were found.[334]

Since the shredder, or cutter as it had been called, was found under floorboards of an area that was home to both sets of occupants, it is not possible to be certain when the fragments of plait were put there. The convicts were allowed to make plaits and sew them into hats for their own wear and for sale, but so were the women who entered later. Among the many fragments of four-end rustic plaits discovered was a single piece of double splint plait made from a cereal crop straw. One paper detailing

Whilst this North American tool would be quick and efficient for splitting palm, to split a straw, the stem first had to be split and flattened. At Framingham Historical Society, Massachusetts one example, still with the start of the plait, has been split with one of these tools.

the archaeological investigations indicated that the women may have been repairing as well as making plaits for hats and baskets.[335] As with the American comb shown in the *Leslie* illustration, this tool would have been used in a similar manner; the cabbage tree palm leaf being drawn across the cutting blades. Since this find is the only currently known example, it is impossible to ascertain if there were variations in design. Sue Brian, an Australian researcher and maker, provided two references: 'Each section, which was about an inch or so in width, was split up into strips of a uniform width by means of sharp pieces of tin inserted in a board. Then these strips were plaited into sennit by hand which occupied a long time before sufficient could be made.'[336] The second reference was from the *Sydney Morning Herald*: 'The leaf was then split into narrow strands of equal width by means of a home-made splitter consisting of a short light wooden haft, into the end of which were inserted peg-tooth points, or teeth, filed from stay busks, the implement thus resembling a miniature rake in appearance, six inches in length.'[337]

Called a shredding tool, it was used to split cabbage tree palm leaves (Livistona australis). *It was found with fragments of a four-end rustic plait under the floors of Hyde Park Barracks, Sydney.*

Chip plane and width cutter

While much detail was given on the preparation of cereal crop straws, the preparation of chip is not recorded in any detail, which is surprising since it must have provided a regular trade in plaiting areas. Peter Debaufre was granted a patent in 1769 for the 'engines or tools for the shaving, cutting and preparing of wood for making of hats and bonnets of the same sort as those which are imported…from Leghorn and other parts of Italy.'[338] After describing the equipment for which no drawings were provided, he then proceeded to describe the loom on which the chip strips were to be woven. The Society of Arts awarded a prize of 25 guineas for 'tools for cutting chips for making chip hats to Mr Robert Galloway' in 1775. No surviving correspondence has been found that could provide information about the tools.

The plane, in the background, and the willow-chip width-maker, in the forefront of the image, consist of a brass holder containing several blades that are separated by removable plates so the spacing can be adjusted. These two objects were used at Aston Clinton, Buckinghamshire until the end of the 1800s.

Notes made at the time of acquisition of a chip plane, a width cutter and a plait from Walter Gray, a plait dealer, stated that 'the wood was worked when green and sappy. The width maker was run down the blocks about a yard long, the shavings were detached with the plane.'[339] The strip width varied from between 1 mm to 10 mm.

In Germany, Switzerland and North America many examples of mills attached to benches still survive while in Great Britain those which attach to a wall are the only known type.

Mills, mangles and rollers

While bleaching and dampening softened the splints, pithier ones might have cracked and broken during plaiting. A splint mill was used to soften the straws after splitting. Milling did not remove the pith, it compressed it, making the splint more pliable. A second type of mill was for flattening and improving the finished plait. Although the splint mill could also be used for both purposes, early versions of the plait mill could only mill plait. The difference between the two is in the construction of the rollers. The splint mill had smooth rollers, and the plait mill rollers incorporated cleverly carved grooves, which while guiding the finished plait through, ensured a plait with a decorative head could pass through without flattening it. Museum collections include more examples of splint mills than plait mills, which is understandable given the versatility of the splint mill and the fact that until the 1860s many plaiters worked within family groups making plaits and hats.

The straw mill design is very similar throughout the British plaiting districts. Two rollers were held in place within the frame and pressure was exerted downwards onto the top roller by means of a wooden screw. A wooden handle attached to the lower roller was turned to feed the splints or plaits between them. In Great Britain the mill was commonly attached to the door frame in the workroom or plaiter's house, but in Europe and North America it was more common for it to be designed into a freestanding bench that could be sat at while the work was done. Mills were expensive, making it unlikely, particularly later in the 1800s as the trade began to fail, that a plaiter could afford to purchase one, but there is evidence they were shared.

Origins of the mill

The earliest record found mentioned repair of a plaiting mill at Caddington workhouse in Bedfordshire in June 1771.[340] The London and Dublin Societies account of 1805 did not mention mills even though it went into considerable detail about the manufacture of plaits. Lamborn wrote in 1859 that 'when the plait is finished, it is passed between a pair of small wooden rollers, called a plait mill to make it flat and hard. When these mills were introduced in 1807, they were called box mills, and cost 7s 6d each.' In 1820 mills were recorded as being part of the inventory in the Edlesborough Workhouse, Buckinghamshire.[341] Lamborn does appear to have collected much of his information from Edlesborough, Buckinghamshire, and Dunstable, Bedfordshire. *The Saturday Magazine*, 1833,[342] mentioned that 'Before working up the splints or straws into plat, those which are more or less curved or hollow, are flattened. This was attempted to be done by the common rolling pin, but latterly by an instrument of work called the plat mill; made generally of deal, but sometimes of box-wood. The straw is put between the cylinders of this mill, and worked two or three times through it, by which the splints become flat, and are easy to work. The plat-mill in use at present is soon put out of order; and an acceptable service would be rendered to several English counties by the improvement of this simple but important machine.'

The Workwoman's Guide stated that the mill should be made of the strongest oak or boxwood. It questioned if 'glass rollers would produce a higher finish,' and provided advice on how to position the mill 'fastened to the side of some chest, press, or door . . . proper height from the floor for convenience. From three feet and a half to four feet and a half is about the best distance. It should be placed in a situation where the handle may have free play.'[343]Although other woods such as oak were used, the frame was commonly made of beech and the rollers of boxwood.[344]

Mills were the work of local wood workers and sold at plait markets, where the plaiter could also purchase a splitter. Without mentioning her sources, or providing dates, Jean Davis in her research notes,[345] stated that 'Benjamin Barber, who lived in Tring, had a brother who was a blacksmith and together they adapted the mill principle into a mangle for clothes, unheard of at that time and in that place. . .' She continued: 'Austin's made mills as well as splitters and the Austin mark may be found on the wooden frame above the handle. Other mill manufactures included Reynolds of Chesham, R. Bland of Luton, Barrett of Luton, R. Carn of Smithfield and there were no doubt many more.' There were, including Bigg, Andrews and Spratley, but most mills were unmarked by their maker.

The European and North American mills worked in the same way as the British type; however, there are a few examples with three rollers instead of two, one being in the collection of Museo Onsernonese, Switzerland.

These are three types of mills used in the straw hat industry. The splint mill with its flat rollers, the plait mill with its grooved rollers and a metal mill made by a Luton company, Moody.

Plait mill

Inwards[346] explained that 'In hand sewing times it (milling) was an absolute necessity, as it imparted a requisite pliability to the somewhat harsh fibres and permitted their easier adjustment in sewing to the requirements of the shape. It also, on those plaits which had "heads", accentuated the difference between the head and the foot, giving a greater boldness of effect. Generally, these rollers were designed and cut to take all widths of plait, and the "trolls", as the individual grooves were designated, were made with a double recess, the smaller one which permitted the head of the plait to escape the pressure exerted on the foot.'

Change was necessary following the introduction of the much harder Chinese plaits. Wooden mills were no longer strong enough for the work and they became unreliable, breaking frequently. Inwards wrote that 'When the extra demand for machine-made hats arose, it was found that the harsher plaits from China were too wearing on the wooden rollers, and mills made from iron were produced.' The metal mills were designed differently, having two narrow rollers of significantly different diameters that were without grooves. To enable the plait to pass between them without falling off the edge, an adjustable guide was fixed beside the lower roller and could be adjusted so the patterned edge of a plait was held clear whilst the body of the plait was compressed. To maintain the necessary factory production speed, some mills were driven by steam or gas.

This variation with two handles was used in Parkdale, Nova Scotia in the 1800s. The plait shown opposite was also made in the Lunenburg County.

The *Luton Illustrated magazine*, which was possibly published in the 1890s, featured articles about Arthur Barrett: 'Block and Plait Mill Manufacturer, Inventor of Improved Plaiting Machines,'[347] Messieurs Janes Brothers: 'Makers and Repairers of Straw Hat Machines and Plait Mills,' and Mr John Spratley who is listed as a 'Marquee and Tent Provider.' The article tells us that 'Mr Barrett has an old established reputation, his improved plait mill, block turning appliances, etc., being recognised as the best in the trade both in design, material and workmanship.'[348] The article on the Janes Brothers included a drawing of their metal mill.

'The company was only established six years ago but has succeeded in building up a business of decidedly more than average importance in supplying plait sewing machines, plait mills and kindred adjuncts. Janes Bros., were the original inventors of the famed "Stanley" Plait Mill, an appliance which by its compactness, efficiency, durability and simplicity of arrangement, has won golden opinions from workers in straw of every sort and condition. One of the principal advantages exhibited by this machine over all others is to be found in the circumstances that whilst constructed throughout of iron and steel, and entirely devoid of any intricate gearing, it can be adjusted to suit any width of plait and head,[349] and will stand the heat of the factories and the wear and tear of the hard plait now used without splitting or getting out of order. It is capable of milling over twenty four inches every revolution, and at £1.15s, which is Messrs. Janes Bros. price to the trade, it may be fairly said to constitute the cheapest and most desirable plait mill extant.'

Rollers and rolling pins

In Essex various sizes of rolling pins were used to soften the splints and to improve the appearance of the finished plaits. The rolling would have been done on a hard surface. Rowe[350] and other sources stated that the hard surface was usually the plaiter's half yard board which was also used for measuring the plaits.

This rolling pin was used to flatten and improve finished plaits in Finchingfield, Essex.

This elaborately trimmed silk reticule with straw products was made in the early 1800s. The side shown has delicate split straw plaits, some incorporating straw threads, and loom-made braids comprising horsehair, plaits and straw threads. There is an insert of fine Italian plait stitched edge to edge. (CTLC 2022/75)

CHAPTER EIGHT

DEVELOPMENT OF PLAIT PATTERNS

'The varieties are endless. Florentine dealers have exhibited more than 7,000 different patterns' was a statement made in a millinery book published in 1918.[351] While that number probably included machine-made braids, it was possibly accurate if variations of plait width, combinations of materials and colourways were included. The European industry was a complex and integrated system of trading with many countries having several centres of industry amd producing plaits made from numerous materials. There was also allied production that included hat trimming products made in Switzerland, Italy and Germany, and loom-made straw braids made in Switzerland and Italy. This latter trade also appeared for a few decades in England and the United States.

Although information about these industries survives in hats, plaits, images and documents, to conclusively prove the provenance of some plaits will probably be impossible. That any consideration of the development of plaits can be made is entirely due to the existence of museum collections and the careful documentation of their curators. The largest collections of straw plait, braid and loom-made braid samples are those of the CTLC. There is probably the largest collection of hat trade sample books in the world in Strohmuseum im Park, Wohlen, Switzerland. The Swiss traders of Wohlen not only traded with other cantons, and set up factories and partnerships with Italian companies, they also relied on material suppliers and other plaiting centres to supply plait. Luton, Bedfordshire was another global centre of trade, buying in materials, plaits and other hat products. This knowledge is vital since at least some of the plaits collected and held in museum collections may be there due to this international trade.

To establish the origins of any product it is essential to analyse the source of the acquisition and the information provided at that time, but even then, further research may still be required. The surviving evidence shows us that the pattern and colour of plaits and braids were copied extensively throughout Europe. When China and Japan entered the market, pattern copying accelerated. Another method of identifying plaits is to closely examine the material that has been plaited. The first plaiting materials were a cereal crop straw, chip or palm. Then loom-woven tapes and lames made from a variety of materials were introduced into the industry by the Swiss, Italian and French traders from the 1820s. In the last decade of the 1800s and into the 1900s, manmade fibres were introduced. The material that a plait or braid is made from, whilst not being an infallible test for dating, can provide additional information.

Plaits before 1800

As far as can be ascertained, until the end of the 1700s, English plait was made using whole cereal crop straw, from imported Tuscan straws, or from wood chip. There were other materials occasionally used such as paper, however it is unclear if this was anything other than a limited genteel occupation. A straw helmet in the collections of the Costume Institute, New York is said to date from the 1500s. The hat's base is made from plaited whole straw that has been knitted together edge to edge, and the decorative trimmings comprise velvet shapes decorated with metal spangles and wire that are edged with two-straw and three-straw plaits. The brim edge is trimmed with a four-end rustic plait.[352] The four-end rustic plait was also known as English pearl, but is has not been established if the name defined one being made from whole straw and the other from split straw. Rustic is still made around the world from whatever local material is available and is known by a wide variety of names, including saw tooth, fishtail and edging; it is known as sinnet in Australia.[353]

Both the two-end plaits, sometimes referred to as tortillon, and three-end plaits, referred to as cordinet, appear to be amongst the earliest made in many European centres and New England. Their names become confused in accounts and sometimes cordinet was called cord and in other accounts both types were called cordinet. Today the two-end plait used to decorate the women's hats of Montehermosa, Spain is known as cord. While use of these two plaits appears to have begun as a purely decorative feature, later in the 1800s, as the demand for new novelty in available patterns increased, both were incorporated into plaits and into a range of other straw products. The rustic plait was used as a trimming on the straw helmet held in the collections at the Costume Institute and was widely used in the construction of hats during the 1700s.

Chip had been imported into this country since at least the beginning of the 1700s and such was the quantity of imports, claimed to come from Holland, it was mentioned in the 1719 petition. Dony argued that it was more likely that the plaits were being imported from Italy: 'The industry around the area of Modena, Italy is well documented as being a production centre of chip plaits.'[354] John Pepperell of Totnes in Devon was awarded ten guineas for chip hats made at his 'manufactory in Totness.' It was commented that in 1774 he was awarded 30 guineas for having established this manufactory.[355] It is unclear whether the chip was being loom-woven into willow squares, plaited, or both.

Above and left: Probably made in the Low Countries, this bergère hat dates from the mid 1700s. The four-end rustic plait has been made using split straws. (CTLC 1994/248)

This bonnet was made by a woman called Mary Glenister in about 1852. It is made from Tuscan plait which has been sewn to shape. (CTLC 1/99/41)

Ida Gandy wrote of the willow trade in the village of Aldbourne, Wiltshire and described weaving the chip strips into willow squares, 'two-foot square.' In 1851 133 willow weavers are listed in the village, having been established there in 1842. At least one family in the village were trading directly with London, where trade directories appear to indicate a willow square making and willow hat making trade of some size in the 1700s and into the 1800s.[356]

William Corston, writing in 1805, stated that Dunstable plaits of seven ends had been made for upwards of a century.[357] While it may have only been introduced into Dunstable at the beginning of the 1700s, it was undoubtedly made elsewhere in much earlier times alongside a flat plait made from nine ends which can be found used in the construction of chip hats from the 1700s. The thirteen-end plait was being made by the 1700s in Italy.

Although the introduction of a splitter might provide a means of dating any split straw plait to the late 1700s or early 1800s, it is not an infallible test. Some hats from the 1700s were made from split straw, and references stated that before the introduction of the splitting tool, straw was cut into narrow slivers or splints with a knife.[358]

Development in the 1800s

British Patents provide a good source for identifying the date of introduction of new ideas, although it is often unclear how successful some inventions were, and if they were ever incorporated into the hat industry. An increase in the number of patents that relate to the preparation of straw and the way it is plaited occured in the early years of the 1800s, which is a time that corresponds to the growth of the straw plaiting industry in Great Britain and Europe. Edward Simpson and Caleb Ibester took out a patent on 8 May 1800 which claimed that 'a new and improved manufacture of straw plait made of split straw, presenting only the outside surface of the straw to the eye.' To make the plait, one must '"split and fold" the straw "to the size wanted," when "the outside surface of the straw only will present itself to the eye."' It also described the split straw being stuck onto silk, paper or wood which was then made into plaits.[359] The patent did not explain how the straw was split. This method of adhering straw to silk must have been of some interest since in 1815, when a woman named Grace Elizabeth Service was granted a patent for a similar process involving gauze.[360] Plaits made from the splints showed both the pearlescent inside of the straw stem and the shiny outside. When worked into a pattern, the effect was striking and very different from those plaits made using whole straw, chip or palm. Split straw plaits also provided a novel visual change from the much-admired Italian thirteen-end plait.

Tansley stated that, when the seven-end split straw plait was introduced in the first years of the 1800s, it created a sensation and for a time commanded up to 12 shillings (60p) as score. He wrote that many amusing stories about the excitement at that time had been handed down and retold one of 'persons called "dealers" collecting it of the plaiters at five yards a time, meeting them on their way to market as early as three or four o'clock in the morning.'[361] He mentioned that other kinds of patterns were introduced: 'rustic pearl, Italian (made from 11 ends) diamond plait and other fancy kinds of plait.' Plaits in the collection held at Orkney Museum, Kirkness include varieties of diamond plait and others that could be described as fancy plaits. Fancy plait was a generic term used in the trade to describe any elaborate plait. It does not indicate any specific plait pattern, material or technique, and by the late 1800s and into the 1900s, the term applied to a wider range of hat products.

Uriah Lane took out a patent in 1822 for a thirteen-end plait, where the single splints were all faced in one direction so that the shiny side of the straw faced outward.[362] The method of plaiting was given in detail, and the patent specification included diagrams that showed it was made in the Italian fashion, with a long stitch on each edge to enable sewing together edge to edge. It is unknown how successful this plait was since split straw is fundamentally weaker and less flexible than whole straw, and more susceptible to breakage when made into a hat. *The Penny Cyclopaedia* published an article entitled 'Straw Platting' in 1842 which raised concerns about the weakness of split straw plait.[363] Rather than seeing the beauty of the shiny and satin appearance of the splints when made into a plait, in its attempt to promote Tuscan straw plaits, the article implied disapproval of the appearance of split straw plait. It continued by saying articles made from split straw were inferior to those of whole straw. These assertions had been taken from the *Transactions of the Society of Arts* where the preface of the 1822 volume stated that 'During the war from which we have not long emerged, the use of hats and bonnets of split wheaten straw was general among the females of every rank, the relative fineness of the platting, and delicacy of colour, forming the chief distinction between the high and the low-priced ones . . . on the resumption of commerce hats of Leghorn plat found an easy entrance into the country . . . met with rapid sale . . . from their real and incontestable superiority, both in the beauty of material, in the fineness of workmanship and durability, over the straw hats of native make.'[364] The writer claimed that demand for the home-produced hats had declined, leaving many out of work. The Society of Arts offered many prizes for the best copies of Leghorn, and several individuals such as Corston, Parry and Cobbett, turned their attention to perfecting an English version to compete with the Italians.

An 1838 government report stated that bent work, a plait made with grasses or imported Italian straws, was the best paid, the bents being supplied to plaiters by dealers. Four types of plaits, Devon, old Dunstable, Luton and pattern plait, were listed as being made in the Ampthill Union, Bedfordshire, and Tuscan or Leghorn plait was also recorded.[365] Variegated plait was mentioned but no description was given. Children were said to have made coloured plaits or white straw plaits. Reference to white plaits were frequently made in the first half of this century, but without further explanation to what white referred to. Frederick Davis may provide the accurate answer in his account of the trade written in 1855. When discussing the use of chip, he referred to the products as white chips.[366] Chip does have a white appearance, and this could have been used descriptively. In the *Second Report of the Children's Employment Commission*, 1843, one of the commissioners, E J White, stated that 'though the term "straw plait" is commonly used, in consequence of straw being the material in most use, other materials, such as crinoline, wood are employed in the same way or for the same purpose. Much of this "fancy work" is made up in the east of London,' which is an area of research awaiting exploration.

Throughout the course of the industry's history, writers showed no consistency in their application of descriptive words, seemingly using them randomly, which leads to considerable confusion when trying to interpret accounts. Leghorn and Tuscan require some explanation. The Italian trade was not based in the town of Leghorn or Livorno, that was the port of export for the products. As explained in Chapter Two, the centres of straw production were in numerous villages around Florence and in other regions of Italy. Italian exports came into English and American ports having passed through the port of Livorno or Leghorn which is the connection. For clarity it is important to also realise that, just as there was never a Dunstable bonnet (although bonnets were made in Dunstable), there was not a specific Leghorn bonnet shape. The Italians produced many types of products, each with individual names, therefore while Leghorn can be used as a generic term, it should not define a type or style of hat, bonnet or plait pattern. Good practice would be to specify the product that the term Leghorn or Tuscan is being referred to, and when a product from another region has been identified, to indicate that information. This would allow the development of a clearer understanding, not only of the Italian industry and of the number of regions involved in Italian plaiting and hat manufacture, but also of the object being examined.

Plait patterns in the 1800s

Thomas Waller was a Luton manufacturer and trader who made many unsuccessful attempts to recreate the Italian plait before finally visiting Tuscany in 1825 to discover the secrets of the straw and plait. In 1826 he was granted a patent for using wheat straw from Tuscany, plaited, twisted or woven, in the same manner as English straw. His invention was to only use the top section of the stem nearest the ear rather than the whole top section which was usual practice. In Italy this top section is called the *punte*, or point. Rather than applying this idea to English straw, his intention was to use his imported Italian straw to produce the English plaits being commonly made in plaiting areas. He claimed in his patent specification that the Tuscan straw was stronger than English straw. It is unclear whether the straw was to be imported readily cut as per his instruction, or if preparation would be undertaken in Dunstable and Luton. He had the idea that the English method of stitching the plait by overlapping, rather than the knitting practised by the Italians, could be unpicked without damage and 'made up again into forms suitable to the prevailing fashion, or fancy of the wearer.'[367] Waller excluded using the Tuscan straw for making English Leghorn, probably realising others were already producing this product and patents exist already. His specification listed the types and commonly-used names of plaits in the trade at that time. This provides an insight into those being used in the trade and these are listed in the comparative table on pages 122–3.

Five other accounts have been added to the table containing Waller's list. A correspondent writing in *The Saturday Magazine* article stated that 'of the different plats, which are numerous, the principal are the following. . .'[368] and *The Workwoman's Guide* included a long list of plaits as well. Robert Slater, a London hat trader, wrote an insightful account published in McCulloch's dictionary of commerce.[369] It included a list of plaits being made for the trade and added the date of introduction of three. Frederick Davis[370] included a list of five plaits which he claimed were being made within the last 30 years then stated that 'since then an almost endless variety of patterns has been invented.' Finally, Charles Lamborn's 1859 book, *Dunstaplelogia*,[371] gave information about the plaits, some of which is not supported elsewhere but may reflect those circulating in Dunstable at the time of his writing. Comparison of the lists is interesting, but is also puzzling to be showing variations in plait names over three decades while not indicating if the patterns and materials were the same. This may indicate name variations between towns but may also tell us something of the people supplying the information. Waller was a trader and manufacturer, Slater a trader, but the others only appear to be acting as recorders of the industry. It is intriguing, and not explained, why none of them made any reference to the types of plait being made before the 1800s, especially since straw plaiting had been established in the area from at least the late 1600s.

By the time of these accounts, regardless of patterns, plaits fall into three general classifications: whole straw, which includes the imitation Tuscan or Leghorn plait; single splint, made with split straw; and double splint, made with two split straws paired either with the shiny outside, or matt inside of the splint showing.

CHRONOLOGY OF INTRODUCTION

Plait patterns recorded from 1826–1859

Waller (1826)	**The Saturday Magazine** (1833)	**The Workwoman's Guide** (1838)	**Slater** (1839)	**Davis** (1855)	**Lamborn** (1859)
Whole Dunstable (Noted as the original product)	Dunstable or whole straw	Whole Dunstable 6p per score Fine whole Dunstable 2s 3d per score Patent Dunstable 2s 6d per score	Whole Dunstable	Whole straw or Dunstable	Whole Dunstable
					Luton double seven and coarser than patent Dunstable
		Fine seven plaits			
Luton twist		Luton Dunstable 1s 4d per score			
Broad Luton twist					
			Split straw (1800)	Split	Split (1809) Seven ends
Double seven-split	Double seven (wetted and laid together and worked double)	Double seven	Patent Dunstable or double seven Luton (1825)	Patent split	Patent Dunstable or double seven
	Fine seven				
				Improved	
	Devonshire (seven straws)	Devonshire of seven and eight	Devonshire (1820)	Devon	Devonshire (1829) Seven split straws
Double eleven	Double eleven	Bedford Leghorn 4s 0d per score	Bedford Leghorn		Bedford Leghorn Eleven double splints
		The double eleven			
		Tuscan ends 3s 0d per score	Italian		Italian Eleven split straws
Whole Dunstable nine-ends					
Whole Dunstable eleven-ends	Eleven straw	The eleven straw			
Whole Dunstable thirteen-ends					
Whole Dunstable fifteen-ends					
	Backbone (also worked in seven)				

Plait patterns recorded from 1826–1859

Waller (1826)	The Saturday Magazine (1833)	The Workwoman's Guide (1838)	Slater (1839)	Davis (1855)	Lamborn (1859)
	Lustre (seventeen straws)	The lustre, or shining of seventeen straws			
	Wave (twenty-two straws)				
	Diamond (twenty-three straws)	Diamond of twenty-three straws		Diamond	
	Rustic (four coarse straws)	Rustic plaits 6d per score			
	Pearl (four small straws)				
		Mixture plaits 1s 2d to 2s 0d. per score			
		Back bone straw			
		The wave of twenty-two (the straws appear as if worked one way)			
				Rutland	
				Coburgh	
				Satin	
				Loop-edge	
				Honey-comb	
				Bird's-eye	
				Dyed plaits of fancy colours	
				Rice plait	

Dunstable and Luton plaits

All sources agree that the first plait was called Dunstable, made with seven whole straws, and which can be used to show how a basic pattern develops through time. Beginning as a Dunstable whole straw plait probably made with folded edges, during the early years of the 1800s it was then made with single splints. Lamborn wrote: 'Dunstable, the first introduced, plaited with seven entire straws; split straws introduced in 1809.' A wider seven-end single splint plait known as banding was used to strengthen a hat's brim edge or the join between crown and brim. Next came the idea to pair the single splints to make a plait known as double seven or patent Dunstable. *The Saturday Magazine* clearly described the patent Dunstable as 'two splints laid together with their inside surfaces towards each other.' Also known as improved plait, it was not considered as good as that made with Italian whole straw for two major reasons. First, it required a great amount of skill to perfectly match the splints, and second, the inner pith side of the straw would often show through, thus spoiling the finish. William Cobbett was deeply critical of English improved plaits, favouring the

Italian plaits made from specially grown fine straw, 'there was a roundness in them that gave light and shade to the plait, which could not be given by our flat bits of straw.'

The Luton plait appears very similar to the Dunstable, but Lamborn stated that it was coarser than the Dunstable 'formed of double seven.' Like the Dunstable plait it is apparent it could be made with whole straw or with double splints. What made it sufficiently different from Dunstable to warrant another name is unknown. Perhaps it was simply the geographic location of its making.

The next evolution was to incorporate a twisted stitch along the head causing the name to change to Dunstable twist, whipcord or cord. Tansley stated that it was introduced in about 1846 and whipcord referred to the fast whipping movement made by the plaiter to create the stitch. In his 1943 book Thomas Hennell showed a drawing of a seven end that he stated was known as 'beady head' in parts of Hertfordshire, but gave no indication of how many years the name had been used in that village. Listing the plaits has identified a problem that is all too common in charting the development of plait patterns: cord, also used as a shortening of the name cordinet, is now also being used for a seven-end plait.

Devon

The plait called Devon creates more questions. The Devon plait was said by Lamborn to have been introduced in 1829 and was made with seven split straws, while Waller claimed that it was introduced in 1809 by Frederick Brown who generated an income of £10,000 in one year from this plait. Dony included a photograph of what he described as a Devon split plait made in China in the 1900s. It was made with seven single splints and both the head and foot edges were folded. *The Workwoman's Guide* listed the Devonshire plait being made with seven or eight ends, the latter number contradicting accounts. Currently there is no consistent evidence to explain what made Devon different from a seven-end split straw plait. John Dony could not establish a link between this plait, and the apparently limited industry carried out in villages on Dartmoor during the 1800s, which he said produced small amounts of poor quality plait. Other sources stated that the plaits were also made in the Exeter area and that the plaiters were very skilled, producing good plaits. The plaiting of wood chip was established in Totnes, Devon in 1774 and later John Pepperell in his correspondence with the Society of Arts was listed as a manufacturer of chip and straw. The census records of 1841 list between 250 to 500 plaiters in Cornwall, 58 in Devon, 100 to 250 in Somerset and 40 in Dorset.

Rice

Charles Knight described his visit to the Luton warehouses where he saw both English and foreign plaits. He observed the rice plait and said it was made with 'the white inner side of the straw being worked outwards.' Davis said it 'works up into a pearly white, imitating the foreign chip.' 'The beautiful rice straw plait, so much in favour of late years, and which ladies prefer to have for wedding bonnets, at a guinea a piece, was invented and made up by that enterprising manufacturer still living, Mr Blackwell. It is so called simply from its colour, occasioned by working the straws inside out.' Tansley stated that rice plait was made up into a number of different plait patterns made from seven, eleven and fifteen ends, and they were very successful in the trade since they were in demand for wedding bonnets. So it seems the term rice referred to the arrangement of the straw splints rather than to a single plait pattern. The term *paille de riz* appeared in later accounts during the 1800s, and some writers stated that the plait was made from rice straw. This is where confusion arises since in some accounts *paille de riz* does refer to the split straw rice plait while other accounts may refer to a plait made from rice straw. This point was made by Davis in 1855: 'erroneously supposed by many to be produced from the straw of the rice plant.'

Bedford Leghorn, Tuscan, eleven- and thirteen-end

The Workwoman's Guide listed these plaits separately so are they considered to be different products? Lamborn also listed them separately and wrote that 'Bedford Leghorn is formed of twenty-two or eleven double straws, and plaited similar to the Tuscan: and Italian, formed of eleven split straws.'

Thomas Waller made his Leghorn plait using eleven whole Italian *punte* straws, and instead of using the Italian method of joining into the centre, joined along the foot edge, and sewed the plait into a hat by overlapping it. He called this the 'Tuscan Grass Bonnet' which was said to be 'patronised by Queen Adelaide and great numbers were sold . . . at prices from 30s. to 50s.'

The Workwoman's Guide included instructions for making a thirteen-end plait to make a Tuscan hat, 'commonly called a Leghorn bonnet.' It stated that the Tuscan hat, or Leghorn bonnet, could be made with seven, nine or thirteen ends, the latter being the most common. In another section, when writing of the English Leghorn, it was not explained how many straws were used to make this plait. John Parry was awarded a Large Silver Medal by the Society of Arts in 1821 for his enterprises to make a thirteen-end plait from Italian grasses.

Fancy plaits

Apart from rustic or English pearl, the sources quoted so far do not indicate any patterning to the edge of the plait, but at the 1851 Great Exhibition, many firms exhibited straw hats, and while the majority exhibited hats that were made with plain edged plaits, Messieurs Muirs, Connell and Brodie of Luton, who had connections to Scotland, showed a huge range of 'plaits and bonnets manufactured from wheat-straw grown in Bedfordshire' and described some as 'fancy.' These included fancy tulip, Coburg, fancy split and fancy coloured, which may denote that a fancy-edge pattern had been created or that the straw had been combined with another or different material in its plaiting. The term 'fancy plait' is not attributable to any one pattern or material, instead it covers a wide range of products including machine-made and loom-made braids.

Plaits with an edge pattern

In its first year of publication in 1861, *The Queen Magazine* included an account which appears to repeat Tansley's information presented to the Society of Arts the previous year. Tansley's knowledge of the trade enabled him to provide a lengthy account of the introduction of plaits into the industry. Starting with the introduction of the split straw plait, he stated that 'similar plaits and trimming followed.' He provided some understanding of the earliest plaits, making a distinction between patent and 'improved' by saying that improved was broader than patent while being made using the same number of paired splints.

'Between the years 1844 and 1850, other and more important plaits were invented. An idea occurred to a straw plaiter of turning the straw on the upper edge in such a manner to form a bead or pearl along the edge at every other straw, and a new plait was formed,' wrote Tansley. We now have a date for the introduction of the pearl plait into the trade of the south east Midlands. As to whether it was the invention of a local plaiter, or had been copied from a sample of foreign plait, may never be known. He wrote that the plait developed into a one-, two- and three-pearl plait. The three purl was also known as rock or Cobourg. At some later time the spelling of pearl changed to purl and the one-purl plait also became known as notch. The spelling of Cobourg later changed to Coburg. It would appear that these names refer to the pattern head or edging stitch rather than to the number of working ends used to make the plait. Surviving pieces of plaits indicate that a three-purl plait would often be made using seven, eight or nine ends, whereas a Coburg would be made using 11 or more.

He then described the making of moss plait which is a variation of the purls. Examples of moss plait in the CTLC are variations of the pearl or purl plaits, but by inserting a pin, hairclip or wire, the edge loops are both more prominent and straighter than the pearl plait which has a scalloped edge.

The satin piping or Vienna plait has every outside straw on the head edge worked over the wire. Later this plait would become known as piping or liseret. 'Feather-edge' had an edge imitating a feather while 'Brussels' was an eleven-end plait with an open lattice work centre and another called 'bird's eye' had a similar appearance. No specifically named examples of bird's-eye plaits survive, but one in the collection of plaits held in the Orkney Museum collections may be an example of this pattern. *The Cassell's Family Magazine* published an article, 'Plait and Plaiters in 1882', which included a drawing of plaiters splitting, milling and plaiting in a plait school. Less obvious to a casual glance is the border representing types of plait and a small drawn insert of named plaits. They are: 'Pearl whole straw' (four-end rustic), 'Whole Straw Whipcord Edge' (seven-end twist), 'Double 7, 2 Notch' (two-purl), 'Double 7 Whipcord Edge' (seven-end, double splint, twist edge) and 'Tuscan with Bird's eye open work.' The article later stated that 'sometimes a strip of cane was inserted in the middle and pulled out as the work proceeded; this produced a kind of open pattern or "bird's eye."' An example of what may be a double splint, eleven-end bird's eye plait is held in the collections of Saffron Walden Museum, Essex.

In various Historical Societies in New England there are surviving examples of plaits, hats, bonnets and tools, and perhaps the largest and best documented of these is held in the Framingham Historical Society, Massachusetts. The display includes a variety of patterned whole and split straw plaits made between 1830–99 with the majority made in the period 1840–50. The range of patterns represent those being made throughout Europe. Additionally, there are bundles of finished plaits including one pattern that incorporates dyed straw. Not only do these plaits show the variety of patterns known by the plaiters, but they also show the skills of the plaiters. Some of the plait names seem to be specific to the United States such as 'California', and would be known as a feather plait in England.

The last types of plaits mentioned by Tansley were coloured plaits which he implied were made in large quantities: 'seven and eight straws . . . composed of coloured and white straws mixed together, and made in a variety of patterns. The plaits being cheap and bonnets made from them . . . great quantities of plait used, and employed numbers of children in the plaiting districts.'

When Austin published his account of the straw trade in Luton in 1871, he included a list of some towns and villages – which he said were the centre of the straw district – and of the plaits being made there, presumably at that time. Thanks to the account of Tansley, whilst some puzzles remain, many of the plait names listed can now be recognised.

However, there are two questions which may continue to provide mystery to the origins of plait patterns. Some have city or district names which may or may not hold some indication of their origin such as Vienna, Brussels and Coburg. Another confusing name yet to be understood is the use of 'China' that appears as a prefix to many patterns.

Thomas Austin's list of patterns made in plaiting villages and towns	
Bedfordshire	
Ampthill	Narrow improved or double-straw for plaits for dyeing.
Houghton Regis	All kinds of Devons and fine split plaits.
Eaton Bray	Plaits are chiefly collected by the Plait Dealers, among them being some very good qualities of Twist, and children-made mixed colour plaits, as well as some superior qualities of coloured plaits.
Totternhoe	It is also noted for children-made mixed coloured plaits, and for Devons of all qualities.
Shefford	Chiefly narrow Twist plait of good and inferior qualities with a sprinkling of medium Devons.
Breachwood Green, Offley, Lilley	Plain and Twist whole straw.
Buckinghamshire	
Ivinghoe	Prevailing kinds are narrow Twist, of good and inferior makes, and Rustic and mixed coloured plaits.
Chesham	Known for its Devons, fine Split, besides Moss edge, Vienna. This latter is now not much in request.
Berkhamsted and neighbourhood	The chief sorts are China pearl, Rock, Coburg and Moss edge of both good and medium qualities.
Hertfordshire	
Tring and Hemel Hempstead	All kinds of plait of a medium quality, and a good share of the better descriptions.
St. Albans	Twist, Devons, and Improved plaits of all qualities.
Hitchin including Biggleswade	Broad Twist, all kinds of medium Twist ranging from inferior to a better (but not the best) quality. Plain improved, lower, and inferior Devons or single-straw plaits.
Essex	
Plaits in the Essex district, while more or less inferior in quality and colour to those produced in this district (Bedfordshire, Buckinghamshire and Hertfordshire) have similar peculiarities or specialities in different neighbours.	

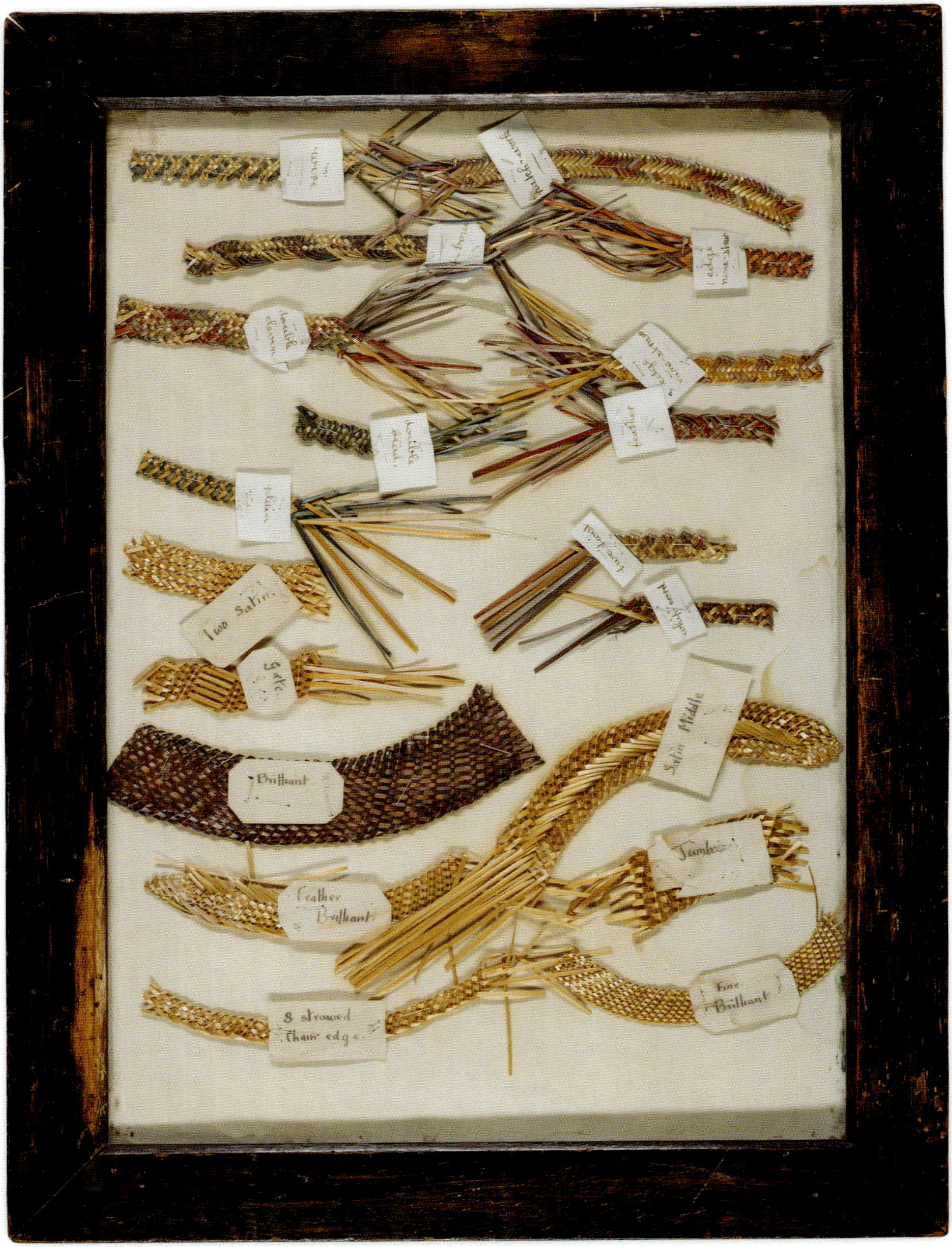

This is one of two sheets of plaits made in the village of Aldbury before 1913. The patterns represent those being made in the village.

Brilliant plait

This extraordinary plait is said to have been introduced in 1850, but whether the pattern was the same as the one which dominated the later industry is unclear. This plait was to carry the stumbling English industry into the 1900s, but ultimately could not save it. The Brilliant plait was either made with single or doubled splints and varied in width according to the number of splints used. Examples made from 8–24 splints survive in various collections. The splints were faced to only show the shiny side on the face and the pith side on the obverse. The vertical splint folded backwards and forwards over a diagonal splint which, by delicate manipulation of the fingers, stayed on its edge to create a faceted surface. The *Hatters' Gazette* printed a statement in 1902 by a Luton plait dealer, probably Walter Gray: 'Whereas a few years ago I could go to Tring market and buy a thousand scores weekly of English brilliant, I now find it difficult to obtain 250 yards fortnightly.' He may have seen a decline from the heyday of his trade in the 1880s, but it was still being made in considerable quantities. His anxiety to obtain as many plaits as possible was due to a new trend in fashion. The *Hatters' Gazette* had first reported an increasing demand for the plait, and indicated the difficulty of finding enough skilled workers to make some with the best quality. 'There are plenty of them who can plait the inferior kinds, but for these there is less demand and prices are poor.' Having kept the pattern alive in villages around Tring, Wilstone, Cheddington, Pitstone and Marsworth, the demand came from Paris fashion houses who were 'inundating local houses with orders for it.' Interest seems to have lasted until about 1911 when criticism begins to appear in the *Hatters' Gazette* with reports that the plait was 'tender and brittle.'

There were many different patterns, such as matchbox, feather and ventilated, and coloured splints could be introduced to create colourways. The shiny face and matt obverse was not suitable for some hat designs, so to please the trade the plait was made with pairs of splints with the shiny side facing outwards so both sides of the plait had the same sheen, making it more durable. The Brilliant plait was made in Buckinghamshire and Hertfordshire until the 1930s, and even in the 1960s and early 1970s old ladies in Buckinghamshire villages such as Wigginton would demonstrate how to make the plait to any interested person.

Copying plaits

Over the centuries the production of plaits has always involved an interchange of ideas. Copying was rife since hats and plaits were objects of fashion, and patterns would change with great frequency. 'A new design is kept secret, for its value lies in its novelty. Directly it is copied and becomes common, its power to command a price and market is lost,' was a comment written in 1898. Two years later the *Hatters' Gazette* included a statement: 'Luton has recently been almost besieged by the representatives of Swiss houses, who are showing their fancy patterns for the next season. On examination of the hundreds of designs that any respectable Swiss firm would send out, one cannot but be impressed by their variety and artistic effect.' The correspondent when asked how such a selection is achieved was told that 'some half-a-dozen of the most skilful workwomen are employed continuously for five or six months in attaining these results.'

Sample books dating from 1853 at Strohmuseum im Park, Wohlen, Switzerland show that the Swiss plaiters of that time were producing numerous edge patterns, using dyed straws to great effect and including a wide range of materials with the straw.

Many plaits contained in the Swiss sample books are also found in several English museum collections. While some of these examples may be Swiss or German in origin, others have undisputed provenance linking them with specific plaiters or villages in England. It is remarkable to observe the way in which not only the pattern was copied, but also the width and colours of the straw. In the Swiss sample books, pieces of certain plaits had been cut off, or completely removed. This could have been done for a wide variety of reasons including being secretly taken to be copied by a competitor.

As the 1800s ended the Japanese and Italian plaiters were still producing novel ideas. The Japanese plait patterns had captivated the hat trade and many of their patterns were copied. The books published as part of the attempts to revive the plaiting industry in England contained instructions on how to copy the simpler Japanese patterns, concentrating on mixing whole and split straws and combining wide and narrow working ends. A German book of 1898 described a range of Swiss, Belgium, Italian, English, Chinese and Japanese plait patterns and colourways.

The top sample was made in Ballinger, Buckinghamshire in about 1889 and the one below appears in Swiss sample books dating from one year earlier. Is this an example of copying? (CTLC 1993/180, CTLC 1997/17/1)

The woman is plaiting palm rather than wheat straw, which is faster to work up into plait and easier to prepare. The photograph was probably taken in the early 1900s.

CHAPTER
NINE

PREPARING TO PLAIT

The first part of this book provided an understanding of how plaiters, and those who supplied materials to them, worked in the past. However, although that knowledge and those skills were almost forgotten, the techniques and plait patterns can be recreated and live on for future generations by using surviving evidence. During the heyday of the industry, plaiting materials and patterns were about exploration and experimentation, and this chapter provides the necessary information to find and prepare suitable plaiting materials in readiness to begin making the plaits in Chapter 10.

Foraged fibres are particularly suitable for plaiting. Whatever the plant material being collected, obtain the landowner's permission before harvesting. Suitable plants may be growing wild but make certain that you are not trying to gather a species protected by local laws.

Finding plaiting materials

Wheat, rye, oats and barley are cropped at different times throughout Europe and North America, and it may also be possible to find a source of suitable rice straw in the southern states of the US. Although not wholly definite, it can be generalised that rye straw will be more easily available in cooler climates and wheat and oats in warmer climates. Suppliers of corn dolly/wheat weaving or thatching straw will sell varieties with a long, hollow top stem and a thin wall. A straw's top section, measured from just below the grain head to the first joint or leaf node, should measure from between 30–45 cm (12–18 in.). Modern cereal varieties are grown for seed rather than the stem, and have been hybridised to shorten growth and strengthen the stem. Many varieties have a stem with a solid or thick pithy wall. Despite its shortness, provided the straw has a hollow stem and is flexible, some modern varieties can still be plaited. You need to harvest when the grain is at the soft flour stage. When the seed is split, the inside is moist and floury; you can check for ripeness by looking at the top leaf node, a little greenness should remain amongst the brown. Avoid decorative floristry straw as it may have a wiry or solid stem that will be too difficult to plait.

The availability of suitable types of palm also varies according to geographic location; there are too many to be listed. Talk to makers or groups in your area, or simply experiment. It is essential to learn how to harvest to avoid damaging the plant's growing heart. Careless harvesting may kill the plant meaning that you will lose your source.

Suitable varieties of meadow grass are normally ready for harvest in the early summer. Some grasses are better than others for plaiting so be prepared to experiment. Those which feel wiry, even while they are still green, are normally more difficult to plait so find grasses with hollow stems in the top and second joints. Collect the grasses just after the seed head has flowered and before it turns brown. Cut off the entire length of the stem just above ground level. Do not do any preparation until it has been bleached or dried. Keep varieties separate.

Water grasses such as sedges and rush will also plait successfully. Rush can be purchased, but when making narrow plaits, request a bolt of finer stems. Many types of leaves are suitable for plaiting including maize leaves.

Willow, birch or poplar skein are the closest equivalent to traditional wood chip. Skeins are the shaved lengths of a whole willow stem in various widths and thickness, so choose the thinnest possible ones as they will be more flexible.

Experiment with paper tapes, yarns and any material that can be cut or shredded into even-width strips, or as the Japanese did, you could be even more adventurous and try plaiting with strips of uneven width. Use scraps of fabric, new or recycled, manmade or natural. Plaiters have used a myriad of different materials in the past, so be adventurous, and have fun.

Just some of the many materials that can be plaited.

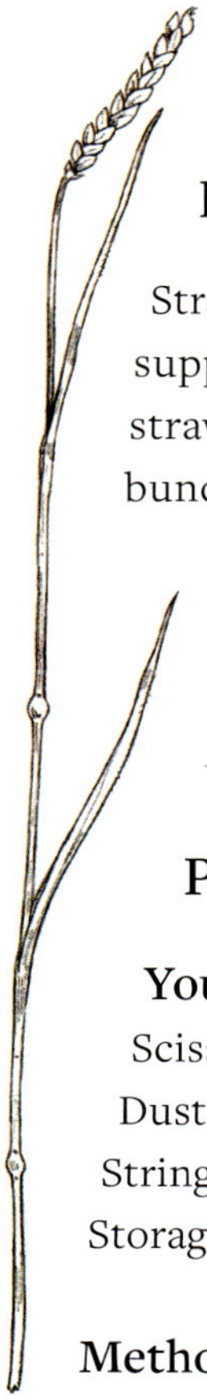

Preparing cereal crop straw

Straw is usually purchased as a sheaf, but some suppliers will sell bundles of ready-prepared straw. Usually, ready-prepared means that the bundle will only contain the top joint, which may or may not have had the outer leaf removed, and may or may not have the head in place.

Preparing a sheaf

You will need:

Scissors
Dust sheet
String or cord
Storage container

Method

1. Draw a single straw from the bound sheaf and look along the stem. From the grain head, moving down the top stem, you will see a leaf growing out from the first leaf node or joint. The leaf covers the lower section of the stem length. This top section is the best plaiting straw.
2. Cut off the top section of stem just above the leaf node, on the head side. A cut on the correct side of the joint will allow the leaf to slide off the stem.
3. Cut off the seed head.
4. Depending upon variety the second section below the leaf node, and above the next, can sometimes be used for making split straw plaits.
5. Cut off the top leaf node, cut the lower end above the next leaf node. The leaf will slide off the stem.
6. Keep the first and second sections in separate bundles.
7. Work through the sheaf until all the straws are cut.

Preparing plaiting lengths

Method

1. Cut off the grain or seed head, if not already removed.
2. Examine the stem, the section closest to the head was not protected by the leaf so is of a darker colour with a slightly rougher surface. This section, the *punte*, produces the finest plait. The section covered by the leaf is shinier, smoother, has a larger diameter and is slightly tougher to plait. This is the *pedale*.
3. If the stem is long enough, cut it in two at the point where the leaf no longer covers the stem. This should give you two lengths of about 23 cm (9 in.) each.
4. If the stem is only long enough to provide one section, then discard the thinnest and thickest ends of the straw, leaving only the central section.

Sorting

To achieve an even plait, sorting is essential. An average sheaf will produce four to six different diameters from fine to thick. If you intend to make a lot of plaits, then it is possible to make a replica of the original straw sorter by inserting various sizes of metal mesh into a frame, but with practice, the straw can be quickly sorted by hand. An alternative is to use a knitting needle gauge as a measure.

Method

1. Take a small bundle of straws and hold it in one hand.
2. Taking a straw at a time, arrange into groups of a similar diameter. Assess similar diameters by looking at the midpoint of the length.
3. Bundle into individual groups and label the size.

This rare example of Italian punte *plaiting straws may date to the early 1800s. The end where the head has been cut off can be seen.*

Splitting straw

Historically many plaits were made using splints (split straws) between 1–2 mm wide, therefore a plaiter had several splitters with different numbers of cutting fins. With their current limited availability, a splitter with six cutting fins is the most practical purchase. However, it may be necessary to have a three or four-fin splitter. Straw can be split when dry or damp, but this will vary according to variety.

Method

1. Make certain the stem end is cut straight.
2. Push the guide point of the splitter into the hollow stem. Adjust the positioning so the cutting fins are at a right angle to the stem. This is important since if held at an angle the splints will cut to uneven widths.
3. Push the straw onto the cutting fins until about 5 cm (2 in.) passes through or over.
4. Evenly grasp the splints then pull with constant effort until all the length is split. Make certain the straw is pulled in a straight line over the cutting fins.

Milling

Milling compresses the inside pith surface of the straw splints to make them more flexible. Without milling, even damp splints may crack when plaited. Whole straw is not normally milled before plaiting. In the past, plaiters used a wooden mill; an old mangle would be a suitable alternative, although a rolling pin works well too.

Method

The splints can be milled while damp or dry. Method for using a rolling pin:

1. Place a small bundle of straw splints onto a hard, flat surface. Make certain none are twisted or bent.
2. Applying firm, even pressure roll across the bundle making certain the entire length of splint goes under the roller.
3. It will be necessary to roll the splints several times until they feel soft and flexible. They will begin to curl and become glossier.

If using a mill: Pass a small bundle of splints through the rollers starting with a light roller pressure, then increase the pressure on subsequent rolling.

Preparing palm leaves

According to type, first remove the tough section of the central vein or edges before bleaching (for some it should be done after bleaching). Experiment to see which method works best for your variety. Plunge into boiling water, the required length of time varies according to the variety, then hang them in the sunshine to dry and bleach.

You will need:

Protective clothing, gloves, eye protection, mask
A container large enough to fit the leaves, such as a large sink or a large fish kettle
Weight
Long-handle tongs or similar
Draining racks

Caution: This method involves the use of boiling water.

Method

1. Long leaves can be loosely rolled then placed into the container.
2. Carefully pour the boiling water to cover the leaves, avoid splashing.
3. Keep them submerged.
4. Depending on both the weather and variety of palm, bleaching may take 10 days.
5. Once dry and appropriately bleached, the leaves can be left whole until required.
6. Splitting palm leaves can be done with scissors, a knife or a pin using the grain of the leaf to guide the cut.
7. Tie into bundles, label and store.

Cabbage tree palm leaves drying.

Bleaching

Bleaching will not remove spots or blemishes from straws, so discoloured straws are best saved for dyeing. The easiest bleaching method is to use the power of the sun, but this may not always be possible or practical. Other methods involve the use of chemicals and should only be undertaken with great care and after suitable safety precautions are in place. The most accessible bleaching agent is hydrogen peroxide. Chlorine bleaches are unsuitable as they cause the straw to yellow and become brittle. The traditional bleaching method using sulphur is not included since the fumes are noxious and the process requires implementation of many health and safety precautions.

Sun bleaching grasses

This ancient method of lightening straw can be used for many types of straw, but the method may need adjustment according to the type. While straw can be plaited when green, the stems will shrink as they dry, causing unattractive gaps and weakness in the plait. William Cobbett's method of sun bleaching is simple to repeat, but do not be alarmed by squeaking noises when the grass is in the water, it is only air escaping from the stems. After removing them from the water Cobbett instructed to lay the grasses onto a lawn. This is not recommended since the hot bundles will scorch the grass. Instead lay the bundles on a flat hard surface or drying rack.

You will need:

Protective clothing, gloves, apron, eye protection
Fine string to tie the grasses into bundles
A heat-proof container long enough to fit the whole length of grass without bending
Weights
Tongs
A drying rack

Caution: This method involves the use of boiling water.

Method

1. Place the harvested grasses into a suitably sized container.
2. Carefully pour over enough boiling water to cover the grasses.
3. If necessary, keep them submerged by carefully lowering a weight onto the grasses.
4. Leave for 10–15 minutes according to quantity.
5. Carefully remove the weight.
6. Using tongs, carefully lift out the grasses and leave them to drain and cool.
7. Once cool spread them out on racks for air to circulate, then place in a light bright area such as a conservatory or greenhouse.
8. They can be left outside in the sun or spread onto a hard surface, but should be brought in at night to prevent damage from any dew or condensation. Do not leave out in the rain.

Alternative method

Some experimentation may be required to find which method is best for different varieties.

Method

1. Spread the straws on a rack, or tightly tie into a bundle of a diameter of no more than 6–7 cm (2 –2.5 in.) at the opposite end to the heads.
2. Place the rack or hang the straws in a sunny spot such as a conservatory or greenhouse. Avoid exposure to condensation, dew or damp.
3. As the stems dry, tighten the tie each day and turn the bundle from inside to out, bringing grasses in the centre to the outside.
4. Depending on weather conditions they will gradually turn from green to a pale cream colour in about 10 days.

Preparing grasses into plaiting lengths

This preparation method has to happen after bleaching and applies to both forms of sun bleaching.

Method

1. Cut the head off.
2. Cut the top section, just above the leaf node, and slide off the leaf.
3. The second joint of the grass stem may also be prepared by cutting between the first and second nodes, then slide off the leaf.
4. Tie into bundles, keeping the sections separate, label and store until required.

Bleaching with hydrogen peroxide

Liquid hydrogen peroxide is successfully used by hairdressers and can bleach straw. The higher-strength solution of 60 volume liquid (18%) works most effectively, but local regulations may mean that only lower volumes are available for general purchase, and will take longer to bleach the straw, perhaps overnight.

You will need:

Protective clothing, gloves, eye protection, mask
Container such as a fish kettle with a lid
Weights
Tongs
Drying rack
Soft cloth
Fine string to tie the straw into bundles

Caution: This process must be done in a well ventilated area and safety clothing must be worn. Any splashes of hydrogen peroxide should be immediately and thoroughly rinsed with cold water.

Method

1. Before bleaching wash the straw in hot soapy water to remove any surface dirt, rinse thoroughly and drain.
2. Carefully pour the hydrogen peroxide into the container. Do not overfill the container.
3. Gently, and without splashing, lower the straws into the liquid.
4. Completely immerse the straw, using a weight if necessary.
5. The length of time needed to bleach the straws will vary. Check after 30 minutes and then at regular intervals.
6. Leave in the solution until the straw is a pale yellow or cream colour. Do not attempt to leave until almost white as many types of straw will be unworkable.
7. When the straw has achieved the desired colour use the tongs to lift it out. Drain and thoroughly rinse.
8. Spread out on a drying rack or flat surface.
9. When dry, polish with a soft dry cloth, tie into bundles, label and store until required.

Dyeing

When yellow and red are mixed they produce orange, and when yellow and blue are mixed, they produce green, so the straw was traditionally bleached before dyeing to remove the yellow tint. Bleaching first also makes it easier to obtain paler colours. Interesting shades can be achieved by varying the strength of dye solution and immersion time, but to achieve strong colours it may be necessary to reduce the dye's dilution. Home dyeing is not an exact science, so experimentations are necessary. To ensure replication, always keep a note of the method used.

Commercial dyes

Use a dye product recommended for colouring cotton or linen. The dyeing effect will vary according to the water used; hard water will inhibit the uptake of dye, therefore some manufacturers recommend the addition of a water softener. It may not be necessary to add salt to the dye solution. The duration of the immersion will vary according to the type of straw. Fine cereal crop straw will tolerate less exposure to simmering water than tough palms.

You will need:

Protective clothing, gloves, apron, eye protection, mask
Straws cut to required length
Detergent
Large container, such as a fish kettle with lid
Weight
Commercial dye, sufficient for the weight of the straws being dyed
Gloves
Long-handle tongs
Draining racks

Caution: Always work in a well-ventilated area. Dyes stain so protect surfaces and clothes, and wear gloves. If there is a danger of splashing, then wear eye protection. Masks are essential when using dry powder dyes.

Method

1. Using hot soapy water wash the straws to remove surface dirt and grease.
2. Rinse then allow to drain until there is no surplus water.
3. Prepare the dye solution according to the manufacturer's instructions.
4. Carefully lower the straw into the dye liquor.
5. Heat the dye solution, cover the pan and maintain a simmer.
6. Turn the straw occasionally, avoiding splashing.
7. Leave until the desired colour is obtained which can be from 10–40 minutes depending on the colour required, quantity and type of straw.
8. Remove the dye bath from the heat.
9. Either allow the straw to cool in the dye liquor or carefully remove and place in a large container or sink allowing it to drain.
10. The same dye liquor can be re-used but must be used within two days.
11. Rinse the straw thoroughly to remove loose dye.
12. Spread out and allow to dry.
13. Safely dispose of the spent dye liquor according to local authority recommendations.
14. Before using the straws wipe with a soft cloth, taking care not to crush the stem. This removes any loose dye, and depending on the type of straw, polishes it too.

Natural dyes

These may be less light resistant, fading quickly when exposed to strong sunlight, but can produce a strong colour on cereal crop straw. They work more effectively on straws that have first been bleached. As there are many available natural dyes, you should spend some time experimenting and keeping records of dye solutions and timings. Begin with household items such as tea, coffee grounds and turmeric, but also vegetables and fruits like onions, beetroots, red cabbages, elderberries and blackberries. Most types of straw will not require the addition of a fixative, however, should you find difficulty in achieving deep colours, it may be worth experimenting to see if it makes a difference. Also experiment with cochineal, logwood, madder, woad and fustic. Follow the supplier's instructions for preparation.

You will need:

Protective clothing, gloves, apron, eye protection
Selected vegetables, fruit or bark

Saucepan, large enough for preparing the dye liquor
Straw
A large container, such as a fish kettle with lid
A weight
Long-handle tongs
Gloves
Draining racks

Caution: The dye solution stains, so protect work surfaces and yourself when using them. Work in a well-ventilated area.

Method

1. Cut the vegetables, fruit or bark into small pieces and place in a pan.
2. Add water to a ratio of 1:1 but not more than 1:2.
3. Bring the pan to the boil and simmer for one hour, or until the liquor is a strong colour.
4. Strain the liquor and pour it into the dyeing container.
5. Add the straw using a weight to make certain it is fully submerged.
6. Bring the dye liquor to a fast simmer and cover the container.
7. Check the straw regularly and leave until the required colour is achieved.
8. The straw can be left in the dye liquor until cool.
9. Carefully remove the straw from the dye liquor.
10. Drain and rinse the straw.
11. It may be possible to reuse the same dye liquor on the same day.

Edible food colouring

Use liquid rather than gels or oil-based food colourings. They give a stronger colour when applied to previously bleached straw. Straws can be submerged or stood upright in the food colouring. This latter method allows the colour to be drawn up through the stem by capillary action resulting in some interesting effects. Food colouring can be painted onto absorbent plaiting materials.

You will need:

Protective clothing, gloves, and apron
Liquid food colouring
Straw
A container suitable for laying the straw flat or a bottle with a wide opening and lid.
Gloves
Draining racks

Caution: Food colourings will stain, so protect work surfaces and yourself when using them.

Method

1. Pour sufficient food colouring for the quantity used into the container.
2. Either lay or stand the straw in the liquid.
3. Leave until the required colour is achieved. This can happen within minutes if dyeing thin bleached straw, or 24 hours or longer for thicker, older and tougher stems.
4. To achieve an even colour regularly turn the straw to ensure that the straws are fully submerged.
5. Once the desired colour is obtained, remove the straw.
6. Rinse thoroughly.
7. Spread out and dry on racks.
8. It may be possible to reuse the food colouring for subsequent batches.

Create colour combinations

First stand the straw stems in red, rinse and allow them to drain. Then, while slightly damp, place them in blue. The capillary action within the stem will create areas of red, blue and some purple hues. Colouring first with blue then yellow will produce blue, yellow and green effects. Combining yellow and red will produce yellow, red and orange effects. Mixing several food colours together before immersing the straw will create a dark brown or black colour.

Miss Emily's Eleven String, 2006, from an original coloured pencil drawing by K Smith, Nassau, The Bahamas. International artist K Smith pays tribute to the hard-working hands of the late Miss Emily Rolle, a native straw worker from Cat Island, The Bahamas. She is here shown plaiting eleven pieces of silver top palm.

Plaiting technique

Plaits are made by hand using as few finger movements as possible and with small working moves. Not only does this allow the plaiter to develop speed, it also prevents undue strain on the hands. With experience, a plaiter's hands become their eyes, so while working it is not necessary to constantly look at the plait; thumbs and fingertips sense the moves. Plaiting is comparable to knitting, where to produce a neat and even work, the maker develops an understanding of the pattern and maintains a constant tension and rhythm.

Basic directions:

1. After setting up, hold the working ends so they are equally balanced between the thumb and first two fingers of each hand. Plaiting suits both left- and right-handed people.
2. The straws are positioned with the working ends pointing upwards so the plait grows downwards.
3. The working moves are made close to the point of working and the hands remain quite still while the fingers work.
4. Lift and position the working ends into the pattern sequence by flexing just enough to allow the moving end to slip through the gap.
5. Keep the two working groups at a constant angle as work progresses. This angle maintains the plait's tension. Varying the angle will change the tension creating an untidy and possibly unstable plait.
6. New straws should be kept close by and ready to be joined into the length. Traditionally plaiters wrapped the straws or splints in a cloth or paper and held them under their left arm.
7. As the plait length increases it should be coiled into a ring or around a board to protect it from accidental damage and to keep it flat.

Plaiting rhymes

In the past, as plaiters learned their skills, they used rhymes to help them to maintain a regular rhythm that matched their working speed. Two rhymes used in the British plaiting industry survive, but neither provide for joining into the plait. Both versions of the seven-end plait are correct since the method changes over time.

English pearl or four-end rustic

'Criss-cross patch and then a twirl, twist it back for English pearl.'

Seven-end plait

'Over one, under two, pull it tight and that'll do.'

This rhyme also appears as:
'Under one, over two, pull it tight and that'll do.'

Using the plait

Depending on the pattern and material, plaits can be stitched into any shape: round, oval, rectangular, square and even triangular or diamond.Plaits can be woven through supporting structures or woven into a sheet. Provided the plaits are well made, they can be used in a wide range of ways.

Preparing

Before using the plait make certain that all the speel and set-in ends have been clipped off. Then mill to flatten and improve the appearance, taking care not to flatten a decorative edge. Do not stretch the plait since it may distort the pattern and cause joins to come apart.

Sewing thread

While any type can be used it is generally better to use a thread of a natural fibre when sewing plant materials. Manmade and nylon threads can tear plaits. Sewing thread can be dyed to match the straw. As a rule, construction stitches should not be obvious, so consider selecting an appropriate gauge of thread for the size of the plait.

Damping

Depending on the project the plait should probably be damped, especially when it must be tightly coiled to start a button. Wrap in a warm damp cloth and leave until the plait is flexible. Do not over wet.

Sewing

Many projects begin with a button. This was often children's work, and they would hand stitch and coil the plait to a disc of about 4 cm (1.5 in.) before handing it over for sewing. For a round shape, the button should be round, and for an oval, the button should be oval.

The shape of button must be adjusted according to the crown shape.

You can either stitch the plait together:

Edge to edge:
For suitable plaits use either the Italian *remaille* or knitting method. You can also use a zigzag stitch, machine or hand stitching which is best suited to plaits made with a speelless join, or those joined into the body.

Overlapping:
The foot edge must be on the inside of the curve and will be under the next row of plait. Overlap about ⅓ of the plait width in each circuit.

Willow and straw plait basket filled with a range of Saxon plaits made in the 1800s.

CHAPTER
TEN

PLAIT INSTRUCTIONS

To reflect the range of patterns produced, plaits from many centres as well as some of the common variations observed in surviving examples are included, which means that there are variations within the instructions. These are deliberately included to enable accurate replication of the plaits, to provide authentic knowledge and to give the opportunity for maximum skills development.

Information sources

Instructions were passed on through plaiting communities or were learnt by copying samples provided by their plait dealer. Only three instruction books written while the plaiting industry was still alive are known to exist. *The Workwoman's Guide*[372] includes instructions for making plaits using between three and 16 working ends. All but one of the plaits, a rustic, have straight edges. A round spiral plait used to decorate hats is included. The *First Course of English Straw Plaiting*, followed by the Second Course book published the following year in 1895, were part of the efforts to revive the English plaiting industry.[373] These books incorporate patterns being made in Japan but only provide instructions for patterns using between three and seven ends. None of the books provide instructions for joining.

Plait structure

Virtually, all plaits have three parts:

Foot: The outside stitch is folded flat. It usually incorporates joins.

Body: Working moves create a pattern. It can contain joins.

Head: This is the decorative edge and never incorporates joins.

Depending on its final use, the plait should be a long, continuous piece maintaining a constant width. This is achieved by using short, matched lengths of the plaiting material. New ends regularly replace the old and must be added in a regular sequence. Whichever joining method is chosen it should be used for the whole length. The surplus section of the old and new ends, known as the set-ins (set-outs) and speels, are only clipped when the required length is complete. Once clipped the plait should be milled, taking care not to damage any decorative head pattern. After damping, the plait is ready to use.

The instructions

Each set of instructions contains three sections:

Setting up

This example of tartan plait shows how the plaiter started. The method could vary from plaiter to plaiter and according to the type of plait.

The plaiting lengths are folded in sequence to create the correct number of working ends. Individual plaiters adopted their own way of setting up and the instructions provide a variety of techniques. In time you may develop your own method for setting up more complex plaits.

When making a plait that required a greater number of ends, plaiters often set up a seven- or nine-end plait then gradually added new lengths until the correct number of ends were in place, usually within the first 5 cm (2 in.) of working. To create a specific colour-way pattern, the same method was used with coloured lengths added in the required order. A few examples of plaits made in the early 1900s started by tying lengths together, and although not common practice, it can be an easier method when learning.

Working

The sequence repeats until the required length is made and is only interrupted by the joining sequence. According to the pattern type, the directional move of the outside working end may affect the side of the plait facing. When the outside end is moved over, the wrong side of the plait faces. When the end is moved under, the right side is facing. This also varies whether the foot edge is on the left or right.

Joining

Joining new working ends into the plait is made in three specific ways:

- Along the foot edge
- Into the body, which is a method known as speelless
- A weak join into the very centre of the plait as found in the thirteen- or fifteen-end Tuscan plait.

Joins are never made into the plait's decorative head. Once a joining method is selected then it should be continued for the entire length.

For some projects the speelless method may be preferable since joins along the foot edge are inherently weak. However, when coiled to shape the foot is on the inside of the curve and the stitches are compressed. Stitching by overlapping further strengthens the joins.

Spacing joins evenly along the plait length creates the strongest plait and allows the plaiter to maintain a rhythm without losing speed. Plaiters appear to have adopted their own spacing rhythm which varied from every other stitch to every sixth stitch.

Some Chinese plaits were joined in sets and runs, that is to add new ends one after the other until all

Made in Breachwood Green in 1897. Note how evenly the joins are made along the foot edge.

are renewed, but this was considered to produce an inferior, weaker plait.

When setting the new end in leave about 2 cm (1 in.) of both old and new ends protruding to ensure they do not slip out of place.

Finishing the plait

Once the plait length was completed and clipped, the plait was wound into a piece or link that could be tied with a splint. Very few lengths with their splint knots survive.

Take one of the inside ends of a working group, wind it around the opposite group, and tuck through the winding thereby holding in place. If preferred the working ends can be secured by tying, but take care not to distort the plait. Alternatively, the ends can be clamped as once dry they will stay in place, but be aware they will move when damped. For patterns where the finishing method varies, a specific method is provided. Once the set-in and speel ends are clipped off the plait can be milled.

Damping

All natural materials require moistening before use. Traditionally plaiters would keep a pot of water by them to moisten their straws. The time it will take to achieve perfect flexibility will vary according to plant type. The general rule is that the plaiting material must bend without cracking. Only dampen as many plaiting lengths as required in one working session. Repeated dampening will spoil the colour and may make the lengths more difficult to work.

Whole straws and thicker materials may take about 10–15 minutes in warm water, longer in cold water. Do not place in water that is hotter than hand hot. Bleached and dyed straws will take less time to dampen.

Split straw or splints, willow skein (depending on thickness), palm leaves and fine grasses may only require immersing for five minutes.

Rush and some sedges are the exception and may need to be left in a wet towel overnight to absorb moisture into their centre.

Wrap the plaiting lengths in a cloth to retain their moisture. If they dry out, dip into and out of warm water or spray the working ends.

Double splints can be worked with either their shiny or matt (pith) side facing outwards. In the past plaiter's passed the pairs through their mouths so saliva held them together, but since this is unhygienic and unsafe, instead damp the splints in water and press them together before using them immediately.

Developing skills

Ideally to develop plaiting skills this chapter should be worked through from beginning to end. The plaits in the trade staples sections are the easiest to make as they have folded edges and show how to create a twist-head. These provide opportunity for the development of finger memory and manipulative skills.

Where possible, the simplest plait is the first one of each section and the most complex is the final one.

Each plait is placed within its historical context, but this should not restrict experimentation and use of other materials. For that reason, each set of instructions simply says whether the plait is best made using a round or flat plaiting material.

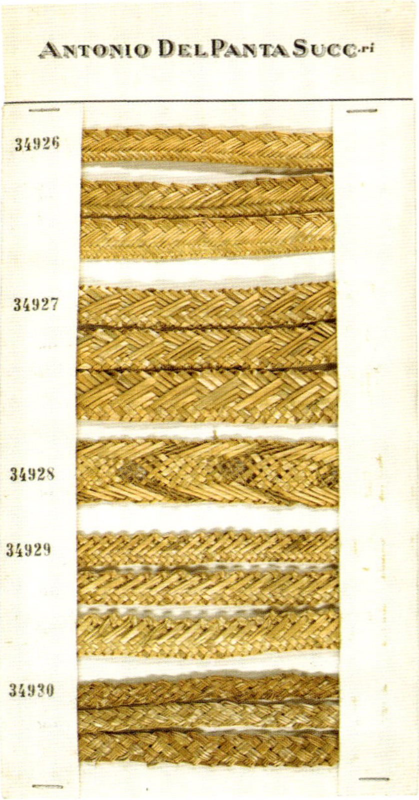

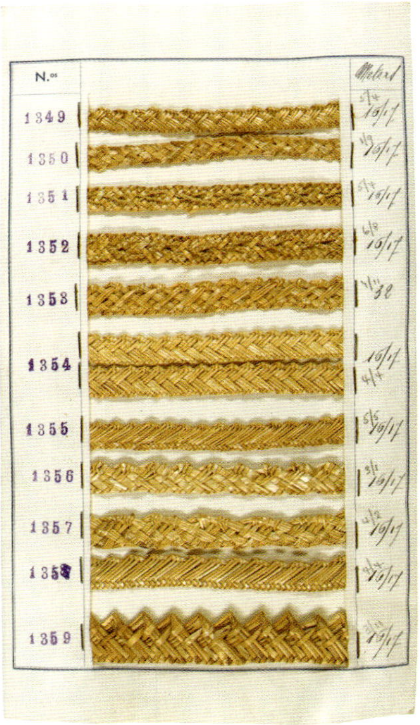

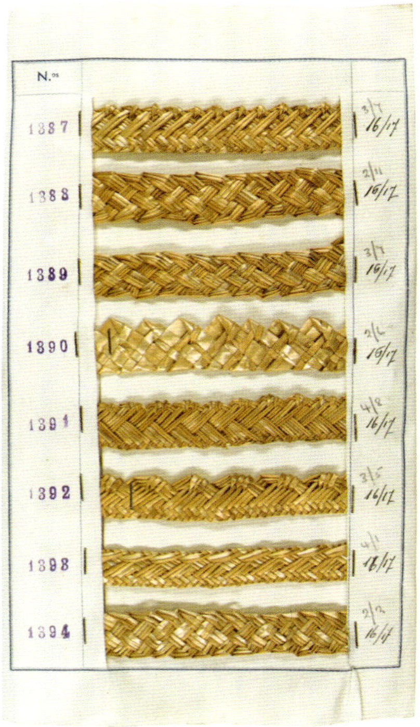

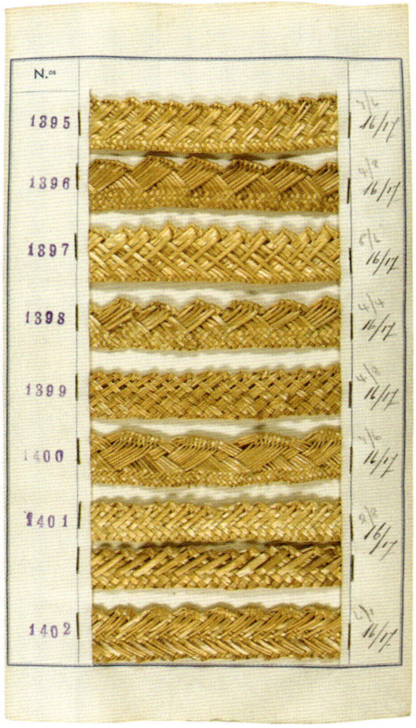

Likewise, although the original plait may have been made with narrow strips, it can often be made using wider ones, or by mixing narrow and wide ones within one pattern. Once a plait has been mastered there is no reason why its pattern cannot be varied by adding a different head edge to the body, increasing the number of working ends or adding some colour.

The overarching message is that while these instructions provide historical context, you are free to adapt and experiment. That is how the original industry developed and it is important that this enterprising spirit should continue.

Always make a note of the plait length you have made and how long it took you to make it. Not only does this ensure that a project can be repeated, but it also enables an accurate pricing of future commissions.

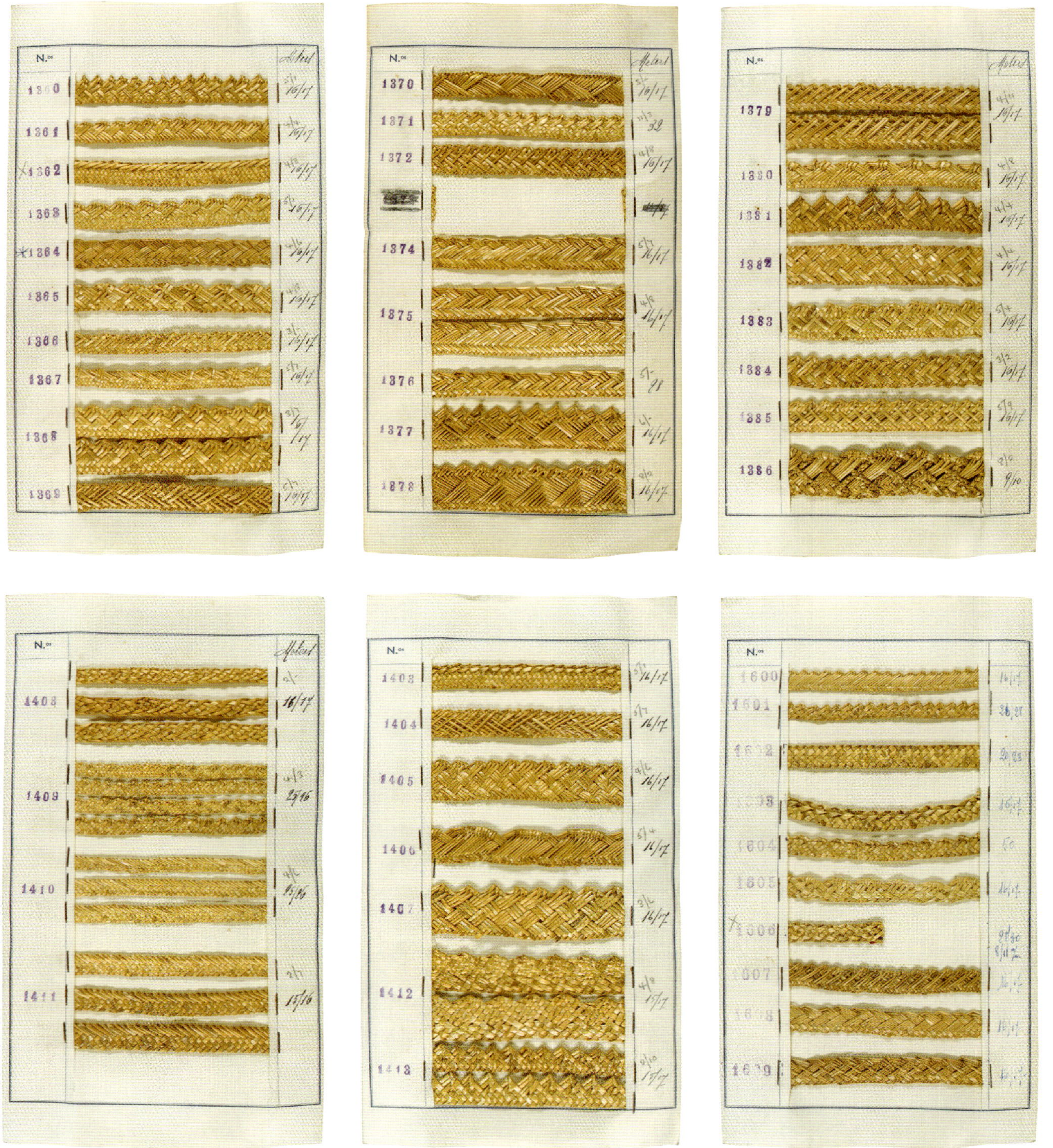

These sample cards show some of the plaits offered by an Italian dealer between 1920–35. This chapter includes a range of plaits in their simple forms. Once the basic techniques are learned the pattern possibilities are endless. (CTLC 1985/61)

From the mid 1950s this women's hat is made with three-end chip plait that has been painted with a floral pattern. (CTLC 2011/52)

Trade Staples – Three, Five and Seven Ends

This section includes some of the most common plaits. Work through these the plaits in this section using the basic hand movements so the holding strategies and joining sequences can be mastered. Balance the plait between both hands only using the first two fingers of each and use a thumbnail to crease the straw before it is folded. This creasing movement is essential to create a straight edge. Always remember to set up the lengths so the working ends are unequal.

Three-end plait

The original plait

Source: CTLC 40/70/61b

Origins: Japan

Production date: *c.* 1910

Type of straw: Barley straw, double splints

Splint width: 5 mm

Plait width: 8 mm

Plaiting direction: During working the back of the plait faces the maker and the front side faces away. The foot is on the right and the head on the left. When completed the front side of the plait has the head on the right and the foot on the left.

Joining: Along foot edge.

Background information: This basic three-end plait regained popularity in the hat industry of the twentieth century, but its origins are centuries earlier. This universal plait pattern was a major export product from China and Japan where it was made from wheat, barley, wood chip or bast. The original plait was made using pairs of splints but it can be worked with single splints or whole straws.

What to use: This can be made with all types of straw.

You need: Two plaiting lengths.
Additional lengths for joining.

Setting up

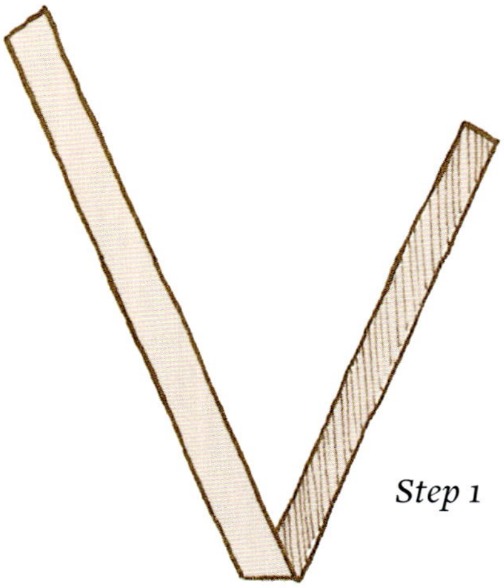

Step 1

Step 1: Off centre fold the left-hand end of the first length towards you and diagonally upwards to form a V. The ends should point to about 11 o'clock and 1 o'clock, an angle of about 45 degrees. Press the fold.

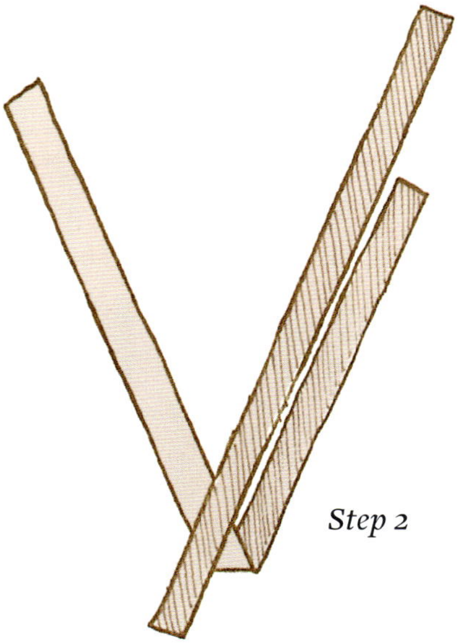

Step 2

Step 2: Take a second length. Place it in front of the V and between the two ends. A short end protrudes downwards, and the long end is placed parallel to the 1 o'clock end, the right-hand end.

You now have three working ends.

Working

The creasing before folding creates the straight edges and maintains a constant angle between the two working ends.

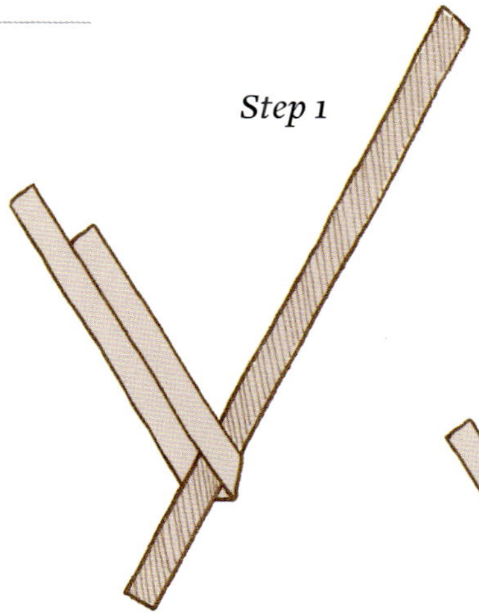

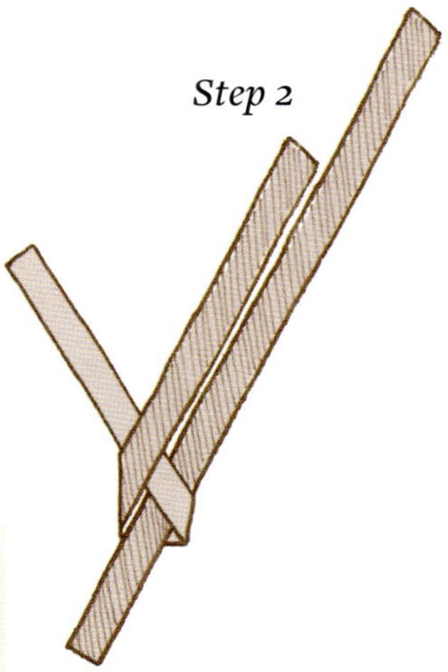

Step 1: Push your thumbnail into the outside right-hand end to create a crease then fold the straw to the left so it lays inside the left-hand end. Lightly press the fold.

There are two ends on the left.

Step 2: Push your thumbnail into the outside left-hand end to create a crease. Fold the outside right-hand end to lay inside of the V, the left-hand straw. Lightly press the fold.

There are two ends on the right and one on the left.

Continue the working sequence until the shortest end needs a new length added.

The working sequence is:
Right: over one, into the middle
Left: over one, into the middle

Joining

It is important to evenly match the size of straw or splint. Joins should be spread out along the plait. With practice you will develop a joining pattern, adding a new end every few moves. If joins are made on consecutive moves the plait will be weak and may come apart in use. The joins must always be made when there are two ends on the right and the end to be joined is in the centre.

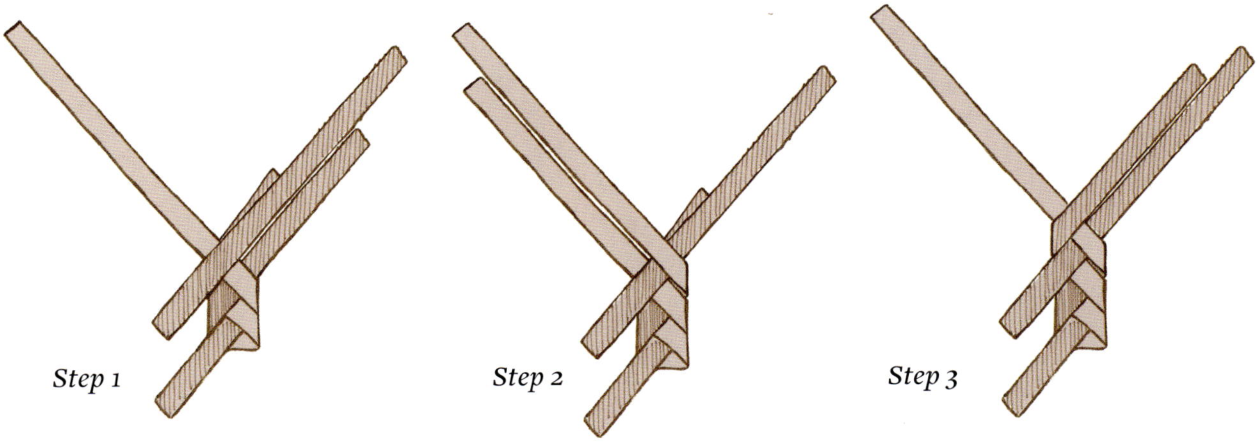

Step 1: Lay the new end over the inside right-hand end. Leave a short length of the straw protruding to the left.

Step 2: Using the creasing move, fold the outside right-hand end over the old and new ends. It lays to inside the left-hand end. Lightly press the fold.

Step 3: Fold the outside left-hand end to inside the right-hand end. Lightly press the fold. At the next move leave behind the old end and continue plaiting until the next join is required.

Variation: Mottled plait

The basic plait diagrams are shown in two shades to represent the inside and outside of the splints. Hold a single splint with its shiny side facing. Off centre fold left-hand end diagonally upwards and to about 11 o'clock so the matt side is facing. Add the second length with the shiny side facing upwards. The plait will have the shiny side of the plait forming the head and the matt side of the plait along the foot edge.

Five-end plait

The original plait

Source: CTLC 40/70/61a

Origins: Japan

Production date: *c.* 1910

Type of straw: Barley straw, whole

Splint width: 2 mm

Plait width: 5 mm

Plaiting direction: During working the back of the plait faces the maker and the front side faces away. The foot is on the right and the head on the left. When completed the front side of the plait has the head on the right and the foot on the left.

Joining: Along foot edge.

Background information: This appeared in *The Workwoman's Guide* but was not more widely used until the 1890s when various designs appeared from Japan and Europe. Instructions for making the five-end plaits worked with a variety of decorative head patterns were included in the 1895 instruction books which were written in attempts to revive the plaiting industry. Although it is unclear whether production continues today, a whole straw five-end plait was still being made in China until the 1960s.

What to use: This can be made with all types of straw.

You need: Three plaiting lengths.
Additional lengths for joining.

Setting up

Arrange so the ends are different lengths.

Step 1: Take one length and hold it horizontally so it lays from 9 o'clock to 3 o'clock.

Take a second length. Hold it diagonally in front of the horizontal length to lay at an angle of about 20 degrees, the top section will lay at a point between 2 and 3 o'clock.

Take the lower end, currently laying between 8 and 9 o'clock, and fold upwards and behind the horizontal length to lay at between 1 and 2 o'clock.

Press the fold.

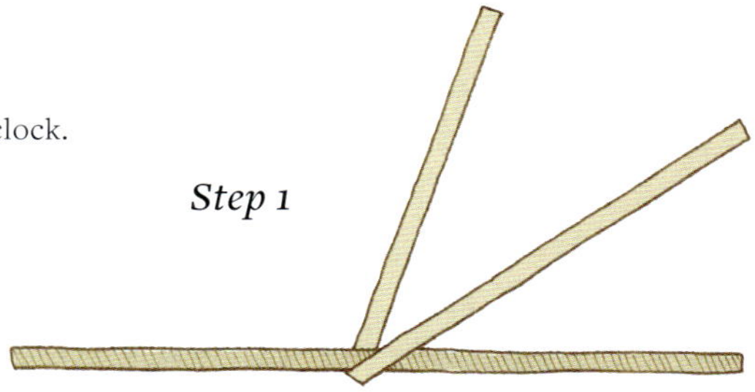

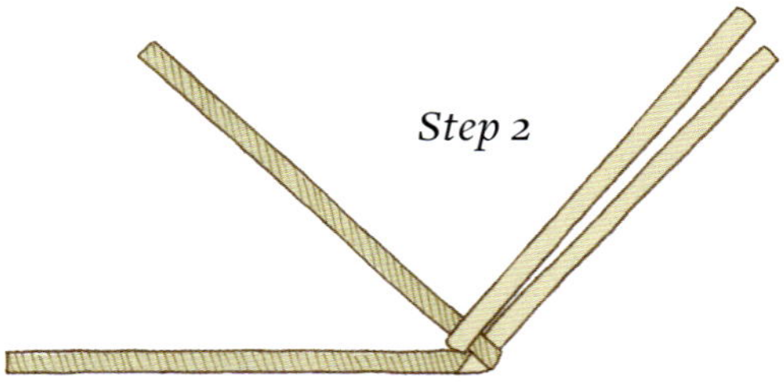

Step 2: Fold the right-hand, 3 o'clock horizontal end, towards you and then diagonally over the first end of the right-hand diagonals and under the second of the same group.

Step 3: Take a new working length and lay it in front of the group, short end pointing to between 4 and 5 o'clock and the long end between the two left-hand ends to lay to about 10 o'clock. This length provides the fifth working end.

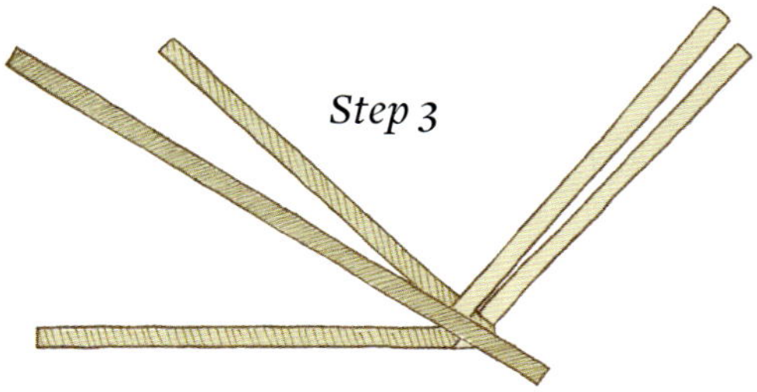

Step 4: Take the left-hand horizontal end, fold it towards you and then diagonally over the newly added end, and under the second of the left-hand group.

There are three ends on the right and two on the left.

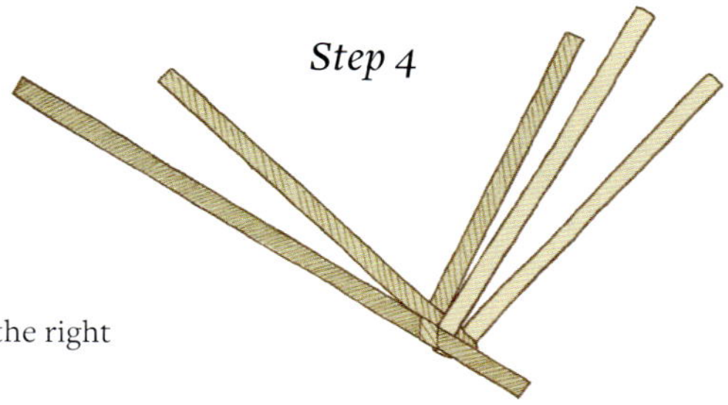

Working

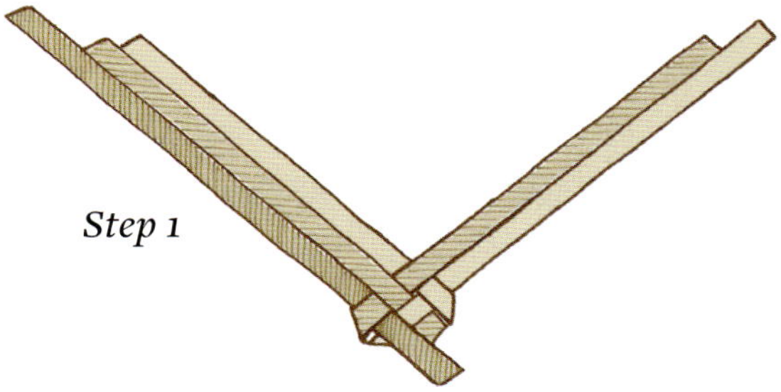

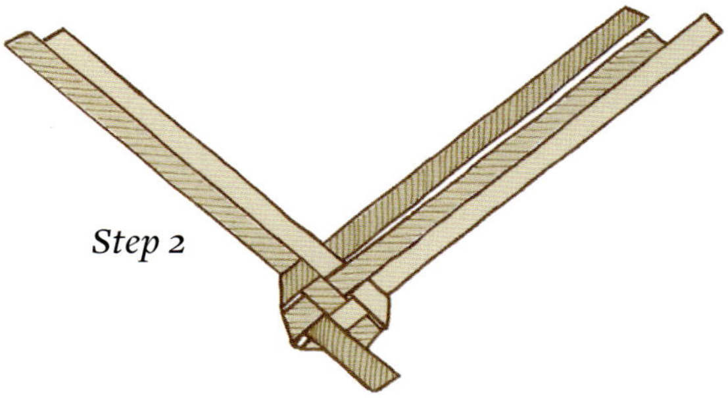

Step 1: Take the outside straw of right-hand group, bring it towards you and then diagonally over the first and under the second end of the right-hand group.

The end has moved over one, under one.

Step 2: On the left-hand side take the outside end of the group fold it towards you then diagonally over the first and under the second left-hand end. It now lays to the inside of the right-hand group. The end has moved, over one, under one.

The working sequence is:
Right: Over one, under one
Left: Over one, under one
Continue the working sequence until joining begins.

Joining

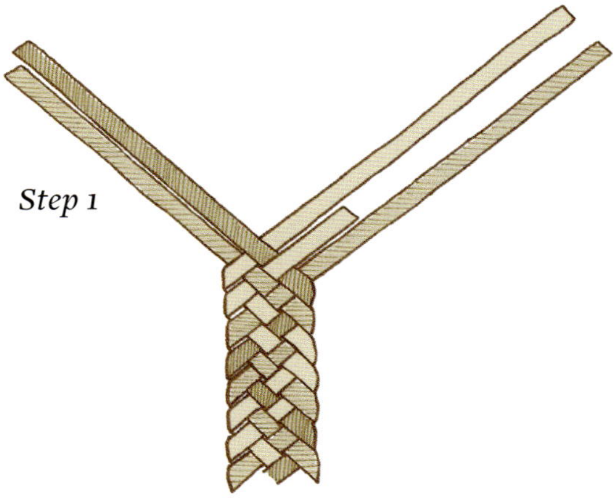

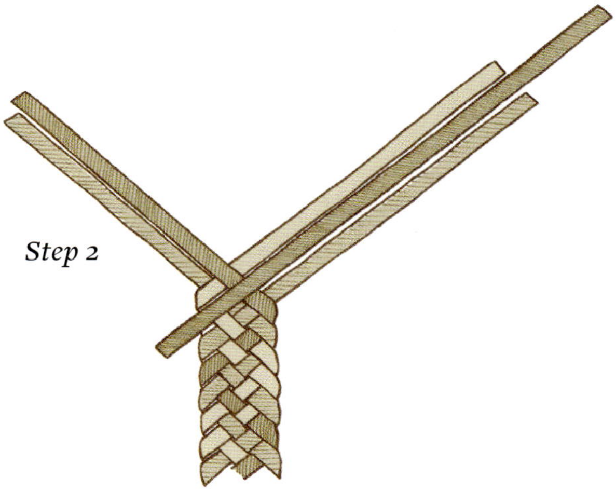

Step 1: The end to be joined must be the centre of of one of the three in the right-hand group.

Step 2: Lay the new end over the short end, leaving a short length protruding to the left. Fold the outside right-hand end, over the new and old ends, then under the inside end. Continue the working sequence leaving behind the old end and only working the new at the next right-hand move.

Begin the joining process before the working ends get too short so that the joining sequence can be evenly spaced.

Variation: Twist head

The head edge can be finished with a twist stitch as shown in this Japanese plait from about 1910 made using barley straw. Instructions for forming the twist, page 155. (CTLC 40/70/61c.)

Seven-end whole straw plait with twist head

The original plait

Source: CTLC 81/30

Origins: Breachwood Green, Bedfordshire

Production date: *c.* 1897

Type of straw: Wheat straw, whole

Straw width: 2–3 mm

Plait width: 15 mm

Plaiting direction: During working the back of the plait faces the maker and the front side faces away. The foot is on the right and the head on the left. When completed the front side of the plait has the head on the right and the foot on the left.

Joining: Along foot edge.

Background information: The seven-end plait with a folded head was probably one of the earliest patterns, but it was the twist edge version that was the most important staple product of the 1800s. The twist edge was known by a variety of names most commonly, cord, whipcord, or beady head. This example is recorded as being called old English. Creating the beautifully even twist edge requires practice, so persevere.

What to use: This can be made with all types of straw but to create the twist edge is most successfully worked with a flexible round straw.

You need: Four plaiting lengths.
Additional lengths for joining.

Setting up

Arrange so the ends are different lengths.

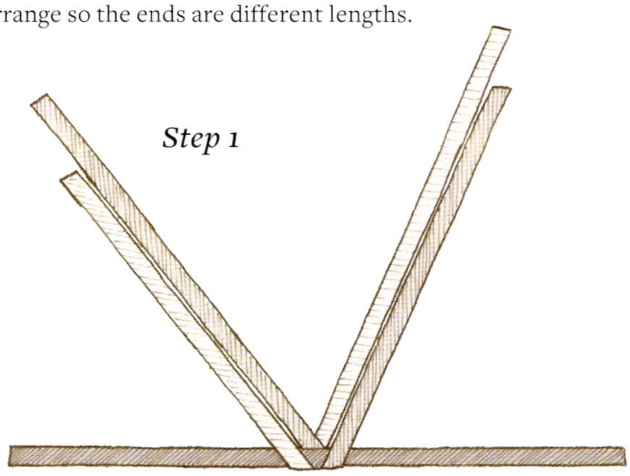

Step 1: The diagram shows the first three elements for positioning the ends.

Hold one length horizontally, from 9 o'clock to 3 o'clock.

Hold a second length diagonally in front of the horizontal length, pointing from about 2 o'clock to 8 o'clock.

Fold the lower end of this length behind the horizontal to lay at about 10 o'clock. Press the fold.

Take the third end. Hold it diagonally to the inside of the diagonal right-hand end. Fold the lower section upwards to lay to the outside of the left-hand diagonally. Press the fold.

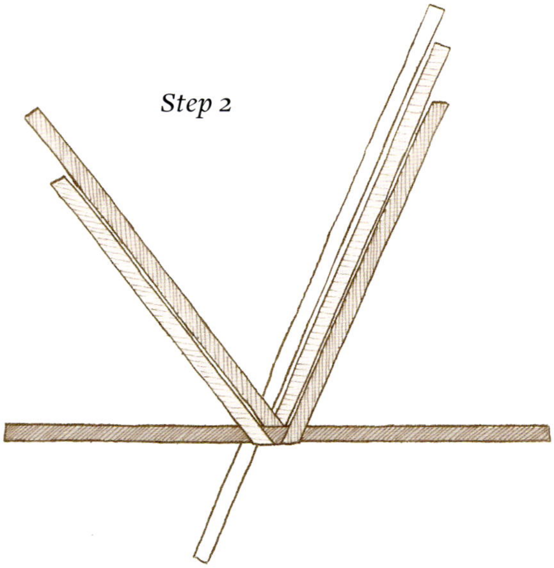

Step 2: Take the fourth end and place it behind the horizontal to lay to inside the right-hand group. Leave a short length protruding from below the horizontal length.

Working

These instructions are for a twist head. For a folded head use the folding movement as made along the foot edge.

There are four ends to the right and three to the left.

Step 1: Take the outside, lowest end of the right-hand group bring it towards you then diagonally upwards, over one, under two. It lays to the inside of the left-hand group.

Step 2: For the first working move only count the left-hand horizontal end, pointing to 9 o'clock, as the outside end. Count the adjacent diagonal of the left-hand group as the second.

For all subsequent moves the outside end will lay parallel to the rest of the group and the adjacent end, second end from the outside, will provide the necessary resistance for creating the twist.

Take the second end from the outside, move it slightly sidewards so it moves away from the other two diagonal ends in the left-hand group. Hold it in place.

Using the second end to provide a resistance for the move, twist the lowest, outside end of the left-hand group diagonally, over one, under two to lay to the inside of the right-hand group. The outside end should form a crease as it moves across but to achieve that the end must not turn on itself.

The working sequence is:
Right: over one, under two
Left: over one, under two

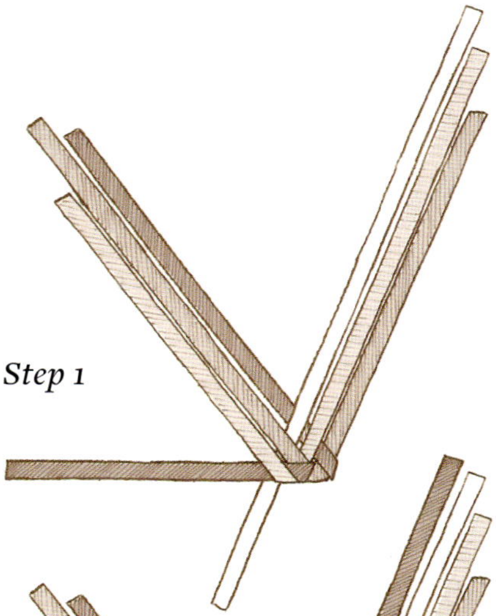

Step 1

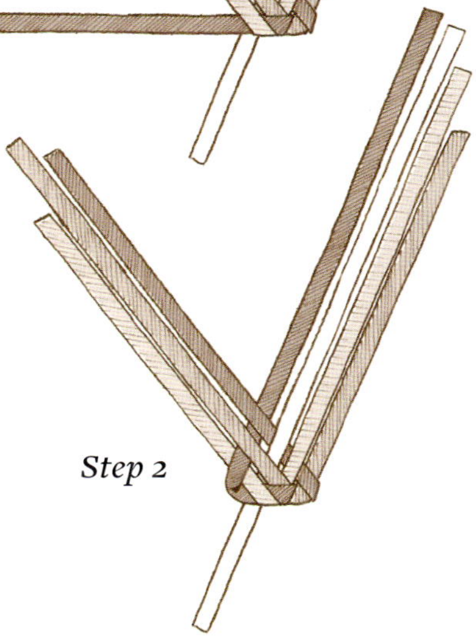

Step 2

Joining

Plan to begin the joining sequence after the first three or four working sequences which will allow subsequent joins to be spaced evenly along the length.

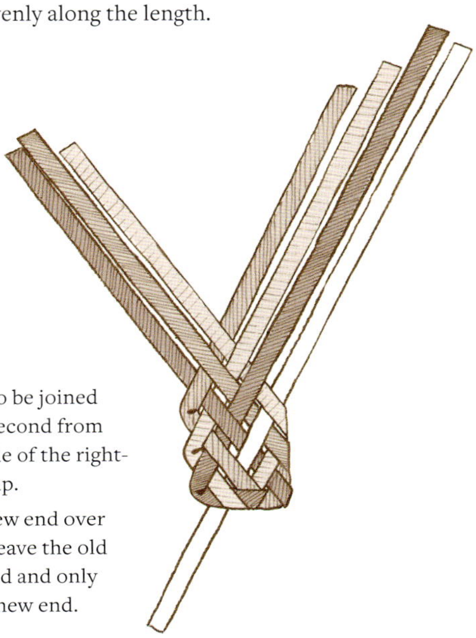

The end to be joined must be second from the outside of the right-hand group.

Lay the new end over the old. Leave the old end behind and only work the new end.

Variations:

The Workwoman's Guide published in 1840 included instructions for a checkerboard pattern. To create this pattern at setting up step 2 it is necessary to hold the fourth end in front of the other ends and to the inside of the right-hand group so it can be locked in place at the first working step.

The working sequence is: Right-hand group, over one, under one, over one
Left-hand group, over one, under one, over one
The head can be created with either a folded or twist head.

Smooth bend

During the 1800s, when this English plait had a folded head it was known as smooth bend. The example shown was one of the early imports from China in 1879. If you look closely, you will see the joins are made into the body of the plait, a method called speelless, *page 288.* (CTLC 49/70/61)

Seven-end single splint plait

The original plait

Source: CTLC 3/99/41

Origins: Dunstable, Bedfordshire

Production date: before 1881

Type of straw: Wheat straw, single splints

Splint width: 1 mm

Plait width: 5 mm

Plaiting direction: During working the back of the plait faces the maker and the front side faces away. The foot is on the right and the head on the left. When completed the front side of the plait has the head on the right and the foot on the left.

Joining: Along foot edge.

Background information: It is rare to have the name of a plaiter and although the CTL records say it was made by Mary Glenister living in Dunstable national census records may indicate she lived in Luton and was a bonnet sewer not a plaiter. The collection holds bonnets attributed to her therefore this may have been a plait she used rather than one she made. We will never know.

What to use: This can be made with all types of flat straw, but to create the shiny and matt effect it should be made with single splint wheat or rye straw.

You need: Four plaiting lengths.
Additional lengths for joining.

Setting up

Arrange so the ends are different lengths.

The diagram shows all stages for setting up and is the same method as for the seven-end whole straw. To create the plaits characteristic pattern the splints must be positioned as indicated.

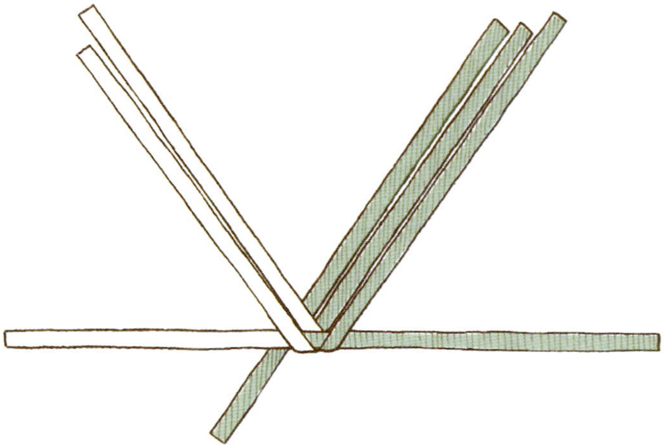

Hold one length horizontally, from 9 o'clock to 3 o'clock. Just off centre, twist the length on itself so the right-hand, 3 o'clock end has the shiny side facing towards you and the left-hand, 9 o'clock end has the matt side facing.

Hold a second length diagonally in front of the horizontal length, pointing from about 2 o'clock to 8 o'clock. The shiny side of the length must be facing.

Fold the lower end of this length behind the horizontal to lay at about 10 o'clock. Press the fold. The left-hand diagonal will have the matt side facing you.

Take the third end. Hold it diagonally, with the shiny side facing to the inside of the diagonal right-hand end. Fold the lower section upwards to lay to the outside of the left-hand diagonal. Press the fold.

Take the fourth end and place it behind the horizontal with the shiny side facing to lay inside the right-hand group. Leave a short length protruding from below the horizontal length.

The right-hand group has four ends with their shiny side facing and the left-hand group, three ends with their matt side facing.

Working

Step 1

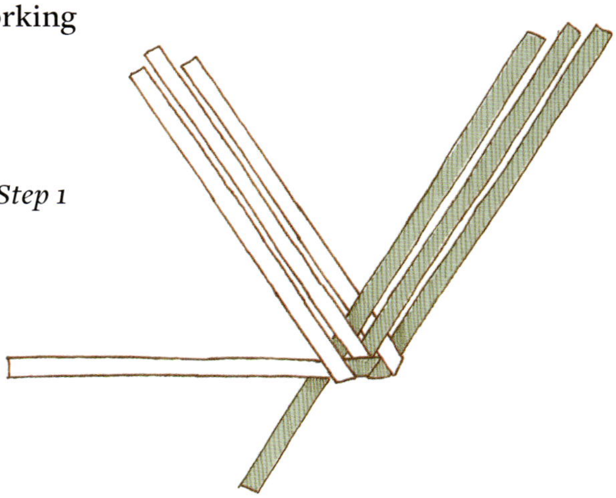

Step 2

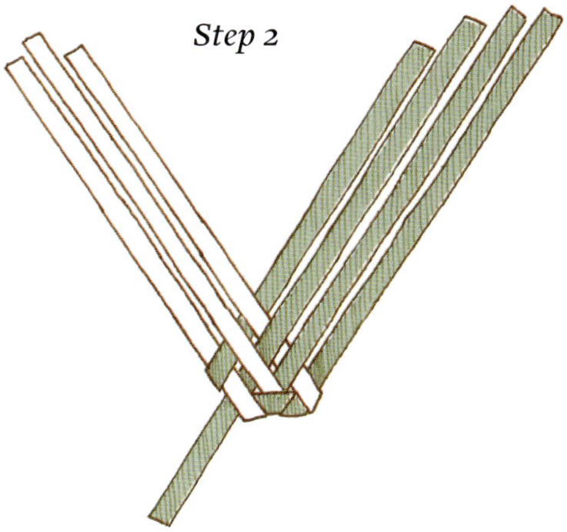

Step 1: Take the outside, lowest end of the right-hand group towards you then diagonally upwards, over one, under two. It lays to the inside of the left-hand group with its matt side facing.

The move is over one, under two.

> **The working sequence is:**
> Right: over one, under two
> Left: over one, under two

Step 2: Take the outside, lowest end of the left-hand group towards you then diagonally upwards, over one, under two. It lays to the inside of the right-hand group. The shiny side of this end will be facing.

Continue working until joining begins.

As the pattern forms the head will be shiny, the body has a row of matt and a row of shiny. The foot edge is matt.

Joining

Plan to begin the joining sequence after the first three or four complete working sequences.

The end to be joined must be second from the outside of the right-hand group as shown in the diagram.

Lay the new end over the old remembering to have the shiny side facing you. Leave the old end behind and only work the new end.

The diagram also shows an earlier join in the length with the set in laying over the body of the plait and speel protruding from behind the foot edge.

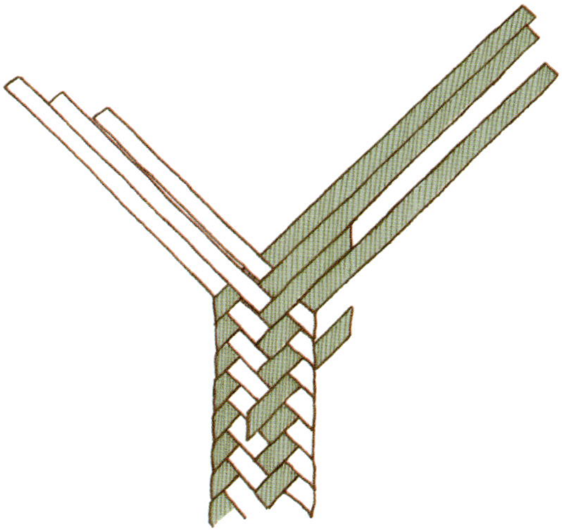

Variation: Plum pudding

This copy of a plait made in about 1850 by Mrs Eldridge, Ballinger, Buckinghamshire is made with five bleached, one red, and one blue splint. It is set up with seven undyed ends then on the third working move on the foot edge, the undyed end is replaced with the red splint. After two more moves on the foot edge the blue splint is added. (CTLC 5/284/32)

Women's boater hat, made in Luton of railroad plait in about 1902. (CTLC 237/33)

Seven-end double splint, rail, or Luton rail

The original plait

Source: CTLC 11/284/32

Origins: Ballinger, near Great Missenden, Buckinghamshire

Production date: Around 1850

Type of straw: Wheat straw, double splints

Splint width: 1–1.5 mm

Plait width: 6-7 mm

Plaiting direction: During working the back of the plait faces the maker and the front side faces away. The foot is on the right and the head on the left. When completed the front side of the plait has the head on the right and the foot on the left.

Joining: Along foot edge.

Background information: Commonly called Luton railroad it was made in many English villages, Switzerland, Germany, and probably in Belgium. There were many pattern colourways. During the 1800s the plaiters passed the pairs of splints through their mouths since their saliva held the lengths together as if lightly glued. For this pattern both edges are folded.

What to use: This can be made with all types of flat straw, but to create the pattern requires a length with one colour on one side and a different one on the other.

You need: Eight plaiting lengths, four dyed and four undyed. Additional lengths of both colours for joining.

Setting up (method 1)

The lengths are set up ready to work using the seven-end whole and single splint methods, however since the lengths are worked as pairs beginners may have some difficulty in keeping them in order. If you do find it problematic use the second method for setting up.

Damp the lengths and pair an undyed to a dyed length. The damping will hold them together.

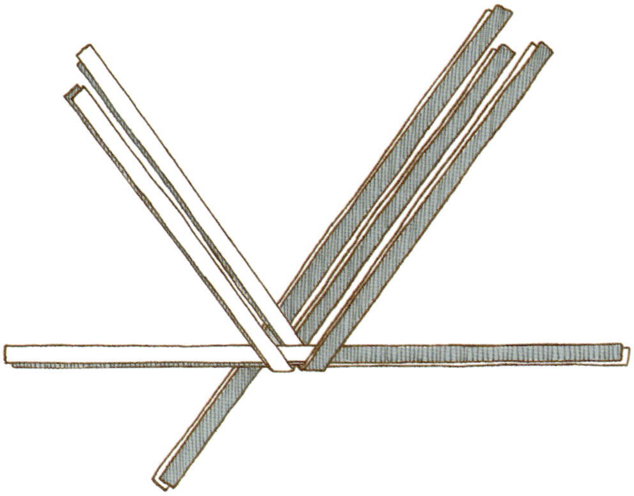

The diagram shows all stages for setting up and is the same method as for the seven-end whole straw. To create the plaits characteristic pattern the pairs of splints must be positioned as indicated with the dark splint of the pair facing in the right-hand group and the undyed facing in the left-hand group.

Hold one pair of splints horizontally, from 9 o'clock to 3 o'clock. Just off centre, twist the pair on themselves so the right-hand, 3 o'clock end has the dyed splint facing towards you and the left-hand, 9 o'clock end has the undyed splint facing.

Hold a second pair diagonally in front of the horizontal length, pointing from about 2 o'clock to 8 o'clock. The dyed splint must be facing.

Fold the lower end of this pair behind the horizontal to lay at about 10 o'clock. The left-hand diagonal will have the undyed splint facing you. Press the fold.

Take the third pair. Hold diagonally, with the dyed side facing to the inside of the diagonal right-hand end. Fold the lower section upwards to lay to the outside of the left-hand diagonal. Press the fold.

Take the fourth pair and place them behind the horizontal with the dyed splint facing to lay to the inside of the right-hand group. Leave a short length protruding from below the horizontal length.

The right-hand group will have four ends with their dyed splint facing, and the left-hand group three ends with the undyed splint facing.

Setting up (method 2)

For this second method begin by setting up single dyed splints then add the undyed splints as a joining sequence. Only the fourth length is immediately added as a pair but could also be introduced as a single splint and its pair added as part of the sequence.

Step 1

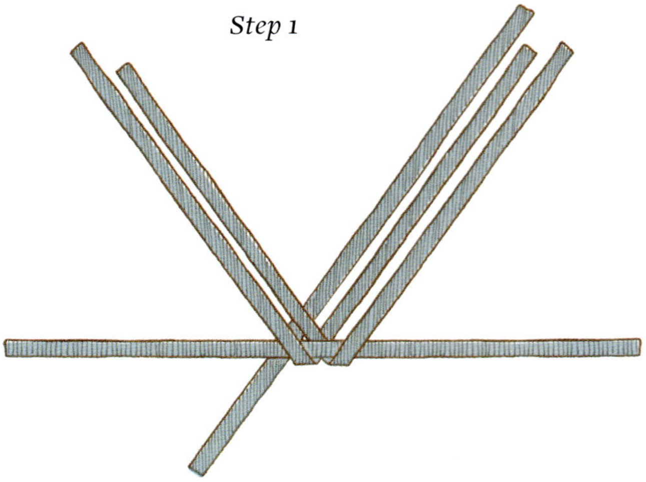

Step 1: Set up the ends following the seven-end single splint setting up instructions, so the right-hand group shows the shiny side, and the left-hand group shows the matt. The fourth length can be added as a pair which is shown in the diagrams.

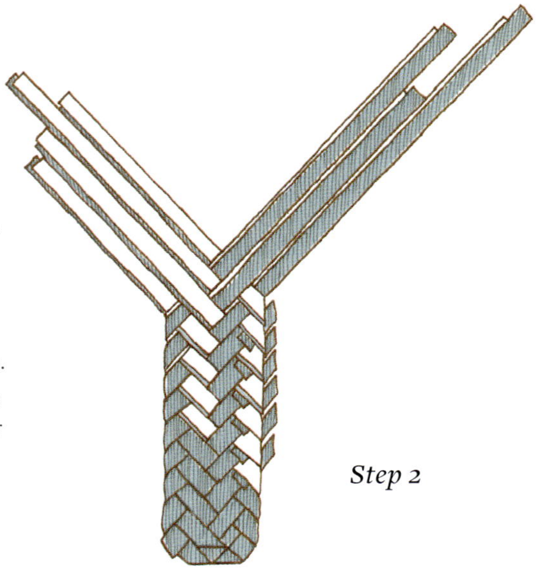

Step 2

Step 2: To create the pattern within a minimum of stitches the undyed splint must be added at every foot edge working move until all the ends are paired undyed to dyed with their shiny sides outwards.

Make three complete working sequences with the single dyed splints.

Begin introducing the undyed splint at each working step 1 using the joining method described for the whole straw and single splint patterns.

When all the undyed splints have been introduced the right-hand group will have three ends with their dyed facing and the left-hand group, four ends with the undyed splint facing you.

Check that all pairs have their shiny side facing outwards.

Working

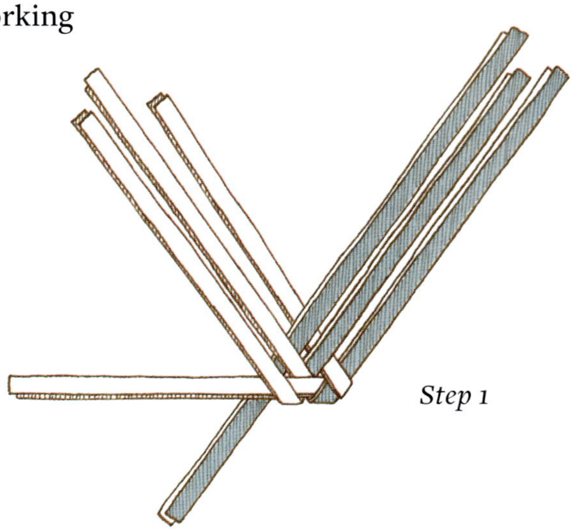

Step 1

Step 1: The diagram shows the pairs set up when beginning with Setting up method 1.

Take the outside, lowest pair of the right-hand group towards you then diagonally upwards, over one, under two. The pair lays to the inside of the left-hand group with the undyed splint facing.

Step 2: Take the outside, lowest pair of the left-hand group towards you then diagonally upwards, over one, under two. It lays to the inside of the right-hand group with the dyed splint facing.

The working sequence is:
Right: over one, under two
Left: over one, under two

Step 2

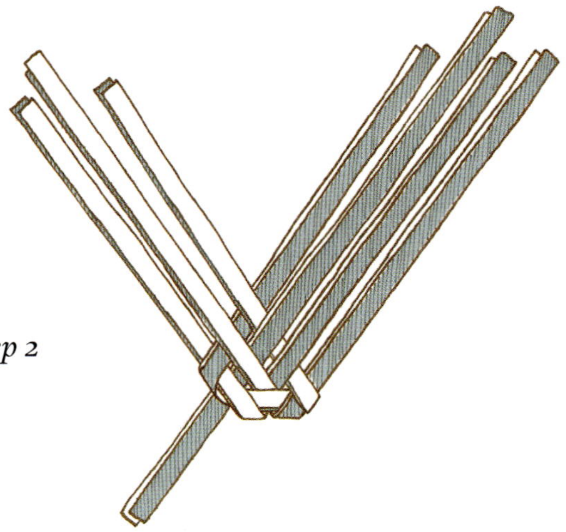

Joining

Plan to begin the joining sequence after the first three or four working sequences which will allow subsequent joins to be spaced evenly along the length.

The pair to be joined must be second from the outside of the right-hand group.

Lay the new pair over the old. Leave the old pair behind and only work the new pair.

Variation: Tartan

Described as a version of English twist this example was made in the 1800s in the village of Bledlow Ridge, Buckinghamshire. Now faded, the original colours were purple and green. To recreate the pattern, pair the splints as matching colours with three paired purple and one paired green. When setting up, place the green pair as the horizontal length so there are five purple and two green working ends. (CTLC 8/284/32)

Baker boy hat. Model: Klay Evaorl
Lucy Barlow created this dramatic oversize hat using a nine-end plait (pattern variation two) and a plain seven-end plait for the brim. Both plaits were made by Veronica Main using durable paper tape.

Trade Staples – Nine and Eleven Ends

This section includes plaits made in Italy and copied in Great Britain as part of the encouragement for plaiters to imitate. Made using fine straws, the beauty of the Tuscan and Leghorn plaits lay within their simplicity and perfect execution. Surviving plait examples are often a natural colour, although in the period 1820–30 fashion trends called for them to be dyed black. Whilst the inclusion of colour is not traditional there is no reason why it should not be since adding colour offers great design opportunities.

Nine-end plait

The replica plait

Source: Copy made from original instructions

Origins: *The Workwoman's Guide*

Production date: Around 1838

Type of straw: Originally rye or wheat. The replica uses paper knitting tape

Straw width: 4 mm

Plait width: 25 mm

Plaiting direction: During working the back of the plait faces the maker and the front side faces away. The foot is on the right and the head on the left. When completed the front side of the plait has the head on the right and the foot on the left.

Joining: Along foot edge.

Background information: *The Workwoman's Guide* did not specify the type of straw therefore assuming it was intended to copy Italian plaits then it was probably made from fine whole straws or grass. This plait can be made from any material. Three variations for this plait are included in *The Workwoman's Guide*. The main instructions show pattern one and the other two are included in the variation section.

What to use: All types of straw.

You need: Five plaiting lengths.

Setting up

Arrange so the working ends are different lengths.

Hold one length horizontally, from 9 o'clock to 3 o'clock. Hold a second length diagonally in front of the horizontal length, pointing from about 2 o'clock to 8 o'clock. Fold the lower end of this length behind the horizontal to lay at about 10 o'clock. Press the fold.

Take the third length. Hold it diagonally behind the horizontal and to the inside of the diagonal right-hand group. Fold the lower end upwards to lay to the outside of the left-hand diagonal. Press the fold.

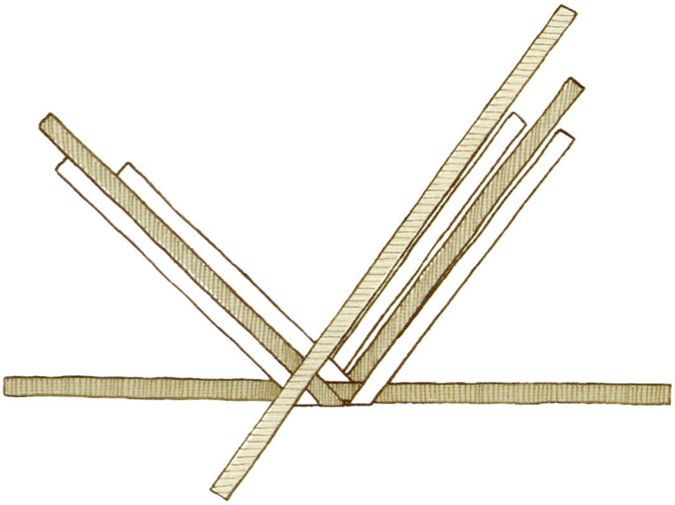

Take the fourth length. Hold it diagonally behind the horizontal and to the inside of the diagonal right-hand group. Fold the lower section upwards to lay to the outside of the left-hand diagonal. Press the fold. Take the fifth end and place it diagonally in front of the group to lay to inside the four right-hand ends. Leave a short length protruding from below the horizontal length.

Working

There are five ends to the right and four to the left.

Step 1

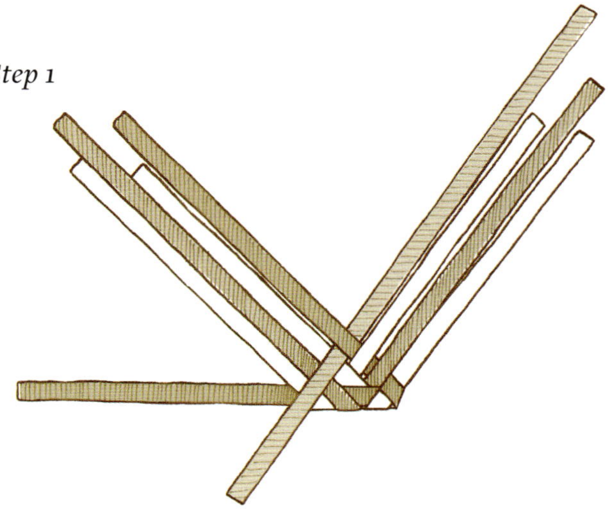

Step 2

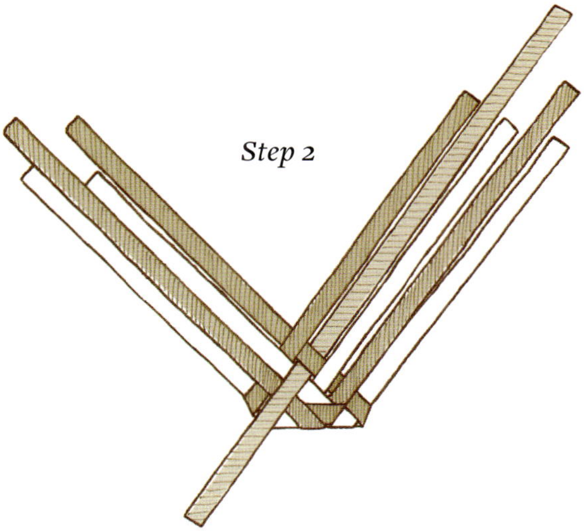

Step 1: Take the lowest outside right-hand end diagonally, over one, under two, over one. It lays to inside the left-hand group.

Step 2: Take the lowest outside left-hand end diagonally, over one, under two, over one. It lays to inside the right-hand group.

Continue working until joining is required.

The working sequence is:
Right: over one, under two, over one
Left: over one, under two, over one

Joining

Plan to begin the joining sequence after the first three or four working sequences which will allow subsequent joins to be spaced evenly along the length.

The end to be joined must be second from the outside of the right-hand group.

Lay the new end over the old. Leave the old end behind and only work the new end.

Variations

Pattern one (top)

The working sequence is:
Right-hand group, over one, under one, over one, under one.
Left-hand group, over two, under one, over one, under one.
Join along the foot or into the body.

Pattern two (below)

The working sequence is:
Right-hand group, over one, under one, over two.
Left-hand group, under one, and over two.
Join along the foot or into the body.

Eleven-end – checkerboard pattern

The replica plait

Source: Copy made from original instructions

Origins: *The Workwoman's Guide*

Production date: Around 1838

Type of straw: Wheat straw, whole

Straw width: Unknown, example 1 mm

Plait width: Unknown, example 16 mm

Plaiting direction: During working the back of the plait faces the maker and the front side faces away. The foot is on the right and the head on the left. When completed the front side of the plait has the head on the right and the foot on the left.

Joining: Along foot edge.

Background information: The checkerboard pattern is still commonly made in the Caribbean using palm and incorporating dyed lengths to create a range of colourways. These instructions follow those in *The Workwoman's Guide*, but it should be noted that where it is being made today the working sequence always begins with the outside end moving under.

What to use: This can be made with all types of straw.

You need: Six plaiting lengths.
Additional lengths for joining.

Setting up

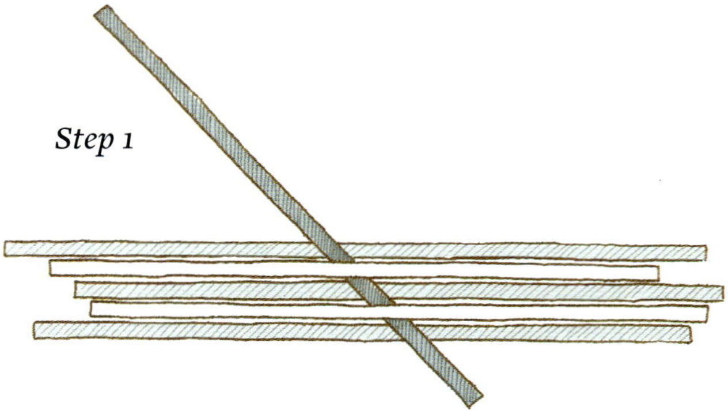

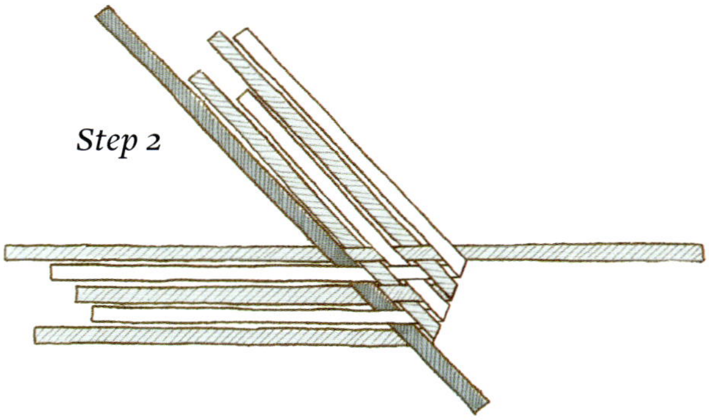

Step 1: Take five of the lengths and arrange side by side horizontally, their ends pointing from nine o'clock to three o'clock.

Insert the sixth end diagonally so it lays from about 5 o'clock to 11 o'clock. The length passes over the lowest horizontal length then over, under, over, under, over.

Adjust the length so the diagonal crosses slightly off centre and the ends are different lengths. Leave a short length of the diagonal protruding below the horizontal group.

Step 2: The diagram shows four consecutive moves.

Take the right-hand end of the lowest length. Fold it upwards, towards you, then diagonally over the next, then under, over, under through the rest of the group. It lays parallel to the right of the diagonal length.

Take the new lowest end and repeat, taking it over and finally under over the remaining ends of the group until it lays to the right of the two diagonals.

Repeat twice until four of the five right-hand ends lay diagonally to the left.

One horizontal end remains on the right.

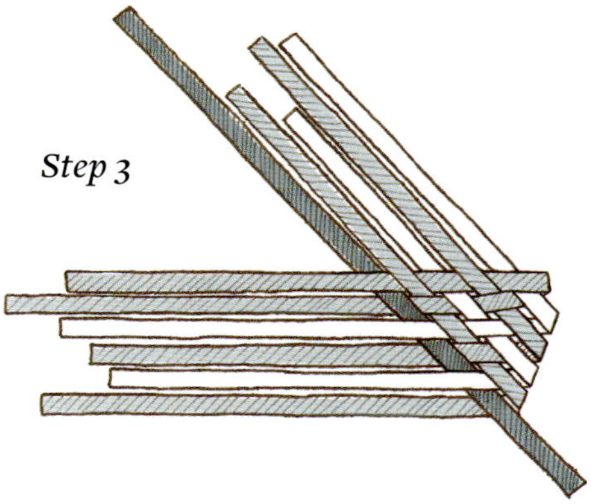

Step 3: Take the remaining right-hand horizontal end, fold it towards you and then horizontally over, under, over, under, over through the left-hand diagonals. It now lays parallel at the top horizontal left-hand group.

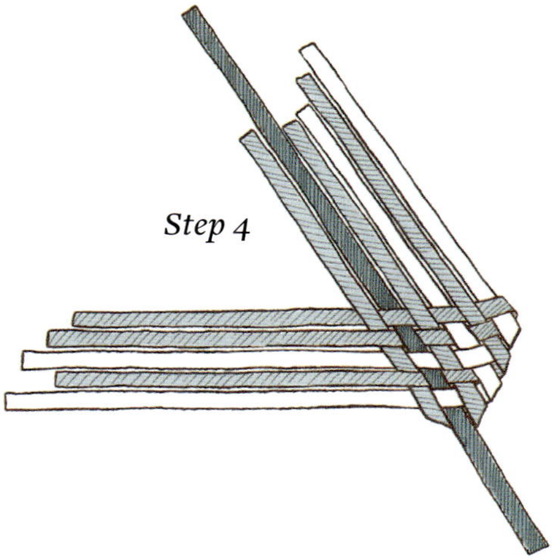

Step 4: Take the lowest end of the left-hand horizontal group. Fold it towards you then diagonally over, under, over, under, over through the other ends of the group. It now lays parallel to the left of the diagonal group.

There are now six ends in the diagonal group and five ends in the horizontal group.

Working

To begin the working steps, rotate the whole piece clockwise so the left-hand group points towards about ten o'clock and right-hand group to about 2 o'clock.

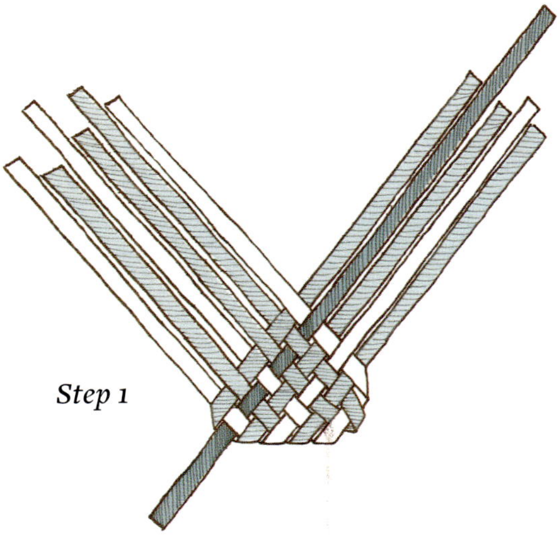

Step 1: Take the lowest end of the right-hand group, fold it towards you and then diagonally over one, under one, over one, under one, over one. It lays to the inside of the left-hand group.

There are five ends in the right-hand group and six ends in the left-hand group.

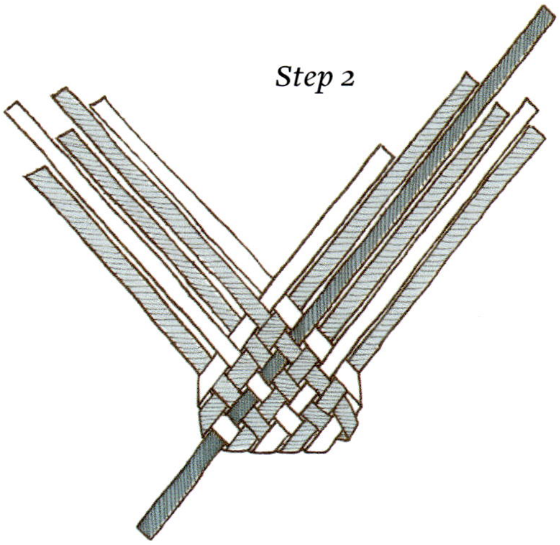

Step 2: Take the lowest end of the left-hand group, fold it towards you and then diagonally over one, under one, over one, under one, over one. It lays to the inside of the right-hand group.

There are five ends in the left-hand group and six ends in the right-hand group.

Continue the working sequence until joining begins.

The working sequence is:
Right: over one, under one, over one, under one, over one
Left: over one, under one, over one, under one, over one

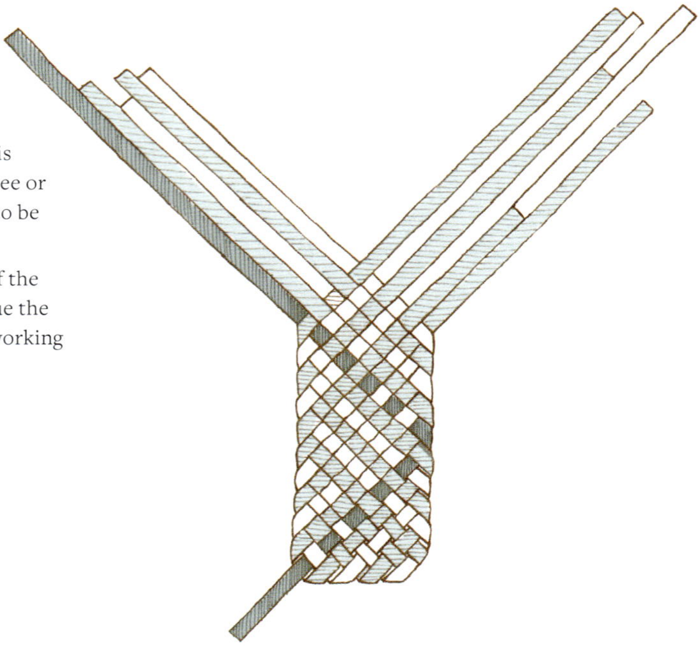

Joining

Since the plait incorporates a greater number of ends it is essential to begin the joining sequence after the first three or four working sequences which allows subsequent joins to be spaced evenly along the length.

The end to be joined must be second from the outside of the right-hand group. Lay the new end over the old. Continue the working sequence leaving the old end behind and only working the new end.

Made in 1886, this pork pie toque hat provides a conundrum. Records say the plait is called Rutland. It is clearly an eleven-end checkerboard however the following eleven-end Tuscan plait was also sometimes called Rutland plait. (CTLC 5/211/32)

Eleven-end Tuscan

The original plait

Source: CTLC 45/27

Origins: Luton, Bedfordshire

Production date: Around 1777

Type of straw: Recorded as bents and possibly made from imported Italian straws

Straw width: 1 mm

Plait width: 6 mm

Plaiting direction: During working the back of the plait faces the maker and the front side faces away. The foot is on the right and the head on the left. When completed the front side of the plait has the head on the right and the foot on the left.

Joining: Along foot edge.

Background information: Thought to have been made by Mrs Cawdell during the 1770s it was described as Tuscan plait. It differs from the Leghorn plaits later in this section as it is joined along the foot edge. Use of the term Tuscan may refer to the pattern or indicate it was being commonly made using Italian straw.

What to use: This can be made with all types of straw.

You need: Six plaiting lengths.
Additional lengths for joining.

Setting up

Although this method of setting up can be faster some ends will be out of position for the first few moves therefore be prepared to adjust them to be able to create the correct working sequence.

Step 1

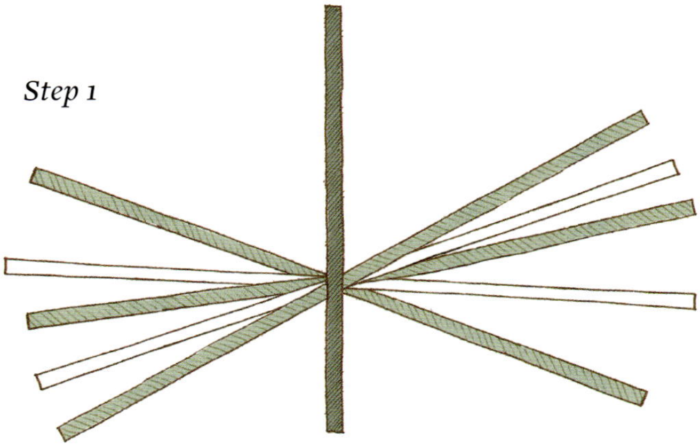

Step 1: Take five of the working lengths and just off centre arrange them one on top of the other with their ends pointing horizontally, left to right.

Take the sixth end and leaving a short length protruding below the centre hold it in front of the group at the point where all the lengths cross.

Step 2

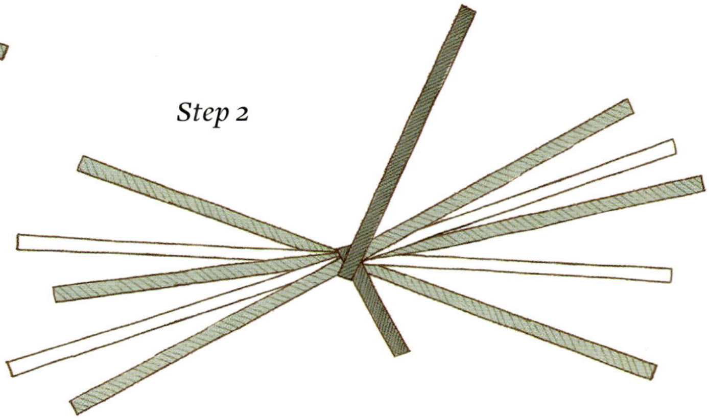

Step 2: Fold the long end of the sixth length away from you, behind the group and vertically downwards to lay to the left of the short end of the same length.

Fold the long left-hand end of the vertical length to the right so it lays to the inside of the right-hand group.

Arrange the horizontal lengths so the working ends are different lengths.

Step 3

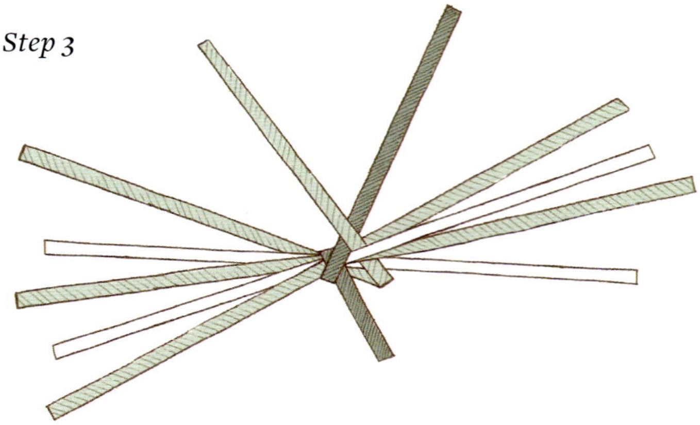

Step 3: Take the lowest end of the right-hand group and fold it towards you, then diagonally over one, under two and over two. It now lays to the inside of the left-hand group.

Step 4

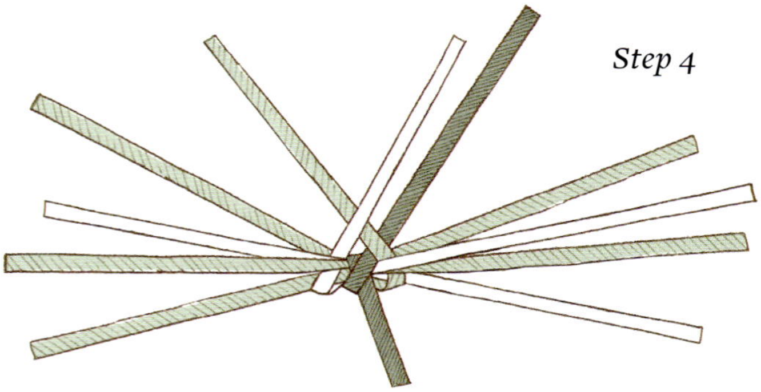

Step 4: To correctly make this move the second lowest end must be moved to the outside of the group so it becomes the lowest end.

Take the lowest end of the left-hand group and fold it towards you then diagonally over one, under two and over two. It now lays to the inside of the right-hand group.

Working

Step 1

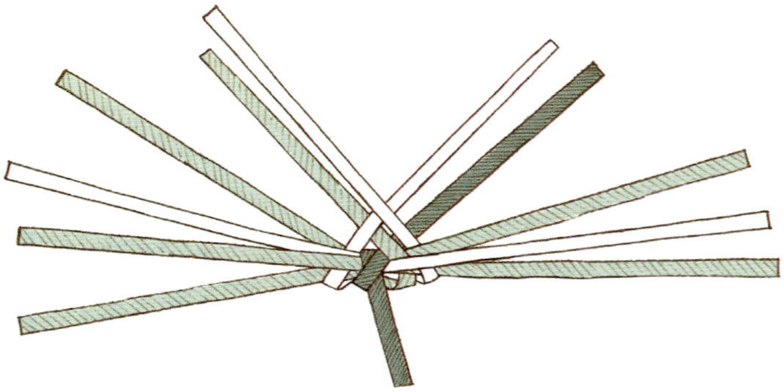

Step 1: Take the lowest end of the right-hand group, fold it towards you and then diagonally over one, under two, over two. It lays to the inside of the left-hand group.

There are five ends in the right-hand group and six ends in the left-hand group.

Step 2

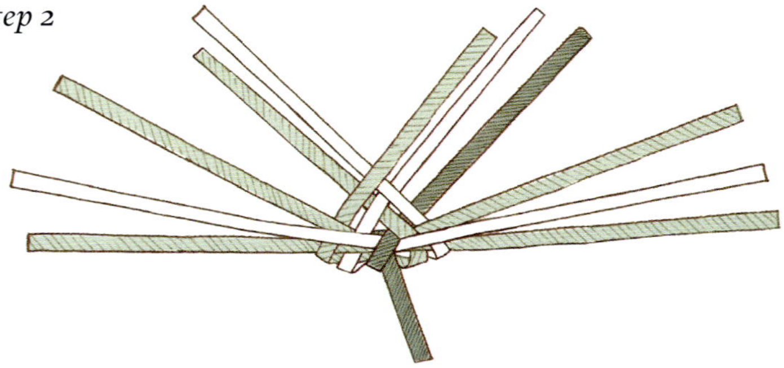

Step 2: Take the lowest end of the left-hand group, fold it towards you and then diagonally over one, under two, over two. It lays to the inside of the right-hand group.

There are five ends in the left-hand group and six ends in the right-hand group.

Continue the working sequence until joining begins.

The working sequence is:
Right: over one, under two, over two
Left: over one, under two, over two

Joining

Since the plait incorporates a greater number of ends it is essential to begin the joining sequence after the first three or four working sequences which allows subsequent joins to be spaced evenly along the length.

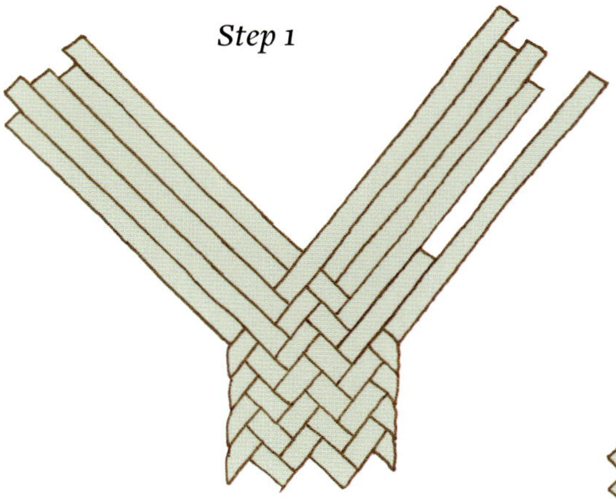

Step 1: The end to be joined must be second from the outside of the right-hand group.

Step 2

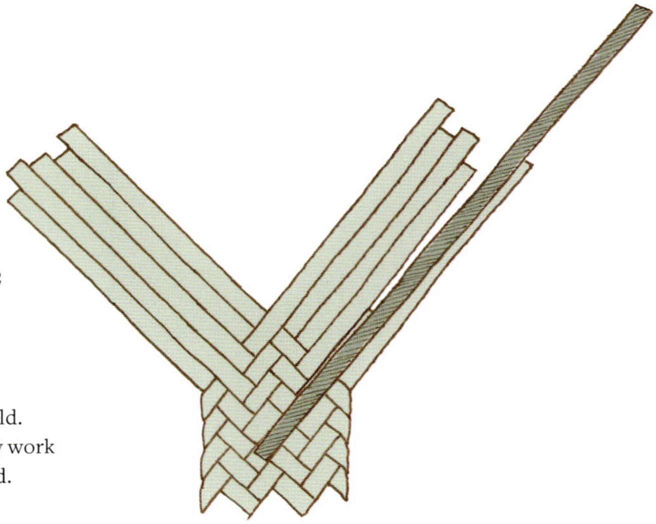

Step 2: Lay the new end over the old. Leave the old end behind and only work the new end when it is next moved.

Variation: Rutland plait

This double splint plait with a twist edge pattern is called Rutland and is associated with Essex. Create the pattern by setting up four pairs of dyed ends in the same group. Set up and add them in as you work. (CTLC 5/211/32)

Variation: Single eleven

Made by one of the last plaiters, Hannah Freeman, Finchingfield, Essex in the early 1930s. The original red is now faded to orange. The by then elderly Hannah was making pattern examples for Thomas Bagshawe. To create the pattern, there must be one dyed end in both working groups. (CTLC BL/34/33)

Eleven-end – English Leghorn

The original plait

Source: CTLC 7/211/32

Origins: Felstead, Essex

Production date: 1800s

Type of straw: Wheat, whole or Italian grasses

Straw width: 1 mm

Plait width: 7 mm

Plaiting direction: During working the back of the plait faces the maker and the front side faces away. The foot is on the right and the head on the left. When completed the front side of the plait has the head on the right and the foot on the left.

Joining: Into the body.

Background information: Joining differs from the eleven-end Tuscan although the pattern is the same. To create the characteristic strong head and foot edges, joins are made into the body. The single edge stitch means it is difficult to stitch together edge to edge so it was sewn into the hat shape by overlapping. This pattern with its method of joining was also made in other European centres.

What to use: This can be made with all types of straw.

You need: Six plaiting lengths.
Additional lengths for joining.

Setting up

Any method for setting up can be used to begin this version of the plait. The diagrams shown follow the neatest way of beginning. It may be easier to lay the lengths on a flat surface until the steps are memorised by your fingers.

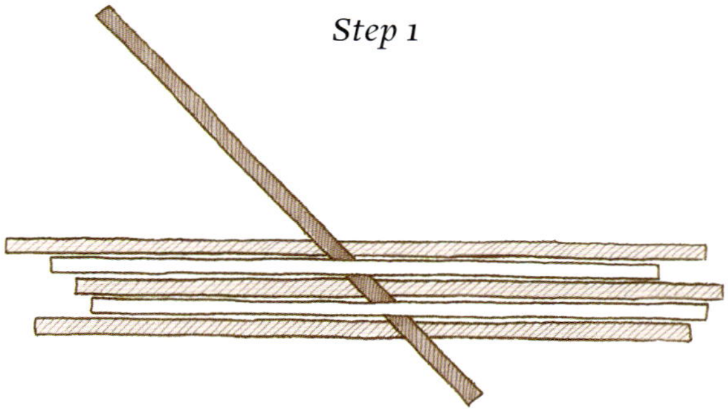

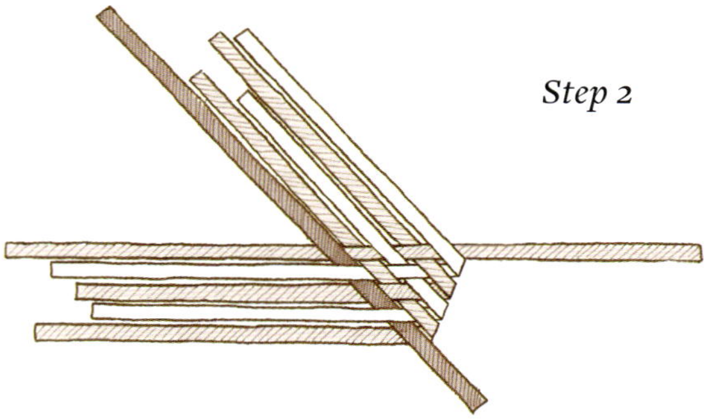

Step 1: Take five of the lengths and arrange side by side horizontally, their ends pointing nine o'clock to three o'clock.

Insert the sixth end diagonally pointing from about 5 o'clock to 11 o'clock and leaving only a short length protruding below the horizontal lengths. The long end passes over the lowest length then under, over, under, over the remaining horizontal lengths.

Adjust the diagonal length so it crosses slightly off centre and arrange the horizontal lengths, so the ends are different lengths.

Step 2: The diagram shows four consecutive moves.

Take the lowest length of the right-hand group. Fold it upwards, towards you, then diagonally over the next, then under, over, under through the rest of the group until it lays parallel to the right of the diagonal length.

Take the new lowest end and repeat, taking it over, under so it lays to the right of the two diagonals.

Repeat these moves until four of the five right-hand ends lay diagonally to the left.

There is one horizontal end on the right.

Step 3

Step 3: Take the remaining right-hand horizontal end, fold it upwards and then horizontally over, under, over, under, over through the left-hand diagonals. It now lays parallel to the top horizontal left-hand group.

Step 4

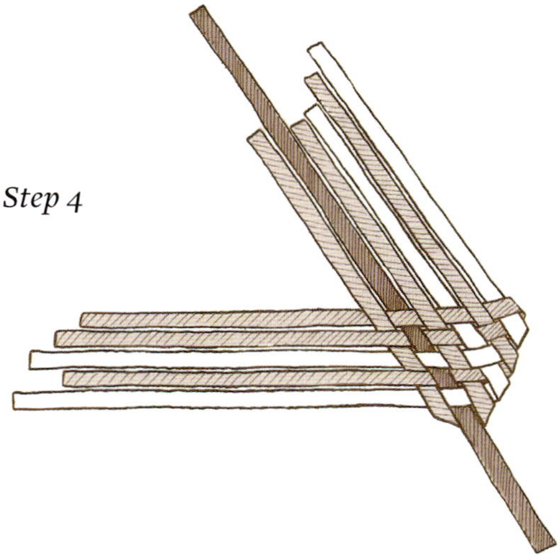

Step 4: Take the lowest end of the left-hand horizontal group. Fold it towards you then diagonally over, under, over, under, over through the other ends of the group. It now lays parallel to the left of the diagonal group.

There are now six ends in the diagonal group and five ends in the horizontal group.

Working

To begin the working steps, rotate the whole piece clockwise so the left-hand group points towards about 10 o'clock and the right-hand group points to about 2 o'clock.

Step 1

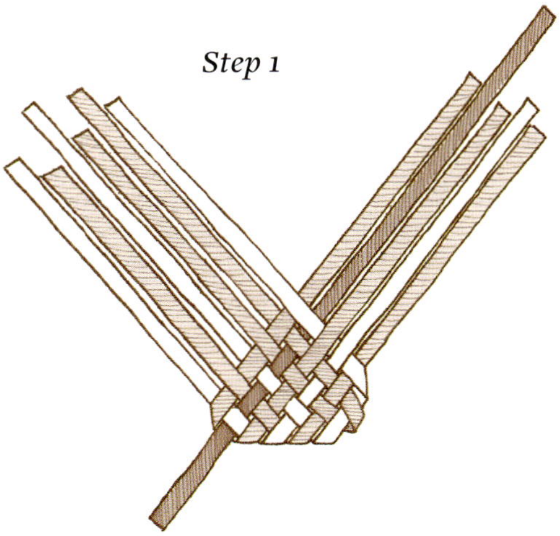

Step 1: Take the lowest end of the right-hand group, fold it towards you and then diagonally over one, under two, over two. It lays to the inside of the left-hand group.

There are five ends in the right-hand group and six ends in the left-hand group.

Step 2

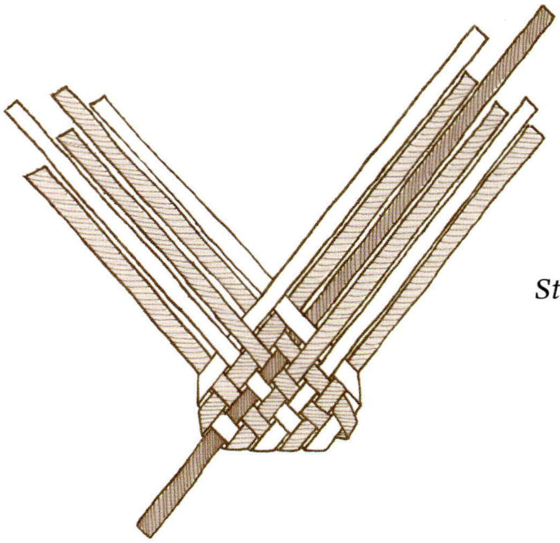

Step 2: Take the lowest end of the left-hand group, fold it towards you and then diagonally over one, under two, over two. It lays to the inside of the right-hand group.

There are five ends in the left-hand group and six ends in the right-hand group.

Continue the working sequence until joining begins.

> **The working sequence is:**
> Right: Over one, under two, over two
> Left: Over one, under two, over two

Joining

It is essential to begin joining after the first three or four working sequences to allow subsequent joins to be spaced evenly along the length.

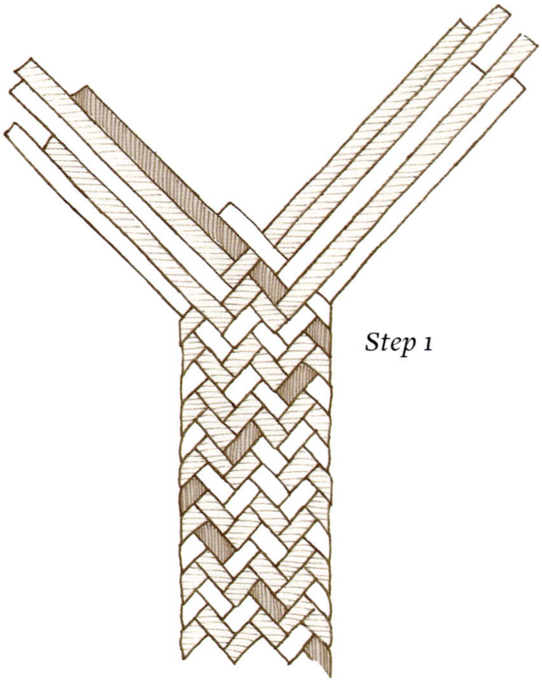

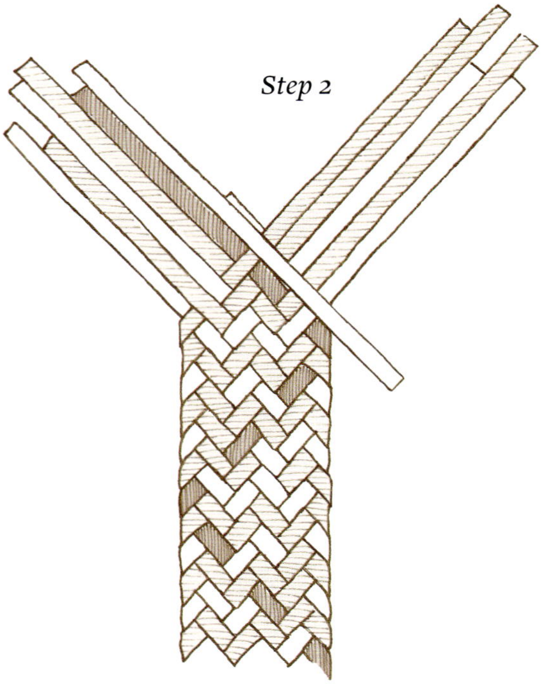

Step 1: The end to be joined must be the last one moved in the right-hand group, working step 1. It is the short end laying to the inside of the left-hand group.

Step 2: Insert the new end over the old following the same working sequence. Leave the old end behind and only work the new end.

Try to leave about three complete working sequences between joins.

Variation

Made from split straws following the English Leghorn pattern this wide plait known as Banding was used to strengthen brims and the insides of hat crowns. This example was made in canton Freiburg, Switzerland in the late 1800s or early 1900s. (CTLC 1997/17/11)

Eleven-end Italian Leghorn

The original plait

Source: CTLC 1a/19/28

Origins: Italy

Production date: Late 1800s or 1900

Type of straw: Italian grasses

Straw width: 1 mm

Plait width: 9 mm

Plaiting direction: During working the back of the plait faces the maker and the front side faces away. The foot is on the right and the head on the left. When completed the front side of the plait has the head on the right and the foot on the left.

Joining: Into body. Also known as speelless.

Background information: This was recorded as Italian Leghorn, collected in 1900, used to make hats and trimmings. Both the foot and head edge are made with a long stitch to facilitate sewing edge to edge. The method of joining makes this plait special to Italy and another reason why it was so highly prized. Joins are arranged so the set-in and speels only show on the back of the plait, leaving the face wonderfully neat.

What to use: This can be made with all types of straw.

You need: Six plaiting lengths.
Additional lengths for joining.

Setting up

Any method for setting up can be used to begin this version of the plait. The diagrams shown follow the neatest way of beginning. It may be easier to lay the lengths on a flat surface until the steps are memorised by your fingers.

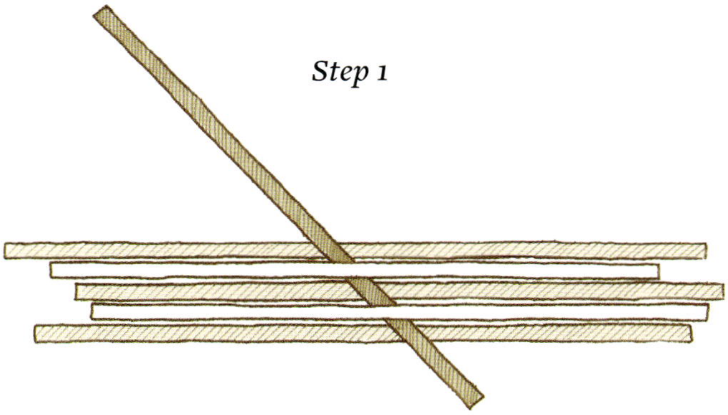

Step 1: Take five of the lengths and arrange side by side horizontally, their ends pointing nine o'clock to three o'clock.

Insert the sixth end diagonally pointing from about 5 o'clock to 11 o'clock and leaving only a short length protruding below the horizontal lengths. The long end passes over the lowest length then under, over, under, over the remaining horizontal lengths.

Step 2: The diagram shows four consecutive moves.

Take the right-hand end of the lowest length, the one next to the diagonal. Fold it upwards, towards you, then diagonally over the next, then under, over, under through the rest of the group until it lays parallel to the right of the diagonal length.

Take the new lowest end and repeat, taking it over, under, over so it lays to the right of the two diagonals.

Repeat these moves until four of the five right-hand ends lay diagonally to the left.

There is one horizontal end on the right.

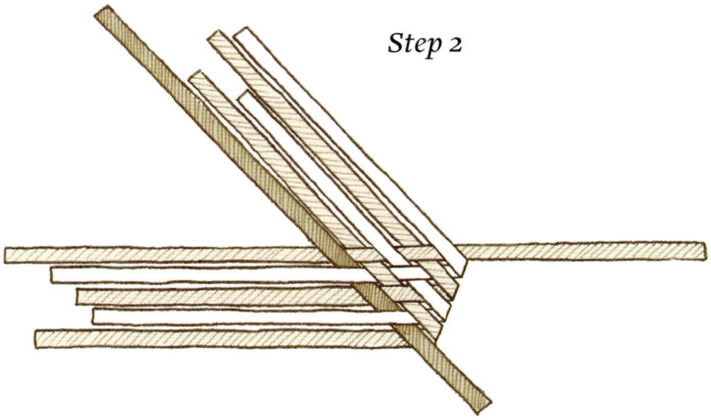

Step 3

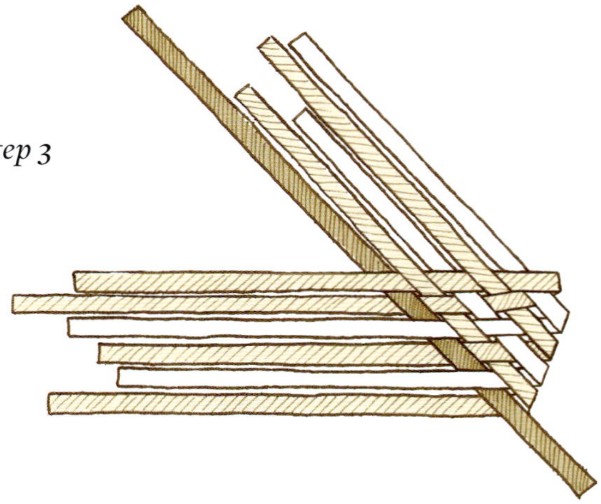

Step 3: Take the remaining right-hand horizontal end, fold it upwards and then horizontally over, under, over, under, over through the left-hand diagonals.

It now lays parallel to the top horizontal left-hand group.

Step 4

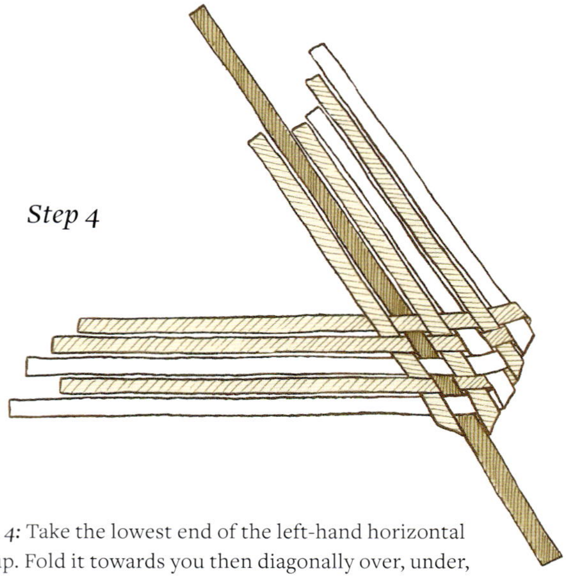

Step 4: Take the lowest end of the left-hand horizontal group. Fold it towards you then diagonally over, under, over, under, over through the other ends of the group. It now lays parallel to the left of the diagonal group.

There are now six ends in the diagonal group and five ends in the horizontal group.

Working

To begin the working steps, rotate the whole piece clockwise so the left-hand group points towards about 10 o'clock and the right-hand group points to about 2 o'clock.

Step 1

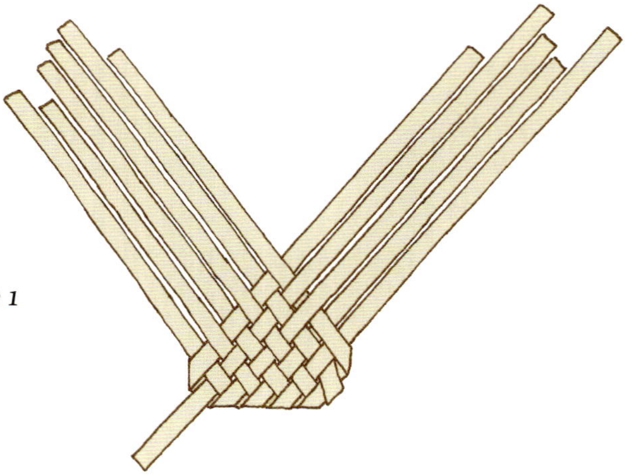

Step 1: Take the lowest or outside end of the right-hand group, fold it towards you and then diagonally over two, under two, over one. It lays to the inside of the left-hand group.

There are five ends in the right-hand group and six ends in the left-hand group.

Step 2

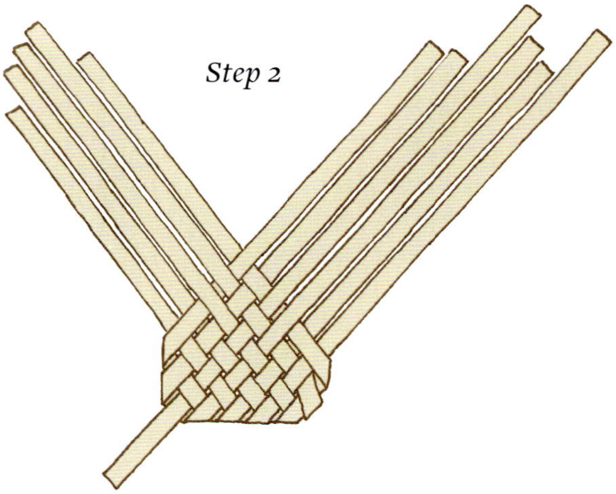

Step 2: Take the lowest or outside end of the left-hand group, fold it towards you and then diagonally over two, under two, over one. It lays to the inside of the right-hand group.

There are five ends in the left-hand group and six ends in the right-hand group.

Continue the working sequence until joining begins.

The working sequence is:
Right: over two, under two, over one
Left: over two, under two, over one

Joining

It is essential to begin the joining sequence after the first three or four working sequences to allow subsequent joins to be spaced evenly along the length. This method of joining is a little more involved than those used so far since the old end must be moved and kept on the side facing you.

Step 1

Step 1: The end to be joined must be the last one moved in the right-hand group. It must be the short end laying to the inside of the left-hand group.

Insert the new end over the old inserting it over two, under two, over one.

Step 2

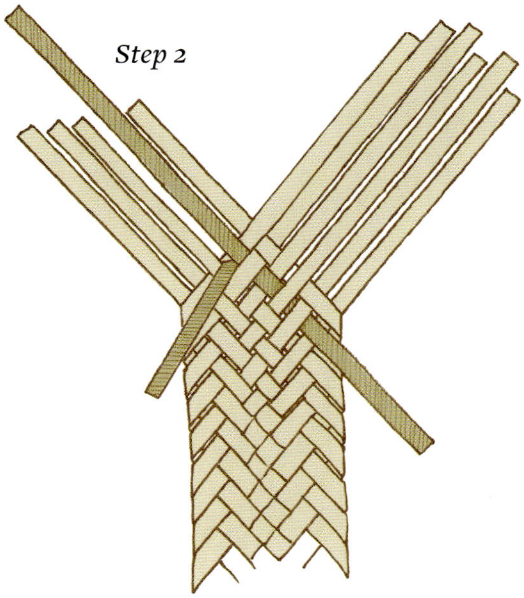

Step 2: Make the next working move with the outside end of the left-hand group.

Make the next working move with the right-hand group.

On the next left-hand working move take care to pass the end under both old and new ends of the newly joined end.

Fold the old end towards you and then diagonally against the adjacent end so it then points outwards to the left. To ensure the ends of the left-hand group do not move out of alignment it will be necessary to compress the old end as it moves to the back of the plait.

Make the next left-hand move using more pressure to keep the ends in alignment and to prevent a gap occurring.

Continue working until the next join is required.

Try to leave about three complete working sequences between joins.

Plaits made using 5 mm wide machine-made hemp braid. Hand stitched. The decorative edge is a four-end plait. Made by Veronica Main.

Trade Staples – Basic Plaits

This section includes an eclectic group of plaits, some first made in the 1800s and some still being made today. The four-, six- and eight-end plaits were less commonly used but provide a useful addition to a plaiter's repertoire as they form the basis for various decorative head patterns featured in later sections. The fifteen-end plait is still being made in the Bahamas where colour is introduced into the patterns. First made in Italy in the early 1800s, the thirteen- and fifteen-end plaits were either made a single stitch or double edge stitch to enable sewing together edge to edge.

Four-end plait

The replica plait

Source: Copy made from original instructions

Origins: Unknown

Production date: *c.* 1838

Type of straw: Wheat, whole

Straw width: 2 mm

Plait width: 6 mm

Plaiting direction: During working the back of the plait faces the maker and the front side faces away. The foot is on the right and the head on the left. When completed the front side of the plait has the head on the right and the foot on the left.

Joining: Along foot edge.

Background information: Instructions for making this plait appear in *The Workwoman's Guide* and the plait shown is a reproduction made using those instructions. The four-end is not commonly found in the construction of surviving hats from the 1800s and it is not until the 1890s that various versions of this plait appear amongst the many patterns made using barley straw in Japan.

What to use: This can be made with all types of straw.

You need: Two plaiting lengths.
Additional lengths for joining.

Setting up

Arrange so the ends are different lengths.

Take one straw, hold it horizontally so it aligns from 9 o'clock to 3 o'clock.

Take the second straw. Hold it diagonally in front of the horizontal straw to lay at an angle of about 20 degrees, the top section will lay at a point between 2 o'clock and 3 o'clock.

Take the lower end, currently laying between 8 o'clock and 9 o'clock, and fold away from you then behind the horizontal straw to lay at between 1 o'clock and 2 o'clock. Press the fold.

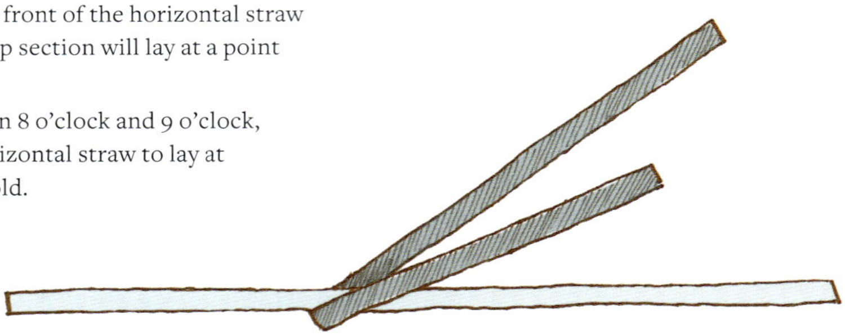

Variations

This Japanese barley straw version of the four-end plait is made with a twist edge. (CTLC 40/70/61R)

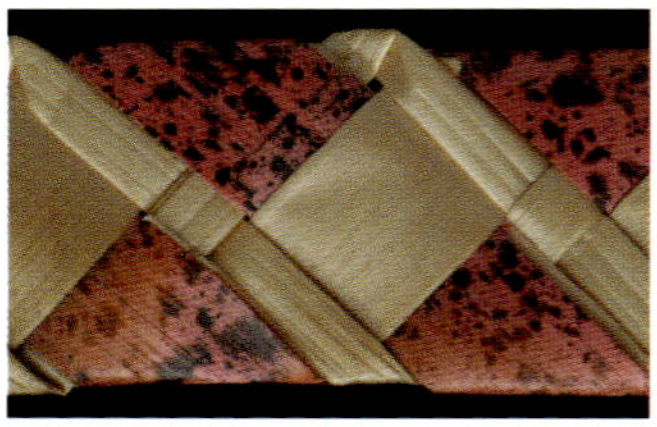

Made for an Anglo-Japanese exhibition of 1910 this shows the extraordinary dye skills of Japanese companies. Two pairs of 10 mm wide speckle-dyed and plain split have been worked with two, 4 mm wide whole straws. To create the pattern, set up the right-hand group in the following sequence: Outside end, whole straw, middle end, dyed and natural wide pair. Inner end, whole straw. The single end on the left-hand side is the wide pair. (CTLC 40/70/61Z)

Working

Step 1

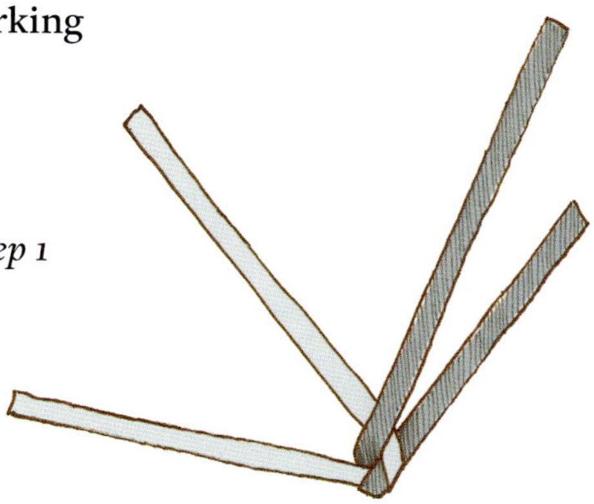

Step 1: Take the outside straw of right-hand group.

Take the end at 3 o'clock and fold it towards you and then diagonally over then under the right-hand ends. It will now lay to the inside of the left-hand or 9 o'clock end.

The end has moved over one, under one.

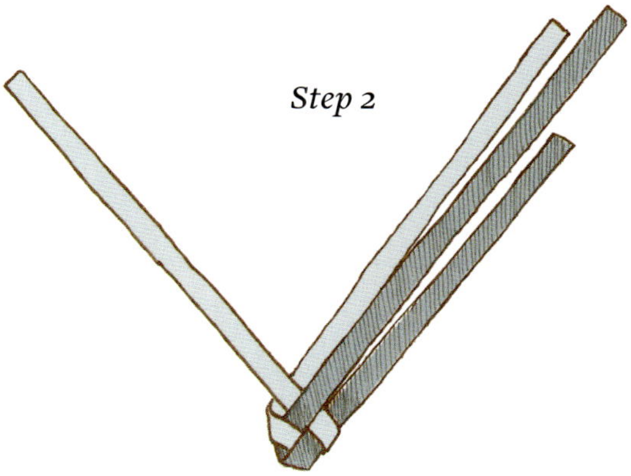

Step 2: The right-hand working end needs to be carefully folded into its position to maintain the angle between the two working groups.

On the left-hand side take the 9 o'clock end and fold it diagonally away from you, under the second left-hand end using it to provide a resistance to the moving end.

The outside end now lays to the inside of the right-hand group.

Continue the working sequence until joining begins.

> **The working sequence is:**
> Right: Over one, under one
> Left: Under one

Joining

The short end to be joined must be in the centre of the three of the right-hand group.

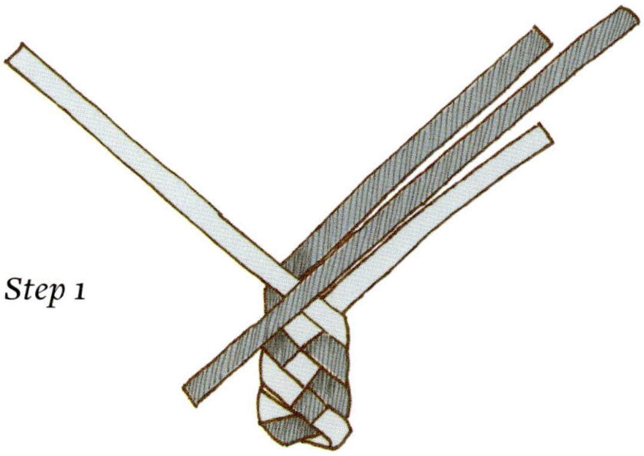

Step 1: Lay the new end over the short end, leaving a short length protruding to the left.

Fold the outside end on the right, over one then under one.

Fold the outside end of the left-hand group under one.

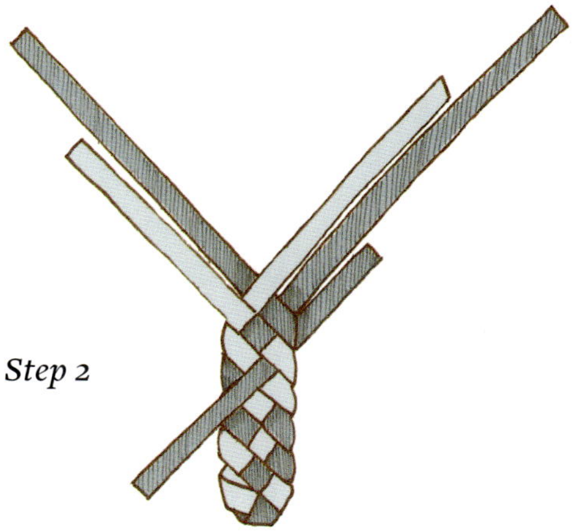

Step 2: Fold only the new end diagonally over one under one to lay to the inside of the left-hand diagonal end.

Continue the working until the next join is required.

It is better to begin the joining process before the working ends get too short so that the joining sequence can be evenly spaced.

Six-end plait – Sixes

The original plait

Source: CTLC 1993/178/5

Origins: Kimpton or Breachwood Green, Hertfordshire

Production date: 1850 onwards

Type of straw: Wheat, whole

Straw width: 2 mm

Plait width: 12 mm

Plaiting direction: During working the back of the plait faces the maker and the front side faces away. The foot is on the right and the head on the left. When completed the front side of the plait has the head on the right and the foot on the left.

Joining: Along foot edge.

Background information: Worked in a variety of colourways it was widely made in Hertfordshire and Bedfordshire. This example was found in the loft of a house in Kimpton, Hertfordshire thought to have been the home of a plait dealer. In 1948 examples of the same six-end pattern were found in the bricked-up compartment of another Kimpton house also thought to have belonged to a plait dealer. The pattern is worked with four dyed and two bleached ends and was worked with either a folded or twist head edge.

What to use: Whole straws, splints, or flat straws.

You need: Four plaiting lengths, four dyed and two undyed. Additional lengths for joining.

Setting up

Arrange so the ends are different lengths. The working ends must be arranged so the two colours alternate across the final six ends. If making this as a single colour plait then set up with one rather than two lengths for the horizontal length.

Step 1: Take a length of a lighter colour, hold it horizontally so it aligns from 9 to 3 o'clock.

Take a second length of the darker colour, overlap one end over the first length. The inner ends must overlap by about 2cm (0.75"). The two ends must have the darker length on the left and the lighter on the right.

Take a length of the darker colour. At the central point where the horizontal ends overlap hold the length diagonally in front of the horizontal pointing to about 1 o'clock. Fold the lower section away from you, behind then diagonally to lay at about 11 o'clock. Press the fold.

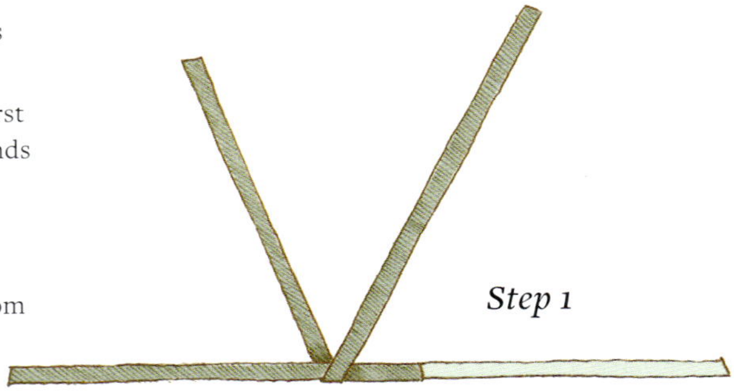

Step 1

Step 2: Take a length of the lighter colour. Hold it diagonally behind the horizontal ends so the top section lays to the inside of the right-hand diagonal, the darker length.

Fold the lower section of the length towards you and diagonally upwards to lay to the outside of the left-hand darker diagonal end. Press the fold.

Fold the two short ends from the overlapped section of the horizontals down to hang below the horizontal length.

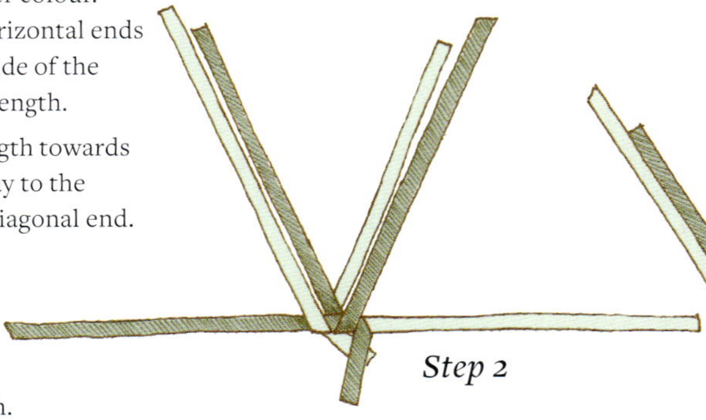

Step 2

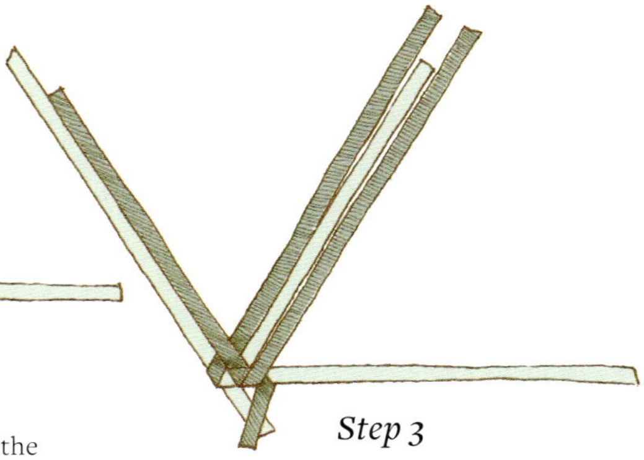

Step 3

Step 3: Take the outside left-hand diagonal at 9 o'clock, over one, under one to lay to the inside of the right-hand group. There are now four ends in the right-hand group.

Working

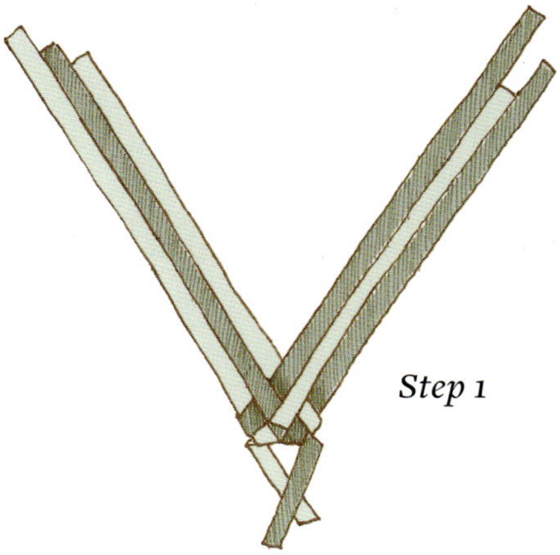

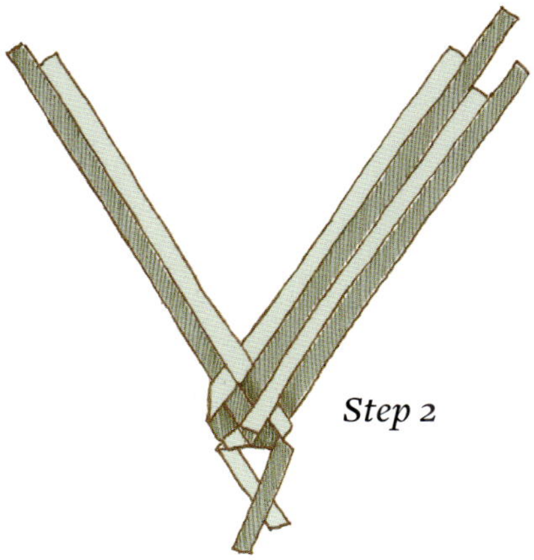

Step 1: Take the right-hand horizontal end, fold it towards you then diagonally over the first and under the other two ends of the right-hand group to lay inside the left-hand group. The end has moved over one, under two.

The working sequence is:
Right: Over one, under two
Left: Over one, under one

Step 2: Take the outside end of the left-hand group, fold it towards you then diagonally over the first and under the second end of the left-hand group. It now lays to the inside of the right-hand group. The end has moved over one, under one.

Continue the working sequence until joining begins.

Joining

Begin the joining process before the working ends get too short so that the joining sequence can be evenly spaced.

At working step 2, when there are four ends in the right-hand group, the end to be joined is next to the outside end.

Lay the new end over the old, leaving a short length of the new length protruding to the left.

Fold the outside right-hand end, over one, under two.

Continue the working sequence leaving behind the old end and only working the new at the next right-hand move.

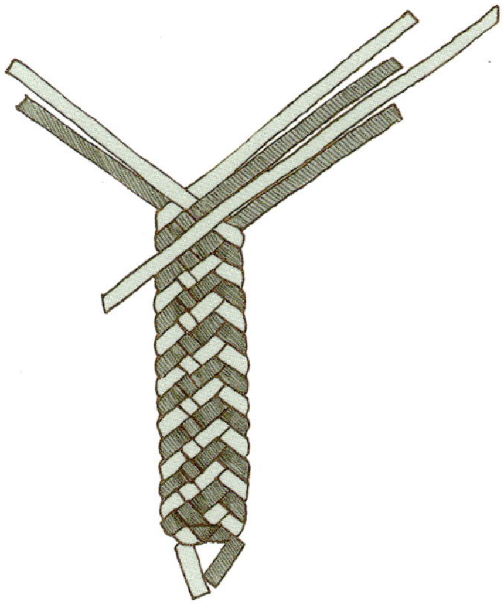

Variation

This was found in the bricked-up compartment of a Kimpton house. The same pattern called Sixes was made by Mrs Andrews, Eaton Bray for a 1934 Women's Institute exhibition display. (CTLC 5/17/48)

Eight-end Aldbury plain

The original plait

Source: CTLC Aldbury plait sample panel

Origins: Aldbury, Hertfordshire, England

Production date: *c.* 1913

Type of straw: Wheat, double splints

Splint width: 1.5–2 mm

Plait width: 5 mm

Plaiting direction: During working the back of the plait faces the maker and the front side faces away. The foot is on the right and the head on the left. When completed the front side of the plait has the head on the right and the foot on the left.

Joining: Along foot edge

Background information: With age the straws now appear to be black and undyed but close examination shows the dark straws were originally dark blue. Instructions for an eight-end plait were included in *The Workwoman's Guide* so can be dated to 1838.

What to use: This can be made with all types of straw but to create the twist edge should be made with a flexible round straw.

You need: Four plaiting lengths, two of one colour and two undyed.
Additional lengths of correct colours for joining.

Setting up

Arrange so the working ends are different lengths. If you wish to recreate the colourway then set up the ends so they are alternate colours..

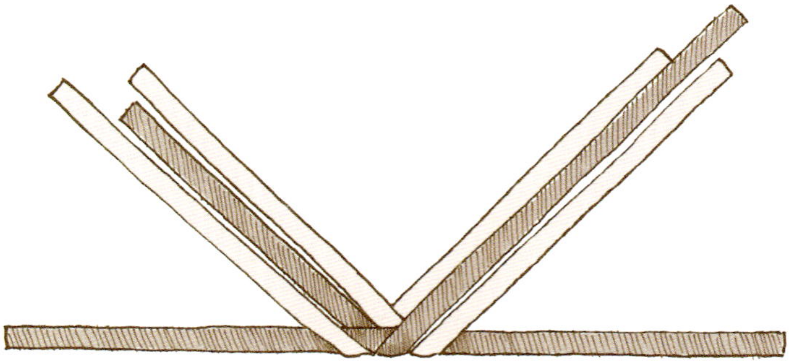

The diagram shows all the elements of setting up the ends ready to begin working.

Hold one length horizontally, from 9 o'clock to 3 o'clock.

Hold a second length diagonally in front of the horizontal length, pointing from about 2 o'clock to 8 o'clock. Fold the lower end of this length behind the horizontal to lay at about 10 o'clock. Press the fold.

Take the third length. Hold it diagonally in front of the horizontal length and to the inside of the diagonal right-hand end. Fold the lower section upwards to lay to the outside of the left-hand diagonal. Press the fold.

Take the fourth length and place it behind the horizontal to lay to the inside of the right-hand group. Fold the lower end diagonally upwards to lay to the outside of the two left-hand diagonals.

There are four ends pointing to the right and four to the left.

Working

To recreate the Aldbury plain pattern use the same folding movement for both foot and head edge.

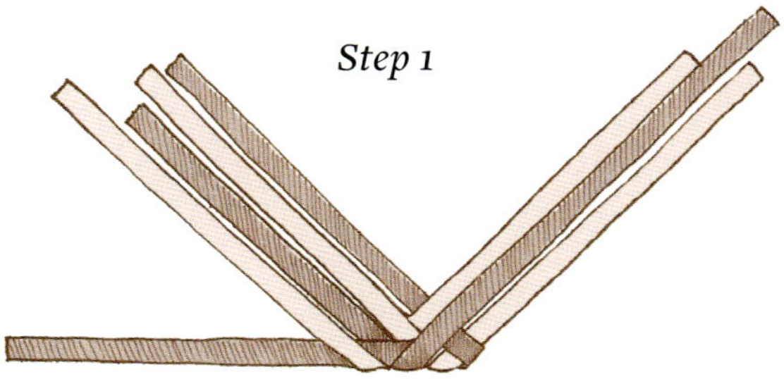

Step 1: Take the outside, lowest end, horizontal of the right-hand group towards you then diagonally upwards, over one, under two. It lays to the inside of the left-hand group.

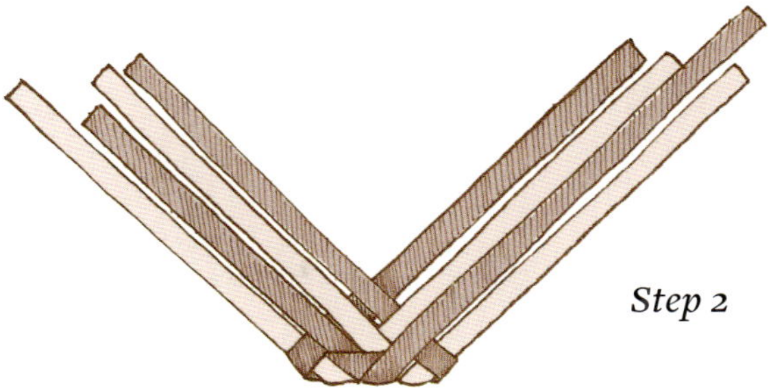

Step 2: Fold the lowest, outside end of the left-hand group towards you and then diagonally, over one, under three to lay to the inside of the right-hand group.

Continue the working sequence until joining begins.

The working sequence is:
Right: Over one, under two
Left: Over one, under three

Joining

Plan to begin the joining sequence after the first three or four working sequences which will allow subsequent joins to be spaced evenly along the length.

The end to be joined must be second from the outside of the right-hand group.

Lay the new end over the old. Leave the old end behind and only work the new end.

The Workwoman's Guide gave two variations of pattern both of which produce a chevron.

Version One
Right-hand group: Over one, under two
Left-hand group: Over two, under two

Version Two
Right-hand group: Over one, under one, over two.
Left-hand group, Under one, and over two.

Variations

Made near Florence Italy in about 1882, this version has a twist head. Remember that to create the twist, you use the adjacent end to provide resistance as the outside end is moved. Do not twist the outside end on itself as it moves. (CTLC 2/70/61A (8))

This version was also being made in Italy around 1882. To create the pattern the working lengths have been set up with two dyed lengths adjacent in each group. When set up is completed the ends in both working groups should be, dyed, dyed, undyed, undyed. (CTLC 2/70/61A (5))

Thirteen-end Italian Leghorn

The replica plait

Source: Copy made from original instructions

Origins: *The Workwoman's Guide*

Production date: *c.* 1838

Type of straw: Wheat, whole or Italian grasses

Splint width: Unknown, example 2 mm

Plait width: Unknown, example 15 mm

Plaiting direction: During working the back of the plait faces the maker and the front side faces away. The foot is on the right and the head on the left. When completed the front side of the plait has the head on the right and the foot on the left.

Joining: Into body.

Background information: The author of *The Workwoman's Guide* felt this plait was so important they devoted a complete section to comment on how to make it. They wrote that the plait was to be made with the finest whole straws and the tress (plait) to make a Leghorn bonnet was formed of seven, nine or generally thirteen ends. The instructions are not clear in explaining the method of joining and so a modification of the eleven-end Italian Leghorn joining method is used to ensure both ends from the join are on the same side of the plait.

What to use: This is best made using fine whole straws, but the pattern can be created with all types of straw.

You need: 13 plaiting lengths.
Additional lengths for joining.

Setting up

These instructions follow those given in *The Workwoman's Guide* but any method for setting up can be used.

Tie together the thirteen ends close to one end of the lengths.

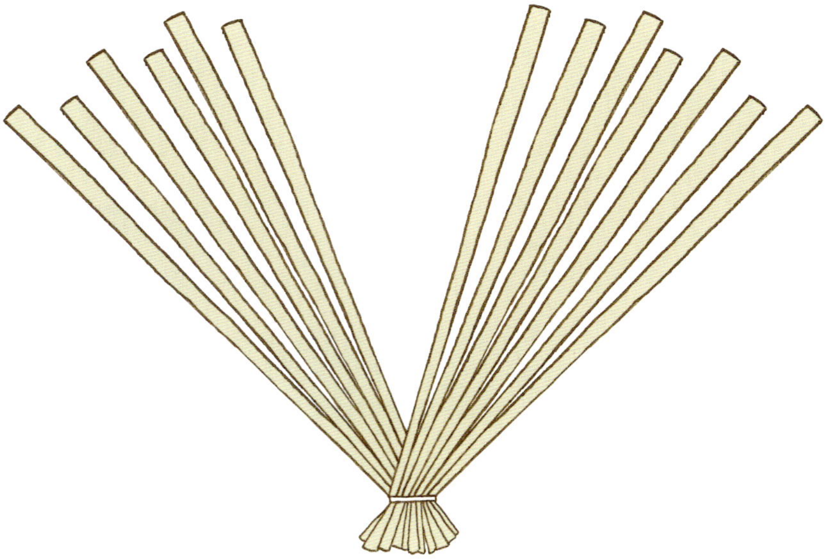

Working

Separate the straws so a group of six ends point to the left and seven ends form a group pointing to the right. As much as is possible, within each group spread the ends out to lay side by side. The first few moves will be untidy until the ends are all in their correct places.

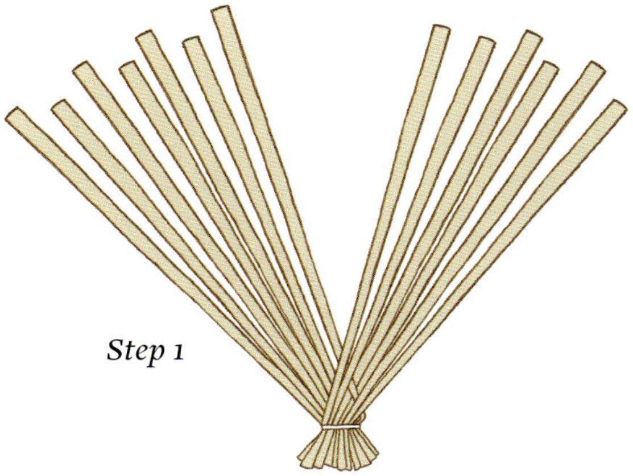

Step 1

Step 1: Take the lowest end of the right-hand group, fold it away from you and then diagonally under two, over two, under two. It lays to the inside of the left-hand group.

There are six ends in the right-hand group and seven ends in the left-hand group.

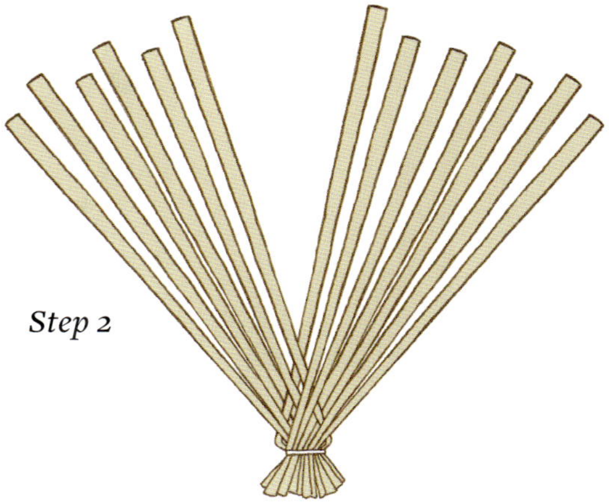

Step 2

Step 2: Take the lowest end of the left-hand group, fold it away from you and then diagonally under two, over two, under two. It lays to the inside of the right-hand group.

There are six ends in the left-hand group and seven ends in the right-hand group. Continue until joining begins.

The working sequence is:
Right: under two, over two, under two
Left: under two, over two, under two

Joining

It is essential to begin the joining after the first three or four working sequences to allow even spacing along the length. To create joins that don't distort the pattern requires a little practice.

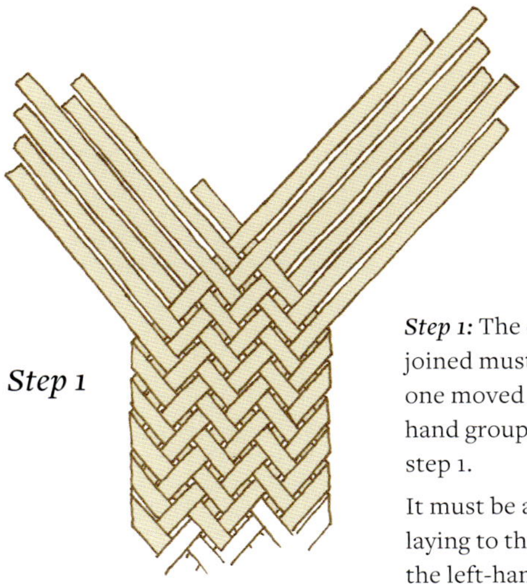

Step 1

Step 1: The end to be joined must be the last one moved in the right-hand group, working step 1.

It must be a short end laying to the inside of the left-hand group.

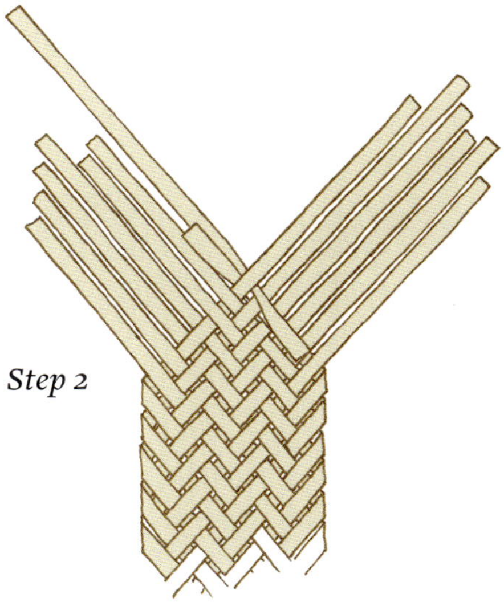

Step 2

Step 2: Insert the new end over the old end and under the last two ends of the right-hand group. The new end lays partly under and partly alongside the short end. Both ends need to be compressed so they do not create a bulge in the pattern.

Make the next left-hand move, compressing the two inside ends of the left-hand group. Joins were normally made every second or third right-hand move. Try not to join consecutively.

Fifteen-end plait – Wave

The original plait

Source: CTLC Aldbury plait sample panel

Origins: Aldbury, Hertfordshire, England

Production date: 1913

Type of straw: Wheat, double splints

Splint width: 2 mm

Plait width: 19 mm

Plaiting direction: During working the back of the plait faces the maker and the front side faces away. The foot is on the right and the head on the left. When completed the front side of the plait has the head on the right and the foot on the left.

Joining: Into body or speelless.

Background information: Included in *The Workwoman's Guide* there are methods for a twill and a checkerboard pattern. The version shown, called Wave was made using double splints, that is pairs of splints with the shiny side facing outwards. For first attempts it is easier to use whole straw. Today this plait is being made in the Bahamas where plaiters use varieties of local palm leaf and incorporate colour to create patterns. Start this plait with longer plaiting lengths since it takes a few moves to set up.

What to use: Can be made with all types of straw.

You need: Eight plaiting lengths.
Additional lengths for joining.

Setting up

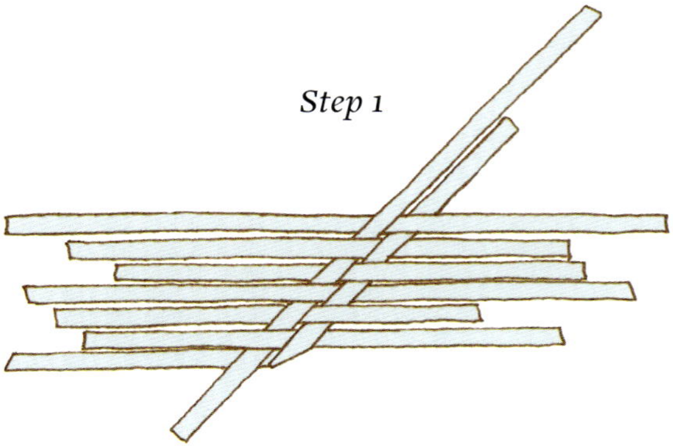

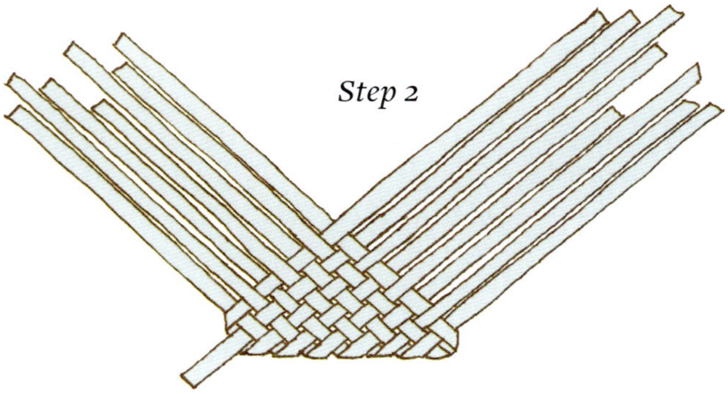

Step 1: Take seven of the lengths and arrange side by side horizontally, their ends pointing nine o'clock to three o'clock.

Insert the eighth length diagonally pointing from about 7 o'clock to 1 o'clock, leaving only a short piece protruding. The long end passes over the lowest length then in sequence under, over the remaining horizontal lengths.

Adjust the diagonal length so it crosses slightly off centre and arrange the horizontals, so they are different lengths.

Take the right-hand end of the lowest length. Fold it upwards, towards you, then diagonally in sequence over, under through the rest of the group until it lays parallel to the right of the diagonal.

Step 2: The diagram shows the completed stage and the whole piece has been rotated to its working position.

Take the lowest right-hand end, fold it upwards, then towards before taking it diagonally in sequence, over, under the rest of the group.

Repeat with the remaining right-hand ends, finally taking the last right-hand horizontal through the group to lay to inside the left-hand horizontal group.

Take the lowest left-hand end and take it, over, under through the left-hand ends.

Rotate the plait so the two groups lay at about 10 and 2 o'clock.

There are eight ends in the right-hand group and seven in the left-hand group.

Working

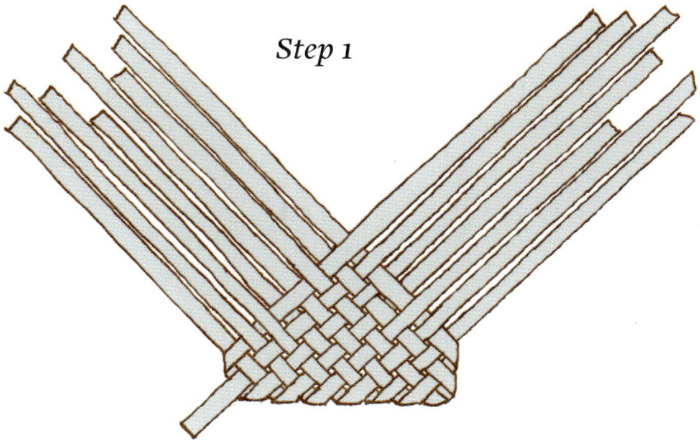

Step 1: Take the lowest end of the right-hand group, fold it towards you and then diagonally over one, under two, over two, under two. It lays to the inside of the left-hand group.

There are seven ends in the right-hand group and eight ends in the left-hand group.

Step 2: Take the lowest end of the left-hand group, fold it towards you and then diagonally over one, under two, over two, under two. It lays to the inside of the right-hand group.

There are eight ends in the right-hand group and seven ends in the left-hand group. Continue until joining begins.

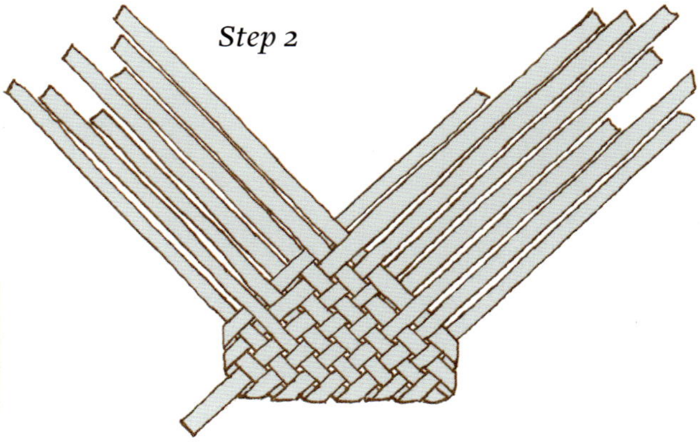

The working sequence is:
Right-hand side: over one, under two, over two, under two
Left-hand side: Over one, under two, over two, under two

Joining

It is essential to begin joining after the first three or four working sequences to allow even spacing along the length.

Choose a method of joining best suited to the final use of the plait. Joins can be made along the foot edge or into the centre of the plait using the method provided for the thirteen-end plait, see page 187.

Variations

Made in the Bahamas by Rosemary Brice, Peas 'n' Rice is made on most Islands and as the name suggests it refers to a local food. Dried palm or banana leaf is used to give the contrast colour. Set up the ends so the dyed and undyed ends alternate within the left and right-hand groups.

Take thru is less popular but still made on Long Island. To create the checkerboard pattern, use a working sequence of over, then under in sequence through both the left and right-hand groups.

This Luton Borough Police helmet from 1876 was worn in the summer months. Helmets made from straw were worn in many English towns and cities until the 1930s. (CTLC 78/27)

Rustic Plaits

Rustic plaits probably date back to the 1600s and today are still being made around the world. According to its location of making, the four-end version is known by a variety of names including sawtooth, fishtail, edging and Jacob's ladder, names which describe its serrated foot and head. This plait is fast to make and is structurally strong, so is used to make a wide variety of practical items from table mats to bags, hats, including boater hats for men, women, and children.

Four-end Rustic or English pearl

The original plait

Source: CTLC 1/346/33

Origins: Switzerland

Production date: *c.* 1931

Type of straw: Racello – artificial silk and cellophane tape

Straw width: 4 mm

Plait width: 21 mm

Plaiting direction: During working the back of the plait faces the maker and the front side faces away. The foot is on the right and the head on the left. When completed the front side of the plait has the head on the right and the foot on the left.

Joining: Horizontally or diagonally along foot.

Background information: Although now commonly known as rustic, during the 1800s in Great Britain it was called English pearl and said to have had a plaiting rhyme associated with its making (see page 140), and the pattern was the second learnt by children. When the Japanese entered the market in the late 1800s it was one of their main products, made using whole straw and split straw. In the early 1900s they began to make a wider version of the plait for lady's hats.

What to use: This can be made with all types of straw but worked best with a flat type.

You need: Two plaiting lengths.
Additional lengths for joining.

Setting up

Arrange so the ends are different lengths.

Step 1: Take one straw, hold it horizontally so it aligns from 9 o'clock to 3 o'clock.

Take the second length. Hold it diagonally in front of the horizontal length to lay at an angle of about 45 degrees, the top section will lay at a point between 1 and 2 o'clock.

Take the lower end, currently laying between 7 and 8 o'clock, and fold upwards behind the horizontal length to lay at between 10 and 11 o'clock. Press the fold.

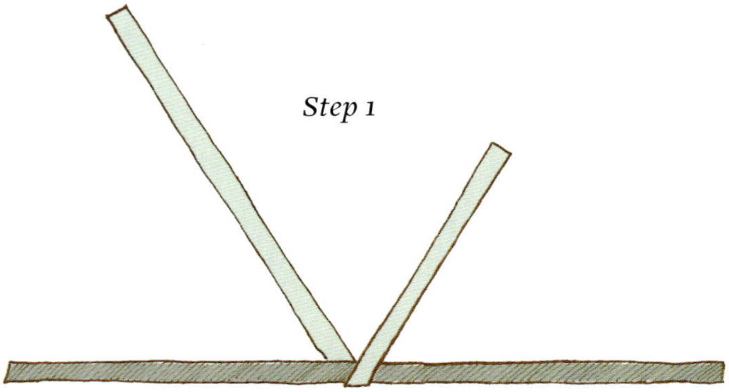

Step 1

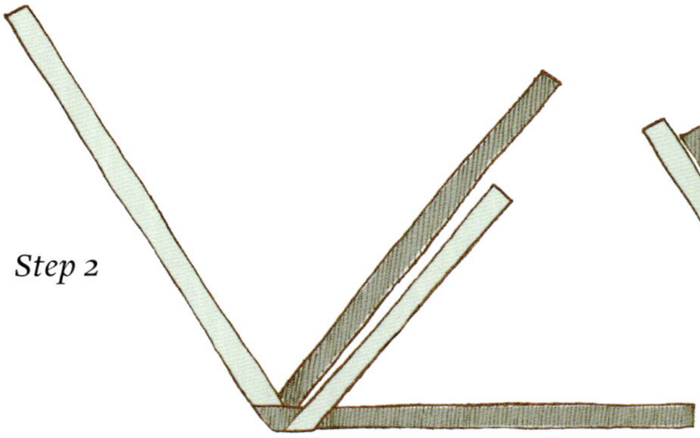

Step 2

Step 2: Fold the left-hand end that is at 9'clock behind the end other left-hand end then diagonally to lay on the inside of the end between 1 and 2 o'clock on the right. Press the fold.

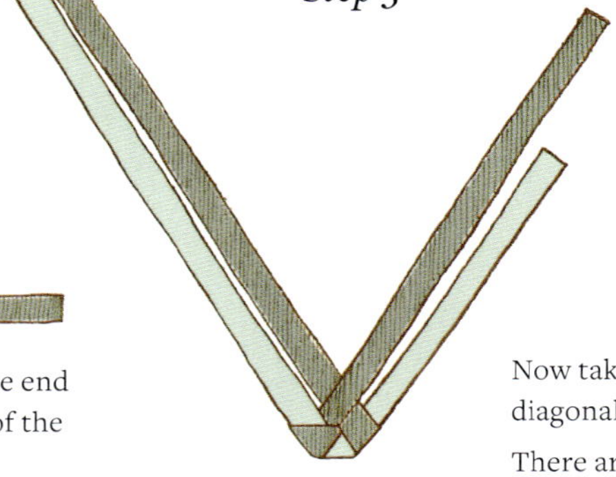

Step 3

Step 3: Take the horizontal end that is at 3 o'clock, bring it towards you then fold diagonally upwards so it points to between 10 and 11 o'clock.

Now take the end under the inside diagonal end. Press the fold.

There are two ends in each group.

Working

Step 1: Stay on the right-hand side. This move will complete the first point on the right.

Take the outside diagonal straw and fold to a horizontal position pointing to 9 o'clock. Now pass the same end behind the outside left-hand diagonal end. Slide the working end downwards into the plait to reduce any gap.

The working end has passed horizontally over two and under one.

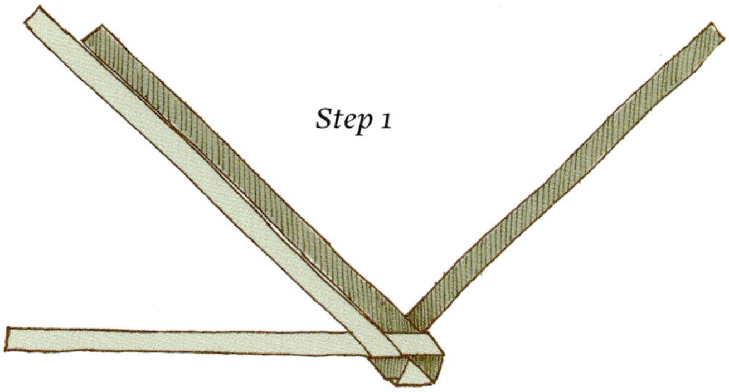

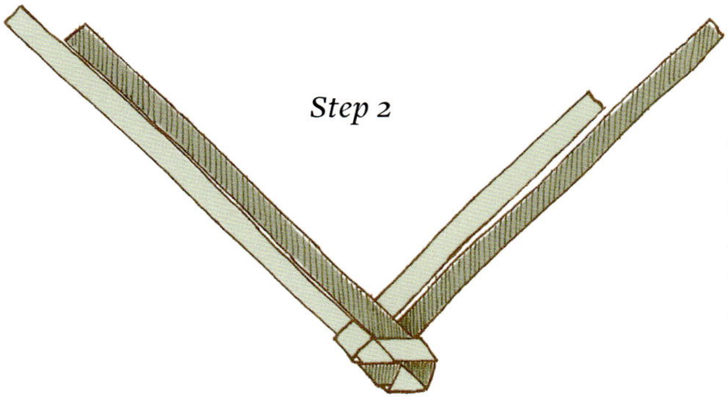

Step 2: The next move is made with the last worked end and will form the first half on the point on the left.

Take the horizontal end at 9 o'clock and fold it over the first and under the second diagonal left-hand ends. Press the fold. The working end has passed over one, under one.

Step 3: Stay on the left-hand side. This move will complete the point on the left-hand side.

Fold the outside diagonal end towards you and fold it horizontally to point to 3 o'clock. Now pass the end behind the outside right-hand end.

Slide the working end downwards into the plait to reduce any gaps. Press the fold.

The working end has passed horizontally over two and under one.

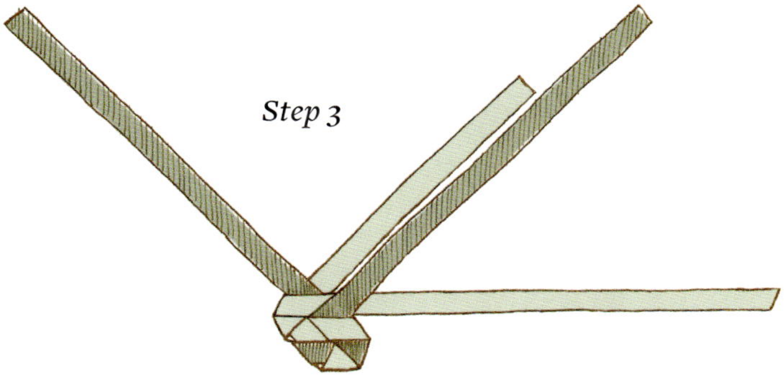

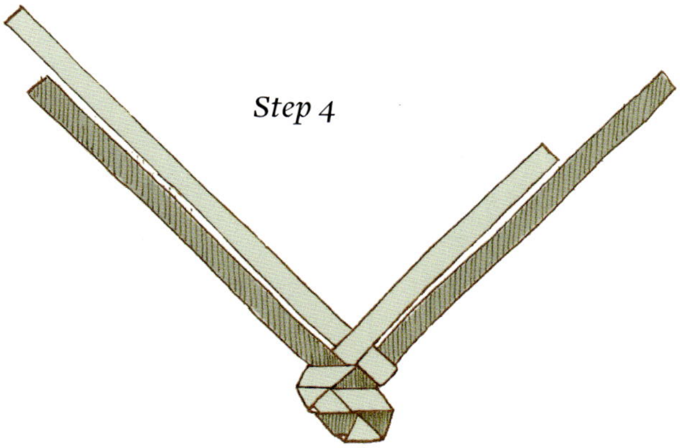

Step 4: Fold the horizontal end laying at 3 o'clock towards you then diagonally upwards to lay to the inside of the left-hand diagonal end. Take it behind the inside diagonal end. Press the fold.

The end has passed over one, under one.

Continue the working sequence until the ends need joining.

The working sequence is:
Right: Horizontally over two, under one
Left: Same end diagonally over one, under one
Left: Horizontally over two, under one
Right: Same end diagonally over one, under one

Joining

New ends can be added both horizontally and diagonally. Start the joining process early so they are spaced evenly along the plait. Never make two joins on the same point and always join on the foot, right-hand side.

Method 1

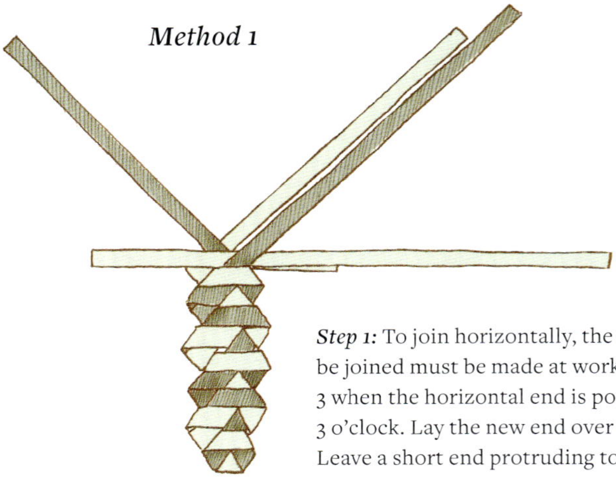

Step 1: To join horizontally, the end to be joined must be made at working step 3 when the horizontal end is pointing to 3 o'clock. Lay the new end over the old. Leave a short end protruding to the left.

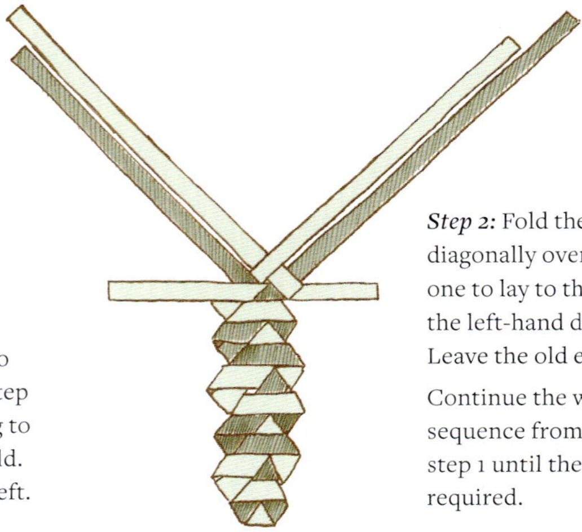

Step 2: Fold the new end diagonally over one under one to lay to the inside of the left-hand diagonal end. Leave the old end behind.

Continue the working sequence from working step 1 until the next join is required.

Method 2

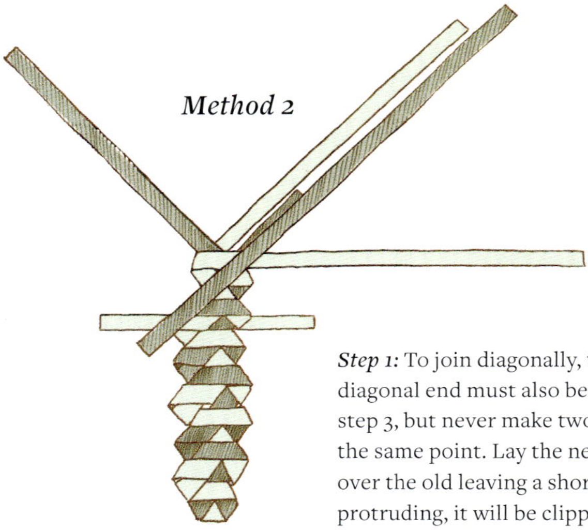

Step 1: To join diagonally, the diagonal end must also be at working step 3, but never make two joins on the same point. Lay the new end over the old leaving a short end protruding, it will be clipped off later.

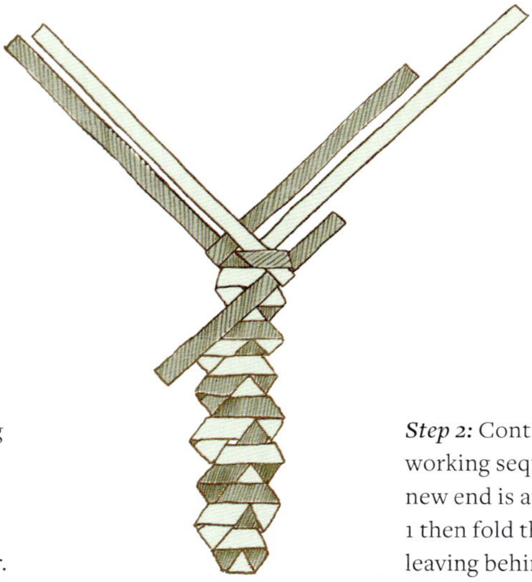

Step 2: Continue the working sequence until the new end is at working step 1 then fold the new end leaving behind the old.

Working with split straw

At setting up, step one twist the horizontal straw so the shiny side faces upwards on the end pointing to 3 o'clock and the matt side faces upwards from mid-point the half pointing to the left. As you work the shiny ends will face you as they point to the right and the matt will face on the left.

Variation

Exhibited at an Anglo British, Japanese exhibition in 1910, this may have been intended as a trimming since the outside straw twists on both edges. To create the twist along the head, at working steps 2 and 3 twist the straw sideways into position rather than folding. (CTLC 40/70/61N)

Six-end twill rustic

The replica plait

Source: Appears in the Second Course of English Chip and Straw plating

Origins of pattern: Possibly Japan

Date of introduction: Pre 1895

Type of straw: Wheat straw. The original was made from wood chip

Plait width: 10 mm

Straw width: 2 mm

Plaiting direction: During working the back of the plait faces the maker and the front side faces away. The foot is on the right and the head on the left. When completed the front side of the plait has the head on the right and the foot on the left.

Joining: Horizontally or diagonally along foot.

Background information: There is no clear indication when this plait was introduced into the industry but it does appear on Chinese and Japanese plait sample cards from the early 1900s. Depending upon the chosen plaiting material this plait may be less suitable for hat construction but is ideal for trimmings, bags and baskets.

What to use: This can be made with all types of straw but you may prefer the finished effect when worked with a flat straw. This example is made from split wheat straw which produces a lightweight and delicate plait.

You need: Three plaiting lengths.
Additional lengths for joining.

Setting up

Arrange so the ends are different lengths.

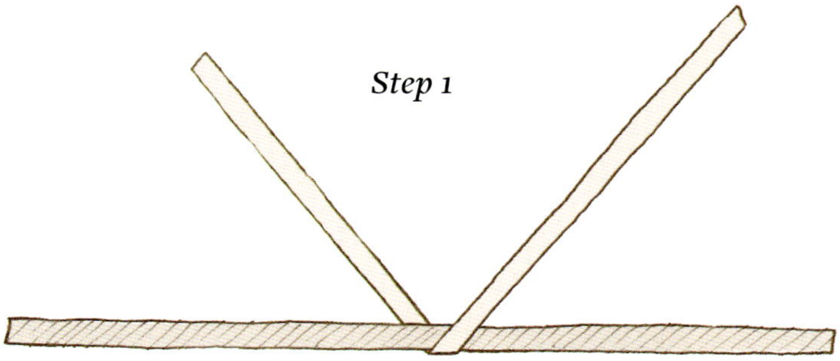

Step 1: The instructions are written for using any plaiting material. If using split straw, then set up so the matt face of the splint is visible along the foot side and the shiny side along the head when in the working position.

Take one length, hold it horizontally so it aligns from 9 o'clock to 3 o'clock.

Take the second length. Hold it diagonally in front of the horizontal straw to lay at an angle of about 45 degrees, the top section will lay at a point between 1 and 2 o'clock.

Take the lower end, currently laying between 7 and 8 o'clock, and fold upwards behind the horizontal straw to lay at between 10 and 11 o'clock. Press the fold.

Step 2: Take the third length and place it to lay parallel to the inside, the left-hand side of the first right-hand diagonal.

Fold the lower end behind and then upwards behind the horizontal end to lay parallel to the outside, left-hand side of the first left-hand diagonal.

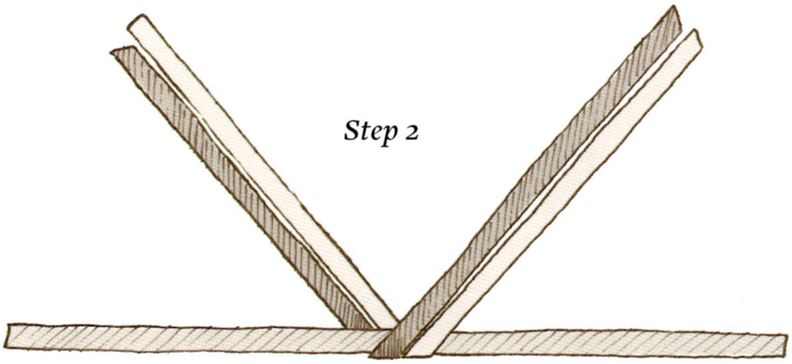

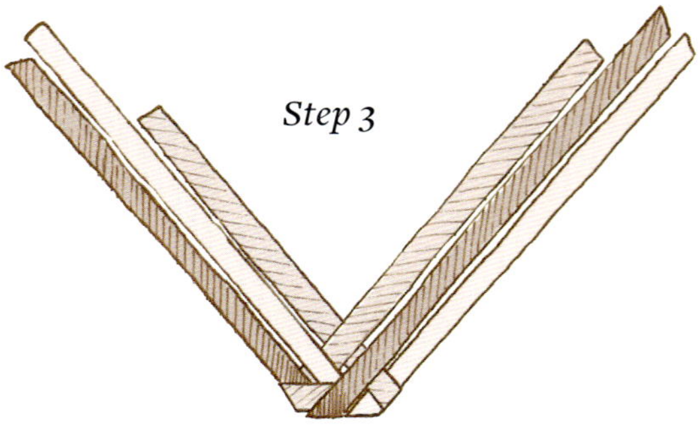

This diagram shows two moves. Fold the left-hand horizontal end that is at 9 o'clock behind the two left-hand ends diagonally to lay parallel on the inside of the two diagonal ends on the right. Press the fold.

Fold the right-hand horizontal end that is at 3 o'clock forward, towards you and then diagonally over one and under two. There are three ends in each group.

Working

Step 1: Stay on the right-hand side. This move will complete the first point on the right.

Take the outside diagonal straw fold to a horizontal position pointing to 9 o'clock.

Now pass it over four diagonal ends and under the outside end.

Slide the working end downwards into the plait to reduce any gaps.

The working end has passed horizontally over four and under one.

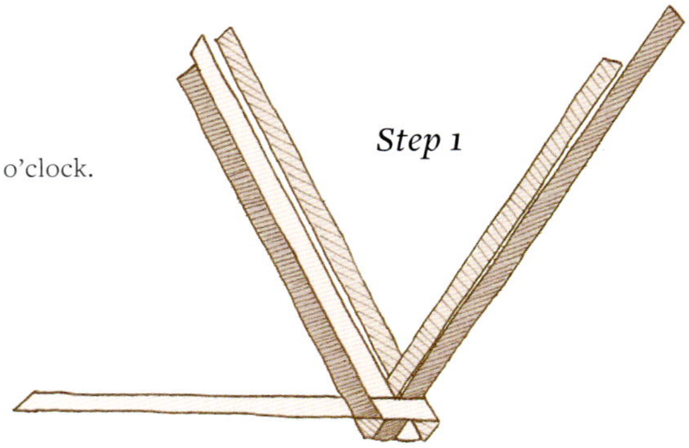

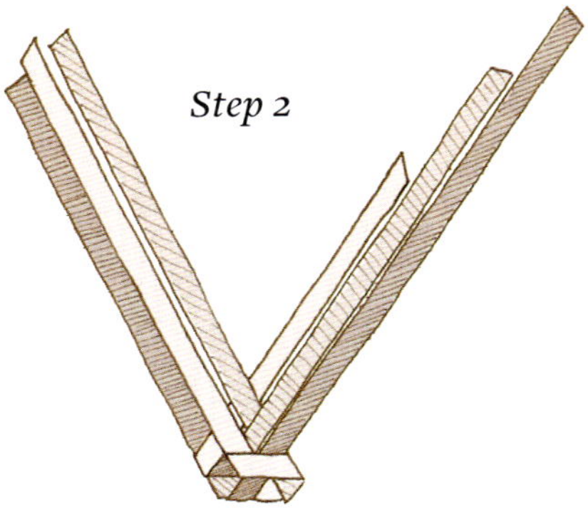

Step 2: The next move is made with the last worked end and will form the first half on the point on the left.

Take the horizontal end at 9 o'clock and fold it over the first and under the next two diagonal left-hand ends. Press the fold.

The working end has passed over one, under two.

Step 3: Stay on the left-hand side. This move will complete the point on the left-hand side.

Fold the outside diagonal end towards you and fold it horizontally to point to 3 o'clock.

Now pass the end over four diagonal ends and under one.
Slide the working end downwards into the plait to reduce any gaps.
Press the fold.

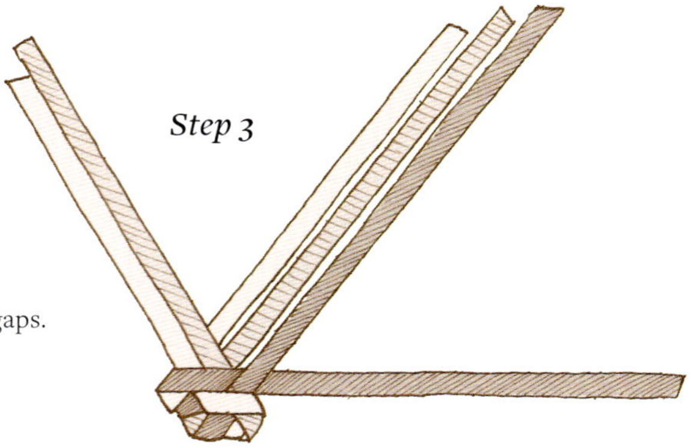

Step 4: Fold the horizontal end laying at 3 o'clock towards you then diagonally upwards to lay to the inside of the left-hand diagonal ends. Take it over the outside then behind the next two diagonal ends. Press the fold.

The end has passed over one, under two.

Continue the working sequence until the ends need joining.

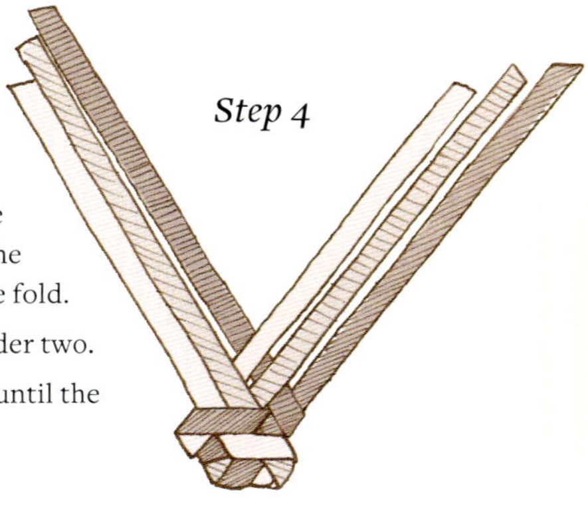

The working sequence is:
Right: Horizontally over four and under one
Left: Same end diagonally over one, under two
Left: Horizontally over four and under one
Right: Same end diagonally over one, under two

Joining

Joins can either be made horizontally or diagonally but always along the foot edge. Never make both joins on the same point as it will weaken the plait. Always begin the joining process while the working ends are quite long as this allows you to plan the joins, spacing them evenly along the length.

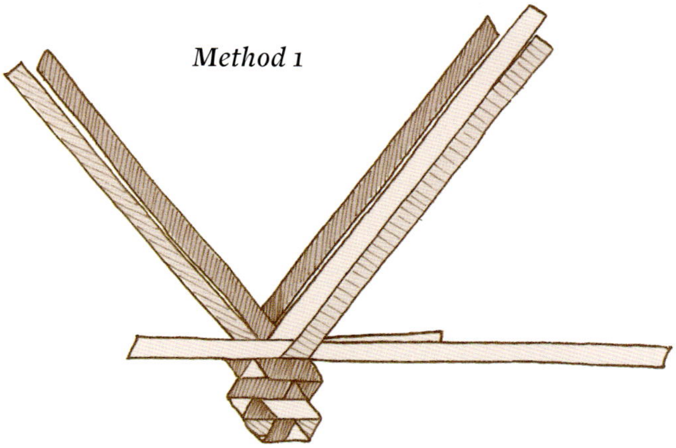

Step 1: To join horizontally, the new end must be inserted when the old end is at 3 o'clock, working step 3. Lay the new end over the old leaving a short end protruding towards 9 o'clock.

Step 2: Only fold the new end diagonally over one under two to lay to the inside of the left-hand diagonal end. Continue the working sequence until the next join is required.

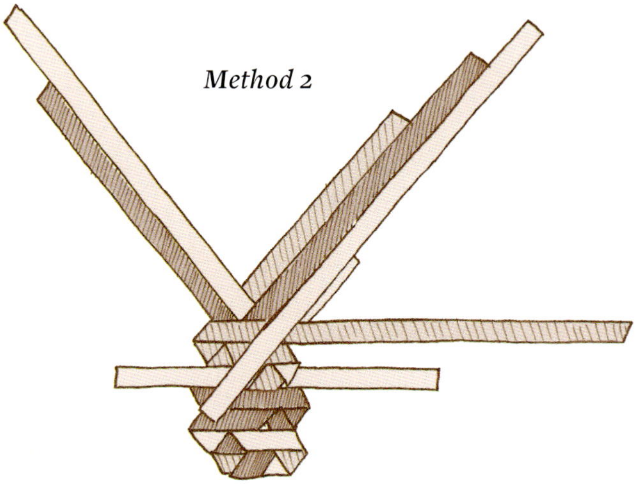

Step 1: To join a new end diagonally the short end to be joined must the outside diagonal end of the right-hand group, working step 2. Lay the new end over the old leaving a short end protruding from the plait.

Step 2: Continue the working sequence until the new end is folded horizontally to the left, then leave behind the old end.

Six-end checkerboard rustic

The replica plait

Origins of the pattern: Currently unknown

Date of introduction: Currently unknown

Type of straw: Wheat, whole

Straw width: 3.5 mm

Plait width: 15 mm

Plaiting direction: During working the back of the plait faces the maker and the front side faces away. The foot is on the right and the head on the left. When completed the front side of the plait has the head on the right and the foot on the left.

Joining: Horizontally or diagonally along foot.

Background information: This pattern doesn't appear on plait dealers' sample cards until the early 1900s and may have been introduced from Japan, China, or both. According to the type of straw used you may find when setting up this plait that the ends do not neatly align. Once the first complete working sequence has been finished, they will sit correctly.

What to use: This can be made with all types of straw but works best with a flat type.

You need: Three plaiting lengths.
Additional lengths for joining.

Setting up

Arrange so the ends are different lengths.

Step 1: Take one length, hold it horizontally so it aligns from 9 o'clock to 3 o'clock.

Take the second length. Hold it diagonally in front of the horizontal straw to lay at an angle of about 45 degrees, the top section will lay at 2 o'clock.

Take the lower end, currently laying at 8 o'clock, and fold upwards behind the horizontal length to lay at 10 o'clock. Press the fold.

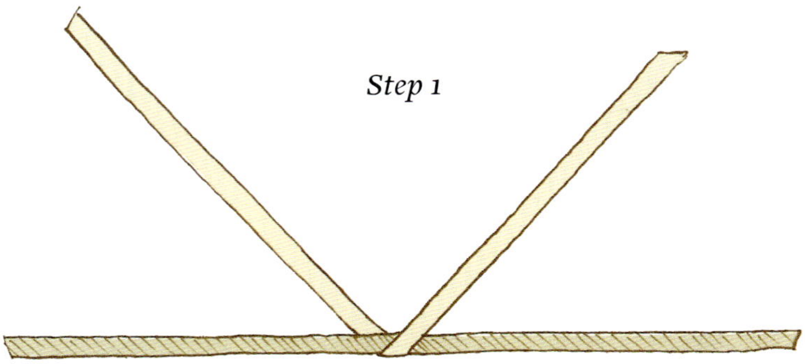

Step 2

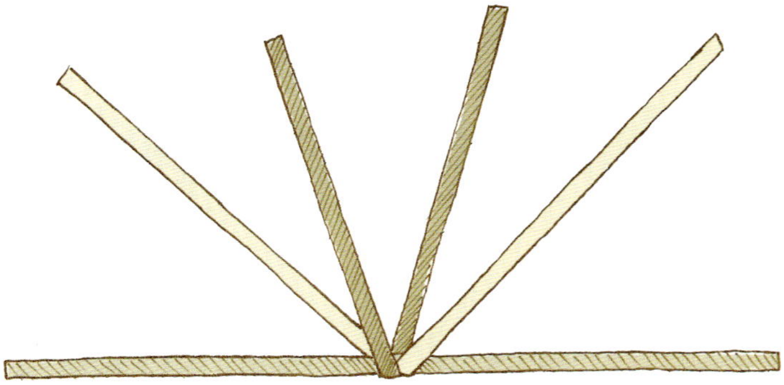

Step 2: Take the third length and place it behind the horizontal end. It lays diagonally inside the right-hand diagonal pointing to about 1 o'clock.

Fold the lower end towards you and then upwards to lay to the inside of the left-hand diagonal end, pointing to about 11 o'clock. Press the fold.

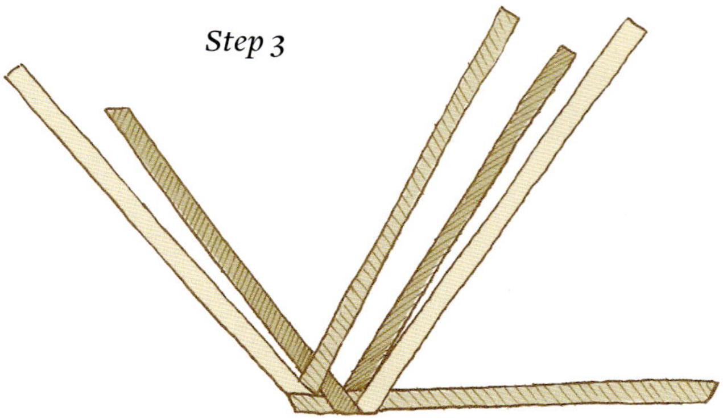

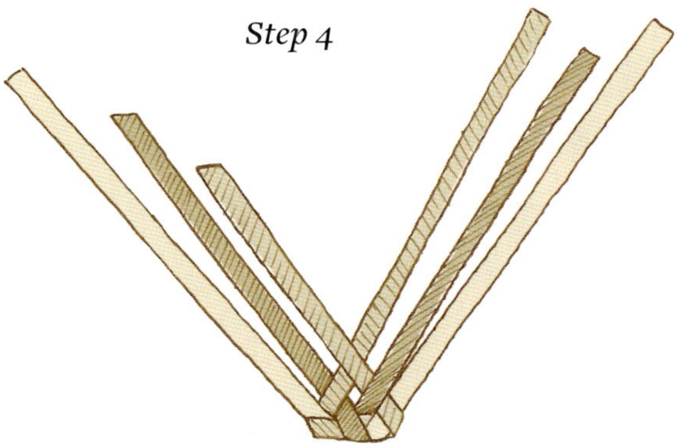

Step 3: Fold the left-hand horizontal end that is at 9 o'clock away from you and then under and over the second end in the left-hand group. It will lay inside the right-hand group.

Step 4: Fold the right-hand horizontal towards you then diagonally upwards, then over, under over the ends. It will lay to the inside of the left-hand group.

Working

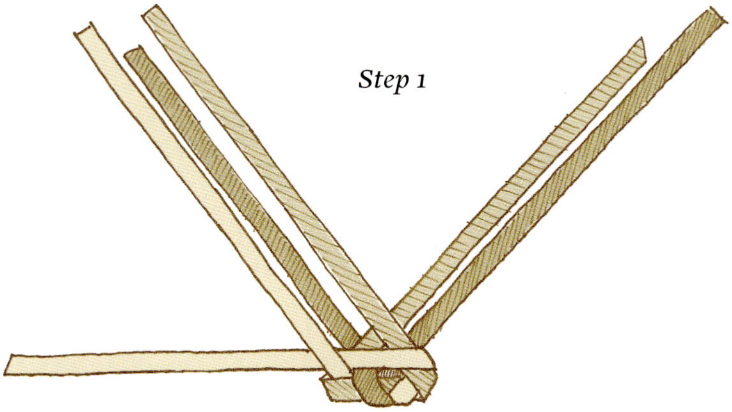

Step 1: Stay on the right-hand side. This move will complete the first point on the right.

Take the outside diagonal straw fold to a horizontal position pointing to 9 o'clock.

Now pass the end behind the outside left-hand diagonal end.

Slide the working end downwards into the plait to reduce any gaps.

The working end has passed horizontally over four and under one.

Step 2: The next move is made with the last worked end and will form the first half on the point on the left.

Take the horizontal end, at 9 o'clock, fold it over the first, under the second and over the third ends in the diagonal group. It will lay to the inside of the right-hand group. Press the fold.

The working end has passed over one, under one, over one.

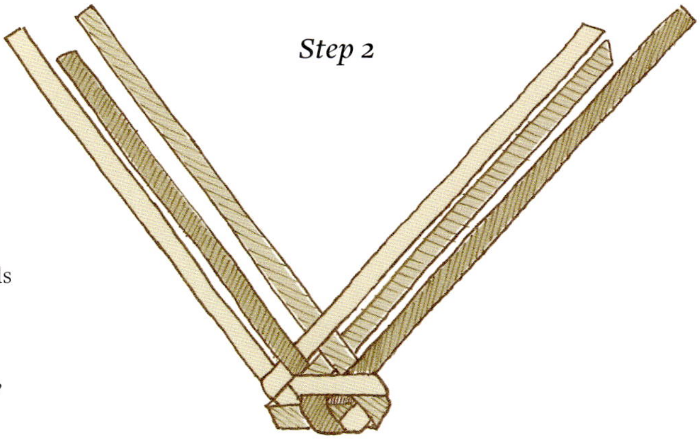

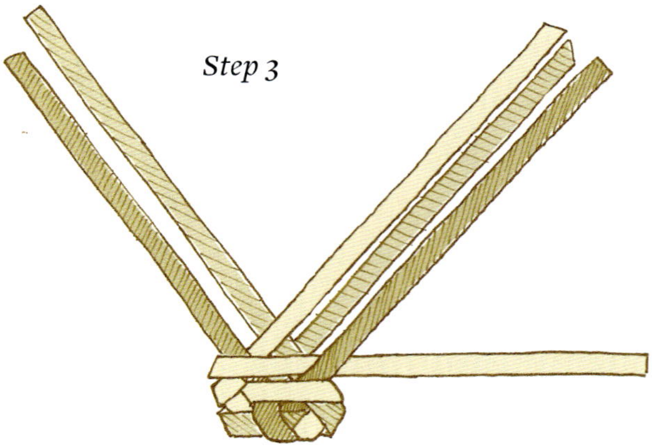

Step 3: Stay on the left-hand side. This move will complete the point on the left-hand side.

Fold the outside diagonal end towards you and fold it horizontally to point to 3 o'clock.

Now pass the end behind the outside right-hand end.

Slide the working end downwards into the plait to reduce any gap. Press the fold.

The working end has passed horizontally over four and under one.

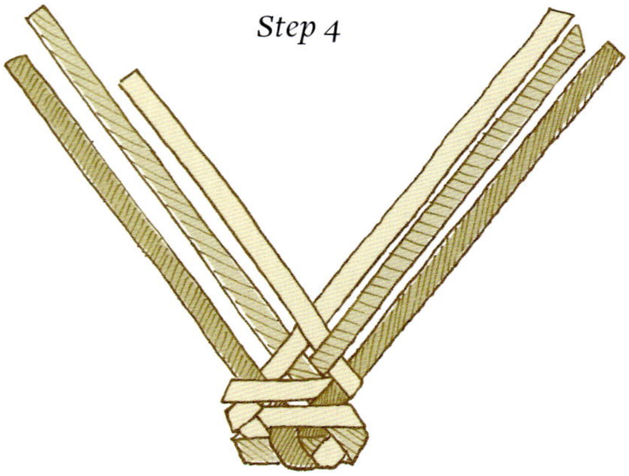

Step 4: Fold the horizontal end laying at 3 o'clock towards you then pass it over one, under one and over one. It will lay to the inside of the left-hand diagonal group. Press the fold.

The end has passed over one, under one, over one.

Continue the working sequence until the ends need joining.

The working sequence is:
Right: Horizontally over four and under one
Left: Same end diagonally over one, under one, over one
Left: horizontally over four and under one
Right: Same end diagonally over one, under one, over one

Joining

Follow the joining instructions for the six-end rustic twill, joining horizontally at working step 4, or diagonally at working step 3. Remember to follow the checkerboard sequence when working the new end into the plait.

Eight-end checkerboard rustic

The replica plait

Origins of the pattern: Currently unknown

Date of introduction: Currently unknown

Type of straw: Wheat, whole

Straw width: 3 mm

Plait width: 20 mm

Plaiting direction: During working the back of the plait faces the maker and the front side faces away. The foot is on the right and the head on the left. When completed the front side of the plait has the head on the right and the foot on the left.

Joining: Into body.

Background information: Still made in the Bahamas and other Caribbean islands it is also historically associated with the palm-leaf industry of the south-eastern seaboard of the USA, but less common in Europe. In the Bahamas when the reverse side is used as the face it is called Jacobs Ladder. When the more commonly used checkerboard face is intended for the right side it is called Jacobs Ladder reversed.

What to use: This can be made with all types of straw but works best with a flat type.

You need: Four plaiting lengths.
Additional lengths for joining.

Setting up

This method of setting up can also be used for the six-end checkerboard rustic, follow setting up steps one to five. Arrange so the ends are different lengths.

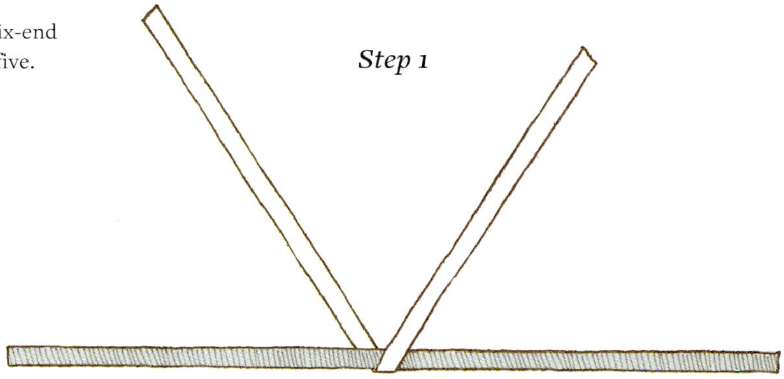

Step 1: Take one length, hold it horizontally so it aligns from 9 o'clock to 3 o'clock.

Take the second length. Hold it diagonally in front of the horizontal length to lay at an angle of about 45 degrees, the top section will lay at 2 o'clock.

Take the lower end, currently laying at 8 o'clock, and fold upwards behind the horizontal length to lay at 10 o'clock. Press the fold.

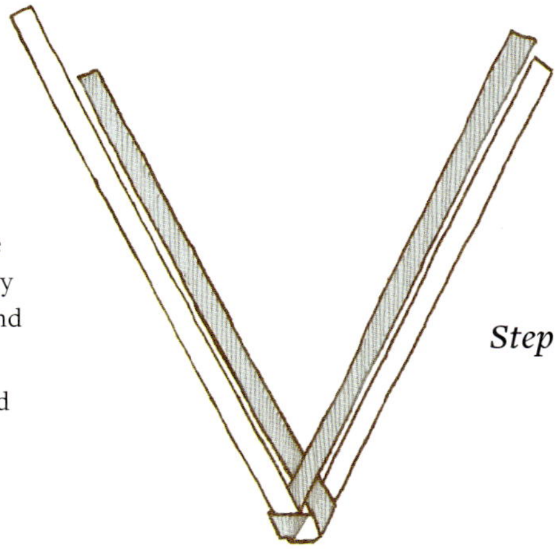

Step 2: Take the 9 o'clock end, fold the end away from you and then diagonally under to lay to the inside the right-hand diagonal end. Press the fold.

Fold the 3 o'clock end towards you and then over and under the to lay inside the left-hand diagonal.

Step 3

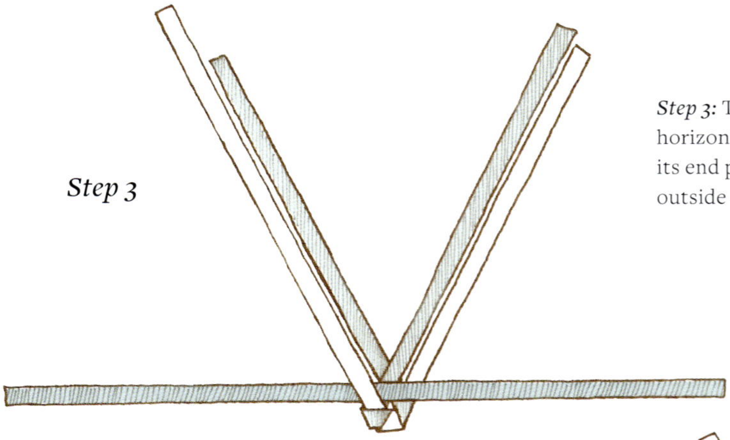

Step 3: Take a new length. Hold it horizontally in front of the plait then slide its end pointing to 9 o'clock, under the outside diagonal of the left-hand group.

Step 4

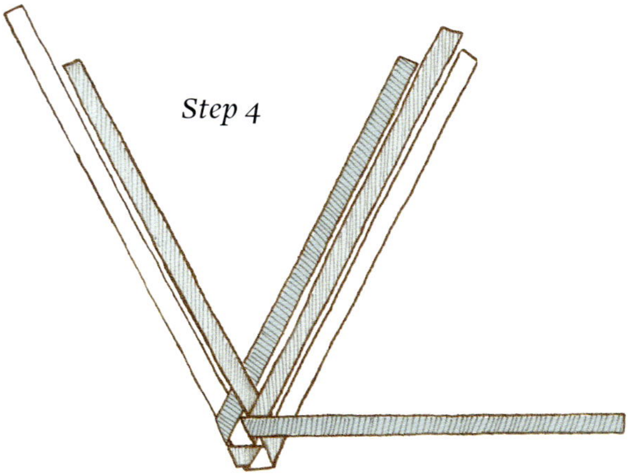

Step 4: Fold the left-hand horizontal end towards you then diagonally over then under the two ends in the left-hand group to lay to inside the right-hand group.

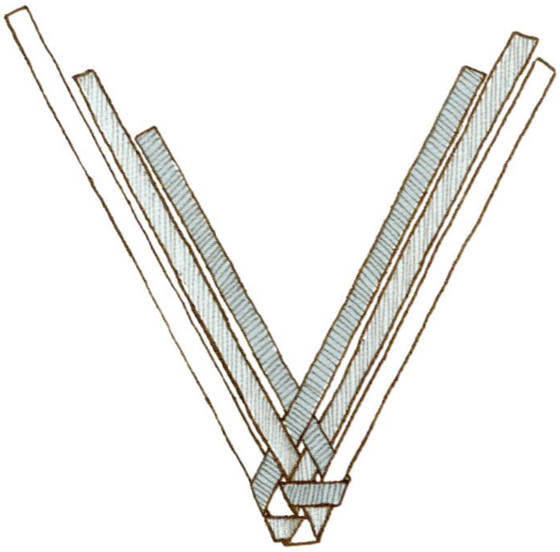

Step 5

Step 5: Take the horizontal end pointing to 3 o'clock and fold it away from you then diagonally under, over, under the other three ends of the right-hand group. It now lays inside the left-hand group. There are now six working ends.

Step 6

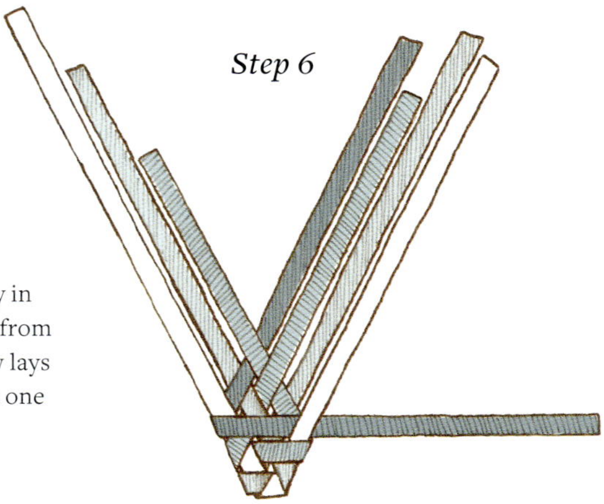

Step 6: Take a new length. Hold it horizontally in front of the plait. Fold the 9 o'clock end away from you then diagonally under, over, under. It now lays to the inside of the right-hand group. There is one horizontal end pointing to 3 o'clock.

Working

Step 1

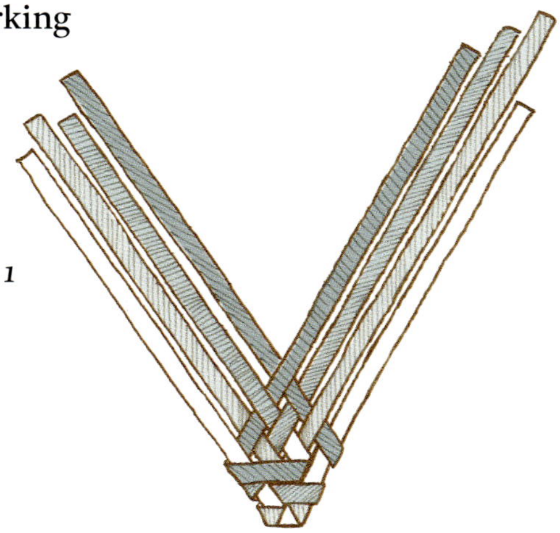

Step 2

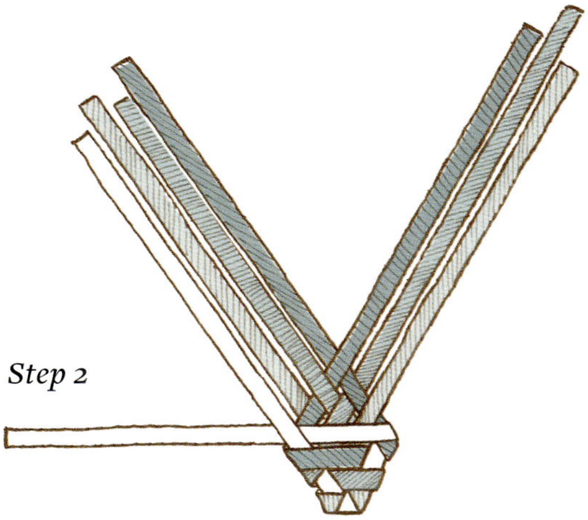

Step 1: Fold the horizontal end laying at 3 o'clock towards you then pass it over one, under one, over one, under one. It will lay to the inside of the left-hand diagonal group. Press the fold.

The end has passed over one, under one, over one, under one.

Step 2: Stay on the right-hand side. This move will complete the first point on the right.

Take the outside diagonal length fold to the horizontal position pointing to 9 o'clock.

Now pass the end behind the outside left-hand diagonal end.

Slide the working end downwards into the plait to reduce any gaps.

The working end has passed horizontally over six and under one.

Step 3

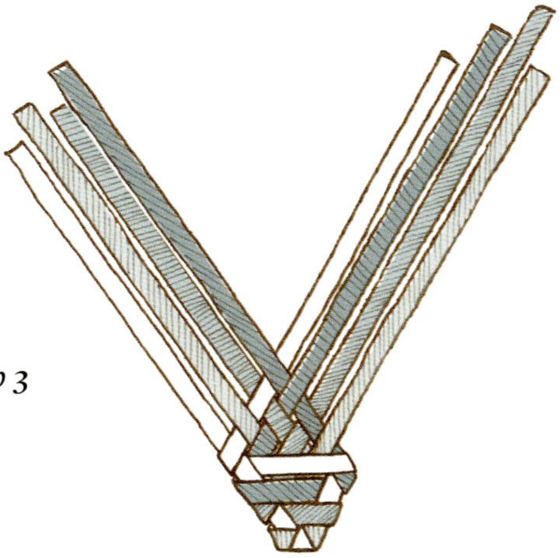

Step 4

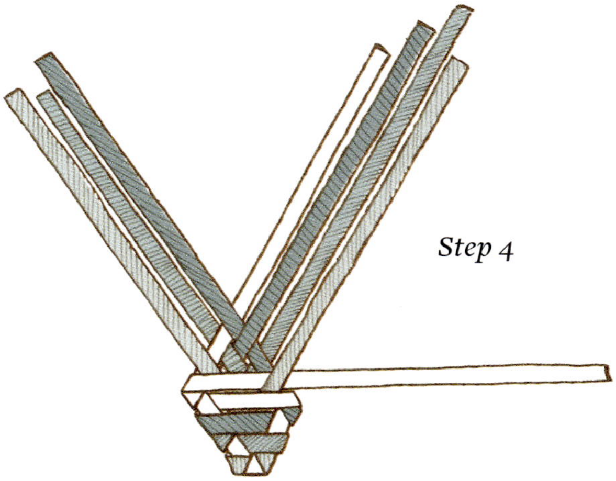

Step 3: The next move is made with the last worked end and will form the first half on the point on the left.

Take the horizontal end at 9 o'clock and fold it over, under, over and under the left-hand diagonal group. It will lay to the inside of the right-hand group. Press the fold.

The working end has passed over one, under one, over one, under one.

The working sequence is:
Right: Horizontally over six and under one.
Left: Same end diagonally over one, under one, over one, under one.
Left: Horizontally over six and under one.
Right: Same end diagonally over one, under one, over one, under one.

Step 4: Stay on the left-hand side. This move will complete the point on the left-hand side.

Fold the outside diagonal end towards you and fold it horizontally to point to 3 o'clock.

Now pass the end behind the outside right-hand end.

Slide the working end downwards into the plait to reduce any gap. Press the fold.

The working end has passed horizontally over six and under one.

Continue the working sequence until the ends need joining.

Joining

Join either horizontally or diagonally as for other rustic plaits.

Four-end rustic flat foot

The original plait

Source: CTLC 10/31/41

Origins: Japan

Production date: Early 1940s

Type of straw: Barley, whole

Splint width: 4 mm

Plait width: 22 mm

Plaiting direction: During working the back of the plait faces the maker and the front side faces away. The foot is on the right and the head on the left. When completed the front side of the plait has the head on the right and the foot on the left.

Joining: Into body as part of working.

Background information: The flat foot version of the rustic plait became popular in the early 1920s for making men's boaters. The split straw produced a lightweight hat that was easier to sew to shape. Using barley straw, the Japanese made it in a variety of flat foot widths and qualities. Its working method is quite different as a new length is joined every working sequence and it is made with short lengths.

What to use: This can be made with all types of straw but works best with a flat type.

You need: Two plaiting lengths.
Additional short lengths for joining.

Setting up

Arrange so the ends are different lengths. The plait starts with the same steps as the four-end rustic.

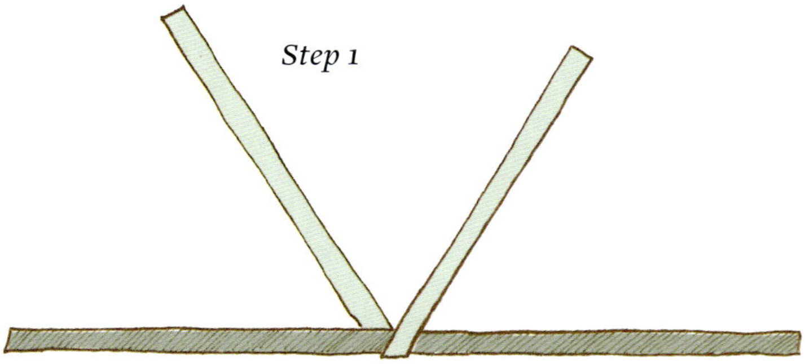

Step 1: Take one straw, hold it horizontally so it aligns from 9 o'clock to 3 o'clock.

Take the second straw. Hold it diagonally in front of the horizontal straw to lay at an angle of about 45 degrees, the top section will lay at a point between 1 o'clock and 2 o'clock.

Take the lower end, currently laying between 7 o'clock and 8 o'clock, and fold upwards behind the horizontal straw to lay at between 10 o'clock and 11 o'clock. Press the fold.

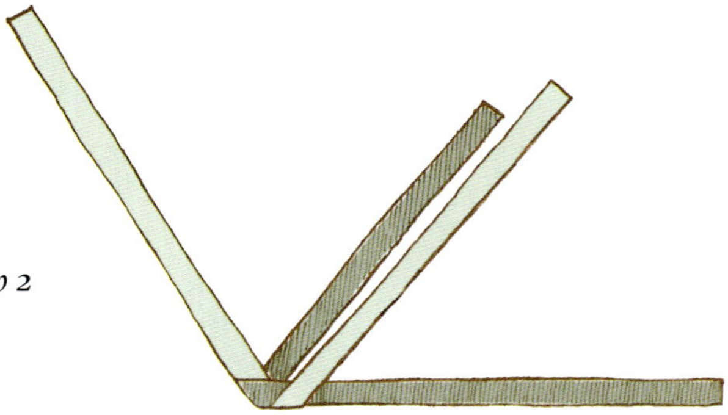

Step 2: Fold the left-hand horizontal end that is at 9 o'clock behind the other left-hand end then diagonally to lay on the inside the end at between 1 and 2 o'clock on the right. Press the fold.

Step 3: Take the horizontal end that is at 3 o'clock, bring it towards you then fold diagonally upwards so it points to between 10 o'clock and 11 o'clock.

Now take the end under the inside diagonal end. Press the fold.

There are two ends in each group.

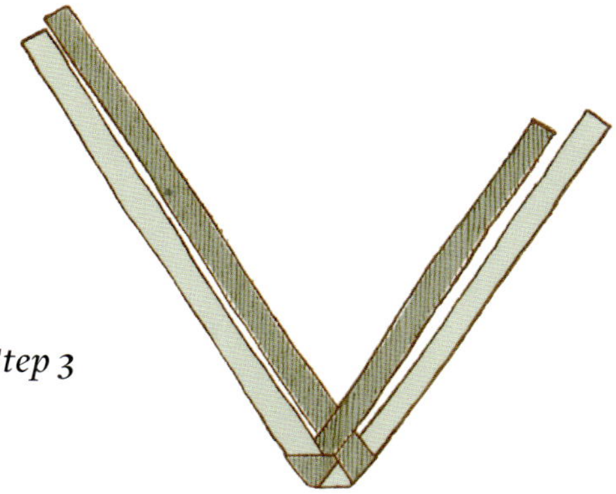

Step 3

Working

Step 1: Take a new plaiting length. Slide it under the outside left-hand end to lay horizontally. The long section of the new end points to 9 o'clock. The short end points to 3 o'clock.

The plait now has five working ends for the next two steps.

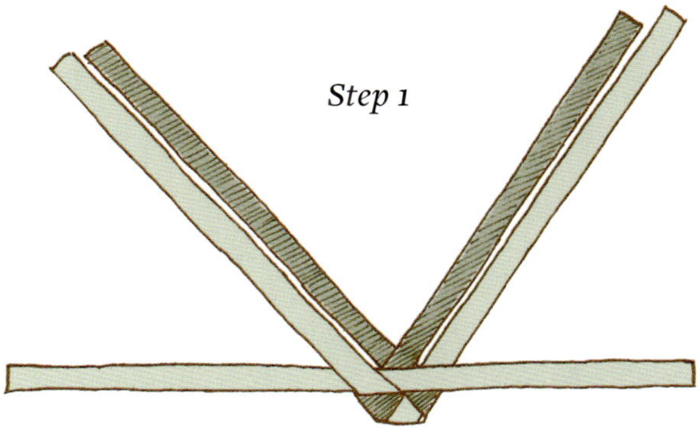

Step 1

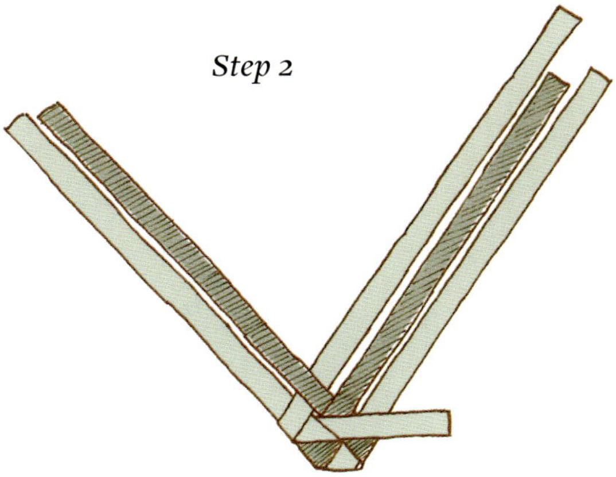

Step 2

Step 2: This move is made with the newly inserted end and will form the first half of the point on the left.

Take the horizontal end at 9 o'clock and fold it over the first and under the second diagonal left-hand end. Press the fold.

The working end has passed diagonally over one, under one.

Step 3: Stay on the left-hand side. This move will complete the point on the left-hand side.

Fold the outside diagonal end towards you and fold it horizontally to point to 3 o'clock.

Now pass the end over two, under one and over the outside end of the right-hand group.

Slide the working end downwards into the workings to ensure it is not visible on the plait face. Press the fold.

The working end has passed horizontally over two and under one, over one.

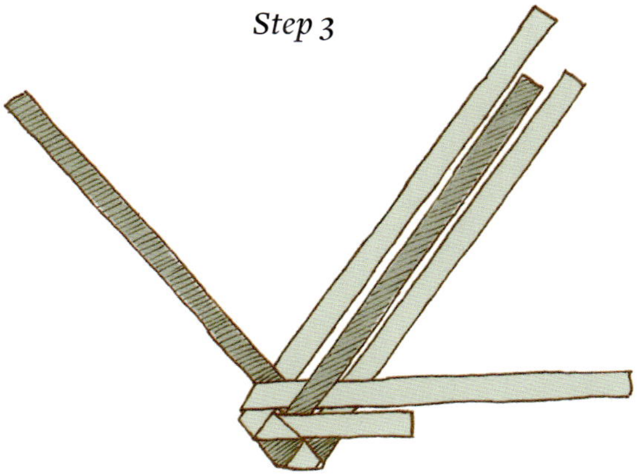

Step 3

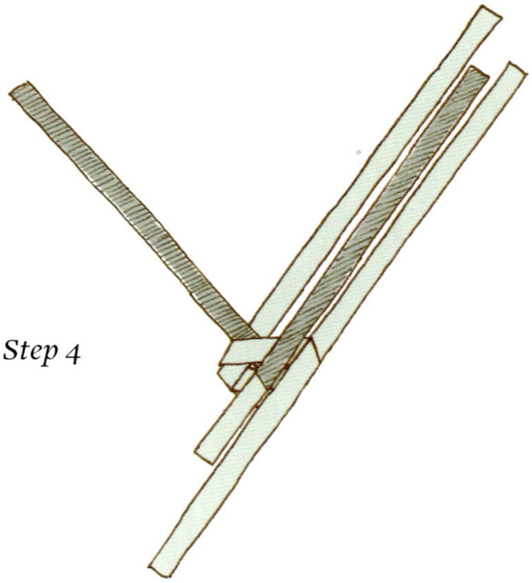

Step 4: Fold the last worked horizontal end at 3 o'clock towards you and then down to point to about 7 o'clock. This end is no longer worked, and the plait is now restored to four ends.

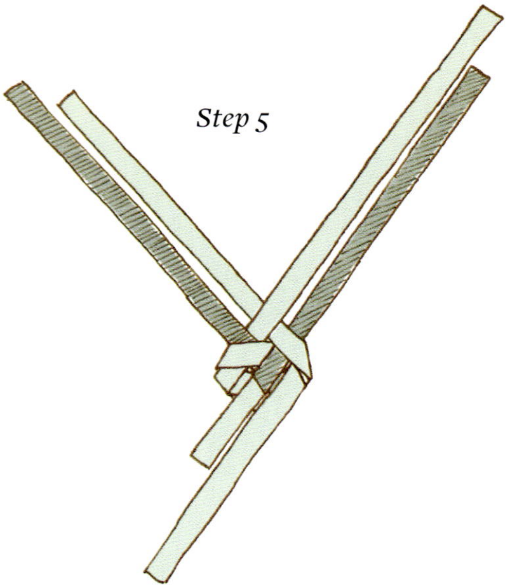

Step 5: This move creates the flat stitch on the foot edge. Make certain the end that was just folded out of the way does not distort this move.

On the right-hand side fold the outside end towards and then fold over one, under one to lay to the inside of the left-hand diagonals.

Continue the working sequence inserting a new length each time.

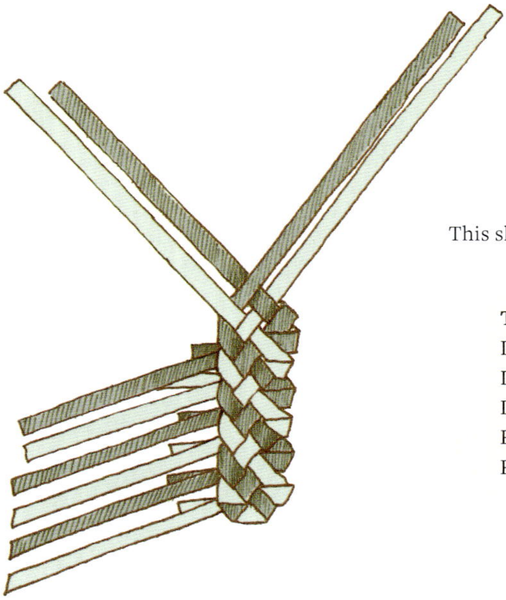

This shows the right side of the plait.

The working sequence is:
Left: Insert new end under outside end.
Left: New end over one, under one.
Left: Outside diagonal, over two, under one.
Right: Fold the last worked end towards the start of the plait.
Right: Over one, under one.

We will never know if this child's dolls' cradle was made as a commercial item or for the workers own children. Using scraps from the workroom and hand sewn it is a work of great skill. (CTLC 360/66)

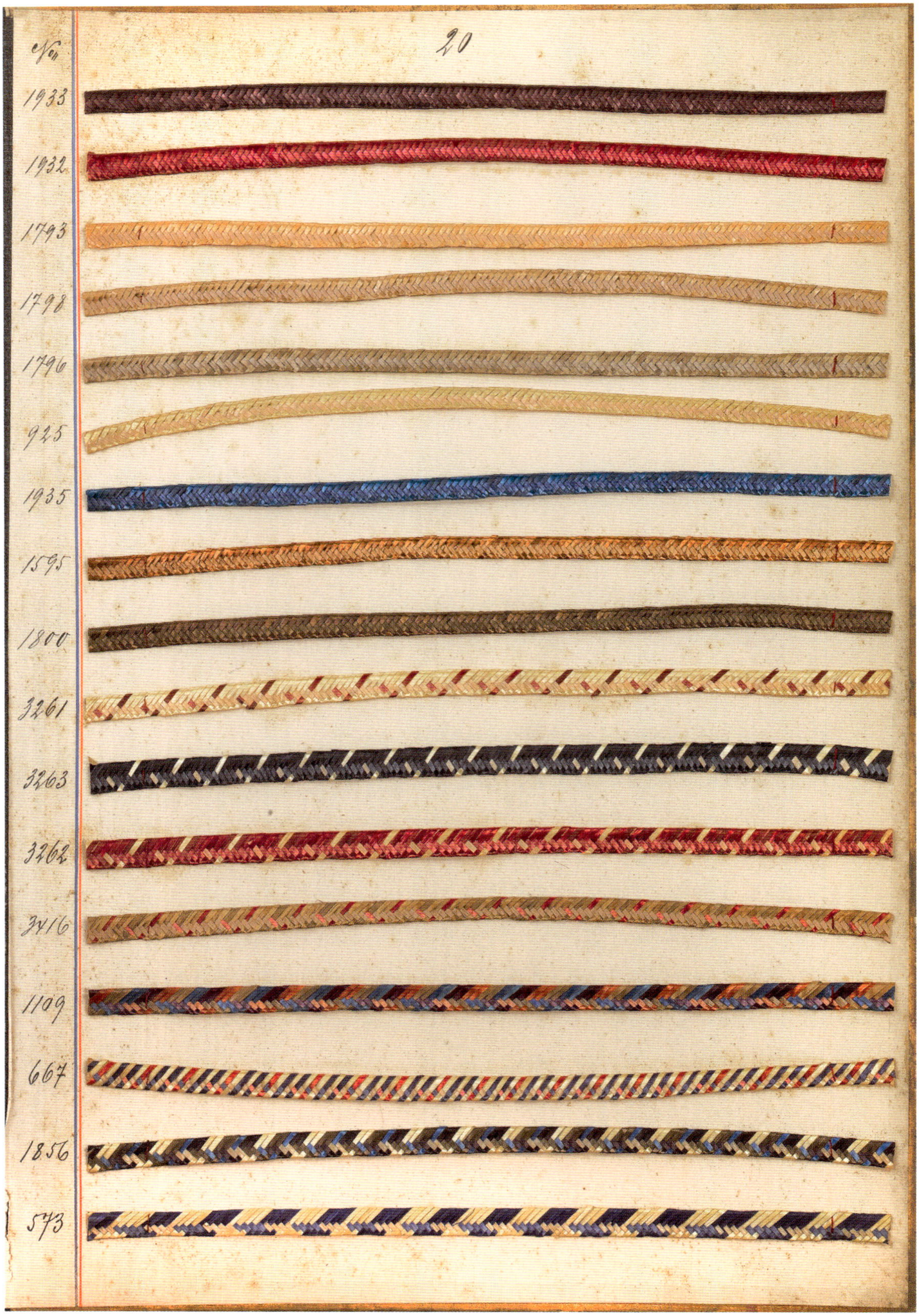

This sample sheet is from pattern books of the Eduard Treutler straw hat factory and dates to the second half of the 1800s. It includes split straw piping plaits in a range of vibrant colours.

Piping and Porcupine

In the early 1800s piping was commonly made as a very narrow plait but in the 1880s wider whole straw patterns came to England from Italy. In the English trade these were known as Under Ten or Under Eleven, the working ends being indicated by the number. In these wider versions the form was removed allowing the head to spread. By the early 1900s piping became known as Liseret, which may be an Anglicisation of the French term *liseré*. The final plait in this section, Porcupine became popular at the end of the 1800s.

Six-end plait piping

The original plait

Source: CTLC1/562/39

Origins: Totternhoe, Bedfordshire

Production date: *c.* 1830

Type of straw: Wheat straw, single splint

Splint width: Less than 1 mm

Plait width: 5 mm

Plaiting direction: During working the back of the plait faces the maker and the front side faces away. The foot is on the right and the head on the left. When completed the front side of the plait has the head on the right and the foot on the left.

Joining: Along foot edge.

Background information: This is part of a group of plaits made in about 1830 by the same plaiter and she may have known it as Vienna or satin piping. Her original example retains the 1 mm softened splints used as the form. The width of the form alters the overall plait width and affects the visual appearance. The form should only be fractionally wider than the working ends.

What to use: Whole straws, splints, or flat plaiting materials.

You need: Three plaiting lengths, each one a minimum 25 cm long.

Additional shorter lengths for joining.

A form or splints, a little wider than the working ends and minimum 12 cm long.

Additional lengths for joining onto the form.

Setting up

The three lengths should be held with their matt side facing towards you and then each is folded off centre, to give six working ends of different lengths.

Step 1: Hold the form vertically at 12 o'clock to 6 o'clock.

Take the first folded working length and place it so the matt side passes behind the form and the shiny side passes in front. Both ends point to the right.

Place the second folded working length above the first, closer to 12 o'clock, with the matt side passing behind the form and the shiny in front.

Repeat with the third working length. There are now six working ends pointing to the right, and a sequence from bottom to top of under, over, under, over, under, over the form. The faces of the working ends alternating matt then shiny.

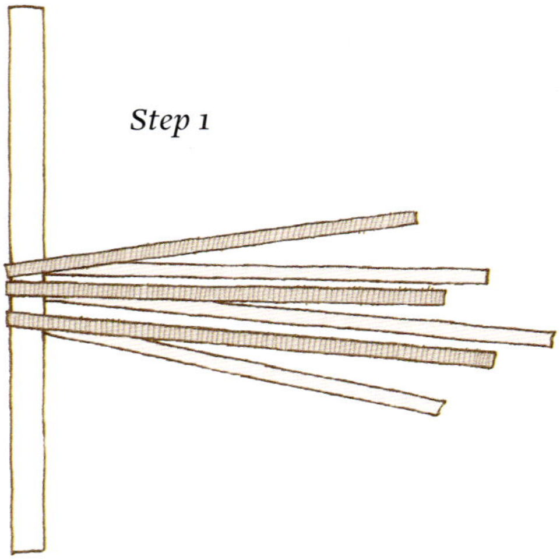

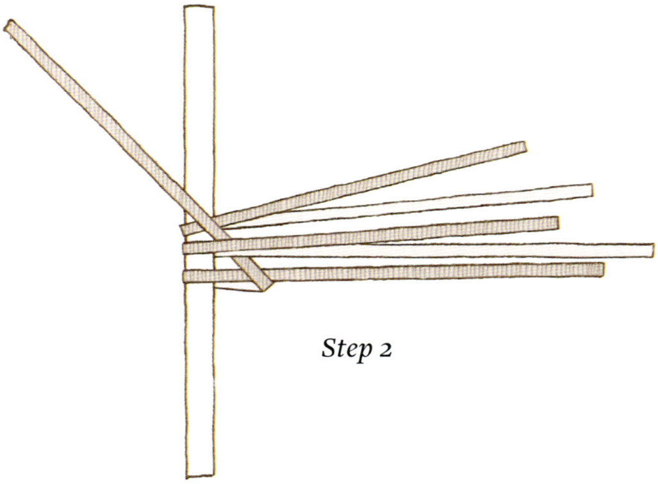

Step 2: Take the lowest end, closest to 6 o'clock fold it, as shown in the diagram, at a point away from the right-hand edge of the form.

Take the same end diagonally over one, under two, then in front of the form and last pair of ends. It now lays diagonally to the left.

There is one end to the left of the form and five to the right.

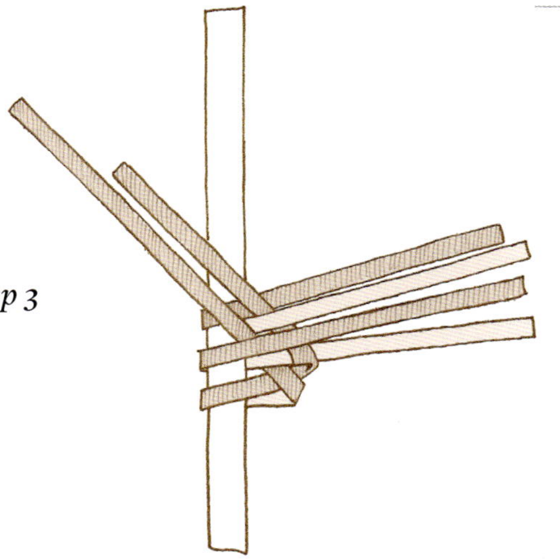

Step 3

Step 3: Repeat with the next lowest outside right-hand end. Instead of folding twist the end so the shiny side is facing you during the move.

Take it diagonally over one and under two then in front of the form. It now lays inside the other left-hand end and with the shiny side facing.

There are two on the left and four ends on the right.

Step 4: Take the lowest right-hand end, fold towards you and then diagonally over one, under two then in front of the form to lay to the inside of the left-hand group.

There are now three ends on the left of the form and three to the right.

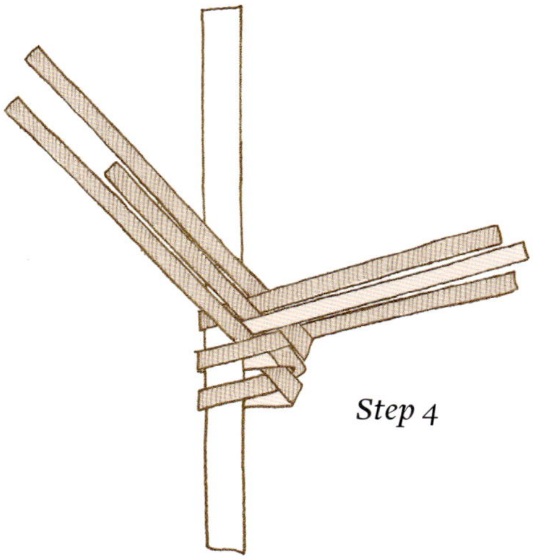

Step 4

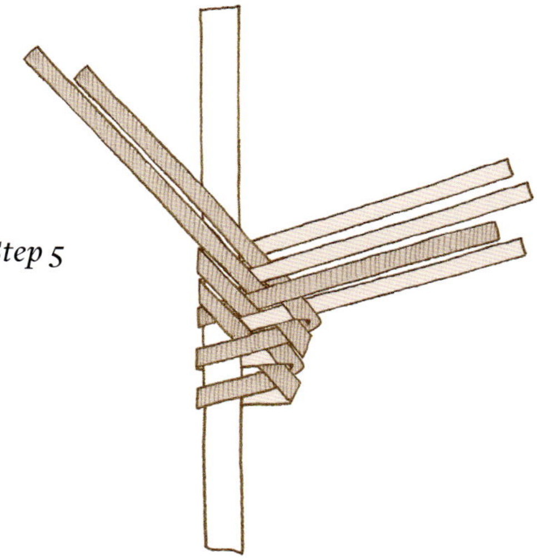

Step 5

Step 5: The diagram shows three moves.

Take the lowest left-hand end and fold it diagonally behind the form to lay to the inside of the left-hand group.

There are two ends on the left and four on the right.

Take the lowest right-hand end, twist it towards you so the shiny side stays uppermost, then position it diagonally over one, under two then in front of the form to lay to the inside of the left-hand group.

Take the lowest left-hand end and fold it diagonally behind the form to lay to the inside of the right-hand group.

There are two on the left and four on the right. One last right-hand end still needs to be turned to face correctly.

Step 6: The diagram shows two moves.

Take the outside end of the right-hand group fold towards you, then take it diagonally over one, under two to lay inside the left-hand group.

Fold the lowest or outside left-hand end diagonally behind the form to lay inside the right-hand group.

Take the outside end of the right-hand group, twisting it so the shiny side stays uppermost then take it diagonally over one, under two to lay to the inside of the left-hand group.

There are three ends in each group.

All the ends of the right-hand group now lay with the matt side facing and all ends of the left-hand group have the shiny side facing.

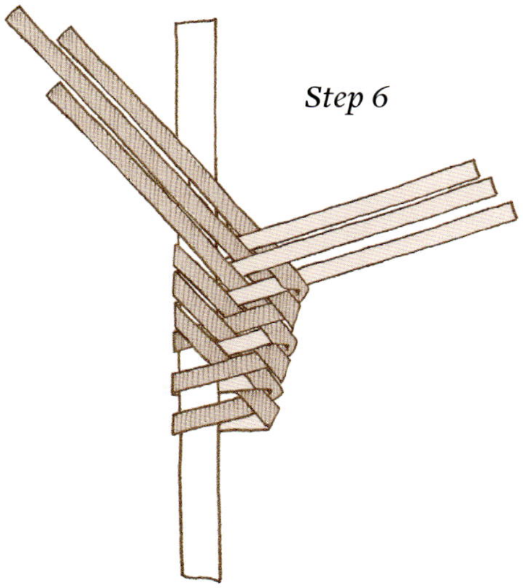

Step 6

Working

Step 1

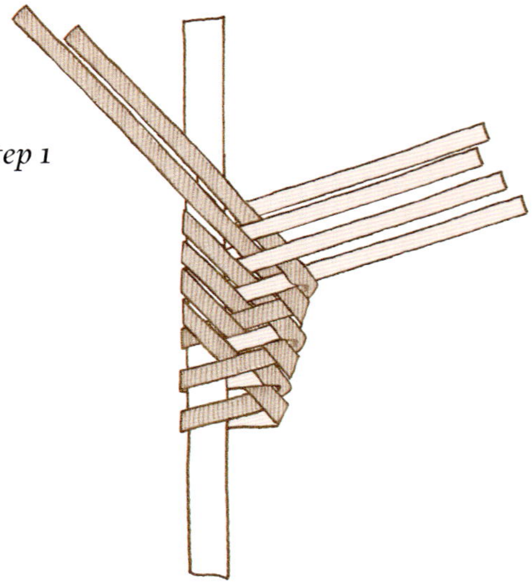

Step 2

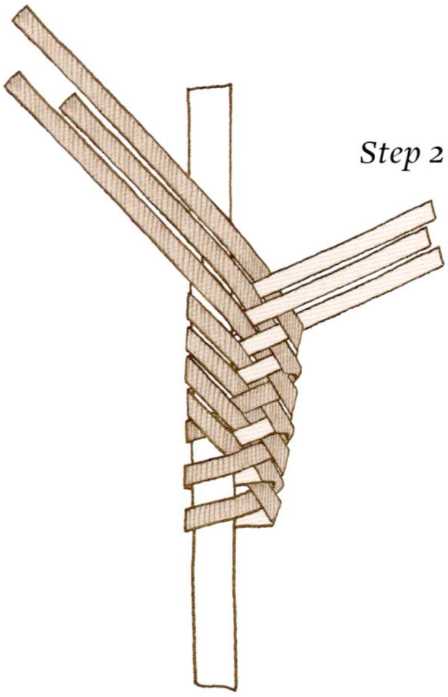

Step 1: Fold the lowest left-hand end behind the form to lay to the inside of the right-hand group. There are four ends on the right and two on the left.

Step 2: Take the lowest end of the right-hand group, fold it towards you and then diagonally over one, under two, then in front of the form to lay alongside the top left-hand end.

There are three ends in the left-hand group and three in the right-hand group.

Repeat from working step 1 until joining begins.

The working sequence is:
Right: Over one, under two to lay to top of left-hand group.
Left: Around and behind the form to the inside of the right-hand group.

Joining

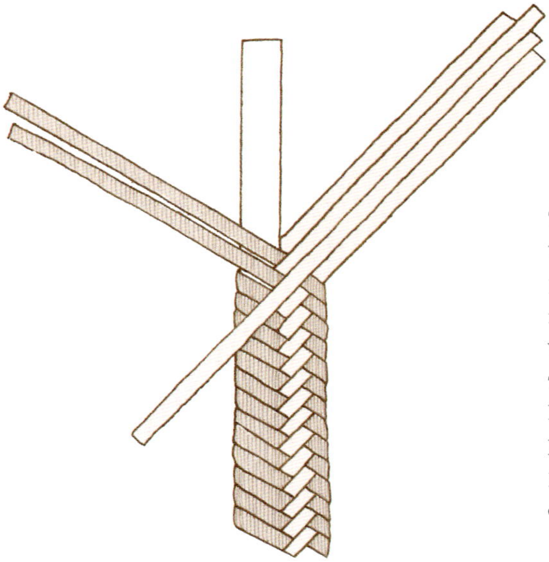

The end to be joined is next to the outside end of the right-hand group.

Lay the new end over the old ensuring its face matches the face of the old end. Continue the working steps.

To join onto the form carefully slide a prepared new length over the end of the original form. It should pass under at least 6 stitches of the head.

Press and flatten the section where the form overlaps to avoid a bulge.

Seven-end piping

The original plait

Source: CTLC 1997/16/1

Origins: Vallée du Geer, Belgium

Production date: Early 1900s

Type of straw: Wheat straw, single splint

Splint width: 1.5–2 mm

Plait width: 5 mm

Plaiting direction: During working the back of the plait faces the maker and the front side faces away. The foot is on the right and the head on the left. When completed the front side of the plait has the head on the right and the foot on the left.

Joining: Along foot edge.

Background information: Until the early 1900s Belgian straw plaiters were renowned for their high-quality split straw plaits, including piping which they made in a range of colours. This pattern was also being made in canton Fribourg, Switzerland in the later 1800s possibly indicating the patterns popularity within the hat trade. The splints used for the form remains in the plaits head edge, so it is important to make certain they are soft and flexible.

What to use: Whole fine straws, splints, or flat straws.

You need: Three different colour plaiting lengths, each one a minimum 25 cm long.
One plaiting length minimum 15 cm long, undyed colour.
Additional shorter lengths for joining.
A form a little wider than the working ends and minimum 12 cm long.
Additional lengths for joining onto the form.

Setting up

The three lengths should be held with their matt side facing towards you and then each is folded off centre, to give six working ends of different lengths. Set up as for six-end piping. The seventh end is added once the first six ends are secured, and colour pattern established.

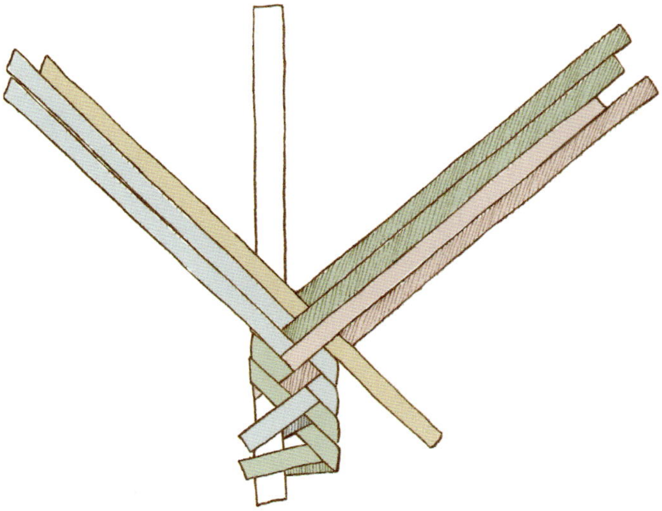

The diagram shows the three folded lengths already set up. There will be two ends in the left-hand group and four in the right-hand group.

Insert the seventh end, shiny side upwards if using split straw. If using another material but following the original colourway then add an undyed colour length.

Take the new end and pass it diagonally over the outside end of the right-hand group then under two and in front of the form to lay inside the left-hand group.

There are three ends in the left-hand group, with the shiny side facing.

On the right there is still one end with the shiny side upwards and this must be turned at its next move.

Working

Step 1

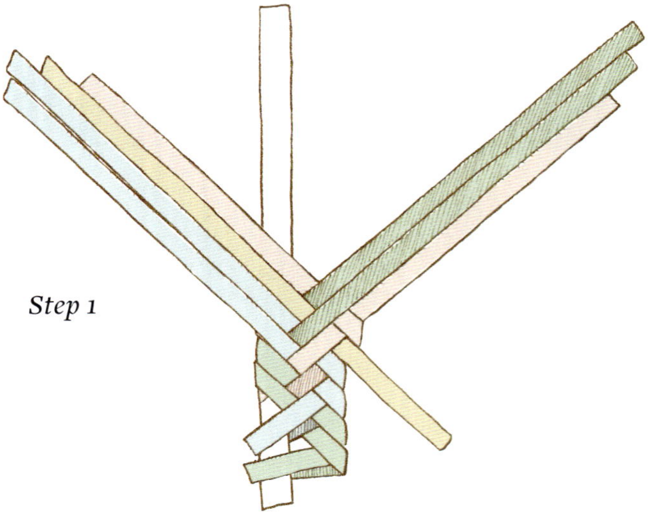

Step 2

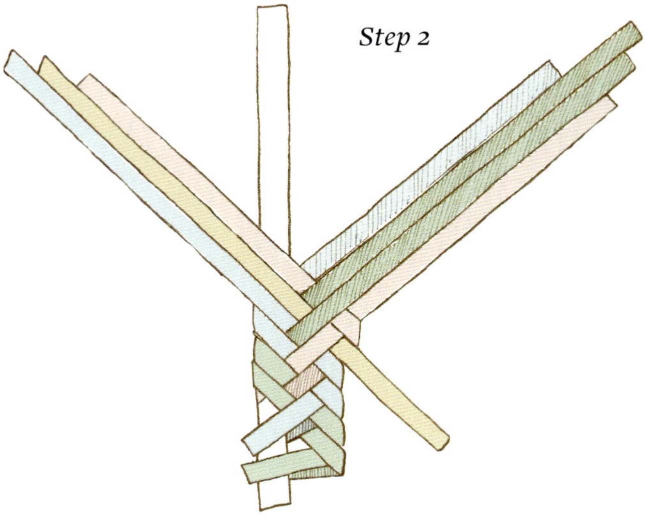

Step 1: Ignoring the short end of the newly added length, fold the outside right-hand end towards you and then diagonally over one, under two to lay to inside the left-hand group.

There are four ends in the left-hand group and three in the right-hand group.

Step 2: Take the lowest end of the left-hand group, fold it away from you and then diagonally behind the form to lay to the inside of the right-hand group.

It will take a few moves to establish the correct angles for the left and right-hand groups.

Avoid leaving gaps between the head stitches, but do not allow them to overlap.

Repeat until joining begins.

The working sequence is:
Right: Over one, under two, in front of the form.
Left: Fold back, diagonally behind the form to lay inside the right-hand group.

Joining

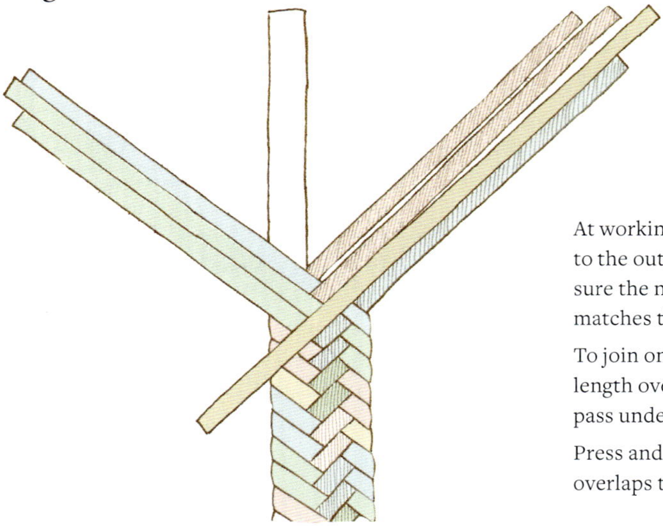

At working step 2 the end to be joined must be next to the outside end of the right-hand group, making sure the new end lays over the old ensuring it matches the pattern.

To join onto the form carefully slide a prepared new length over the end of the original form. It should pass under at least six stitches of the head.

Press and flatten the section where the form overlaps to avoid a bulge.

Ten-end piping

The original plait

Source: 1993/180

Origins: Ballinger, Buckinghamshire

Production date: *c.* 1880

Type of straw: Wheat straw, single splints

Splint width: 2 mm

Plait width: 19 mm

Plaiting direction: During working the back of the plait faces the maker and the front side faces away. The foot is on the right and the head on the left. When completed the front side of the plait has the head on the right and the foot on the left.

Joining: Along foot edge.

Background information: Made by Sarah Halse this may have been exhibited at a major hat trade exhibition in Glasgow in the 1880s but was she copying a plait being made in canton Fribourg, Switzerland? An almost identical example is in a Swiss plait dealer's sample book. The British name of this plait may be one bar, which at that time is frequently mentioned in the trade press. The form used to make this pattern is said to have been a whalebone or baleen from a corset. It is removed from the finished plait.

What to use: Whole fine straws, splints, or flat plaiting materials.

You need: Four undyed plaiting lengths, each one a minimum 25 cm long.
One plaiting length minimum 25 cm long, dyed.
Additional shorter lengths for joining.
A form a little wider than the working ends and minimum 15 cm long.

Setting up

The plait can be set up using the methods for six-end piping, but these instructions give an alternative where the ends are added and worked in move by move. If using a split straw and following the colour pattern then remember to twist the ends of the right-hand group so the matt side faces upwards, as required in the method for setting up the six and seven-end piping.

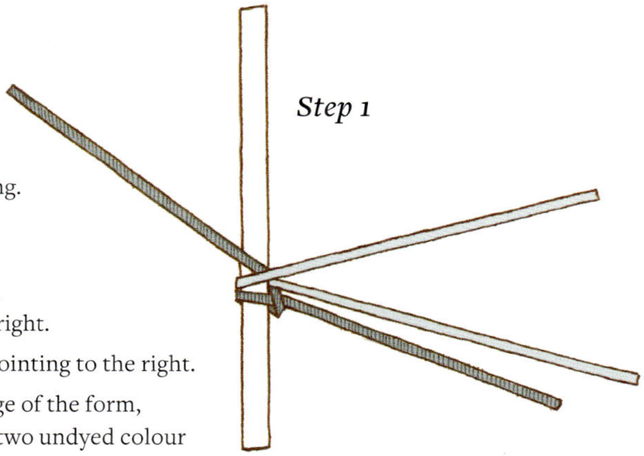

Step 1: The diagram shows two moves.

Hold the form vertically. Place the coloured straw, off centre behind the form.
Fold the left-hand end around the front of the form so both ends point to the right.

Repeat with an undyed colour length. There are four ends of unequal length pointing to the right.

Take the lowest right-hand end, fold it at a point away from the right-hand edge of the form, towards you and then diagonally, over the next coloured straw and under the two undyed colour ends, then in front of the form to lay to the left of the form.

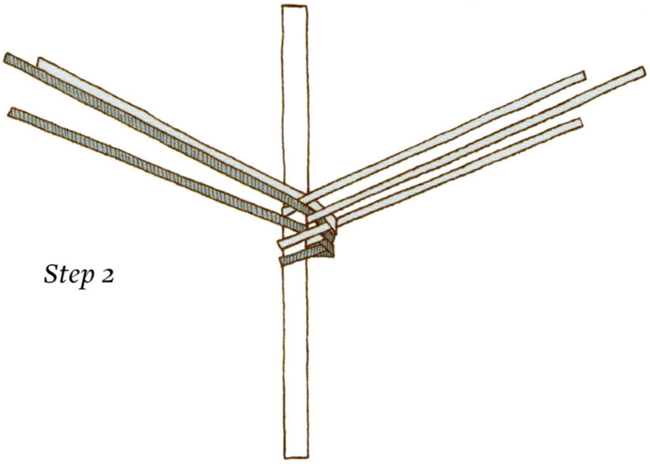

Step 2: The diagram shows three moves.

Add a new length, folding around the form so both ends point to the right.

Take the lowest right-hand end and fold it towards you at a point away from the right-hand edge of the form. It then passes diagonally to the left, over one and under two then in front of the form.

Note that both ends of this length are in front of the form.

There are two ends on the left and four ends to the right.

Take the lowest right-hand end and fold it diagonally over one, under two so it lays to the inside of the left-hand group.

There are three on the left and three on the right of the form.

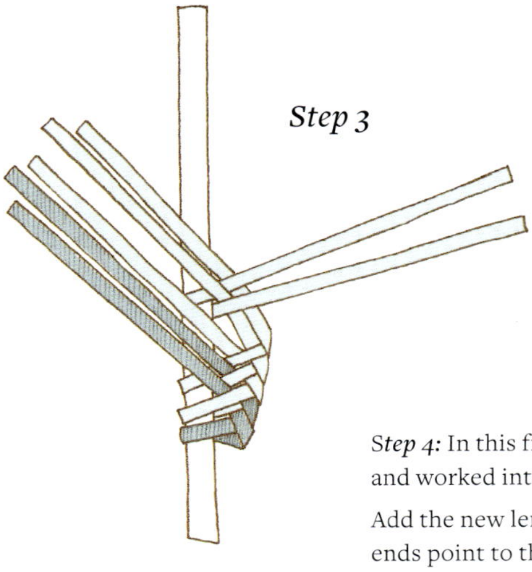

Step 3: The diagram shows three moves.

Add a new length, folding around the form so both ends point to the right.

Take the lowest right-hand end of the group and fold it diagonally towards the left passing over one and under two to lay to the inside of the left-hand group.

There are four ends on the left and four on the right.

Fold the lowest right-hand end diagonally over one, under two.

There are five on the left and three on the right.

Step 4: In this final step the last length is added and worked into the plait.

Add the new length, folding off centre so both ends point to the right. There are five ends in the right-hand group.

Take the lowest end of the right-hand group, fold it diagonally, over one, under two to lay to the inside of the left-hand group.

There are six ends on the left and four on the right of the form.

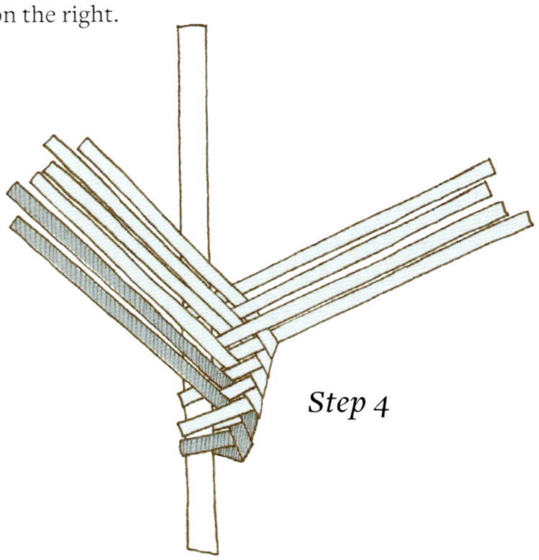

Working

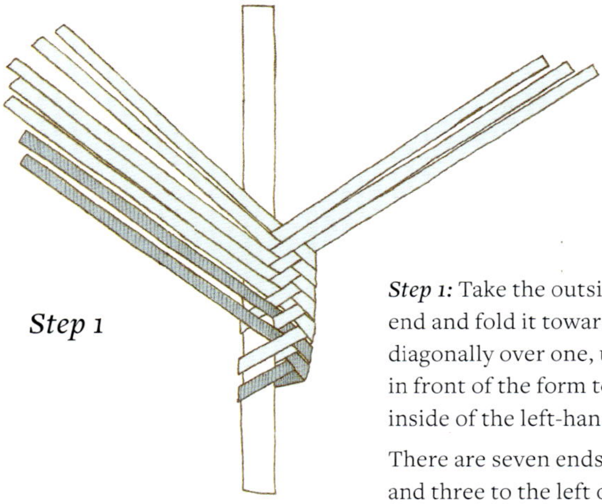

Step 1: Take the outside right-hand end and fold it towards you then diagonally over one, under two and in front of the form to lay to the inside of the left-hand group.

There are seven ends on the right and three to the left of the form.

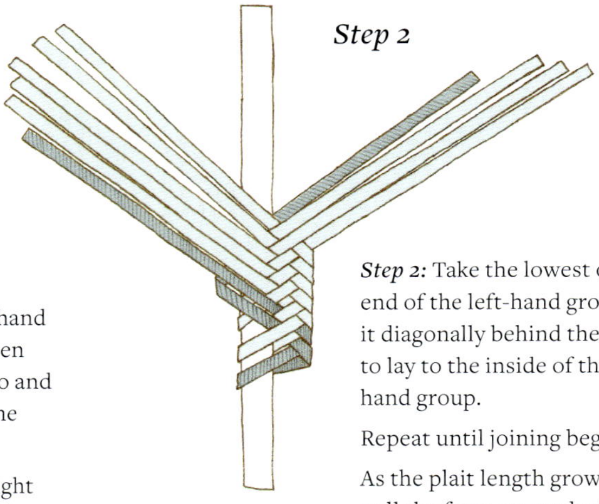

Step 2: Take the lowest outside end of the left-hand group fold it diagonally behind the form to lay to the inside of the right-hand group.

Repeat until joining begins.

As the plait length grows gently pull the form upwards through the plait.

The working sequence is:
Right: Over one, under two, in front of the form to lay inside the left-hand group.
Left: Fold backwards, behind the form to the inside of the right-hand group.

Joining

The end to be joined must be next to the outside end of the right-hand group. Make sure that the new end covers the old and ensure that the length matches the pattern. Space out the joins and avoid making them on consecutive stitches.

Eleven-end under plait

The original plait

Source: CTLC 2/70/61D

Origins: Near Florence, Italy

Production date: *c.* 1882

Type of straw: Wheat straw, whole

Splint width: 2 mm

Plait width: 8.5 mm

Plaiting direction: During working the back of the plait faces the maker and the front side faces away. The foot is on the right and the head on the left. When completed the front side of the plait has the head on the right and the foot on the left.

Joining: Along foot edge.

Background information: Writing in *Straw Hats,* Harry Inwards mentioned a range of fashionable Under Plaits. Differing from piping plaits in two ways, the direction of straws forming the head lay in a different direction and within the body of the plait there is an extra locking stitch not found in piping plaits. Inwards writes of the head being worked over a suitable template of bone, metal or any thin hard-wearing material which is removed leaving the "heads in the air".

What to use: Whole fine straws.

You need: Five plaiting lengths, each one a minimum 25 cm long.
One plaiting length minimum 25 cm long.
Additional shorter lengths for joining.
A form a little wider than the working ends and minimum 15 cm long.

Setting up

Step 1: The diagram shows three moves.

Hold the form vertically.

Take three lengths. In turn place each one behind the form. Fold each one off centre so the ends point to the right of the form.

Arrange and hold the ends in position so they are alternately behind and in front of the form as for the piping plaits.

There are six ends on the right.

Fold the lowest end, the one coming from behind the edge of the form, towards you then diagonally over one, under two over one then behind the form. The end now points to the left. For the diagonal end to cross correctly the fold must be made a short distance to the right of the form as shown.

Repeat folding the lowest right-hand end towards then diagonally over one, under two, over one then behind the form. It lays to the inside of the first left-hand end.

There are now two ends on the left and four on the right of the form.

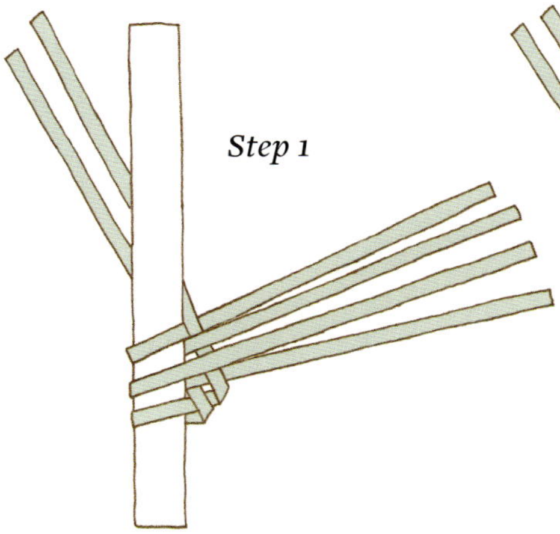

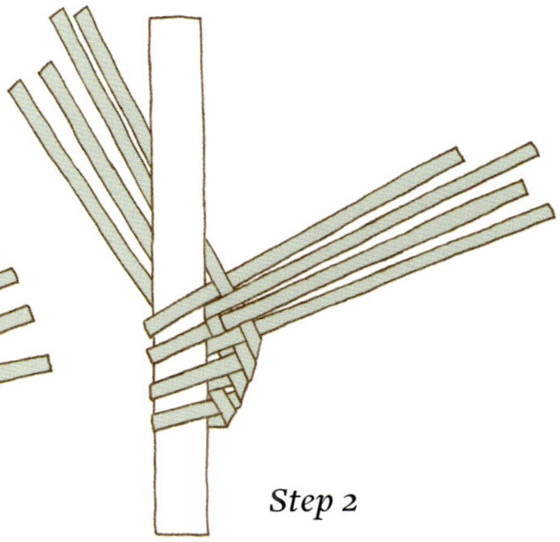

Step 2: The diagram shows three moves.

Add a new length, holding it behind the form, then fold the left-hand end to the right. Keep the section of the newly added length that comes from behind the form below that passing in front.

There are six ends on the right and two on the left.

Fold the lowest right-hand end towards you then diagonally over one, under two, over one then behind the form to lay to the inside of the two left-hand ends.

Repeat with the lowest end on the right, taking it over one, under two, over one, behind the form to lay to the inside of the left-hand group.

There are now four ends on the right and four on the left.

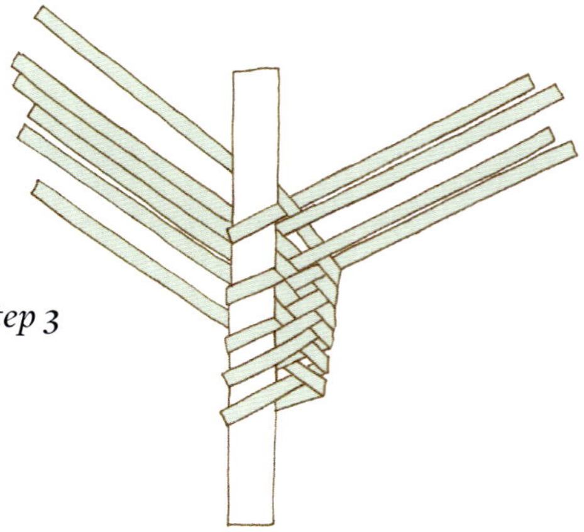

Step 3

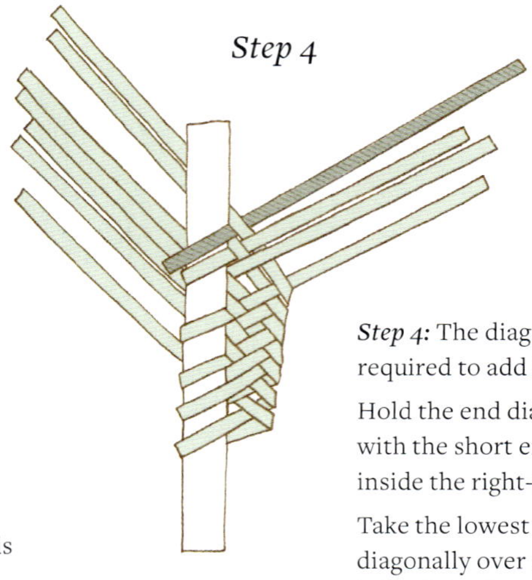

Step 4

Step 3: The diagram shows three moves.

Add a new length folding off centre as before so both ends point to the right.

Take the lowest right-hand end, fold it diagonally over one, under two, over one, then behind the form to lay to the inside of the left-hand group.

Repeat with the lowest right-hand end taking it over one, under two, over one then behind the form to lay to the inside of the left-hand group.

There are now four ends on the right and six on the left.

Step 4: The diagram shows the two moves required to add the eleventh working end.

Hold the end diagonally in front of the form with the short end to left and long end to inside the right-hand group.

Take the lowest right-hand end and fold it diagonally over one, under two, over one, behind the form to lay to inside the left-hand group.

There are now eleven working ends, four on the right and seven on the left of the form.

Working

As the working sequence continues the angle of the ends will gradually arrange themselves more accurately to form the pattern. The head can be created by simply folding the straw as it passes around the form, but the original patterns incorporated a twist. Use the left-hand edge of the form to provide a gentle resistance against the working end during the twisting move.

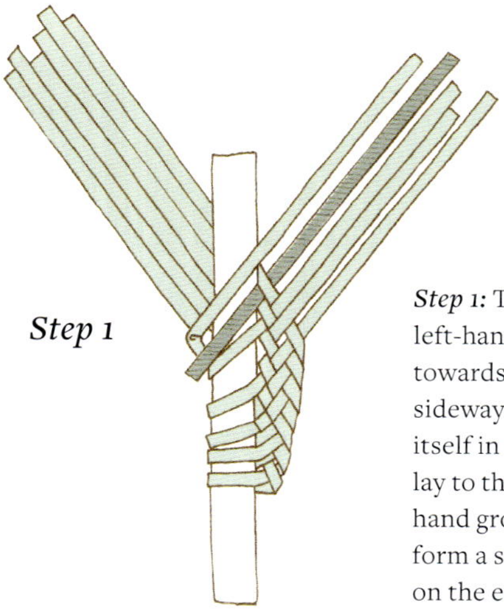

Step 1

Step 1: Take the lowest left-hand end, bring it towards you, then diagonally sideways without turning on itself in front of the form to lay to the inside of the right-hand group. The move will form a slightly raised crease on the edge.

There are five ends on the right and six to the left of the form.

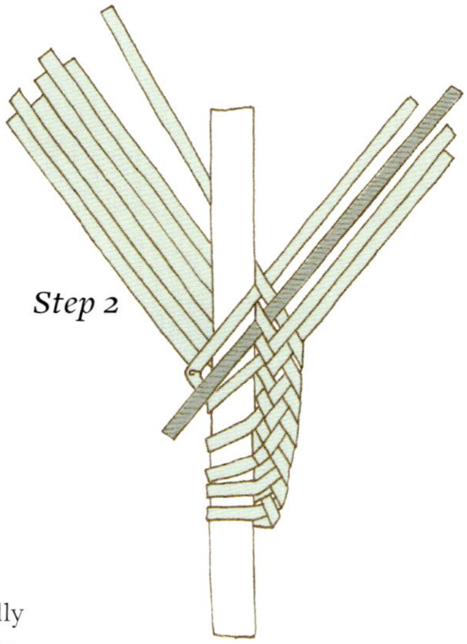

Step 2

Step 2: Take the lowest right-hand end fold it diagonally over one, under two, over one then behind the form to lay to inside the left-hand group.

There are four ends on the right and seven to the left of the form.

Continue the working moves until joining begins.

As the plait grows gently pull the form upwards. The finished plait will gradually come off the form.

The working sequence is:
Left: Towards then diagonally to create a twist to lay inside the right-hand group.
Right: Lowest end, over one, under two, over one, behind the form to lay inside the left-hand group.

Joining

Start joining as soon as possible and take care to space out the joins. Avoiding making joins on consecutive stitches.

The end to be joined must be next to the outside end of the right-hand group.

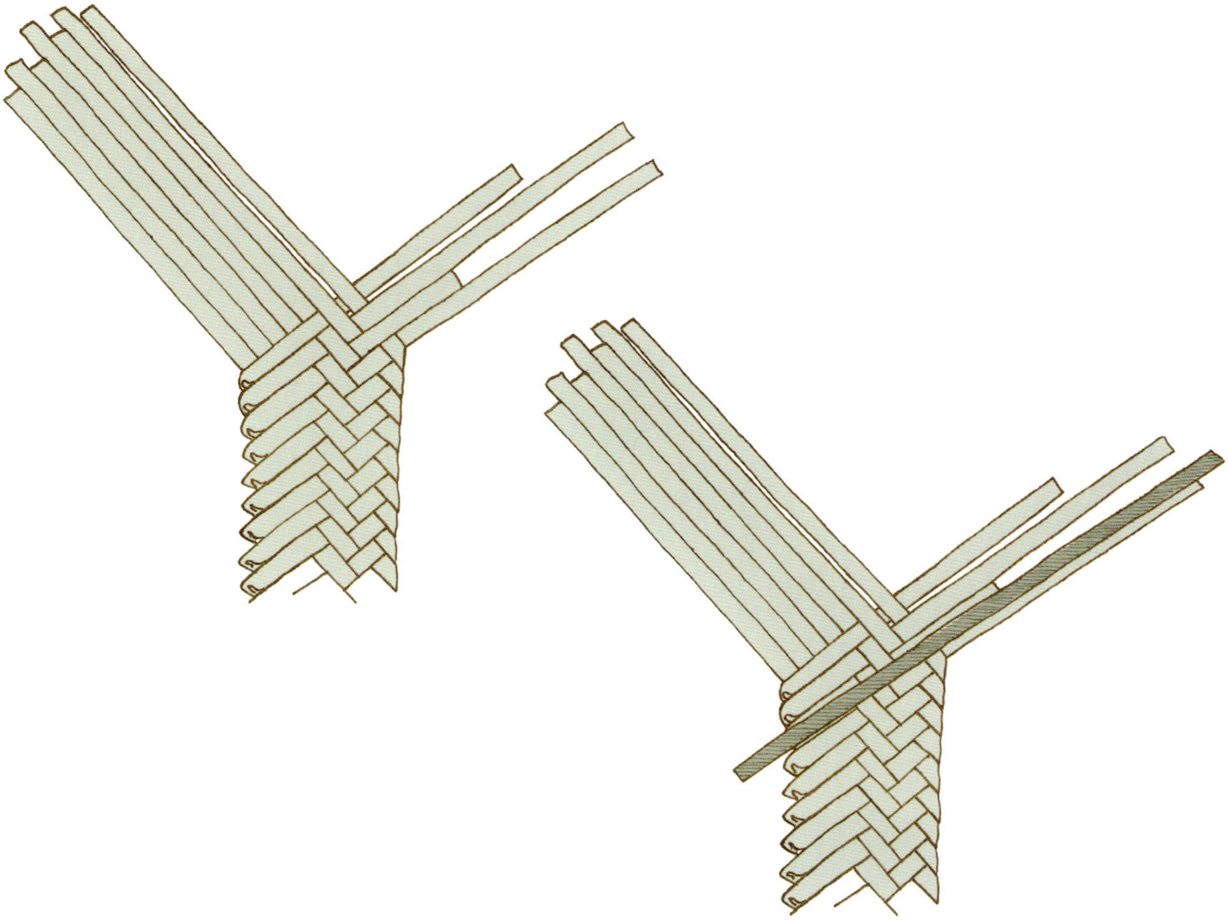

Seven-end porcupine plait

The original plait

Source: CTLC 1993/173/1A

Origins: Kimpton/Breachwood Green, Hertfordshire

Production date: 1880-1900

Type of straw: Wheat straw, whole

Splint width: 3 mm

Plait width: 19–20 mm

Plaiting direction: During working the back of the plait faces the maker and the front side faces away. The foot is on the right and the head on the left. When completed the front side of the plait has the head on the right and the foot on the left.

Joining: Along foot edge.

Background information: Thomas Hennell included a drawing of porcupine plait commissioned from a Hertfordshire straw plaiter in *Change in the Farm* published in 1933, however he did not name the village. These instructions are based on two surviving examples and when examining them, their unevenness may indicate they were made free hand. The head pattern can be worked around a form.

What to use: Whole straws.

You need: Four plaiting lengths.
Additional lengths for joining.
A form about 3 mm wide, 15 cm long.

Setting up

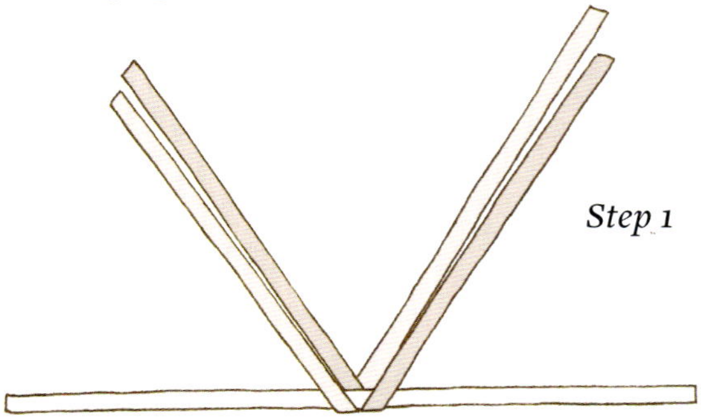

Step 1: The diagram shows five moves.

Hold one length horizontally, from 3 o'clock to 9 o'clock.

Take a new length and place it diagonally in front of the horizontal, making certain it is off centre. The end should point from approximately 2 o'clock to 8 o'clock.

Fold the 8 o'clock end diagonally upwards behind the horizontal length. It should lay at about 10 o'clock.

Take a new length and hold it diagonally behind the horizontal length to lay to the inside of the first right-hand diagonal. It will also lay at about 2 o'clock to 8 o'clock.

Fold the lower section, at 8 o'clock, diagonally upwards, in front of the horizontal length to lay to the outside of the left-hand diagonal.

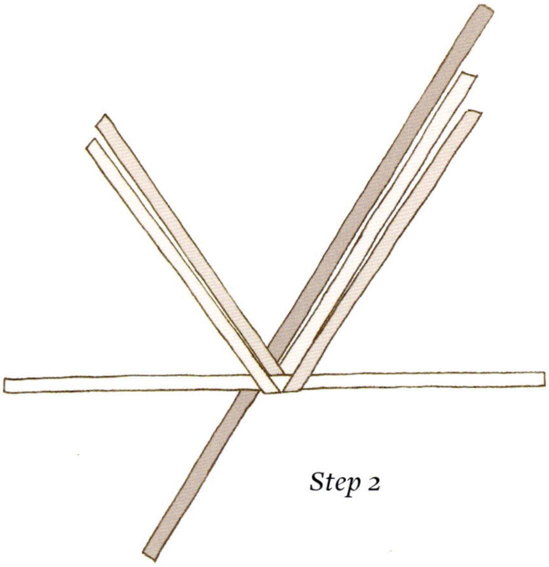

Step 2: Hold a new length diagonally off centre behind the horizontal to lay inside the two right-hand ends. Leave a short piece of the length protruding below the horizontal length.

Step 3

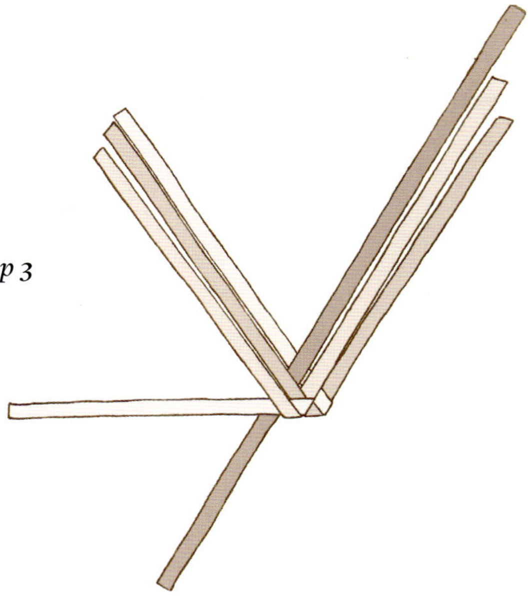

Step 3: Fold the right-hand horizontal end, that is at 3 o'clock, towards you then diagonally over one, under two. It now lays to the inside of the left-hand group.

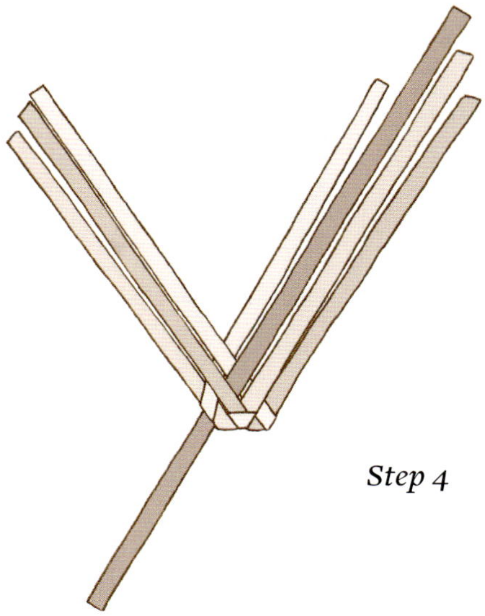

Step 4

Step 4: Fold the left-hand horizontal end, that is at 9 o'clock, towards you and then diagonally over one, under two. It now lays to the inside of the right-hand group.

There are four ends in the right-hand group and three ends in the left.

Working

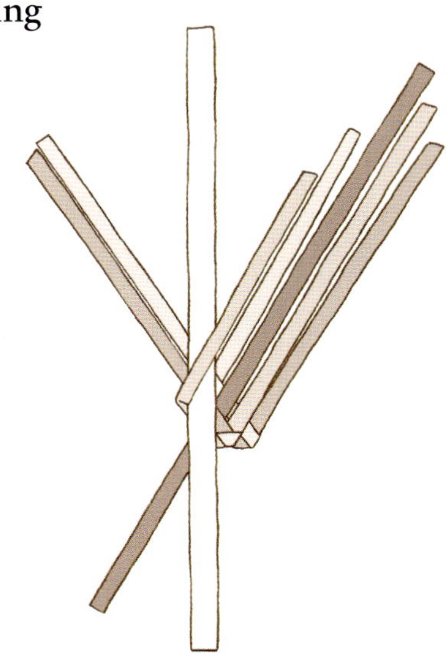

Step 1

Step 1: Hold the form in front of the plait, lining up the left-hand of the form to the left-hand edge of the plait.

Take the lowest end of the left-hand group and fold it towards you then diagonally in front of the form to lay to the inside of the left-hand group. As the end is moved hold the straw so it does not turn on itself, this will cause it to crease.

There are five ends in the right-hand group and two ends on the left

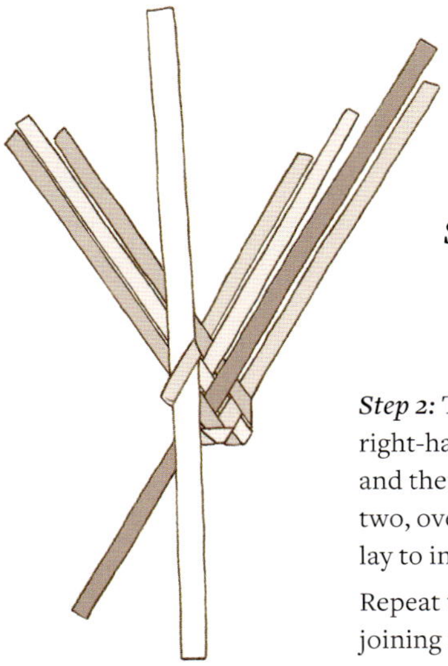

Step 2

Step 2: Take the lowest end of the right-hand group, fold it towards you and then diagonally, over one, under two, over one then behind the form to lay to inside the left-hand group.

Repeat the working sequence until joining is necessary.

The working sequence is:
Left: Lowest end, twist diagonally in front of the form to lay inside the right-hand group.
Right: Lowest end towards you then diagonally over one, under two, over one, behind the form to lay to the inside of the left-hand group.

Joining

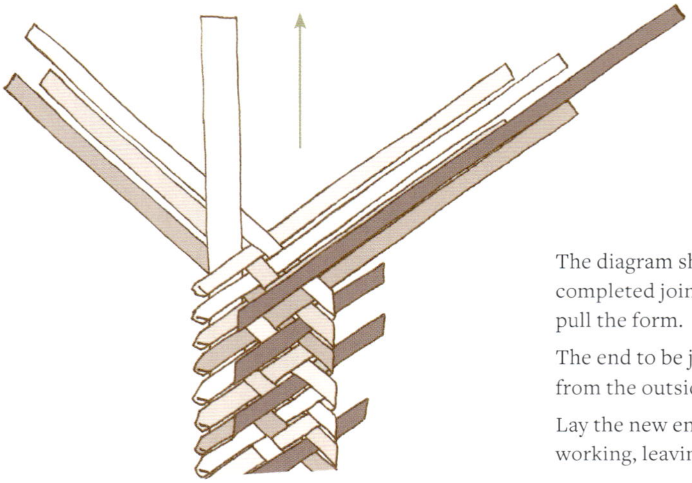

The diagram shows a sequence of several completed joins, and the direction to gently pull the form.

The end to be joined must be the second end from the outside of the right-hand group.

Lay the new end over the old and continue working, leaving the old end behind.

Plaiters worked to the strict requirements of the plait dealers. Commissioned plait had to be made to a specified size and the dealer would check using a micrometer or gauge. These gauges were also used to check imported plaits. The measurements are in millimetres. (CTLC X147, CTLC 1/42)

Plaited using colourful hemp tapes this bonnet dates to the 1880s and shows how a simple twist edge can be made to look spiked when made with a stiffer material. (CTLC 1999/76)

Created by Luton milliner Trudy Comfort. The plaits are a one-purl and seven-end plait made from machine-made hemp braid by Veronica Main.

Purl and Moss

These patterns were called head, notch, scallop, bead, rock or simply referred to the number of notches; one-purl, two-purl, and three-purl. One example made in Aldbury, Hertfordshire was called Lucy. In 2021, one-purl or notch plait was still being commercially made in China. To make a moss-edge pattern, a hair pin, a needle or wire is inserted along the head to create a line of raised loops rather than a characteristic scallop. The original examples shown in this section are made using double splints but can be made using whole straws or any flat plaiting material.

Seven-end purl, one head

The original plait

Source: CTLC 157/41

Origins: Bedfordshire

Production date: 1867 or 1878

Type of straw: Wheat straw, double splints

Splint width: less than 1 mm

Plait width: 4 mm

Plaiting direction: During working the back of the plait faces the maker and the front side faces away. The foot is on the right and the head on the left. When completed the front side of the plait has the head on the right and the foot on the left.

Joining: Speelless, into body or on foot edge.

Background information: The plait shown was exhibited at an exhibition in Paris either in 1867 or 1878 and was commissioned by a Dunstable hat manufacturer, Welch. The original example is described as "one purl speckled" which refers to the colour pattern created by the dyed splints. The purl can be worked once as explained in these instructions or repeated as described in variations.

What to use: This can be made with all types of straw.

You need: Four plaiting lengths.
Additional lengths for joining.

Setting up

Arrange so the ends are different lengths. The method of setting up is the same as that used to set-up a seven-end plait.

Step 1: Hold one length horizontally, from 9 o'clock to 3 o'clock.

Hold a second length diagonally in front of the horizontal length, pointing from about 2 o'clock to 8 o'clock.

Fold the lower end of this length behind the horizontal to lay at about 10 o'clock. Press the fold.

Take the third end. Hold it diagonally behind and to the inside of the diagonal right-hand end. Fold the lower section upwards to lay in front and to the outside of the left-hand diagonal. Press the fold.

Take the fourth end and place it behind the horizontal to lay inside the right-hand group. Leave a short length protruding from below the horizontal length.

Step 1

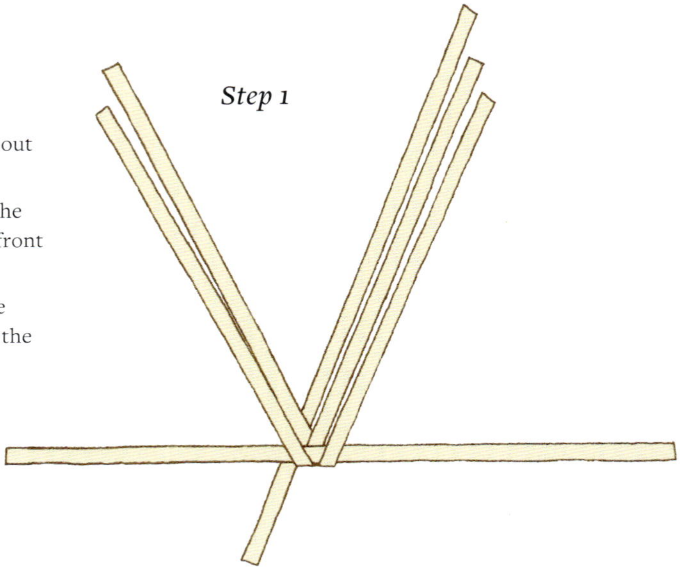

Step 2

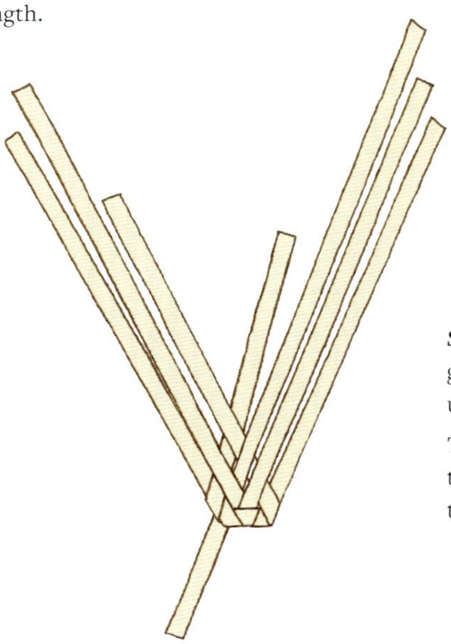

Step 2: Take the outside, lowest end of the right-hand group towards you then diagonally upwards, over one, under two. It lays to the inside of the left-hand group.

Take the outside, lowest end of the left-hand group towards you then diagonally upwards, over one, under two. It lays to the inside of the right-hand group.

Working

Step 1: Take the outside, lowest end of the right-hand group towards you then diagonally upwards, over one, under two. It lays to the inside of the left-hand group.

There are three ends on the right and four on the left.

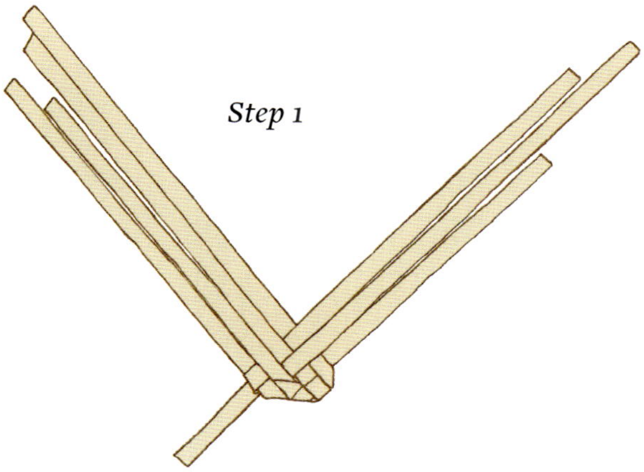

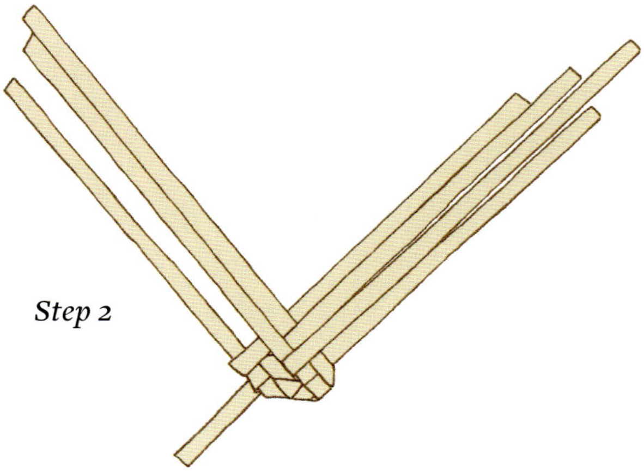

Step 2: In this move the outside end must be held firm to provide the support for formation of the notch stitch.

Hold the outside, lowest end of the left-hand group in place. This will act as the carrier for the notch.

The notch is made in one continuous move.

Take the second from outside end away from you out to the left, then twist it completely around the outside, carrier, end until it lays at the front of the plait.

Join it back into the body by taking it diagonally under the two remaining left-hand ends. It lays to the inside of the right-hand group.

Step 3: Take the outside, lowest end of the right-hand group towards you then diagonally upwards, over one, under two. It lays to the inside of the left-hand group.

There are three ends on the right and four on the left.

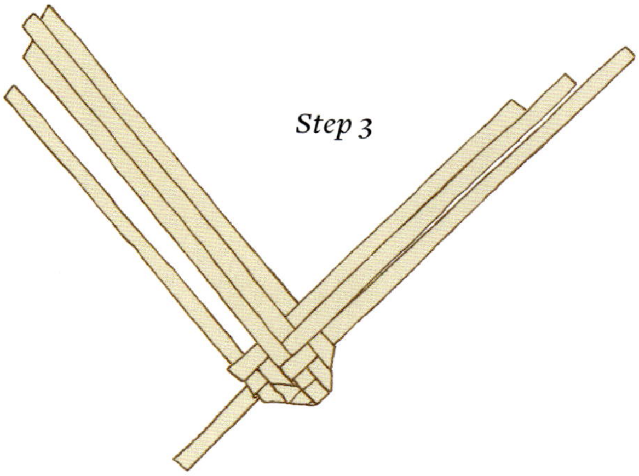

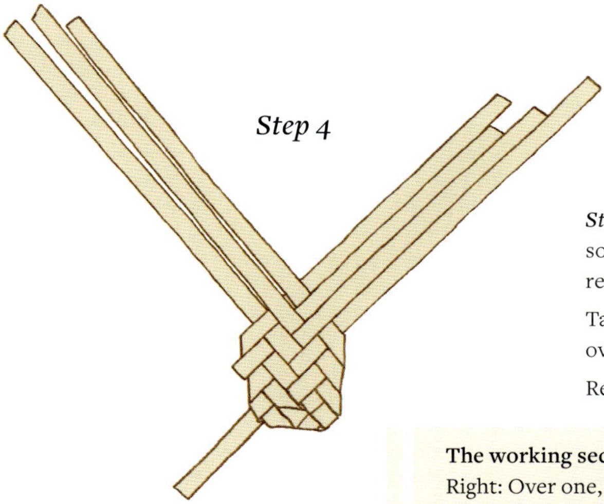

Step 4: In this move the carrier end is now secured into the body. In some extant examples of purl plait the end is turned on itself as it re-joins the body and in others it remains flat.

Take the outside left-hand end, the carrier, bring it towards you then over one, under two. It lays to the inside of the right-hand group.

Repeat until joining begins.

The working sequence is:
Right: Over one, under two
Left: Second from outside around the outside end, back into body, under two
Right: Over one, under two
Left: Outside carrier end back into the plait, over one, under two.

Joining

New ends can be added either along the foot, laying the new end over the second from outside end of the right-hand group, or by using a method called speelless joining. This places the join in the centre of the body. These instructions are for creating a speelless join.

The end to be joined must be the end laying to inside the left-hand group.

Insert the new end over the old, following the sequence, over one, under two.

Continue working, leaving the old end behind.

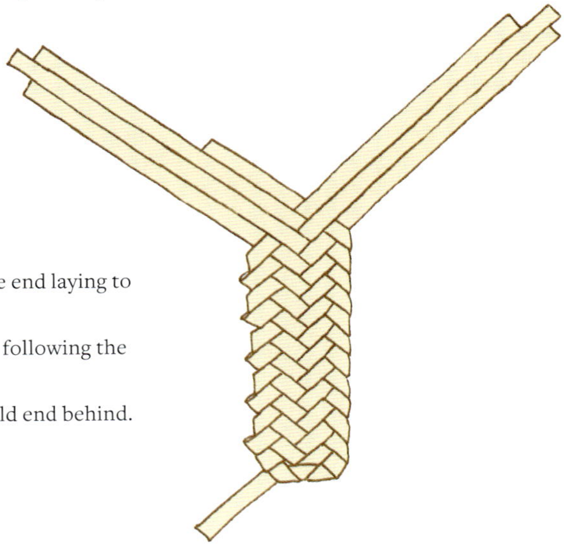

Variations

For a two-purl pattern make two notches before returning the outside carrier straw into the body. The example shown was made in Italy in 1882 using fine Italian straw and incorporates two dyed and five undyed ends. Set up so the dyed end forms the carrier end. (CTLC 2/70/61A)

This example was made in China in the early 1900s. It is unusual to find an example of this Chinese plait made with double splints as it is normally made from whole straws. (CTLC 14/31/41)

Seven-end moss-edge, three notch

The original plait

Source: CTLC 2/147/36

Origins: Essex

Production date: pre 1875

Type of straw: Wheat straw, double splints

Splint width: 1–1.5 mm

Plait width: 8 mm

Plaiting direction: During working the back of the plait faces the maker and the front side faces away. The foot is on the right and the head on the left. When completed the front side of the plait has the head on the right and the foot on the left.

Joining: Along foot edge.

Background information: While moss stitch plait was frequently mentioned in documentation very few known examples survive. Without precise provenance they may have been confused with purl patterns or over the years the notches may have become distorted making them unidentifiable. The moss edge is made around a hair pin or wire to create the loops. During the first few moves the pin can be difficult to control but once secured by previous stitches it becomes much easier.

What to use: This can be made with all types of straw.

You need: Long wire, hair pin or darning needle.
Four plaiting lengths.
Additional lengths for joining.

Setting up

Arrange so the ends are different lengths. The method of setting up is that used to set-up a seven-end plait.

The diagram shows several steps.

Hold one length horizontally, from 9 o'clock to 3 o'clock. Hold a second length diagonally in front of the horizontal length, pointing from about 2 o'clock to 8 o'clock.

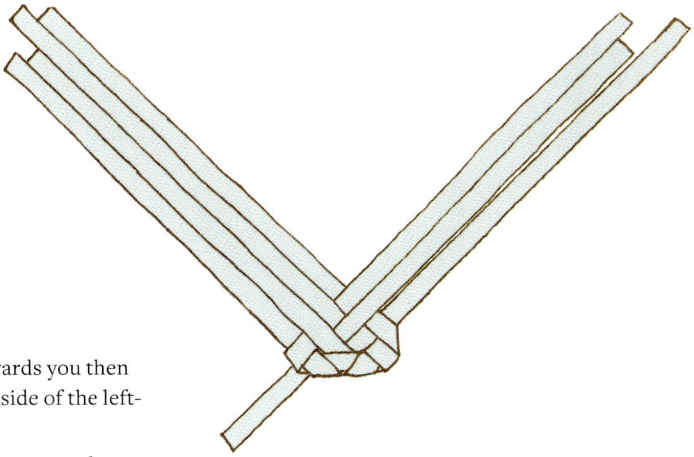

Fold the lower end of this length behind the horizontal to lay at about 10 o'clock. Press the fold.

Take the third end. Hold it diagonally behind and to the inside of the diagonal right-hand end. Fold the lower section upwards to lay in front and to the outside of the left-hand diagonal. Press the fold.

Take the fourth end and place it behind the horizontal to lay inside the right-hand group. Leave a short length protruding from below the horizontal length.

Take the outside, lowest end of the right-hand group towards you then diagonally upwards, over one, under two. It lays to the inside of the left-hand group.

Take the outside left-hand end and take it diagonally over one, under two so it lays to inside the right-hand group.

Take the outside right-hand end and move it over one, under two.

There are three ends on the right and four on the left.

Working

Hold the needle vertically alongside and slightly to the outside of the head. Hold the outside diagonal left-hand end in front of the needle. The remaining three ends of the left-hand group are also in front of the needle.

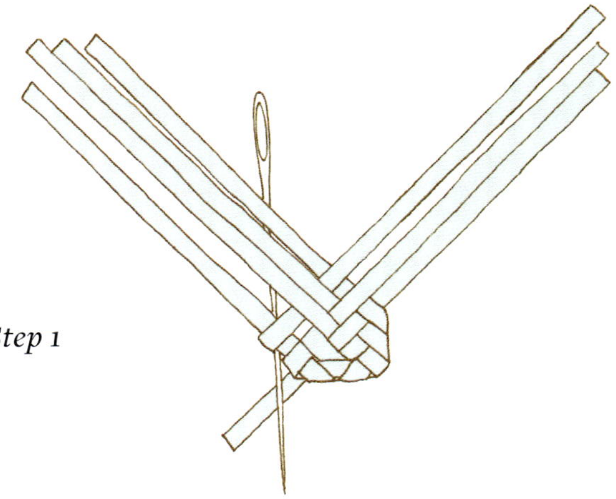

Step 1

Step 1: Take the second from outside end of the left-hand group away from you, behind the needle then twist it around the outside, carrier end and needle until it lays at the front of the plait.

Join it back into the body by taking it under the two remaining left-hand ends. It lays to the inside of the right-hand group.

Take the outside, lowest end of the right-hand group towards you then diagonally upwards, over one, under two. It lays to the inside of the left-hand group.

There are three ends on the right and four on the left.

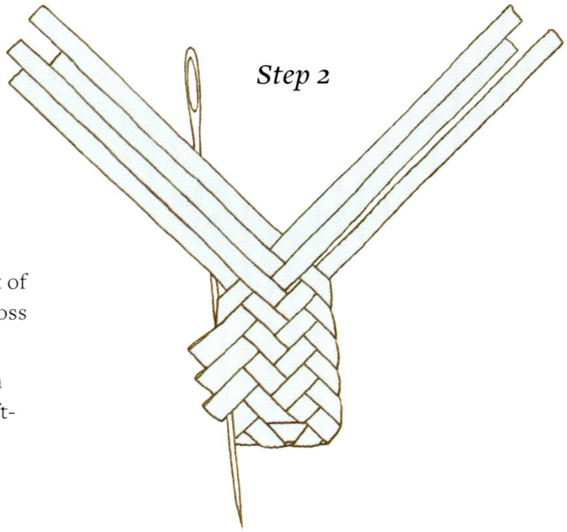

Step 2

Step 2: Repeat step one until three notches have been formed.

Now the carrier end is returned into the body.

Take the outside left-hand end bring it towards you, keeping it in front of the needle then take it diagonally over one, under two. It will slide across to the right of the needle and lay to the inside of the right-hand group.

Take the outside, lowest end of the right-hand group towards you then diagonally upwards, over one, under two. It lays to the inside of the left-hand group.

There are three ends on the right and four on the left.

Repeat until joining begins.

The working sequence is:
Right: Over one, under two.
Left: Second from outside end around the needle and back into the plait under two.
Right: Over one, under two
Repeat to make three notches
Left: Bring the carrier end back into the plait, in front of the needle, then over one, under two.

Joining

New ends can be added either along the foot, laying the new end over the second from outside end of the right-hand group, or by using speelless joining which places the join in the centre of the plait body. To make a speelless join the short end must be the end laying to the inside of the left-hand group.

Variations

As with purl plaits the number of notches, beads or loops created can be varied. The plait can be made with whole or split straw and coloured straw can be introduced. The size of the notch can be varied according to the thickness of the needle or wire used.

Seven-end buttonhole plait

The original plait

Source: CTLC Aldbury plait sample panel

Origins: Aldbury, Hertfordshire

Production date: *c.* 1913

Type of straw: Wheat straw, double splints

Splint width: 1 mm

Plait width: 11 mm

Plaiting direction: During working the back of the plait faces the maker and the front side faces away. The foot is on the right and the head on the left. When completed the front side of the plait has the head on the right and the foot on the left.

Joining: Along foot edge.

Background information: The village of Aldbury seems to have been a centre for making many versions of purl plait not recorded elsewhere. This plait is a basic three-notch plait however after the final notch is worked the carrier end is left out while three stitches are made along the head. This sequence creates a loop which does look like a buttonhole.

What to use: This can be made with all types of straw.

You need: Four plaiting lengths.
Additional lengths for joining.

Setting up

Arrange so the ends are different lengths. Use the method for setting up a seven-end plait.

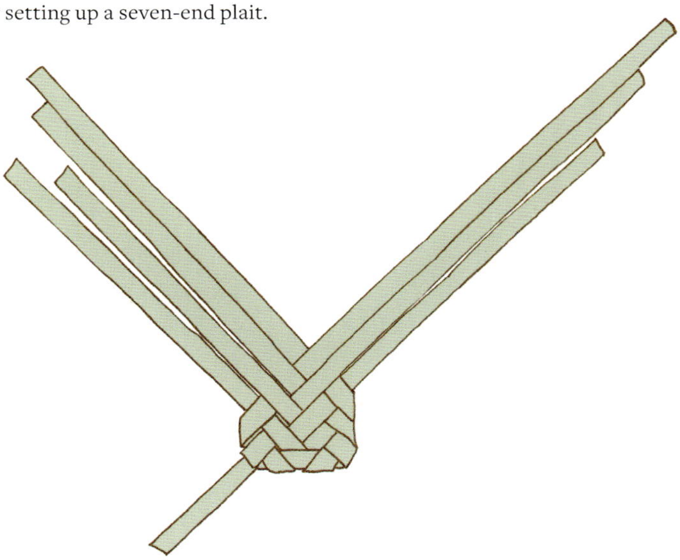

Hold one length horizontally, from 9 o'clock to 3 o'clock.

Hold a second length diagonally in front of the horizontal length, pointing from about 2 o'clock to 8 o'clock.

Fold the lower end of this length behind the horizontal to lay at about 10 o'clock. Press the fold.

Take the third end. Hold it diagonally behind and to the inside of the diagonal right-hand end. Fold the lower section upwards to lay in front and to the outside of the left-hand diagonal. Press the fold.

Take the fourth end and place it behind the horizontal to lay to inside the right-hand group. Leave a short length protruding from below the horizontal length.

Take the outside, lowest end of the right-hand group towards you then diagonally upwards, over one, under two. It lays to the inside of the left-hand group.

Take the outside, lowest end of the left-hand group towards you then diagonally upwards, over one, under two. It lays to the inside of the right-hand group.

Make another stitch on the right, then on the left and finally again on the right. There are three stitches on the foot and two on the head.

There are three ends in the right-hand group and four in the left.

Working

The working sequence begins by creating the first series of three notches along the head.

Step 1: In this move the outside left-hand end must be held firm to provide the support for the notches.

Hold the outside, lowest end of the left-hand group in place.

In one continuous move take the second from outside end away from you then out to the left. Twist it completely around the outside carrier end until it lays at the front of the plait.

Secure the notch by taking it under the two remaining left-hand ends. It lays to the inside of the right-hand group.

Take the outside, lowest end of the right-hand group towards you then diagonally upwards, over one, under two. It lays to the inside of the left-hand group.

There are three ends on the right and four on the left.

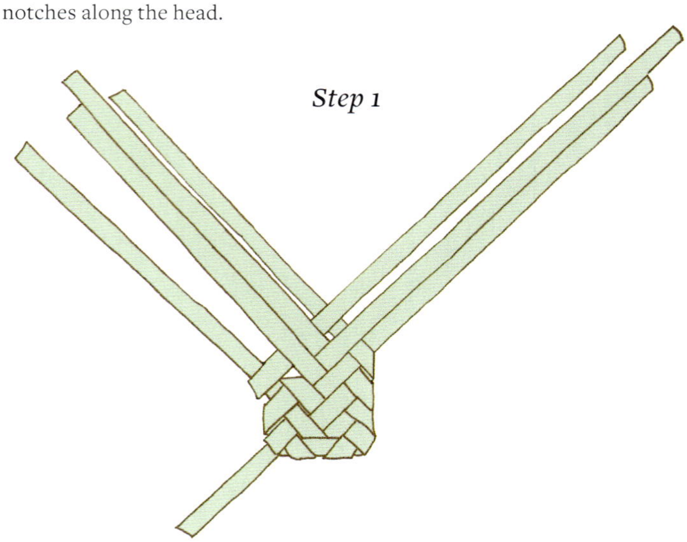
Step 1

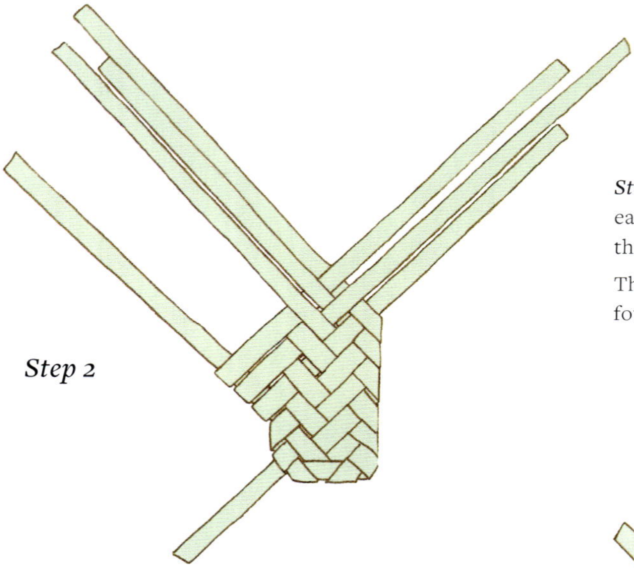
Step 2

Step 2: Repeat until there are three notches. After each left-hand move remember to make a move on the right, over one, under two.

There must always be three ends on the right and four on the left after a notch is made.

Step 3: Ignore the outside left-hand end that the notches were formed around.

Take the lowest of the group of three left-hand ends fold it away from you then diagonally behind the plait then under two, so it lays to inside the right-hand group.

On the right-hand edge make a stitch, over one, under two.

The fold must form a straight edge.

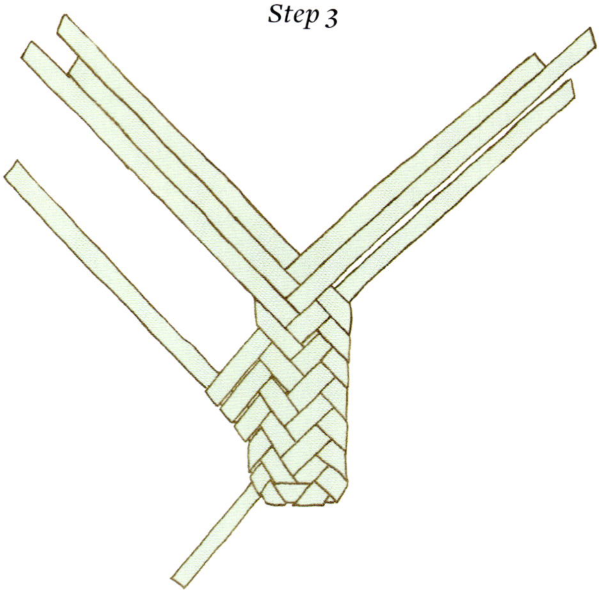
Step 3

Step 4: Repeat this step twice more, folding a left-hand end then making a right-hand move until there are three stitches along the head.

There are three ends in the right-hand group and four in the left-hand group.

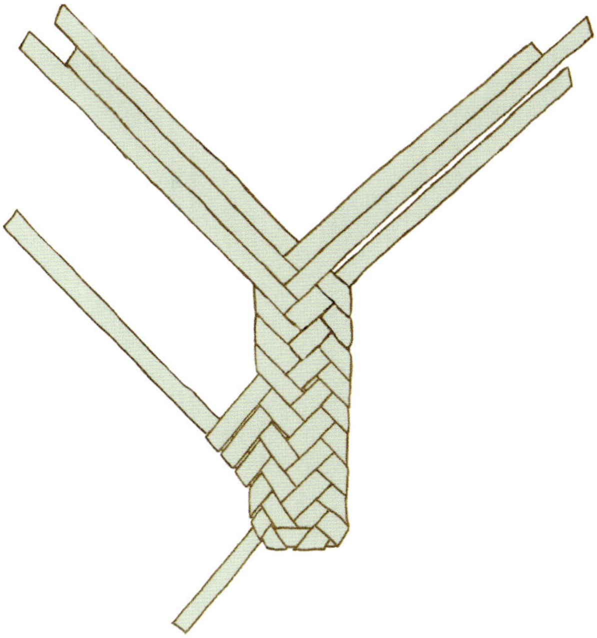

Step 4

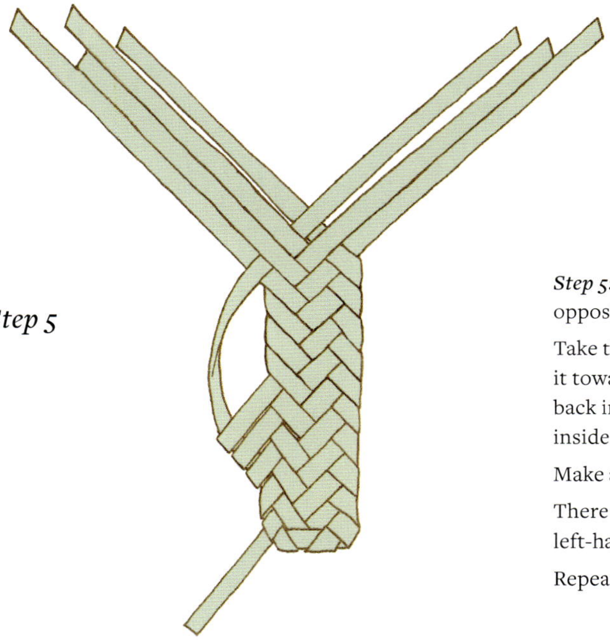

Step 5

Step 5: In this step the working end is turned on itself, so its opposite side faces upwards as it returns into the body.

Take the outside left-hand end that carries the notches. Bring it towards you then gently turn the end as it moves diagonally back into the body passing over one, under two. It lays to the inside of the right-hand group.

Make a stitch on the right, over one, under two.

There are three ends in the right-hand group and four in the left-hand group.

Repeat the working sequence until joining begins.

The working sequence is:
Right: Over one, under two
Left: Take the second from outside end around the outside end return it into the body, under two.
Right: Over one, under two
Repeat until there are three notches. There are four ends on the left and three on the right.
Repeat the sequence folding the lowest left-hand end until three stitches are formed.
Left: Take the outside carrier end back into the body, over one, under two.

Joining

This pattern is best joined along the foot edge. The end to be joined must be second from the outside of the right-hand group. Insert the new end, following the sequence, over one, under two so the long end lays over the old. Continue working, leaving the old end behind.

Nine-end purl loop

The original plait

Source: CTLC Aldbury plait sample panel

Origins: Aldbury, Hertfordshire

Production date: *c.* 1913

Type of straw: Wheat straw, double splints

Splint width: 2 mm

Plait width: 12 mm

Plaiting direction: During working the back of the plait faces the maker and the front side faces away. The foot is on the right and the head on the left. When completed the front side of the plait has the head on the right and the foot on the left.

Joining: Along foot edge.

Background information: In this striking variation also made in Aldbury, a single stitch has been added to the head after the notch is made and before the carrier end returns into the body. This plait can be made with other numbers of notches or with an extra stitch to create a longer loop. The instructions given are for recreating this colourway, but it can be made with undyed straw or with whole straws.

What to use: This can be made with all types of straw.

You need: Five plaiting lengths. Two dyed and three undyed lengths comprising pairs of splints faced shiny side outwards.
Additional lengths for joining.

Setting up

To create this colourway the fifth length is added after the first moves have been made each side. It is inserted so it lays diagonally pointing from 5 o'clock to 11 o'clock to inside the left-hand group. It is important to arrange the lengths so the working ends are different lengths.

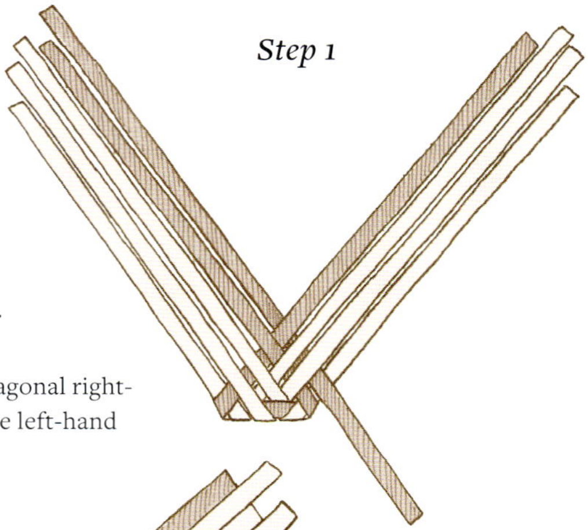

Step 1

Step 1: Hold one dyed length horizontally, from 9 o'clock to 3 o'clock.

Hold a second undyed length diagonally in front of the horizontal length, pointing from about 1 o'clock to 7 o'clock.

Fold the lower end of this length behind the horizontal to lay at about 11 o'clock. Press the fold.

Take a third undyed length. Hold it diagonally behind and to the inside of the diagonal right-hand end. Fold the lower section upwards to lay in front and to the outside of the left-hand diagonal. Press the fold.

Take a fourth undyed length and hold it diagonally behind and to the inside of the diagonal right-hand ends. Fold the lower section upwards to lay in front and to the outside of the left-hand diagonal. Press the fold.

Take the outside, lowest end of the right-hand group towards you then diagonally upwards, over one, under two. It lays to the inside of the left-hand group.

Take the outside, lowest end of the left-hand group towards you then diagonally upwards, over one, under three. It lays to the inside of the right-hand group.

Insert the fifth end placing it diagonally towards the left. It passes over one, under three to lay to inside the left-hand group. Leave a short length protruding from below the horizontal length.

There are four ends to the right and five ends to the left.

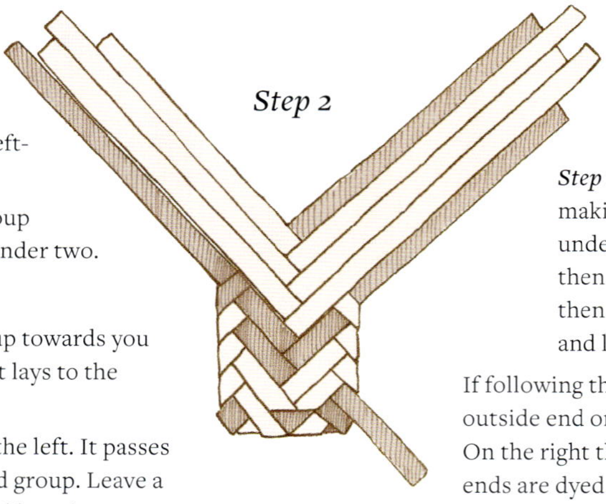

Step 2

Step 2: Lock in the ends by making another over one, under three moves on the left, then on the right, the left and then twice more on the right and left.

If following the colour pattern, the outside end on the left is the dyed end. On the right the outside and inside ends are dyed.

There are five ends in the right-hand group and four in the left-hand group.

Working

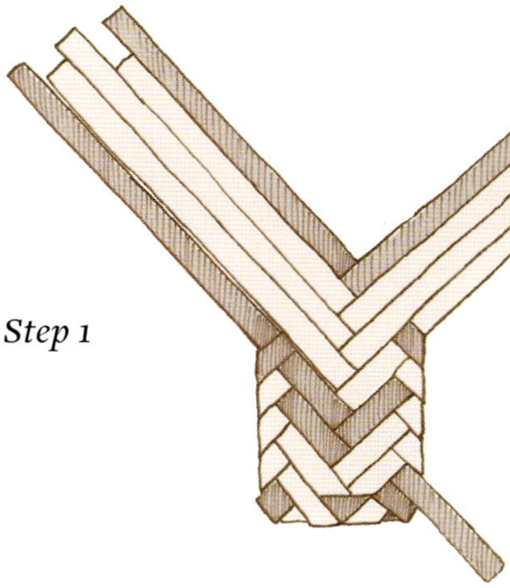

Step 1

Step 1: Take the outside, lowest end of the right-hand group towards you then diagonally upwards, over one, under three. It lays to the inside of the left-hand group.

There are four ends on the right and five on the left.

The working sequence is:
Right: Over one, under three
Left: Second from outside around the outside, back in under three.
Right: Over one, under three
Left: Second from outside around the outside, back in under three.
Right: Over one, under three
Left: Fold the second from outside end diagonally under to lay inside the right-hand group.
Right: Over one, under three
Left: Bring the carrier back into the body, over one, under three.

Joining

New ends can be added either along the foot, laying the new end over the second from outside end of the right-hand group, or by using speelless joining (see page 288).

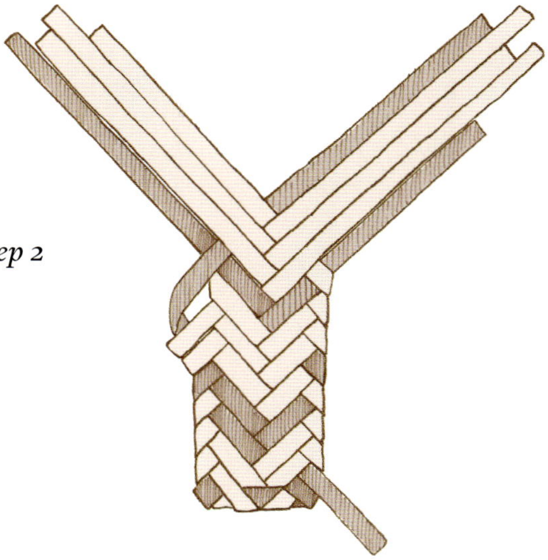

Step 2

Step 2: The diagram shows the completed pattern.

Create the first notch.

Hold the outside, lowest end of the left-hand group in place. If you are following the colourway then this will be a dyed end and will act as the carrier for the stitches.

Take the second from outside end away from you then twist it completely around the carrier end until it lays at the front of the plait.

Join it back into the body by taking it under the three remaining left-hand ends. It lays to the inside of the right-hand group.

Make a right-hand move, over one, under three.

There are four ends on the left and five ends on the right.

Create the second notch.

Take the second from outside end away from you then twist it completely around the carrier end until it lays at the front of the plait.

Join it back into the body by taking it under the three remaining left-hand ends.

Make a right-hand end move over one, under three.

Make the spacing stitch on the left.

Take the second end from the outside under three, the carrier is the outside end.

Make a right-hand end move over one, under three.

Next bring the carrier end back into the group.

Take the outside end diagonally over one, under three. There are five ends to the right and four to the left.

Continue the working sequence until joining is required.

Variation

This rare example of a four-purl plait was made in Buckinghamshire. It is 22 mm wide. Recorded as an imitation plait which may have been assigned by Thomas Bagshawe who applies the term to some double splint plaits. (CTLC 4/284/32)

Eleven-end purl Coburg

The original plait

Source: CTLC 4/284/32

Origins: Buckinghamshire

Production date: Late 1800s, early 1900s

Type of straw: Wheat straw, whole or Italian grasses

Splint width: 2 mm

Plait width: 12 mm

Plaiting direction: During working the back of the plait faces the maker and the front side faces away. The foot is on the right and the head on the left. When completed the front side of the plait has the head on the right and the foot on the left.

Joining: Along foot edge.

Background information: The name Coburg may refer to the British Royal family, or it may indicate that the pattern originated in Germany. The latter suggestion is less likely since Coburg is some distance from currently known German plaiting areas, but perhaps more information about the German industry awaits discovery. A two-purl edge is added to a body of an eleven-end twill pattern and new ends set in every third move.

What to use: This can be made with all types of straw.

You need: Six plaiting lengths.
Additional lengths for joining.

Setting up

The setting up begins in the same way as for an eleven-end plait using the folding method, pages 175–6.

Step 1: The diagram shows the completed setting up process.

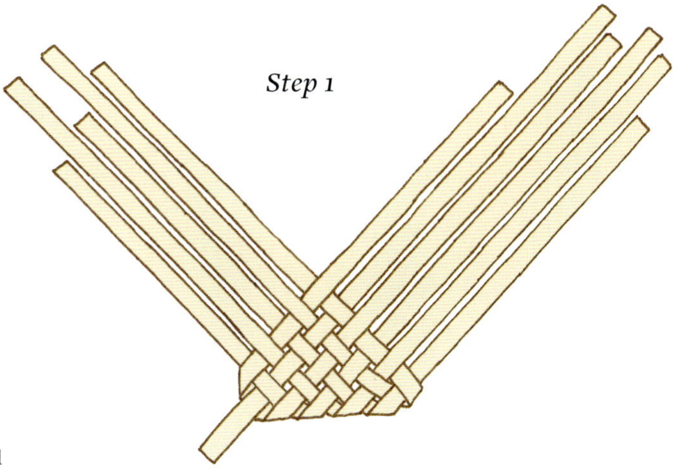

Take five of the lengths and arrange side by side horizontally, their ends pointing nine o'clock to three o'clock.

Insert the sixth length diagonally long end pointing to 11 o'clock and the short protruding length below the horizontal lengths to 5 o'clock. The long end passes over the lowest length then under, over, under, over the remaining horizontal lengths.

Adjust the diagonal length so it crosses slightly off centre. Arrange the horizontals, so the ends are different lengths.

Take the right-hand end of the lowest length, the one next to the diagonal. Fold it upwards, towards you, then diagonally over the next, then under, over, under through the rest of the group until it lays parallel to the right of the diagonal length.

Take the new lowest end and repeat, taking it over, under so it lays to the right of the two diagonals. Repeat these moves until four of the five right-hand ends lay diagonally to the left.

There is one horizontal end on the right.

Take the remaining right-hand horizontal end, fold it upwards and then horizontally over, under, over, under, over through the left-hand diagonals. It now lays parallel to the top horizontal left-hand group.

Take the lowest end of the left-hand horizontal group. Fold it towards you then diagonally over, under, over, under, over through the other ends of the group. It now lays parallel to the left of the diagonal group.

There are now six ends in the diagonal group and five ends in the horizontal group.

Rotate the plait so the two groups lay at about 10 and 2 o'clock.

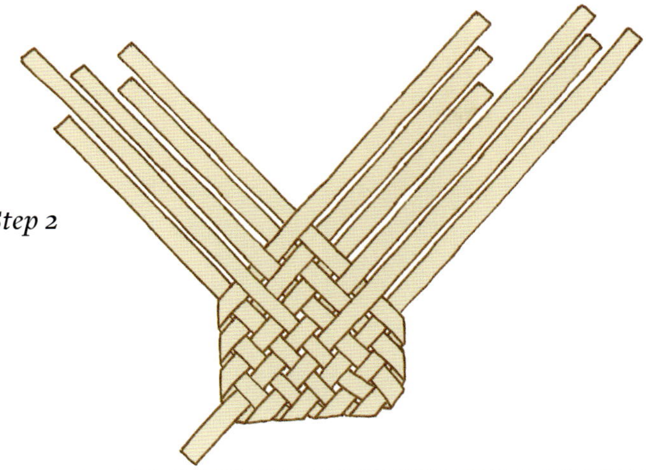

Step 2

Step 2: Fold the outside right-hand end diagonally over one, under two, over two. It lays to inside the left-hand group.

Fold the outside left-hand end diagonally over one, under two, over two. It lays to inside the right-hand group.

Repeat on the right and then on the left. There are six ends in the right-hand group and five in the left-hand group.

Working

Step 1: Fold the outside right-hand end, over one, under two, over two.

Make the first notch on the head edge.

Take the second from outside end, curling it away from you then out to the left and around the outside end so it lays in front of the plait. Now pass the end under two, over two. It lays to inside the right-hand group.

Repeat these two moves once more to make the second notch.

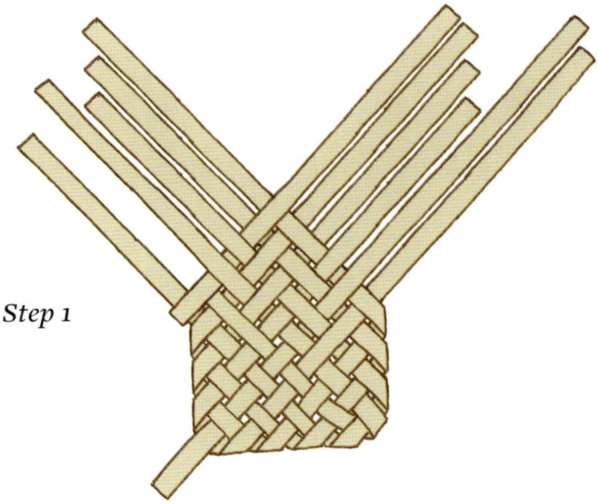

Step 1

Step 2

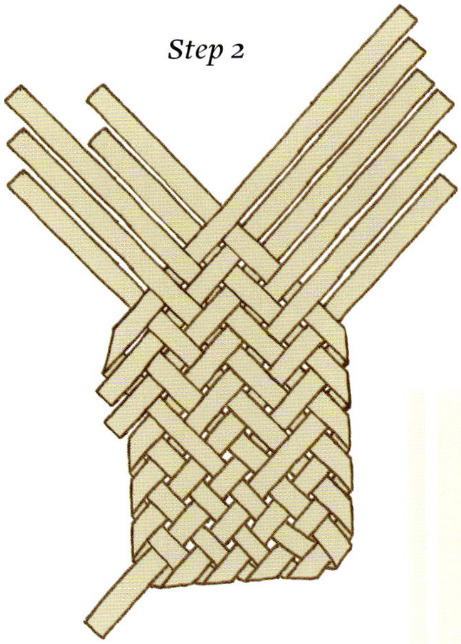

Step 2: Fold the outside right-hand end, over one, under two, over two.

Now bring the carrier end back into the group.

Take the outside end and fold it over one, under two, over two so it lays to the inside of the right-hand group. In this pattern the end returns into the body without any gap.

Repeat from working step 1 until joining is required.

The working sequence is:
Right: Over one, under two, over two.
Left: Second from outside around the carrier, back into body, under two, over two.
Right: Over one, under two, over two.
Left: Second from outside around the carrier, back into body, under two, over two.
Right: Over two, under two, over two.
Left: Carrier end back into body, over one, under two.

Joining

Join along the foot edge. The end to be joined must be the second from the outside end of the right-hand group. Lay the new end over the old leaving a short length protruding.

Willow basket finished with home grown bamboo made by Hilary Burns MBE. Her original design incorporates a variation of a five-end Vandyke plait made by Veronica Main using willow skein.

Batwing or Vandyke

Commonly found in plait sample books associated with Germany, Italy, Switzerland from the 1860s onwards, their popularity in the 1880s may have been due to the influence of Japanese imports. The name batwing, sometimes written as batswing, appeared later in the 1800s and the pattern may still be commercially made in China today. Patterns in this section offer opportunities to use other plaiting materials and for mixing narrow and wide plaiting lengths.

Five-end Vandyke

The replica plait

Source: Original instructions in Second Course of Straw and Chip Plaiting

Origins: Unknown

Production date: pre 1895

Type of straw: Wheat straw, whole or chip

Splint width: 3 mm and 5 mm

Plait width: 23 mm

Plaiting direction: During working the front of the plait faces the maker. The head is on the right and the foot on the left.

Joining: Along foot edge.

Background information: This was the first pattern in the *Second Course of English Straw and Chip Plaiting* book. The instructions are for using wide and narrow plaiting lengths of chip with one coloured length to provide an accent. The reproduction is made with willow skein and a narrow whole wheat straw. To faithfully recreate the pattern these instructions follow the method given in the original instruction book.

What to use: Best made with flat plaiting materials. The original pattern used four wide strips of chip and one of thin strip of chip.

You need: Five plaiting lengths.
Additional lengths for joining.

Setting up

Step 1: Take two lengths, close to their ends and with the long section of each pointing to about 10 o'clock and 2 o'clock respectively, cross left over right.

Take the long end of the right-hand length, fold it towards you and downwards, over the front of the left-hand diagonal at the point where they cross so it lays at about 6 o'clock. Immediately fold the same end up behind the crossover point and then diagonally to the right, back into its 2 o'clock position.

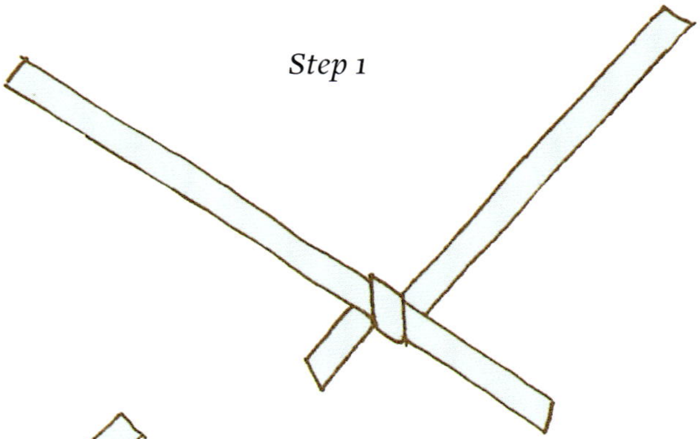

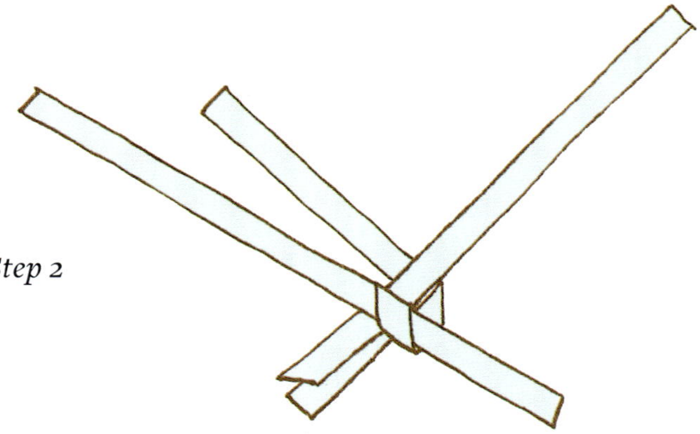

Step 2: Add a third length, placing it behind the crossover and with the long end pointing to the right. It lays inside the first right-hand end.

Take the outside right-hand end under one to lay diagonally to inside the left-hand long end.

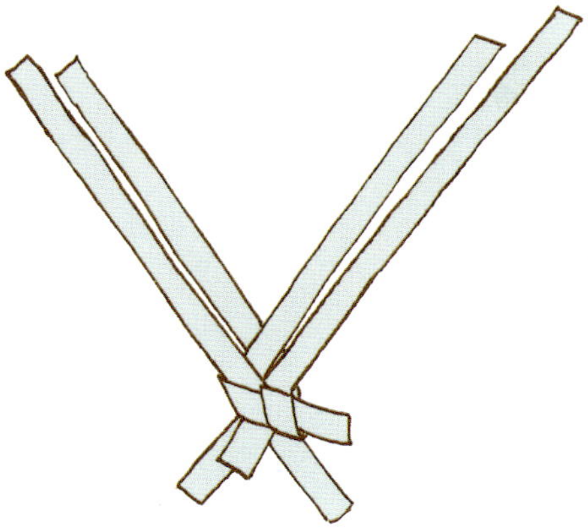

Step 3

Step 3: Insert a fourth end on the left, behind the crossover and in between the two existing left-hand ends.

Take the outside end under one, over one. There are two ends on the right and two on the left.

Step 4: Placing it behind the group, insert the thin whole straw in between the two diagonal right-hand ends. Take the outside right-hand end diagonally under one, over one to lay to inside the left-hand group. There are two ends on the right and three on the left.

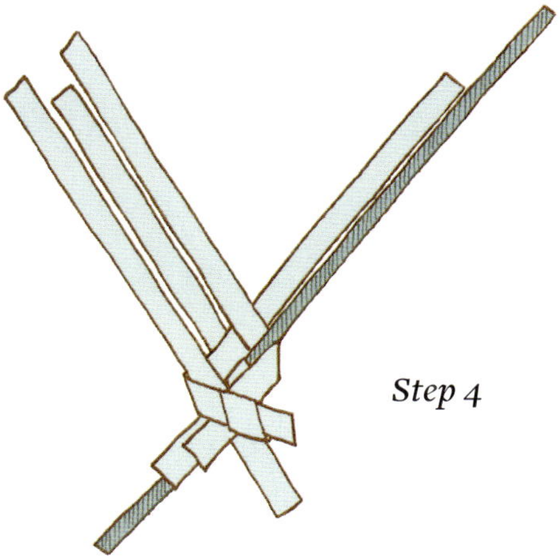

Step 4

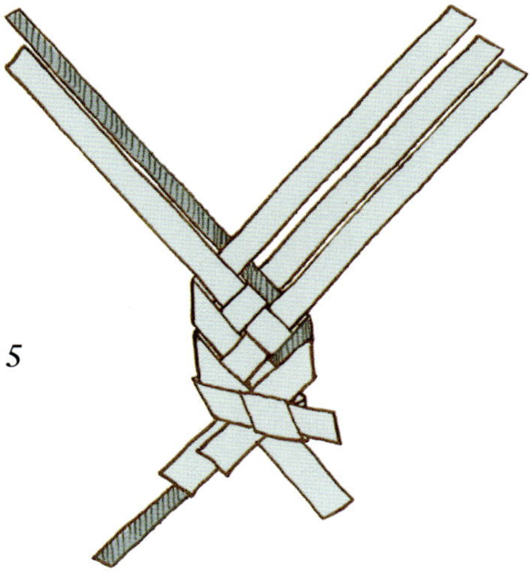

Step 5

Step 5: The diagram shows three steps.

Take the outside left-hand end, move it diagonally under one, over one to lay inside the right-hand group.

Take the outside right-hand end diagonally under one, over one.

Take the outside left-hand end under one, over one.

There are three wide ends on the right and two on the left. The dyed, thin single end is the inside end of the left-hand group, and the wide one is outside.

Working

Step 1: This move creates the first stitch of the Vandyke point.

Hold the outside right-hand end in place. Take the middle end of the right-hand group and fold it towards you, diagonally downwards and outwards to point to about 4 o'clock. Now roll it behind the outside end and diagonally to the left, passing it over one. It lays to inside the left-hand group.

Take the outside left-hand end diagonally under one, over one to lay inside the right-hand group.

There are three ends on the right and two on the left.

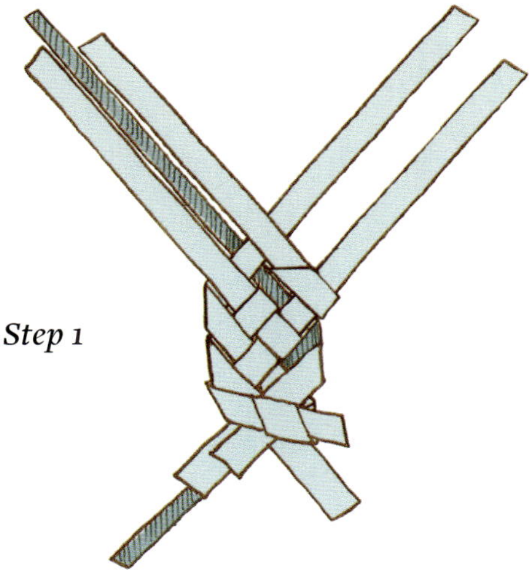

Step 1

Step 2

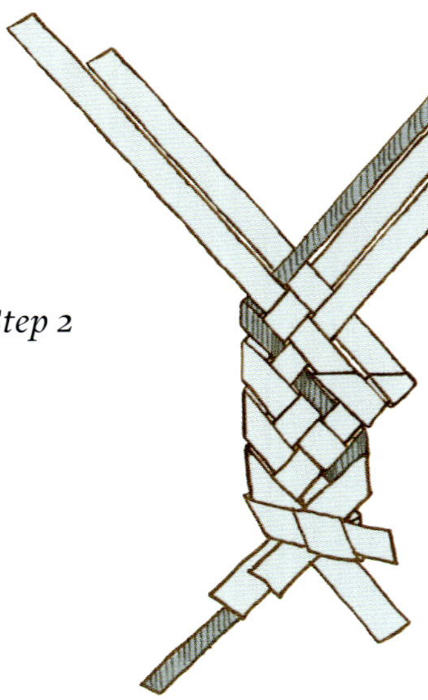

Step 2: This move completes the point. Take the outside right-hand end and roll it towards you, diagonally downwards and outwards towards 4 o'clock. Roll it behind itself and diagonally towards the left. Adjust so it forms a tight point.

Take the end under one, over one so it lays to inside the left-hand group. Take the outside left-hand end, under one, over one.

Step 3

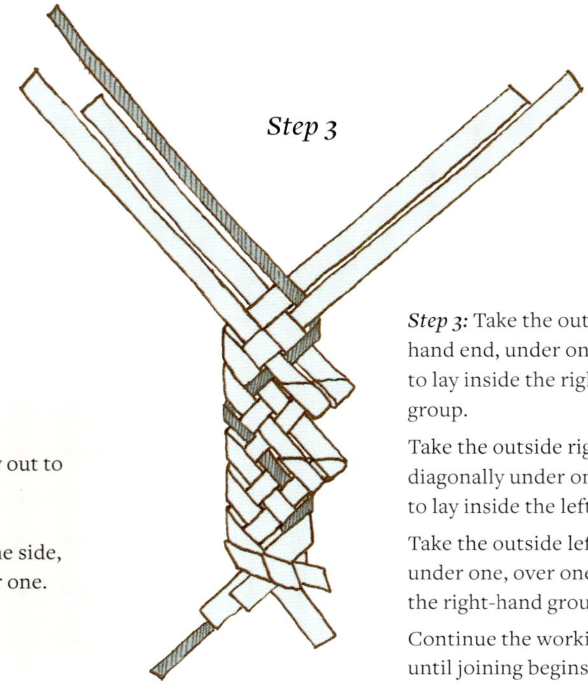

The working sequence is:
Right: Second from outside, towards you, diagonally out to the side, roll around, back into the body over one.
Left: Under one, over one
Right: Outside end towards you, diagonally out to the side, roll it to create a tight point, back into the body over one.
Right: Narrow end, under one, over one.
Left: Under one, over one.

Step 3: Take the outside left-hand end, under one, over one, to lay inside the right-hand group.

Take the outside right-hand end diagonally under one, over one to lay inside the left-hand group.

Take the outside left-hand end under one, over one to lay inside the right-hand group.

Continue the working sequence until joining begins.

Joining

Joins are made on the foot edge which is on the left. The short end to be joined is the inside end of the right-hand group and the new end is inserted after the final move with the old end.

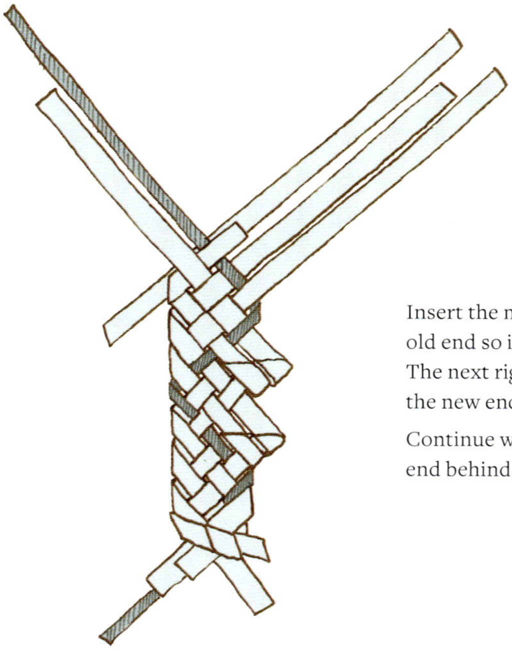

Insert the new length under the short old end so it continues the pattern. The next right-hand move locks in the new end.

Continue working leaving the old end behind.

Seven-end split straw Vandyke

The original plait

Source: CTLC 1997/17/2

Origins: Possibly canton Fribourg, Switzerland

Production date: 1864

Type of straw: Wheat straw, double splints

Splint width: 1–1.5 mm

Plait width: 12 mm

Plaiting direction: During working the front of the plait faces the maker. The head is on the right and the foot on the left.

Joining: Along foot edge.

Background information: This plait may have first been made in Switzerland in 1864 where sample books included vibrant colourways that showed off the newly introduced chemical dyes. The original plait was made with pairs of splints faced undyed to dyed so to create this specific pattern, the splints must be twisted along the foot. This creates a ridge, however, but if the straw is sufficiently soft it does not create problems when stitched together by overlapping.

What to use: This can be made with all types of straw.

You need: Four plaiting lengths of double splints each pair faced undyed to dyed.
Additional lengths for joining.

Setting up

Damp the lengths and pair an undyed to a dyed length. The damping will hold them together.

Step 1: The diagram shows all stages for setting up. To create the original plait's characteristic pattern the pairs of splints must be positioned as indicated with all the dyed splints facing.

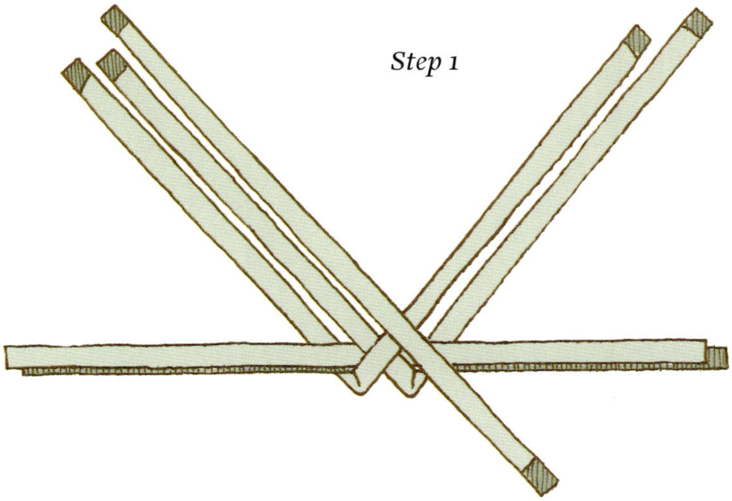

Hold one pair of splints horizontally, from 9 o'clock to 3 o'clock. Just off centre, the dyed side is facing.

Hold a second pair diagonally behind the horizontal length, pointing from about 2 o'clock to 8 o'clock. The dyed splint must be facing.

Fold the lower end of this pair in front of the horizontal to lay at about 10 o'clock. Twist the left-hand diagonal pair so the dyed splint is facing. Press the fold.

Take the third pair. Hold diagonally in front of the horizontal, with the dyed side facing to the inside of the diagonal right-hand end.

Fold the lower section upwards and behind the horizontal to lay to the outside of the left-hand diagonal and twist so the dyed splint is facing. Press the fold.

Take the fourth pair, dyed splint facing, and place them in front of the horizontal to lay to the inside of the left-hand group. Leave a short length protruding from below the horizontal length.

There are four ends on the left and three on the right. The dyed length is facing on all seven-ends.

Step 2

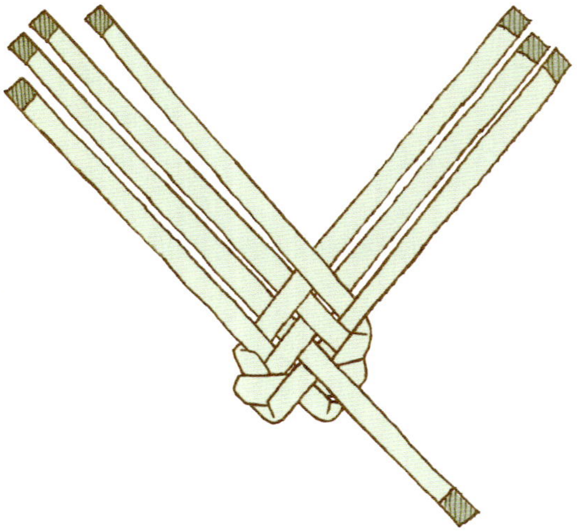

Step :2 In these moves the twisted head and foot are created.

Take the outside left-hand horizontal, twist, using the adjacent pair of splints for resistance then take the pair diagonally under one, over two to lay to the inside of the right-hand group.

Take the outside right-hand horizontal, twist, using the adjacent pair of splints for resistance then take the pair diagonally under one, over two to lay to the inside of the left-hand group.

Repeat on the left and again on the right. There are four ends on the left and three on the right.

Working

During working make certain the dyed splint of each pair is always facing.

Step 1

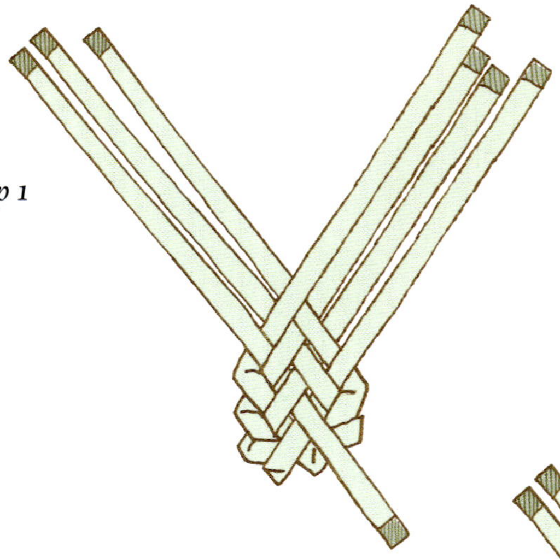

Step 1: Take the outside left-hand pair, twist, using the adjacent pair for resistance diagonally under one, over two to lay to inside the right-hand group.

There are four ends on the right and three on the left.

Step 2: In this move the first stitch of the point is created.

Take the second from outside right-hand pair fold them diagonally downwards and out to the side so they point to about 4 o'clock.

Hold the outside, carrier end in place, now roll the pair behind and diagonally to the left. It passes over two and lays inside the left-hand group.

Take the outside left-hand end, twist, and take the pair under one, over two, under one to lay to the inside of the right-hand group.

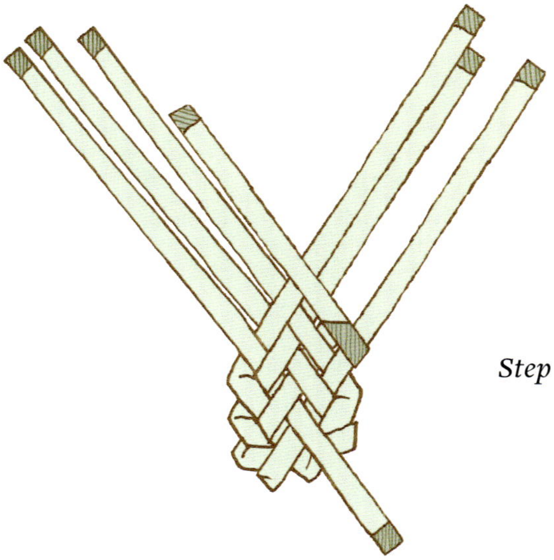

Step 2

Step 3

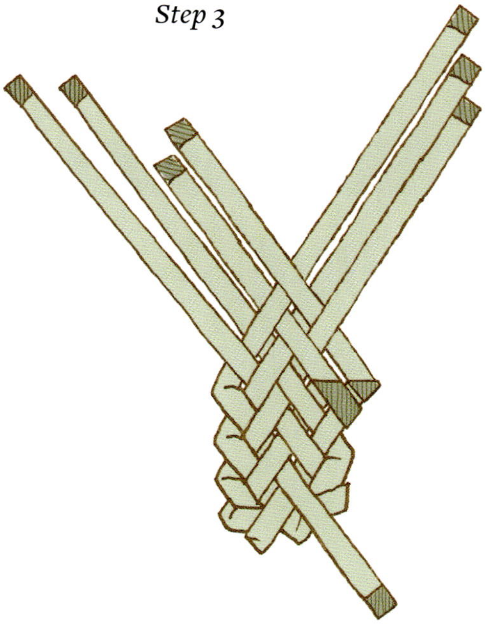

Step 3: In this move the Vandyke point is completed.

Take the outside right-hand pair, twist them outwards and towards 4 o'clock then roll them behind and diagonally towards the left. They pass under one, over two.

Continue the working moves from step 1.

The working sequence is:
Left: Outside end, twist, then under one, over two.
Right: Second from outside, towards you, diagonally outwards, roll over then back into the body over two.
Left: Outside end, twist then under one, over two, under one.
Right: Outside end, towards you, diagonally outwards, roll on itself then back into the body under one, over two.

Joining

The new end is inserted from the left, so the short end protrudes from the left-hand edge. The end to be joined must be the inside end of the right-hand group.

Take the new end pass it behind the old end and take it under one, over two, under one. It is now concealed behind the old end.

Leave behind the old end when the new end is worked.

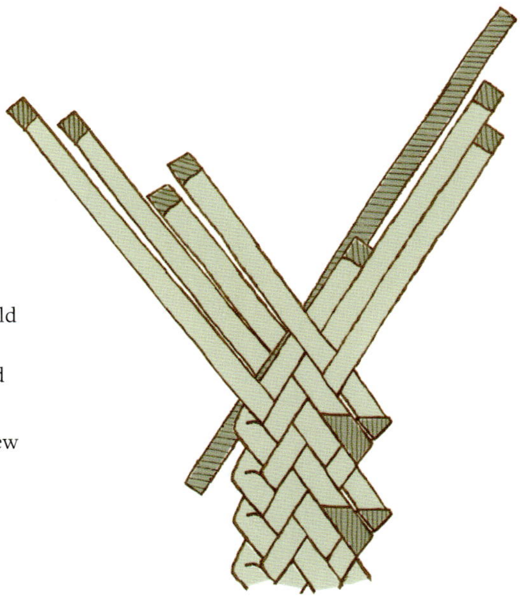

Seven-end Vandyke and twist

The original plait

Source: CTLC 1997/74/1

Origins: canton Fribourg, Switzerland

Production date: 1890s

Type of straw: Wheat straw, double splints

Splint width: 2 mm

Plait width: 13.5 mm

Plaiting direction: During working the plait's face is towards you. The foot is on the right and the head on the left, the outside end moves under. New ends must be added from behind.

Joining: Along foot edge.

Background information: This pattern was found in a Swiss plait sample book dating to the 1890s. The use of narrow and wide pairs of splints indicates the influence of Japanese patterns coming into Europe at that time. The single turn of the Vandyke point is made using a wider straw of a different colour. In between the points the head has a twist edge to create a contrasting feature.

What to use: This can be made with all types of straw.

You need: Four plaiting lengths of double splints, three narrow and one wide. Each pair is the same colour and faced shiny side outwards.
Additional lengths for joining.

Setting up

These adapted instructions enable the required under move of the outside stitch. Damp the lengths and if using splints pair them. The damping will hold the splints together.

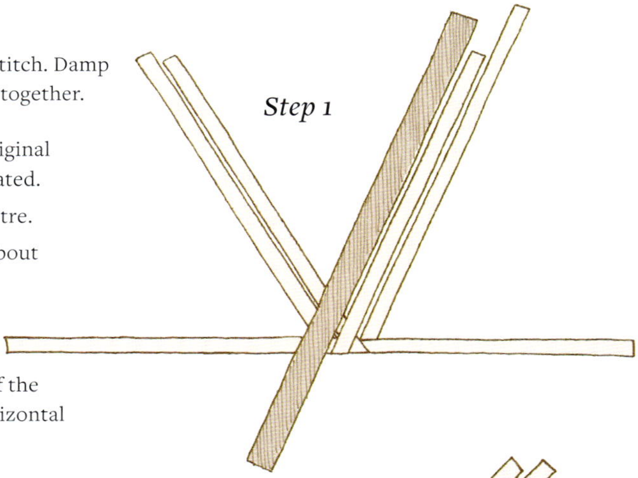

Step 1: The diagram shows all stages for setting up the ends. To create the original plait's characteristic pattern the pairs of splints must be positioned as indicated.

Hold one pair of splints horizontally, from 9 o'clock to 3 o'clock. Just off centre.

Hold a second pair diagonally behind the horizontal length, pointing from about 2 o'clock to 8 o'clock.

Fold the lower end of this pair diagonally upwards, in front of the horizontal to lay at about 10 o'clock. Press the fold.

Take the third pair. Hold diagonally in front of the horizontal to the inside of the diagonal right-hand end. Fold the lower section upwards and behind the horizontal to lay to the outside of the left-hand diagonal. Press the fold.

Take the fourth pair, a wide splint, and place in front of the horizontal to lay to the inside of the left-hand group. Leave a short length protruding from below the horizontal length.

There are three ends on the right and four on the left.

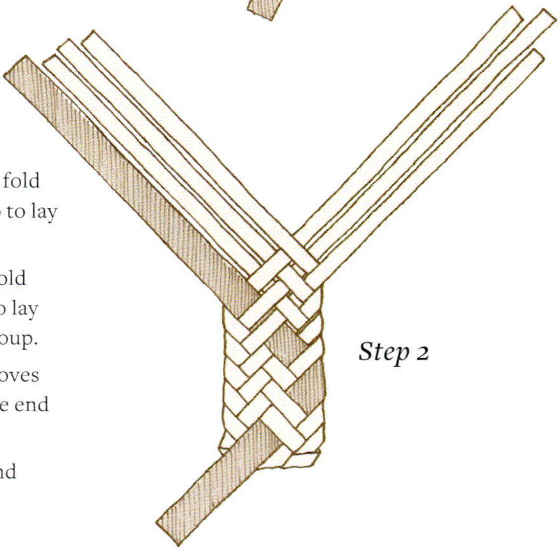

Step 2: The diagram shows all the moves required to position the wide splint ready for working.

Take the outside right-hand horizontal end, fold it diagonally under one, over two to lay to the inside of the left-hand group.

Take the outside left-hand horizontal, fold diagonally under one, over two to lay to the inside of the right-hand group.

Take the outside right-hand end, fold it diagonally under one, over two to lay to inside the left-hand group.

Take the outside left-hand end, fold diagonally under one, over two to lay to the inside of the right-hand group.

Repeat the right and left-hand moves until the wide straw is the outside end of the left-hand group.

There are four ends on the left and three on the right.

Working

Step 1: Take the second from outside left-hand end, fold towards you, diagonally downwards and out to the side so it points to about 8 o'clock. Now roll it behind and diagonally to the right. It passes under one, over two to lay inside the right-hand group.

Take the outside right-hand end, under one, over two.

Roll the wide outside end to a point then pass it under one, over two.

Take the outside right-hand end under one, over two.

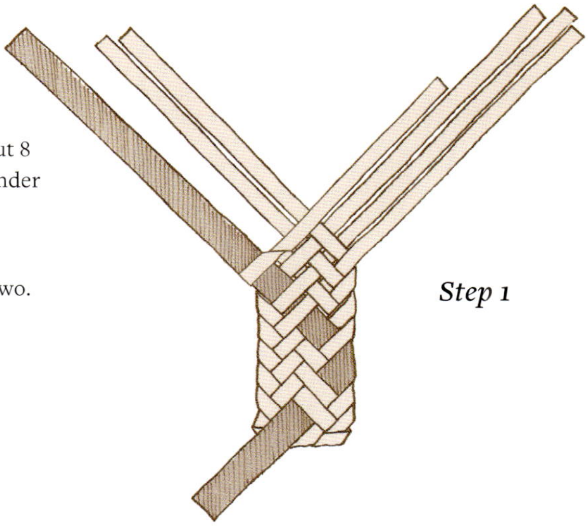

Step 1

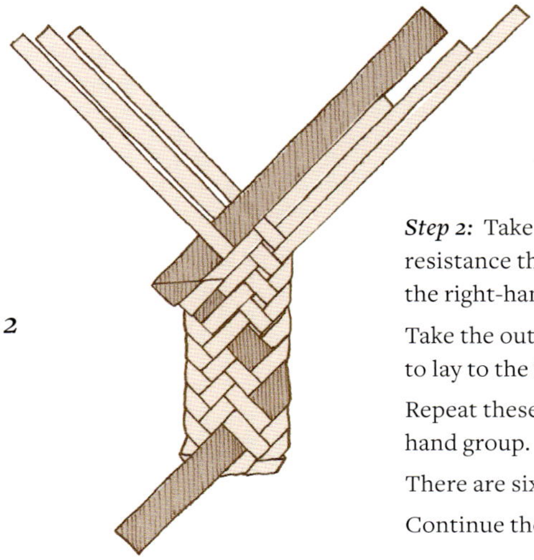

Step 2

Step 2: Take the outside left-hand end, twist, using the adjacent end for resistance then take it diagonally under one, over two to lay to inside the right-hand group.

Take the outside right-hand end fold it diagonally under one, over two to lay to the inside of the left-hand group.

Repeat these moves until the wide end is the outside end of the left-hand group.

There are six twist stitches between the points. The foot edge is folded.

Continue the working sequence from step 1.

The working sequence is:
Left: Second from outside end, towards you, diagonally outwards, roll on itself, back into body, under one, over two.
Right: Under one, over two.
Left: Outside wide end, roll to point, back into body under one, over two.
Right: Under one, over two.
Left: Twist stitch, under one, over two.
Right: Under one, over two.
Repeat the last two moves five times. The wide end will be the outside left-hand end.

Joining

The new end is inserted from the right and the short end protrudes from the foot edge on the left. The end to be joined must be the inside end of the left-hand group.

Take the new end pass it behind the old end and take it under one, over two. It is now concealed behind the old end. Continue the working sequence leaving behind the old end when both old and new reach the outside of the left-hand group.

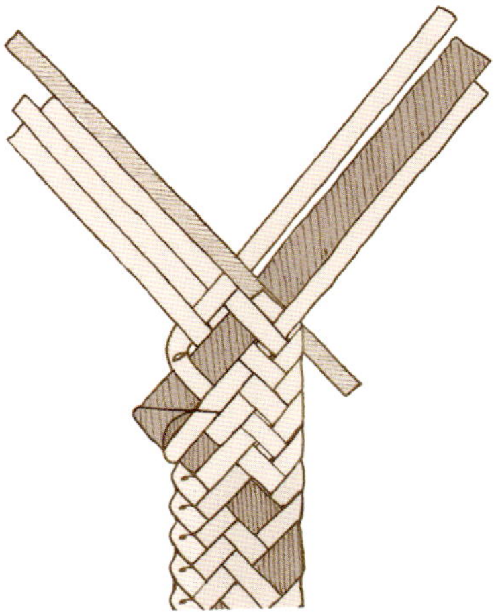

Seven-end Vandyke and purl

The replica plait

Source: Original instructions in Second Course of Straw and Chip Plaiting

Origins: unknown

Production date: pre.1895

Type of straw: Original pattern made with chip

Splint width: 3 mm and 5 mm

Plait width: 29 mm

Plaiting direction: During working the front of the plait faces the maker. The head is on the right and the foot on the left.

Joining: Along foot edge.

Background information: This pattern appeared in the *Second Course of English Straw and Chip Plaiting*. The original instructions required the Vandyke point to be made from a wide chip length and the purl from finer ones. This example uses two lengths of paper tape and five thinner whole wheat straws. There is one variation from a standard purl pattern, rather than immediately returning into the body, the carrier end twists on itself before returning into the plait.

What to use: This can be made with all types of straw.

You need: Four plaiting lengths three thin and one thick. Additional lengths for joining.

Setting up

The original instructions for setting up were lengthy therefore these instructions use the over, under folding method since this method immediately sets the lengths into the correct sequence.

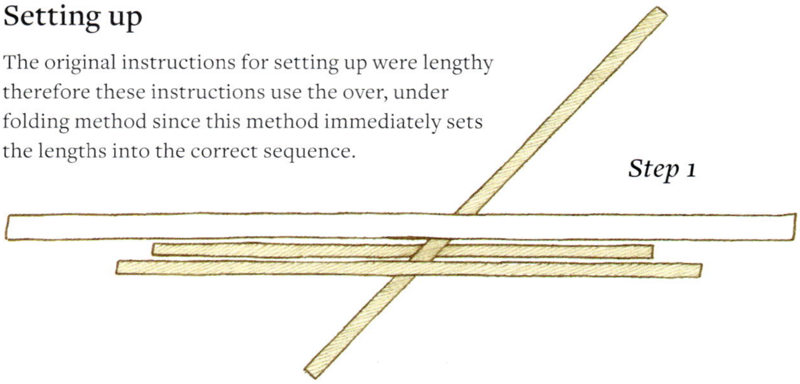

Step 1

Step 1: Lay two thin lengths horizontally. Lay the thick length above them.

Off centre pass the third thin length diagonally, under one, over one, under one. A short end protrudes, pointing to about 7 o'clock and its long end points to about 1 o'clock.

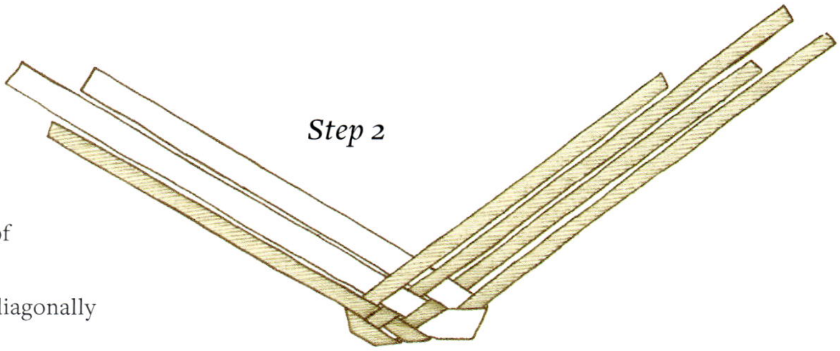

Step 2

Step 2: The diagram shows all the setting up moves. The ends have been rotated to their working position.

Take the lowest right-hand horizontal and fold it diagonally under one, over one to lay to the right of the diagonal.

Take the lowest right-hand horizontal and fold it diagonally under one to lay to the right of the diagonal.

Take the last right-hand horizontal end, the thick length, and fold it diagonally on itself and then under the rest of the diagonal group, under one, over one, under one.

Take the outside left-hand end and pass it under one, over two to lay to the inside of the right-hand group.

Rotate the ends so the left-hand group points to about 10 o'clock and the right-hand group to about 2 o'clock. There are four ends on the right and three on the left.

Step 3: In this step several stitches are made to put the ends into their correct positions for working the pattern sequence.

Take the outside right-hand end diagonally, under one, over two to lay inside the left-hand group.

Take the outside left-hand end diagonally, under one, over two to lay inside the right-hand group.

Repeat until the two wider ends are adjacent to each other on the right-hand edge. They are ready to create the first Vandyke point.

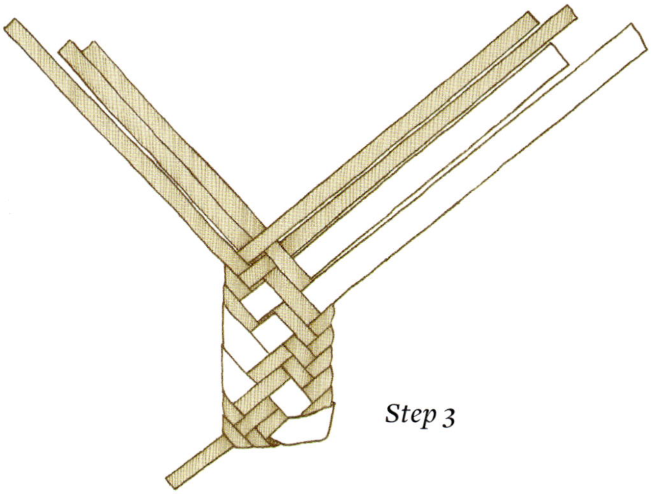

Step 3

Working

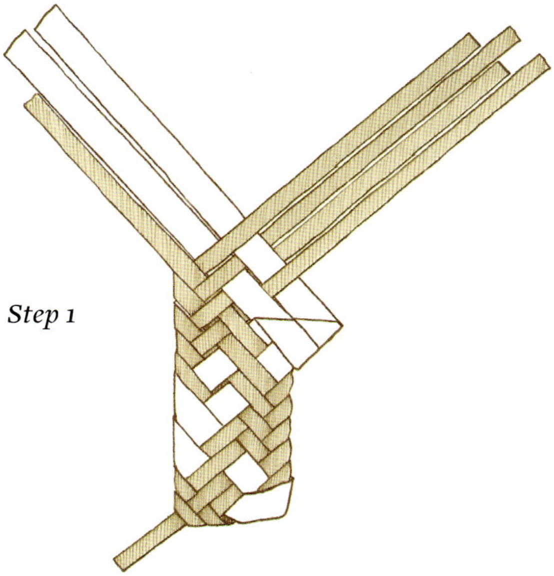

Step 1

Step 1: In this move the Vandyke point is created. The diagram shows both moves.

Take the second from outside right-hand end fold it diagonally downwards and out to the side to point to about 4 o'clock. Bring it back into the body, over two to lay to the inside of the left-hand group.

Take the outside left-hand end and fold it away from you then diagonally under one, over two to lay inside the right-hand group.

Now create the second stitch of the point.

Take the remaining wide right-hand end twist it towards you then diagonally on itself to form a tight point. Return it into the body, under one, over two.

Take the outside left-hand end and fold it diagonally under one, over two to lay inside the right-hand group.

The Vandyke point is complete. There are four ends in the right-hand group and three in the left.

Step 2: The next moves create the purl sequence.

Use the outside end as the carrier for the purl stitches. Take the second from outside right-hand end and, fold the end diagonally towards you out to the side, then roll it behind the carrier. It now returns into the body passing over two to lay to the inside of the left-hand group.

Take the outside left-hand end and fold it diagonally under one, over two to lay inside the right-hand group.

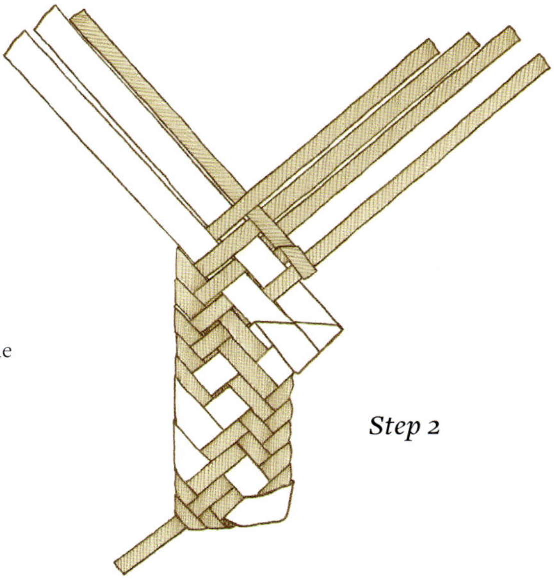

Step 2

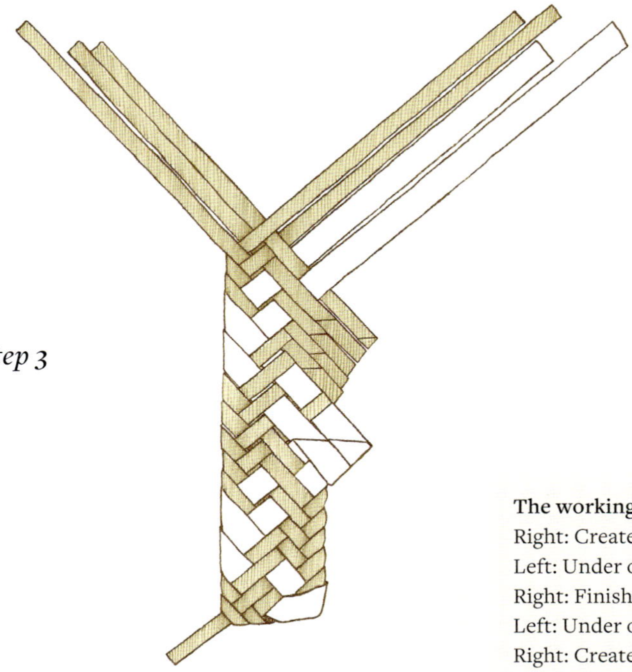

Step 3

Step 3: Repeat until there are a total of four purl stitches.

The next move creates a point on the carrier end as it returns into the body.

Fold the outside end towards you then diagonally outwards to about 4 o'clock. Roll it on itself to form a tight point. Bring it diagonally back into the body, passing it under one, over two to lay to inside the left-hand group.

Take the outside left-hand end and fold it diagonally under one, over two to lay inside the right-hand group.

There are four ends on the right and three on the left. The two wide ends are the two outside ends of the right-hand group.

Repeat the working sequence until joining begins.

The working sequence is:
Right: Create first stitch of the Vandyke point.
Left: Under one, over two.
Right: Finish the Vandyke point.
Left: Under one, over two.
Right: Create the first stitch of the purl sequence.
Left: Under one, over two.
Repeat last two moves until there are four pearl stitches.
Right: Take the outside end, roll it on itself to make a point bring it back into the body.
Left: Under one, over two

Joining

The new end is inserted from the left and the short end protrudes from the foot edge. The end to be joined must be the inside end of the right-hand group.

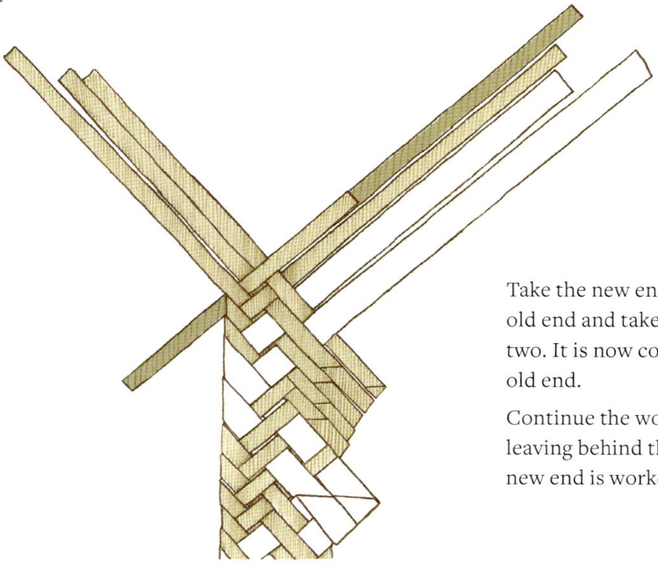

Take the new end pass it behind the old end and take it under one, over two. It is now concealed behind the old end.

Continue the working sequence leaving behind the old end when the new end is worked.

Eight-end batwing

The original plait

Source: CTCL 12/31/41B

Origins: China

Production date: Early 1900s

Type of straw: Wheat straw, whole

Splint width: 15.5 mm

Plait width: 2 mm

Plaiting direction: During working the front of the plait faces the maker. The head is on the right and the foot on the left.

Joining: Along foot edge.

Background information: Usually made from whole straw the pattern was made using seven, eight or nine ends. The number of stitches in the point also varied but is not necessarily related to the number of ends. The plait varied, sometimes joins being made on the foot and in other examples joined in the body, speelless.

What to use: This can be made with all types of straw.

You need: Four plaiting lengths.
Additional lengths for joining.

Setting up

The original instructions for setting up were lengthy therefore these instructions use the over, under folding method since this method immediately sets the lengths into the correct sequence.

Step 1: The diagram shows all the steps required for setting up.

Hold one length horizontally.

Take a second length, hold it diagonally behind the horizontal length so it is pointing to the left. Fold the lower end towards you and diagonally upwards to the right.

Add a third length, placing it in front of the horizontal and to the right of the left-hand diagonal. Fold the lower end up behind the horizontal to lay to the right of the right-hand diagonal.

Add a fourth length in front of the horizontal and to the right of the two left-hand diagonals. Fold the lower end up behind the horizontal to lay to the right of the two right-hand diagonals.

Take the left-hand horizontal end, fold it diagonally under one, over two to lay inside the right-hand group.

Take the right-hand horizontal end and fold it diagonally under one, over three to lay to the inside of the left-hand group.

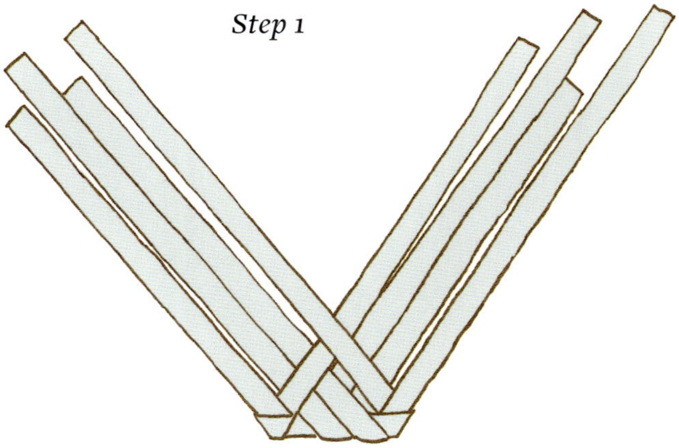

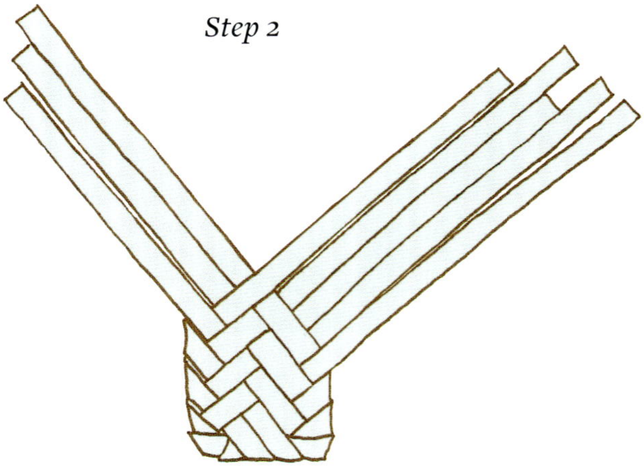

Step 2

Step 2: These moves arrange the ends ready for working.

Take the left-hand horizontal end, fold it diagonally under one, over two to lay inside the right-hand group.

Take the right-hand horizontal end and fold it diagonally under one, over three to lay to the inside of the left-hand group.

Take the left-hand horizontal end, fold it diagonally under one, over two to lay inside the right-hand group.

Take the right-hand horizontal end and fold it diagonally under one, over three to lay to the inside of the left-hand group.

Take the left-hand horizontal end, fold it diagonally under one, over three to lay inside the right-hand group.

There are three ends on the left and five on the right.

Working

Step 1: In this move the first stitch of the point is created.

Take the fourth from outside right-hand end, fold it diagonally towards you and out to the side to point to about 4 o'clock.

Hold the outside carrier ends in place. Roll the end behind and diagonally to the left. It passes under three, over one to lay inside the left-hand group.

Take the outside left-hand end under one, over two to lay to the inside of the right-hand group.

There are three ends on the left five on the right, note the gap on the right.

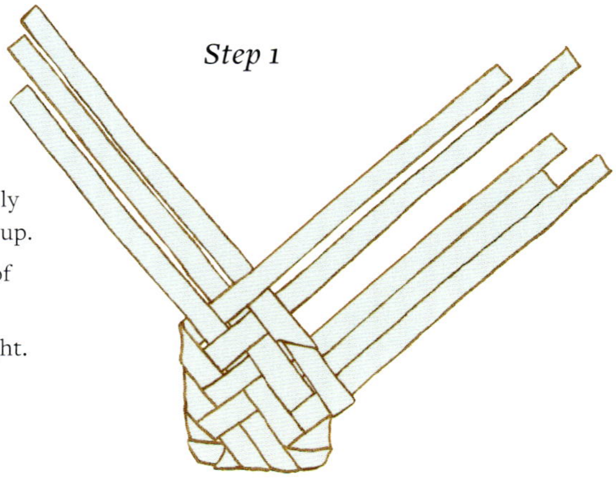

Step 1

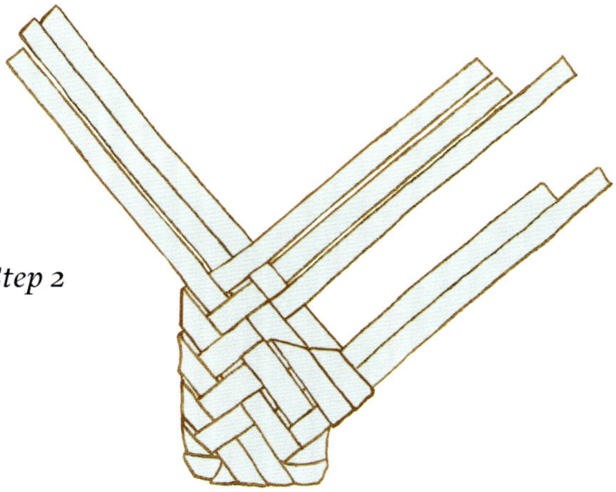

Step 2

Step 2: Take the third from outside right-hand end. It is the end below the gap. Fold it diagonally towards you and out to the side to point to about 4 o'clock.

Hold the outside end in place now roll the end behind and diagonally to the left. It passes under three, over one to lay inside the left-hand group.

Take the outside left-hand end under one, over two to lay to the inside of the right-hand group.

Step 3: Take the second from outside right-hand end. Fold it towards you then diagonally out to the side to point to about 4 o'clock.

Hold the outside, carrier end in place, now roll the end behind and diagonally to the left. It passes under three, over one to lay inside the left-hand group.

Take the outside left-hand end under one, over two to lay to the inside of the right-hand group.

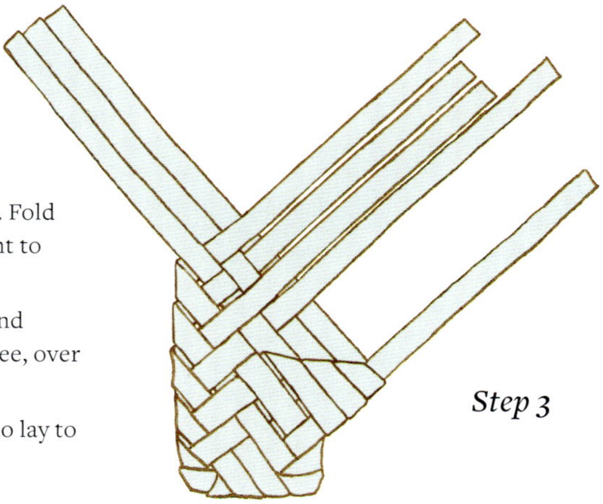

Step 3

Step 4

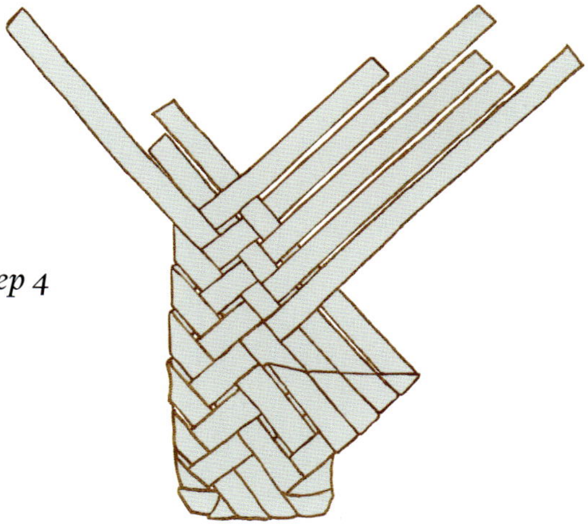

Step 4: This move makes the final stitch of the point.

Take the outside right-hand end. Fold it diagonally towards you and out to the side to point to about 4 o'clock.

Now roll the end behind and diagonally to the left. It passes under three, over one to lay inside the left-hand group.

Take the outside left-hand end under one, over two to lay to the inside of the right-hand group.

There are three ends on the left and five on the right.

Continue the working move until joining begins.

The working sequence is:
Right: Fourth end from outside, round the carrier ends, back into body, under three, over one.
Left: Under one, over two.
Right: Third end from outside, round the carrier, back into the body, under three, over one.
Left: Under one, over two.
Right: Second end from outside, round the carrier, back into the body, under three, over one.
Left: Under one, over two.
Right: Take the outside end, roll it on itself to make a point, back into the body, under three, over one.
Left: Under one, over two.

Joining

Start joining early and join regularly. Insert the new end from the left, it must be the inside end of the right-hand group.

Insert the new end behind the old, following the old end's move of under one, over two.

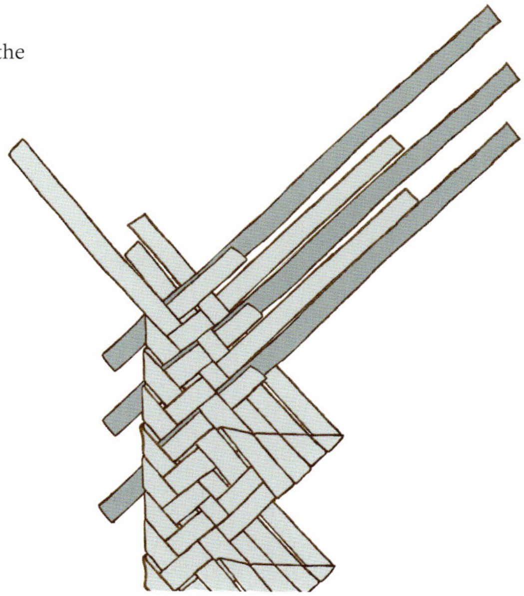

This basket from 1933 was made in the village of Finchingfield, Essex. It may have been made by Hannah Freeman for Thomas Bagshawe. The plait patterns are diamond and wisp. (CTLC 3/284/32)

Feather and Wisp

Feather and wisp plaits were popular patterns made throughout Europe and Great Britain during the 1800s and into the early 1900s. To classify as a feather edge plait the splints gently curve while in a wisp plait they often bend. Either made with undyed or combinations of coloured ends the many patterns were created by differently configurating the lengths during the setting up. There were also many adaptations of the feather head, with various numbers of feathers being made and feathers and wisps or folds being combined.

Eight-end Aldbury feather

The original plait

Source: CTLC Aldbury plait sample panel

Origins: Aldbury, Hertfordshire

Production date: *c.* 1913

Type of straw: Wheat straw, double splints

Splint width: 2 mm

Plait width: 12 mm

Plaiting direction: During working the back of the plait faces the maker and the front side faces away. The foot is on the right and the head on the left. When completed the front side of the plait has the head on the right and the foot on the left.

Joining: Along foot edge.

Background information: Made in Aldbury it is another example shown on the panels and whilst it is still possible to see the original red, the second colour has faded to bronze. There are some indications that the straws may have originally been blue. The instructions are for creating this pattern however the plait can be made with one colour or with undyed lengths.

What to use: This is best made using a flat straw.

You need: Four plaiting lengths, two of one colour and two undyed.
Additional lengths of correct colours for joining.

Setting up

Arrange so the working ends are different lengths. If you wish to recreate the colourway then set up the lengths so they are alternate colours.

Step 1: The diagram shows all stages of setting up the eight ends.

Hold one length horizontally, from 9 o'clock to 3 o'clock. Hold a second length diagonally in front of the horizontal length, pointing from about 2 o'clock to 8 o'clock.

Fold the lower end of this length behind the horizontal to lay at about 10 o'clock. Press the fold.

Take the third end. Hold it diagonally behind the horizontal length and to the inside of the diagonal right-hand end. Fold the lower section upwards to lay to the outside of the left-hand diagonal. Press the fold.

Take the fourth length and place it behind the horizontal to lay to the inside of the right-hand group. Fold the lower end diagonally upwards in front of the horizontal to lay to the outside of the two left-hand diagonals.

Step 1

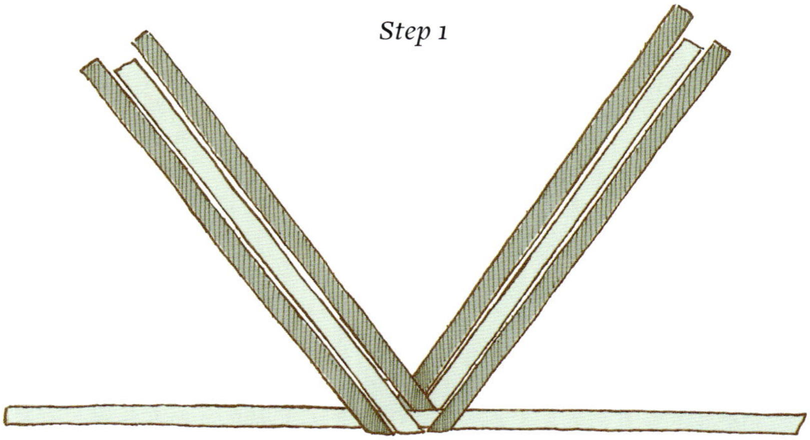

Step 2

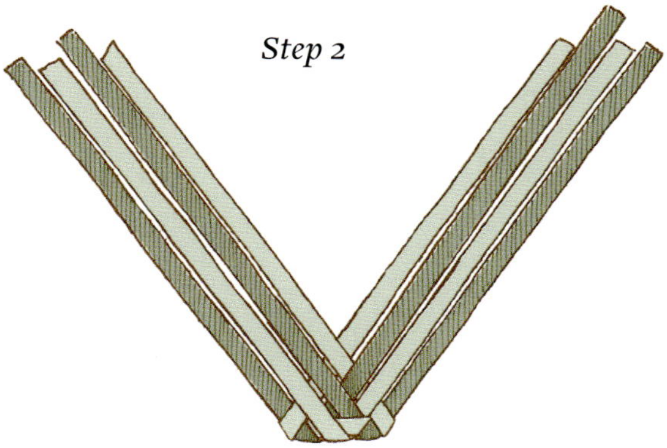

Step 2: This step begins to lock in the ends.

Take the right-hand horizontal end, fold it towards you then diagonally over one, under two to lay to the inside of the left-hand group.

Take the left-hand horizontal end and fold it towards you then diagonally over one, under three to lay inside the right-hand group.

There are four ends in each group.

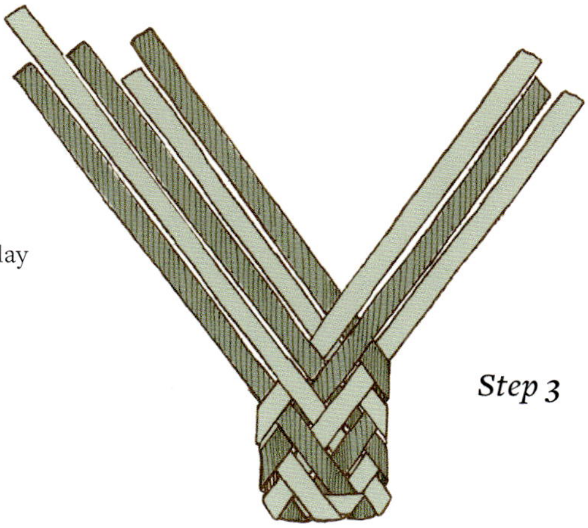

Step 3

Step 3: Take the lowest right-hand end diagonally over one, under two to lay to the inside of the left-hand group.

Take the lowest left-hand end, diagonally over one, under two, over one.

Take the lowest right-hand end over one, under two.

Take the lowest left-hand end, diagonally over one, under two, over one.

Take the lowest right-hand end over one, under two.

There are three ends on the right and five on the left.

Working

The first feather pattern will have loose stitches as they enter the body. This will correct itself in the subsequent moves.

Step 1

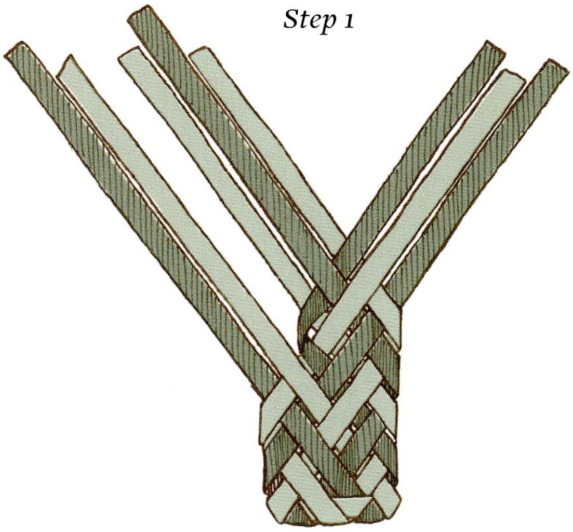

Step 1: This move forms the shortest stitch of the feather.

On the left-hand side, take the third end from the outside of the group curve it so it moves diagonally, over one to lay to the inside of the right-hand group.

Outside right-hand end over one, under two to lay to the inside of the left-hand group.

Step 2

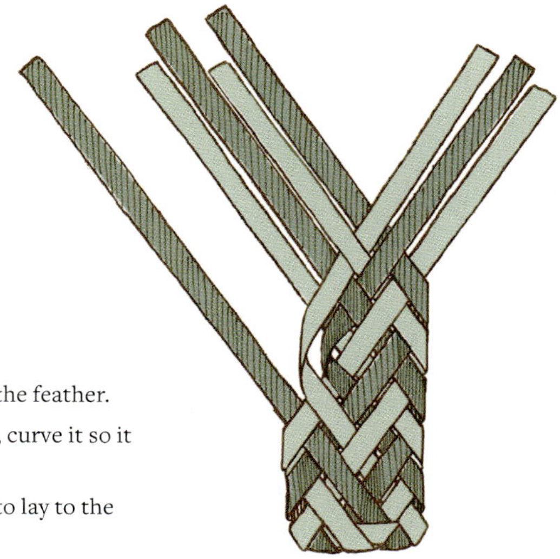

Step 2: This move forms the middle stitch of the feather.

On the left take the second from outside end, curve it so it moves diagonally over two, under one,

Outside right-hand end over one, under two to lay to the inside of the left-hand group.

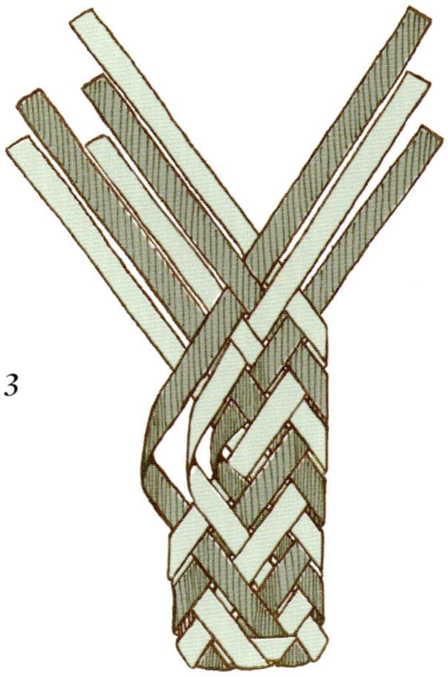

Step 3

Step 3: This move forms the longest stitch of the feather pattern.

Take the outside left-hand end, curve diagonally over three, under one to lay to the inside of the right-hand group.

Outside right-hand end over one, under two to lay to the inside of the left-hand group.

Continue the working sequence until joining begins.

The working sequence is:
Left: Third from outside, curve back into body, over one.
Right: Over one, under two.
Left: Second from outside end, over two, under one.
Right: Over one, under two.
Left: Outside end, over three, under one.
Right: Over one, under two.

Joining

Join along the foot edge.

The end to be joined must be second from the outside of the right-hand group.

Lay the new end over the old. Leave the old end behind and only work the new end.

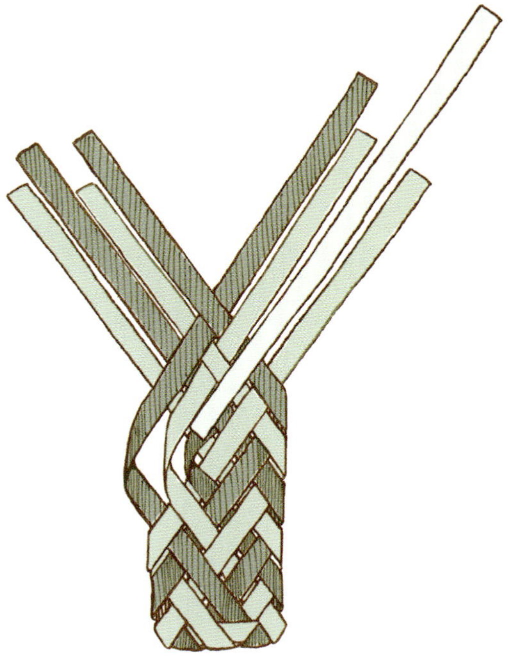

Variation

This eight-end version of the feather plait was found in a cottage in the village of Edlesborough, Buckinghamshire and may have been made at the end of the 1800s. To create the colourway the dyed lengths have been faced to an undyed length. The plait is 8mm wide and the splints are 1–1.5 mm. (CTLC 435/59)

Ten-end feather

The original plait

Source: CTLC 4/147/36

Origins: Essex

Production date: *c.* 1913

Type of straw: Wheat straw, double splints

Splint width: 1–1.5 mm

Plait width: 9 mm

Plaiting direction: During working the back of the plait faces the maker and the front side faces away. The foot is on the right and the head on the left. When completed the front side of the plait has the head on the right and the foot on the left.

Joining: Along foot edge.

Background information: Said to have been made in an unnamed Essex village before 1875, it came from the stock of a plait dealer working in Essex and Luton, J.J. Linsell. Ten-ends seem to have been a popular number of ends to use and on this example there are four feathers. They create a distinctive head and rather than having a gap between them, the plaiter has laid feathers on each other.

What to use: This is best made using a flat straw.

You need: Five plaiting lengths.
Additional lengths for joining.

Setting up

The instructions use the folding method for setting up. Remember to arrange so the working ends are different lengths.

Step 1: The diagram shows all the moves to set up the ends.

Hold the five lengths horizontally, from 9 o'clock to 3 o'clock.

Take the lowest right-hand end and fold it upwards, over, under, over, under the four left-hand horizontals.

Repeat with the remaining three ends until there is one right-hand horizontal.

Fold the last right-hand horizontal over, under, over, under so it lays to the top of the left-hand horizontal group.

Rotate clockwise so that the left-hand group points to about 10 o'clock and the right-hand group to about 2 o'clock.

Step 1

Step 2

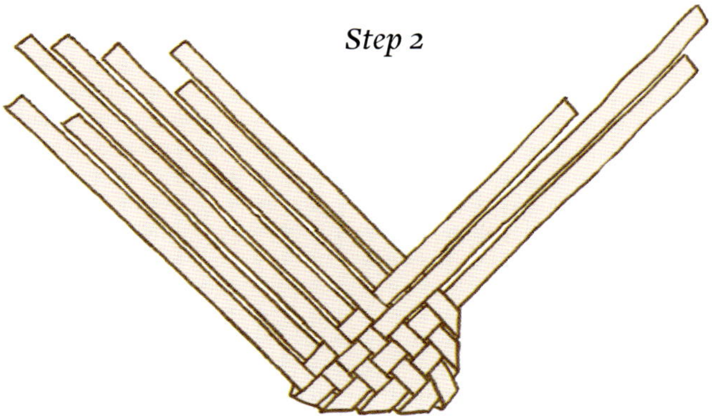

Step 2: This move arranges the ends ready for working.

Take the lowest left-hand end, under, over, under, over, under so it lays to the inside of the right-hand group.

Take the lowest right-hand end diagonally over one, under three to lay to the inside of the left-hand group.

Take the lowest right-hand end diagonally over one, under two to lay to the inside of the left-hand group.

There are three ends on the right and seven on the left.

Working

Step 1: This move forms the first and shortest stitch of the feather.

On the left-hand side, take the fourth end from the outside of the group. Curve it then take it diagonally, over one, under two to lay to the inside of the right-hand group.

Outside right-hand end over one, under two to lay to the inside of the left-hand group.

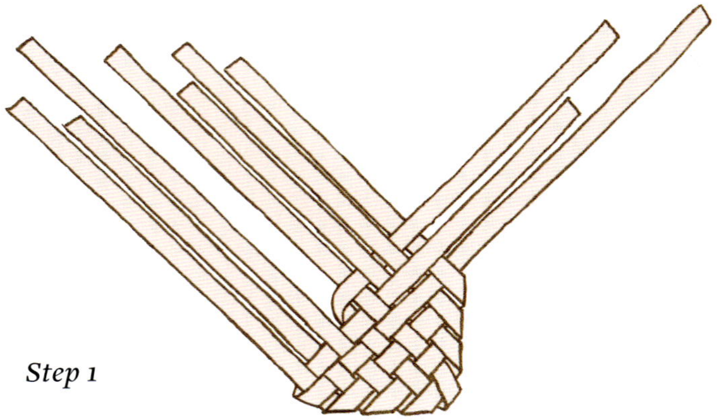

Step 1

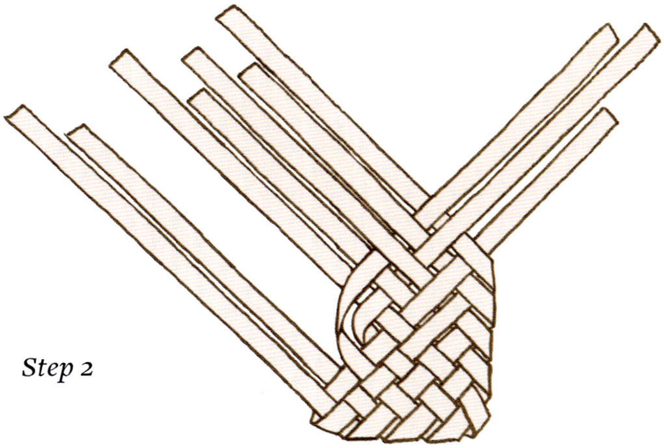

Step 2

Step 2: Form the second feather.

Take the third from outside end, curve it towards you and then diagonally over two, under two so it lays to the inside of the right-hand group.

Outside right-hand end over one, under two to lay to the inside of the left-hand group.

Step 3

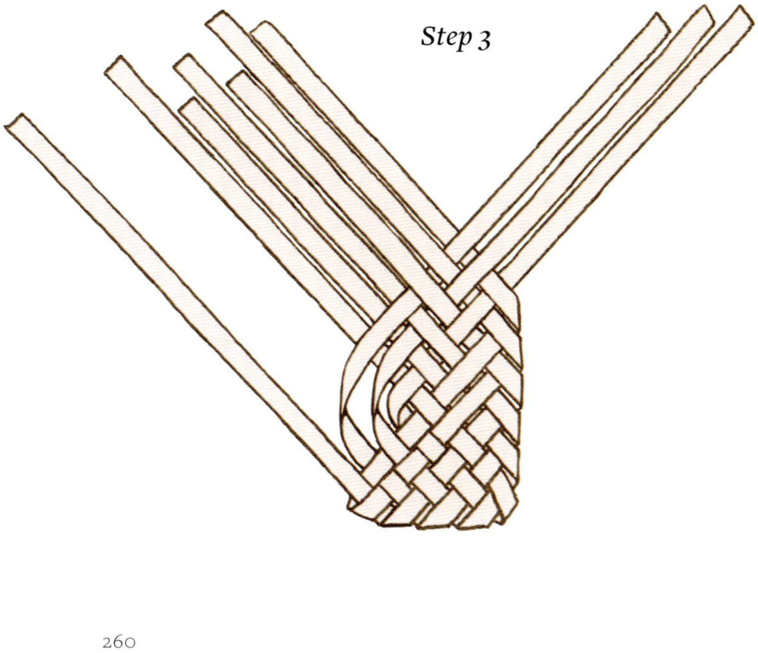

Step 3: Form the third feather.

Take the second from outside left-hand end, curve it then bring it diagonally over three, under two to lay to the inside of the right-hand group.

Take the lowest right-hand end over one, under two to lay to the inside of the left-hand group.

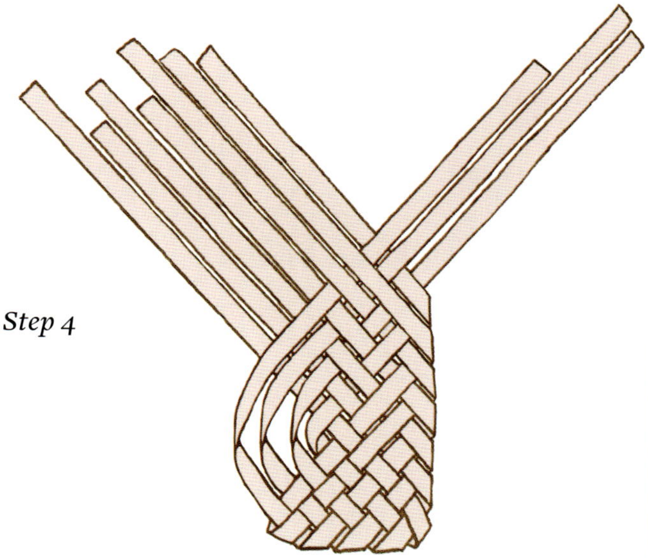

Step 4

Step 4: Form the fourth and longest feather.

Take the outside left-hand end and curve it diagonally over four, under two to lay to the inside of the right-hand group.

Outside right-hand end over one, under two to lay to the inside of the left-hand group.

Continue the working sequence until joining begins.

The working sequence is:
Left: Curve fourth straw over one, under two.
Right: Over one, under two.
Left: Curve third straw in over two, under two.
Right: over one, under two.
Left: Curve second straw over three, under two.
Right: over one, under two.
Left: Curve outside end, over four, under two.
Right: over one, under two.

Joining

Join along the foot edge. The new end to be joined must be the second from outside of the right-hand group.

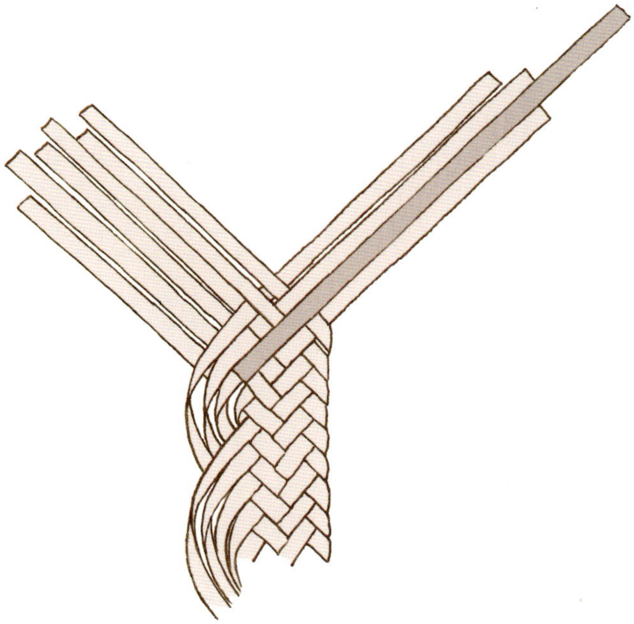

Variation

Made in Castle Hedingham, Essex in about 1866 this is a development of the rail pattern. There are five stitches for the feather and the first stitch is folded tightly so it creates what looks like a purl stitch. To create the colourway and pattern effect a dyed splint has been faced to an undyed splint. The plait is 9mm wide and made with ten ends. (CTLC 4/211/32)

Nine-end single splint wisp

The original plait

Source: CTLC BL/35/33

Origins: Essex

Production date: *c.* 1933

Type of straw: Wheat straw, single splints

Splint width: 1–3 mm

Plait width: 15 mm

Plaiting direction: During working the back of the plait faces the maker and the front side faces away. The foot is on the right and the head on the left. When completed the front side of the plait has the head on the right and the foot on the left.

Joining: Along foot edge.

Background information: Not all plaits were beautifully made, sometimes they were made as quick demonstration, or they were made by an elderly plaiter whose fingers no longer worked so well. This plait was made in 1933 when Hannah Freeman was 72 years old. She was recorded as also making the wisp using ten ends. To create the wisp she worked the pattern around a 'rush which had to be kept at the back'.

What to use: To create the mottled effect, use split wheat or rye straw, but it can be made with all types of flat straw.

You need: Five plaiting lengths.
Additional lengths for joining.

Setting up

To make this as a mottled plait take care to arrange the ends with the shiny side facing upwards in the right-hand group and the matt side facing upwards in the left-hand group.

Step 1: The diagram shows all the ends in place and adds the additional steps required when making a mottled plait.

Hold one length horizontally, from 9 o'clock to 3 o'clock with the shiny side facing. Off centre, twist the left-hand end so the pith side is facing.

Hold a second length diagonally in front of the horizontal length, pointing from about 1 o'clock to 7 o'clock. Fold the lower end of this length behind the horizontal to lay at about 11 o'clock. Press the fold.

Take a third length. Hold it diagonally behind and to the inside of the diagonal right-hand end. Fold the lower section upwards to lay in front and to the outside of the left-hand diagonal. Press the fold.

Take a fourth length and hold it diagonally behind and to the inside of the diagonal right-hand ends. Fold the lower section upwards to lay in front and to the outside of the left-hand diagonals. Press the fold.

Insert the fifth end placing it diagonally towards the right inside the right-hand group and to the front of the group. Leave a short length protruding from below the horizontal length.

There are five ends to the right and four to the left.

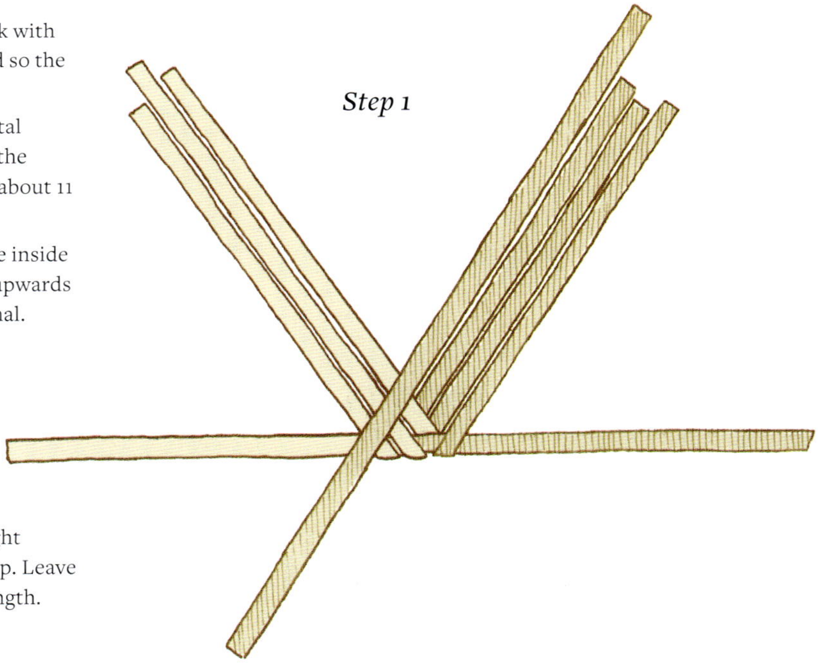

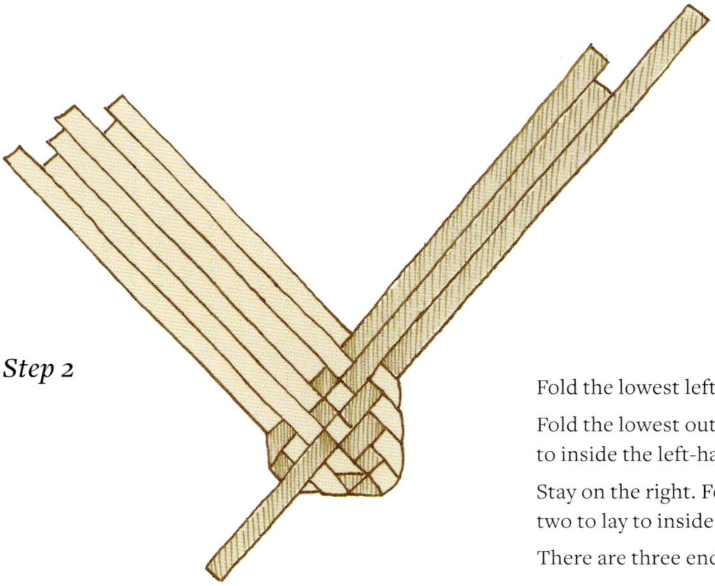

Step 2

Step 2: Take the outside, right-hand horizontal end towards you then diagonally upwards, over one, under two, over one. It lays to the inside of the left-hand group.

Take the left-hand horizontal towards you then diagonally upwards, over one, under two, over one. It lays to the inside of the right-hand group.

Fold the lowest right-hand end diagonally over one, under two, over one.

Fold the lowest left-hand end diagonally over one, under two, over one.

Fold the lowest outside right-hand end, over one, under two, over one to lay to inside the left-hand group.

Stay on the right. Fold the lowest outside right-hand end, over one, under two to lay to inside the left-hand group.

There are three ends in the right-hand group and six in the left-hand group.

Working

The pattern is formed by folding the straws to create the wisp rather than turning as with a feather edge.

Step 1: Take the fourth end from the outside of the left-hand group, curve it towards you and then diagonally over one, under one so it lays to inside the right-hand group.

Fold the outside right-hand end over one, under two to lay inside the left-hand group.

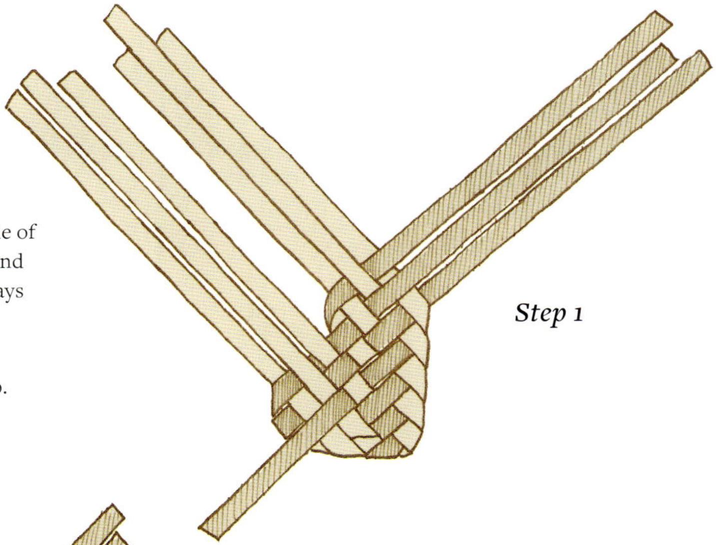

Step 1

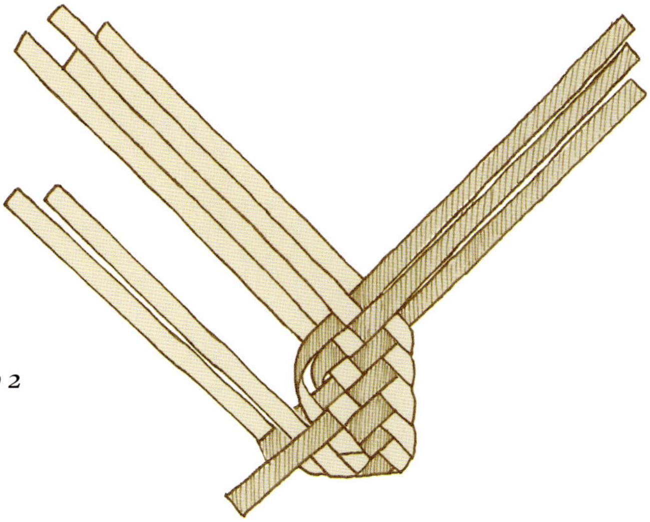

Step 2

Step 2: Take the third end from the outside of the left-hand group, curve it towards you and then diagonally over two, under one to lay to inside the right-hand group.

Fold the outside right-hand end over one, under two to lay inside the left-hand group.

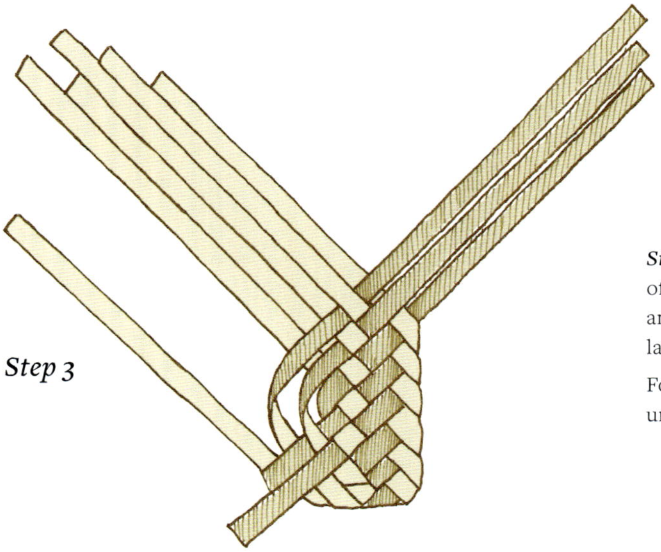

Step 3

Step 3: Take the second end from the outside of the left-hand group, curve it towards you and then diagonally over three, under one to lay to inside the right-hand group.

Fold the outside right-hand end over one, under two to lay inside the left-hand group.

Step 4: Take the outside left-hand end and curve it diagonally over four, under one to lay inside the right-hand group.

Fold the lowest right-hand end over one, under two to lay inside the left-hand group.

Continue the working sequence until joining begins.

The working sequence is:
Left: Curve fourth over one, under one.
Right: Over one, under two.
Left: Curve third over two, under one.
Right: Over one, under two.
Left: Curve second, over three, under one.
Right: Over one, under two.
Left: Curve outside end, over four, under one.
Right: Over one, under two.

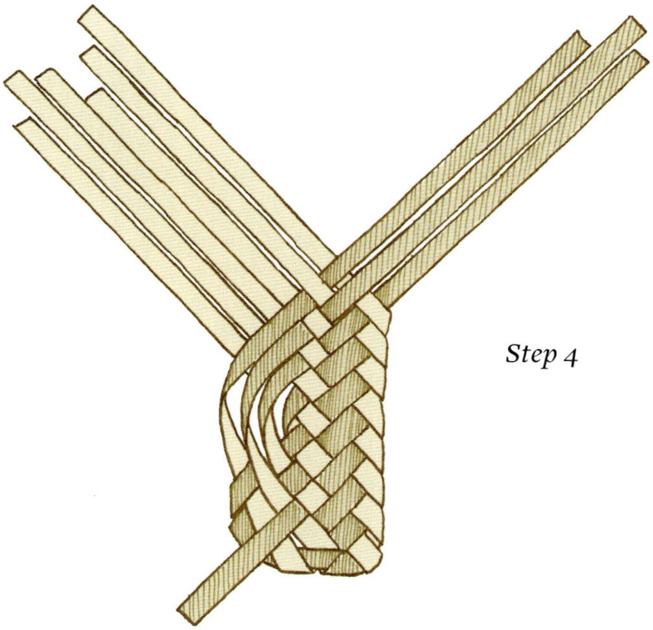

Step 4

Joining

New ends can be added either along the foot, laying the new end over the second from outside end of the right-hand group, or by using speelless joining over the inside end of the left-hand group.

Nine-end double splint wisp

The original plait

Source: CTLC 1997/69/1

Origins: Switzerland

Production date: 1864

Type of straw: Wheat straw, double splints

Splint width: 1 mm

Plait width: 8 mm

Plaiting direction: During working the front of the plait faces the maker. The foot is on the right and the head on the left. On each side the outside end moves under.

Joining: Along foot edge.

Background information: Made in about 1864 in Switzerland and perhaps in Germany, the colourway of this double splint plait may reflect the excitement within the fashion world for mauve. Since hats and bonnets needed to match the outfit, it is not surprising plaits that incorporated mauve began to appear. The pattern is achieved by setting up five pairs of splints with mauve and brown, and the remaining four are paired brown to brown.

What to use: To create this pattern, use split wheat or rye straw, but it can also be made with all types of flat straw.

You need: Five plaiting lengths. If making with double splints, five pairs brown to brown and five pairs brown to mauve. The pairs have their shiny side outwards. To set up the pattern set up with five pairs of brown, then add the purple in sequence.
Additional lengths of the correct colours for joining.

Setting up

This is set up a little differently. The plait begins with only eight-ends, the ninth end is added later.

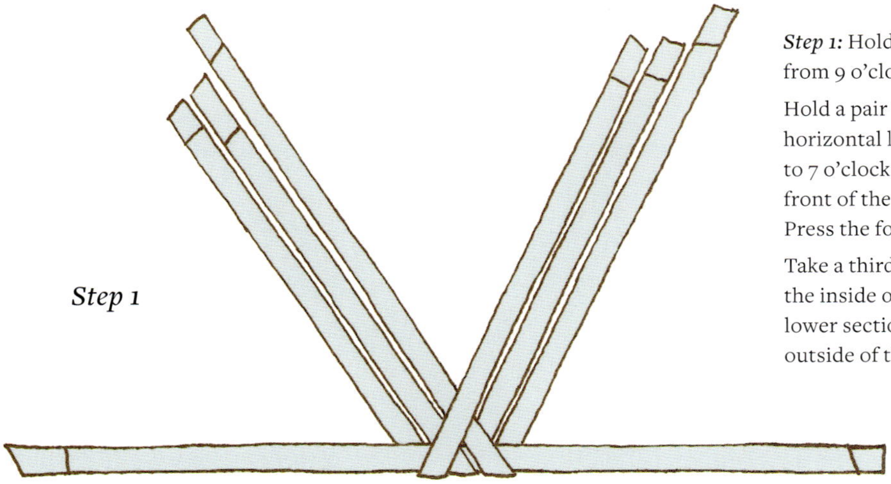

Step 1

Step 1: Hold one pair of brown splints horizontally from 9 o'clock to 3 o'clock.

Hold a pair of brown splints diagonally behind the horizontal length, pointing from about 1 o'clock to 7 o'clock. Fold the lower end of this length in front of the horizontal to lay at about 11 o'clock. Press the fold.

Take a third pair hold it diagonally behind and to the inside of the diagonal right-hand end. Fold the lower section upwards to lay in front and to the outside of the left-hand diagonal. Press the fold.

Take a fourth pair, hold diagonally in front and to the inside of the diagonal right-hand ends. Fold the lower section upwards to lay behind and to the outside of the left-hand diagonals. Press the fold.

There are four ends to the right and four to the left.

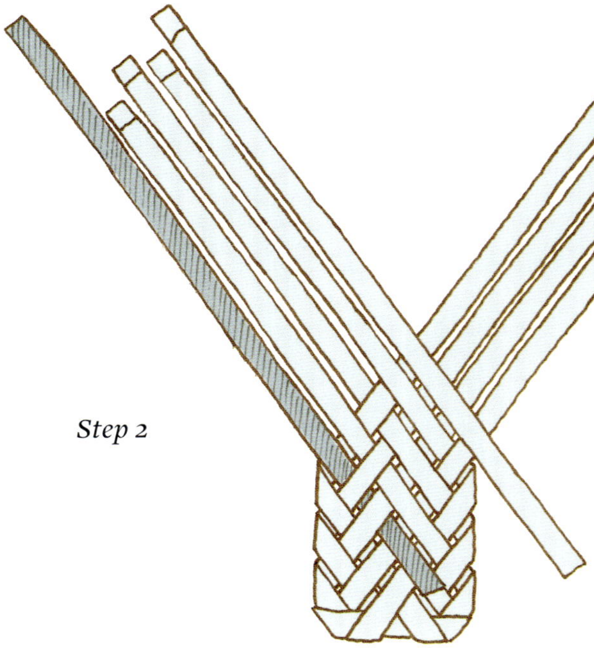

Step 2

Step 2: Take the outside, left-hand horizontal end away from you then diagonally, under one, over two. It lays to the inside of the right-hand group.

Take the right-hand horizontal away from you then diagonally upwards, under one, over three. It lays to the inside of the left-hand group.

Fold the lowest left-hand end diagonally under one, over two.

Fold the lowest right-hand end diagonally under one, over three.

Fold the lowest left-hand end diagonally under one, over two.

Fold the lowest right-hand end diagonally under one, over three.

Fold the lowest left-hand end diagonally under one, over two.

Fold the lowest right-hand end diagonally under one, over three.

In the next move one of the outside left-hand pair of splints is replaced with a purple splint.

Slide a purple splint over the top splint and under the two body stitches. Clip off the original top brown splint, leaving the original lower splint of the pair in place.

Insert the ninth working end, inside the left-hand group. The long end points to about 10 o'clock and the short end protrudes to the right of the plait. It is not yet locked in place.

Working

To form the wisp the pair of splints is gently folded rather than curved. During the first moves the original pairs of brown splints are replaced with brown and purple, with the purple facing upwards.

Step 1: Take the second end from the outside of the left-hand group, fold it away from you and then diagonally under one, over two to lay to inside the right-hand group.

Fold the lowest right-hand end under one, over three to lay inside the left-hand group.

The next move forms the first wisp.

Take the lowest outside left-hand end and fold it diagonally away from you under two, over two to lay inside the right-hand group.

Fold the lowest right-hand end under one, over three to lay inside the left-hand group.

The third of the five purple splints must be added to the left-hand group. The five purple lengths will be set into the left-hand group alternately.

Add a purple splint to the third from outside left-hand end. Clip off the original top brown splint, leaving the original lower splint of the pair in place.

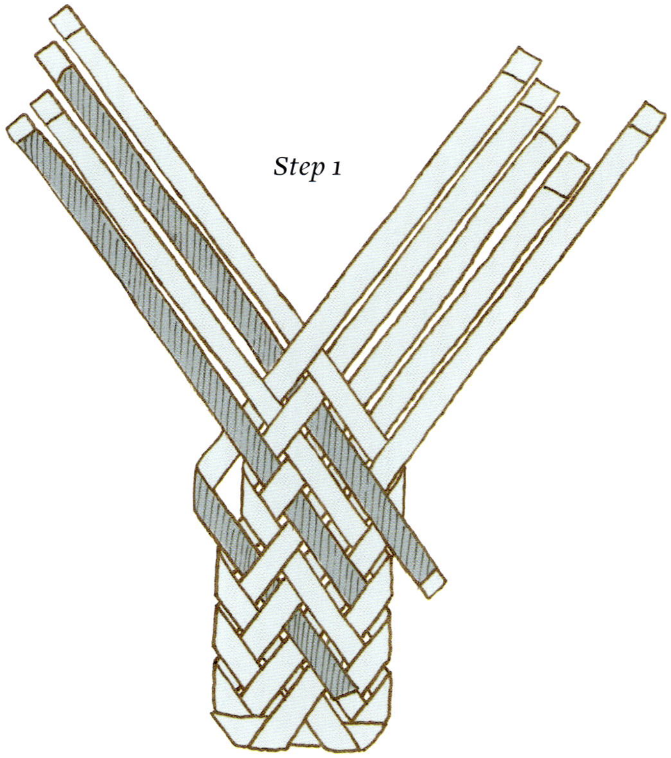

Step 1

Step 2: Repeat the sequence until all five purple splints have replaced the original brown pair. Then continue the sequence without changing the colours, only joining with the correct combination of pairs. The diagram shows all five purple splints added and the purple stitch on the right of the body starting to show.

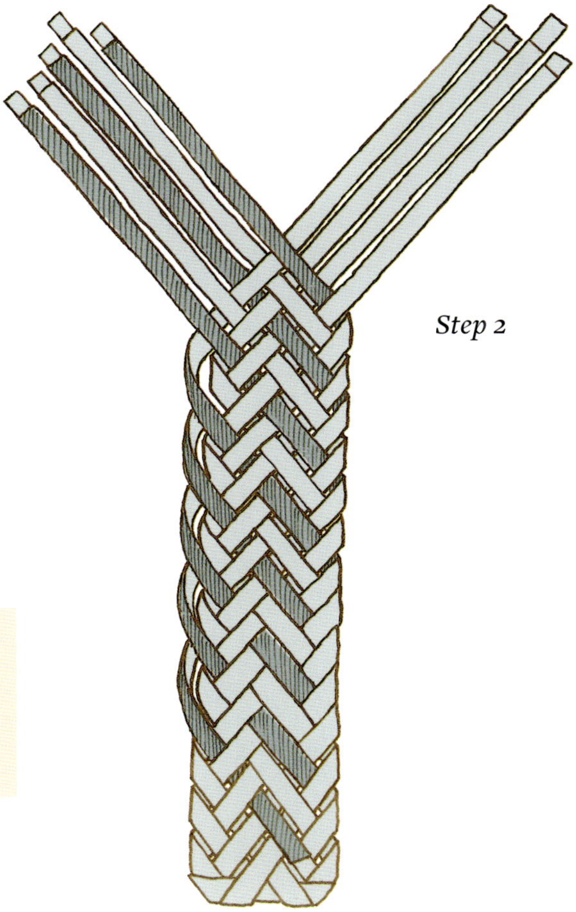

Step 2

The working sequence is:
Left: Second from outside, under one, over two.
Right: Under one, over three.
Left: Form the wisp. Outside end, under two, over two.
Right: Under one, over three.

Joining

New ends can be added either along the foot, laying the new end over the second from outside end of the right-hand group, or using a speelless join where the short end must be the inside end of the left-hand group.

Seventeen-end single splint, satin wisp

The original plait

Source: CTLC 1997/71/2

Origins: Switzerland

Production date: 1800s.

Type of straw: Wheat straw, single splints

Splint width: 1 mm

Plait width: 15 mm

Plaiting direction: During working the front of the plait faces the maker. The foot is on the right and the head on the left and on each side the outside end moves under.

Joining: Along foot edge.

Background information: Made in Switzerland and perhaps in Germany in the 1880s it may also have been made using chip. The single splints create an elaborate and dramatic pattern. The edge pattern contains a small edge variation which is not included in the instructions. The first wisp is folded, the second wisp is also folded but is made longer and more pointed, so it hides behind the third and fourth which are curved to be more feather-like.

What to use: Can be made with all types of straw but to make this pattern use single splints.

You need: Nine long plaiting lengths.
Additional lengths for joining.

Setting up

If preferred the plait can be set up by tying together seventeen plaiting lengths, then setting twelve ends to the left and five to the right. To create the single splint pattern of matt and shiny set up so all ends in the right-hand group have the shiny side upwards and all the ends of the left-hand group have the matt side facing upwards.

Step 1: Take eight of the lengths and arrange side by side horizontally, their ends pointing nine o'clock to three o'clock.

Insert the ninth end diagonally pointing from about 5 o'clock to 11 o'clock, leaving only a short length protruding from the bottom of the group. The long end passes under the lowest length then in sequence, over, under the remaining horizontal lengths.

Adjust the diagonal length so it crosses slightly off centre and arrange the horizontals, so they are different lengths.

Take the lowest left-hand end fold it away from you, then diagonally in sequence under, over through the rest of the group until it lays parallel to the left of the diagonal. Repeat with the next four left-hand ends.
Take the fifth end over the last end.

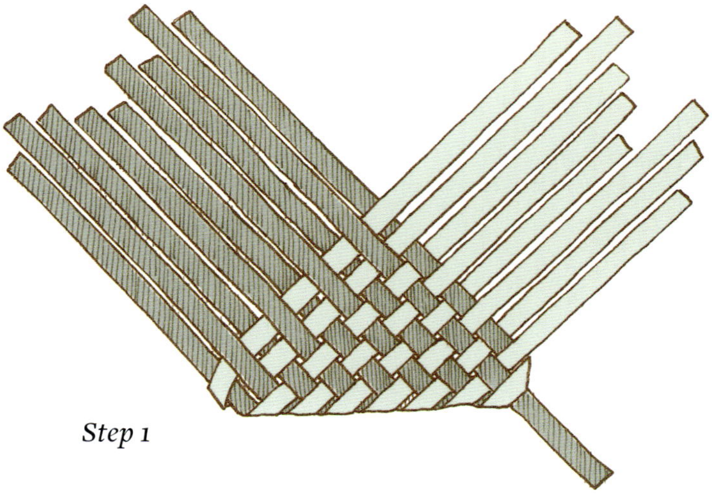

Step 1

Take the lowest right-hand end and fold it diagonally away from you under, over, under, over, under over, under two to lay to inside the left-hand group.

Rotate the plait so the two groups lay at about ten o'clock and two o'clock.

There are eight ends in the right-hand group and nine in the left-hand group. The shiny outside of the straw faces you in the right-hand group, and the matt side faces in the left-hand group.

Step 2

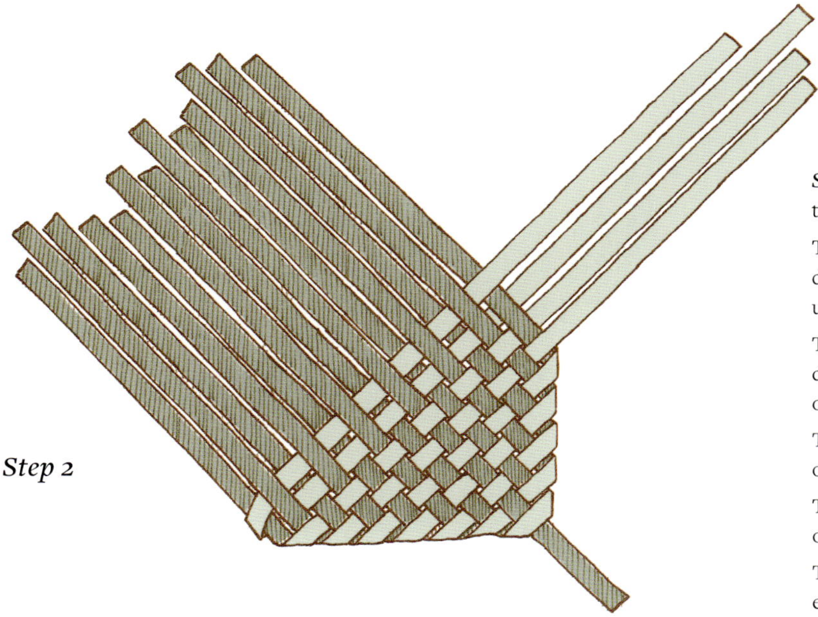

Step 2: Only work the right-hand group to set up the ends ready for working.

Take the lowest outside right-hand end, fold it diagonally away from you, under one, over one, under one, over one, under one, over two.

Take the lowest outside right-hand end, fold it diagonally, under one, over one, under one, over one, under two.

Take the lowest outside right-hand end, under one, over one, under one, over two.

Take the lowest outside right-hand end, under one, over two, under one.

There are four ends on the right and thirteen ends on the left.

Working

The ends will not be in their final positions until the first working sequence is completed.

Step 1

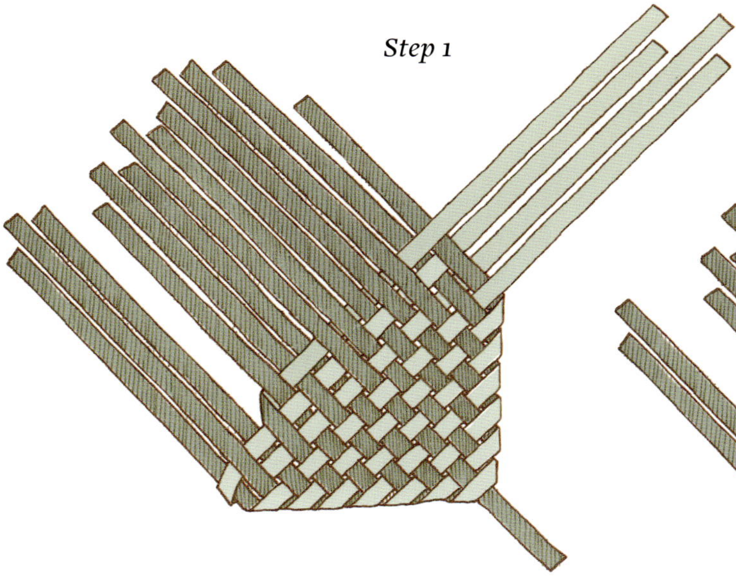

Step 2

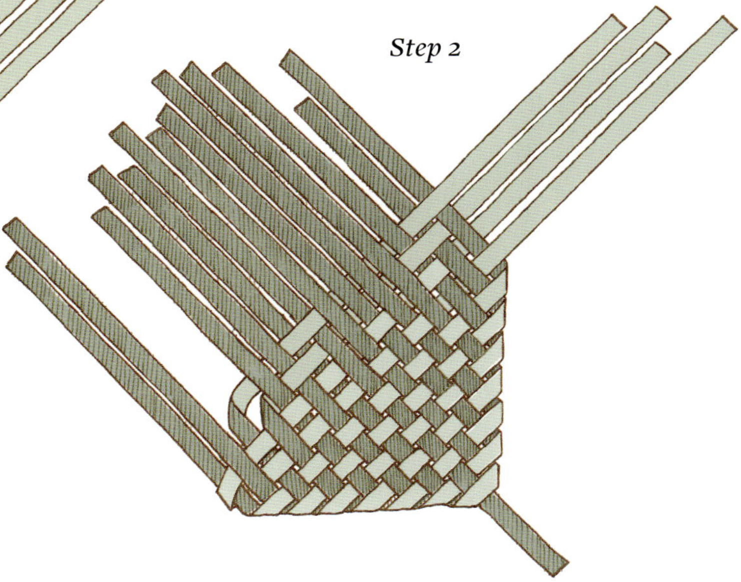

Step 1: This move is on the left. Take the fourth end in from the outside end. Curve it diagonally away from you, under one, over two, under five, over two.

Take the lowest right-hand end diagonally under one, over two, under one.

There are four ends in the right-hand group and thirteen ends in the left-hand group.

Step 2: Take the third from outside end of the left-hand group, curve it away from you then diagonally under two, over two, under five, over one. It lays to the inside of the right-hand group.

Take the lowest right-hand end diagonally under one, over two, under one.

Step 3: Take the second from outside end of the left-hand group, curve it away from you, under three, over two, under five, over one.

Take the lowest right-hand end diagonally under one, over two, under one.

Step 3

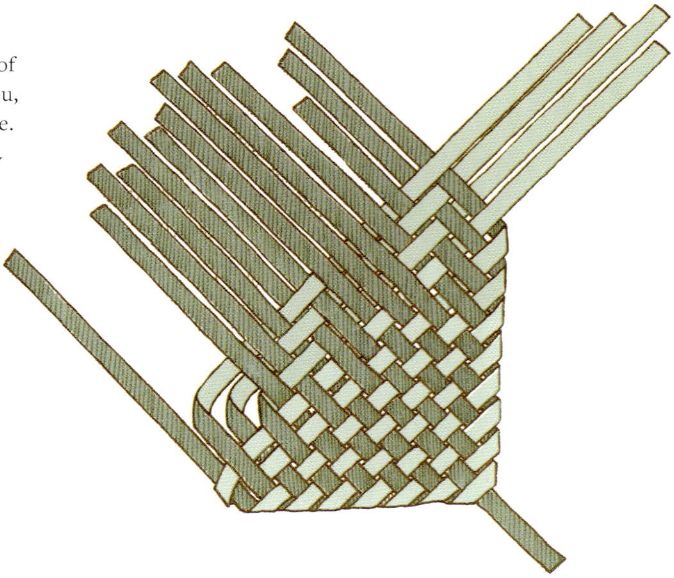

Step 4

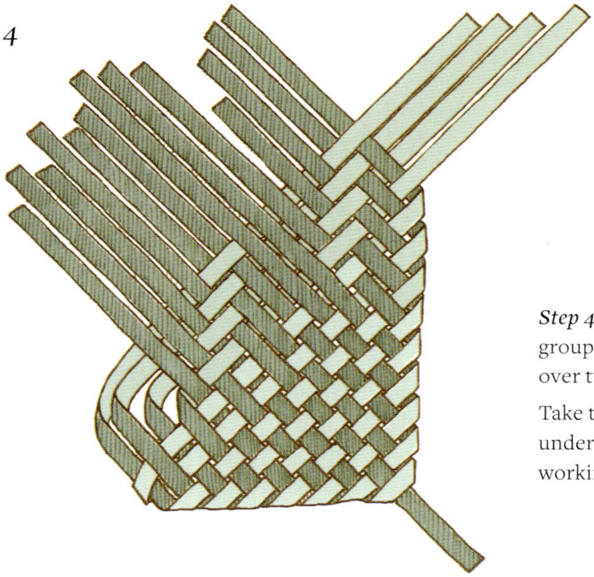

Step 4: Take the outside end of the left-hand group, curve it away from you, under four, over two, under five, over one.

Take the lowest right-hand end diagonally under one, over two, under one. Continue the working sequence until joining begins.

The working sequence is:
Left: Fourth end in from outside curve away from you and diagonally, under one, over two, under five, over two.
Right: Under one, over two, under one.
Left: Third end in from outside, curve away from you and diagonally, under two, over two, under five, over one.
Right: Under one, over two, under one.
Left: Second end in from outside, curve away from you and diagonally, under three, over two, under five, over one.
Right: Under one, over two, under one.
Left: Outside end, curve away from you and diagonally, under four, over two, under five, over one.
Right: Under one, over two, under one.

Joining

It is essential to begin joining after the first three or four working sequences to allow even spacing along the length.

The original plait is joined using the speelless method as shown, but joins can be made along the foot.

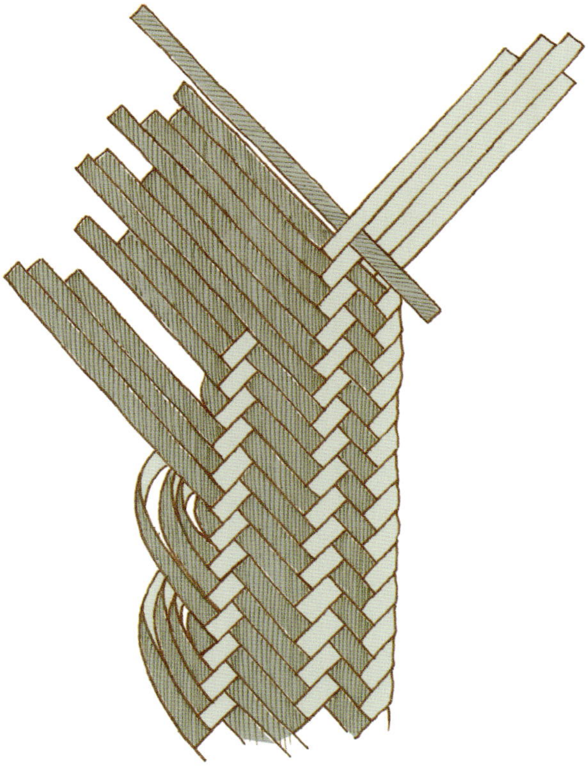

Even the plainer plaits can be stitched together in ways that make a basic shape intriguing. This hat from 1855 is recorded as being made from English China Purl. (CTLC 102/37)

Purchased in Caussade, France in the early 2000s, this man's boater made from Italian straw diamond pattern was stitched on an Anita machine. It has an inner layer made from seven-end plait to provide strength.

Diamond and Wave

Diamond and wave may be some of the earliest fancy patterns. Currently there are no clues as to where they were first introduced but they were made throughout Europe and North America. Diamond patterns were still made in Italy in the early 1900s. They can be made using whole straws, single splints and double splints, choices that are encompassed in the selection of plaits in this section. As in defining the different between feather and wisp there is a similar difficulty between diamond and wave patterns.

Thirteen-end single splint diamond

The original plait

Source: CTLC BL/33/33a

Origins: Finchingfield, Essex

Production date: 1930s

Type of straw: Wheat straw, single splints

Splint width: 1–2 mm

Plait width: 16 mm

Plaiting direction: During working the back of the plait faces the maker and the front side faces away. The foot is on the right and the head on the left. When completed the front side of the plait has the head on the right and the foot on the left.

Joining: Along foot edge.

Background information: This is another example of a plait made by Hannah Freeman in about 1933. The pattern was created by using single splints of wheat straw to produce a mottled effect. She used a range of domestic fabric dyes and laundry blue bags, then dip-dyed which colours the pith but does not penetrate the outer shiny side of the straw.

What to use: All types of flat straw.

You need: Seven plaiting lengths.
Additional lengths for joining.

Setting up

If making this as a mottled plait take care to set up the lengths so the shiny side of the right-hand group face upwards and in the left-hand group, the matt side face upwards. These instructions use the folding method to set up the ends.

Step 1: Hold six lengths horizontally, matt side upwards. Take the seventh length, with the shiny side upwards, and move it diagonally through the horizontal ends, over, under, over, under, over, under. The diagonal end lays towards about 1 o'clock with the short end protruding towards about 7 o'clock.

Fold the lowest right-hand horizontal end towards you then diagonally, over, under, over, under, over. It lays parallel to the right of the diagonal length.

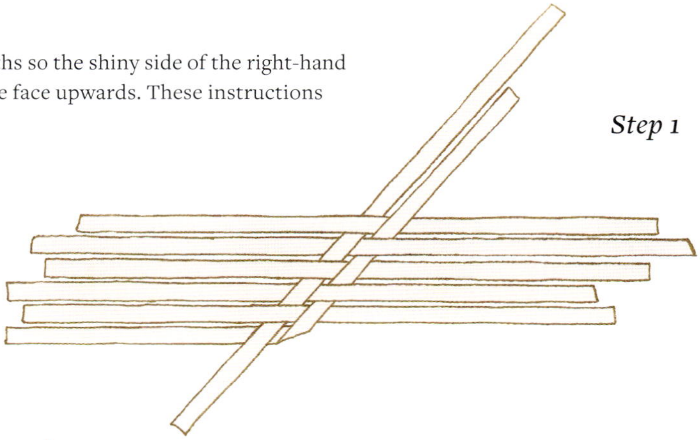

Step 1

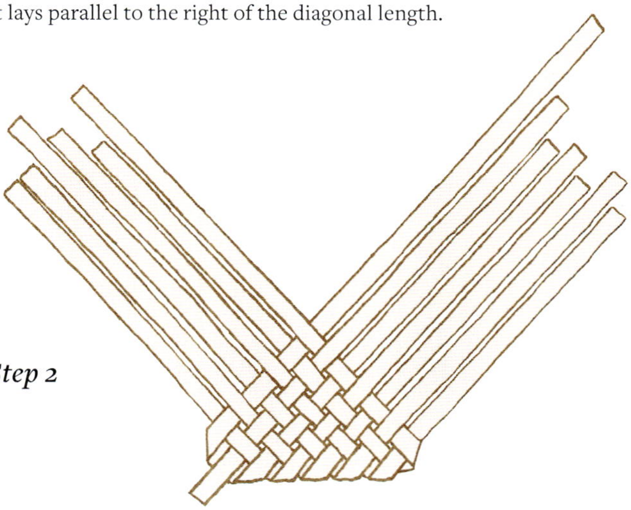

Step 2

Step 2: Take the lowest right-hand end, fold it towards you then diagonally, over, under, over under. It lays parallel to the two diagonal ends.

Repeat the folding movements with the right-hand ends until only one remains.

Fold the last right-hand end on itself then pass it, over, under, over, under, over, under the diagonal ends.

Take the lowest left-hand end, fold it on itself then over, under, over, under, over, under until it lays to inside the right-hand ends.

There are seven ends in the right-hand group with the shiny side facing and six in the left-hand group.

Working

Step 1: Take the outside right-hand end, fold it towards you and then diagonally, over one, under two, over three.

Take the outside left-hand end, fold it towards you and then diagonally, over one, under two, over two, under one.

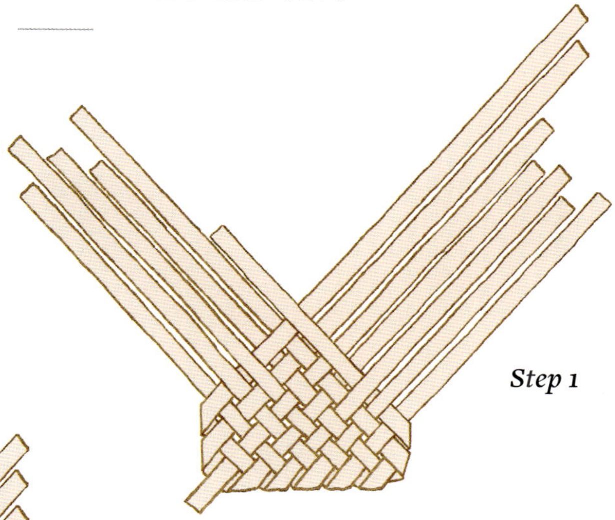

Step 1

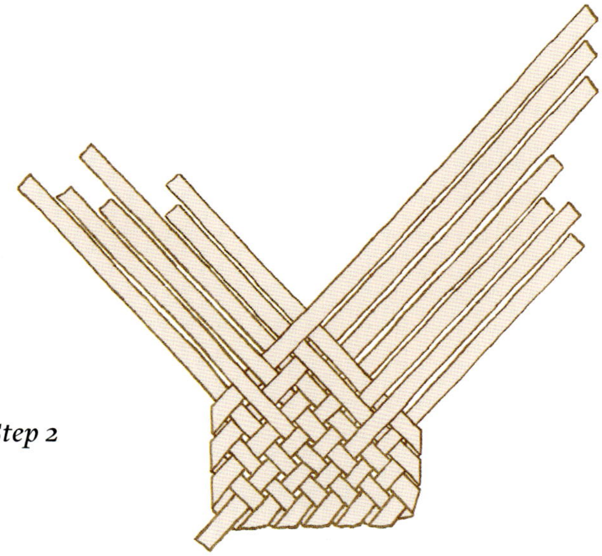

Step 2

Step 2: Take the outside right-hand end, fold it towards you and then diagonally, over one, under two, over three.

Take the outside left-hand end, fold it towards you and then diagonally, over one, under two, over three.

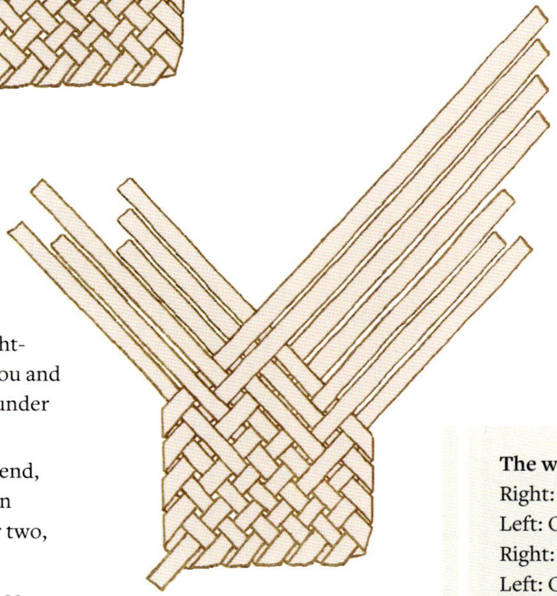

Step 3

Step 3: Take the outside right-hand end, fold it towards you and then diagonally, over one, under two, over two, under one.

Take the outside left-hand end, fold it towards you and then diagonally, over one, under two, over three.

Repeat the working sequence from step 1.

The working sequence is:
Right: Over one, under two, over three.
Left: Over one, under two, over two, under one.
Right: Over one, under two, over three.
Left: Over one, under two, over three.
Right: Over one, under two, over two, under one.
Left: Over one, under two, over three.

Joining

Join along the foot edge by laying the new length over the short old end which should be second from the outside of the right-hand group.

Thirteen-end single splint diamond with three-purl head

The replica plait

Source: CTLC 7/284/32

Origins: Ballinger, Buckinghamshire

Production date: 1850

Type of straw: Wheat straw, single splints

Splint width: 1.5 mm

Plait width: 12 mm

Plaiting direction: During working the back of the plait faces the maker and the front side faces away. The foot is on the right and the head on the left. When completed the front side of the plait has the head on the right and the foot on the left.

Joining: Along foot edge.

Background information: When Mrs Eldridge made this plait in about 1850, she set a master class for others to follow. I advise today's maker to feel confident with making both a three-purl head, and the thirteen-end diamond plait before tackling this pattern. A three-purl head has four moves whereas the diamond plait has a pattern repeat of four to complete the pattern so the two run out of sequence. It takes three completed purls before the working sequence repeats.

What to use: All types of flat straw.

You need: Seven plaiting lengths. Additional lengths for joining.

Setting up

If making this as a mottled plait take care to set up the lengths so the shiny side of the right-hand group face upwards and in the left-hand group, the matt side face upwards. This plait is set up using the same method as the thirteen-end single splint diamond.

Step 1: Hold six lengths horizontally, matt side upwards. Take the seventh length, with the shiny side upwards, and move it diagonally through the horizontal ends, over, under, over, under, over, under. The diagonal end lays towards about 1 o'clock with the short end protruding towards about 7 o'clock.

Fold the lowest right-hand horizontal end towards you then diagonally, over, under, over, under, over. It lays parallel to the right of the diagonal length.

Step 1

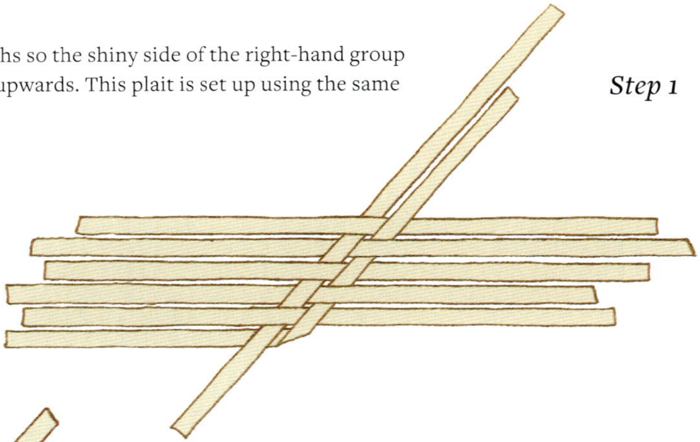

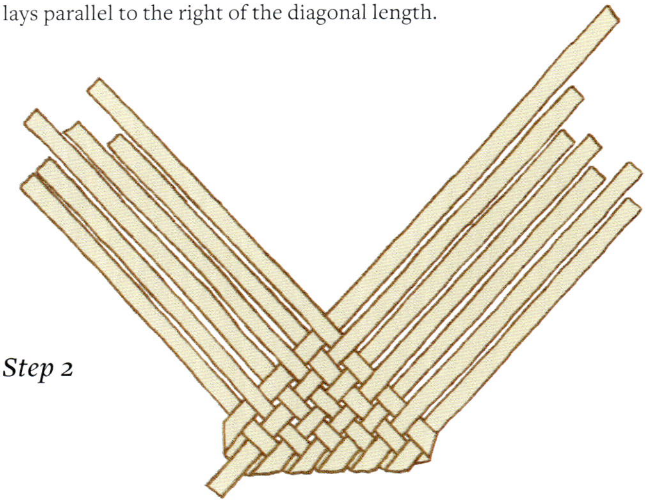

Step 2

Step 2: Take the lowest right-hand end, fold it towards you then diagonally, over, under, over under. It lays parallel to the two diagonal ends.

Repeat the folding movements with the right-hand ends until only one remains.

Fold the last right-hand end on itself then pass it, over, under, over, under, over, under the diagonal ends.

Take the lowest left-hand end, fold it on itself then over, under, over, under, over, under until it lays to inside the right-hand ends.

There are seven ends in the right-hand group with the shiny side facing and six in the left-hand group with the matt side facing.

Working

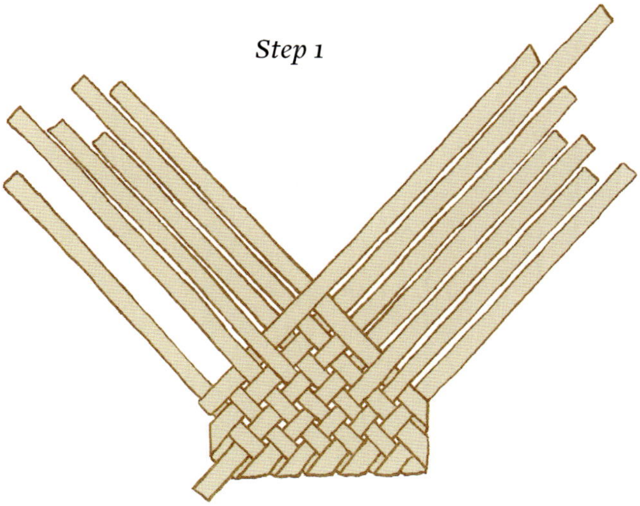

Step 1

Step 1: First purl, first stitch.

Take the outside right-hand end, fold it towards you and then diagonally, over one, under two, over three.

Take the second from outside left-hand end, fold it away from you and then around the outside left-hand end. Bring it back into the plait diagonally, under two, over three.

Step 2

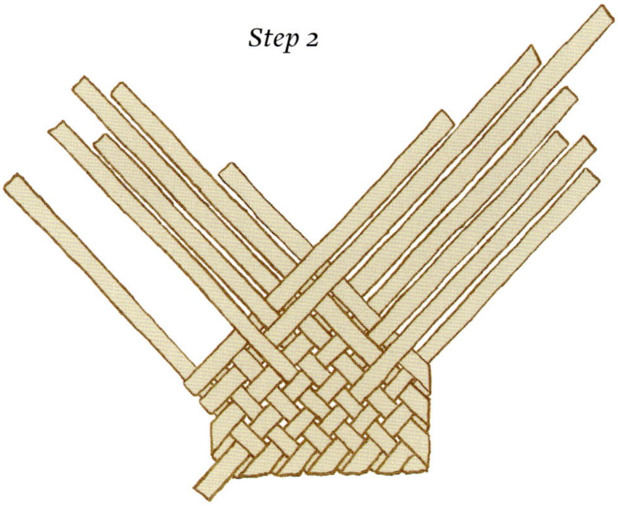

Step 2: First purl, second stitch.

Take the outside right-hand end, fold it towards you and then diagonally, over one, under two, over two, under one.

Take the second from outside left-hand end, fold it away from you and then around the outside left-hand end. Bring it back into the plait diagonally, under two, over three.

Step 3

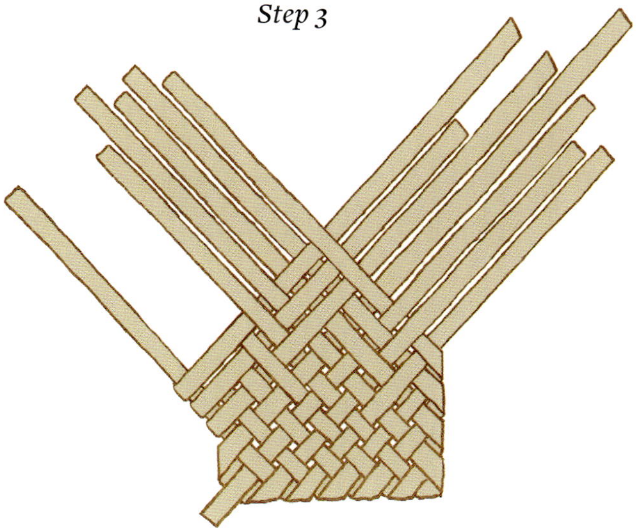

Step 3: First purl, third stitch.

Take the outside right-hand end, fold it towards you and then diagonally, over one, under two, over three.

Take the second from outside left-hand end, fold it away from you and then around the outside left-hand end. Bring it back into the plait diagonally, under two, over two, under one.

Step 4

Step 4: First purl, return of carrier stitch.

Take the outside right-hand end, fold it towards you and then diagonally, over one, under two, over three.

Take the outside left-hand end, fold it towards you and then bring it back into the plait diagonally, over one, under two, over three.

Second purl, first stitch.

Take the outside right-hand end, fold it towards you and then diagonally, over one, under two, over two, under one.

Take the second from outside left-hand end, fold it away from you and then around the outside left-hand end. Bring it back into the plait diagonally, under two, over three.

Second purl, second stitch.

Take the outside right-hand end, fold it towards you and then diagonally, over one, under two, over three.

Take the second from outside left-hand end, fold it away from you and then around the outside left-hand end. Bring it back into the plait diagonally, under two, over two, under one.

Second purl, third stitch.

Take the outside right-hand end, fold it towards you and then diagonally, over one, under two, over three.

Take the second from outside left-hand end, fold it away from you and then around the outside left-hand end. Bring it back into the plait diagonally, under two, over three.

Second purl, return of carrier into plait.

Take the outside right-hand end, fold it towards you and then diagonally, over one, under two, over two, under one.

Take the outside left-hand end, fold it towards you and then bring it back into the plait diagonally, over one, under two, over three.

Third purl, first stitch.

Take the outside right-hand end, fold it towards you and then diagonally, over one, under two, over three.

Take the second from outside left-hand end, fold it away from you and then around the outside left-hand end. Bring it back into the plait diagonally, under two, over two, under one.

Third purl, second stitch.

Take the outside right-hand end, fold it towards you and then diagonally, over one, under two, over three.

Take the second from outside left-hand end, fold it away from you and then around the outside left-hand end. Bring it back into the plait diagonally, under two, over three.

Third purl, third stitch.

Take the outside right-hand end, fold it towards you and then diagonally, over one, under two, over two, under one.

Take the second from outside left-hand end, fold it away from you and then around the outside left-hand end. Bring it back into the plait diagonally, under two, over three.

Third purl, return of carrier into plait.

Take the outside right-hand end, fold it towards you and then diagonally, over one, under two, over three.

Take the outside left-hand end, fold it towards you and then bring it back into the plait diagonally, over one, under two, over two, under one.

Continue from working step 1.

The working sequence is:
Right: Over one, under two, over three.
Left: Second from outside away, around carrier end, diagonally under two, over three.
Right: Over one, under two, over two, under one.
Left: Second from outside away, around carrier end, diagonally under two, over three.
Right: Over one, under two, over three.
Left: Second from outside away, around carrier end, diagonally under two, over two, under one.
Right: Over one, under two, over three.
Left: Outside carrier end back into body, over one, under two, over three.
Right: Over one, under two, over two, under one.
Left: Second from outside away, around the carrier end, diagonally under two, over three.
Right: Over one, under two, over three.
Left: Second from outside away, around carrier end, diagonally under two, over two, under one.
Right: Over one, under two, over three.
Left: Second from outside away, around the carrier end, diagonally under two, over three.
Right: Over one, under two, over two, under one.
Left: Outside carrier end back into body, over one, under two, over three.
Right: Over one, under two, over three.
Left: Second from outside away, around carrier end, diagonally under two, over two, under one.
Right: Over one, under two, over three.
Left: Second from outside away, around carrier end, diagonally under two, over three
Right: Over one, under two, over two, under one.
Left: Second from outside away, around carrier, diagonally under two, over three.
Right: Over one, under two, over three.
Left: Outside carrier end back into body, over one, under two, over two, under one.

Joining

Begin adding new lengths early in the plait. Join along the foot edge by laying the new length over the short old end which should be second from the outside of the right-hand group.

Seventeen-end English wave

The original plait

Source: CTLC *96/29*

Origins: Aldbury, Hertfordshire.

Production date: late 1800s

Type of straw: Wheat straw, double splints

Splint width: 1.5 mm

Plait width: 18 mm

Plaiting direction: During working the back of the plait faces the maker and the front side faces away. The foot is on the right and the head on the left. When completed the front side of the plait has the head on the right and the foot on the left.

Joining: Along foot edge.

Background information: Although called English Wave, this pattern, made in a variety of colourways, was found in Swiss and German sample books. Making was not confined to Aldbury as surviving examples were made in Essex. Note that the pattern on the front does not look the same as the back where there is one long stitch in each pattern sequence.

What to use: All types of flat straw.

You need: Nine pairs of splints faced dyed to undyed. Additional lengths for joining.

Setting up

If creating the colourway of the original plait take care to set up the lengths so the dyed splint of the pair faces upwards in the right-hand group and in the left-hand group, the undyed splint of the pair faces upwards. These instructions use the folding method to set up the ends.

Step 1

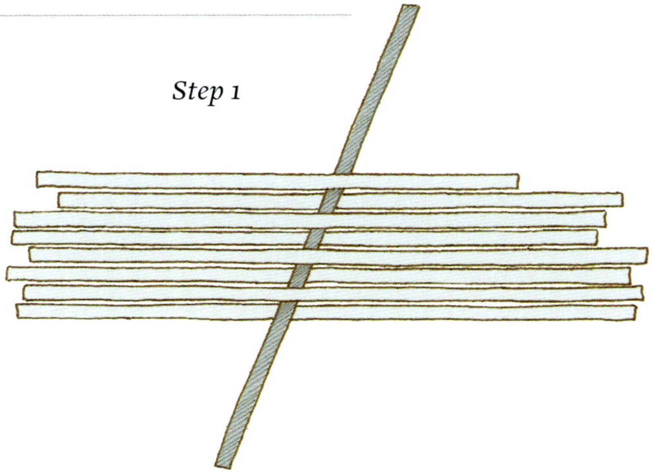

Step 1: Hold eight paired lengths horizontally with the undyed splint upwards. Take the seventh length, with the dyed splint of the pair facing upwards, and move it diagonally through the horizontal ends using an over, under sequence.

The diagonal end lays towards about 1 o'clock with the short end protruding towards about 7 o'clock.

Step 2

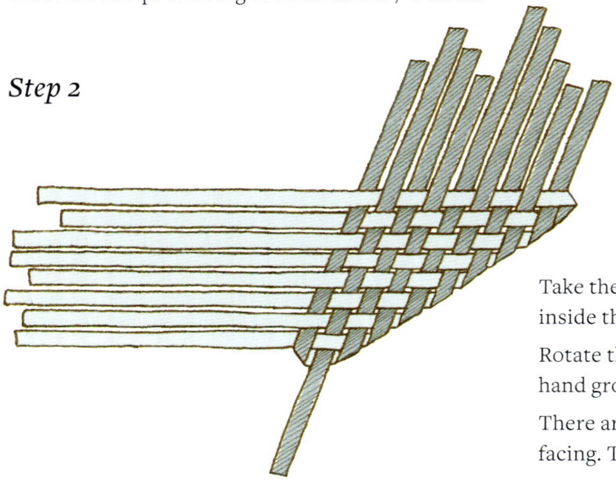

Step 2: Take the lowest right-hand end, fold it towards you then in sequence diagonally, over, under the ends until it lays parallel to the two diagonal ends.

Repeat the folding movements with the right-hand ends taking the ends over, under until only one end remains.

Fold the last right-hand end on itself then pass it in sequence over, under the diagonal ends.

Take the lowest left-hand end, fold it on itself then over, under until it lays to inside the right-hand ends.

Rotate the plait so the right-hand group points to about 1 o'clock and the left-hand group to about 11 o'clock.

There are nine ends in the right-hand group with the dyed splint of the pair facing. There are eight in the left-hand group with the undyed splint facing.

Working

Step 1

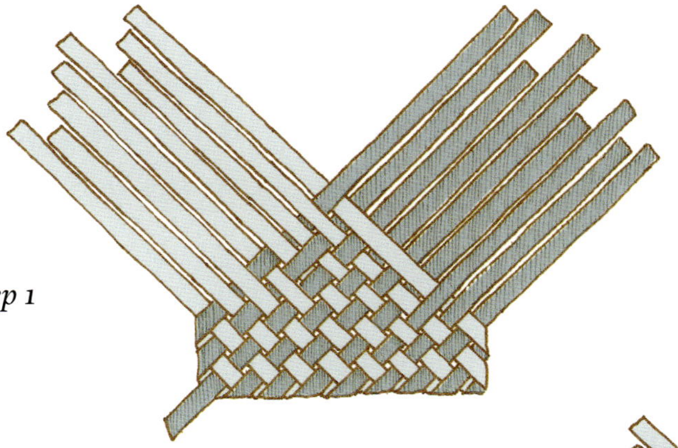

Step 1: Take the outside right-hand end, fold it towards you and then diagonally, over one, under two, over five.

Take the outside left-hand end, fold it towards you and then diagonally, over one, under two, over one, under three, over one.

Step 2

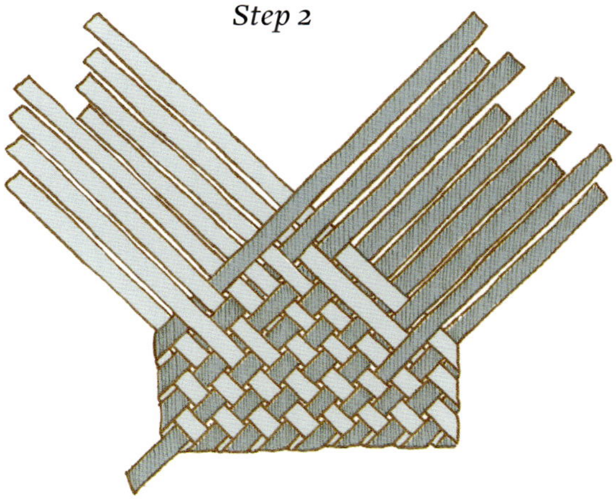

Step 2: Take the outside right-hand end, fold it towards you and then diagonally, over one, under two, over three, under two.

Take the outside left-hand end, fold it towards you and then diagonally, over one, under two, over five.

Step 3

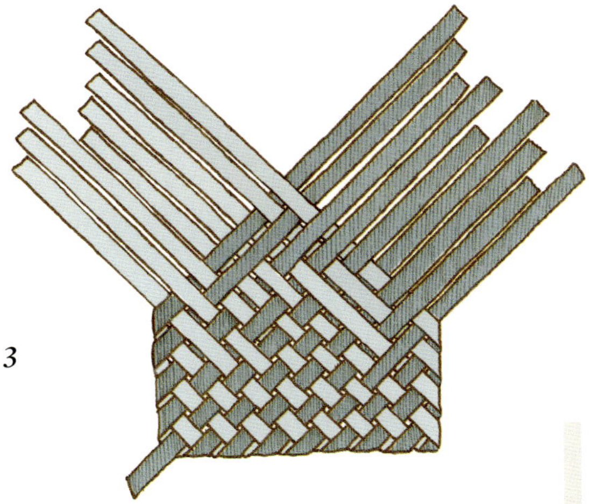

Step 3: Take the outside right-hand end, fold it towards you and then diagonally, over one, under two, over one, under three, over one.

Take the outside left-hand end, fold it towards you and then diagonally, over one, under two, over three, under two.

Repeat the working sequence from step 1.

The working sequence is:
Right: Over one, under two, over five.
Left: Over one, under two, over one, under three, over one.
Right: Over one, under two, over three, under two.
Left: Over one, under two, over five.
Right: Over one, under two, over one, under three, over one.
Left: Over one, under two, over three, under two.

Joining

Join along the foot edge by laying the new pair over the short old pair which should be second from the outside of the right-hand group. In some on the surviving examples one of the splints has been joined into a pair rather than always joining a pair at the same time.

Fourteen-end diamond with twist head

The original plait

Source: CTLC 1985/62 (12E)

Origins: Italy

Production date: 1920-1935

Type of straw: Wheat straw, whole

Splint width: 1 mm

Plait width: 18 mm

Plaiting direction: During working the back of the plait faces the maker and the front side faces away. The foot is on the right and the head on the left. When completed the front side of the plait has the head on the right and the foot on the left.

Joining: Along foot edge.

Background information: Diamond patterns were widely made around Florence from the early 1880s, however this example is thought to have been made between 1920 and 1935 and not available to the Luton hat trade after 1945. To make this plait the working ends are not evenly grouped; there are twelve ends in the right-hand working group and only two in the left-hand group. The head's twist pattern is not locked in place until the diamond sequence is complete.

What to use: All types of straw.

You need: Seven whole straws.
Additional lengths for joining.

Setting up

These instructions use the folding method to set up the ends, however if preferred the ends could be tied together.

Step 1: Hold seven lengths horizontally.

Take the lowest right-hand end fold it towards you and then diagonally over, under the remaining horizontal lengths so it lays towards the left at about 10 o'clock.

Repeat with the remaining right-hand ends until only one remains.

Take the remaining right-hand end, fold it towards you and then in sequence, fold it over, under the remaining right-hand ends so it lays to inside the left-hand group.

Step 1

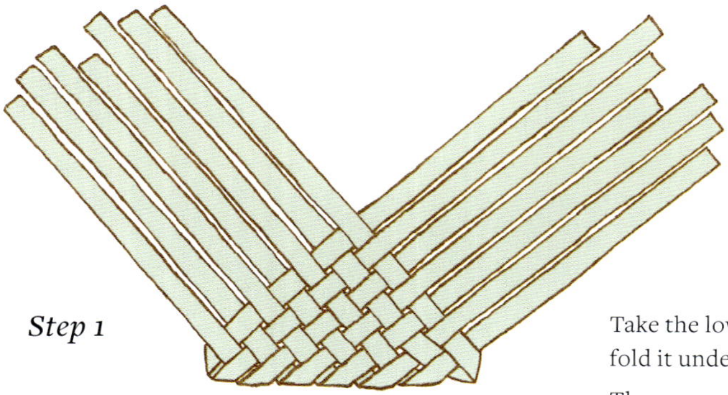

Take the lowest left-hand end, fold it away from you and then in sequence fold it under, over the remaining ends in the left-hand group.

There are seven ends in each group.

Step 2

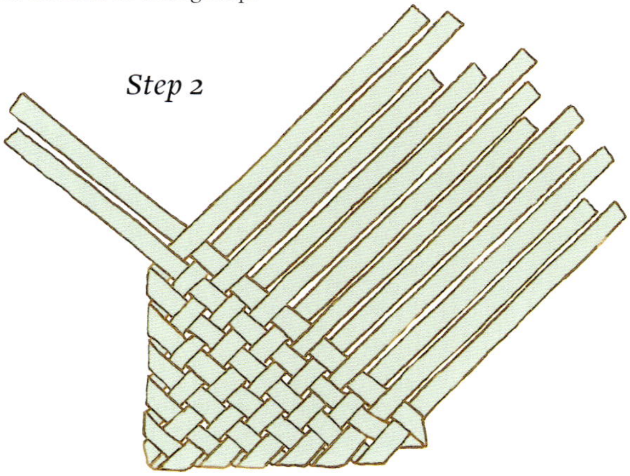

Step 2: Take the lowest left-hand end, fold it away from you then in sequence diagonally, under, over, the left-hand ends until it lays parallel to the two diagonal ends.

Repeat the folding movements with the left-hand ends taking the ends over, under until two ends remain in the left-hand group.

There are twelve ends in the right-hand group and two in the left-hand group.

Working

The working rhythm is different from other plaits, the ends forming the head edge are not secured until each diamond pattern is completed.

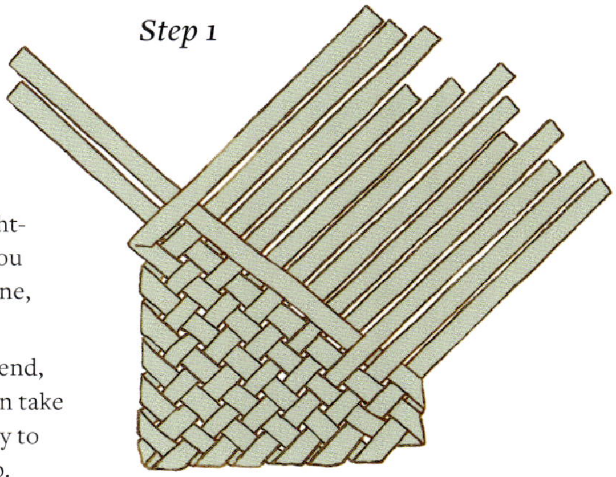

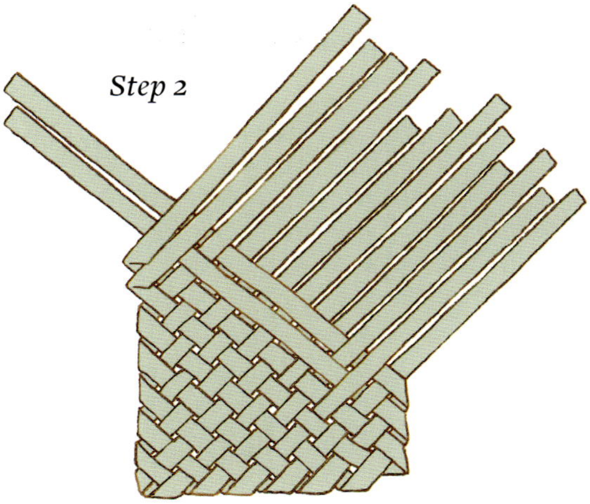

Step 1: Take the outside right-hand end, fold it towards you and then diagonally, over one, under two, over eight.

Take the outside left-hand end, form a twist stitch, and then take it diagonally, over two to lay to inside the right-hand group.

Step 2: Take the outside right-hand end, fold it towards you and then diagonally, over one, under two, over six, under two. The long stitch returns into the body under the same end as the previous stitch.

Take the outside left-hand end, form a twist stitch, and then take it diagonally, over two to lay to inside the right-hand group.

Step 3: Take the outside right-hand end, fold it towards you and then diagonally, over one, under two, over four, under four.

Take the outside left-hand end, form a twist stitch, and then take it diagonally, over two to lay to inside the right-hand group.

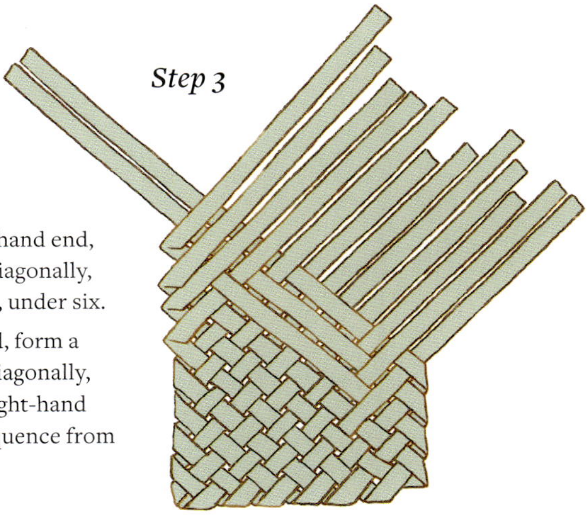

Step 4: Take the outside right-hand end, fold it towards you and then diagonally, over one, under two, over two, under six.

Take the outside left-hand end, form a twist stitch, and then take it diagonally, over two to lay to inside the right-hand group. Repeat the working sequence from step 1.

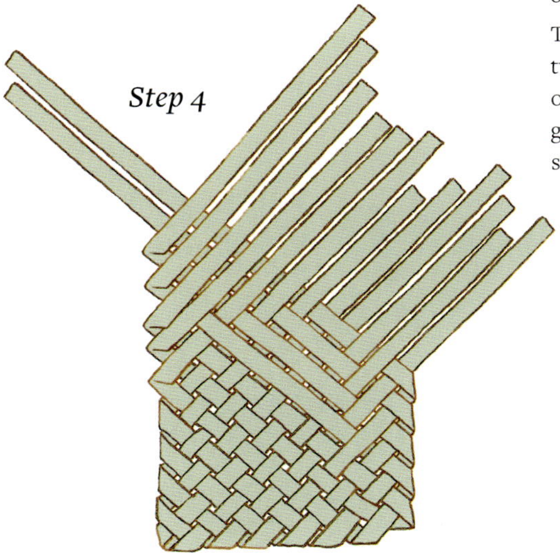

The working sequence is:
Right: Over one, under two, over eight.
Left: Twist, over two.
Right: Over one, under two, over six, under two.
Left: Twist, over two.
Right: Over one, under two, over four, under four.
Left: Twist, over two.
Right: Over one, under two, over two, under six.
Left: Twist, over two.

Joining

It is important to evenly space joins. Join along the foot edge by laying the new end over the short old end which should be second from the outside of the right-hand group.

Sixteen-end diamond

The original plait

Source: CTLC 1985/62 (12A)

Origins: Italy

Production date: 1920-1935

Type of straw: Wheat straw, whole

Splint width: 1 mm

Plait width: 18 mm

Plaiting direction: During working the front of the plait faces the maker. The foot is on the left and the head on the right.

Joining: Along foot edge.

Background information: This pattern appeared amongst samples of plaits made in the Orkney isles during the 1800s and from the 1880s appeared to be a popular Italian product. In the early 1900s, the Italian sample books included pieces where colour had been introduced. This plait does not have a prominent foot edge so when used for a hat was stitched edge to edge using an Anita, zigzag stitch machine, a method which also strengthens the otherwise weak join.

What to use: All types of straw, fine round wheat, rye, and grasses work best.

You need: 16 lengths.
Additional lengths for joining.

Setting up

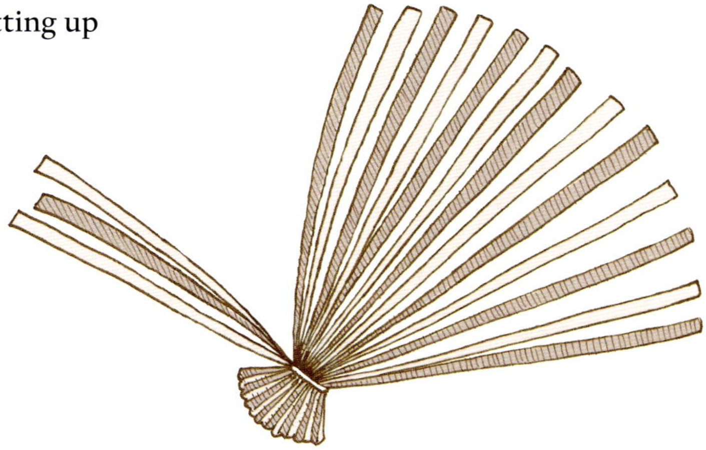

Step 1: Tightly tie together sixteen lengths close to one end. Divide the group so thirteen ends are in the right-hand group and three in the left-hand group.

Working

As you become more familiar with the working sequence your fingertips will tell you if a length has moved to a wrong place, but until then check both the front and back of the plait since the unlocked ends can move out of place.

Step 1: To create the twist stitch, hold the second from outside end to provide resistance for the outside end to move against. Depending on the straw it may also be necessary to make a little crease to the inner side of the length with your fingernail.

Take the outside right-hand end and use a sideways movement to create a neat twist. Then fold it diagonally under one and over the remaining ends.

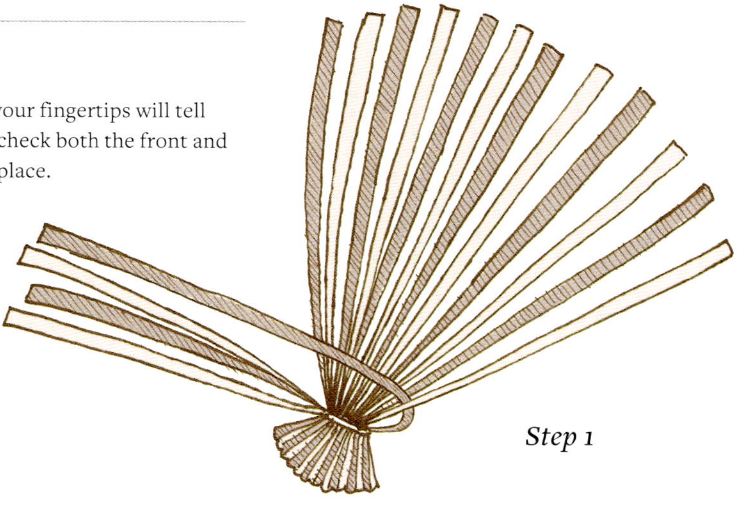

Step 1

Step 2: Take the outside right-hand end, make a twist stitch then move it diagonally under one and over the remaining ends in the group.

Repeat until only three ends remain in the right-hand group.

There are now thirteen ends in the left-hand group and three in the right-hand group. The ten ends laying across the body form the diamond pattern. They are locked in place in the next move.

Now work the left-hand foot edge.

Take the outside left-hand end fold it away from you under one and over the remaining ends in the group to lay to the inside of the right-hand group.

The left-hand edge is the foot, therefore fold the ends instead of creating a twist.

Repeat until only three ends remain in the left-hand group.

If thicker straws are used there may be a pattern distortion as the working move changes to the opposite edge. To counter this gently press the straws so working ends can pass over without rising upwards.

Repeat the sequence working alternate sides.

Step 2

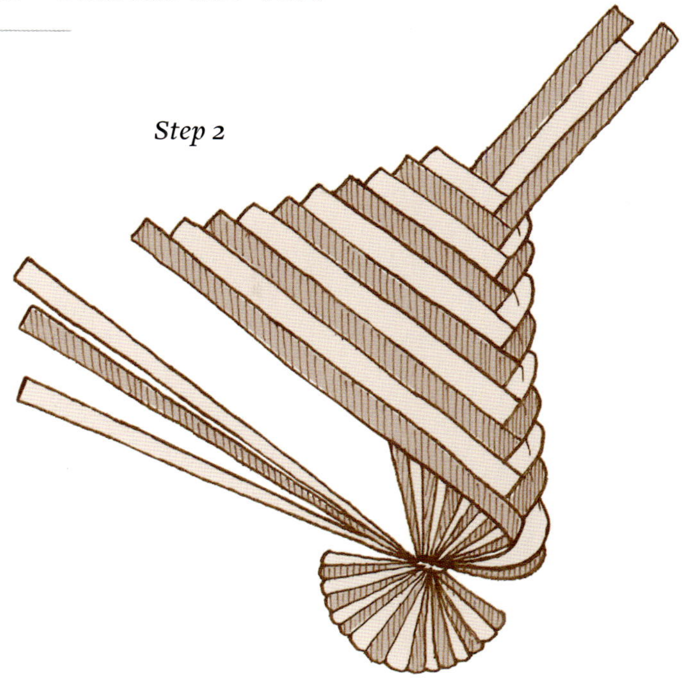

The working sequence is:
Right: Under one, over the remaining ends.
Repeat until three ends on one side.
Left: Under one, over the remaining ends.
Repeat until three ends on one side.

Joining

The plait's structure means joins are weak so avoid joins in consecutive moves and leave longer than usual set in and speel ends and leave clipping until the length is complete.

The short end must be the outside end of the left-hand group.

Take the outside short end, fold it away from you, under the next and over the remaining ends in the left-hand group.

Place the new end under the last moved end, taking it across the remaining ends in the group. Take care to keep the old and new ends together.

When the old and new ends reach the outside of the right-hand group having been locked in place by the last right-hand move, fold the old end back on itself diagonally towards about 8 o'clock.

Only work the new end.

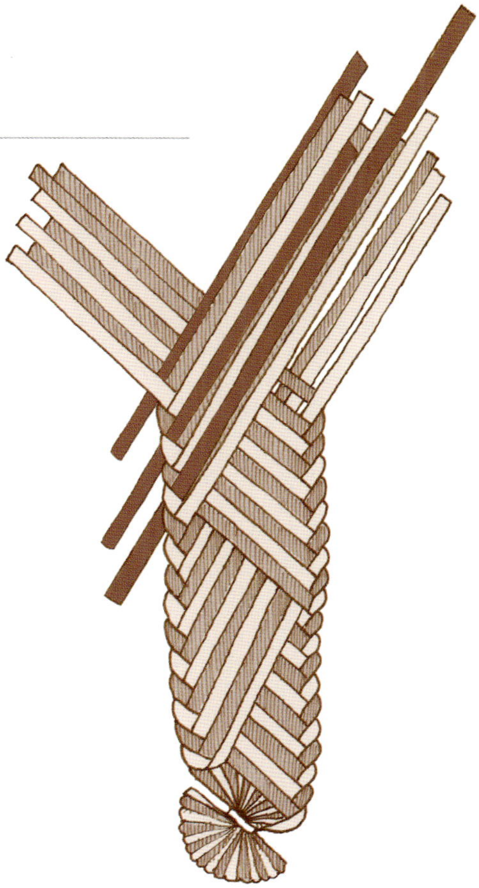

Museum of London 35:13. This exceptionally rare bonnet is from a Brilliant plait that is interspaced with seven-end plait to add strength. It dates to 1888. The inside nape edge is finished with a three-purl plait.

Brilliant

To make a good plait depends upon the preparation of the straw, the method of holding the working ends, their angle, and stitch tension all working in harmony. Even then the working end that crosses the body on its edge to give the facetted pattern may not always lay as it should. Practice regularly until it can be made with relaxed hands and mind. The English pattern was made in Switzerland, Germany, and Belgium but they also produced a version that was more forgiving for the plaiter with its tighter stitches and crossing end laying flat.

Eight-end Brilliant with double splints

The original plait

Source: CTLC 1997/17/4

Origins: Switzerland

Production date: Late 1800s

Type of straw: Wheat straw, double splints

Splint width: 3 mm

Plait width: 20 mm

Plaiting direction: During working the front of the plait faces the maker. The foot is on the right and the head on the left.

Joining: Along foot edge or on crossing end.

Background information: This pattern provides an easier introduction for learning the intricacies of turning the ends to keep the crossing splint on edge. All plaits require an ability to be able to adjust angles and tensions according to the straws being worked, but this is particularly pertinent for Brilliant plaits. Not all surviving examples are perfect, the crossing end sometimes flattened or turned on itself when worked by even the best plaiters.

What to use: All types of flat straw.

You need: Four pairs of splints, two pairs dyed and two pairs undyed.
Additional lengths of correct colours for joining.

Setting up

Arrange so the working ends are different lengths. If you wish to recreate the colourway then set up the ends so they are alternate colours.

Step 1: Hold one pair horizontally, from 9 o'clock to 3 o'clock.

Hold a second pair diagonally in front of the horizontal length, pointing from about 2 o'clock to 8 o'clock. Fold the lower end of this pair behind the horizontal to lay at about 10 o'clock. Press the fold.

Take the third pair and place it behind the horizontal to lay to the inside of the right-hand pair. Fold the lower end diagonally towards you to lay to the outside of the left-hand diagonal.

Take the fourth pair. Hold them diagonally in front of the horizontal pair and to the inside of the diagonal right-hand ends. Fold the lower section behind the horizontal to lay to the outside of the left-hand diagonals. Press the fold.

Take the outside right-hand horizontal pair and fold them diagonally towards you and over one, under one, over one. Take the outside left-hand horizontal pair and fold them diagonally away from you so they pass under one, over one, under one, over one.

There are four pairs in each group.

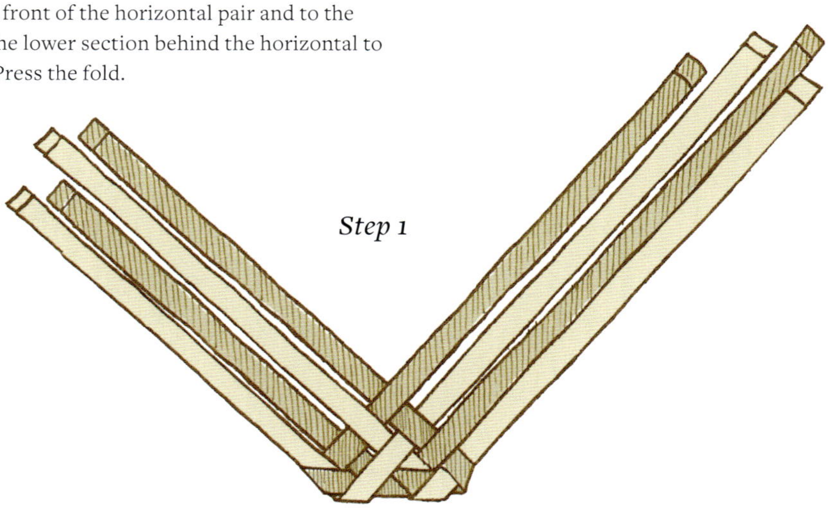

Step 2

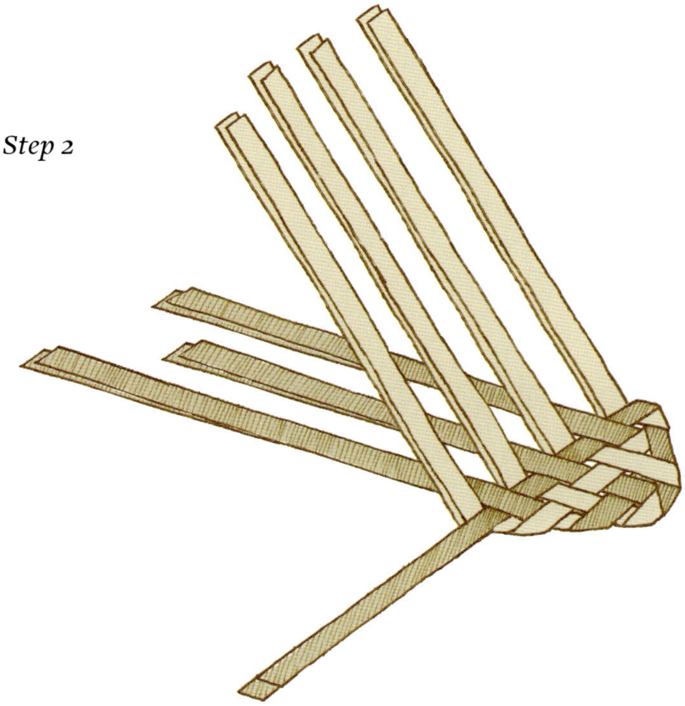

Step 2: Take the outside left-hand pair fold away from you and then diagonally under one, over one, under one to lay to inside the right-hand group.

Take the outside left-hand pair and fold away from you then diagonally under one, over one to lay to inside the right-hand group.

Take the outside left-hand pair and fold diagonally under so it lays inside the right-hand group.

There are seven-pairs of ends on the right and one on the left.

Starting from the right of the right-hand group, fold the outside pair towards you, the next away from you, repeating so four are towards you and three away. The pairs should be positioned to form a V with an angle of about 45 degrees. If turned sideways the forward group will be at about 2 o'clock and the back group at about 10 o'clock.

Working

To keep the crossing pair on its edge requires a counter-twist with the left-hand end that emerges from the plait twisting backwards and as it reaches the right, twisting towards you.

Step 1: Take the outside left-hand pair, twist it gently away from you and then lay it between the ends, twisting it towards you and holding so the crossing end is on edge. Hold the crossing end in place between the V of the two groups.

Step 1

Step 2: Working from the right, fold the pairs so those at the front pass to the back and those at the back fold to the front. Remember to keep them in a V-shape with an angle of about 45 degrees.

The next move maintains the correct number of ends in the front group. The crossing pair is held in place on its edge. Without disturbing it move the free end downwards to join the front group.

There are three pairs towards you and four pairs away from you. The crossing pair is gently held in position within the V.

Continue the working sequence.

The working sequence is:
Left: Twist outside end onto its edge, lay across the other ends.
Right: Working from the right fold the ends in the front group to the back and those in the back group to the front.
Right: Carefully twist the loose end of the crossing end to join the front group.

Step 2

Joining

When looking at various examples of Brilliant plaits it is apparent that plaiters joined onto the crossing end and onto the vertical ends. Joining onto the crossing end is easier when learning these plaits.

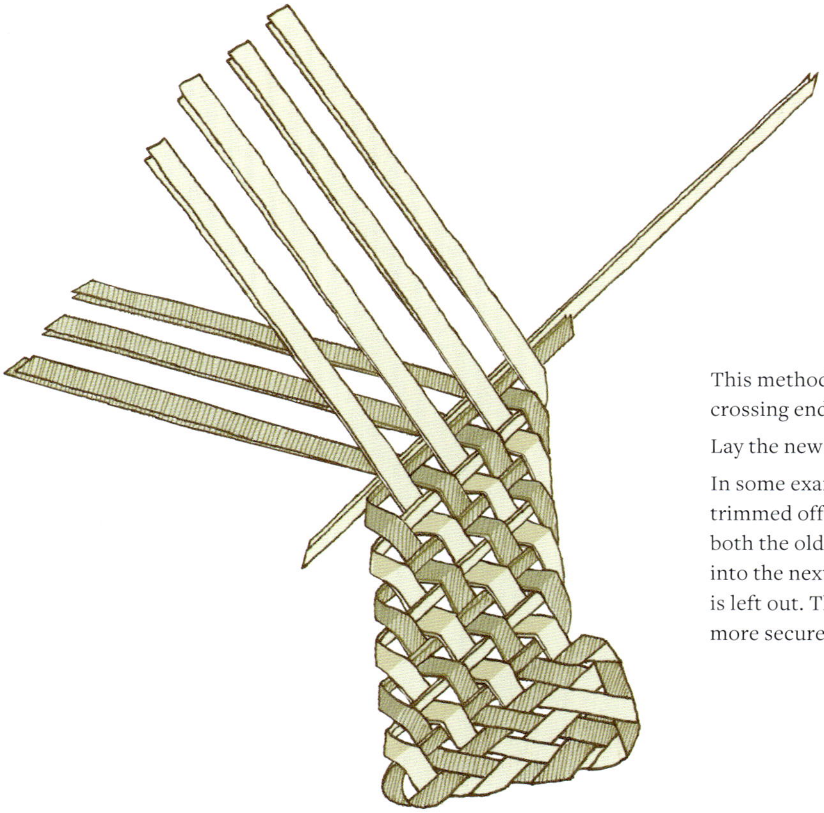

This method is for joining onto the crossing end.

Lay the new end over the short old end.

In some examples the old end is trimmed off at the edge, while in others both the old and new ends are worked into the next moves before the old end is left out. The latter method produces a more secure plait.

Eight-end Brilliant with feather edge

The original plait

Source: CTLC 9/28

Origins: Luton, Bedfordshire

Production date: 1926

Type of straw: Wheat straw, single splint

Splint width: 2 mm

Plait width: 8 mm

Plaiting direction: During working the front of the plait faces the maker. The foot is on the right, and head on the left.

Joining: Along foot edge or on crossing end.

Background information: The name of the plaiter who made this plait has been lost, but the story of where and when she made it survives. It was made while she was sitting on a horse-drawn waggon which was part of a 1926 Jubilee procession in Luton. The celebration was to mark Luton's fifty years as a municipal council and four ladies representing the industry sat in front of a mock thatched cottage.

What to use: All types of flat straw.

You need: Four lengths.
Additional lengths for joining.

Setting up

The splints must be set up, so the right-hand group has the shiny side facing upwards and the left-hand group has the matt side facing upwards.

Step 1: Hold one length horizontally, from 9 o'clock to 3 o'clock. Shiny side facing upwards.

Hold a second length diagonally in front of the horizontal length, pointing from about 2 o'clock to 8 o'clock. The shiny side must be facing. Fold the lower end of this length behind the horizontal to lay at about 10 o'clock. Press the fold.

Take the third length and place it behind the horizontal to lay to the inside of the right-hand end. Shiny side facing. Fold the lower end diagonally towards you to lay to the outside of the left-hand diagonal.

Take the fourth length, shiny side facing. Hold it diagonally in front of the horizontal length and to the inside of the diagonal right-hand ends. Fold the lower section behind the horizontal to lay to the outside of the left-hand diagonals. Press the fold.

Take the outside right-hand end and fold it diagonally towards you and over one, under one, over one. Take the outside left-hand end turn it so the shiny side is facing then fold it diagonally away from you, so it passes under one, over one, under one, over one.

There are four ends in each group, with shiny side facing in the right-hand group and the matt side in the left-hand group.

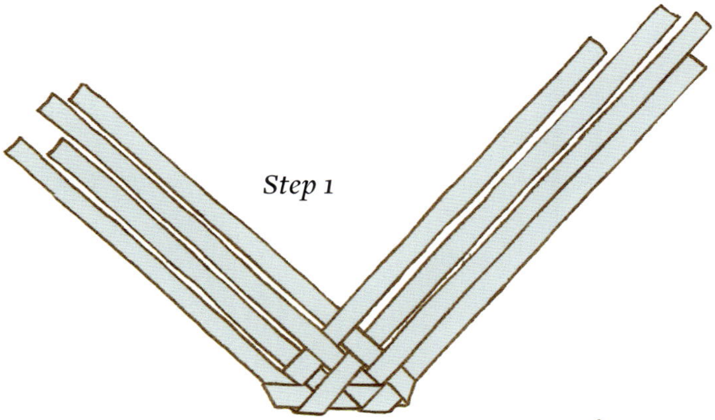

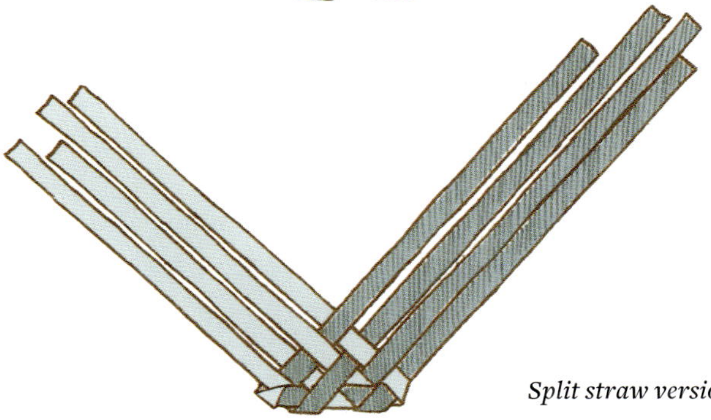

Split straw version

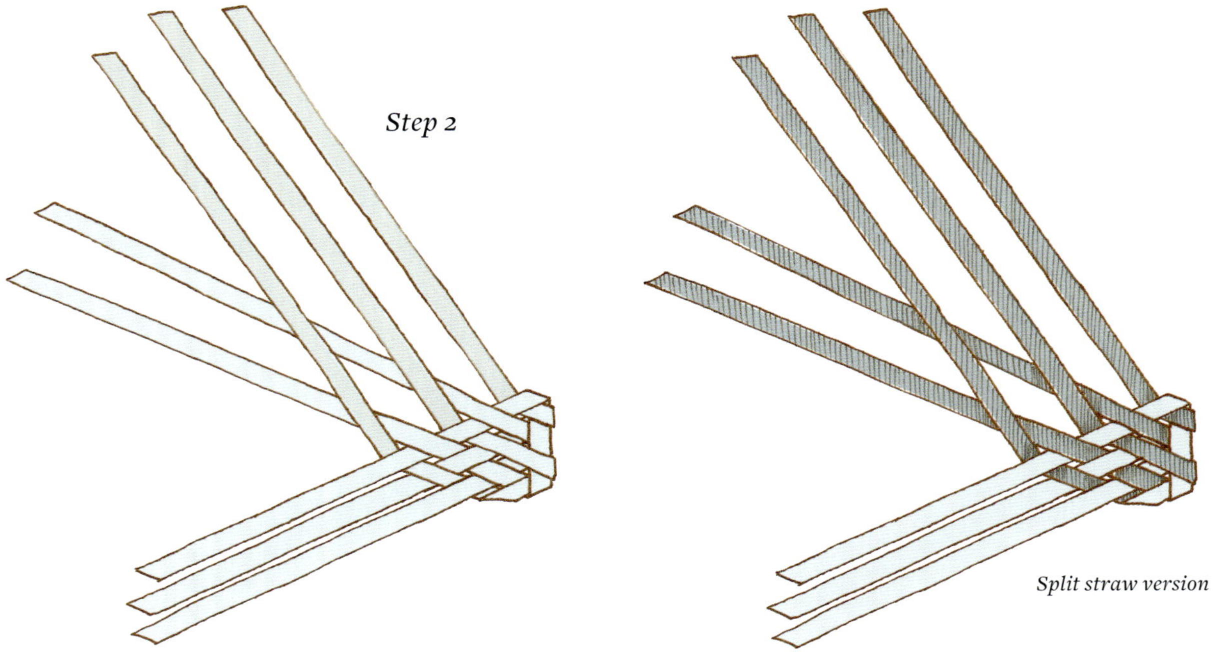

Step 2: Take the outside left-hand end and fold it diagonally under one, over one, under one.

There are five-ends on the right and three on the left.

Starting from the right of the right-hand group, fold the outside end towards you, the next away from you, repeating so three are towards you and two away. The ends should be positioned in a V-shape, with an angle of about 45 degrees. The forward group will be at about 2 o'clock and the back group at about 10 o'clock.

Working

The number of ends in the back and front groups will alternate during the working sequence.

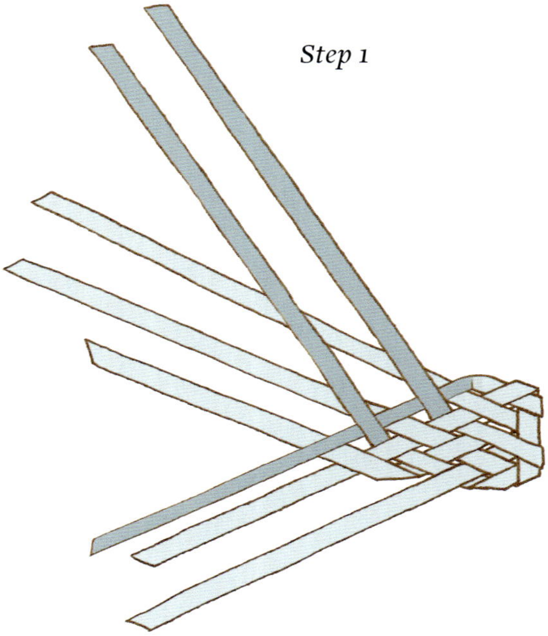

Step 1: Fold the middle end of the left-hand group diagonally upwards, over the top left-hand end. Twist it so the shiny side faces upwards.

Take the outside right-hand end, twist it gently towards the left so it lays between the ends of the V. Holding the crossing end on its edge, gently twist the long end away from you so the end stays on its edge.

Step 2: Working from the right, fold the ends so those at the front of the V pass to the back and those at the back fold to the front. Remember to keep the crossing ends upwards in their 45 degree V-shape. Gently hold the crossing end on its edge.

Take the lowest left-hand end, fold it diagonally upward, over the other two in the group. It points away from you, over the crossing end with its shiny side facing.

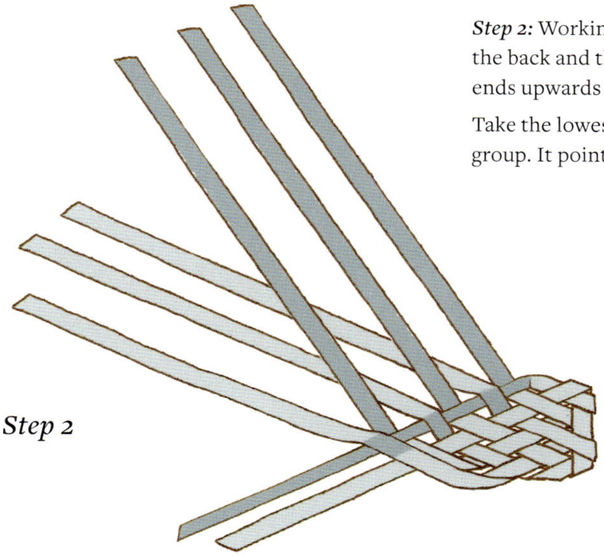

Step 2

Step 3: Take the outside right-hand end and lay it across the V-shape, over the crossing ends. It lays to the left. There are now three ends in the left-hand group.

Working from the right, fold the forward ends back and the backwards ends forwards to hold the crossing end in place.

Continue the working sequence until joining begins.

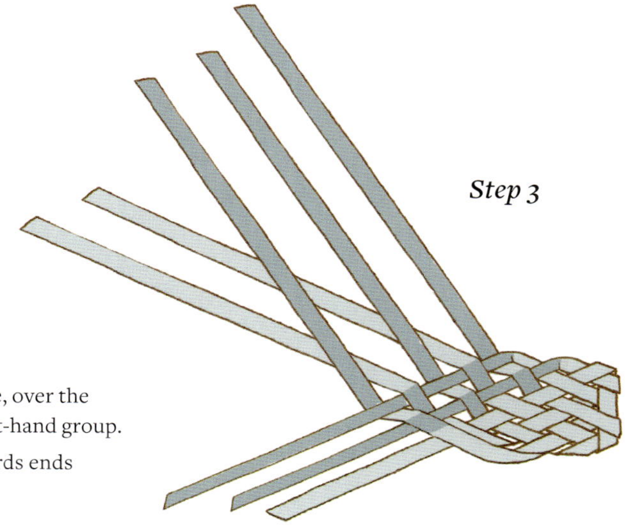

Step 3

The working sequence is:
Left: Middle of outside group, over top end, twist so the shiny side faces.
Right: Outside end on its edge across the V to lay to the top of the left-hand group.
Right: Move the back ends of the V to the front and those at the front to the back.
Left: Lowest of outside group, over next two ends, shiny side facing.
Right: Outside end on its edge across the V to lay to the top of the left-hand group.
Right: Move the back ends of the V to the front and those at the front to the back.

Joining

The original example provides no indication of the joining method therefore to develop a range of joining methods the instructions use a diagonal join, however, joining onto the crossing end can also be used.

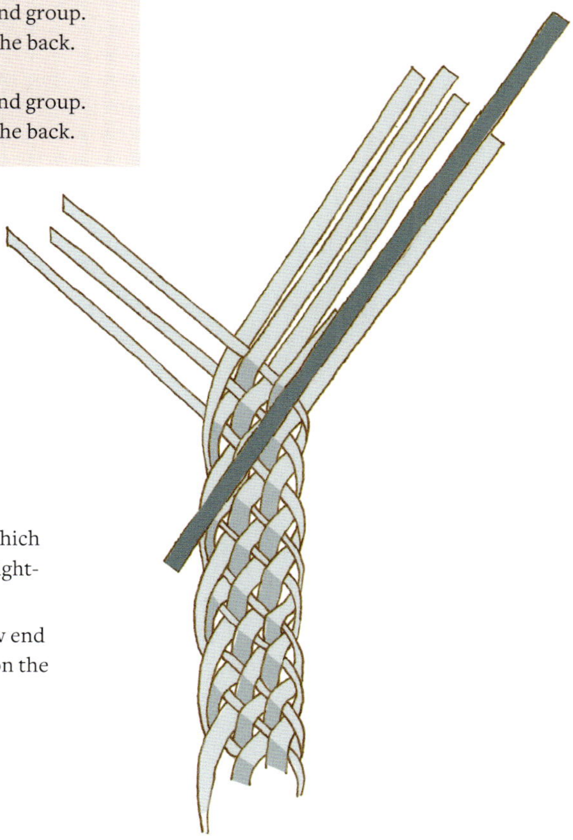

Lay the new end over the short old end which must be second from the outside of the right-hand group.

Work the two ends together until the new end is locked in place and can be clipped off on the backside of the plait.

Sixteen-end Brilliant

The original plait

Source: CTLC 10/28

Origins: Luton area, Bedfordshire

Production date: 1885

Type of straw: Wheat straw, single splint

Splint width: 1–1.5 mm

Plait width: 15 mm

Plaiting direction: During working the front of the plait faces the maker. The foot is on the left and the head on the right.

Joining: Along foot edge or on crossing end.

Background information: This example was made for an exhibition held in the Luton Plait Halls in 1885, a major exhibition attended by Royalty and staged to promote the straw hat industry and straw plaiting. Prizes were awarded to local plaiters and although it cannot be proved the quality of the plait shown indicates it may have been a prize winner.

What to use: This can be made with all types of flat straw.

You need: Eight lengths.
Additional lengths for joining.

Setting up

Set up so all the ends in the right-hand group have the shiny side facing and those in the left-hand group have the matt side facing.

Step 1: Hold the eight lengths horizontally with their matt side facing upwards.

Take the lowest right-hand end, fold it towards you then in sequence diagonally, over, under the ends until it lays towards about 2 o'clock.

Repeat the folding movements with the right-hand ends taking the ends over, under until only one end remains.

Fold the last right-hand end forward to lay parallel to the previous right-hand end. Then fold it on itself, forming a small point so it then passes in sequence over, under the diagonal ends.

Take the lowest left-hand end, fold it on itself to form a small point, then under, over until it lays to inside the right-hand ends.

There are eight ends in both groups. The ends in the right-hand group have the shiny side facing upwards and the left-hand group with the matt-side facing upwards.

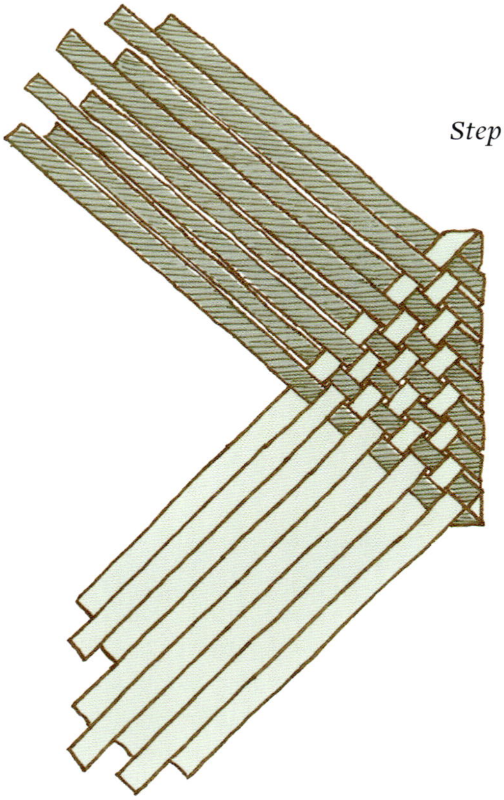

Step 1

Step 2: Take the outside left-hand end and fold it away from you then diagonally under and over until it lays to the inside of the right-hand group.

Repeat until only one end remains in the left-hand group. Rotate the starting group so the left-hand end points to about 8 o'clock.

Step 2

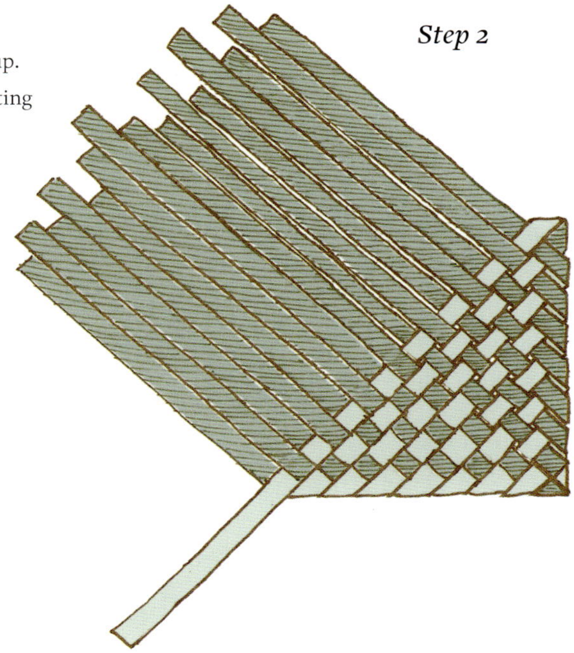

Step 3

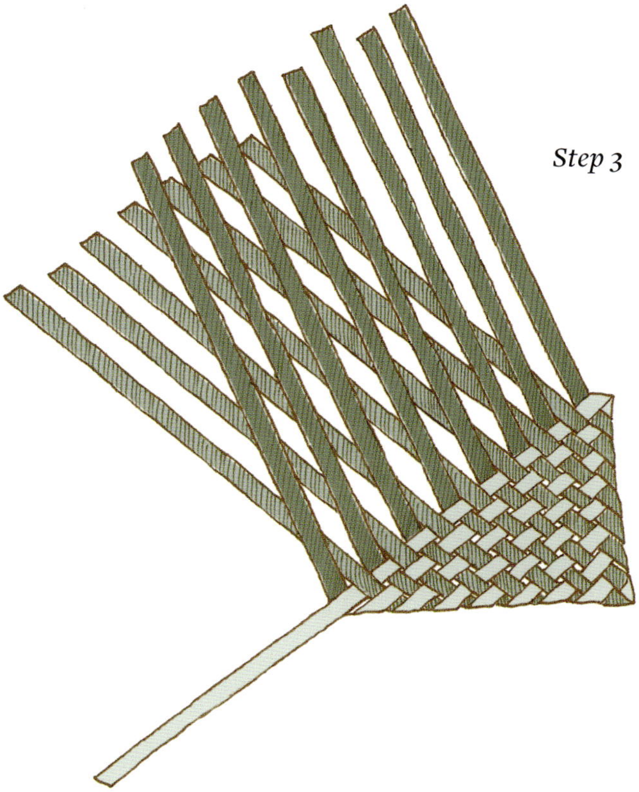

Step 3: Working from the right towards the left, fold the outer end forward, the next backwards and keep them in a V-shape with an angle of about 45 degrees. There are seven in the back group and eight in the front group. One end points to the left.

Working

The ends should maintain an upwards angle to form a V with an angle of about 45 degrees. As they change position from front to back try not to compress the crossing end. There is a temptation to tighten the plait to hold the crossing end in place, but it will create an unattractive plait and will be counterproductive. With practice you will find the correct tension and learn how to adjust according to the materials.

Step 1

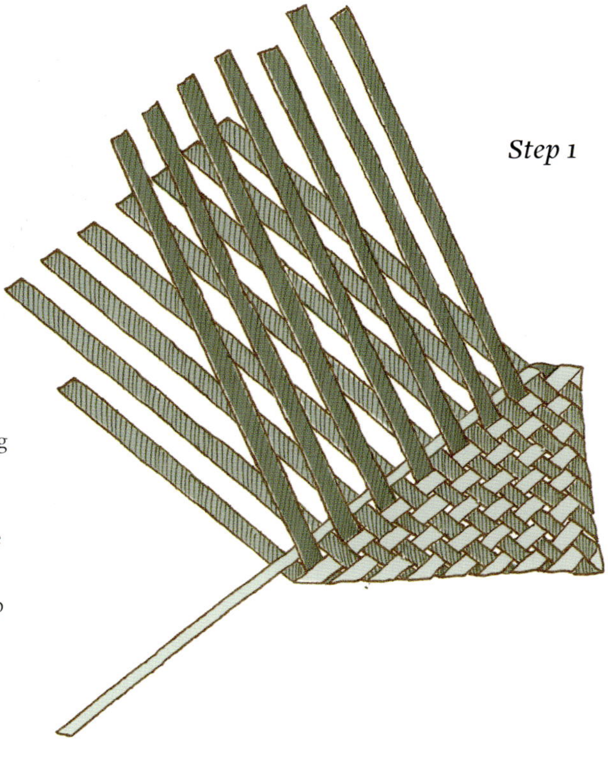

Step 1: Take the end that crossed and without disturbing the part that crosses between the folded ends, twist it upwards to join the right-hand end of the front group.

Take the right-hand end, twist it diagonally towards the left passing between the V-shape group of ends.

Make a gentle counter twist on the crossing end to keep it on its edge with the shiny side facing.

Step 2

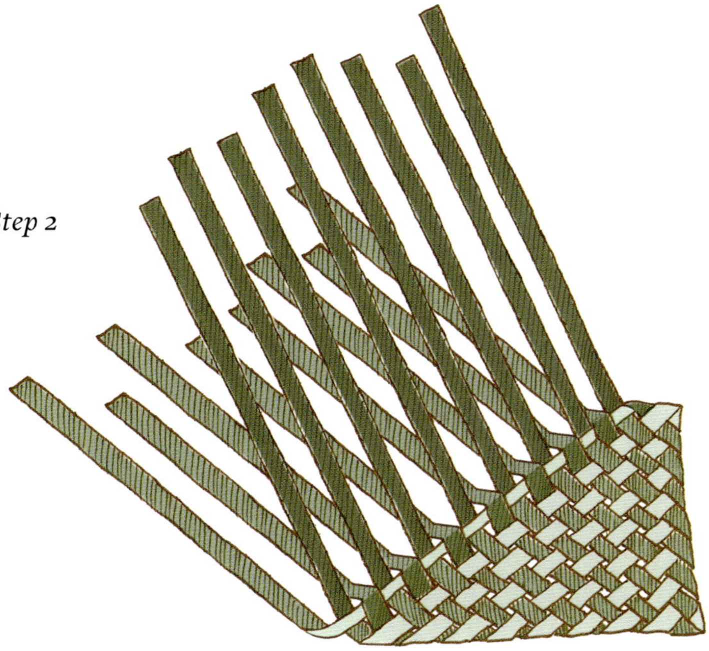

Step 2: Fold the ends so the ones at the back fold to the front and those at the front fold to the back. Maintain the V-shape to about 45 degrees. They now hold the crossing end in place.

Continue the working sequence until joining begins.

The working sequence is:
Left: Carefully fold the outside end upwards to join the back group of the V.
Right: Outside end on its edge across the V to lay to the left.
Left: Fold the ends at the back of the V to the front and those at the front to the back.

Joining

The new end can be introduced as the crossing end or into the main group. The diagram shows joining into the V-shape group.

Hold the new end behind the second from outside on the left. Work both ends together leaving behind the old end the next time it is folded forward.

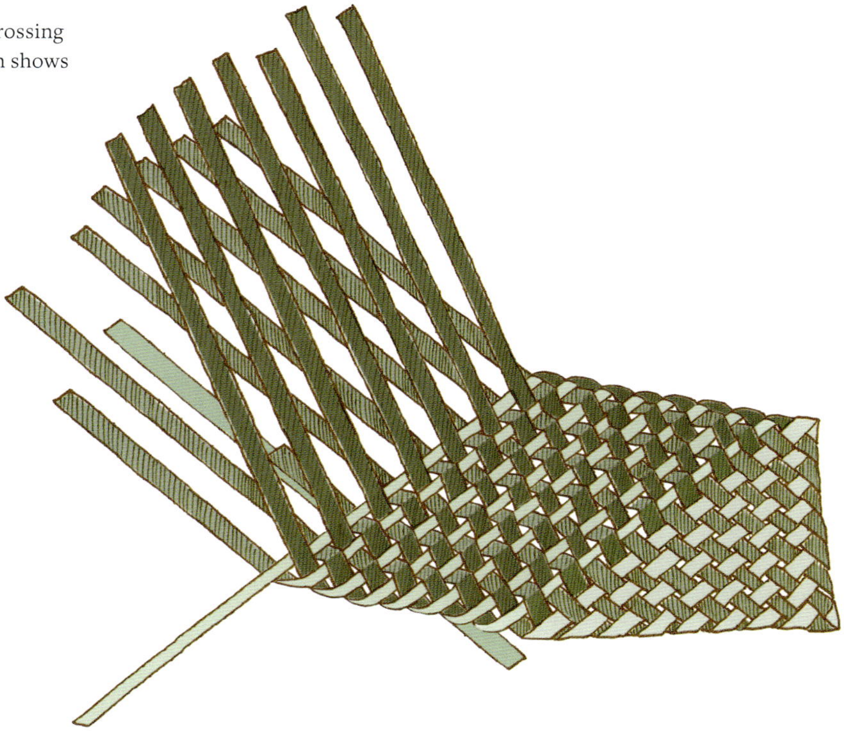

Twelve-end Brilliant gate

The original plait

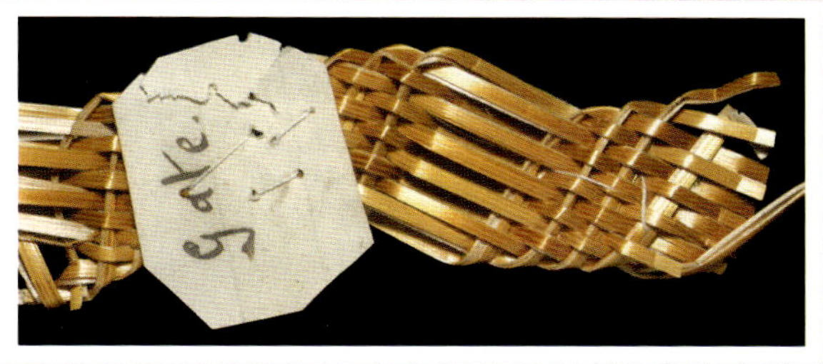

Source: CTLC Aldbury plait sample panel

Origins: Aldbury, Hertfordshire

Production date: 1913

Type of straw: Wheat straw, double splints

Splint width: 1–2 mm

Plait width: 19–20 mm

Plaiting direction: During working the front of the plait faces the maker. The foot is on the left and the head on the right.

Joining: Along foot edge or on crossing end.

Background information: This pattern was more commonly called matchbox signifying that a piece of wooden matchbox was used as the form to create the spacing. It is unclear why this pattern was called gate; it may simply be a local name. The variation section shows a pattern that was made in Switzerland. This is another Brilliant pattern that was made with various numbers of working ends and in a variety of colourways.

What to use: All types of flat straw.

You need: Six pairs of splints.
Additional lengths for joining.
A form. The size used for the original plait was a rectangle approximately 16 mm x 25 mm and 3 mm thick.

Setting up

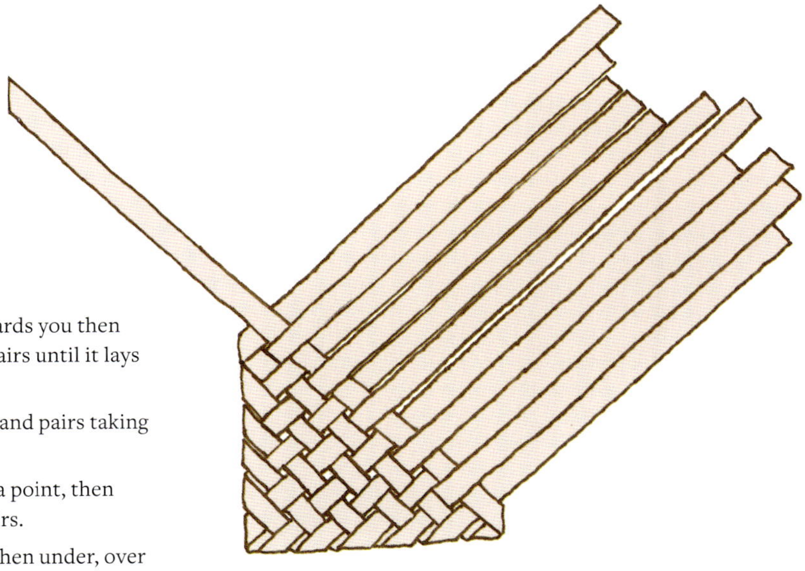

Hold the six paired lengths horizontally.

Take the lowest right-hand pair, fold them towards you then in sequence diagonally, over, under the other pairs until it lays towards about 2 o'clock.

Repeat the folding movements with the right-hand pairs taking them over, under until only one pair remains.

Fold the last right-hand pair on itself to create a point, then pass it in sequence over, under the diagonal pairs.

Take the lowest left-hand pair, fold it on itself then under, over until it lays to inside the right-hand pairs.

There are six pairs in each group.

Take the outside left-hand pair and fold it diagonally under and over until it lays to the inside of the right-hand group.

Repeat until one pair remains in the left-hand group.

Working

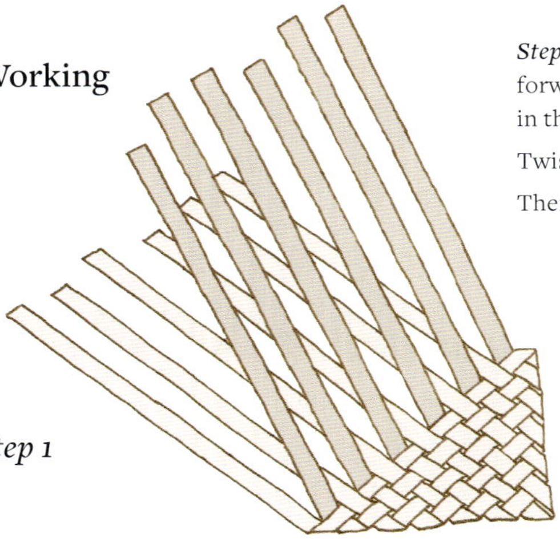

Step 1

Step 1: Starting from the right-hand side, fold the pairs at the back of the V forward, and those at the front back. Six are in the front group of the V and five in the back group of the V.

Twist the outside left-hand pair under and upwards to join the back group.

There are now six in each group.

Step 2

Step 2: Take the outside right-hand pair of the front group, take it on its edge across the V. Make a gentle counter twist on the crossing end to keep it on its edge. Hold the crossing end in place.

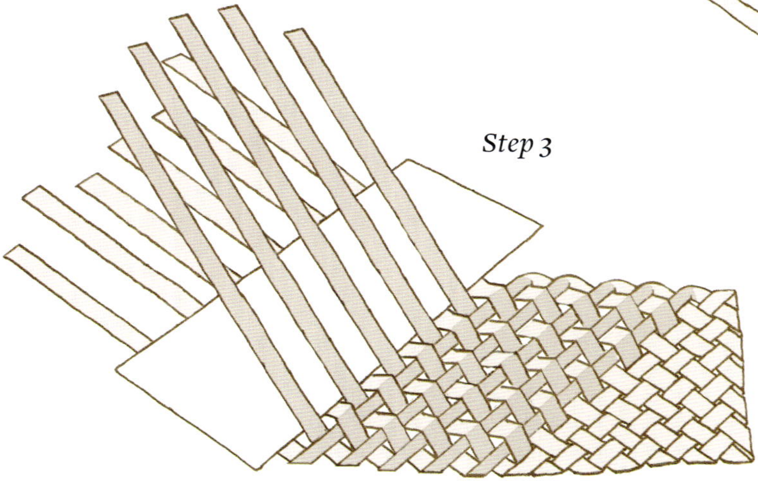

Step 3

Step 3: In this step the form is added. This move is only made every fifth row of the pattern.

Follow working steps 1 to 2 until four rows are made. After working step 2 insert the form.

Fold up the ends in the front group of the V over the form and cross them over the top of the V to the back. Fold the ends at the back of the V over the back of the form and bring them to the front over the top.

This move holds the form in place.

Continue from working step 1.

The working sequence is:
Right: Fold the ends at the back of the V to the front and those at the font to the back.
Left: Twist the outside end upwards to join the back group.
Right: Outside end on its edge across the V.
Work four rows, insert the form then repeat the sequence.

Joining

A more secure join will be achieved by restricting joins to the section of plait. The method used on the original plait is not obvious they can be added to the vertical ends of the V or to the crossing end.

Variation

Made in Switzerland in about 1894, sample books in the Strohmuseum im Park archive show that this pattern was made in a great number of colourways. Look carefully at the example shown and you will see a join onto a vertical working end. The crossing ends are flat. (CTLC 1997/75/3)

Sixteen-end Brilliant, satin-middle

The original plait

Source: CTLC Aldbury plait sample panel

Origins: Aldbury, Hertfordshire

Production date: 1913

Type of straw: Wheat straw, single splints

Splint width: 1.5–2 mm

Plait width: 25 mm

Plaiting direction: During working the front of the plait faces the maker. The foot is on the left and the head on the right.

Joining: Along foot edge.

Background information: Another popular version of the Brilliant pattern that can be worked with different numbers of ends. The central satin-middle pattern is found in a wide variety of plaits, not only made in England, but throughout Europe. Setting up the plait is a lengthy process, but once done the working sequence is easy to follow.

What to use: All types of flat straw.

You need: Eight lengths.
Additional lengths for joining.

Setting up

Set up so all the ends in the right-hand group have the shiny side facing and those in the left-hand group have the matt side facing.

Step 1: Hold the eight lengths horizontally with their matt side facing upwards.

Take the lowest right-hand end, fold it towards you then in sequence diagonally, over, under the ends until it lays towards about 2 o'clock.

Repeat the folding movements with the right-hand ends taking the ends over, under until only one end remains.

Fold the last right-hand end on itself to create a neat point then pass it in sequence over, under the diagonal ends.

Take the lowest left-hand end, fold it on itself to create a point then under, over until it lays to inside the right-hand ends.

There are eight ends in both groups. The ends in the right-hand group have the shiny side facing upwards and the left-hand group with the matt-side facing upwards.

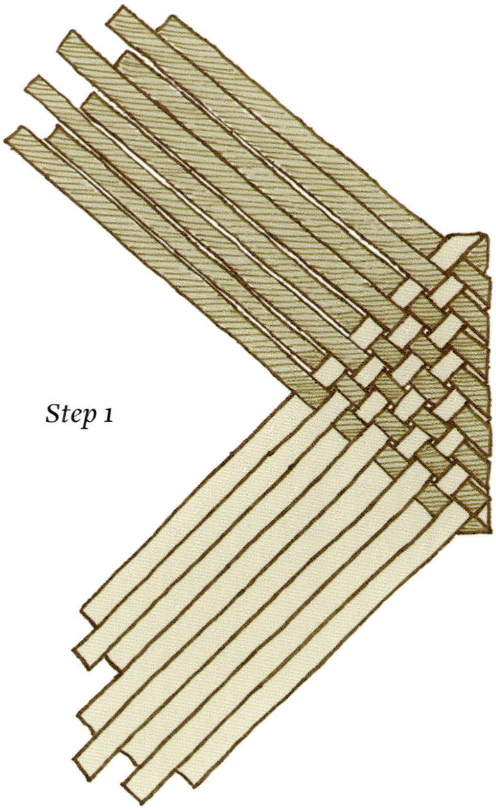

Step 1

Step 2: Take the outside left-hand end and fold it diagonally under and over until it lays to the inside of the right-hand group.

Repeat until five ends remain in the left-hand group.

Fold the left-hand vertical end downwards, over five left-hand horizontal ends. This forms the first stitch of the satin pattern.

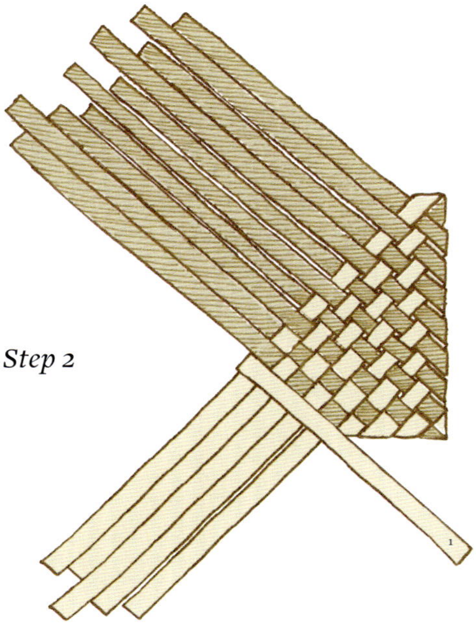

Step 2

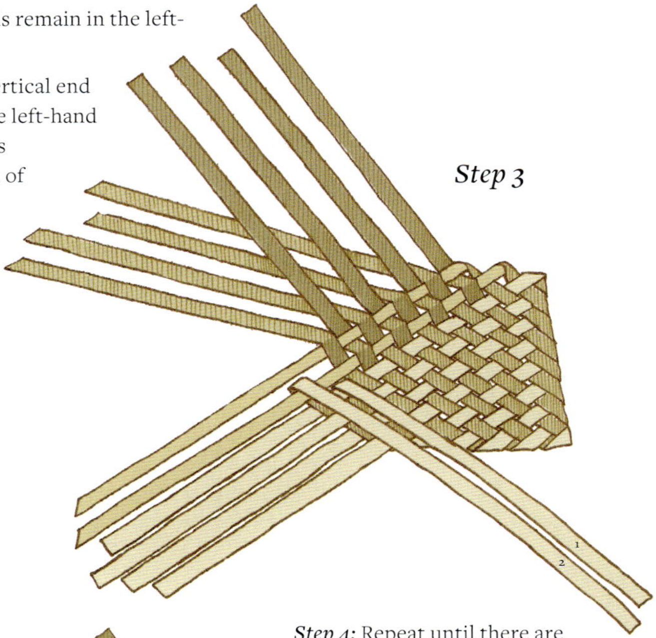

Step 3

Step 3: Fold the lowest end of the horizontal left-hand group and take it under, over the other ends to lay to inside the right-hand group.

Working from the right towards the left, fold the outer end forward, the next backwards.

Do not move the two left-hand ends of the verticals as these will form the satin stitches.

Twist the outside right-hand end so the shiny side faces outwards. Holding it on its edge bring it between the group so it lays to the top of the left-hand group.

Fold the outside left-hand end towards you and downwards to lay parallel to the other ends. This forms the next stitch of the satin pattern.

Working from the right-hand side fold the ends in the front group of the V to the back and those at the back to the front.

Step 4: Repeat until there are still five ends in the left-hand horizontal group, the first five ends of the left-hand diagonal group are folded downwards to form the stitches of the satin pattern.

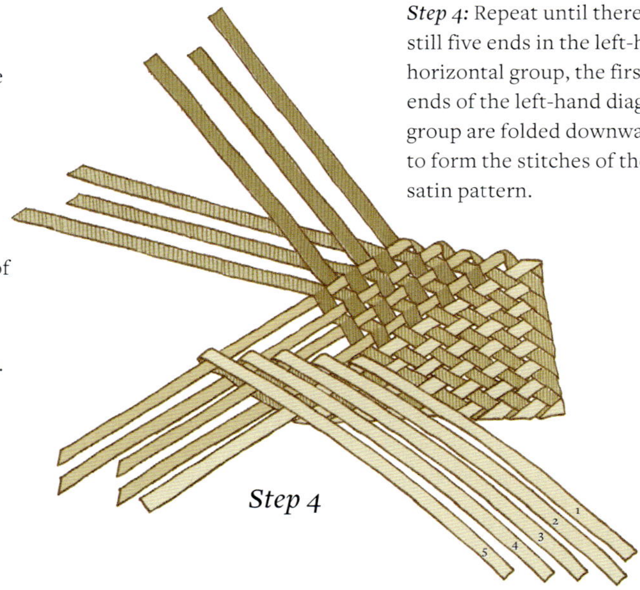

Step 4

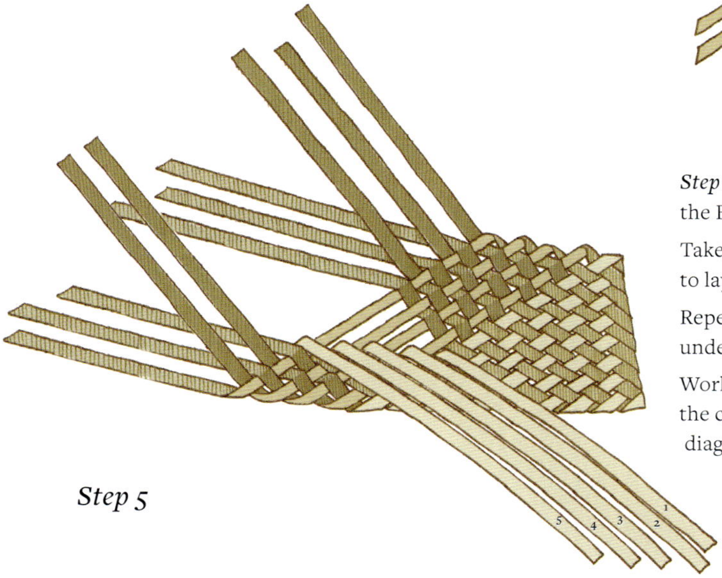

Step 5

Step 5: In this move the left-hand horizontal group is set up to start the Brilliant pattern to the left of the satin stitches.

Take the lowest left-hand horizontal, fold it under, over, under over to lay diagonally towards about 1 o'clock.

Repeat until only one horizontal end remains on the left, then fold it under and diagonally upwards to lay parallel to the other ends.

Working from the left fold the ends backwards and forwards over the crossing end. To the left of the five satin stitches there are two diagonal ends upwards and three downwards.

To the right of the five satin stitches there are three diagonal ends upwards and three downwards.

Working

The group of five ends for the satin stitches are worked between the left and right-hand groups of Brilliant stitches each side of them. As you work the lowest satin stitch will re-join the right-hand group. The lowest of the left-hand group of Brilliant stitches will join the satin group.

Step 1: Take the outside right-hand end, twist it diagonally towards the left passing across the two sets of V ends. Make a gentle counter twist on the crossing end to keep it on its edge. Hold the crossing end in place.

Make the next stitch in the satin group. The satin stitches are the central groups of ends pointing downwards.

Fold the right-hand end of the group satin stitches upwards. It will now join the right-hand Brilliant section.

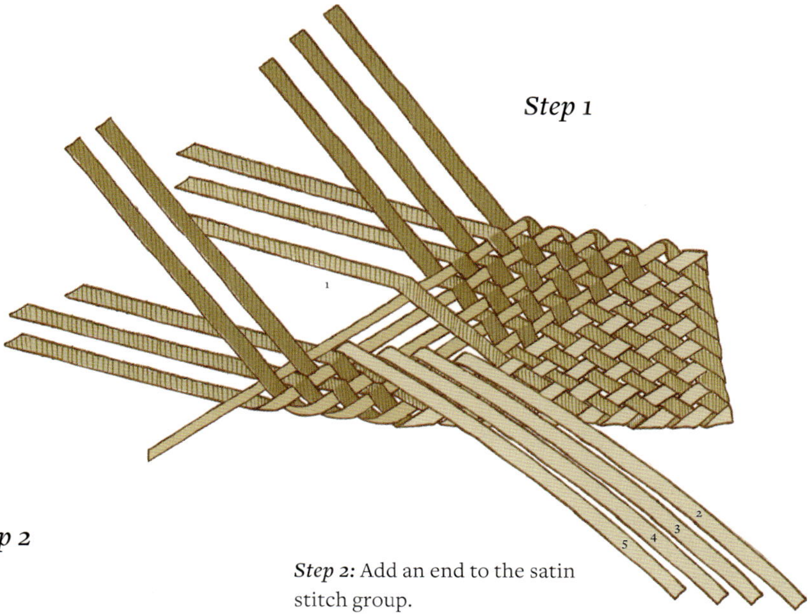

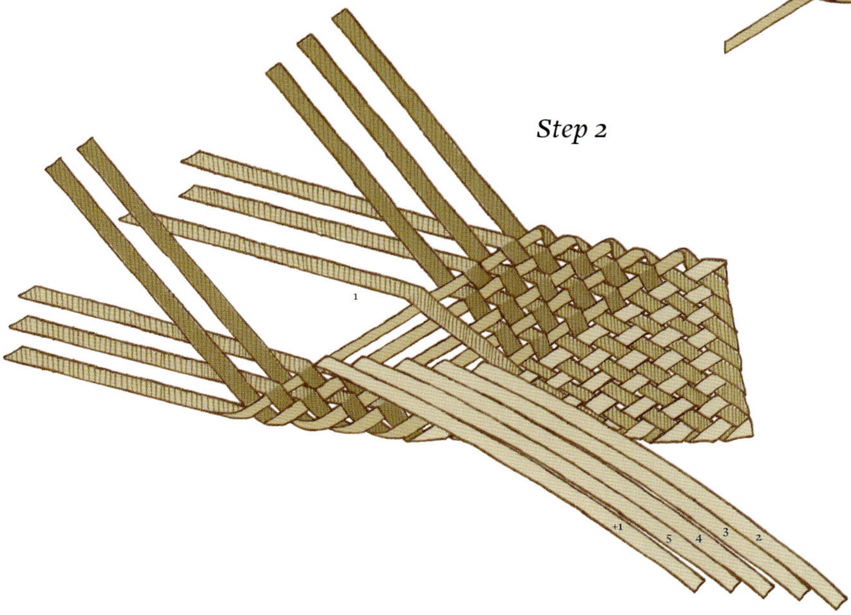

Step 2: Add an end to the satin stitch group.

Take the innermost end of the left-hand V section fold it towards you and then downwards. It becomes a new end in the group of five satin stitches.

Working from right to left, fold the ends of two groups of V. Bring the ones at the back of the V to the front and those at the front to the back. They now hold the crossing end in place.

Fold the outside left-hand end, which just crossed the body, upwards so there are three ends at the back of the left-hand V and two at the front.

Continue the working sequence.

The working sequence is:
Right: Take outside right-hand end across the two V group ends.
Right: Fold the right-hand end of the satin group upwards.
Left: Fold the innermost end of the left-hand V section downwards.
Right: Working from the right fold the ends in the back of the V to the front and those at the front to the back.
Left: Fold the outside left-hand crossing end upwards to join the back of the left-hand V.

Joining

The method used on the original plait appears to be unconventional. The new end was added to the head edge then, both the old and new ends form the crossing stitch, before the old end is left out on the foot edge.

Insert the new end with the shiny side upwards, behind the outside right-hand end so it tucks under the previous row. Take both ends across the plait. Leave the new end out when the new end is folded upwards.

This hat from the late 1700s is made from rag paper. Four-end rustic plaits form the body, and the rosette trimmings, which are also made from paper, are two-end plaits. The hat is lined with green silk. It is attributed to the Duchess of Somerset. (CTLC 221/53)

Trimmings

This section includes some of the earliest known plaits commonly used as trimmings for a wide range of items from the 1600s. Perhaps originating in Europe, by the later 1800s they had spread around the world and as they did plaiters adapted their own methods of making the plaits at speed. Until the mid 1900s five-end spiral plaits were made in Italy and Eastern Europe to be made into bags and baskets. It is difficult to comprehend the quantities produced by plaiters and the products' importance to world fashion and commerce.

Two-end plait

The replica plait

Origins: Originally made in Europe

Production date: From the 1600s onwards

Type of straw: Unknown

Splint width: Unknown

Plait width: Unknown

Plaiting direction: The direction of turning will depend upon the maker's method.

Joining: Body

Background information: Now commonly called two-straw during the 1800s it was recorded as cordinet. The secret of success for this triangular plait is to keep the angle of the working ends at a constant one hundred and twenty degrees. The instructions show the positions at twelve, eight and four o'clock, but the plait can be worked at any one hundred and twenty degree clock face combination that provides a comfortable working hand hold. The plait can be worked clockwise or counter-clockwise. Adjust the plait's tension by altering how close to horizontal the working end is folded. Folding closer to horizontal makes a tighter plait.

What to use: This was commonly made with fine whole rye or wheat straws and split straws. You can use either whole straws or narrow flat tape.

You need: One plaiting length.
Additional lengths for joining.

Setting up

Fold the plaiting length off centre.

Hold the length so it points from 12 to 6 o'clock. Fold the lower end under and position at 4 o'clock. The ends must be uneven lengths.

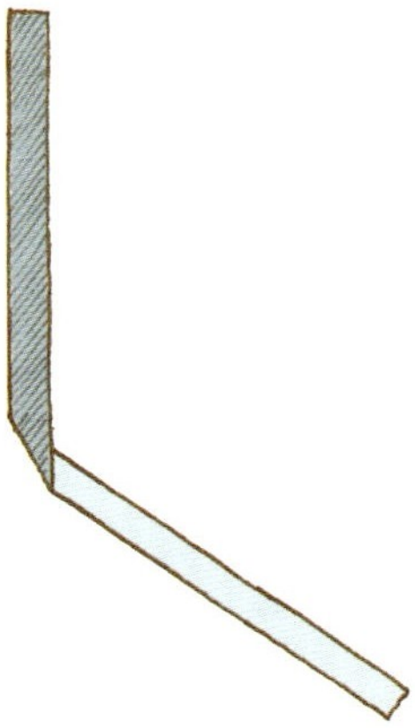

Working

Step 1

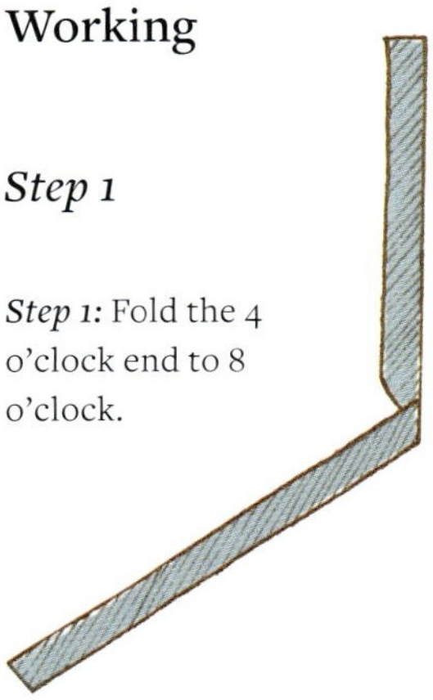

Step 1: Fold the 4 o'clock end to 8 o'clock.

Step 2

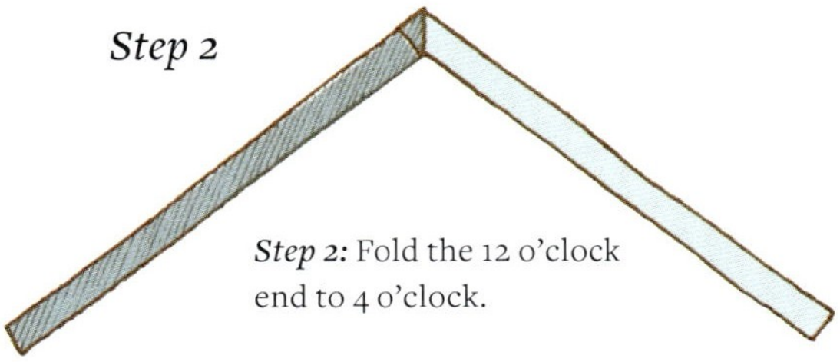

Step 2: Fold the 12 o'clock end to 4 o'clock.

Step 3

Step 3: Fold the 8 o'clock end to 12 o'clock. Continue the working sequence until the ends need joining.

The working sequence is:
4 o'clock to 8 o'clock.
12 o'clock to 4 o'clock.
8 o'clock to 12 o'clock.

Joining

The secret of joining is to evenly match the size of straw or splint. Begin joining when the shortest end is in the 12 o'clock position and the second end is at 4 o'clock.

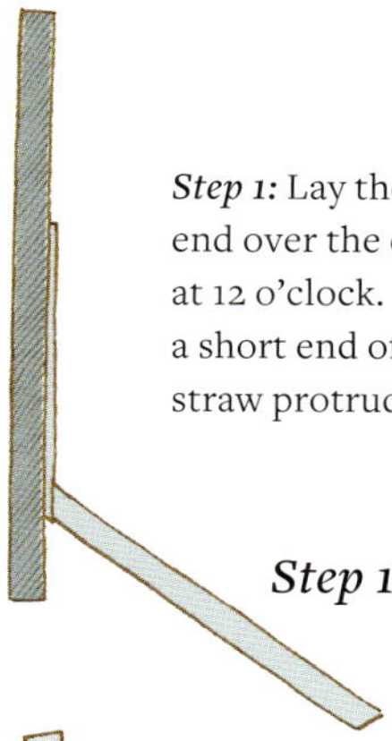

Step 1: Lay the new end over the old end at 12 o'clock. Leaving a short end of the new straw protruding.

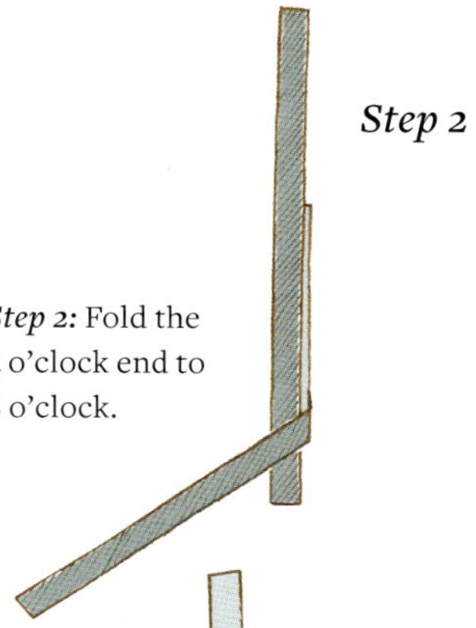

Step 2: Fold the 4 o'clock end to 8 o'clock.

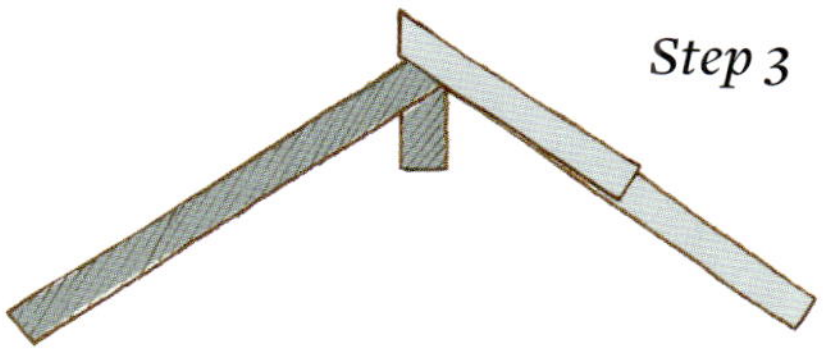

Step 3: Fold the new and old 12 o'clock straws to 4 o'clock. The old end is on top of the new.

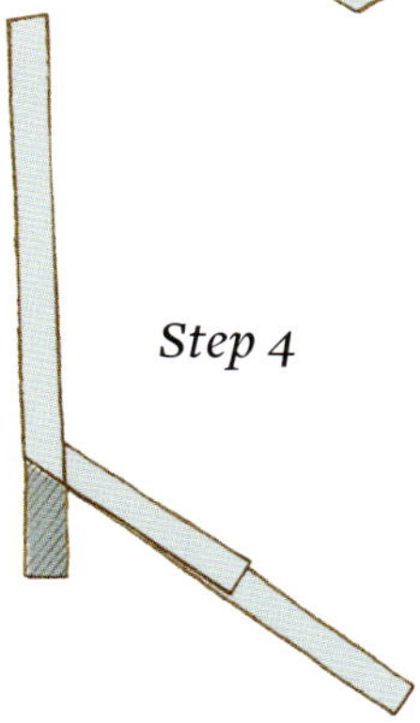

Step 4: Fold the 8 o'clock to 12 o'clock.

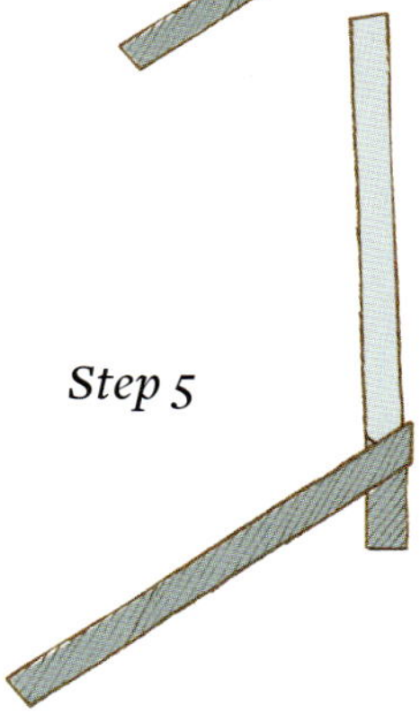

Step 5: Fold both old and new ends from 8 o'clock to 4 o'clock. The short old end is under the new end.

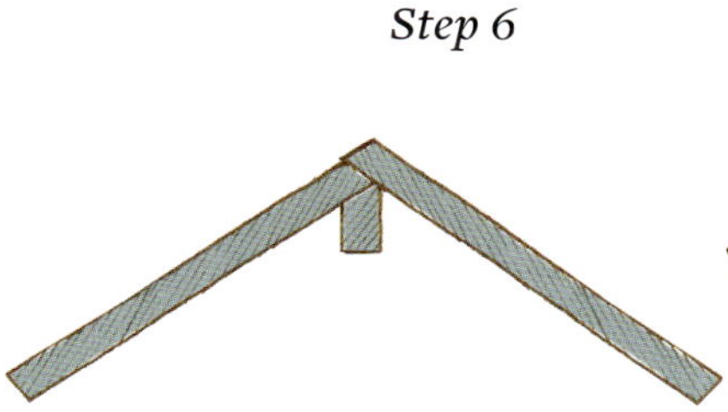

Step 6: Fold the 12 o'clock straw to 4 o'clock.

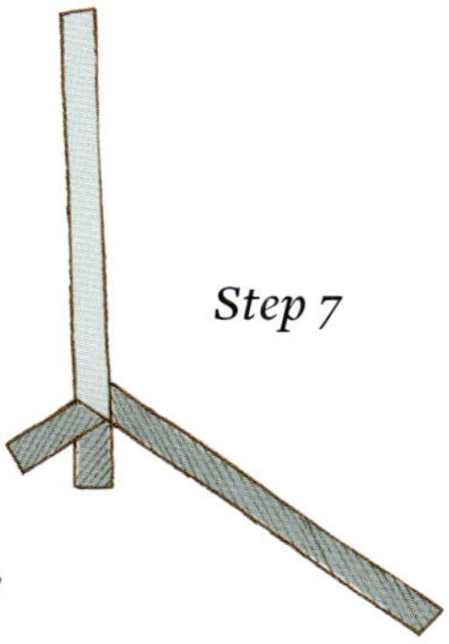

Step 7: Fold only the new end from 8 o'clock to 12 o'clock, leaving the old end behind. Continue the working sequence until the next join is required.

Variations

These two plaits were made in Edlesborough in about 1865 by a lady called Catherine Newman. Both are made with doubled splints, but the cordinet two-bow pattern is made with the shiny side of the straw facing outwards and the cordinet three-bow pattern is made with the rice of matt side of the straw facing outwards. If you look closely, it is possible to see glimpses of the shiny side.

This Five bow cordinet is said to have been commonly made in villages around Dunstable, Bedfordshire in the 1880s, but this example is thought to have been made in 1913. (CTLC 44/35)

Sometimes the pattern was added to a simple plait, in this case to form a pattern called eyelet. The image shows part of a longer length, made somewhere near Luton, Bedfordshire in the 1890s. (CTLC 43/35)

Three-end ring, version one

The original plait

Source: CTLC 1997/61/1B

Origins: Switzerland

Production date: 1800s

Type of straw: Rye straw, single splints

Splint width: 2 mm

Plait width: 4 mm

Plaiting direction: During working the back of the plait faces the maker. The foot is on the right and the head on the left. If making a plait with split straw the matt side will be facing.

Joining: Along foot edge.

Background information: The pattern is made using split straw which makes is lighter and more flexible. To create a plait with a shiny face and matt obverse it is important to set up the ends as shown in the diagrams. The characteristic twist edge keeps the splints facing in the correct direction. Ring plaits were made from a wide variety of materials, from chip to fabric tapes.

What to use: This was commonly made with fine whole rye split straws You can use any flat tape.

You need: Two plaiting lengths.
Additional lengths for joining.

Setting up

The instructions are for working with split straws.

Step 1: Hold one length with the shiny side facing, horizontally from nine o'clock to three o'clock.

Take the second end shiny side facing and place it, off centre, diagonally in front of the horizontal length to lay towards about 2 o'clock. It lays close to the left-hand end of the horizontal length.

Fold the lower end away from you and upwards behind the horizontal length to lay to about 10 o'clock.

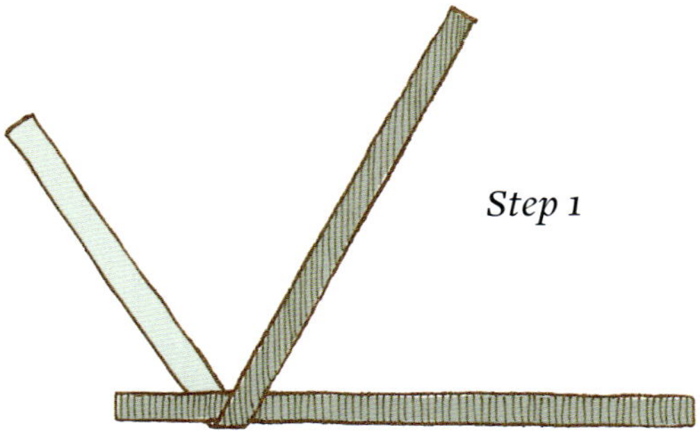

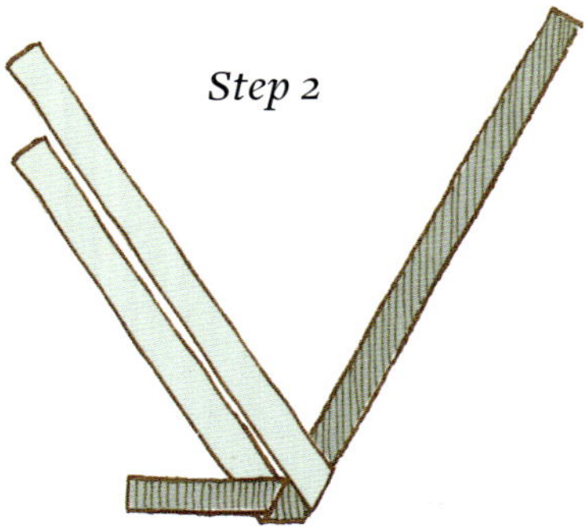

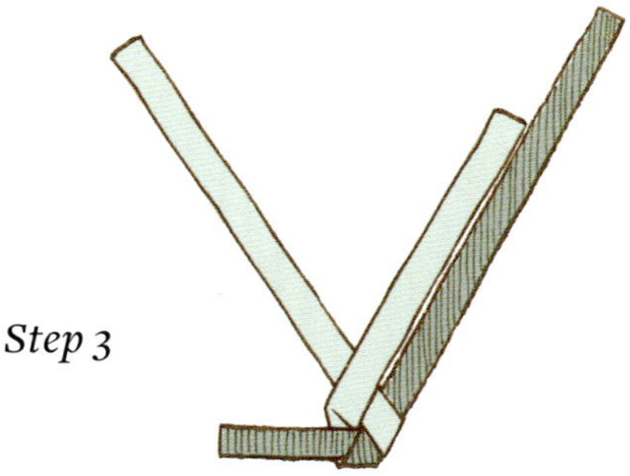

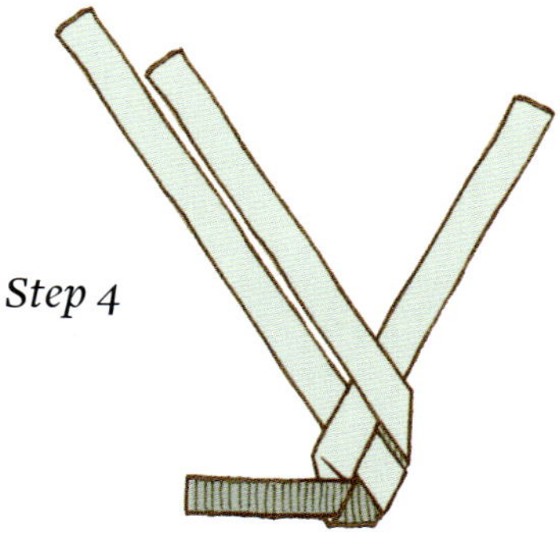

Step 2: Fold the right-hand horizontal end diagonally towards you and into the centre of the V. It lays parallel to the left-hand diagonal end.

Step 3: In this move the end is twisted to keep the matt side facing.

Using your fingernails make a crease and twist, then slide the end to the right to lay inside the V. The end lays parallel to the outside right-hand diagonal.

Step 4: Fold the outside right-hand end to lay inside the left-hand end of the V.

Working

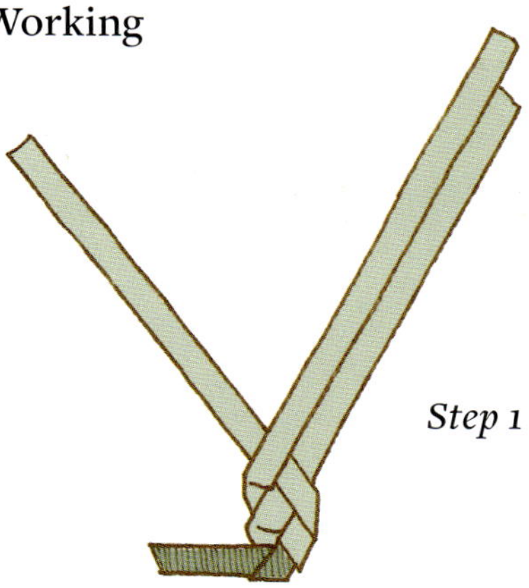

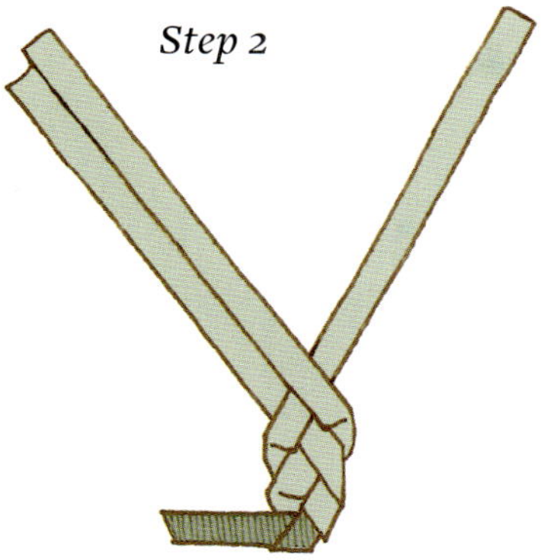

Step 2: Take the outside right-hand end, using your fingernails, make a twist, and lay the end to the inside of the left-hand group.

Continue the working sequence until the ends need joining.

Step 1: Take the outside left-hand end, using your fingernails, make a twist, and lay the end to the inside of the right-hand group.

The working sequence is:
Left: Outside end, twist, lay to inside of the right-hand diagonal end.
Right: Outside end, twist, lay to inside of the left-hand diagonal end.

Joining

Make the joins when the short end is to the inside of the right-hand group. Try to spread joins evenly along the length.

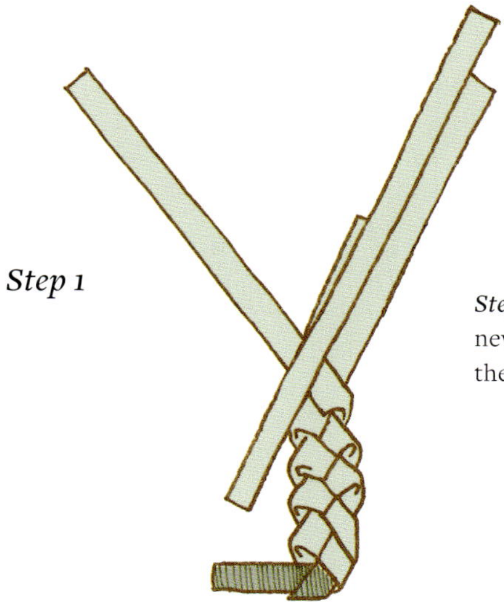

Step 1: Lay the new end over the old end.

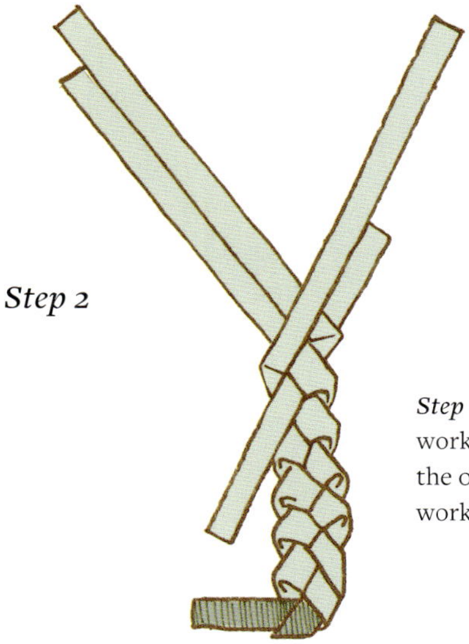

Step 2: Continue working, leaving behind the old end, and only working the new.

This silk bonnet, elaborately trimmed with three-end ring plaits, dates from around 1806. No other information about its maker or wearer survives which is sad since it must have been important in someone's life.

Three-end ring, version two

The original plait

Source: 1997/61/1A

Origins: Switzerland

Production date: unknown

Type of straw: Rye straw, single splints

Splint width: 2 mm

Plait width: 4 mm

Plaiting direction: During working the back of the plait faces the maker. The foot is on the right and the head on the left.

Joining: Along foot edge.

Background information: The pattern is made by positioning the working ends at one hundred and twenty degrees so that in cross-section the plait is shaped like a rhombus. The ends form a central line along the plait. Some plaiters held the ends at right angles, 9 o'clock, 12 o'clock and 3 o'clock and while the plait is very similar, the stitches are looser.

What to use: This was commonly made with fine whole rye split straws. You can use any flat tape.

You need: Two plaiting lengths.
Additional lengths for joining.

Setting up

Step 1: Hold one length with the matt side facing, vertically from 6 o'clock to 12 o'clock.

Place the second end diagonally behind the vertical. It points from 2 o'clock to 8 o'clock.

Fold the 8 o'clock end from 8 o'clock to 4 o'clock. The shiny side of this end faces.

Step 1

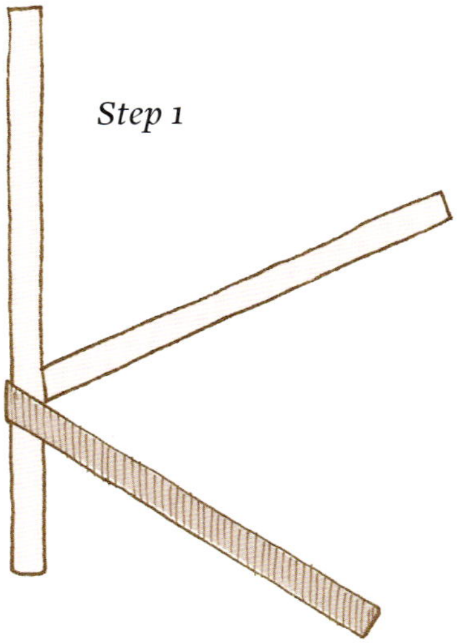

Step 2

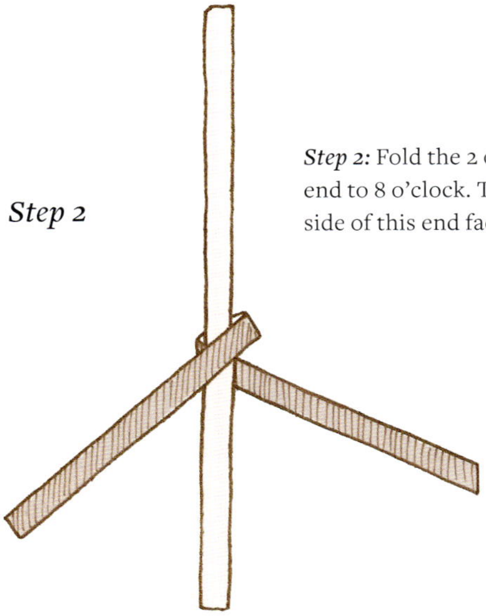

Step 2: Fold the 2 o'clock end to 8 o'clock. The shiny side of this end faces.

Step 3: Fold the 4 o'clock end to the right-hand side of the 12 o'clock end. They must lay parallel.

Step 3

Working

Step 1: Fold the left-hand 12 o'clock end to 4 o'clock.

Step 1

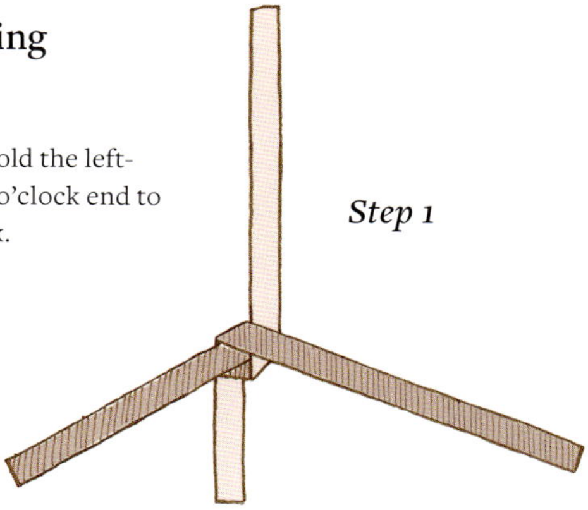

Step 2

Step 2: Fold the 8 o'clock end to the left of the other 12 o'clock end.

Step 3

Step 3: Fold the right-hand 12 o'clock end to 8 o'clock.

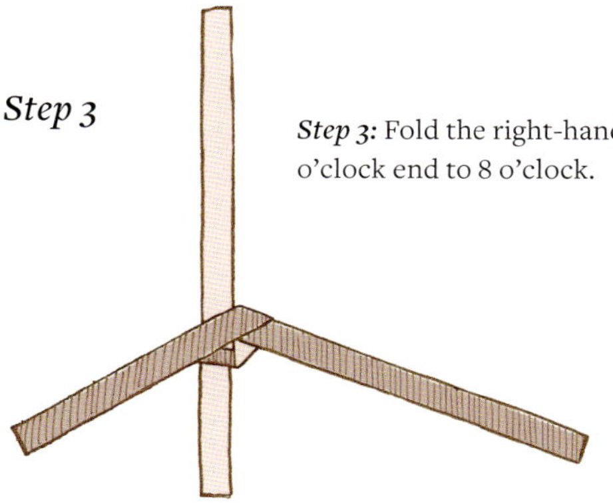

Step 4

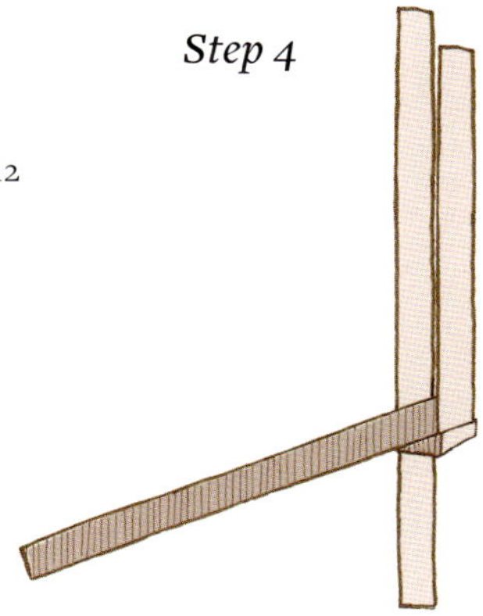

Step 4: Fold the 4 o'clock end to the right-of the 12 o'clock end.

Continue the working sequence until the ends need joining.

The working sequence is:
Left-hand 12 o'clock end to 4 o'clock.
8 o'clock end to left- of 12 o'clock end.
Right-hand 12 o'clock end to 8 o'clock.
4 o'clock end to right of 12 o'clock end.

Joining

Start the joining process early so they can be regularly spaced. The end to be joined must be at 8 o'clock.

Step 1: Lay the new end over the short end that points to 8 o'clock. The short end points to 2 o'clock and the long to 8 o'clock. There are two ends at 8 o'clock.

Step 1

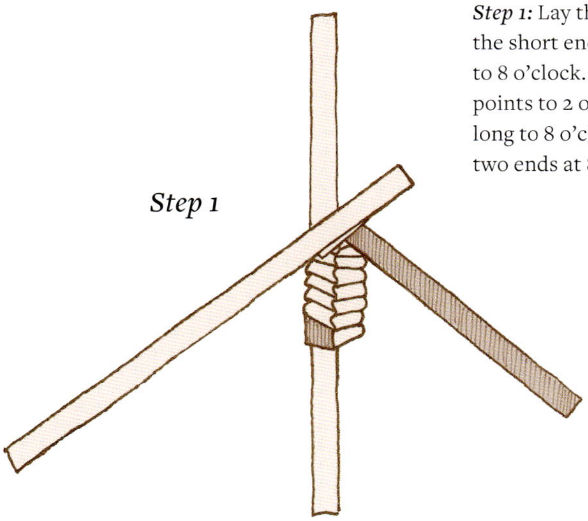

Step 2

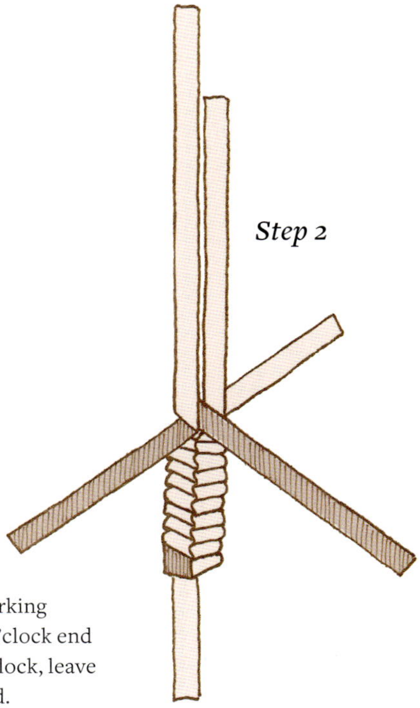

Step 2: Continue the working sequence. When the 8 o'clock end folds to the left of 12 o'clock, leave the short old end behind.

Four-end *gufenring*

The original plait

Source: 1997/61/2

Origins: Switzerland

Production date: 1800s

Type of straw: Rye straw, single splints

Splint width: 2 mm

Plait width: 6 mm

Plaiting direction: During working the front of the plait faces the maker. The foot is on the right and the head on the left.

Joining: Along foot edge.

Background information: The pattern can be dated to the early 1800s but may have been made much earlier. The name of these looped plaits varies according to the pattern and are perhaps influenced by Swiss cantonal dialect. One book written in 1896 calls this pattern 'huffenring.' *Hufen* is the German word for hoofs.

What to use: This was commonly made with fine whole rye split straws. You can use any flat tape.

You need: Two plaiting lengths.
Additional lengths for joining.

Setting up

If you look at the diagram, you will see the first length has been carefully folded to form a point. This allows the ends to lay side by side with the shiny side of both facing.

Step 1: Take the first length with the shiny side facing, fold it off centre so both ends lay at 12 o'clock with both shiny sides facing.

Take two lengths, lay one on top of the other, both with matt side facing.

Insert the pair between the fold of the first end. The short end is to the left of the 12 o'clock ends and the long ends of the pair at 4 o'clock. Check that the left-hand 12 o'clock end is in front of the inserted pair.

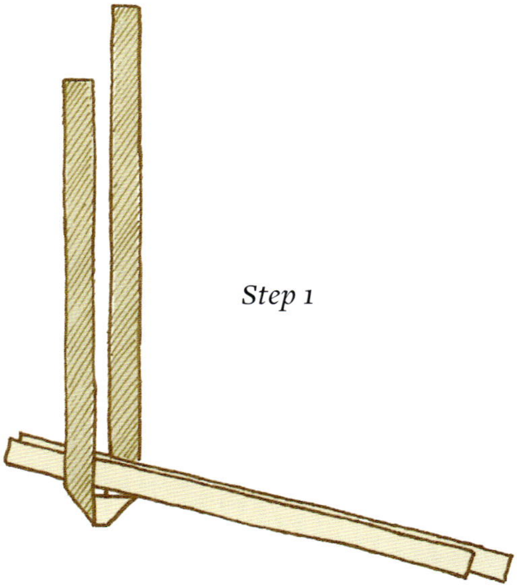

Step 1

Step 2

Step 2: The diagram shows four moves.

Fold the right-hand 12 o'clock end to 8 o'clock.

Fold the pair of ends at 4 o'clock to the right of the 12 o'clock end.

Fold the left-hand from 12 to 4 o'clock.

Fold the 8 o'clock end to the left-hand 12 o'clock.

Working

Step 1

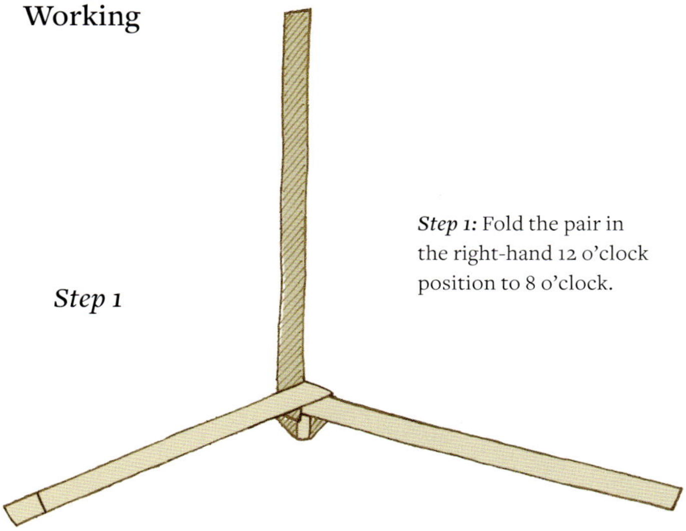

Step 1: Fold the pair in the right-hand 12 o'clock position to 8 o'clock.

Step 2

Step 2: Fold the 4 o'clock end to the right of the 12 o'clock end.

Step 3

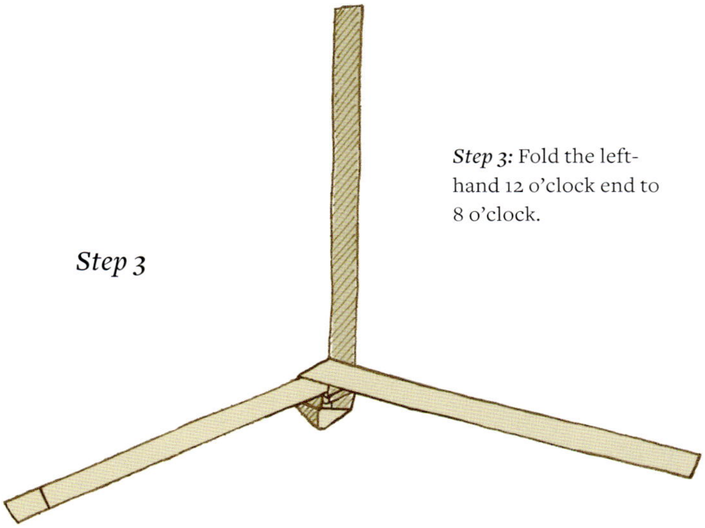

Step 3: Fold the left-hand 12 o'clock end to 8 o'clock.

Step 4

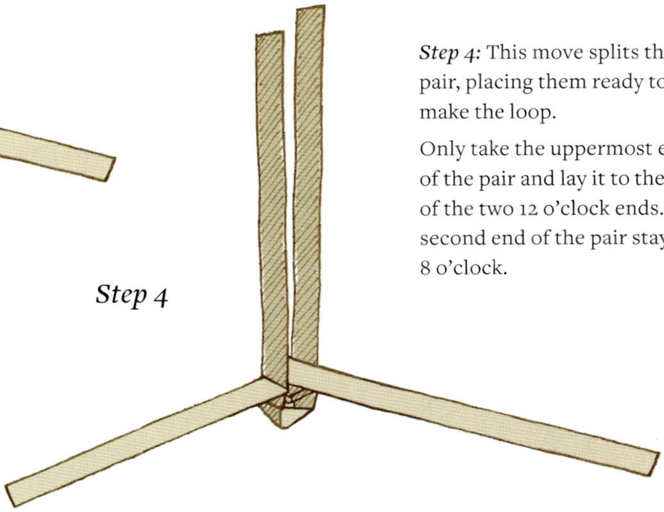

Step 4: This move splits the pair, placing them ready to make the loop.

Only take the uppermost end of the pair and lay it to the left of the two 12 o'clock ends. The second end of the pair stays at 8 o'clock.

Step 5

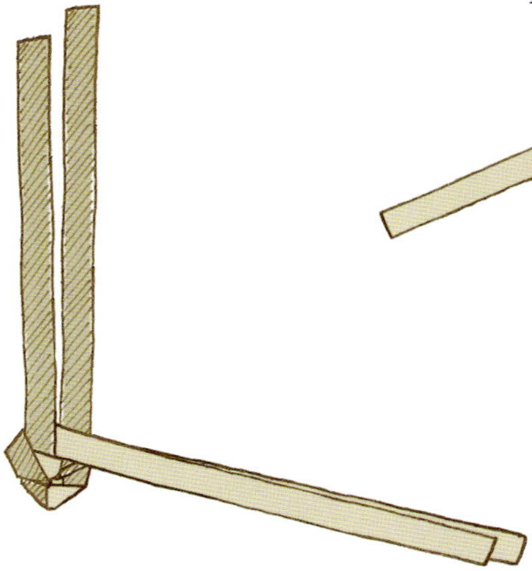

Step 5: This move creates the loop.

Take the end at 8 o'clock, twist it on itself, keeping the shiny side upwards and lay it on top of the 4 o'clock end. The matt side faces.

Step 6: The diagram shows four completed moves.

Fold the right-hand 12 o'clock end to 8 o'clock.

Fold the pair at 4 o'clock to the left-hand of the 12 o'clock ends.

Fold the left-hand 12 o'clock end to 4 o'clock.

Fold the 8 o'clock end to the left of the 12 o'clock end.

Continue the working sequence until the ends need joining.

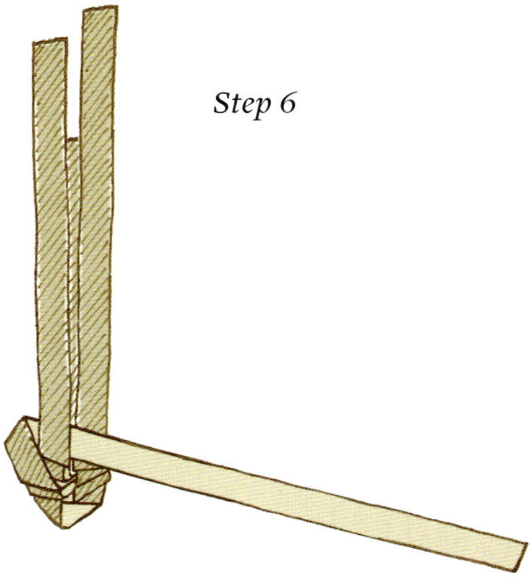

Step 6

The working sequence is:
Pair at right-hand 12 o'clock to 8 o'clock.
4 o'clock to right of 12 o'clock.
Left-hand 12 o'clock end to 8 o'clock.
8 o'clock top end of pair, to left-hand 12 o'clock.
8 o'clock end twist behind the 12 o'clock to lay on top of 4 o'clock end.
Right-hand 12 o'clock end to 8 o'clock.
Pair at 4 o'clock to left-hand of 12 o'clock.
Left-hand 12 o'clock end to 4 o'clock.
8 o'clock end to left of 12 o'clock end.

Joining

Start the joining process early so they can be spaced.

The end to be joined must be at 4 o'clock.

Lay the new end over the old. The short end points to 2 o'clock and the long end to 4 o'clock.

Leave the old end behind when that move is made.

Five-end cord

The original plait

Source: CTLC 1/19/28B

Origins: Italy

Production date: 1800s

Type of straw: Italian straw, whole

Straw width: 1 mm

Plait width: 10 mm

Plaiting direction: The spiral works anticlockwise.

Joining: Into body

Background information: This plait appeared in *The Workwoman's Guide* where it was called "hollow spiral work" and can be made with up to twenty-one ends. It was also made using four-ends which produced a triangular plait with an elongated spiral pattern. The spiral can be worked clockwise or counter-clockwise. The plait was sometimes worked around a thin straw, wire or stick which could be left in place when made up.

What to use: Fine whole straws, preferably with a hollow stem.

You need: Three plaiting lengths.
Additional lengths for joining. Scissors.

Setting up

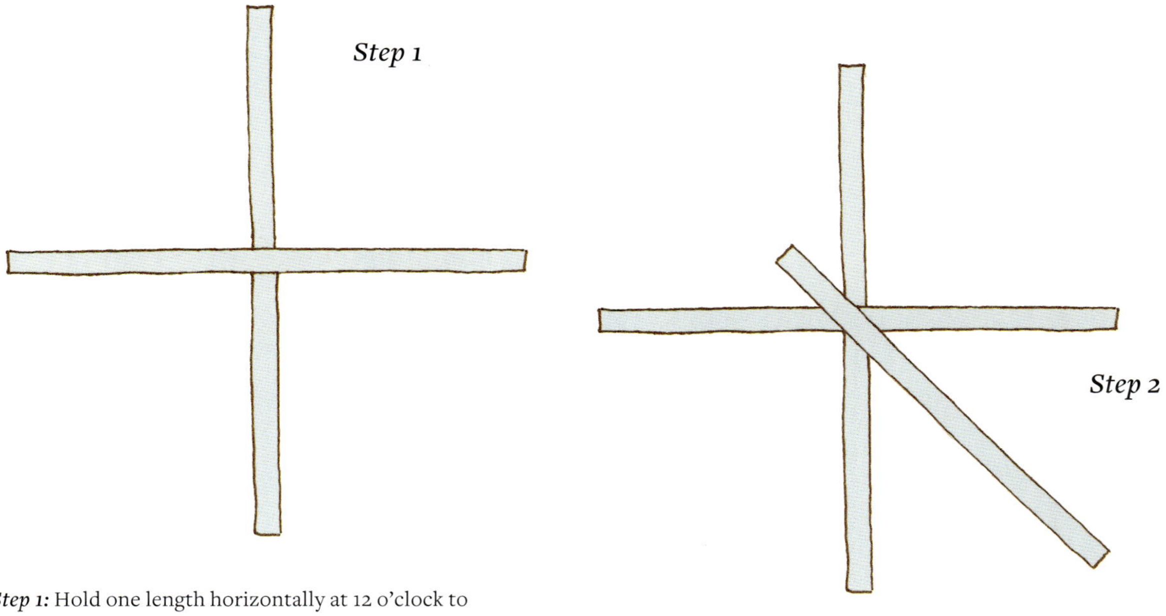

Step 1: Hold one length horizontally at 12 o'clock to 6 o'clock.

Take a second length and place it at right angles crossing over the first. The four ends are at 12, 9, 6 and 3 o'clock.

Step 2: Add the third length to intersect the 3 o'clock and 6 o'clock ends.

Fold the short end of the third length downwards away from you. It remains under the plait as work progresses.

Working

Each working move is described as a fold, but to create even stitches and work in a rhythm break the single move into five stages. First bring the working end towards you. Fold it upwards to vertical. Hold the end it will move over in place. Fold the end over.

Step 1

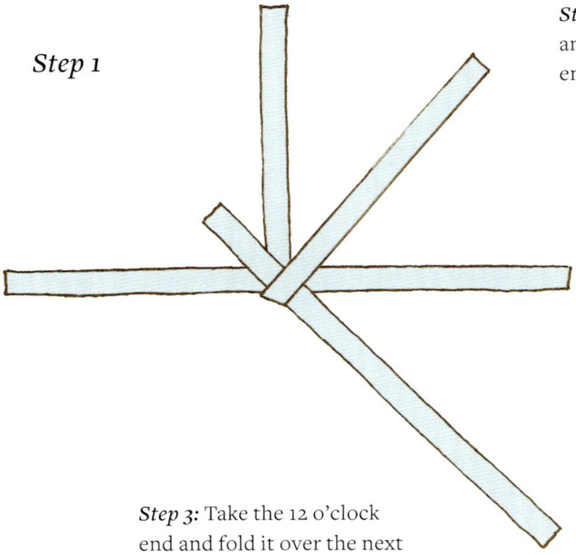

Step 1: Take the 6 o'clock end and fold it over the next two ends. It will lay at 1 o'clock.

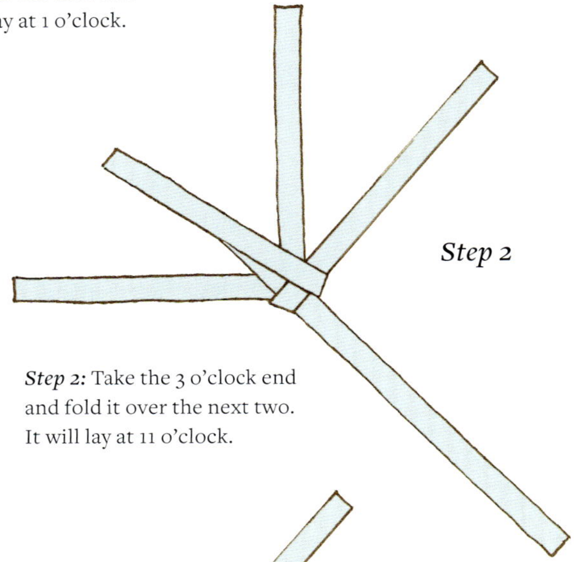

Step 2

Step 2: Take the 3 o'clock end and fold it over the next two. It will lay at 11 o'clock.

Step 3: Take the 12 o'clock end and fold it over the next two so it lays in the 7 o'clock position. Turn the plait.

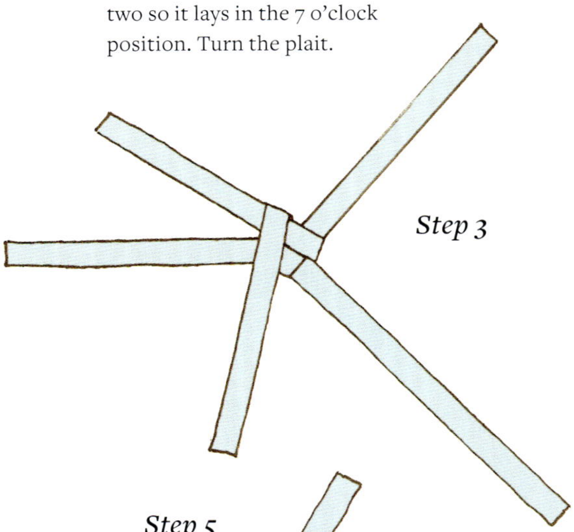

Step 3

Step 4: Take the 9 o'clock straw and fold it over the next two. It will lay at 4 o'clock.

Step 4

Step 5

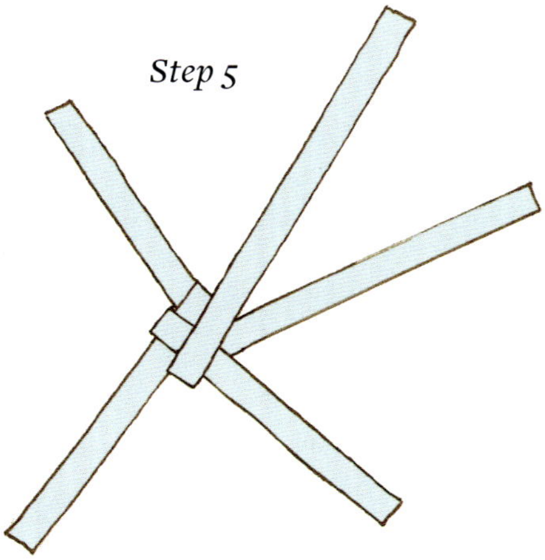

Step 5: Take the end that was at 5 o'clock and fold it over the next two ends.

As you work the straws form a square shape. Continue the working sequence until joining begins.

The working sequence is:
Take the end behind the last moved end over the next two. Once the working sequence has been learned develop the practice of turning the whole plait, one quarter turn clockwise, so the move is always made in the same position.

Joining

It is important to spread the joins out along the length. Two methods of joining were used. The easiest is to insert the new end into the hollow of the old ensuring the new end is inserted as far as possible in to the old. When using extremely thin straws, plaiters overlapped the old over the new end. The new and old ends protruded from the plait during working, then clipped off when the required length was complete.

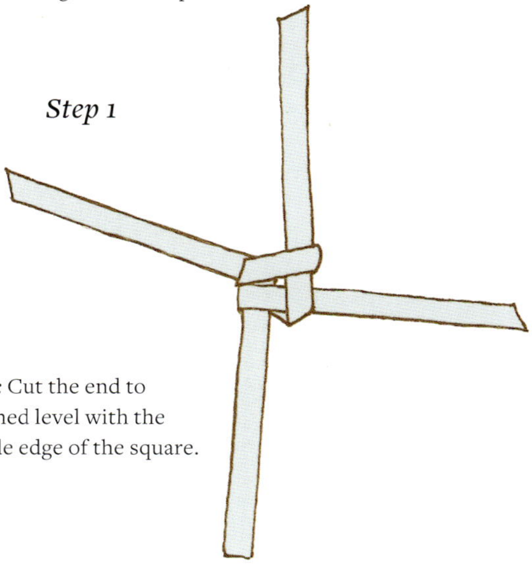

Step 1: Cut the end to be joined level with the outside edge of the square.

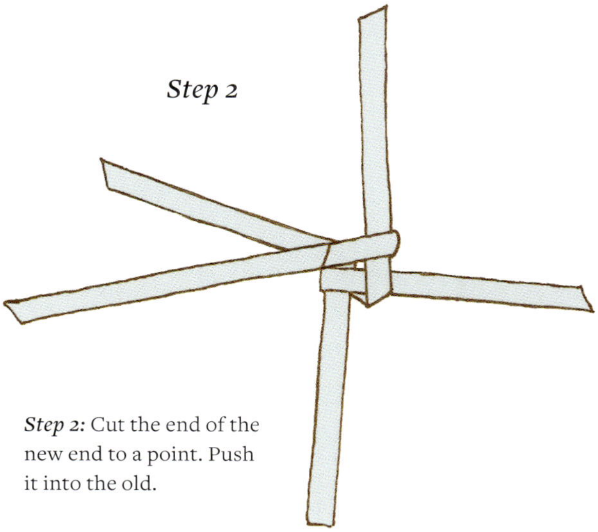

Step 2: Cut the end of the new end to a point. Push it into the old.

Finishing

Slide the loose end, the last end worked, between two rows of plait.

Found in a Bedfordshire house, this decorative spiral plait hat band from the late 1800s has a tassel and decorative bosses made from two-end plait. (CTLC 5/35/59)

Push pull plait

The original plait

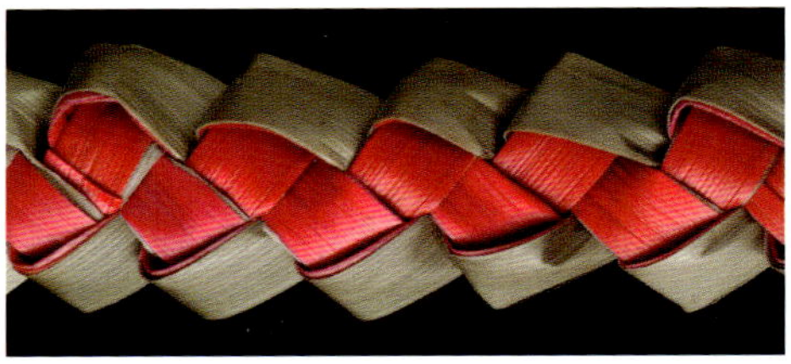

Source: CTLC 1997/76/4

Origins: possibly Japan

Production date: 1880s

Type of straw: Possibly barley straw, double splints

Splint width: 5 mm

Plait width: 20.5 mm

Plaiting direction: This plait is made with the right side facing you and there is no head or foot.

Joining: Into body

Background information: This pattern, which is a chain sinnet made with 'broad chip,' appeared in the 1895 *Second Book of Plaits* where it is called the 'Ninth pattern.' In an American publication about palmetto braiding, it was called 'push pull braid' and was recommended for trimming hats and baskets. It appeared again in the 1960s, this time made from lengths of ready-made plait and braid. In the Bahamas it is called Shark's tooth.

What to use: Use flat flexible types of straws, or ready-made plait, braid, or strips of fabric.

You need: To make a continuous length cut two pieces each four times longer than the finished length required. When using short lengths of straw select two pieces minimum 30 cm (12 in.) plus additional strips for joining.

Setting up

According to how you intend to use the finished length choose the appropriate sequence. Use method 1 if you want to make a loop where the start can easily be joined to the final stitches. Use method 2 to make a straight length.

Method 1

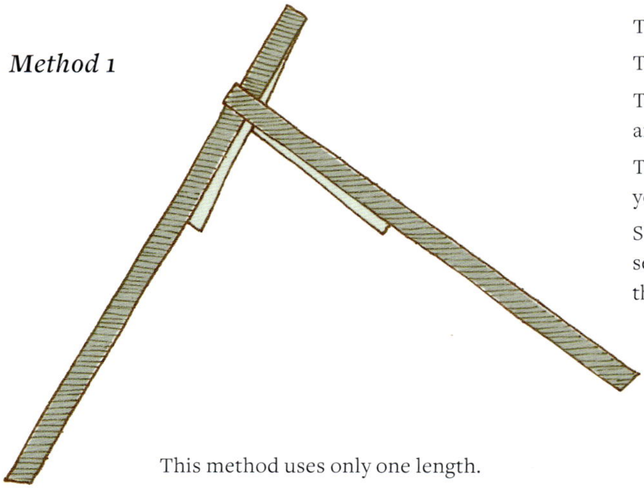

This method uses two lengths.

The diagram shows three moves.

Take one length, fold with the long length towards you and a short end behind.

Take a second length and fold with the short end towards you and the long end behind.

Slide the first length through between the fold of the second. The first length lays with the loop at 1 o'clock and the long end at 7 o'clock.

Method 2

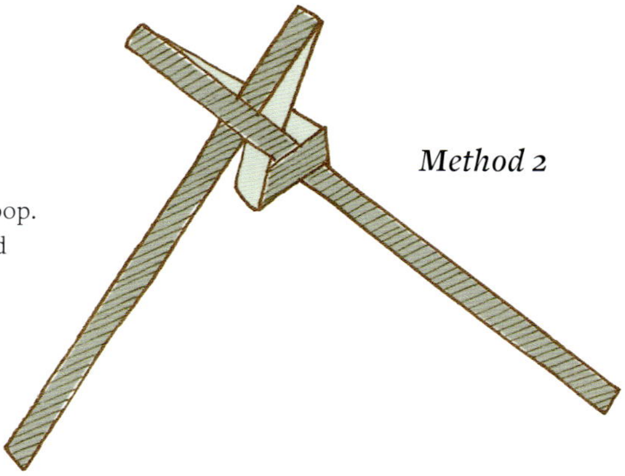

This method uses only one length.

Take one length softly fold in half.

Make a loop by crossing the ends right over left to make a loop. The left-hand end is pointing to 5 o'clock and the right-hand end to 7 o'clock.

Take the left-hand end and make a loop close to the centre point with the long end facing.

Slip the second loop through the first from back to front.

Pull on the right-hand end to tighten the first loop.

Working

Step 1: Take the right-hand end and with the long end towards you make a loop. Lift the long end upwards, curl with the long end facing.

Slide the new loop through the left-hand loop from right to left.

Gently pull on the long left-hand end until the loop holds the new loop in place. You can also pull on the back of the previous loop.

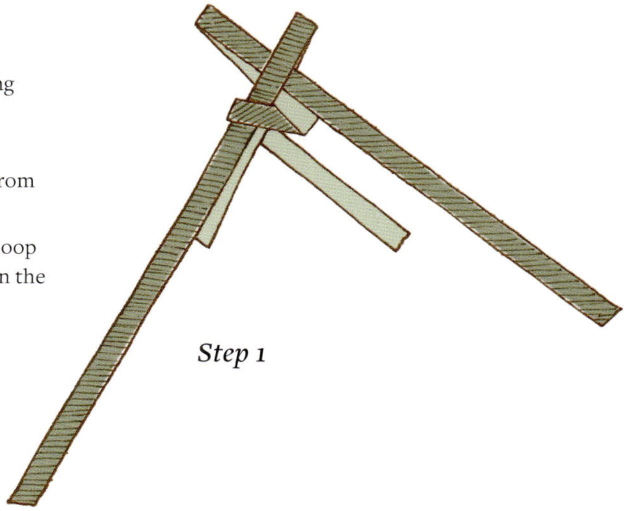

Step 1

Step 2

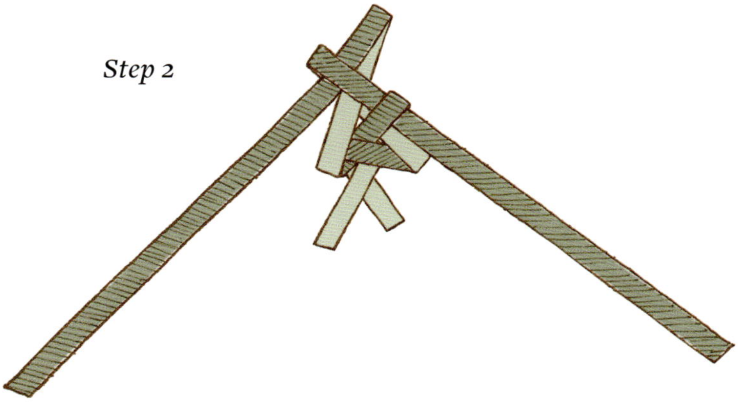

Step 2: Make a new loop with the left-hand end. Lift the long end upwards, curl towards you with long end facing, then slide from front to back through the previous loop.

Gently pull the long right-hand end until it grips the new loop. Make any adjustments to tighten the loops so they stay in place.

Continue the sequence taking care to make certain the straw lays neatly and the tension is even.

The working sequence is:
Right: Make a loop.
Left: Put the right loop through the left.
Tighten the loops.
Left: Make a loop.
Right: Put the left loop through the right.
Tighten the loops.

Joining

The method is shown for joining on the left-hand side but is the same method when making joins on the right.

Step 1

Step 1: Fold back the end to be joined. Take a new end and insert into the gap under the previous loop.

Step 2: Fold the short end back to lay on top of the new end and make a loop with both the old and new ends.

Slide it through the right-hand loop. Gently tighten the right-hand loop.

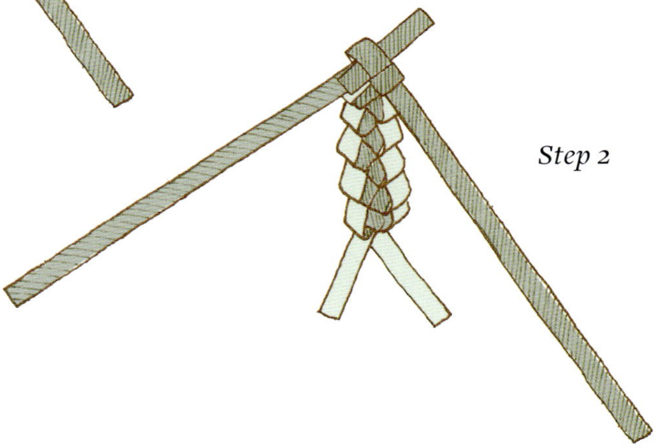

Step 2

Step 3

Step 3: Make a new loop with the right-hand end.

Step 4

Step 4: Make a loop with the old and new left-hand ends.

Continue working. The short old end is left behind on the wrong side and can be clipped off later.

Finishing

To finish as a loop, feed the last ends through the first so they continue the pattern. Pull the stitches tight. To finish as a length, fold the end of the last loop to the wrong side of the plait and feed the end back into a previous loop. Now repeat with the other end. Pull the threaded ends tight.

Thought to have been made in Essex in the early 1900s, this basket incorporates five-end and four-end spiral plaits. Baskets, boxes and reticules were also made in large quantities in Italy during the 1800s. Today spiral work is widely made into bags and baskets in Eastern Europe. (CTLC 386/33)

ENDNOTES

1 John Dony, *A History of the Straw Hat Industry*, Bamforth Press, 1942, p.18.
2 Page W. Denizations and Naturalisations (Huguenot Society) Volume VIll., p.136.
3 John Dony, *A History of the Straw Hat Industry*, Bamforth Press, 1942, p.17.
4 Agnes Strickland, *Lives of the Queens of Scotland and English Princesses*, 1852, Volume 3, p.187.
5 Despite their extensive research the pamphlet by Mrs Mooney was not located and its authenticity could not be verified. They found no evidence of local plaiters with family origins in Lorraine, neither did they find evidence of any significant straw plaiting industry in that region of France in the late 1500s. By the time Agnes Strickland was writing she may have been aware that Nancy in Lorraine was an important area of straw hat production and a competitor posing threats to certain aspects of the British straw industry.
6 The Bedfordshire Herald, The *Visit of the Prince*, 6 December 1878, p.7.
7 William Page, *The Victoria History of the County of Bedford*, Archibald Constable, 1908, p.119.
8 Ralph Thorsby, *Ducatus Leodiensis*, 1715, p.211–12.
9 Plet is assumed to be plait.
10 Dony writes that this account relates to her work in 1639 yet the original account does not appear to include this information.
11 Arthur Vaisey, *An Abstract of the title of the Rt Hon Lord Rothschild to the market tolls of Tring*, 1900. The document is held a Hertfordshire Archives and Local Studies, Hertford. I am indebted to Tim Amsden of Tring for providing this information.
12 Thomas Baskerville's *Journeys in England*, 1681, Vol. 8, App.2.
13 The Newcastle Courant, Saturday 24 September 1714. https://www.britishnewspaperarchive.co.uk and John Dony, *A History of the Straw Hat Industry*, Bamforth Press, 1942, p.27.
14 J. Oldmixon, *A History of England in the Reigns of King William and Queen Mary, Queen Anne, King George I*, 1735, p. 755.
15 Daniel Defoe, *Tour Through England and Wales*, 1725, Volume 2, p.114.
16 *The Agreeable Historian or The Complete English Traveller*, 1746, Volume 1, p.2.
17 *The Agreeable Historian or The Complete English Traveller*, 1746, Volume 1, p.2.
18 John Dony, *A History of the Straw Hat Industry*, Bamforth Press, 1942, p.29.
19 William Corston, *Papers in Manufactures*, 1805, p.223–32.
20 Patents Office Specifications, 1826, No.5335.
21 Thomas George Austin, *The Straw Hat Trade*, O'Doherty Printer and Publisher, 1871, p.38.
22 László L. Gróf, *Children of Straw*, Barracuda Books, 1988, p.30.
23 The Workwoman's Guide, *On Straw Plaiting*, London, 1838, p.288.
24 The Queen Magazine, *Dunstable and Straw Manufacture*, November 1861, p.179–80.
25 *An Account of the Work-Houses in Great Britain in the year*, 1724, Luton 1786, p.87.
26 John Dony, *A History of the Straw Hat Industry*, Bamforth Press, 1942, p.75, footnote 6.
27 Kuhn, et al. *Strohzeiten*, AT Verlag, 1991, p.117–18.
28 Exhibition catalogue, *Straw into Gold*, 2016–7, p.36.
29 Major Burns, *Second Report from the Commissioners on the Employment of Children*, 1843.
30 Joseph Lancaster, *Improvements in Education*, Collins and Perkins, 1807, p.102–20.
31 Belfast Monthly Magazine, Volume VIll, January to June 1812, p.25–7.
32 London and Dublin Societies for Bettering the condition of the poor; Relating to schools for the Education of children of the lowest classes. Part ll, 1807.
33 Hatters' Gazette, *Straw Plaiting*, January 1882, p.27. Reporting J.E. Cussans, History of Hertfordshire.
34 *Report from the Select Commissioners on the Poor Laws*, 1838.
35 George Culley *First Report of the Commissioners on the Employment of Children, Young Persons and Women in Agriculture*, 1867–8.
36 J.E. White, *The Second Report of the Children's Employment Commission, Report on the plaiting and bonnet-sewing industries in South Bedfordshire*, 1864.
37 *First Report of the Commissioners on the Employment of Children, Young Persons and Women in Agriculture*, 1868, p.205. The correspondence dates to 1864.
38 *Report from the Select Commissioners on the Poor Laws*, 1838.
39 Ibid.
40 P.P. 1867–8, XVll, App. Pt. 2, p.515.
41 *First Report of the Commissioners on the Employment of Children, Young Persons and Women in Agriculture*, 1868, p.207. Evidence of H. Veasey of Woburn, Bedfordshire, August 31, 1864.
42 Tuberculosis and smallpox were commonplace in these times meaning warm, overcrowded rooms were of concern.
43 Ibid. p.547.
44 Beadon v Parrott. *The Law Reports of the Queen's Bench, Vol. Vl*, Michaelmas 1870 to Trinity 1871.
45 *First Report of the Commissioners on the Employment of Children, Young Persons and Women in Agriculture*, 1868, p.205–7
46 Charles Knight, *British Almanac and Companion*, 1861, p.8.
47 *Report from the Select Commissioners on the Poor Laws*, 1838.
48 Thomas George Austin, *The Straw Hat Trade*, O'Doherty Printer and Publisher, 1871, p.19.
49 Charles Knight, *British Almanac and Companion*, 1861, p.10–11.
50 Thomas Austin, *The Straw Hat Trade*, O'Doherty Printer and Publisher, 1871, p.36–7.
51 Patrick Neill, *A Tour through the Orkneys*, 1806, p.71.
52 McCulloch's *Statistical Account of the British Empire*, 1839, Vol. 1, p.729.
53 Journal of the Society of Arts, December 1860, p.74.
54 John Dony, *A History of the Straw Hat Industry*, Bamforth Press, 1942, p.59.
55 Alexander Fenton, *The Northern Isles*, John Donald Publisher, 1978, p.270–2.
56 A.J. Tansley, *On the Straw Plait Trade*, Journal of the Society of Arts, 1860, p.71.
57 Her name appears spelt in a variety of ways, Sibella, Sybella and Sybilla.
58 Anna Saskia Wolsak, *Bonnet, and Wine: The Cultural History of the Bermuda Palmetto*, 2017, p.69–72.
59 Ibid. p.66.
60 Michael J. Jarvis, *"In the eye of all trade": Maritime revolution and the transformation of Bermudian Society, 1620–1800*, William and Mary College VA, 1998, p.289, 594–6.
61 Pat 1716/GB403.
62 Christine MacLeod, *The 1690s Patents Boom: Invention or Stock-Jobbing?* Economic History Review, 2nd series, issue 39, p.551.
63 Anna Saskia Wolsak, *Bonnet, and Wine: The Cultural History of the Bermuda Palmetto*, 2017, p.72.
64 Ibid. p.65.
65 Cunnington and Beard, *A Dictionary of English Costume*, A.C. Black, 1960, p.16.
66 Old Bailey Records online https://www.oldbaileyonline.org/ (Accessed June 2022.) The Court records also mentioned theft of Chip and Leghorn plait and hats.
67 These are held at Hatfield House, Culture Trust Luton, Hereford Museum, Costume Institute, New York, Colonial Williamsburg. A sixth hat may be in a French collection.
68 Anna Saskia Wolsak, *Bonnet, and Wine: The Cultural History of the Bermuda Palmetto*, 2017, p.78.
69 Official Descriptive and Illustrated Catalogue of the Great Exhibition, Spicer and Clowes, *Colonies and Dependencies, Bermudas*, 1851, p.971.
70 Ibid. p.78.
71 Ibid. p.77.

72 Kim Outten and Grace Turner, *Straw Work: A Case Study of Continuity & Change*, Festival of American Folklife, Smithsonian Institution, 1994, p.70–2.
73 http://creativenassau.com/strawwork. Accessed April 2022.
74 Anna Saskia Wolsak, *Bonnet, and Wine: The Cultural History of the Bermuda Palmetto*, 2017, p.66.
75 The Great Industries of the United States, *Hats and their Manufacture,* 1872, p.732.
76 Thomas Dublin. "Rural Putting-Out Work in Early Nineteenth-Century New England: Women and the Transition to Capitalism in the Countryside". *The New England Quarterly* 64, no. 4 (1991): 531–73. and Transforming Women's Work, Cornell University Press, 1994.
77 Ibid. p.549.
78 Unpublished research by Katherine Morris, Librarian, Phinehas S. Newton Library, Royalston, Massachusetts.
79 Rebecca Henning, *From Cuba to Amherst,* https://consecratedeminence.wordpress.com/2016/05/28/from-cuba-to-amherst/ Accessed April 2022.
80 Margaret Weaver, Municipal Historian and Kathleen Flaherty, Reference Librarian *at Killingly Historical & Genealogical Center*, Danielson, CT provided access to the samples and research into the Kies family.
81 Caroline Sloat, *"A great help to many families", Straw Braiding in Massachusetts before 1825,* The Dublin Seminar for New England Folklife Annual Proceedings 1988, p.89–100.
82 Barbara Gorely Teller, *Million dollar business,* The Wellesley Townsman, 1982, published in six parts between November and December.
83 Ibid, part 2.
84 Edgar Potter, *Who Made the First Straw Bonnet in Massachusetts?* Old-Time New England, Vol. Xl no. 2, 1920, p.73.
85 Documents held at Old Colony Historical Society, Taunton, Massachusetts.
86 *An Essay on the Manufacture of Straw Bonnets*, Providence, Barnum Field & Co 1825.
87 Transactions of the Society of Art, Manufactures and Commerce, Vol.34, 1821, p.217–22.
88 *Transactions of the Society of Art, Manufactures and Commerce*, Vol.43, 1824, p.16–21.
89 S. W Adams and Henry R. Stiles, *The History of Ancient Wethersfield*, Vol. 1, New England Press, 1909, p.650–1.
90 They married on 9 November 1820.
91 List of Patents for Inventions and Designs issued in the United States from 1790 to 1847, Washington, 1847, p.77. The patent is listed under the names Garden Wells and Sophia Wells and simply lists Hats, bonnets, of grass.
92 Melissa Josefiak, *Sophia Woodhouse's Grass Bonnets,* Wethersfield Historical Society. Accessed April 2022. https://www.wethersfieldhistory.org/articles/sophia-woodhouses-grass-bonnets/
93 Boston Commercial Gazette, *Domestic Imitation Leghorn Bonnet*, 2 August 1821, p.1.
94 New England Farmer, *On the Manufacture of Grass and Straw Bonnets,* Boston, Vol.2, 1824, p.308–9.
95 William Tufts Brigham, *Baltimore Hats Past and Present*, 1890, reprint 2018, p.63–6.
96 Hatters' Gazette, *The Mackinaw Hat,* November 1914, p.587–9.
97 Hatters' Gazette Diary, *Varieties of Straw Plait,* 1913, p.60, example 13.
98 Ibid. p.33.
99 Joleen Gordon, *Handwoven Hats*, Nova Scotia Museum, 1981, p.22.
100 Official Catalogue of the *Great Exhibition of the Works of Industry of all Nations*, Spicer, 1851, p.171
101 Joleen Gordon, *Handwoven Hats*, Nova Scotia Museum, 1981, p.25–7.
102 Gustave Pierotti, *La Paglia in Toscana*, Edizioni Dell'ente per le Attivita, Firenze, 1927, p.13 and note p.65.
103 Ibid. p.18–21.
104 D.E. Colnaghi, *Report on the Florentine Straw Industry* 1886 (Parliamentary Paper, lxvii).
105 Gustave Pierotti, *La Paglia in Toscana,* Firenze, 1927, p.15.
106 Diana and Tony Webb, *The Anglo-Florentines*, Bloomsbury Publishing, 2019, chapter 13.
107 Hatter's Gazette, *Straw Hat Industry in Tuscany* 1896, p.261–4.
108 Gustave Pierotti, *La Paglia in Toscana,* Edizioni Dell'ente per le Attivita, Firenze, 1927, p.24.
109 T.G. Austin, *The Straw Trade 1871,* Luton: Patrick O'Doherty, 1871, p.7.
110 Angelo Naldi, *L'avvento della treccia di paglia nella nostra montagna,* online blog, published 10 April 2013. Accessed May 2022.
111 Gustave Pierotti, *La Paglia in Toscana,* Edizioni Dell'ente per le Attivita, Firenze, 1927, p.24–5.
112 Olivia Rucellai, *La Paglia Intrecci Svizzeri a Firenze*, Edizioni Polistampa, 2001, p.20.
113 John Dony, *A History of the Straw Hat Industry*, Bamforth Press, 1942, p.193–4.
114 Giovanni Bianconi, *L'industria della paglia in Onsernone,* Folklore Svisse, volume 52, 1–4, 1962, p.9.
115 Museo Onsernone, Onsernone: das Tal und sein Museum, p.36.
116 *Manufacture de la paille Musée du pays et Val de Charmey*, 1996, p.8–10.
117 Planfayon French. Plaffeien German.
118 Joseph Reichlen, *L'Industrie des Pailles Tressées,* La Gruyère Illustrée, 1891, p.29.
119 Various accounts indicate that in this period it was only possible to dye straw black.
120 Many are displayed at the Sensler Museum at Tafers.
121 Constant Delacaux, Schweiz Archiv für Volkskunde, Band XLIII, *La tressage de la paille au Pays-d'Enhaut,* 1946.
122 Dr. Hans Lehmann, *Die Aargauische Strohindustrie,* Larl Bührer, 1896, p.46.
123 M. Bruggisser & Co., *Centenary Yearbook*, 1812–1912. No publisher, no page numbers. The account additionally lists seven-ends, straw cords and four-ends.
124 Ibid, p.34–6 and p.45–9.
125 Ibid.
126 Gottlieb Rodel, *Die Strohindustrie im aagauischen und luzernischen Seetal, Von den Anfängen der Freiämter Strohflechterie*, Buchor. Freiämter Zeitung A.G., Wohlen,1951, p.9–10.
127 Hatters' Gazette, *Straw Plaiting in Germany*, December 1897, p.665–7.
128 Norbert Döll, *Strohhutindustrie zu Lindenberg/Allgäu*, Volkskunst, 8.2 1985, p.5.
129 The warrant was renewed in 1777.
130 Mart. Koelbl, Hundert Jahre Ullgäuer Strohhut-Industrie, Adolf Schwarz, Lindenberg im Ullgäu, 1923, p.34.
131 Hatters' Gazette, *Straw Plaiting in Germany*, December 1 1897, p.665–667.
132 Georg Grübel, et al, *Chapeau: Das Westallgäu behütet die Welt: Die Geschichte der Hutproduktion in Lindenberg und Umgebung,* Kunstverlag Josef Fink, 2015.
133 Charles Dickens, *Business in the Black Forest,* All Year Round, 26 April 1862, p.163–4.
134 Girl's Own Paper, *Girl-Life in the Black Forest*, 1885 Annual, p.740–4.
135 Hatters' Gazette, *Straw Braiding in the Black Forest*, 1886, p.87–8. It previously appeared in Hat, Cap, and Fur Trade journal.
136 Museum der Strohverarbeitung, Kapellenweg 2, 27239 Twistringen, Germany. Deutsches Hutmuseum Lindenberg, Museumsplatz 1 88161 Lindenberg.
137 Hatters' Gazette, *Fortunes with Straw Foundations*, February 1898, p.77.
138 National Gallery, London. Inventory number: NG776. Location in Gallery: Room 55.
139 Syson L. & Gordon D. Pisanello: Painter to the Renaissance Court. National Gallery/Yale, p.140.
140 National Gallery, London. Inventory number: NG186. Location in Gallery: Room 63.
141 Ibid.
142 Hatters' Gazette, *Belgium Straw Workers*, October 1885, p.569.
143 L'industrie chapeliére dans la Vallée du Geer, 1950. p.7.
144 Ibid, p.9.
145 John Dony, *A History of the Straw Hat Industry*, Bamforth Press, 1942, p.17.
146 Daniel Loddo, *Al païs de la phlhòla*, C.O.R.D.A.E./La Talvera -A.L.C.O.C., 1999, p.66.
147 Ibid, p.75.
148 Hatters' Gazette, *Foreign notes*, February 1905, p.91.
149 https://montehermosocultural.blogspot.com/2014/06/mitos-origenes-

y-realidades-sobre-la.html *La gorra de Montehermoso: mitos, orígenes y realidades*, accessed April 2022.

150 Ruth Matilda Anderson, *Spanish Costume: Extremadura*, Hispanic Society of America, 1951, p.117–29.

151 http://carlosehistorias.blogspot.com/2013/08/desfile-de-traje-de-palha-para-promover.html *Desfile de «Traje de Palha» para promover uma das maiores tradições de Fafe*, accessed April 2022.

152 Veronica Main, *We are Born in Straw: Straw Plaiting and Hat Making in Transylvania*, Journal of Ethnological Studies 2000–1, vol. 39, p.75–90.

153 The Hatter and Umbrella Trade Circular, *Chinese Straw Plait*, December 1873, p.367.

154 The Hatter and Umbrella Trade Circular, *Luton and Dunstable*, March 1874, p.80.

155 Now known as Guangzhou.

156 These are the current names of the Chinese provinces.

157 The *Schantung Eisenbahn Gesellschaft*, Shantung Railway Company was opened in 1904.

158 Now known as Yantai. Another port used by the British was Tientsin now known as Tianjin.

159 Journal of the Royal Society of Arts, *Chinese Straw Braid*, p.935–6.

160 Laichow is the romanticised name of Laizhou. The city is still known today as Capital of Handmade Straw Crafts in China.

161 Journal of the Royal Society of Arts, *Chinese Straw Braid*, p.936.

162 Hatters' Gazette, *The English and Italian Straw Plaiting Industries*, October 1888, p.529.

163 Hatters' Gazette, *The Straw Plait Trade of China*, November 1903, p.592.

164 In the 1800s its length varied throughout China. In the plaiting districts it was about 14 inches.

165 Ibid.

166 Hatters' Gazette, *Trade Reports*, November 1887, p.633–44.

167 Hatters' Gazette, *The Straw Braid Trade in China*, September 1889, p.372.

168 Hatters' Gazette, *The Straw Braid Trade in China*, November 1885, p.265.

169 Hatters' Gazette, *the Trade in Straw Goods*, November 1892, p.569.

170 Catherine Robinson, *Imports, Mechanisation and the Decline of the English Plaiting Industry: the View from the Hatters' Gazette, Luton 1873–1900*, University of Hertfordshire, 2016, p.113.

171 Tatsuaki Morimoto, *Development of the straw braids in modern Japan-A case study in Okayama prefecture*, 2018. Accessed online April 2022. https://ousar.lib.okayama-u.ac.jp/ja/list/nii_types/Journal%20Article/p/550/item/55748

172 Consular Reports of the United States, *Report from Kanagawa*, no. 49, January 1885, p.72.

173 John Dony, *A History of the Straw Hat Industry*, Gibbs, Bamforth & Co., Luton, 1942, p.87.

174 Hatters' Gazette, *Japanese Straw Plait*, September 1887, p.506.

175 Hatters' Gazette, *Foreign Notes*, September 1888, p.480.

176 Hatters' Gazette, *The Straw Trade*, August 1901, p.416.

177 Diplomatic and Consular Reports, *Trade of Chefoo*, 1898, p.8.

178 Tatsuaki Morimoto, *Development of the straw braids in modern Japan-A case study in Okayama prefecture*, 2018. Accessed online April 2022. https://ousar.lib.okayama-u.ac.jp/ja/list/nii_types/Journal%20Article/p/550/item/55748

179 Catherine Robinson, *Imports, Mechanisation and the Decline of the English Plaiting Industry: the View from the Hatters' Gazette, Luton 1873–1900*, University of Hertfordshire, 2016, p.99.

180 Tatsuaki Morimoto, *Development of the straw braids in modern Japan-A case study in Okayama prefecture*, 2018. Accessed April 2022. https://ousar.lib.okayama-u.ac.jp/ja/list/nii_types/Journal%20Article/p/550/item/55748 p.395.

181 Hatters' Gazette, *The Luton and St Albans Hat Trade*, February 1900, p.393.

182 Hatters' Gazette, *The Quality of China Straw Plait*, November 1899, p.633.

183 Hatters' Gazette, *The Japan-British Exhibition*, September 1910, p.505.

184 Hatters' Gazette, *The Luton and St Albans Hat Trade*, February 1900, p.401.

185 Hatters' Gazette Diary, *British Straw Hat Trade Conditions*, February 1913, p.53.

186 He was a senior manager for Vyse & Co.

187 Charles Freeman, *Luton and the Hat Industry*, Luton Museum, 1953, p.25.

188 Hatters' Gazette, *Luton's Straw Industry Illustrated, Machinery in the Luton Hat Trade*, June 1908, p.306.

189 There is contrary evidence about the date. Harry Inwards, *Straw Hats*, 1922, p.21. states 1870 but Jas. Saunders, *Reminiscences of the Straw Trade*, The Luton News Almanac, 1914, p.8 and 15 says 1874. Accounts also vary whether the hats were stitched on a Singer or Willcox and Gibbs chain stitch machine.

190 A 10 Guinea did at first cost ten guineas, but the name 17 Guinea was introduced to identify the improved version.

191 John Dony, *A History of the Straw Hat Industry*, Bamforth, 1942, p.116.

192 Harry Inwards, *Straw Hats*, Pitman, 1922, p.22.

193 Hatters' Gazette, *Sewing Machines and the Straw Hat Industry*, October 1888, p.525.

194 Jas. Saunders, *Reminiscences of the Straw Trade*, The Luton News Almanac, 1914, p.8 and 15.

195 Ibid.

196 Hatters' Gazette, September 1888, p.iii.

197 Block makers create the form needed to shape the hat.

198 Transactions of the Society of Arts, 1815, Vol.33.

199 Illustrated London News, *Luton and the Straw Plait Industry*, 7 December 1878, p.453.

200 Also called hat press or panning machine.

201 Hatters' Gazette, *The Straw Hat Industry*, July 1882, p.295.

202 Hatters' Gazette, *The Plaiting of Straw Hats*, July 1901, p.371.

203 Hatters' Gazette, *The Straw Industry*, January 1894, p.38.

204 Hatters' Gazette, *Straw Plaiters' Earnings*, May 1894, p.245.

205 Hatters' Gazette, *Trade Reports, St Albans*, June 1877, p.134.

206 Kreischa, Dippoldiswalde and Radeberg.

207 Norbert Döll, *Strohhutindustrie zu Lindenberg/Allgäu*, Volkskunst, 8.2 1985, p.5.

208 Olivia Rucellai, *La Paglia Intrecci Svizzeri a Firenze*, Editioni Polistampa, 2001, p.24.

209 Linari describes peasants as being farm workers who plait in their spare time or in the winter months rather than those whose living depends upon it.

210 A.G. Linari, British Consular Report, *The Straw Hat Industry of Tuscany*, 1897. p.9. Linari does qualify that of the men most are involved in growing or preparing the straw.

211 Ibid. p.27.

212 Joseph Reichlen, *L'Industrie des Paille Tressées*, La Gruyére Illustrée, 1891, p.29.

213 Manufacture de la paille Musée du pays et Val de Charmey, 1996, p.11.

214 Hatters' Gazette, *Review of the Straw Trade for 1881*, January 1882, p.23.

215 Hatters' Gazette, *Luton and the Straw Plait Trade*, July 1885, p.403.

216 Hatters' Gazette, *The Luton Plaiting Industry*, April 1891, p.192.

217 Hatters' Gazette, *The Luton Straw Industry*, January 1899, p.192.

218 Hatters' Gazette, *Technical Education for Bedfordshire*, August 1891, p.416.

219 Hatters' Gazette, *Technical Education in Straw Plaiting*, July 1893, p.374.

220 Hatters' Gazette, *Straw Plaiting in South Beds.*, January 1896, p.374.

221 Bedfordshire County Council, *Report upon the Work of the Year 1896–7*, p.24.

222 Bedfordshire County Council, *Report upon the Work of the Year 1896–7*, p.24.

223 Colonial Williamsburg Costume and Textile Collections, object number 1953-868. Attributed to England 1745–5 and described as woven horsehair with all over repeat of four squares arranged in a small cross.

224 Arthur Young, *General View of the Agriculture of the County of Hertfordshire* 1804, David and Charles reprint, 1971, p82.

225 Edwin Grey, *Cottage Life in a Hertfordshire Village*, Fisher Knight, 1935, p.74.

226 George Meason, *The Official Illustrated Guide to the Great Northern Railway*, London, 1861, p.27–9.

227 John Dony, *A History of the Straw Hat Industry*, Bamforth, 1942, p.52, note 3.

228 Chalkey Gould, *Straw Plaiting – A Lost Essex Industry*, The Essex Naturalist, 1905.

229 John Dony, *A History of the Straw Hat Industry*, Bamforth, 1942, p.62, note 1. He writes, Wilshere's account was written when plait was still commanding a good price and there was an economic incentive for

farmers to grow plaiting straw.
230 William Wilshere, *The Commonplace Book of William Wilshere written between the years of 1754–1824.* 1816.
231 James Caird, *English Agriculture in 1850–51,* 1853, p.453–4.
232 William Cobbett, *The Cottage Economy,* 1979 ed, p.176. Society of Arts, 1860, p.75. Hatters' Gazette, 1886, p.364.
233 Triticum Turgidum is Emmer wheat.
234 W. Salisbury, *Material used in Tuscany for Plat,* Transactions of the Society of Arts, Vol. 43, 1824, p.21–2.
235 Thomas Coryat, *Coryat's Crudities:* hastily gobbled up in five months travels in France, Italy, &c., 1611, p.82.
236 William Cobbett, *Cobbett's Political Register,* Vol. 67, p.390.
237 Now known as Rothamsted Research. Edwin Grey, *Cottage Life in a Hertfordshire Village,* Fisher Knight, 1935, 117.
238 William Corston, *An account of a substitute for Leghorn plait for hats, etc.* Journal of Natural Philosophy, 1811.
239 A Lady, *The Workwoman's Guide,* Simpkin Marshall, 1840 edition, p.281.
240 John Shirreff, *A General View of Agriculture of the Orkney Islands,* 1814, p.163.
241 James and Andrew Muir, *British Leghorn,* Transactions of the Society, Vol.45, 1827, p.161.
242 William Cobbett, *The Cottage Economy,* 1822, 1979 ed, p.168.
243 Maria Edgeworth, *Works of Maria Edgeworth, Harry and Lucy, Concluded,* Vol. VIII Boston, 1825, p.129–31.
244 Maria Emirena Tozzi Bellini, *La Manifattura della Paglia nel Novecentro,* Edizioni Polistampa, 2007, p.146.
245 Known in the United States as bass wood.
246 Gottlieb Rodel, *Von der alten Friämter Stroh-Handflechterei zur modernen Hutgeflechindustrie,* 1960.
247 Ibid. p.66.
248 Abaco Sun, *Grasping at Straws: Plaiting a Path Out of Poverty,* May 14, 2014, https://abacosun.com/2014/05/14/bahamian-straw-hats/ Accessed April 2022.
249 The Cornwall Chronicle, Tasmania, 20 January 1847, Advertisement, p.57. https://trove.nla.gov.au/newspaper/article/65942185?searchTerm=cabbge%20tree%20hats%20hat Accessed April 2022.
250 The Cornwall Chronicle, Tasmania, 20 January 1847, Advertisement, p.57. https://trove.nla.gov.au/newspaper/article/65942185?searchTerm=cabbge%20tree%20hats%20hat Accessed April 2022.
251 International Exhibition 1862 Medals and Honourable Mentions, London, 1862, p.292.
252 British Patent Specifications, Wearing Apparel, Division 1, Head Coverings, No. 2765, George Simmonds, May 19, 1804.
253 British Patent Specifications, Wearing Apparel, Division 1, Head Coverings, No.2985, Robert Bowman, October 30, 1806.
254 Los Angeles County Museum of Art, Costume Council Fund no. M.64.85.4
255 Notes from the late J. Rudolf Isler, Wohlen, Switzerland.
256 Frederick Davis, *Luton, Past and Present: its History and Antiquities* Luton 1874, p.23.
257 William Wilshere, *The Commonplace Book of William Wilshere written between the years of 1754–1824.* 1817.
258 Foreign Office Miscellaneous Series, *Straw Hat Industry of Tuscany,* 1897, p.5.
259 Consul-General Colnaghi, *Florentine Straw Industry,* 1887, reported in Journal of Society of Arts, London, May 1887, p.692.
260 William Wilshere, *The Commonplace Book of William Wilshere written between the years of 1754–1824.*
261 Frederick Davis, *Luton, Past and Present: its History and Antiquities* Luton 1874, p.23.
262 The Saturday Magazine, *Straw-Platting,* January 1833, Vol.2, p.30.
263 London and Dublin Societies for Bettering the Condition of the Poor, Vol.4, Appendix 3, p.82.
264 A.J. Tansley, *Straw Platting,* The Saturday Magazine, Volume 2, January to June 1833. p.30.
265 The Saturday Magazine, *Straw-Platting,* January 1833, Vol.2 p.29.
266 Consul-General Colnaghi, *Florentine Straw Industry,* 1887, reported in Journal of Society of Arts, London, May 1887, p.692–3.
267 Museo della Paglia e dell'Intreccio, Signa, Italy.
268 Roberto Lunardi, *Condizioni della Industria Fiorentina delle Trecce e dei Cappelli di Paglia nel 1896,* Editioni Polistampa, 2003, p.54.
269 W.S. Campbell, *The Parramatta River and Its Vicinity, 1848–1861* read at the Royal Australian Historical Society May 27, 1919.
270 William Cobbett, *English Straw Plat,* Cottage Economy, 1822, 1971 reprint, p.151.
271 Joseph Lucas, *Kalm's Account of his visit to England on his way to America in 1748,* MacMillan, 1892, p.337–8.
272 A Lady, *On Straw Platting,* The Workwoman's Guide, 1840 reprint, p.281.
273 Veronica Main, *We are Born in Straw,* Folk Life, Journal of Ethnological Studies, Vol. 39, 2000–1, p81.
274 Mr. James Martin, Bleacher, Dyer, etc., Hitchin Road, High Town, *A descriptive Account of Luton Illustrated,* no date, p40.
275 Harry Inwards, *Straw Hats,* Pitman, 1922, p.60.
276 The Hatters' Gazette, 1 June 1905, p.336.
277 *Lye & Sons, Limited, 1857–1937.* Copy held in the Culture Trust Luton Collections.
278 Monopol was the trade name for the Lye bleach.
279 *A Descriptive Account of Luton Illustrated,* no date, p.31
280 Hatters' Gazette, *The Practical Straw Dyer,* May 1, 1894, p.246.
281 Information provided by Sue Brian in Australia and Rosemary Brice in the Bahamas.
282 Ernest Fevenc, *The Decay of the Cabbage-Tree,* Evening News, 7 November, 1896, p.10.
283 Litmus is also known as orchil or cudbear.
284 *To Dye Straw of Different Colours,* The Lady's Monthly Museum and School of Arts, No.1, January 1799, p.55.
285 Harry Inwards, *Straw Hats,* Pitman 1922, p.52.
286 Skilbeck Brothers Limited, *Dyewood and Mordants,* 1977, 16 pages, company publication. Skilbeck appear to have been suppliers to the trade of dyestuffs, etc., and were based in London.
287 Small beer was a diluted beer.
288 *Straw Plait Manufacture and Trade,* The Penny Cyclopaedia, vol.23, 1842, p.111.
289 J.J. Kershaw, *Reminiscences of the Straw Trade,* 1937, p.11.
290 The Hatters Gazette, January 1887
291 George Gage, British Patent Specifications, Division 1, Head Coverings, page 230, 1860, August 15, no.1977.
292 The late Tony Horn former Chairman of Baxter Hart & Abraham and Barford Brothers in conversation with Veronica Main 1990s.
293 Harry Inwards, *Straw Hats,* Pitman, 1922, p.57.
294 Mary Farnell, *The Neglected Aylesbury Prune,* Buckinghamshire Countryside, December 1977.
295 Thomas Bagshawe and Charles Freeman, *The Romance of the Straw Hat,* Luton, 1933.
296 Bagshawe Collection Archive, Culture Trust Luton Collections. Accessed with the kind permission of the Bagshawe family.
297 Denis Diderot and Jean le Rond d'Alembert, *Encyclopédie ou Dictionnaire raisonné des sciences, des arts et des métiers,* Vol. 4, Plate 10, Paris, 1765. The drawing first appears in the 1751 edition as Plate 3, Cabinet Marquetry Tools.
298 The tool was later transferred to the collections at Moot Hall, Elstow, Bedfordshire.
299 Journal of the Society of Arts and the Institutions in Union. Volume 9, From 23 November 1860 to 15 November 1861.
300 It is important to note that whilst references call the prisoners French men from many countries were held in the various depots.
301 Peterborough Museum and Art Gallery, accession number PETMG: E523.
302 The Man-Milliner, *European Magazine, and London Review,* Vol. 3, January 1783, p.13 and February 1783, p.91.
303 *Straw-Plat Manufacture and Trade,* The Penny Cyclopaedia of the Society for the Diffusion of Useful Knowledge, Volume 23, 1842, p.108–9.
304 In the Luton publications *The Romance of the Straw Hat,* and all subsequent versions of *Luton and the Hat Industry,* Bagshawe and Freeman incorrectly use the date 1795 which has led to it being incorrectly used in other publications.
305 Arthur Young, *General View of the Agriculture of the County of Hertfordshire,* David and Charles reprint 1971,1804, p.223.

306 Quarter Session Rolls 1804, Bedfordshire and Luton Archives and Records Service (BLARS).
307 Reports of the London and Dublin Societies for Bettering the Condition of the Poor; Relating to Schools for the Education of Children of the Lowest Class, Part 11, published 1807.
308 Patent Specifications. Wearing Apparel. Division 1 Head Coverings, May 8, 1800. Number 2399.
309 *Straw-Plaiting,* The Saturday Magazine, second volume, January to June 1833, 26 January, page 30.
310 Charles Lamborn, *The Dunstapelogia*, 1859, p.151–2.
311 Marian Nichols, former Principal Keeper, Luton Museum and friend of John Dony.
312 Gottlieb Rodel, *Die Strohindustrie im aarguaischen un luzernischen Seetal,* 1950, p.47.
313 Rev. I. Taylor, *Dunstable - Straw Work,* Scenes of British Wealth in Produce, Manufacturers and Commerce, 1825, p.21–2.
314 M.N.C. Seringe, *Mémoire sur la Culture et Emploi ds Céreales,* Mémoires de la Société Royale D'Agriculture, Histoire Naturelle, Et Arts Utitilities of Lyon, Lyon, 1828. P.117–20. Plate 2.
315 *Girl-Life in the Black Forest,* The Girl's Own Paper, October 1885, p.742–3.
316 http://www.strohmanufactur.de/strohflechterei/strohflechtertei-frueher/ Accessed April 2022.
317 Johann Carl Leuchs, *Werfertigung der Strohüte,* Handbuch fur Fabrikanten, Nürnberg, 1821, p.47–8.
318 *Ottmar Reich Hundert Jahre,* 1938, p.28.
319 A Lady, *The Workwoman's Guide*, Simpkin, Marshall and Co., 1840 edition, p.281.
320 Edmund St, Carleton Place, ON K7C 3E8, Canada.
321 I. Chalkley Gould, *Straw Plaiting - A Lost Essex Industry*, Essex Naturalist, 1905, p.187.
322 Miller Christy, Victoria County History, *Industries*, Volume 2, 1907, p.375.
323 R.W. Rowe, *The Art of Straw Plaiting in Essex*, Essex Countryside, Volume 13, April 1965, p.349.
324 *Plait and Plaiters*, Cassell's Family Magazine, E. Clarke, 1882, p.76–7.
325 *Straw-Plaiting,* The Saturday Magazine, second volume, January to June 1833, 26 January, p.30.
326 Mart. Koelbl, *Hundert Jahre Ullgäuer Stroh-Industrie 1814 - 1913*, Adolf Schwarz Lindenberg im Ullgäu, 1923, p.8.
327 Jean Davis, *Straw Plait*, Shire Publications, 1981, p.11.
328 *Ottmar Reich Hundert Jahre,* 1938, p.29.
329 Louis Edgar Andés, *Die Verarbeitung des Strohes zu geflehten und strohhüten,* Leipzig, 1898, p.61.
330 *The Hatters' Gazette, Straw Plaiting in Germany, December 1897, p.666.*
331 Caroline Sloat, *House and Home,* The Dublin Seminar for New England Folklife Annual Proceedings, Boston University, 1988, p.93, footnote 13.
332 Johann Carl Leuchs, *Werfertigung der Strohüte,* Handbuch fur Fabrikanten, Nürnberg, 1821, p.47–8.
333 Penny Crook and Tim Murray, *An Archaeology of Institutional Refuge, The Material Culture of the Hyde Parks Barracks, Sydney, 1848–1886,* Historic Houses Trust of NSW publications, Vol.12, 2006, p.18.
334 Peter Davies, Penny Crook, Tim Murray, Studies in Australasian Historical Archaeology 4, *An Archaeology of Institutional Confinement,* Sydney University Press, 2013, p. 114.
335 Davies, Crook, Murray, *An Archaeology of Institutional Confinement,* Studies in Australasian Historical Archaeology 4, Sydney University Press, 2013. Crook and Murray, *An Archaeology of Institutional Refuge, The Material Culture of the Hyde Park Barracks, Sydney 1848–1886,* Vol. 12 of the Archaeology of the Modern City Series, Historic Houses of NSW Publication, 2006.
336 W.S. Campbell, Extract from Mrs Felton Mathew's Journal (1848–61) read at the Royal Australian Historical Society May 27, 1919.
337 *Cabbage Tree Hats - A Lost Industry,* The Sydney Morning Herald, 2 November 1929.
338 British patent, no. 922, March 21 1769.
339 Culture Trust Luton Collections, Wardown House Museum and Gallery, accession no: LTNMG 97/29.
340 Bedfordshire County Records Office, P35/12/9
341 László Gróf, *Children of Straw*, Barracuda Books, 1988, p.26.
342 *Straw-Plaiting,* The Saturday Magazine, second volume, January to June 1833, 26 January, p.30.
343 Ibid. p.280.
344 Harry Inwards, *Straw Hats*, Pitman, 1922, p.82.
345 Her research notes are held in the Culture Trust Luton Collections.
346 Harry Inwards, *Straw Hats*, Pitman, 1922, p.82.
347 The Culture Trust Luton collection includes five mills marked Barrett.
348 *Descriptive Account of Luton Illustrated*, W.T. Pike, Brighton, p.34–8.
349 Head refers to the decorative edge of a plait.
350 R.W. Rowe, *The Art of Straw Plaiting in Essex*, Essex Countryside, Volume 13. April 1965, p.349.
351 Charlotte Rankin Aiken, B.A. *The Millinery Department,* Department Store Merchandise Manuals, Ronald Press, New York, 1918, p.12.
352 Costume Institute accession number 32.132. Credit Line: Rogers Fund, 1932.
353 Information kindly provided by Sue Brian of Gunning, NSW, Australia who has undertaken considerable research into the method of making the traditional cabbage tree hats and now teaches the skills.
354 John Dony, *A history of the Straw Hat Industry*, Bamforth Luton, 1942, page 26, footnote 3.
355 Summary Account of Rewards, Society of Arts, 1775 to 1782, p.149–50. The Royal Society of Arts archive holds correspondence with Pepperill.
356 Ida Gandy, The Heart of a Village: Intimate History of Aldbourne, 1975, p.47–8.
357 William Corston, *Transactions of the Society,* Society of Arts, Vol. 23. London, 1805, p. 221, 223–51.
358 A.J. Tansley, *On the Straw Plait Trade,* Journal of the Society of Arts, Vol. 9, December 21, 1860 p.70.
359 British Patent Specifications, Wearing Apparel, Division 1, Head Coverings, No.2399, May 8, 1800.
360 British Patent Specifications, Wearing Apparel, Division 1, Head Coverings, No.3930, August 12, 1815.
361 A.J. Tansley, *On the Straw Plait Trade,* Journal of the Society of Arts, Vol. 9, December 21, 1860 p.70.
362 British Patent Specifications, Wearing Apparel, Division 1, Head Coverings, No.4719, October 18, 1822.
363 The Penny Cyclopaedia, *Straw-Plat Manufacture and Trade,* Vol.23, 1842, p.109.
364 Transactions of the Society of Art, Vol.40, 1822, Preface, page xii–xiii.
365 *Report from the Select Commissioners on the Poor Laws*, 1838, paragraph 8150, 8155 and 8156.
366 Frederick Davis, *History of Luton,* Luton 1855, p.158.
367 Repertory of Patent Inventions, Vol.9, 1830, p.83–5.
368 The Saturday Magazine, *Straw Platting,* January to June Vol.2, 1833, p.29–31.
369 J.R. McCulloch, *A Dictionary of Commerce and Commercial Navigation,* Hats (Straw), Robert Slater, p.632–5.
370 Frederick Davies, *History of Luton*, Luton, 1855, p.158–9.
371 Charles Lamborn, *The Dunstaplelogia*, Dunstable, 1859, p.149.
372 A Lady, *The Workwoman's Guide*, Simpkin, Marshall and Co., 1840 edition.
373 Mrs Hughes and Mrs and Misses Batchelor, *First Course in Straw Plaiting*, E.J. Arnold, Leeds, 1894 and 1895.

CONVERSION TABLES

LENGTH

Millimetres to inches

mm	inch as decimal	inch as fraction
1	0.04	1/32
2	0.08	3/32
5	0.20	3/16
6	0.24	1/4
10	0.39	3/8
12	0.47	15/32
12.5	0.49	1/2
15	0.60	9/32
20	0.80	25/32
25	0.98	31/32
25.4	1.00	1
30	1.18	1 3/16

Feet/yards/mm/cm/m

feet	inches	mm/cm/m
1 foot	12 inches	305/30.5
3 feet or 1 yard	36 inches	914/91
3 feet 3 inches	39 inches	1000/100/1

Plait length measurements

Half-score	10 yards/30 feet/360 inches	914 cm
Score	20 yards/ 60 feet/720 inches	1,829 cm

MONEY

Four farthings = one penny (d)

Two half-pennies commonly called a ha'penny = one penny

Three pennies commonly called thruppence (3d)

Six pennies commonly called sixpence (6d)

Twelve pennies = one shilling (1s)

Twenty four pennies = two shillings (2s 0d)

Thirty pennies or two shillings and six pence commonly called half crown (2s 6d)

240 pennies or 20 shillings = one pound (£1)

One guinea = one pound, one shilling (£1.1s)

Pre-decimal £/shilling/pennies	Decimal £/pence
1/4d	0.5p
1/2d	1p
1d	2p
12d or one shilling	5p
24d or two shillings	10p
Ten shillings	20p
One pound	50p

QUANTITY

One dozen	12
Score	20
Gross or twelve dozen	144

WEIGHT

Pounds (lbs)	Grammes (g) /Kilograms (kg)
1lb	450 g
1 hundredweight (cwt) = 112 lbs	50.4 kg
1 quintal (metric unit) = 220.4 lbs	100 kg

All conversions are approximate

GLOSSARY

A

A1 — Trade name of a straw bleach used in the hat industry.

B

Banding — Length of plait used to strengthen a hat's brim edge. Normally made with seven or nine ends, single splints with a folded foot and head edge.

Bast — Inner fibrous plaiting or weaving material taken from under the plant bark of a wide variety of plant sources.

Bead — See Notch.

Beady head — Name given to twist edge plait in Hertfordshire.

Bents — A name for meadow grass, or used to signify imported Italian plaiting straws.

Bleaching box — Box or barrel that straw was placed in for bleaching.

Block — Form of wood, plaster, composition, or aluminium over which a hat or bonnet is stretched and pressed to its required shape and size.

Blocking — Mechanical process of shaping of the hat over a former either by hand or machine.

Body — Central section of a plait or braid which carries the pattern and may incorporate joins.

Bonnet — Covers the head, frames the face, and has a tye, usually under the chin.

Bordüre — Term used in Switzerland to describe a loom-made braid. *Bigherini* (Italian).

Braid — An interlacing structure made on a machine such as a mechanical braiding machine or loom.

Brazilian hat — Hat woven from palm, similar to a Panama hat's construction. See Capeline.

Brilliant — Plait pattern made with an even number of straws. The crossing end is kept on edge to create a facetted effect.

Brimstone — Flowers of sulphur, used for bleaching straw.

Bundle — Quantity of prepared stubs or pipes sold to plaiters. Frequently the size of two hand spans or 15 cm (6 in.) diameter.

Butt — Lower end of the top section of a plant stem. Closest to the leaf node.

Button — Central starting point of sewn plait on the top of a hat crown. Normally hand sewn to the size of 'a half crown' (35 mm). In the hat trade people who made the buttons were known as, "Button sewers". They were often children working for their mothers.

C

Cabbage tree — Livistona australis palm. Grows in the coastal regions of Australia. Used to make the iconic Cabbage tree hat.

Cable edge — Brim edge of a boater hat. A cane wrapped with plait is inserted between the two layers of the brim. Also known as cane edge.

California — Type of loop edge plait pattern. A sample dated 1850 is at Framingham Historical Society, Massachusetts, USA.

Canton — Term used to describe the first imported plaits from China. The port of exit from China was Canton (Guangzhou).

Capeline — A woven cone shape. Also known as a hood or flare.

Cereal crop straw — Plaiting material applies to wheat, rye, barley, oats, and rice.

Chad or chard pot — Pot or tin filled with hot coals or embers and placed under the plaiter's chair and skirts to provide warmth in the winter months. Also called a dicky pot.

Chain edge — Pattern effect on head of a plait. The outside straw along the head edge is returned into the body of the plait in alternate movements.

Cheen or chine — Bedfordshire term for a straw splitter. Pronounced as sheen. Also called machine or engine.

China — Name for seven-end plait.

Chinese nettle — General name for the plant from which ramie is obtained.

Chip — Material used to make a plait. Wood planed from a tree and used green. The source may be poplar, willow, or larch. Also called wood chip. Sometimes loosely referred to as bast.

Clip or Clipping — Process to cut off ends left from the joining process once the plait is finished.

Coburg — Also see purl. In Italy the plait is called Coburgo. Also spelt as Cobourg.

Cord — Another term for the seven-end plait whipcord pattern. Also used to describe the Tuscan spiral plait used as a trimming.

Cordinet — Term used to describe a cord which outlines a decorative pattern. Usually applied to a two or three-end plait. Also spelled, cordonnet and cordinette.

Crin — Originally natural horsehair. From the early 1900s made from viscose, pyroxylin, and now polyester. Also refers to a machine-made open-weave braid.

Crinol — Artificial horsehair or fibre.

Cuba bast — Fibre obtained from hibiscus elatus. Immersed in acid to burn away the soft tissue, leaving only the skeletal or fibrous parts. Introduced into the European hat industry in about 1895.

D

Dealer — Either a straw dealer who sold the plaiting straws, or a plait dealer who purchased plait and sold it on to the hat manufacturers.

Devon — Seven-end plait made with single splints. Any association to the county of Devon is unclear but may relate to the enterprises of John Pepperell of Totnes.

Diamond — Trade name of a straw bleach used in the hat industry.

Dicky pot — See Chad or chard pot.

Double splint — Two splints faced together and worked as one plaiting length.

Dunstable — Type of plait. First used to refer to a specific pattern but later often used to describe plaits from the area around the town.

Dunstable bonnet	Straw hat or bonnet made in Dunstable. Not associated with any specific style, material, or method of construction.
Dunstable twist	Seven-end plait made with a twist edge.

E

Ears	Term used in Eaton Bray, Bedfordshire, to describe the fins or blades of a straw splitter.
Edge	Outside stitch of a plait. Can be the foot or head.
Enamel	Outer shiny side of the cereal crop straw stem.
Ends	Number of straws, or splints used to make a plait. Double splints are counted as one.
Engine	See Cheen or Machine.

F

Face	Front of the plait.
Fancy	Generic term to describe an elaborate plait pattern, or a plait made with a combination of materials. Also applys to loom and machine-made braids.
Feather	Pattern where the outside straws are left out for several moves then brought back in sequence to form a patterned edge.
Fioretto	Italian term for a Leghorn hat before blocking, or for a large flop hat.
Flags	Leaf covering the cereal straw stems. Removed before plaiting.
Flats	Refers to Italian hats exported ready sewn, or 'knitted' together.
Foot	Edge of the plait along which joins are made. Usually concealed and strengthened when stitched into a hat or bonnet.

G

Glossy side	Also see Enamel or Shiny side.
Grasses	General term for meadow grasses, water grasses used as a plaiting material. See also Bents.

H

Half yard board	Wooden board to measure finished plait, approximately 46 cm (18 in.) long. Can also be a stick. The length and form of this measuring device varies throughout European plaiting centres and the Far East.
Hank	Measured length of finished plait. Also called a link, piece or skein.
Hat	May or may not entirely cover the head and may be held in place with a head band or length of elastic.
Hatters' Gazette	Trade journal of the British hat trade. Published between 1872 and 1960.
Head	Edge of a plait or braid that is visible when made into a hat, bag, or basket. The head can incorporate a decorative edge. Also used to describe a purl plait, for example one head, two head.
Hemp	See Manila hemp.

I

Imitation	Term for a plait. Used in the early 1900s for plaits made in Buckinghamshire and Bedfordshire. Application unclear but may refer to a plait made with double splints. May also indicate plaiters copied foreign patterns.
Improved	Descriptive term for a plait made with double splints.

J

Jippijapa	Name of a town in Ecuador, but used to describe hats, a hat body or material. The name is spelled in various ways in *Hatters' Gazette* accounts.
Jumbo	Type of wide plait imported from Japan in early 1900s and popular for men's boaters.

K

Knitted or knitting	Used as reference to the sewing together of straw plait. See Maglia and Remaille.

L

Lace straws	Generic term in the British hat industry to describe imports from Italy and Switzerland, includes loom-made and knotted braids.
Laichow	Refers to a type of plait, seven-end whole straw, made near Laichow (Ye Xian) in the province of Shandong, China. Laichow was also a port of export for plait in the 1800s.
Laichow mottled	See Mottled.
Lame(s)	Name for a tape used as a plaiting or braiding product. Known in Switzerland as bandel.
Leghorn	Anglicisation of Livorno. The port used for exporting straw, plaits and hats from Italy. Not a plait or hat production centre. Also used to describe various products; Italian 'flat' where the plaits are sewn edge to edge. (1800s), as a term used for all Italian hats (1900s), and to describe a plait of nine, eleven, thirteen or fifteen ends with folded edges. Also describes a plait with a long stitch on both head and foot to enable stitching or knitting together.
Lima	Prepared natural horsehair.
Link	See Hank.
Linked-up	Neat looping of the plait over the arm while worked. The finished plait may also be put into a link ready for sale. Double link, the finished plait is wound in a figure of eight.
Liseret or Liseré	French word meaning piping. By the 20th century the term is used to describe the English piping pattern. *The Millinery Department* by Charlotte Rankin Aiken (1918) describes Liséré as a shiny, stiff, narrow braid made generally from split straw, but sometimes from whole and imported (into North America) from Switzerland, Belgium, China, and Japan. Erroneously says a three-end liséré from Japan is used extensively.
Loop	Alternative name for the feather edge pattern.
Luton	Plait pattern, type unclear, but possibly a seven-end, courser version of Dunstable.

M

Machine	See Cheen.
Maglia	Italian word meaning knitted, relates to the joining together of Italian plait. See Remaille and Maglia.
Malimpo or Maslimpo	Chinese seven-end plait from that region.
Mangle	See Mill.
Manila hemp	Musa textilis fibres. Introduced to the Swiss hat products industry in the 1820s. Used to create a wide range of products. Also see Sinamay.
Manmade	Natural fibres or materials manufactured into a variety of products.

Matt side	Pith, or rice side of a split straw.
Milan or Maglina	General name for a fine, narrow Italian seven-end plait made from pedal straw, but now also applied to Chinese seven-end whole straw plait.
Mill	Also box mill. Made of wood or metal, used to softened splints and to press finished plait. A plait mill with trolls was used in sewing rooms and factories.
Monopol	Trade name for bleach used in the hat trade.
Moss edge	Plait similar to purl but the head is formed around the outside straw and a hair pin. The resulting edge is straighter than a purl edge
Mottled	Used in the south east midlands to describe a single splint straw plait. Also used in the hat trade to describe Chinese plait, late 1800s and 1900s, made with the whole length of straw stem thus causing a colour variation that is not removed by bleaching.

N

Neora	Ramie tape covered on one side with cellophane. Introduced in the 1920s.
Nip	Term used to describe the part of a plait where the straws too short to work. In use around Tring, Hertfordshire. Can also refer to a twist edge pattern.
Notch or bead	Type of plait with a loop edge. The term was used in Essex. In Framingham Historical Society, Massachusetts a loosely worked example of rustic is labelled notch.

O

Old English	Name for seven-end twist head used in Hertfordshire at the end of the 1800s.

P

Paille de riz	Another name for rice plait.
Palm	Generic term for any local palm leaf or stem for plaiting.
Panama	Name for a woven hat body and finished hat. Traditionally made in Ecuador from toquilla palm, but used as a generic term in the hat trade.
Patent Dunstable	Seven-end plait made using double splints.
Patent Milan	Chinese plait mimicking Milan.
Pearl	English name for a four-end rustic plait.
Pedal or Pedale	Italian term for plait made with the lower section of straw to produce a coarser plait than that made with punte or point straw.
Plait	Originally spelled plat or sometimes plet. Pronounced as in hat. In terms of this book, defines an interlinked product made by hand.
Plait mill	See Mill.
Piece	See Hank or Link.
Pipe	South east midlands name for a whole straw prepared for plaiting. Also called stub.
Piping	See Liseré. A type of plait pattern.
Pith side	See Matt side.
Point	The section of the plaiting straw closest to the head. In Italian, *punte*.
Pottle	Archaic measuring container for half a gallon (Imperial measure).
Punte	See Point.
Purl	Plait with a patterned edge formed by taking a single or double splint or whole straw round a carrier end. The movement can be repeated one to four times to form a scalloped edge.

Q

Quintel	Metric measurement used to weigh bales of straw plait. Equivalent to 100 kg.

R

Racello	Trade name for a tape covered on one side with cellophane. Can be made into various widths and from a range of materials such as artificial silk, ramie, bast or paper. See also Neora.
Raffia	Natural plant material from a palm found in Africa and Madagascar. Also artificial raffia made from paper or an extruded manmade fibre.
Rail or railroad	Plait pattern that uses pairs of undyed and dyed straws to form a pattern.
Ramie	See Chinese nettle. A plant fibre introduced at the end of the 1890s.
Remaille	French word. Also see maglia or a maglia. A method of stitching plaits together, common to Italy. Nowadays in sewing it is called 'ladder' stitch.
Rice plait	Type of plait patterns made with double straws, but with the inner pith side faced outward. May also apply to certain plaits made using rice straw.
Ring plait(s)	Group of plaits first made in France or Switzerland, later made world-wide. Made from chip or single splint.
Rough and Ready	Wide plait made of whole straw popular at the end of the 1800s and early 1900s.
Rustic	See also Pearl or English pearl.
Rustic flatfoot	Version of Rustic where the foot edge is straight. Believed to have originated in Japan at the end of the 1800s. Widely used to make boater hats in the early 1900s.
Rutland	Type of plait pattern, however the exact pattern is unclear.

S

Sala	Type of rush used in Italy for plaiting and weaving.
Score	20 yards of plait. A standard British length.
Set in or set out	Addition into a plait of new working lengths. These are the ends that protrude from the plait and are clipped.
Setting out	Term found in and around Tring, Hertfordshire referring to the joining of ends into a plait.
Sets and runs	Also setts and runs. Method of joining associated with Essex plait in the 1800s. All working ends are joined in close succession then the plait continues without joining until the ends run out. Also joining method found on some Chinese plaits.
Set up or setting up	Arrangement of the plaiting lengths into their working positions ready to start plaiting.
Shiny side	See Enamel.
Sinamay	Woven straw product introduced into the British hat industry in the late 1980s. Made from musa textilis fibres. Also see Manila hemp.
Skein	Section of a Chinese hank of plait. Also see Hank.
Smooth bend	Name used in villages around Luton for a seven-end plait with folded head.

Sorting	Grading the stubs or pipes into similar sizes by passing them through grids. Can be a hand process.
Speckled	Plait made with a combination of undyed, or bleached, and dyed straws to produce a pattern. Also called spotted plaits.
Speelless	Also written as speeless. The method of joining into the body of the plait, rather than along the foot.
Speels	The old working end replaced by the set in or set up.
Splint(s)	Section cut from a length of whole straw.
Splitter	Tool for cutting a stem of straw into splints. Also known as: Machine, cheen, engine, frame. Made in a variety of forms.
Steaming	Refers to bleaching the straw or plait with sulphur. Also called stoving.
Stitch	Term given to a single move within a plait.
Straw	Often used as a generic term in the hat industry. Can encompass many plant, manmade and synthetic fibres.
Straw cutter	Occupation of cutting the cleaned straw into plaiting lengths.
Straw drawer	Occupation of cleaning the sheaves from the field and taking out the straw for re-bundling before it is cut.
Straw hat	Lightweight summer hat made from a variety of methods and wide range of materials.
Straw sorter	Machine for sorting the straws usually through a series of grids. Also, an occupation.
Stringer	Occupation in a dyeing factory. Puts lengths of string through the hanks prior to bleaching or dying so they can be hung up. Often the job of children.
Stub	See Pipe.

T

Tagel	Also tagal or tagle. Machine-made braid originally made from vegetable fibres grown in the district of Tagel, Java. Later from other sources. The name is normally followed by a series of number e.g., 13/2. This indicates thirteen-ends with two fibres in each end. Introduced into the hat industry in the 1900s.
Tapes	See Lames.
Tress	Old fashioned name for plait.
Trimming	Decoration of a finished product.
Tristram Shandy	Zigzag plait pattern made in 1843 and on display in the Framingham Historical Society, Massachusetts.
Troll	Individual grooves in a plait mill roller.
Tubes	See Pipe or Stub.
Turn	The fold or stitch on the plait edge. Attributed to plaiters in Ivinghoe, Buckinghamshire in Joseph Lucas' translation of Pehr Kalm account.
Tuscan	Also appears in documents as Tuskan. There are several definitions. Can apply to the Italian region, a type of plait, a loom made braid, or plaiting straws imported from Italy. May also refer to the spiral cord plait made for trimming and bags. Its use in documentation is not always clear.
Twist	Also nip edge, or cord or whipcord.

U

Under	Type of plait mentioned in *Straw Hats*, by Harry Inwards. In Italy known as *ginocchiello*. A whole straw pattern like piping.
Undyed	Whole plaiting lengths or splint(s) which may be natural or may have been bleached by sulphur. The preparation cannot be determined by examination.
Upping	Term found in the area around Tring, Hertfordshire, referring to making the plait between joins. See setting out and nip.

V

Ventilated	Type of plait with an open-work centre. The spacing may be created by use of a former.

W

Weaving	Made by hand or on a loom. Constructed with a diagonal weave (bias) or has warp and weft.
Whipcord	See Cord.
Widdle-waddle	Also called twiddle-twaddle or twittle-twattle. A type of plait which may have been made with materials other than straw or with lengths of plait.
Willow square	Also willow sheets or woven willow. Loom-woven strips of willow cut then made into a hat or bonnet.
Wood chip	See Chip.
Working ends	Number of ends worked in a plait.
Working lengths	Plaiting lengths folded to give the ends that are worked in the plait.
Woven hat	Method of construction. Starting at the top centre of the crown (the rosette) the fibres are woven on a bias into a basic hat shape which is then blocked. This method was used for making a Brazilian hat. See Capeline and Panama.

Y

Yard stick	Similar to half-yard board, for measuring finished plait.
Yedda or Yeddah	Plant fibre used in the Swiss and Italian hat industries to manufacture lames or tapes and other products.
Yeddo	Fibres of this plant can be used to weave hats. Also a Japanese machine-made braid of the 1900s. Or it can be a type of hat constructed by joining a continuous spiral of whole straws with knotted thread.
Yova	Plant fibre used in the Swiss industry for manufacture into other products.

SELECTED BIBLIOGRAPHY

A

A Lady, *The Workwoman's Guide*, On Straw Plaiting, London, 1838.

Adams Sherman W and Henry R. Stiles, *The History of Ancient Wethersfield*, Vol. 1, New England Press, 1909.

Anderson Ruth Matilda, *Spanish Costume: Extremadura*, Hispanic Society of America, 1951.

Andés Louis Edgar, *Die Verarbeitung des Strohes zu geflehten und strohhüten*, Leipzig, 1898.

Anon, *An Essay on the Manufacture of Straw Bonnets*, Providence, Barnum Field & Co 1825.

Ashley Clifford, *The Ashley Book of Knots*, Faber and Faber, London, 1944 ed.

Austin Thomas George, *The Straw Hat Trade*, O'Doherty Printer and Publisher, 1871.

B

Bagshawe Thomas Wyatt, *The Romance of the Straw Hat*. Luton: Luton Museum and Art Gallery, 1933.

Batchelor, Mrs and Misses, and Mrs Hughes, *First Course in English Straw and Chip Plait*. Leeds: E.J. Arnold, 1894.

Batchelor, Mrs and Misses, and Mrs Hughes, *Second Course in English Straw and Chip Plait*. Leeds: E.J. Arnold, 1895.

Bianconi Giovanni, *L'industria della paglia in Onsernone*, Folklore Svisse, volume 52, 1-4, 1962.

Brigham William Tufts, *Baltimore Hats Past and Present*, 1890, reprint 2018.

British Patent Office, *British Patent Specifications, Wearing Apparel, Division 1, Head Coverings*, 1890.

Bruckman Janilla, *la Paglia di Fiesole*. Florence: Regione Toscana – Giunta regional, 1987.

C

Campbell W.S., *The Parramatta River and Its Vicinity, 1848-1861*, Royal Australian Historical Society, 1919.

Carpenter Kirsty, *The novelty of the French émigrés in London in the 1790s*, University of London Press; Institute of Historical Research, 2013.

Chamberlain Paul, *The Napoleonic Prison of Norman Cross*, The History Press, 2018.

Cobbett William, *Cottage Economy*. Oxford: Oxford University, 1822, 1979 ed.

Cook Viva, Sampley Julia, *Palmetto Braiding and Weaving*, Manual Arts Press, Peoria, 1947.

Crook Penny and Murray Tim, *An Archaeology of Institutional Refuge, The Material Culture of the Hyde Parks Barracks, Sydney, 1848-1886*, Historic Houses Trust of NSW publications, Vol.12, 2006.

D

Davies Peter, Crook Penny, Murray Tim, Studies in Australasian Historical Archaeology 4, *An Archaeology of Institutional Confinement*, Sydney University Press, 2013.

Davis Frederick, *History of Luton*, Luton 1855.

Davis Frederick, *Luton, Past and Present: its History and Antiquities* Luton 1874.

Davis Jean, *Straw Plait*, Shire Publications, 1981.

Delacaux Constant, Schweiz Archiv für Volkskunde, Band XLIII, *La tressage de la paille au Pays-d'Enhaut*, 1946.

Diderot Denis and d'Alembert Jean le Rond, *Encyclopédie ou Dictionnaire raisonné des sciences, des arts et des métiers*, Vol. 4, Plate 10. Paris, 1765.

Dony, John Dr, *A History of the Straw Hat Industry*. Luton: Leagrave Press, 1942.

Dublin, Thomas, *Rural Putting-Out Work in Early Nineteenth-Century New England: Women and the Transition to Capitalism in the Countryside*, The New England Quarterly 64, no. 4, 1991.

Dublin, Thomas, *Transforming Women's Work*, Cornell University Press, 1994.

E

Edgeworth Maria, *Works of Maria Edgeworth, Harry and Lucy, Concluded*, Vol. VIII Boston, 1825.

F

Farnell Mary, *The Neglected Aylesbury Prune*, Buckinghamshire Countryside, December 1977

Fenton Alexander, *The Northern Isles*, John Donald Publisher, 1978.

Fevenc Ernest, *The Decay of the Cabbage-Tree*, Evening News, 7 November 1896.

First Report of the Commissioners on the Employment of Children, Young Persons and Women in Agriculture, 1864.

Freeman, Charles, *Luton and the Hat Industry*. Luton: Luton Museum & Art Gallery, 1953.

G

Gandy Ida, *The Heart of a Village: Intimate History of Aldbourne*, 1975

Gordon Joleen, *Handwoven Hats*, Nova Scotia Museum, 1981.

Great Industries of the United States, *Hats and their Manufacture*, J. B. Burr & Hyde, Hartford, 1872.

Gróf, László, *Children of Straw*. Buckingham: Barracuda, 1988

Edwin Grey, *Cottage Life in a Hertfordshire Village*, Fisher Knight, 1935.

Grübel Georg et al, *Chapeau: Das Westallgäu behütet die Welt: Die Geschichte der Hutproduktion in Lindenberg und Umgebung*, Kunstverlag Josef Fink, 2015.

H

Hatter's Gazette 1872–1959.

Hennell Thomas, *Change in the Farm*, Cambridge, 1936.

I

Inwards Harry, *Straw Hats: Their History and Manufacture*. London: Pitman, 1922.

J

Jarvis Michael J., *"In the eye of all trade": Maritime revolution and the transformation of Bermudian Society, 1620-1800*, William and Mary College VA, 1998.

K

Koelbl Mart., *Hundert Jahre Ullgäuer Stroh-Industrie 1814 – 1913*, Adolf Schwarz Lindenberg im Ullgäu, 1923.

Kuhn D & Wohler A. & Hohl M, Littmann B & Isler J.R. *Strohzeiten* Aargau: AT Verlag, 1991.

L

L'industrie chapeliére dans la Vallée du Geer, 1950.

Lamborn Charles, *The Dunstaplelogia*, Dunstable, 1859.

Lehmann Hans, Dr, *Die Aargauische strohindustrie*, Aarau, Switzerland: Karl Bührer, 1896.

Leuchs Johann Carl, *Werfertigung der Strohüte, Handbuch fur Fabrikanten*, Nürnberg, 1821.

Loddo Daniel, *Al païs de la phlhòla*, C.O.R.D.A.E./La Talvera -A.L.C.O.C., 1999

Lunardi Roberto, *Condizioni della Industria Fiorentina delle Trecce e dei Cappelli di Paglia nel 1896*, Editioni Polistampa, 2003.

M

Mcculloch J. R. *Dictionary Of Commerce*, London: Longman, Rees, Orme, Brown, Green, And Longman, 1832 & 1834.

Mcculloch J. R. *Statistical Account Of The British Empire*, Vol. 1, 1839.

Main Veronica, *Swiss Straw Work: Techniques of a Fashion Industry*, London: Main Collins, 2003.

Main Veronica, *We are Born in Straw: Straw Plaiting and Hat Making in Transylvania*, Journal of Ethnological Studies 200-2001, vol. 39

Morimoto Tatsuaki, *Development of the straw braids in modern Japan-A case study in Okayama prefecture*, 2018. Accessed online April 2022.

N

Neill Patrick, *A Tour through the Orkneys*, 1806,

O

Official Descriptive and Illustrated Catalogue of the Great Exhibition, *Colonies and Dependencies*, *Bermudas*, Spicer and Clowes, 1851.

Outten Kim and Turner Grace, *Straw Work: A Case Study of Continuity & Change*, Festival of American Folklife, Smithsonian Institution, 1994.

P

Paccagnini, Giovanni, (tr. Carroll Jane), *Pisanello*, London: Phaidon, 1973. (tr. 1973).

Patents Office Specifications, Wearing Apparel, London, 1826.

Penny Cyclopaedia. *Straw Plait Manufacture and Trade*, vol.23, 1842.

Pierotti Gustave, *La Paglia in Toscana*, Edizioni Dell'ente per le Attivita, Firenze, 1927.

R

Rankin Aiken Charlotte,B.A. *The Millinery Department*, Department Store Merchandise Manuals, Ronald Press, New York, 1918.

Reichlen Joseph, *L'Industrie des Pailles Tressées*, La Gruyère Illustrée, 1891.

Reports from the Commissioners on the Employment of Children, 1843.

Reports from the Select Commissioners on the Poor Laws, 1838.

Reports of the Commissioners on the Employment of Children, Young Persons and Women in Agriculture, 1864, 1868.

Robinson Catherine, *Imports, Mechanisation and the Decline of the English Plaiting Industry: The View from the Hatters' Gazette, Luton 1873-1900*, University of Hertfordshire, 2016.

Rodel Gottlieb, *Die Strohindustrie im aarguaischen und luzernischen Seetal*, 1950.

Rodel Gottlieb, *Die Strohindustrie im aagauishcen und luzernischen Seetal*, Von den Anfängen der Freiämter Strohflechterie, Buchor. Freiämter Zeitung A.G., Wohlen,1951.

Rodel Gottlieb, *Die Technik in der Freiämter, Seetaler und Obwaldner Strohflechterei*, Bern: Büchler, 1949.

Rodel Gottlieb, *Von der alten Freiämter Stroh-Handflechterei zur modern Hutgeflechtindustrie.*). n.p. 1960.

Rucellai Olivia, *La Paglia Intrecci Svizzeri a Firenze*, Edizioni Polistampa, 2001.

S

Sandford Lettice and Davis Philla, *Decorative Straw work*, Batsford, London, 1964.

Seiler-Baldinger Annemarie, *Textiles a Classification of Techniques.* Bathurst, NSW, Australia: Crawford House, 1994.

Seringe M.N.C., *Mémoire sur la Culture et Emploi ds Céreales,* Mémoires de la Société Royale D'Agriculture, Histoire Naturelle, Et Arts Utitilities of Lyon, Lyon, 1828.

Shirreff John, *A General View of Agriculture of the Orkney Islands,* 1814.

Slater Robert, *A Dictionary of Commerce and Commercial Navigation,* Hats (Straw), J.R. McCulloch, 1839.

Sloat Caroline, *"A great help to many families", Straw Braiding in Massachusetts before 1825,* The Dublin Seminar for New England Folklife Annual Proceedings, 1988.

Sydney Morning Herald, *Cabbage Tree Hats - A Lost Industry,* 2 November 1929.

Syson Luke & Gordon Dillon, *Pisanello: Painter to the Renaissance Court*. London: National Gallery, 2001.

T

Tozzi Bellini Maria Emirena, *La Manifattura della Paglia nel Novecentro,* Edizioni Polistampa, 2007.

W

Ward Mrs Humphrey, *Marcella*, 13th edition 1895.

Webb Diana and Tony, *The Anglo-Florentines*, Bloomsbury Publishing, 2019.

Wolsak Anna Saskia, *Bonnet, and Wine: The Cultural History of the Bermuda Palmetto*, 2017.

Y

Young Arthur, *A Six Month's Tour of the Northern Counties*, Volume 1, 1768.

Young Arthur, *General View of the Agriculture of the County of Hertfordshire* 1804, David and Charles reprint.

PICTURE CREDITS

Carleton Place and Beckwith Heritage Museum 103

Cassell's Family Magazine 17

Creative Nassau Photographer Eric Rose/TRIOM 30, 77, 189

Culture Trust Luton 14, 79, 80, 130, 144, 145, 150, 152, 153, 154, 155, 156, 159, 161, 169, 171, 172, 174, 175, 180, 182, 183, 184, 185, 188, 192, 194, 204, 210, 213, 215, 217, 220, 223, 226, 228, 229, 231, 234, 235, 236, 243, 246, 251, 256, 258, 259, 261, 262, 265, 268, 274, 280, 282, 284, 288, 291, 294, 297, 298, 299, 305, 306, 308, 310, 313, 315, 316, 319

Culture Trust Luton/family of R. Durler 58, 61

Culture Trust Luton/Luton News 12, 62, 65, 85

Culture Trust Luton/Pan3sixty 16, 40, 43, 50, 53, 54, 60, 70, 74, 75, 93, 94, 102, 104, 105, 109, 111, 113, 116, 117, 118, 128, 146–7, 148, 158, 168, 190, 207, 222, 254, 271, 302

Culture Trust Luton. Photographer Shawn Armstrong. Purchased with assistance from the Art Fund 114

Danvers Historical Society, Danvers, Massachusetts 26, 35, 307

Deanie Neuhofer 56

Evlyn McLeod Flewelling and Margo Flewelling. Photographer Jack Butler 38, 103

Frank Leslie's Illustrated Newspaper 106

Heather Beeson 134

Hereford Museum and Gallery, Hereford Museum Service 29

Hilary Burns. Photographer Keith Charles Valler 238

Hyde Park Barracks Archaeology Collection, Sydney Living Museums. Photo (c) Jamie North 108

Jim Cornish 101, 109, 133

K Smith. Miss Emily's String 140

Lucy Barlow (page 162. Model Klay Evaorl) 4, 162

Margaret Weaver/Killingly Historical Society 33

Museum für Sächsische Volkskunst, Dresden 142

Museum of London 71, 286

North Carolina Museum of History 32

Orkney Museum 22

Parkdale-Maplewood Community Museum 112, 113

Rosemary Sault 73

Strohmuseum im Park 45

Schulmuseum, Schmiedeberg 208

Sue Brian. Photographer Daniel Bornstein 78, 135

Tring History Society/Mike Bass 21

Kind permission of T.W. Bagshawe's family/Culture Trust Luton 82, 86, 91, 96, 98, 130

Veronica Main 48, 57, 132, 141, 151, 157, 164, 165, 166, 167, 178, 180, 186, 195, 198, 201, 224, 240, 248, 272, 276, 304

Veronica Main. Photographer Andy at APG Video 98, 102, 107

Veronica Main with kind permission of Jan Huss. Photographer Andy at APG Video 99

INDEX

References to images are in *italics*.